RELIGIOUS THOUGHT IN ENGLAND

FROM THE REFORMATION TO THE END OF LAST CENTURY

A Contribution to the History of Theology

BY THE REV. JOHN HUNT, M.A.
AUTHOR OF 'AN ESSAY ON PANTHEISM'

VOLUME I.

STRAHAN & CO., PUBLISHERS
56 LUDGATE HILL, LONDON
1870

TAYLOR AND CO., PRINTERS,
LITTLE QUEEN STREET, LINCOLN'S INN FIELDS.

PREFACE.

THIS is not a work which requires a long preface. The title-page sufficiently indicates its object. It is not written to promote the interests of any party, and the utmost effort has been made to preserve fairness and impartiality. It is impossible, I apprehend, for any man to write on controverted subjects, even in the way of history, without indicating his own bias. It is not perhaps desirable, for that bias, however little it may appear, is really the stand-point from which he writes, and sometimes the key to his object in writing. I have tried to avoid making inferences, wishing rather to state facts honestly, believing that in every case the inferences which I should make, will be made inevitably by all impartial minds. I am dissatisfied, and I suppose most men are, with the spirit in which the history of religion in England is generally written. If it is the work of a Churchman, it takes the form of a defence of the Church of England; if by a Nonconformist, it is a defence of nonconformity. And thus a subject which, in proper hands, might be prolific for good, is sacrificed to the glorification of a sect or a party. Even the external facts of history refuse to be thus treated, and much more the thoughts which underlie the facts.

There are two views of Christianity distinctly traceable in the history of the Church. They exist more or less in all systems, and often in the same mind. The one receives its highest expression in the Roman claim to infallibility, the other in Bishop Temple's theory of the education of the human race. All questions of Catholicism and Protestantism, the Church and the Bible, in all their varied forms, are ultimately reducible to these two. Neither of them has yet been pressed to its logical result, and it is only in our day that the full antagonism between them begins distinctly to appear. Both theories suppose the Church and the Bible as in some way divine. The difference is, that the Church of Rome claims to be the infallible and sole medium of the divine communications, while the education theory supposes the Divine Being to have revealed Himself at sundry times and in divers manners to all men. The one supposes the Church to be constituted by the Roman hierarchy. The other makes the Church potentially to be co-extensive with the human race, and actually with all men, under all dispensations, who have followed the teaching of the Divine Spirit. In the natural order the theory of infallibility comes first. It is the earliest human idea of revelation. It is, so to speak, a device of the human mind to satisfy its own craving for absolute certainty. The theory of education is of later origin. It is built on observation of the actual history of revelation. It is the theology of experience. The certainty it gives is only moral, throwing men back upon conscience and trust in God. Infallibility offers a ready solution. The education theory bids us learn our lessons, and patiently wait God's time. The claim to infallibility has never been made good to reason. In fact, it has refuted itself. The Council of Trent appealed to the 'unanimous consent of the Fathers.' It has since been proved that the doctrines of the Church of Rome to-day are not those of the ancient Fathers.* To save the infallibility

---

* This is admitted by Dr. Newman, who sets aside the canon of Vincentius Lirinensis, *quod ubique, quod semper, quod ab omnibus, creditum est*. Of this canon Dr. Newman says it is 'hardly available now, or effective of any satisfactory result.'

of the Church, the most advanced theologians of the Church of Rome have adopted the hypothesis of development or progressive revelation. If this is not in itself a confession of fallibility, a new meaning must be put on the word infallible. The Church of England at the Reformation appealed to the Scriptures. Some of the Reformers, as for instance Bishop Jewel, denied that there was any such thing as 'a universal consent of the Fathers.' The appeal to Scripture alone supposed a revelation given once for all. It supposed Christianity to be the absolute religion. But it also implied a progressive development of the human mind in understanding that religion. In the trial of the question which of the two theories agrees best with the facts of Christianity, the history of all Protestant Churches, and especially of the Church of England, must be brought in evidence. What is the result of three centuries of the Reformation? Is it such as to justify the Reformation, and to determine us to go forward? It is true that our progress has been slow. The principle of the Reformation has been itself retarded by Church theories that have no meaning but on the assumption of infallibility. Yet, though slow our progress has been sure. Some great questions have been thought out exhaustively in England, and the last word on them has been said. The Roman Catholic can only taunt us with our divisions, our diversities of opinion, and the extravagancies of some individuals or of some sects. All these things are admitted. They are necessary stages in our religious history. But when the worst has been said, we can comfort ourselves with the fact, that the most absurd sects of Protestantism have taught nothing more irrational than the dogmas of the Church of Rome. In the very theory of the Divine Being progressively educating the human race, it is implied that there are stages of childhood which we have passed. But the theory of infallibility stereotypes our errors, and makes men children for ever.

This work, then, is intended to be a record of progress. It will show how cautiously, and yet how surely, the naturally conservative English mind has been working out its own religious position. At the Reformation we awoke to a higher sense of duty. All the problems of religion, indeed, are not yet solved, but our position to-day is sufficient to convince us that truth is to be found in the path we have chosen.

If there is anything more to be said here, it is a word concerning the execution of this volume. I can scarcely persuade myself that it is entirely free from errors. Much of it was written from notes made from books that were read at different times and in different places. In some cases I may have misunderstood the authors. But I have done my best, and have tried always to state every argument as clearly as if I had been urging it for something which I myself believed. It may be added, that in no case is the information taken at second-hand.

TABLE OF CONTENTS.

CHAPTER I.

	Page
Transubstantiation the culminating heresy of the Church of Rome	1
The Mass its chief act of worship	1
The gulf between the Church of England and the Church of Rome impassable	2
The English Reformation progressive	2
Early Reformed authors	2
Robert Barnes	2
On justification by faith	3
The Sabbath	3
Passive obedience	3
His definition of the Church	4
John Frith	4
Salvation by faith and not by sacraments	4
Simon Fishe	5
His controversy with Sir Thomas More	5
William Tyndale	5
Not patristic	5
On Christ's kingdom	6
His translation of the New Testament attacked by More	6
His theology Augustinian	7
Rejection of the Papal supremacy in England	8
The Ten Articles	8
A gleam of Protestantism	9
'The Institution of a Christian Man'	9
The Church Catholic defined	9
'A Necessary Doctrine and Erudition of a Christian Man'	10
Faith defined	11
Most advanced Protestantism under Edward VI.	11

TABLE OF CONTENTS.

	Page
The Articles of Religion	12
The First Book of Homilies	12
The question of the Royal supremacy	12
Archbishop Cranmer	13
The civil office as sacred as the ecclesiastical	14
His scheme to unite all the Reformed Churches	14
On faith and works	15
The 'Homily on Good Works'	16
On the Sacraments	17
His great controversy on the Eucharist	17
Christ's body occupies a place in heaven	18
John vi. does not refer to the Eucharist	19
Cranmer's language on the Sacraments sometimes perplexing	19
He appeals to the Fathers	20
Explains from Augustine how figures are to be understood	21
Beseeches his readers not to take his figures literally	22
The spiritual union	22
Christ's body spiritual	23
To eat Christ's flesh is to believe	24
Strong language of the Catechism	24
Zwingle never called the Sacrament a *mere* commemoration	25
No propitiatory sacrifice in the Supper	26
No sacrificing priesthood under the Gospel	27
Bishop Ridley	27
Claims the Fathers as on his side	27
Explains the Sacrament of the Supper	28
In what sense the Sacraments confer grace	29
Bishop Latimer	29
Not disposed to cling to the Fathers	29
Sanctions the Augustinianism of Article XIII.	30
Bishop Hooper	30
Differs from Cranmer and Ridley as to the mode of the Reformation	30
More of an innovator	31
Did not reverence the authority of the Fathers	31
Danger of putting the Sacraments in the place of Christ	32
Agreed with Cranmer as to the divine right of the King to be Governor of the Church	32
John Bradford	33
His extreme Calvinism	33
Explanation of the Sacraments	34

TABLE OF CONTENTS.

	Page
John Bradford—*continued*.	
On the Church Catholic	35
Archdeacon Philpot	35
The Church before Luther	35
Romish doctrine has not the consent of all nations	36
Bishop Bonner and the fat capon	36
Roger Hutchinson	37
Scarcely orthodox	37
Defends the Fathers	37
No proper priest in the new dispensation	38

CHAPTER II.

The Church re-established under Elizabeth	39
The new Bishops oppose the ceremonies	40
Bishop Coverdale	41
His translations from the foreign Reformers	41
Holds that the King is above all Bishops	42
Elizabeth's first Bishops	42
Archbishop Parker renews the correspondence with Calvin	42
Barlow the oldest Protestant Bishop	42
Bishop Jewel	43
His 'Apology for the Church of England'	43
Unity no test of truth	44
The Church of England not built on the Fathers but on the Apostles	45
Rome deserted, because in it the waters of life have failed	45
Jewel Zwinglian	45
He defends Calvin	45
Thomas Becon	46
His plain speaking	46
His Presbyterianism	46
Scruples about dresses and ceremonies partly overcome	47
Sampson and Humphreys	47
Parker enforces conformity	47
Convocation about equally divided as to conformity	48
Rise of the Puritans	48
Thomas Cartwright	49
He is the incarnation of Presbyterianism	49
The Bible its own witness	50

	Page
Thomas Cartwright—*continued*.	
No morality but in the Bible	50
His 'Admonition to Parliament'	50
Complains of the severity of the Bishops	50
The Prayer Book not in harmony with the 'Word'	51
Archbishop Whitgift	52
He answers Cartwright's 'Admonition'	52
Defends the order of the Church	52
Denies that the Puritans were persecuted	53
Opposes popular election of ministers	53
The Church free as to rites and ceremonies	53
Denies that Sacraments confer grace	54
Maintains that some must have authority in the Church	54
No special form of Church government binding on us	55
Cartwright defends ruling elders	55
Deacons not preachers	56
Richard Hooker	57
Gives up the divine origin of Episcopacy	57
Defends the divinity of order	58
The Church free as to its polity	59
Defends rites and ceremonies	59
Added nothing to the answers to the Puritans	60
A Rationalist	60
His disputes at the Temple with Walter Travers	61
Reason first and Scripture next	62
Definition of faith	63
Can a Pagan have saving faith?	63
Justification	64
Romish errors on justification	64
Travers on the 'Discipline'	65
Able reply to Hooker—'The Christian Letter'	65
Hooker said to contradict the XXXIX. Articles	66
Whitgift preferred to Hooker	69
Dr. William Covel's 'Defence of the Ecclesiastical Polity'	69
Dr. John Bridges replies to Travers's 'Discipline'	70
The Martin Marprelate Tracts	71
Martin's Epistles reckoned libels	72
Search for Martin	72
He attacks Whitgift	73
And Aylmer	73
Bishop Aylmer plays bowls on Sunday	74

	Page
The Martin Marprelate Tracts—*continued.*	
Aylmer's 'Harborowe for Faithful and True Subjectes'	75
On Church property	76
Martin Marprelate and Bishop Cooper	77
Cooper's 'Admonition to the People of England'	77
Martin replies to it	79
'The Appellation of John Penry'	82
Dr. Some's 'Godly Treatise'	83
He maintains that heretics ought to be compelled to receive the Catholic faith	84
Martin's 'Dialogue'	85
Bancroft preaches against the Martinists	86
Proclaims the divine right of Episcopacy	86
Four marks of heretics	86
Bancroft's 'Dangerous Positions' and 'Survey of the Pretended Holy Discipline'	87
Thomas Bilson	88
His treatise on the 'Perpetual Government of Christ's Church'	88
Uses the Puritan arguments in defence of Episcopacy	89
The twelve apostles and the seventy disciples	90
Whitgift's Calvinism	91
Calvinism of the Church of England	91
Peter Baro's four propositions	92
The Lambeth Articles	93
Lord Bacon	94
Not an indifferent spectator of the religious world	94
Blames the Puritans	94
And the bishops	95
His Church reforms	96
'The Christian Paradoxes'	96
Philosophy and divinity	97
Final causes and physical causes	97
Faith and reason	98
Revelation to be received, not examined	98
Believes in election	99

APPENDIX TO CHAP. II.—MARTIN MARPRELATE TRACTS:—

'Hay any More Worke for a Cooper?'	100
Martin Junior	101

APPENDIX TO CHAP. II.—*continued*.   Page

    Martin answered by Thomas Nash 102
    'Pappe with an Hatchet' 102
    Martin dead 103
    His epitaphs 104
    'Plaine Percivall' 105
    'A Whip for an Ape' 105
    'Marre-Martin' 106
    'Marre Mar-Martin' 106
    Plays against Martin in St. Paul's 107

CHAPTER III.

The Hampton Court Conference 108
    Discussion on Confirmation 109
    Baptism by laymen 110
    Falling from grace 110
    King James on predestination 111
    And on a preaching ministry 112
Dr. John Rainolds 112
Richard Field's 'Book of the Church' 113
    Object of the work 113
    Donatism of the Church of Rome 114
    What is the Church? 114
    The Church in relation to those outside . . . 115
    The Church visible and invisible 116
    Notes of a true Church 116
    Non-Episcopal Churches included in the Catholic Church . 117
    Errors of the Church of Rome 117
    Orders and order 118
    The Church Catholic 119
The Works of King James 119
    His hatred of Arminianism 120
Dean Overall's 'Convocation Book' 120
    The civil ruler above the bishops 121
    Curious arguments for the divine right of kings . . 122
    Pagans included in the Catholic Church . . . 122
    Christ and His Apostles obeyed their temporal governors . 123
    Orders of the Jewish and Christian Churches compared . 123

TABLE OF CONTENTS. XV

	Page
The Works of Bishop Andrewes	124
A curious explanation of the Real Presence	125
Christ's descent into hell	126
Augustine supposed Hades to be the place of the damned	127
His views adopted by Whitgift	127
Bilson supports him	127
And is answered by Hugh Broughton	127
Christ descended not to hell, but to Sheol	128
Archbishop Abbot	128
On the Church	129
The priesthood not the Church	129
The Church consists of those who hold the faith of Christ	130
The Sabbath controversy	131
Decision of the Hampton Court Conference	131
Dr. Bownd's 'True Doctrine of the Sabbath'	132
Quotes Bullinger as saying, 'The Sabbath came in with the first man, and must go out with the last'	133
The Apostles observed the first day of the week	134
The Jewish Sabbath, or seventh day, to be kept holy	135
Theophilus Brabourne's 'Defence'	135
The change of the seventh day to the first a corruption of Popery	136
Bishop White's answer to Brabourne	136
The Sabbath not from the beginning	137
The first Christians kept two days holy	138
The first day appointed by the Church, which is to be obeyed	138
It gives licence for work and sports on Sunday	138
Sacred days and sacred places	139
Dr. Peter Heylin's 'History of the Sabbath'	140
He argues that the Lord's Day is not an Apostolic institution	140
Jewish Sabbatical superstitions	141
The Church before the Reformation Sabbatarian	141
The Sabbath in Scotland	142
Tithes	143
John Selden's 'History'	143
Tithes among the Jews	144
Among the Gentiles	144
No tithes among the first Christians	144
Sir James Sempil defends the divine right of tithes	145
Archdeacon Tillesley's 'Animadversions on Selden's History of Tithes'	146

TABLE OF CONTENTS.

	Page
Arminianism in the Church of England	146
The five points	147
The Church Calvinistic in the beginning of James's reign	148
Prynne's defence of Calvinism	148
Bishop Davenant opposes Arminianism	149
He admits that predestination implies reprobation	150
Richard Montagu's 'Gagg for the New Gospel'	151
And his 'Appello Cæsarem'	151
Did Peter fall from grace?	151
Bishop Carleton opposes Arminianism	152
All doctrinal Calvinists now called Puritans	152
Carleton holds that the doctrine of Calvin is the ancient Catholic doctrine	153
Augustine on sacramental justification	154
Conference on Montagu's books	155
Charges against them	155
The transubstantiation controversy under James and Charles	156
The real presence in the Eucharist	156
The altars taken down at the Reformation	157
The Vicar of Grantham removes the communion table	157
And causes it to be placed altar-wise	158
Christ instituted the sacrament on a table, not an altar	159
Bishop Williams orders the Grantham table to be placed table-wise	159
Dr. Peter Heylin's 'Coal from the Altar'	159
He asserts that the Lord's Supper was called 'the sacrament of the altar' by the Reformers	160
Bishop Williams replies to Heylin	161
Quotes Bishop Ridley	162
Tables or altars in the primitive Church	162
Heylin's 'Antidotum Lincolniense,'—a reply to Bishop Williams	163
Quotes Irenæus that there are sacrifices in the Christian Church	163
Dr. Pocklington pleads for altars	164
Archdeacon Hakewill replies to Heylin	165
The Eucharist an improper sacrifice	166
'Hoc facite'	166
Aquinas' explanation that 'We have an altar' means Christ's cross, generally received by the Church of England	166
Joseph Mede on sacrifices and altars	167

	Page
The transubstantiation controversy—*continued*.	
The Christian altar and the pagan	168
Archbishop Laud	168
Developes Bancroft's theory of Episcopacy, and unites with it Arminianism and the new doctrine of the real presence	168
His 'Conference with Fisher the Jesuit.'	169
How do we know the Scriptures to be divine?	170
The Spirit's testimony to the Scriptures	170
Tradition of the Church	171
The inspiration of the Church	172
Laud a Puritan reversed	172
Archbishop Ussher	172
Opposes Laud	172
A Calvinist	173
The bishop question	173
Leighton's 'Sion's Plea against Prelacy'	173
Bishop Hall and the Smectymnians	174
Jus divinum, what it means	175
Hall undertakes to prove that Episcopacy is divine	176
Apostolic practice	176
Hall's hatred of the Independents	177
He had to lean on an antiquity younger than the Apostolic age	177
Difference between the Apostles and other ministers	177
Timothy and Titus bishops	178
Testimony of the Fathers to Episcopacy	179
No Church without bishops till the invention of the Geneva 'Discipline'	180
Hall answered by 'Smectymnuus'	180
The Episcopal faction in Scotland	181
The Fathers did not use liturgies	181
No diocesan bishops in the early Church	182
Presbyters can ordain without bishops	183
Timothy and Titus not bishops	184
Jurisdiction of bishops from the King	185
Bishop Hall replies to 'Smectymnuus'	185
Prynne's 'Unbishopping of Timothy and Titus'	186
The Archbishopric of Crete	187
John Milton	188
He replies to Hall and Ussher	188

John Milton—*continued*.

	Page
His contempt of the Fathers	188
Worthlessness of Catholic antiquity	189
He finds Church government in the New Testament	190
His work on Christian doctrine	191
Discards reason	191
Begins with the doctrine *of God*	192
An Arminian	192
An Arian	193
On the Sabbath	194
Advocates polygamy	195
A Baptist	195
A Millenarian	195
Conference at the Dean of Westminster's on innovations	196
Proposed changes in the Prayer Book	197

CHAPTER IV.

The Westminster Assembly of Divines	198
Confession of Faith	199
Light of nature	199
Predestination	200
The civil magistrate	201
The Sabbath	202
The Church	203
The Sacraments	203
Church government	204
The members of the Assembly the average good men of their time	205
William Twisse	206
On the 'Decrees'	206
Cornelius Burges	207
On baptismal regeneration	208
Quotes the foreign Reformers and Hooker for baptismal regeneration	209
Daniel Cawdry	210
His controversies with the Independents	210

	Page
The Westminster Assembly of Divines—*continued*.	
Francis Cheynell	211
Writes against the Socinians	211
Accuses Chillingworth of Socinianism	212
The 'Dissenting Brethren'	212
Their objections to the Presbyterian polity	213
Thomas Goodwin on Independency	214
Independent ministers, channels of grace	215
Independency goes further from Presbyterianism	216
The Savoy 'Declaration'	216
Rise of the Baptists	217
John Smyth baptizes himself	217
The Westminster Assembly's Committee on baptism	218
John Tombes' 'Exercitation about Infant Baptism'	218
Arguments for and against infant baptism	219
Evils arising from it	220
Stephen Marshall's Assembly sermon on infant baptism	221
The first Baptist	222
Infants members of the Church	222
Tombes replies to Marshall	223
Quotes the Fathers	224
Baptism delayed in the early Church	225
The seal of the covenant not to be given to all that are in the covenant	226
Marshall replies to Tombes	227
Athanasius and infant baptism	228
Why baptism was sometimes deferred	228
Tombes disputes publicly with Richard Baxter	229
The Baptist heresies	230
What is the real benefit which children receive from baptism?	231
Dr. Featly's 'Dippers Dipt'	232
Jeremy Taylor's 'Discourse on Baptism'	232
Children saved by baptism	233
The untolerated sects	234
The Family of Love	234
Henry Nicholas, of Amsterdam	235
Made one with the Deity	236
The new era	237
The Quakers	238
Logically descended from the Baptists	238

The untolerated sects—*continued*.   Page
    The Quakers—George Fox 238
    Behmenists 239
    Rosicrucians 240
        Dr. Fludd expounds their doctrines . . . 240
        God and Nature one 240
        The two worlds—aerial and temporal . . . 240
        Spirit the catholic element of the universe . . 241
    The Muggletonians 241
        The dispensation of the Spirit 242
        The 'Two Witnesses' 242
        The 'right devil' 243
    The Fifth Monarchy Men 243
        Oliver Cromwell 'the little horn' 243
        John Tillinghast 244
        Charles Feake 244
        Cromwell overcome by the saints . . . 245
    John Bidle—the first of the English Unitarians . . 245
        Denies the personality of the Holy Ghost . . 246
        The Fathers Platonists 247
The Antinomian Controversy 247
    Danger of the Lutheran doctrine of justification by faith . 248
    Dr. Crisp 249
        The free gift 249
        The elect *made* willing 250
        Danger of Calvinism 250
    John Saltmarsh 251
        Free grace 251
    Richard Baxter's 'Aphorisms of Justification' . . 251
        Censured by Calvinists 252
        His 'Scripture Gospel Defended' . . . 253
    Dr. Daniel Williams undertakes a refutation of Crisp's heresies 253
Leaders of the Independents 254
    Lord Brook 254
    Peter Sterry 254
        His mystical theology 255
    John Howe 256
    John Owen 256
        Against the Arminians 257

Leaders of the Independents—*continued.*   Page

  John Owen—*continued.*

      Pillars of his theology 257
      Attacks Walton's Polyglotta 258
    John Goodwin 259
      Contrasted with Owen 259
      An Arminian 260
      His warfare with the Presbyterians . . . 260
      On the Trinity 261
      God never called a Person in the Scriptures . . 261
      Questions the right of the civil magistrate to interfere in religion 262
      His 'Sion College Visited' 262
      'The Pagan's Debt and Dowry' 263
      Defends the execution of Charles I. . . . 264
      Names the Baptists 'The Brethren of the Dip' . 264

Richard Baxter 265
  Difficult to classify 265
  Professes to be a Calvinist, but explains away Calvinism . 265
  Maintains that man can *know* God 266
  Always on the borders of conformity 266
  His 'Treatise of Episcopacy' 267
  Primitive Episcopacy a bishop for every market town . 268
  'Of National Churches' 269
  The civil ruler the proper head of the Church . . 269
  Three kinds of bishops 270
  The first English writer on the evidences . . . 271
  Definition of faith 272
  Proves by miracles that the Scriptures are a revelation from God 273
  Maintains that the miraculous still existed . . . 274
  Manna in England 274
  Fulfilment of prophecy 275
  Witches 275
  Publishes 'The Unreasonableness of Infidelity' . . 276
  Christians the most rational of men 276
  Power of Christianity 277

CHAPTER V.

	Page
Restoration of Charles II.	278
The King finds the Presbyterians the best upholders of his cause	279
The Presbyterians did not renounce the primitive Episcopacy	279
And are satisfied that there should be a Liturgy	280
The King, in his 'Declaration,' promises great reforms	281
Presbyterians offered bishoprics and deaneries	282
The Savoy Conference	282
The Ministers' exceptions to the Prayer-book	283
Special objections	284
Objections to the Offices	285
The Communion	285
Baptism	286
The Catechism	287
Confirmation	287
The Marriage Service	288
The Order for the Visitation of the Sick	288
The Order for the Burial of the Dead	288
The bishops' answer	289
The Prayer Book defended	289
The 'three nocent ceremonies'	290
The special Objections answered	291
All children to be baptized	292
In the Catechism 'inheritors' means 'heirs'	293
Confirmation not a 'corrupt following of the Apostles'	293
In the Burial of the Dead charity recommended	294
The public disputation	295
Things 'sinful' in the Prayer Book	295
The Prayer Book revised by Convocation	296
Bishop Morton	297
Origin of 'The Book of Sports'	297
His 'Catholic Appeal for Protestants' and 'Institution of the Sacrament'	297
Bishop Cosin	298
Reckoned among Laud's supporters	298
His sermon at the consecration of Bishop White	299
On the Sabbath	299
His 'Scholastical History of the Canon of Holy Scripture'	300
On the history of transubstantiation	301

TABLE OF CONTENTS.   xxiii

	Page
Bishop Cosin—*continued.*	
Quotes the foreign Confessions on the real presence	302
The civil ruler's authority in the Church	303
Ordination by presbyters valid	303
Bishop Walton	304
A 'scandalous minister'	304
His 'Biblia Polyglotta'	305
Defends himself against John Owen	305
His hatred of the sects	306
His reception when made Bishop of Chester	306
His consecration and death	307
Bishop Pearson	307
His 'Exposition of the Creed'	307
Definition of faith	308
And of the Church Catholic	308
On the resurrection of the body	309
Bishop Sanderson	309
Not a Puritan, but a Calvinist	310
On the fourth commandment	310
On the civil ruler	311
Dr. Henry Hammond	312
His controversies with the Presbyterians	312
The 'angels' of the churches were bishops	312
St. John calls himself a 'presbyter'	313
Meaning of 'presbyter' in the primitive Church	314
Primacy of Diotrephes	314
The Apostles were bishops	314
The 'angel' addressed as a plurality of persons	315
The seven 'angels' the metropolitans of Asia	316
Christian polity copied from Jewish polity	317
Only bishops and deacons in the early Church	317
Meaning of the word 'bishop'	318
And of the word 'presbyter'	318
Testimony of antiquity to Episcopacy	319
Hammond also engages in the controversy on infant baptism	319
Rests it on the Jewish baptism of infants	320
Baptism a memory of the Deluge	320
Instruction not necessary before baptism	321
Children of believers holy	321
Regeneration in baptism only external	322

	Page
Herbert Thorndike	322
His treatise on 'The Right of the Church in a Christian State'	322
Erastianism of the Long Parliament	323
Church and State connection	323
The origin of the civil ruler's authority in matters ecclesiastical	324
Thorndike's theory of Church and State that of the Presbyterians	324
Distinction between ecclesiastical power and power in ecclesiastical matters	325
The Conformist followed the Puritan in declaring the independence of the Church	326
Archbishop Bramhall	327
Calvinism of the Church of Ireland	328
Bramhall succeeds in getting the Irish Convocation to adopt the XXXIX. Articles	329
Defences of the Church of England	329
What is schism?	330
Schism a *culpable* separation	331
Roman Catholic bishops decreed Henry VIII. 'head of the Church'	331
The Reformation a vindication of our ancient rights	332
Kings of England before Henry VIII. ruled the Church in England	332
Bishop Hopkins	333
On the effect of the death of Christ	333
On baptismal regeneration	333
Jeremy Taylor	334
'The Liberty of Prophesying'	334
There is room in heaven for men of different opinions	335
Heresy an error of the will, not of the intellect	335
How men were called heretics in the early ages	336
'Heretic' only a name to frighten people	336
The development of opinions into heresies	336
Uncertainty of the meaning of the Scriptures should make men tolerant	337
Donatists' interpretations of Scripture	338
Traditional interpretations of Scripture worthless	338
Even tradition of customs contradictory	339
Apostolic traditions now disregarded	339

TABLE OF CONTENTS.

Jeremy Taylor—*continued*.   Page
   Influence of Augustine made doctrines 'Catholic' . . . 340
   Taylor a Rationalist 340
   A semi-Pelagian 341
   His 'Doctrine and Practice of Repentance' . . . 341
   Nature and grace 341
   The law and the gospel 342
   Works necessary as well as faith 342
   Men do not suffer death for Adam's sin 343
   Passages supposed to teach original sin explained . . 344
   Art. IX. explained 344
   Concupiscence is not sin 345
   On Episcopacy 345
   Church government must be in the New Testament . 345
   Bishops in the church of Antioch 346
   On Confirmation 347
   Baptism does not give the Holy Ghost 347
   On 'The Real Presence' 348
   Christ only present in spirit 349
   John vi. does not refer to the Eucharist . . . 349
   John Gaule and Henry Jeanes reply to Taylor on original sin 349
   Jeanes' 'Of Original Righteousness and its Contrary Concupiscence' 350
   Original righteousness something positive . . . 351
   What it is, explained 351
   Is sin natural or accidental to man's nature? . . . 352

Liberty of Conscience literature 353
   Taylor's 'Liberty of Prophesying' 353
   Liberty of conscience always most ardently pleaded for by those to whom it was denied 353
   Samuel Rutherford replies to Taylor 353
   Conscience not man's guide 354
   The Bible and the Church must overrule the conscience 354
   The Church infallible when it declares truth . . 354
   The Church has power to determine what is heresy . 355
   Mental blindness to be punished 356
   Heresy not an innocent error 357
   Toleration implies a sceptical spirit as to revelation . 357
   The magistrate to punish heretics 357
   The meaning of Scripture not uncertain . . . 358

TABLE OF CONTENTS.

Liberty of Conscience literature—*continued*.   Page
    Leonard Busher's 'Plea for Liberty of Conscience' . . 358
    His 'Reasons against Persecution' 359
    'The Ancient Bounds'—an early plea for liberty of conscience 360
    Idolatry not to be tolerated 360
Two theological writers outside ecclesiastical circles . . 361
    Sir Thomas Browne 361
        A half-reasoning, half-believing Christian . . 362
        Does not allow himself to be a heretic . . . 363
        Followed faith or reason just as he fancied . . 363
        On predestination 363
        The book of nature 364
        A believer, after all 365
        And only a philosopher by fits 365
    Sir Matthew Hale 365
        On 'The Origination of Mankind' 366

CHAPTER VI.

Rational theologians 368
John Hales of Eton 369
    Bids 'good night to John Calvin' 370
    On the Lord's Supper 370
    Receives Cranmer's doctrine, but refuses Cranmer's speech . 371
    Crude speeches of the Reformers about the Lord's Supper . 371
    The 'keys' 372
    On schism 372
    On the kingdom of Christ 373
    Not the visible Church 373
    On the Scriptures 374
William Chillingworth 374
    A Rationalist from his youth 375
    Seeks rest in the Church of Rome, and does not find it . 375
    His controversy with Knott the Jesuit . . . 376
    'The Religion of Protestants a Safe Way to Salvation' . 376
    The Church Catholic and the Church of Rome . . 377
    On faith 377
    The Christian life one of the facts of Christianity . . 378

TABLE OF CONTENTS.

	Page
William Chillingworth—*continued.*	
What is the rule or judge of controversies?	378
We must always begin with reason	379
Scripture a rule, not a judge	379
If a rule be plain, a guide is unnecessary	380
Hooker on reason and the Bible	381
The Bible a safe rule without the Church	381
The Roman Catholic must begin with reason as well as the Protestant	382
Protestants are not heretics	382
Thomas Hobbes of Malmesbury	383
A professed believer in Christianity	383
Was Hobbes sincere?	384
Traces the origin of all things to motion	384
The 'Leviathan'	385
The King is God's vicar	385
His laws constitute right and wrong	386
Hobbes' Commonwealth ideal	387
The King prescribes religion and determines canonical writings	387
Bishops are bishops by the grace *not of God but of the King*	388
The sectaries, who worship God according to conscience, are rebels against the Commonwealth	388
Cases in which the sovereign may not be obeyed	389
The Kingdom of Darkness	390
The Pope reigns over it	390
How far Hobbes is orthodox	391
Hobbes and Bishop Pearson	392
How far Hobbes is rational	392
Criticism of the Old Testament	393
How a prophet was to be known	394
On miracles	394
Endless punishment denied	395
The Devil not a person	395
Deliverance from sin	396
The 'Leviathan' a great world of rational theology	396
The light of nature	397
God not personal	398
Nor incorporeal	398
The consubstantiality of mind and matter	399

Thomas Hobbes of Malmesbury—*continued.*

	Page
Cowley's praise of Hobbes' philosophy	399
Lord Clarendon replies to Hobbes	400
Charges Hobbes with writing in favour of Cromwell	401
Archbishop Tenison replies to Hobbes	402
Denies that a thing is made just by God's doing it	403
Archbishop Bramhall replies to Hobbes	403
Calls the 'Leviathan' atheistical	404
Recommends Hobbes to try his government among the savages in America	404
Samuel Clarke replies to Hobbes	405
Also, Bishop Parker	405
He produces arguments in proof of the divine origin of Christianity	406
'The True Effigies of the Monster of Malmesbury'	407
William Pike, Alexander Ross, and Dr. Eachard, on the 'Leviathan'	408
Beneficial influence of the 'Leviathan'	409
Hobbes contradicts his own doctrine by acknowledging laws natural, immutable, and eternal	410

The Cambridge Platonists 410

Dr. Cudworth 410

His 'Treatise concerning Eternal and Immutable Morality'	411
The ancient sceptics said that morality was made by the State	412
Even the will of God cannot make anything contrary to what it is by reason	413
The sceptical moralists among the ancients were also sceptical as to being	414
Reason converses with realities	414
Cudworth's Discourse on the Lord's Supper	415

Henry More 416

Puts on reason as the 'sacerdotal breastplate'	416
Christianity is the only religion which appeals to reason	416
His 'Antidote to Atheism'	417
Superstition begets Atheism	417
Man has an idea in his mind of *what* God is	418
The properties of spirit as intelligible as those of body	418
On the 'Immortality of the Soul'	419

TABLE OF CONTENTS. xxix

	Page
Cambridge Platonists—*continued*.	
Henry More—*continued*.	
On the 'Mystery of Godliness'	419
Mystery defined	420
Plato's Trinity	420
Bishop Wilkins	421
On natural religion	421
Arguments for the existence of Deity	422
Universal belief the result of a universal cause	423
The world had a beginning	423
Duties of natural religion	423
Religion profitable for the life that now is and for that which is to come	424
Can men be saved by natural religion?	425
John Smith	426
His discourse 'Concerning the True Way or Method of Attaining to Divine Knowledge'	426
Divinity a divine life rather than a divine science	426
Truth is known by a faculty within us	427
Four sorts of men	428
Smith's discourse on 'Superstition'	428
Superstition defined as a perversion of the religious instinct	429
His discourse on the 'Immortality of the Soul'	429
Every good man feels that his soul is immortal	430
The resurrection body spiritual and not material	431
Benjamin Whichcot	431
The greatest preacher of the Cambridge school	431
Shaftesbury's preface to Whichcot's Sermons	431
Is goodness eternal, or only constituted by authority?	432
Natural goodness the essence of true religion	432
Virtue brings naturally its own reward, and vice its own punishment	433
Christianity to be tested by reason	434
Truth of two kinds	434
Revealed religion as well as natural is self-evidencing	435
We are not ashamed of the gospel, because it is rational	436
The inseparability of goodness and blessedness, of vice and misery	437
Preaching Christ defined	437
Superstitions connected with the Sacraments	438

	Page
Bishop Cumberland	439
His treatise 'De Legibus Naturæ' in reply to Hobbes	439
Which has the greater certainty, revelation external or internal?	440
Lord Herbert of Cherbury	441
His theology a philosophy	442
The divine love must be universal	443
Five articles of natural religion	444
There is one God	445
He is to be worshipped	445
Chief part of divine worship is virtue joined with piety	445
Repentance a natural duty	446
Rewards and punishments	446
The Gentiles have the law written in their hearts	446
They knew the essential parts of the Christian religion	447
And did not look upon death with terror	448
Religion always corrupted by the priests	449
Herbert does not deny external revelation	450
Has a revelation vouchsafed to him regarding the publication of 'De Veritate'	450
The revelation within has stronger evidence than the external revelation	451
John Locke disputes Herbert's doctrine of *innate ideas*	452
'On the Reasonableness of Christianity'	453
The law of faith	454
Faith defined	454
Can the heathen be saved?	455
Locke on the atonement	455
Thomas Halyburton replies to Lord Herbert	455
Denies that we are judges of what is just in God	456
Daniel Whitby on the necessity of revelation	456
The darkness of Paganism	457
Impurity of Pagan worship	458
Christianity a republication of natural religion with articles of faith added	459
Richard Baxter replies to Lord Herbert	460
Admits that Pagans may be saved	460
On the Scriptures	461
A man may believe one part of the Bible to be God's word and not another part	461
Can Pagans be said to believe?	462

Lord Herbert of Cherbury—*continued.* Page
    The craving for supernatural evidence 463
    No religion is true if the Christian is false 464
    The excellency of the Christian religion its great evidence . 464

APPENDIX.

(A) Theological writings not mentioned in the text . . . 465
(B) The Bishops from 1530 to 1660 468

CHAPTER I.

TRANSUBSTANTIATION.—THE DIFFERENCE BETWEEN THE CHURCH OF ENGLAND AND THE CHURCH OF ROME, NO NARROW INTERVAL.—REFORMATION PROGRESSIVE.—BARNES.—FRITH.—TYNDALE.—DOCTRINAL DOCUMENTS.—CRANMER.—RIDLEY.—LATIMER.—HOOPER.—BRADFORD.—PHILPOT.—HUTCHINSON.

'TRANSUBSTANTIATION (or the change of the substance of bread and wine) in the Supper of the Lord cannot be proved by Holy Writ; but is repugnant to the plain words of Scripture, overthroweth the nature of a Sacrament, and hath given occasion to many superstitions.' The Reformers of the Church of England were guided by a rare instinct when they fastened on Transubstantiation as the culminating heresy of the Church of Rome. This was at once an appeal to reason, and to the Scriptures as interpreted by reason. The change of the substance of bread and wine was a continual miracle which the Church of Rome professed to perform. To disbelieve this change was to distrust the infallibility of the Church, which involved necessarily a rejection of its authority to teach any doctrine not agreeable to Scripture and reason. *The culminating heresy of the Church of Rome.*

In the Church of Rome the Sacrifice of the Mass is the chief act of worship. For this the priesthood exists,—for this the Church exists. If the body and blood of Christ are not really present on the altar, there is no true and proper sacrifice for the priest to make. It follows from this, that there is no true and proper priest,—no true and proper altar. The Church, the ministry, the sacraments *The Mass the chief act of worship in the Church of Rome.*

must be differently regarded the moment we deny a real, that is an actual, presence of the body and blood of Christ.*

The gulf between the Church of England and the Church of Rome impassable.

That the difference between the Reformers and the Church of Rome was no narrow interval, but a great and impassable gulf, was felt and acknowledged by both sides. It was not a mere difference in detail. The first principles from which they started were not the same. The doctors of the Church of Rome still recognized in the Church an infallible authority to which their judgments must yield. The Reformers rejected the living voice, and limited their creed to what was clearly taught in the Canonical writings. In interpreting these writings, they might be guided merely by the individual reason, or they might call to their assistance the judgment of ancient bishops and Fathers; but, in either case, they had separated widely from those who receive implicitly whatever the Church, professing infallibility, agrees to publish as the true teaching of Christianity.

English Reformation progressive.

It was a peculiarity of the Reformation in England that it was gradual. The conservative principle was strong even with those who, in the course of events, became the leaders of the Reformation. The tide of Protestantism rose high before it reached the high places of the Church. Obscure monks and priests, who had perhaps read the works of Wickliffe, or visited Luther in Germany, were marked out as teaching the Reformed doctrines, but as yet these doctrines were far away from the palaces of the King or the bishops; the teachers of them were in exile or in hiding-places, from which they were dragged forth only to receive the martyrs' crown.

Early Reformed authors.

The most eminent of these early Reformers and martyrs, that is, those of them whose writings exist to our times, were Robert Barnes, John Frith, and William Tyndale. The first was prior of an Augustinian Convent in Cambridge.

---

* Dr. Pusey in the *Eirenicon* says that our Article rejects, not the Transubstantiation explained by the Council of Trent, but that of the schoolmen, who said that the bread and wine lost the nourishing qualities natural to them. The Council of Trent affirmed that these qualities remained. The change is not material or natural, but 'hyperphysical.' The 'accidents' remain, and under this word 'accidents' the Church of Rome, according to Dr. Pusey, includes all that we mean by substance. This is very ingenious, but, unfortunately, it was not known at the time of the Reformation.

He had learned the Lutheran doctrine of justification by faith only, and with it the Augustinian views of election, which he held with such logical strictness as to deny that man had any free-will except to do evil. This doctrine of faith he placed in opposition to the *opus operatum* of the Church. Men were to be saved by faith, and not in virtue of the act of the priest. 'Good works,' he said, 'shall be rewarded, but the reward is not the forgiveness of sins. The doers of the law shall be justified, but justification precedes their doings. God justifies His elect, and good works follow as the fruit.'

Justification by faith.

Barnes gave offence to the authorities of the Church by a sermon which he preached in St. Edward's, Cambridge. It was directed against what he regarded as a superstitious observance of days. It referred in the first instance to the supposed sanctity of Christmas Day; but Barnes apparently took the wide ground that all days are alike, including the weekly Sabbath. He maintained that the old command to the Jews, 'Thou shalt observe thy holiday,' was not binding on Christians. He quoted St. Augustine and St. Jerome, as teaching that the Jewish Sabbath was ended. Augustine even calls those Antichrist who say that it is not lawful to work on Sabbath or Sunday. Barnes's argument was not that all days are profane, but that all days are sacred. Christ was born every day. Every day He rose again. Every day He ascended into heaven. The 'Supplication' which he addressed to the King begins with a condemnation of the Church of Rome for claiming to have power over kings to depose them at its will. The king is above the Church. Even wicked kings are to be obeyed. John the Baptist was subject to Herod, and Jesus did not refuse obedience to Pilate. This doctrine was among the articles for which Barnes was condemned. With this he was safe. But he objected to the power and jurisdiction which were possessed by the bishops. He denied that they were an order distinct from presbyters. He said that the Apostolic rule was a bishop for every city. The present bishops professed to be the successors of the Apostles, but the only Apostle whom they followed was Judas. Barnes described them as making merchandise of their sacred offices, wearing mitres

Robert Barnes and the Sabbath.

Passive obedience.

glistening with precious stones, and so luxurious that they had their hands gloved even in the midst of the ceremonies. He defined the Church as the congregation assembled for worship, and again as the glorious Church invisible, which is made clean by the blood of Christ. This was the Church which could not err. His description of the visible Church is almost in the words which were afterwards incorporated into the Articles of Religion. The Church is where 'the word of God is sincerely preached, and the sacraments orderly administered after the blessed ordinance of Christ.' To the Church are committed the *keys*, that is, the ministers preach the mercy of God, and declare forgiveness to them that believe. To preach the word of God is to open heaven. All the members of the Church have the power of the keys, for the Church is built on the confession of the true faith. The members of the Church give to the ministers the exercise of this power, and those who give it can also take it away.

The history of John Frith will ever be remembered, because of the part which Cranmer took in procuring his condemnation and execution. He had embraced the rational views of the sacraments that had been taught by Zwingle. He reasoned that if the body of Christ ascended into heaven, it could not be in the Eucharist, for it was impossible for a body to be in more places than one at one time. Christ is present in the Eucharist, as He was present in the wilderness, when the old fathers did eat His flesh and drink His blood as we do now. They were spiritually nourished by Him. To them that believed He was the bread of life. Frith complained that the error prevailing in his day was too much trust in the outward signs, as if by them was accomplished what could only be done by faith. He denies that the sign gives the Spirit of God or grace. Those that come rightly to baptism have grace already. The ordinance is a witness that they are in a state of grace. The life of a true Christian is a continual baptism. One result of attaching so much importance to the outward sacrament, was the consigning of unbaptized infants to everlasting pain. The difference, according to Frith, did not depend on the mere outward act of baptism, but on our election of

God. Those whom God has chosen He saves by means of faith which He works in them, and not by means of sacraments. No man can be saved without faith, but a man may be saved without baptism.

The 'Supplication of the Beggars,' written by Simon Fishe, led to a controversy about Purgatory. It was answered by Sir Thomas More in his 'Supplication of Souls.' Fishe contrasted the wealth of the monks with the poverty of the multitudes in London, and recommended that the money spent for Souls in Purgatory should be applied to the relief of the destitute. Sir Thomas More represented the Souls in Purgatory lamenting that there was so little faith in the earth, that the relief of destitute bodies should be placed before that of suffering souls. He argued, too, for the necessity of the existence of Purgatory, from the fact that men's sufferings in this life are not sufficient to make satisfaction for their sins. At this point John Frith took up the controversy. With the doctrine of the sufficiency of Christ's atonement, and that faith alone was necessary to receive it, he had a full answer to More's objections. The true Purgatory, he said, is the word of God. Christ makes His Church clean by His word. Faith is the Purgatory of the heart. To take away our infirmities, God nails us to the cross of Christ.

William Tyndale is even better known than Barnes or Frith. His translation of the Bible was the groundwork of that version which was completed under King James, and which is still the authorized version of the Church of England. Tyndale was a thorough Protestant. To him the Church of Rome was the thick darkness, and his only hopes of dissipating it were in the dissemination of the Scriptures. For the Fathers he had no reverence. They had taken liberties with the Scriptures, and prepared the way for their being set aside by the Church of Rome. To the Fathers we owe the senses 'tropological,' 'allegorical,' and 'anagogical,' —twenty doctors expounding one text in twenty ways, as if the only use of the Bible was for men to weave out of it ingenious allegories. 'Understand,' says Tyndale, 'Scripture has but one sense, which is the literal one.' On the sacraments, he avoids the rhetorical and questionable language of the Fathers.* He classes the prelates with the supporters of Antichrist. He calls Confirmation a 'dumb ceremony,' one of 'the rabble of ceremonies' which the bishops had set up, instead of preaching the plain text of God's law. He regarded the laying on of hands as a thing indifferent,—a custom of the Jews, but not necessarily connected with the gift of the Holy Spirit.

On some of the practical questions which were eagerly discussed at a later time, Tyndale has expressed his judgment. Christ's kingdom not being of this world, he thought the officers of the Church should not hold offices of state. A minister of religion, he said, should never be a magistrate, for it is incongruous to his office that he should enforce a law of violence. The King, however, is judge over all. He is God's vicar, responsible to none but God. We are not to judge the King, nor to resist him, for that is to resist God. He is without law, and may do right or wrong, for he is to be judged at another tribunal than ours. This exaltation of the civil ruler had a meaning which it has not to us. The Reformers looked to the King as their only hope of deliverance from the supremacy of the Pope.

When Tyndale published his translation of the New Testament, he found an opponent in Sir Thomas More, who objected not only to his founding the Church on the Bible, but to several words used in the translation. As Tyndale identified the Scriptures with the word of God, he had to show that the Church was begotten by the word. More, on the other hand, had the historical fact that the Church did exist, not indeed before the word, but before the word was written. Tyndale, agreeing with Barnes and Frith about the identity of bishops and presbyters, translated the Greek word for presbyters as 'elders.' They were so called, he said, for their gravity; and, because of their office of overseers, they were called bishops. The word usually translated Church he rendered 'congregation.' The clergy, he said, had appropriated to themselves the term

---

* Here is an illustration of the effects of baptism, 'As a preacher, in preaching the Word of God, saveth the hearers that believe; so doth the washing, as that it preacheth, representeth unto us the promise that God hath made unto us in Christ.'—*Doctrinal Treatises*, Par. Soc. Ed. p. 253.

which by right belonged to all Christians. The visible Church or congregation was fallible, but the elect Church was that which could not err.

The rest of Tyndale's theology is of the darkest kind of Augustinianism, with but few gleams of light. Through the fall of Adam we are all, he says, heirs of the vengeance of God by nature and by birth, even 'in our mothers' wombs we had fellowship with the damned devils.'* It is our nature to sin, as it is that of a serpent to sting. Out of this state of sin and condemnation God has appointed some to eternal life; and when the Gospel is preached, the Spirit enters into these, opens their eyes, and works faith in them. He again compares men by nature to 'wild crab-trees,' of which God chooseth whom He will, and plants them in the garden of His mercy. Consistently with this view of the limitation of the Divine mercy, Tyndale condemns the idea of men working in order to obtain the Divine forgiveness. We are to do what is right without reference to reward, for this alone is true goodness; and we are not to work because of the reward, for that comes not by our merit, but by the free gift in our election. They that are chosen do good, so to speak, spontaneously. It becomes their nature, as it was at first their nature to sin. Of those doctors who make good works necessary to salvation, Tyndale says that they ascribe that to good works which belongs solely to Christ.† The Spirit of God works only in the chosen, and these, as we understand Tyndale, are to be found only among Christians. The moral virtues of the Pagans are declared to be even worse than their sins.‡

---

* Tyndale is sometimes impetuous. His mind was unequal. It wanted logical precision. This exposed him to the criticism of his enemies. But he was simple, earnest, and devout. If his logic is often bad, and his theology sometimes repulsive, they are redeemed by passages that savour of the sincerest piety, such as this, 'Prayer is a moving, a longing, and a desire of the spirit God-ward for that which it lacketh; as a sick man mourneth and soroweth in the heart, longing for health. Faith ever prayeth.'

† Tyndale says of all the schoolmen, they 'agree that no man is saved by Christ but by holy works.' This was an inference which might have been turned against himself. It might have been said Tyndale believed that no man is saved by Christ but only by faith.

‡ 'Thou mayest hereby perceive, that all that is done in the world before the Spirit of God come, and giveth us light, is damnable sin; and the more glorious, the more damnable; so that that which the world counteth most glorious is more damnable in the sight of God, than that which the whore, the thief, or the murderer do.' This is illustrated by the case of Lucretia, who,

CHAP. I.

Rejection of the Papal supremacy in England.

King Henry's quarrel with the Pope was the accidental means of the Reformed doctrines finding favour with the dignitaries of the Church. The King threw off the Papal supremacy, and in this he was supported by all the bishops except Fisher, of Rochester. Some of the bishops were disposed for further reformation, but the rest of them as to doctrine were as much Roman Catholic as they had ever been.* From the time of the rejection of the supremacy of the Pope down to the end of the reign of Edward, we have, in public documents and authorized formularies, the history of all the doctrinal changes from Roman Catholicism to the most advanced expression of Protestantism that the Church of England has ever made. The first of these is the ten articles concerning religion which the King enjoined to be taught by all bishops and preachers.† The object of these articles was to secure unity and quietness among the bishops, for in some of them the leaven of the Reformation had already begun to appear, and all of them had been instrumental in substituting the supremacy of the King for that of the Bishop of Rome. In these articles there is an implicit consciousness that the ground is changed. The King prescribes to the bishops the Bible and the three Creeds as the only source of doctrine and foundation of their faith, calling them the 'infallible words of God.' Those who denied this were declared to be 'members of the devil, with whom they shall perpetually be damned.' The sacrament of Baptism was held necessary to attain everlasting life,—children dying without it could not be saved. Confession to a priest, or the second part of Penance, was declared necessary when it could

The ten articles.

---

in her chastity, sought her own glory, and not God's.'— *Par. Soc. Ed.* p. 183.

Again, Tyndale says, 'Serve God as He hath appointed thee, and not with any good intent or good zeal. Remember Saul was cast away of God for ever for his good intent. God requireth obedience unto His word, and abhorreth all good intents and good zeals which are without God's word.'—*Ibid.* p. 330.

* The leaders on the Protestant side were—
Cranmer, Archbishop of Canterbury.
Goodrich, Bishop of Ely.
Shaxton, Bishop of Sarum.
Latimer, Bishop of Worcester.
Fox, Bishop of Hereford.
Hisley, Bishop of Rochester.
Barlow, Bishop of St. David's.

On the other side were—
Lee, Archbishop of York.
Stokesley, Bishop of London.
Tonstal, Bishop of Durham.
Gardiner, Bishop of Winchester.
Longland, Bishop of Lincoln.
Sherburne, Bishop of Chichester.
Kite, Bishop of Carlisle.

† The title of this document is, 'Articles Devised by the King's Highness,' etc. 1536.

be had, for, by the appointment of Christ, the absolution of the priest was the application of God's promises to the penitent. The words of the priest pronouncing absolution were 'the very words and voice of God Himself, as if He should speak unto us out of Heaven.' The third part of Penance was also declared necessary, that the penitent perform external works of charity and mercy. Transubstantiation was left unchanged. A gleam of Protestantism seemed to fall over the doctrine of justification. It was declared that though contrition, faith, and good works are necessary to the attainment of everlasting life, yet they do not merit salvation. We might pray to saints so long as it could be done without superstition, or so long as we did not think them more merciful than Christ. Images might be erected in churches, especially those of Christ and 'our Lady.' It is, however, allowed that circumstances may arise when it is lawful to destroy them, as we find in the Old Testament. We may pray for the dead, and offer Masses for the repose of their souls, but we do not know where they are. The articles end with a protest against the Bishop of Rome's pardons, the abuses that go under the name of Purgatory, and the supposed value of Masses said at *Scala Cœli*.

Next year, 1537, the bishops published 'The Institution of a Christian Man.' In this book the King's articles were incorporated almost without a change. Besides an exposition of the Apostles' Creed, the seven Sacraments, ten Commandments, *Paternoster* and *Ave Maria*, there is a definition of faith, as 'that singular gift of God, whereby our hearts, that is to say, our natural reason and judgment, is lightened and purified.' The 'faith' apparently refers to certain articles that are to be believed. The descent of Christ into hell is to be interpreted that He went there to 'deliver from thence all the souls of those righteous and good men which, from the time of Adam, died in the favour of God.'

The ascended Christ is declared to be the only Mediator between God and man, and the only Intercessor for them that believe. The most significant part of 'The Institution of a Christian Man' is the definition of a Church, and especially the Church Catholic. As to the King, it is determined that, though he be an overlooker of priests and bishops, he is yet not to 'preach, or teach, or administer sacraments, not to absolve or excommunicate.' The Church is taken in the twofold sense of visible and invisible. Sometimes all who are christened are called the Church, and sometimes only those who are 'chosen and ordained to reign with Christ.' The Catholic Church is 'the elect and faithful people of Christ.' They are 'the temple and habitation of God, the pure and undefiled spouse of Christ, His very mystical body.' With the members of this body there have ever been mixed evil and wicked people; so long as these are not excommunicated, they are accounted of the body. 'Catholic' is defined as that which 'cannot be coarcted or restrained within the limits of any one town, city, province, region, or country, but is spread and dispersed universally throughout the whole world.' The Church of Rome and all other Churches make one spiritual unity, which is founded on faith, hope, and charity, with agreement as to the right doctrine of Christ, and the uniform use of the sacraments.

'A Necessary Doctrine and Erudition.'

In 1543, the King set forth 'A Necessary Doctrine and Erudition of a Christian Man.' This was identical with the 'Institution,' if we except 'A Declaration of Faith' which was prefixed, and two articles added, one on 'Free Will,' and another on 'Good Works.' This book is supposed to be less Protestant than its predecessors. Collyer says that 'it manages with less latitude than the "Institution;" bends to the Six Articles,* and, in some points of controversy, drives further into the doctrines of the Roman communion.' Strype's judgment is different. He says that, 'in the former book, devotion to images, honouring of saints, and praying to images, Masses for the dead, and various Popish rites and ceremonies were commanded and enforced; in this book they spoke more dubiously and warily of, or rejected them; and so for Purgatory, which made one great article in the former book, at the end of it,—it is in this quite left out.' Between the two books there is not much to choose; Strype's view is, on the whole, the more correct, but the historian of facts is rarely to be trusted when he writes of doctrines.

* The 'Six Articles' of 1539 intervene between the 'Institution' and the 'Necessary Doctrine.' They are purely Roman Catholic, maintaining transubstantiation, communion in one kind only, forbidding priests to marry, enjoining clerical celibacy, private masses, and auricular confession.

Strype is wrong in saying that the article on Purgatory is left out in the 'Necessary Erudition.' The title is changed into that 'Of Prayer for Departed Souls,' but the article itself remains unchanged. The prefixed article on 'Faith' is not different in substance, but fuller in its teaching than what appeared in the 'Institution.' Faith is presented under two aspects; the second is that lively faith which is joined with hope and charity. It is identified with the faith described in the eleventh chapter of the Epistle to the Hebrews. The first is simply belief in itself. It is described as a persuasion wrought in man's heart that there is a God, and that the words and sayings of Scripture are infallible truth. It is the belief of what was taught by the Apostles, and confirmed by the universal consent of the Church. 'Here man leaneth not to his natural knowledge which is by reason, but leaneth to the knowledge of faith, as Isaiah saith—"unless ye believe ye shall not understand."' The passage from Isaiah is according to the reading in the Vulgate. It is remarkable that the first rather than the second kind of faith is regarded as 'the gift of God,' and this seems still more strange, when we read further on, that the promises of God are made *on condition* of our believing certain articles of faith. *Good Works* are declared necessary in order to justification. We must bring forth fruit, and yet we are not justified because of the merit of our works, for remission of sins is the gift of God. The article on Free Will is Augustinian, but temperate. It ends with the admonition that preachers are neither so 'to preach the grace of God that they thereby take away free-will, nor on the other side, so to extol free-will that injury be done to the grace of God.'*

CHAP. I.

Faith defined.

In the reign of Edward the doctrines of the Reformers were triumphant in the Church of England. The Prayer Book of 1552, revised with the assistance of Bucer, was more Protestant than any of its predecessors. To this reign, also,

Most advanced Protestantism under Edward.

---

* It has been maintained in our day that all, even the earliest of these documents, are still binding on the Church. If this can be proved, we may get back to the nearest possible point of contiguity with the Church of Rome without being of it. The Reformers and their successors never seem to have imagined that the later formularies did not supersede those that went before.

CHAP. I.

The Articles of Religion.

we owe the Articles of Religion, afterwards reduced from forty-two to thirty-nine,* and drawn almost entirely, as is confessed on all sides, from the Confessions of the Reformed Churches in Germany. To the same date belongs the first book of Homilies. These are not remarkable for any definite statements of doctrine. The authors of them were of widely different sentiments.† From the words of David to Absalom the doctrine of passive obedience is enjoined on all subjects who wish to be good Christians. The King is the anointed—God's lieutenant and vicegerent, whose will we may not in any case resist. It is worth noticing that in the homily on reading the Scripture, it is said that 'in it is *contained* God's true word.' The use of this expression is not frequent in any of the official documents of this era. King Henry, as we have seen, pronounced the Bible, along with the three Creeds, to be 'the infallible words of God.'

Homilies.

The Bible contains *God's word.*

The royal supremacy the most urgent practical question.

At the time of the Reformation, the first question, and practically the most urgent, was that of the royal supremacy. It might seem a matter of little importance whether the Church in England was under the supremacy of the King or the Bishop of Rome. And an indifferent matter it did appear to many of the bishops in King Henry's time; for though the assertion of the royal supremacy was the first step in the Reformation, it did not seem to imply the necessity of separation from the Roman See. But ere the Reformation had far progressed, it was manifest that it involved the wide question of what constitutes a Church. Jurisdiction in all that concerned the temporalities of the Church might be

---

* Archbishop Parker expunged four of the original articles, viz. '10th,' '16th,' '19th,' '41st,' and added four, viz. the present '5th,' '12th,' '19th,' '30th.' The Convocation made further alterations. They erased the latter part of the original third article, the whole of the '39th,' '40th,' and '42nd.' The first of the four expunged was on the will. It was against those who entirely denied the freedom of the will. The next was on the 'Blasphemy against the Holy Ghost,' which was described as 'railing upon the truth of God's word manifestly perceived.' The third was on the law of Moses, declaring the ceremonial law to be ended, but the moral to be still binding. The last was against the Millenarians. The latter part of Article III. was on Christ's 'ghost departing from Him,' and being with the 'ghosts' that were in prison.' Art. XXXIX. was against those who said that the resurrection is past already. Art. XL. was against those who said the soul slept till the resurrection of the body; and Art. XLII. against those who believed in the ultimate salvation of all men.

† Dr. Corrie says that the Homily on Charity was written by Bishop Bonner.

yielded to the King, but if the Church is not built on St. Peter and continued by his successors, the Bishops of Rome, on what is it built, and in whom is it continued? The Reformers had to answer this question, not solely to defend their position, but in order to take up a position at all. In England the question had two well-defined answers. One was that derived from the Reformed Churches on the Continent, that a Church is constituted by men holding Christian doctrines and living Christian lives. Such a community will govern itself by what external forms are most suitable for the time and place in which it exists. The second answer was Cranmer's, which differed from the first only by resting the government of the Church in the King. The State was reckoned the best judge as to what forms of religion would be most suitable to control and develop the spiritual life of the nation. The Reformed Church of England thus became, so far as Cranmer represents it, an Episcopal Church, of which, however, the head is not the bishops, but the civil ruler.

CHAP. I.

Cranmer.

The royal supremacy, in the first instance, was simply a declaration of independence. The King did not mean it for more, neither did those of the bishops who took the oath of supremacy, and yet opposed the Reformation. But with Cranmer it was antagonism to the See of Rome spiritually and temporally. It gave external form to the Church, and established the relation which he thought should always exist between the Church and the State where the sovereign is a Christian. No name was too hideous for the Church of Rome. It was Antichrist. Satan had been let loose upon it, and had ruled over it for five hundred years. Christianity, in its external form, was not to be a union of all Churches presided over by one bishop, to whom it was given not to err in doctrine. The visible Church, Cranmer said, had erred. Christianity was a spirit, and had no external form of divine appointment. The true Church was invisible, not known to men, but known only to God, who searches the hearts of men. This is the Church which cannot err, which is the pillar and ground of truth. This is the Church all whose members are holy, elect, mystical members of the mystical body of Christ. But there is a visible Church consisting of

How much the royal supremacy meant.

good and bad, of men holding and professing the faith. It is the business of Christian princes to give laws to this Church, to appoint its officers, and to see that their functions are duly performed; for all officers of the Church are servants of the State. The civil office was as sacred, in Cranmer's judgment, as the ecclesiastical, and the grace of God promised for the execution of the one as well as of the other. To the King was committed the care of the souls of his subjects as well as the government of their temporal estate. As the Lord Chancellor and other civil officers are appointed to discharge secular duties for the commonwealth, so the Archbishop of Canterbury and the clergy are appointed to discharge the spiritual and the ecclesiastical.* The foreign Reformed Churches mostly adopted the Presbyterian form of government, while Cranmer retained Episcopacy, but he in no way reckoned that bishops were necessary to constitute a Church. In the primitive Church they were the same as presbyters. The bishop, he said, may make a priest, so may the king, and so may the people by their election. The last was the custom of the primitive Church, before princes were converted to Christianity. The Apostles did not appoint other ministers of the Gospel. They recommended such persons as they thought eligible, leaving it to the people to choose or to reject them.

When King Edward died, Cranmer was endeavouring to bring all the Reformed Churches into one communion, each national or provincial Church to retain its own forms and formularies. This fact, had we no other evidence, would be enough to show what were his views of the character and constitution of a Church. From the creeds and standards of the foreign Churches he borrowed the language in which, for the most part, he expressed his own doctrines. True, indeed, these Churches had taken this language from St. Augustine and those Fathers who agreed with St. Augustine, so that in this there was agreement with at least one

---

* 'All the said officers (of state) and ministers (of religion) as well of the one sort as of the other be appointed, assigned and elected in every place by the laws and orders of kings and princes. ... And there is no more promise of God, that grace is given in the committing of the ecclesiastical office, than it is in the committing of the civil office.'—*Cranmer's Works*, vol. ii. p. 102, Jenkyn's Ed.

portion of the early Church. On predestination, free-will, and original sin there is not much in Cranmer, if we except what is said in the Articles and Homilies. On justification by faith he clearly declares for the Lutheran doctrine, that we are justified by faith alone, but with Melancthon's qualification, that it is by a faith which is not alone. The Son of God made 'a sacrifice, satisfaction, or, as it may be called, amends to His Father for our sins to assuage His wrath and indignation.' We have the benefit of this satisfaction by faith; but it is not a faith which makes works unnecessary. It only takes away the necessity of them as meritorious, lest they should be put in the same class with the merits of Christ. It is a faith which includes charity or love. It is, in the end, equivalent to works—that is, to keeping the moral commandments of God. Cranmer reckons the substance of faith to have been embraced in the works which Jesus mentioned to the young man in the Gospel as necessary to be done to inherit eternal life.* We cannot perfectly keep the commandments, but our imperfection is perfected by Christ. His merit serves for our want of merit. We fulfil the law in Him, 'forasmuch as that which our infirmity lacketh, Christ's justice hath supplied.' We are justified by works in the sense that they are the equivalent of faith, and a necessary condition of justification; but when we say by faith alone, we take away the idea of merit on our part, acknowledge that we are unworthy, and resolve salvation solely into the mercy of God.

But the opposition of faith and works had some other relations, which helped to involve this subject in ambiguities almost beyond remedy. The Church of Rome made 'good works' to consist in obeying the commands and traditions of the Church concerning meats and drinks, fastings and pilgrimages.† To these the Reformers had to oppose a sub-

---

* 'So that this is to be taken for a most true lesson taught by Christ's own mouth, that the works of the moral commandments of God are the true works of faith which lead to the blessed life.'—Vol. ii. p. 168.

† Speaking of the controversies between him and the Church of Rome, one of them Cranmer says, is, 'which be the good works and the true service and honour which pleaseth God, and whether the choice of meats, the difference of garments, the vows of monks and priests, and other traditions which have no word of God to confirm them,—whether these, I say, be right good works, and such as make a Christain man, or no.'—Vol. ii. p. 16.

jective faith. They directed the people to Christ, and to the faith and works which He had enjoined, instead of directing them to the Church, with the faith and works which it had enjoined. In doing this they adopted Augustine's language, which had been used against the Pelagians. The Church of Rome had become Pelagian as opposed to Augustinian; but it had also become something worse than Pelagian. The good works which Pelagius inculcated as the conditions or grounds of justification were the moral laws of God; but the good works of the Church of Rome were the traditions of the elders and the commandments of men. Moreover, the language of Augustine, never logical, always exaggerated, and often inconsistent with itself, was an uncertain vehicle for conveying the thoughts of men whose immediate object was to oppose the merit of 'good works' of quite another kind from those to which Augustine's language referred. An instance of the perplexity arising from this is in Article XIII., which says that 'Works done before the grace of Christ and the inspiration of His Spirit are not pleasant to God, forasmuch as they spring not of faith in Jesus Christ.' If they are *good* works, from what else could they spring but the grace of Christ and the inspiration of His Spirit? If they are not *good* works why are they mentioned? The statement, in the latter case, is a mere truism. Clemens of Alexandria, with some other ancient Fathers, ascribe all the goodness of the Pagan philosophers to the grace of God working in them, though they knew not whence it came. The Bishop of Ely thinks that Clemens' doctrine does not interfere with that of the Article. But the Article limits grace and inspiration to those works which 'spring of faith in Christ.' Can the heathen do such works, or can they in any sense be said to have faith in Christ? Clemens would have answered this question, but in a way altogether opposed to the spirit of this Article, which owes its existence to another theology. In the 'Homily on Good Works,' which is said to have been written by Cranmer, we read that the good works of the Pagans, such as feeding the hungry and clothing the naked, were but 'dead, vain, and fruitless works.' They needed *faith* to commend them to God. Had Cranmer been expressing his own judgment, he would have said that the works are equivalent to faith. Had he followed Clemens of Alexandria, he would have explained that philosophy was to the Pagans what the law was to the Jews, or the Gospel to the Christians. But he was following Augustine, who says that such works have not the faith of Christ for their foundation, and therefore they are not good.* In his exposition of the eighty-fourth Psalm, that Father speaks of Christians as typified by *the turtle-dove that hath found a nest where she may lay her young birds.* Jews, Heretics, and Pagans do good works, but they have not found a nest. Their works are not done in the true faith, and, 'therefore, these birds are lost.'

CHAP. I.

Augustine applied the language of Art. XIII. to moral works.

After the Royal supremacy, which, as we have seen, affected the whole constitution of the Church, the next urgent question between the Reformers and the Church of Rome was that of the Sacraments. Cranmer did not object to the number seven, though five of them could not be called sacraments except in an inferior sense. Nor does there appear to have been any difference about Baptism, unless it be that the Roman theologians, while admitting the presence of the Holy Ghost in Baptism, denied that of Christ's humanity, which they reserved for the other sacrament only. This might be construed into a wish on their part to elevate the Communion above Baptism. Cranmer's object was to make them of equal importance and significance. His great controversy was on the Eucharist. It was with this sacrament, he said, that the devil had 'craftily juggled.'† Transubstantiation was the root of the deadly tree of error, the

The Sacraments.

---

* By 'faith of Christ,' Augustine evidently means an objective faith, the belief of a certain creed. Cranmer adopts Augustine's language without Augustine's meaning. It is possible that Augustine would have denied the Church of Rome to be the Church Catholic had he lived in Cranmer's day, but the spirit of his remarks is embodied in the following passage from the notes appended to the Douay version of the New Testament, Rom. i. 17:—'*Liveth by faith.*— That is our faith, that is to say, *the Catholic belief* (saith Augustine) *which maketh us just*, and that by the law of faith, and not by the law of works. Wherefore it ariseth that the Jew, the heathen philosopher, and the heretic, though they excelled in all good works of moral virtue, could not be just, and a Catholic Christian man, living but an ordinary honest life, either not sinning greatly or supplying his faults by penance, is just.' *Saving faith* is here obviously *faith* in the Church of Rome—receiving a certain creed.

† 'The devil, the enemy of Christ and of all His members, hath so craftily juggled herein, that of nothing riseth so much contention as of the holy sacrament.'—Vol. ii. p. 297.

dank bed of the weeds of superstition.* It 'overthroweth the nature of a sacrament,' for a sacrament requires a visible sign of what is signified. But the symbols cease to exist if they are changed into the body and blood of Christ. Cranmer's thorough opposition to the belief of the real presence in the 'sacrament of the altar' in any sense at all approaching the Roman Catholic doctrine, is the only defence that can be made for the language of Article IV., which speaks of Christ having ascended into heaven with 'flesh' and 'bones.' The natural body of Christ, he argued, occupies a *place* in heaven, and therefore it cannot be also present in the bread and wine of the Communion. That body may be glorified; it may have become heavenly and spiritual, but whatever change it has undergone, it is still subject to that law by which it is a body,—that it be in only one place at one time. If it can be predicated of it that it is both in heaven and on earth, or that it is present whenever the priest consecrates the host, it no longer comes under our conception of body. The bread in the Communion is still bread and the wine is still wine, but the body of Christ is in heaven. It was bread which He broke, and not His body; it was wine which He gave His disciples to drink, and not His blood; the signs, but not the things that were signified.† To eat Christ's body, says Cranmer, would be, 'doing something abhorrent to any Christian.' In old times it was a custom to burn what remained of the consecrated elements. If these had become the body of Christ, then the priests who burned them ought, he said, to be called Christ-burners.

Transubstantiation was mainly supported by the words of Jesus—'This is my body;' and by His discourse to the Jews about eating His flesh and drinking His blood, as recorded

---

* 'The very body of the tree, or rather the roots of the weeds, is the Popish doctrine of transubstantiation, of the real presence of Christ's flesh and blood in the sacrament of the altar (as they call it), and of the sacrifice and oblation of Christ made by the priest for the salvation of the quick and dead, which roots, if they be suffered to grow up in the Lord's vineyard, they will overspread the ground again with the old errors and superstitions.'—Vol. ii. p. 289.

† Christ is not to be worshipped, Cranmer says, 'as being corporally in the bread; for He is not in it, neither spiritually, as He is in man, nor corporally, as He is in heaven but only sacramentally, as a thing may be said to be in the figure whereby it is signified.'—Vol. ii. p. 446.

in the sixth chapter of John's Gospel. The words, 'This is my body,' were easily explained by the common use of language. It is just what we should have expected Jesus to have said when He gave His disciples the symbols of that body which was soon to be bruised and broken on the cross, and of that blood which was to be poured out for the life of the world. The discourse in John's Gospel Cranmer at once rejected as having no reference to the sacrament of the Supper; that is, no more than it had to the sacrament of Baptism, or any other religious service in which by a figure of speech we are said to eat Christ's flesh and drink His blood. The words were spoken a year, probably a year and a half, before the institution of the Supper, while Jesus spoke to those present of eating His flesh and drinking His blood then, otherwise they could have no life in them. To suppose that Jesus referred to the Eucharist is to throw an unnecessary veil of mystery over words whose meaning is as plain as the plainest passage in John's Gospel. The Jews murmured when they heard Him speak of their eating His flesh. They thought He spoke of some carnal and corporal eating, such as is implied in transubstantiation. Their error was not less absurd than that of Nicodemus concerning regeneration, who thought that to be born again a man must enter a second time into his mother's womb and be born. Jesus answered them: 'It is the Spirit that quickeneth, the flesh profiteth nothing.' To eat His flesh means to believe on Him.*

John vi. does not refer to the Eucharist.

Cranmer denies that Christ's body and blood are present in the sacraments. They are in heaven, and not upon earth. Yet he says many times over, in language strong, express, and sometimes perplexing, that worthy communicants eat Christ's body and drink His blood. If Christ's body is in heaven, the difficulty of conceiving how it can be present to the faithful and received into their hearts is not less than the difficulty of conceiving it to be in or under the elements. All his arguments drawn from reason against transubstantiation seem to be equally valid against his own doctrine. He

Cranmer's language on the sacraments sometimes perplexing.

---

* 'What need we any other witness when Christ Himself doth testify the matter so plainly, that whosoever eateth His flesh and drinketh His blood hath everlasting life, and that to eat His flesh and to drink His blood is to believe on Him?'—Vol. ii. p. 426.

explains that Christ's body is eaten *spiritually* and *sacramentally*. The latter word is not definite, but fortunately Cranmer tells us what he means by it. A sacramental eating is an eating of the sign when, by a figure of speech, we are said to eat the thing which is signified. To eat a *body* spiritually is an expression some degrees worse than indefinite. It is a manifest contradiction. To speak of believing on Christ under the figure of eating the bread which came down from heaven, is an intelligible speech, but to eat spiritually something which is corporal and in heaven is not so intelligible. Cranmer's words are, 'We receive the self-same body of Christ that was born of the Virgin Mary, that was crucified and buried, that rose again, ascended into heaven, and sitteth at the right hand of God the Father Almighty.' He repeats frequently that it is the 'very flesh' and the 'very blood' which the worthy communicants receive. As we are *regenerated* in Baptism, so are we nourished by the body and blood of Christ in the sacrament of the Supper. The Holy Ghost *is joined* to the water in baptism not *inaquate*, not made water; and so in the other sacrament, the body of Christ is joined to the bread, but not made bread. These are Cranmer's words; can we find out Cranmer's meaning?

Appeal to the Fathers.

The Church of England at the Reformation appealed to the Fathers. In separating from the See of Rome it did not wish to separate from the Church Catholic. Cranmer quoted many passages from the old Fathers as expressing his doctrine. Chrysostom says, 'That the bread before it be sanctified is called bread, but when it is sanctified by the means of a priest, it is delivered from the name of bread, and is exalted to the name of the Lord's body, although the nature of bread remains.' Ambrose, speaking of the change of the bread into the body of Christ, says that 'God can make things that were before, still to be, and also to be changed into other things.' Augustine says, 'That which you see on the altar is the bread, and the cup which also your eyes do show you. But faith showeth further that bread is the body of Christ, and the cup His blood.' Again, 'There is both the sacrament and the thing of the sacrament, which is Christ's body.' Such passages as these, Cranmer thought, were opposed to transubstantiation. Gardiner quoted others, which he held to teach a real presence of the natural body in the elements. Cyprian said the bread was changed in nature, but not in its outward form. Chrysostom denied that the consecrated bread and wine passed through the œsophagus, or were subjected to the action of the stomach, like other bread and wine, but rather like wax cast into the fire, no substance is left. If the Fathers in such passages as these did not teach transubstantiation, they taught something which might be substituted for it without much danger of the counterfeit being discovered. To most of the passages quoted by Gardiner, Cranmer added the context, which generally modified the meaning. When this was done, he quoted the same Fathers again, with their instructions how these words are to be understood. Tertullian says that Christ meant by the words 'This is my body,' it is a figure of my body. Chrysostom says that bread and wine are the similitudes of Christ's body. Augustine, speaking of the discourse at Capernaum, says that Jesus seems to command a very heinous and wicked thing, and therefore it must be a figure. Again, that 'when Christ gave the sign of His body He did not hesitate to call it His body.' This same Father, at some length, shows how all such speeches are to be understood. Thus on the day before Good Friday, we say, To-morrow Christ suffered His passion. On Easter Sunday we say that this day Christ rose from the dead. Yet He died but once and rose again but once, and that many hundreds of years ago. Augustine says that in the same way we speak of the sacrament of Christ's body as His body, and of the sacrament of His blood as His blood. In Baptism we are said to be buried with Christ, but though the Apostle says *we are*, it is only a similitude. The sacrament of the thing is called by the name of the thing itself. Cranmer concludes that all this language of the Fathers concerning the sacraments, however literal it may seem, must not be taken literally. And the same he wishes to be the case with his own language, when he seems to imply a bodily presence of Christ. He was misunderstood. The Roman Catholics said that he was teaching the doctrine which he opposed. He accused them in return of being ignorant of language. 'In plain speech,'—these are his words—'it is not true that we eat Christ's body and drink

Cranmer, from Augustine, explains how figures are to be understood.

His blood.' These are 'figurative speeches.'* In one place, where he speaks with great decision, he beseeches his readers not to take his words literally, not to suppose that because Christ is not corporally in the visible signs, He is corporally in the persons who duly receive them. He assures them that he means no such thing. The presence of which he speaks is spiritual. It is explained as consisting in the grace, the virtue, and the benefit of that body which was crucified for us and that blood which was shed for us. Why, we may ask, did Cranmer use words which were so often misunderstood, and conveyed to the reader a meaning so different from what he intended? He answers that it was his wish in everything to use the same words and phrases as had been used by the ancient Fathers.†

There seems, however, to have been in Cranmer's mind some vague idea of eating the body and drinking the blood of Christ in some way that was not a figure. 'We receive,' he said, 'Christ's own very natural body, but not naturally, nor corporally.' He took literally the expression that we are members of Christ's body. The union between Christ and believers was to him something so real, that to call it a figure would have seemed to deprive it of reality. It was a bodily union after a spiritual manner. The truest of all unions is doubtless the spiritual, yet, to our sensuous apprehension, that is most real which is corporal. The Church of Rome kept to the literal sense, which to the gross mind is the most real. Cranmer rose above this, and yet to make a spiritual presence real, he seemed to think there was a necessity to speak of it under the figure of a bodily presence. The sun is in heaven, but its influence is upon earth; so the

---

* 'Marvel not, good reader, that Christ at that time spake in figures, when He did institute that sacrament, seeing it is the nature of all sacraments to be figures. And although the Scriptures be full of schemes, tropes, and figures, yet specially it useth them when it speaketh of sacraments.'—Vol. ii. p. 396.

† 'Not only I mean to judge these things as the Catholic Church and the most holy Fathers of old, with one accord, have meant and judged, but also I would gladly use the same words that they used, and not use any other words, but to set my hands to all and singular their speeches, phrases, ways, and forms of speech which they do use in their treatises upon the sacrament.' (Vol. iv. p. 127.) Melancthon said that if the Fathers had known what use was to be made of their language, they would have expressed themselves more guardedly. It should also be noticed that the majority of the passages from the Fathers quoted in the Eucharist controversy were from works that are not now reckoned genuine.

body of Christ is in heaven, yet that which emanates from it, its strength or virtue, is upon earth. When Gardiner took up this controversy with Cranmer, both disputants were soon lost in the questions—what constitutes a body, wherein it differs from spirit, what substance is, and how a substance is to be distinguished from its accidents. The 'corporal' or 'carnal' body with 'flesh' and 'bones' which Cranmer said was in heaven, Gardiner denied to be either in heaven or in the Eucharist. The heavenly body of Christ was spiritual, not corporal. As Gardiner was driven to explain it, the body of Christ was spirit, and the sacramental presence the presence of the substance of spirit under the accidents of bread and wine. Cranmer, on the other hand, denied that he ever meant by corporal and carnal such a gross material body as exists on earth, but he did contend that Christ's body was palpable, visible, circumscribed, and occupying but one place at one time. It was now in heaven. To say that the substance of it can be present under the accidents of bread and wine, is to deny it the qualities of body, and to confound all our ideas of substance. We only know a body from its accidents, and to suppose that the substance of any body is different from what its accidents declare it to be, is to 'mix heaven and earth together.' Gardiner admitted that Christ had a circumscribed body in heaven, but by the power of God, he said, that body was also present in the sacrifice of the Mass. It had rarely been denied by Roman Catholic writers that the wicked as well as the faithful eat the body and drink the very blood of Christ in the sacrament. So far there was a consistent advocacy of a real objective bodily presence. It had been admitted, too, by some Roman theologians, that a mouse, or any such creature, eating the consecrated bread would also eat the body of Christ. Consistently with what he had said about the spiritual substance of body, this was denied by Gardiner, from which it followed that a mouse might make a meal on accidents, leaving the substance untouched.

Cranmer said that the worthy communicants received Christ in the sacrament, but the unworthy only received bread and wine. Had he meant the reception of any corporal substance, his arguments against Gardiner would have

CHAP. I.

Christ's body spiritual.

Can a mouse eat the substance of the consecrated bread?

been valid against himself. But the reception was of something spiritual and by faith in the hearts of believers, not by their mouths as partakers of meats and drinks. And as a man may receive the sacrament without receiving Christ's body, so also may he receive Christ's body without receiving the sacrament.* This is expressed clearly in a neglected rubric at the end of the Service for the Communion of the Sick. To eat Christ's flesh and to drink His blood Cranmer everywhere explains as believing in Christ. The faithful feed upon Christ in their daily lives. In hearing His word preached, in prayer, in praise, in acts of faith, in Baptism as well as in the Supper, they eat His flesh and drink His blood. We receive the body of Christ in Baptism as well as in the Communion, and we are *regenerated* in the Communion as well as in Baptism.† In the sacraments we have visible signs of His invisible presence, but beyond this He is no otherwise present than He is present always with His people to the end of the world. The saints of old time, before His incarnation, were nourished by His body and His blood, even as we are now. They did all, says an Apostle, eat the same spiritual meat and they drank the same spiritual drink, for they drank of the rock that followed them, and that rock was Christ.‡ It is commonly supposed that the Church of England takes a middle view on the Eucharist, between the Roman Catholic and Zwinglian. But this supposition is without foundation, if we are to take Cranmer as representing the Church of England. There are some strong expressions in the Prayer Book; perhaps the strongest are those in the Catechism—where it is said, 'The body and blood of Christ are verily and indeed taken and received by the faithful in the Lord's Supper.' Cardinal Wiseman said that these words were put there to deceive the Catholics. Words equally strong are frequent

---

* 'If Christ had never ordained the sacrament, yet should we have eaten His flesh and drunken His blood, as all the faithful did before the sacrament was ordained, and do daily, when they receive not the sacrament.'—Vol. iii. p. 66.

† 'For what Christian man would say ... that we be not regenerated, both body and soul, as well in Baptism as in the sacrament of the body and blood of Christ?'—Vol. iii. p. 276.

‡ 'The words that I speak unto you are spirit and life.' This is explained, that we eat Christ by faith spiritually, 'in such wise as Abraham and other holy Fathers did eat Him.'—Vol. i. p. 378.

in Cranmer's writings. He himself has told us that they do not mean what they seem to mean, and that they are ignorant of the use of theological language who take such words literally.* They are in no way intended to approach the *real presence*, as taught in the Church of Rome. To put the matter past all doubt, Cranmer at last declares that on this subject he does not differ from Bucer, and that Bucer, in his judgment, did not differ from Œcolampadius and Zwingle. True, this sacrament is no *mere* commemoration. Did Zwingle ever call it so? What necessity or what authority for prefixing the word *mere*? A religious commemoration of so great an event could not be a mere *badge* or *token* of profession. The keeping of such a command as 'Do this in remembrance of me,' could not surely be less a means of God's invisible working in us than any ordinary exercise of religious worship. That Zwingle denied sacramental grace, is the invention of men who have theories to support.† He denied, and so did Cranmer, the notion of grace coming through the sacraments in virtue of their being administered by any particular order of men, or that grace was in any way inseparably connected with the sacraments. Cranmer and Zwingle both agreed that the sacraments were means whereby God works in men invisibly, but not different in kind from other means.‡ If Jesus

Zwingle never called the sacrament a mere commemoration.

---

* Cranmer translated a catechism written by a Lutheran, Justus Jonas, in which were the words, 'with our bodily mouths we receive the body and blood of Christ.' Some objected to the words, and Cranmer called them 'ignorant persons not used to read old ancient authors.' In the first Prayer Book of King Edward, there was a sentence in the consecration prayer in which the priest asked that the bread and wine 'may be unto us the body and blood of Thy most dearly beloved Son, Jesus Christ.' Gardiner claimed this for transubstantiation. To avoid such claims it was omitted at the next revision.

† Calvin blames Luther, Œcolampadius, and Zwingle for the spirit in which they carried on the controversy about the Eucharist. He says that Luther should have abstained from those 'rude similitudes,' meaning the rhetorical expressions of the Fathers. And as to Œcolampadius and Zwingle, he says 'notwithstanding they denied not the verity, yet they did not teach it openly as was becoming. Thus do I understand, that whiles they give themselves studiously and diligently to affirm that the bread and wine were called the body and blood of Christ, because they be signs thereof, they thought not that they ought in the meantime to do this thing also, to add to that they are the signs after such sort that the verity is nevertheless joined unto them. Neither did they declare that they went not about to deface the true communion which the Lord giveth us in His body and blood.'— *Coverdale's Translation of Calvin's 'De Cœna Domini.'*

‡ 'Christ is present in His sacraments, as they (the old writers) teach; also that He is present in His word when He worketh mightily by the same in the hearts of the hearers.'—Vol. iii. p. 38.

Christ is present always and everywhere; if He dwells in the hearts of His people; why should He not be present in the sacrament of Baptism and the ordinance of the Supper?

In denying the *real presence* of the body of Christ, Cranmer was led consistently to deny that there was any proper propitiatory sacrifice in the Lord's Supper. There was but one sacrifice propitiatory, that of Christ, and Christ alone could offer it. One of our Articles pronounces the propitiatory sacrifice of the Mass a *blasphemous fable*,* and the priest who pretends to make it Cranmer calls 'the horrible adversary' of Christ. The word *propitiatory* is taken literally; Christ once for all assuaged God's wrath, and satisfied His justice. The Supper is a memorial of that sacrifice, and is properly called on that account a sacrifice of thanksgiving. It is eucharistic or gratulatory, but not propitiatory. It was explained by Gardiner that the Mass was not an additional offering over and above that of Christ's. The priest there offered Christ, so that it was still the same offering which was repeated. The Mass was called propitiatory because of its connection with the offering on the cross. For Gardiner's side there was the perplexing fact that the sacrifices of the priests under the old law were called propitiatory. Now if the offerings of the Jewish priests, which were but shadows of the offering on Calvary, were called propitiatory, why should not the same word be applied to the memorial sacrifice in the Supper? Cranmer might have so applied it, and pleaded, as he had done in other cases, the language of the Fathers; but here he felt the importance and necessity of contending about a word. He saw that if 'propitiatory' were allowed, even in a figurative sense, to be applied to the sacrifice of the Mass, he would have no words left to distin-

---

* It is true that in our Article the word is plural 'Masses' not 'Mass.' From this Dr. Pusey ('Eirenicon,' p. 25) maintains that the Article does not condemn the 'sacrifice of the Mass' but a habit of trusting to the purchase of Masses when dying, which he says was condemned by the Council of Trent as well as by our Articles. This is very ingenious, but it finds no sanction from Cranmer. He condemns not merely accidental abuses, but the whole doctrine of sacrifice in the Mass as understood by the Church of Rome. Such passages as the following are frequent:—'The Romish Antichrist to deface this great benefit of Christ, hath taught that His sacrifice upon the cross is not sufficient hereunto without another sacrifice devised by him and made by the priest, or else without indulgences, beads, pardons, pilgrimages, and such other pelfrey to supply Christ's imperfection.'—Vol. ii. p. 287.

guish between the offering of Christ and such sacrifices as it is the duty of all Christians to offer. He did not believe in a sacrificing priesthood as distinct from a sacrificing people; and whatever might be pleaded theoretically for a connection of the sacrifice of the Mass with that on the cross, it appeared to him that practically every Mass was a new propitiation.

Bishop Ridley's theology did not differ from Cranmer's. In his examination at Oxford previous to his martyrdom, he defended the same positions as to the Eucharist, and with the same arguments. To separate from Rome was not, he maintained, to separate from the Catholic Church. To make out this, Ridley interpreted a passage of St. Augustine to mean that Africa was not subject to the See of Rome; and he quoted Vincentius Lirinensis, who says that 'when one part is corrupted with heresies we are to prefer the whole world before that part, but if the greatest part be infected then we must turn to antiquity.' With this protest against Rome as a usurper, it was incumbent upon Ridley to show that the Fathers were on his side. He was pressed with the words of Chrysostom, that 'Christ took His flesh with Him into heaven and yet left it on earth; that He sitteth above with His Father, and is handled with the hands of all men at the very same moment of time, and delivers Himself to them that will receive Him.' And again, 'that the blood which is in the cup is the same which flowed from His side, that here we have the Lord on the altar and not in a manger, and that He is handled not by a woman but by a priest.' These words Ridley explained as a presence of Christ's body by grace. His blood indeed was in the cup, even the very blood that gushed from His side, but after the manner of a sacrament. This he explained as Cranmer had done, on the principle that we ascribe to the sacrament what belongs to the matter of the sacrament, and thus we say of the sacrament of the blood that it is the blood. 'It is well then,' cried the examiners; 'we have blood in the chalice.' To which Ridley answered, 'it is true, but *by grace in a sacrament.*' At which words, the historian says, all the people hissed. The same explanation was put on a passage of Augustine when discoursing on Psalm xxxiv. Augustine says of the words, 'He carried himself in his own hands,' this was not true of David but of Christ.* The Council of Lateran said, 'The Lamb of God lieth on the table,' which means, says Ridley, that He is there not corporally but in a mystery, according to His power.

This mysterious presence did not satisfy the examiners. Either the actual body was present or it was not. Transubstantiation might have its difficulties. Its advocates might be drawn into contradictions in its defence. Ridley might ridicule it as he had done under the figure of Christ playing 'bo-peep under a piece of bread'† but he was not to be allowed to speak of a body being present when he only meant that the symbol of it was present.

Following as closely as possible the language of the Fathers, he said that there was a miracle in the Eucharist, for bread which is used to sustain the body becomes food for the soul, that the grace and strength of the body of Christ is the only salvation and life of men; that we worship the symbols when we handle them reverently, and in this sense we adore and worship Christ in the Eucharist. He altogether rejected the imputation that he regarded the Lord's table as nothing different from any other table, or that the sacrament is a bare sign or figure of Christ's death. The symbols are taken from common use, and made the signs of a great and holy thing. Every sacrament has grace. It is, so to speak, an instrument by which God works. But when we say a sacrament *has* grace, we should explain that it has 'not grace included in it, but, to those that receive it well, it is turned to grace. After that manner the water in Baptism hath grace promised, and by that grace the Holy Ghost is given,—not

---

* The passage is 1 Sam. xxi. 13, where in our version it reads, 'He feigned himself mad in their hands.' It relates to David's conduct at Gath, which was also, it is supposed, the occasion of his writing Psalm xxxiv. (Vulgate xxxiii.). Augustine's words are, 'Hoc vero, fratres, quomodo possit fieri in homine, quis intelligat? Manibus suis nemo portatur. Quomodo intelligatur in ipso David secundum literam non invenimus; in Christo autem invenimus. Ferebatur enim Christus in manibus suis cum, commendans ipsum corpus suum, ait, Hoc est meum corpus. Ferebat enim illud corpus in manibus suis.'

It is difficult to know where Augustine got this reading. The Hebrew is יְהֹלֵל בְּיָדָם. The LXX. has παρεφέρετο ἐν ταῖς χερσὶν αὐτοῦ, and the Vulgate 'Collabebatur inter manus eorum.'

† 'Christ shall not come to hide Himself and play bo-peep, as it were, under a piece of bread.' — *Ridley's Works*, Par. Soc. Ed. p. 116.

that grace is included in water, but that grace cometh by water.'*

This use of patristic language, to which Ridley clings, and which was wisely laid aside by Tyndale, only helped to prolong the controversy. The explanations did not satisfy the examiners, who understood the words of Chrysostom and Augustine in a different sense. Ridley connects the sacraments with grace, but only as it was done by Cranmer, and before him by Tyndale. He also connects preaching with grace, and the connection is the same in kind. Sacraments and preaching he puts in one category, comparing them to the beams of Christ, who is the Sun of Righteousness.†

Bishop Latimer was less anxious than either Cranmer or Ridley about adhering to the words of the Fathers. He disposed of them with a sentence of Melancthon's, that if these doctors had known to what use their language was to be applied, they would not have written as they did. He used the favourite terms of his brother Reformers and martyrs about *sacramental* body and eating *sacramentally*. One of the examiners at Oxford asked him where he got these words, for certainly they were not in the Bible. It was only in his examination that he seems to have used them, and then he reminded the examiners that he was an old man, past four score years, that his memory had failed him, and it was a long time since he had been engaged in these

In what sense the sacraments confer grace.

Latimer not disposed to cling to the Fathers.

---

* It is sometimes said that Ridley was less Protestant than Cranmer. This is entirely without foundation. The exaggerated language of the Fathers about the sacraments, which he thought he was obliged to use, he explains as Cranmer had explained it. Palmer, in his book on the Church, says that Cranmer virtually denied the *real presence*. He adds that in this he was unlike Ridley, Ponet, and 'The Necessary Erudition.' This statement is not correct, at least as regards Ridley and Ponet. The views of Ponet are found in King Edward's Catechism, of which he is said to have been the author. There is also a sermon by him on 'The right use of the Lord's Supper.' A copy of this sermon, printed in 1550, is in the British Museum. Long extracts from it will be found in the late Dean Goode's work on the Eucharist. A book on the Lord's Supper, called *Diallacticon Viri Boni*, etc., printed in 1557, has been ascribed to him, but without sufficient reason.

† The account which Ridley gives of the patronage of the Church before the Reformation, will teach us not to wonder at the evils which continued after it. 'When Papistry was taught,' he says, 'there was nothing too little for the teachers. When the bishop gave his benefices to idiots, unlearned, ungodly, for kindred, for pleasure, for service, and other worldly prospects, all was then allowed.'—*Works*, Par. Soc. Ed. p. 332.

studies. Latimer's sermons are practical rather than theological, but whenever he touches on theology his doctrine is that of the most advanced Reformers. The perverse Augustinianism which Cranmer imported into Article XIII. and the 'Homily on Good Works' is fully sanctioned by Latimer. Perfect men among the heathen, he says, who lived uprightly as concerning their outward conversation, 'went to the devil in the end, because they knew not Christ.' He defined the Church in the words of Lyra, as consisting of persons 'in whom abideth the true knowledge and confession of faith.' The sacrificing priesthood which existed under the old law was now, he said, changed into a 'preaching priesthood,' and all Christian men are sacrificing priests. In accordance with this view, Latimer wished that the ministers of religion should always be called ministers and not priests, for while they are called priests there is an implication that they have a sacrifice to offer, different from that which should be offered by all Christian men. The sacraments he denied to be bare signs or mere outward tokens, but as circumcision spoke to the Jews of the circumcision of the heart, so the bread and wine in the Eucharist are lively representations of the breaking of Christ's body and the shedding of His blood. Baptism assures us of the washing away of sins. It tells us that as water purifies the body, so the blood of Christ cleanses the soul.

Hooper, the Bishop of Gloucester, differed with Cranmer and Ridley about wearing the vestments used by the bishops of the Church of Rome. There is distinctly traceable in Hooper a tone or temper different from that by which Cranmer and Ridley were guided. It would be wrong to say that they differed in their views of the Reformation itself, but they did differ as to the mode in which it was to be carried on. Cranmer wished the Reformed service to be so like the Roman that the ignorant multitude might be unconscious of the change. In this doubtless he was supported by Ridley, who seems to have earned a universal reputation for solid learning, prudence and moderation. Hooper had more of the spirit of Tyndale, which in after times was incarnated in the extreme Puritans. He had no reverence for antiquity, and he hated the very garments of the Church of Rome. He was more avowedly an innovator, yet it would be difficult to draw a well-marked line between his theology and that of Cranmer or Ridley. He openly scorned the idea of founding the Church upon the succession of bishops. Truth alone, he said, makes a true Church: agreement with Scripture and the Church of the Apostles. God's word is not bound to the clergy. The doctors and Fathers have no authority but as they preach truth. Christian men have the Scriptures in their hands, by which they are to judge if their teachers are right or wrong. Whoever preaches contrary to God's word is to be rejected, whatever be his place in the Church, and whatever reverence antiquity may have gathered around his name.* He is not to be followed, even should he be Augustine, Tertullian, or an angel from heaven. That the Church of Rome is not a true church, Hooper thought to be sufficiently proved by the lives of many of the Popes. They were evidently not members of God's Church, but 'members of the devil, and the first-begotten of Antichrist.'

In answer to the plea that the ceremonies of the Church of Rome were useful for instructing the ignorant, Hooper argued that a lesson drawn from nature would be more effectual in impressing on their minds the doctrines of Christianity. The ploughman would learn more of Christ's death by the corn that he sows in the field than by the dead posts that hang in the church. The springing up of the grain from the earth would be a more vivid lesson of the resurrection, than the ceremony of pulling a post out of a sepulchre, with priests singing *Christus resurgens*.

---

* 'Leave not,' Hooper says, 'till the matter be brought unto the first, original, and most perfect Church of the Apostles. If thou find by their writings that their church used the thing that the preacher would prove, then accept it, or else not. Be not amazed though they speak of never so many years, nor name never so many doctors. Christ and His Apostles be grandfathers in age to the doctors and masters in learning. Repose thyself only upon the Church that they have taught thee by the Scripture. Fear neither for the ordinary power or succession of bishops nor for the greater part. For if either the authority of bishops or the greater part should have power to interpret the Scripture, the sentence of the Pharisees should have been preferred to that of Zachary, Simeon, Elizabeth, or the blessed Virgin. Consider that many a time the true Church is but a small congregation, as Esay saith,—*Except the Lord had left us a remnant we should have been as Sodom.*' ... 'Beware of deceit when thou hearest the name of the Church. The verity is then assaulted: they call the church of the devil the holy church many times.'— *Early Writings*, Par. Soc. Ed. p. 84.

Danger of putting the sacraments in the place of Christ.

Hooper brought against transubstantiation* the same arguments as the other Reformers. He wished all due reverence to be given to the sacraments. Yet we are to be guarded against ascribing to them what Christ alone can do. He protests fearlessly against the notion that Baptism is necessary to salvation. He could not doubt that the children of Christian parents were saved; and he could see no reason why the mercy of God should not also extend to the children of unbelievers. They have no sin upon them but the original guilt of Adam's transgression. Sacraments he explained as confirmations of Christ's promises, which are already realized by those who receive the sacraments, otherwise the external rite avails nothing. That sacraments are necessary to salvation he calls 'an ungodly opinion that doth deny the mercy of God.' Hooper agreed with Cranmer on the divine right of the King to be governor of the Church. He pleaded

---

* The Roman Catholic argued that the body of Christ being changed after His resurrection it may be in the elements invisibly, after the manner that Christ came among the disciples when the door was shut. To which Hooper answers, 'Wheresoever His body be, it must have the qualities and quantities of a true man. If His body be corporally in the sacrament, and yet without all properties of a true body, this text is false—He *was found in fashion as a man*, likewise this—*He was made in all things like unto His brethren*. They grant that only the spirit of man eateth the body of Christ in the sacrament: then either the spirit of man is turned into a corporal substance or else the body of Christ loseth his corporal substance, and is become a spirit. For it is not possible for the spirit of man to eat corporally a corporal body.'—*Early Writings*, Par. Soc. Ed. p. 68.

Again :—'They make Him there and yet occupy no place: then it is no body, for a true body, physical and mathematical as Christ's body is, cannot be, except it occupy one place. They say I must believe and say with the Virgin, *Ecce ancilla Domini*. I may not seek to know the means how. Well, let them do as much to me in this matter as was done unto the Virgin Mary, and I am content. She could not comprehend how Christ was made man in her belly, yet the effect and corporal nativity of Christ ascertained both her reason and senses that she had borne a true body. It shall suffice me if they make demonstration unto my senses, and warrant my reason, that they have here present a corporal body; how it cometh and by what means, I leave that unto God.'—*Ibid.* p. 69.

Again :—' As soon as they have confessed the bread to be the essential and substantial body of Christ, and the wine His natural blood; they add, *sed invisibiliter et ineffabiliter, et non ut in loco, non qualitative et quantitative.* So doth Thomas Aquinas and Lombertus sophistically dispute the matter. Is it not a wonder that men will not mark what contradiction is in their words? First they say Christ's very natural, corporal, physical, substantial and real body is in the sacrament; the body that died on the cross, was buried, that rose the third day, that was taken into heaven; and yet they make it without quality and quantity. Notice this, a marvellous doctrine, to say that Christ now hath a body that is neither great neither small. Truly if He have now such a body as is invisible without all qualities and quantities, then had He never upon the earth a true body, but a fantastical body as they make Him to have in the sacrament.'—*Ibid.* p. 193.

the example of the Jews. Aaron and his sons had the ministry committed to them, but they never made laws or introduced ceremonies without the sanction of Moses, their prince.*

Cranmer, Ridley, Latimer, and Hooper were prominent in the reign of Edward, as heads of the Church and leaders of the Reformation. When the fires were kindled under Mary to burn Protestantism out of the Church, persecution dragged others into fame. Among these were John Bradford and Archdeacon Philpot. Bradford was a saint more than a theologian. His works are remarkable for the strong expression of what would now be reckoned the worst form of Calvinism. Salvation, he said, could not be free if it did not proceed from election. Divine mercy was not conceivable, if not confined to a chosen few. The elected children alone could magnify this mercy, and they alone could be truly humble for they know that they have not chosen God, but that God has chosen them. Bradford refused to distinguish between the divine foreknowledge and the divine predestination. God's attributes, he said, could not be separated,—His foreknowledge from His wisdom nor His wisdom from His will. Christ Himself has told us that but few are chosen. If God's mercy had extended to all men, then all would have been saved. Where it is said that Christ enlighteneth every man that cometh into the world, Bradford explained that light is given sufficient to make men without excuse. All men, in the Scripture, means all elect men. Though man is

---

* It is a question that has been keenly discussed between Calvinists and Arminians, which side could claim Cranmer, Ridley, Latimer, and Hooper. If the question were to be determined by the general tone and spirit of their writings, there can be no doubt that they were Calvinists. But the task of proving their Calvinism to those who question it, is not so easy. As to Cranmer, if we are to take the notes on the Great Bible known as Cranmer's Bible, to be his, which certainly we ought to do, the question, so far as he is concerned, is settled. He was a moderate Calvinist. In his controversial writings, it is not a subject which he had to discuss directly. The same may be said of Ridley Yet Strype says he and Bradford wrote on predestination and election against the Free Willers, and that Bradford's treatise received the approbation of Cranmer, Ridley, and Latimer. There are passages in Latimer's sermons which distinctly declare him to have been a Calvinist; but he preferred preaching about God's *revealed* will, which concerns our duty, to curious speculations about God's *secret* will, which is beyond our reach. As to Hooper, who certainly had most of the Puritan in him, it is singular how little can be found in his writings to bear on the subject. The passages quoted on the one side by Toplady, and on the other by Archbishop Laurence, do not prove much for either.

without free-will, yet what he does is sin, even as devils sin willingly, though for them to sin is to show their corrupt nature. On questions like these we are not to reason. It is sinful and arrogant to ask—How? Faith in this election, Bradford declared to be the sum of what God requires of us. It is that faith without which it is impossible to please God. The Bible, and not our reason, is the judge of good and evil, virtue and vice. Whatever it commands must be right, whatever it forbids must be wrong. We are to obey its voice as implicitly, and with as an entire negation of our own judgment, as Abraham obeyed, when he was commanded to sacrifice his son.

Explanation of the sacraments.

On the sacraments, Bradford's arguments and illustrations are the same that were common to the other Reformers. The Christian eats and drinks the body and blood of Christ in the Eucharist, but he also has the same spiritual nourishment in hearing the Gospel preached. He quoted St. Jerome, who says, 'We are fed with the body of Christ and we drink His blood, not only in mystery, but also in knowledge of Holy Scripture.' Again Jerome says, 'Christ's flesh and blood is poured into our ears by hearing the word, and therefore great is the peril if we yield to other cogitations while we hear it.' He also quoted Augustine, who says, 'It is no less peril to hear God's word negligently, than so to use the sacraments.' At his examination previous to his martyrdom, Bradford told the Lord Chancellor that he believed Christ's body to be present corporally unto faith in the sacrament. There the worthy receive it, but the unworthy do not receive it, as St. Augustine said of Judas, he received *panem Domini*, the bread of the Lord, but not *panem Dominum*—the bread, the Lord.

The plain declaration that Christ was corporally present in the sacrament might have satisfied the Lord Chancellor, but he could not understand the qualification 'unto faith.' Bradford quoted Augustine, who says that the bread is Christ's body, after the same manner that circumcision is God's covenant, and the sacrament of faith is faith, or as Baptism and the water of Baptism is regeneration. In what sense Bradford took Baptism for regeneration he states in another passage, where he makes it a *declaration* of our adoption, on which we should say with Mary, 'Be it unto me, O Lord, according to Thy word.' It is amazing how well the Reformers explained the Fathers as agreeing with them, but it sometimes required a considerable exercise of ingenuity. Augustine defined the Catholic Church as 'that which has the consent of peoples and nations.' The Archbishop of York,* quoting this definition, asked Bradford how it could agree to his Church. The answer was 'Marry, all people and nations that be God's people have consented with me, and I with them, in the doctrines of faith.' It will not be denied that this answer was clever. It did not satisfy the Archbishop, and it might be an undue exercise of private judgment to say that it would have satisfied St. Augustine.†

Of the writings of Archdeacon Philpot‡ we have almost nothing beyond his examinations, as they are recorded by Foxe. These relate chiefly to transubstantiation, and the question of what constitutes the Catholic Church. Philpot maintained that he was of the Catholic faith and the Catholic Church, the same into which he was baptized, and in which he wished to live and die. He was asked, where his religion was a hundred years ago. He answered in Germany, and divers other places. He said, he agreed with the true Catholic Church, that which was in the time of the Apostles. It was called Catholic though it was not universally received, but because it had the perfect doctrine of Christ, which was to be preached throughout the whole world, which, Philpot said, is Augustine's explanation of Catholic, who, in another place, says the Catholic Church is that which believes aright. The Archbishop of York quoted Augustine against the Donatists, that they had no succession of bishops, and that they wanted universality, being chiefly found in Africa. Philpot denied this to be Augustine's meaning, for to universality he added verity, and he spoke of faithful successors of Peter before corruption came into the Church. He further denied

---

* Heathe.

† It will interest some people to know that Bradford, interpreting Rom. viii. 20, 21, understood the deliverance of the creature from the bondage of corruption to mean the restitution of all the brute creation to life and immortality.

‡ Philpot was Archdeacon of Winchester. Some one called him 'a gentleman,' when Bishop Story cried out, 'A gentleman! he is a vile heretic knave; a heretic is no gentleman.'

the succession of bishops to be an infallible mark by which the Church may be known. There may be a succession of bishops where there is no Church, as at Jerusalem and Antioch. The Archbishop quoted Augustine's four notes of the Catholic Church: consent of all nations—Apostolic See—universality—and the name Catholic. Philpot replied that Rome was not the only Apostolic See, that the faith of the Church of Rome had not the consent of all nations, that the name Catholic did not belong to it, for it differed in almost everything from the Catholic Churches planted by the Apostles. The Church of which he was a member would, he said, be universal if only ten persons belonged to it, because it agrees with the universal Church which the Apostles planted throughout the world. He allowed the Church of Geneva to be Catholic, and its doctrine apostolic, and the same was to be said of the Church of England as it stood in the days of King Edward.

On the doctrine of transubstantiation, Philpot presented the same explanations with which the other Reformers had perplexed their examiners.* A spiritual presence, which in the rhetorical language of the Fathers sounded like a corporal presence, seemed at times to satisfy the two bishops, who were enraged when they found that the meaning was not as they understood it. When Philpot said that Christ was present only to faith, and His body eaten by the worthy receivers alone, Bishop Bonner cried out, 'My Lords, take no heed of him, for he goeth about to deceive you. If I should say to Sir John Bridges, being with me at supper and having a fat capon, "Take eat, this is a fat capon;" although he eat not thereof, is it not a fat capon still?' If this illustration was homely and not too reverent, it had yet the merit of bringing the question to the desired issue. Bonner and his party took figures literally, and this taught Philpot the

* Philpot's explanation of Chrysostom's saying that Christ took His flesh with Him and yet left it behind Him, is worth quoting: 'Christ took on Him our human nature in the Virgin Mary's womb, and through His passion in the same hath united us to His flesh, and thereby are we become one flesh with Him; so that Chrysostom might therefore right well say that Christ ascending took His flesh which He received of the Virgin Mary away with Him, and also left His flesh behind Him, which are we that be His elect in this world, who are the members of Christ, and flesh of His flesh.'

necessity of laying aside figures, and of saying what he had to say in plain words.

The writings of Roger Hutchinson* have an individuality perhaps more marked than those of any of the other theological authors of that time. His editor apologizes for some of his expressions as scarcely within the range of what is considered orthodox. Affliction is spoken of as if it atoned for sin.† Hutchinson, says the editor, was led into one or two such statements by following St. Chrysostom. It is conjectured that these would have been modified had the author seen them in print, but they are in harmony with the tone and character of Hutchinson's mind. He speaks of our bearing other people's sins as Christ has borne ours, and he makes the substance of religion to consist of 'upright conversation and a good life.' Without these, he says we are no more Christians than the Turks, for it is not homilies, nor ceremonies, nor sacraments that make men Christians. Hutchinson denied the existence of any such affections or passions in the Divine Being as anger or mercy. Scripture only uses these modes of speech, because of our weak understandings. Man changes in his relation to God, but God is ever the same. The sun is pleasant to the eye in health, but painful when the eye is diseased; so God is said to be at peace with the righteous, and angry with the sinner. Nothing, says Hutchinson, can properly be spoken of God, for then He would not be unspeakable. Even the intercession of the Holy Ghost is explained, not that He intercedes with the Father, but that He 'stirreth us unto prayer.' The 'unutterable groanings' ascribed to the Spirit are the lamentations of the sinner for his sins.

Hutchinson vindicated, and explained as agreeing with the Reformed faith, the passages from the Fathers most frequently quoted in the Eucharistic controversy. Many, he said, boast and prate about the old Fathers who do not understand the Fathers. He defended as not teaching tran-

---

* Hutchinson died in 1555, just before the martyrdom of the Reformers.

† This is not less orthodox than the passage from St. Cyprian quoted in the Homily on Almsdeeds, 'How wholesome and profitable it is to relieve the needy and help the afflicted, by the which we may purge our sins and heal our wounded souls.'

substantiation the sentence from St. Cyprian,* *Panis non effigie, sed natura mutatur*—the bread is changed not in appearance, but in nature. This sentence surely, if of any authority, must have settled the question for the Roman Catholic side; but Hutchinson argues that as Elijah is said to have changed the nature of iron, meaning thereby the natural property—that which was heavy having become light,—so the bread and wine, which before were food for the body, after consecration become food for the soul.† The distinction between *nature* and *natural property* is a refined distinction. But the meaning plainly is, that as iron was still iron, though the prophet made it to swim, so the bread and wine in the sacrament are still bread and wine, though set aside for a higher service than the nourishment of the body. Hutchinson was a rational Protestant, and what in the present day would be called a sober Church of England man. The Scriptures, he said, allowed three orders of ministers, bishops, presbyters, and deacons; but priest, in the sense of *sacerdos*, is never found in the New Testament, except when applied to the ministers of the Jewish law. This law with its priesthood is now annulled. Christ alone is Priest. There is no priesthood but His, and that which belongs to all Christian men, whether ministers or lay people. They have all but one sacrifice to offer, which is the sacrifice of thanksgiving, and the living oblation of their own bodies.

No proper priest in the new dispensation.

---

* The 'De Cœna Domini' ascribed to St. Cyprian is now reckoned spurious.

† Hutchinson acknowledged some speciality in the sacrament. When Christ said 'This is my body,' He meant more than when He said 'I am the vine.' The bread was a sacrament of His body, but the vine was only a metaphor. The rock was a sacrament, the brazen serpent was a sacrament. They were not accidental symbols or bare metaphors, but specially appointed symbols of Christ.

CHAPTER II.

THE CHURCH UNDER ELIZABETH.—THE CONSECRATORS OF ARCHBISHOP PARKER.—ELIZABETH'S FIRST BISHOPS.—JEWEL.—BECON.—RISE OF THE PURITANS.—GRINDAL, CARTWRIGHT AND WHITGIFT.—HOOKER AND TRAVERS.—DR. JOHN BRIDGES AND MARTIN MARPRELATE.—AYLMER.—BANCROFT.—BILSON.—LORD BACON.

ON the accession of Queen Elizabeth all the bishops, with but one exception, refused to take the oath of the royal supremacy.* Those who opposed the Reformation did not scruple, as we have seen, to take the oath under Henry. Some of them had conformed under Edward, and returned to the Church of Rome under Mary.† The Bishop of Llandaff alone was ready for a change again.

The Reformers who had escaped the Marian persecution returned from exile, and to them the Queen committed the government of the Church. Of these only four were bishops, *The Church re-established under Elizabeth.*

---

* This was Anthony Kitchin, Bishop of Llandaff. Kitchin managed to spoliate the revenues of his see. It is supposed that at last he was deprived. The see is spoken of as vacant two years before his death.—*Archbishop Parker's 'Correspondence,'* p. 208, Par. Soc. Ed.

Two hundred and forty clergymen quitted their livings on the re-establishment of Protestantism, fourteen of whom were bishops. Neal says, 'Most of the inferior beneficed clergy kept their livings through all the reigns.'

Bishop Burnet makes the number who refused to conform, one hundred and ninety-nine. In D'Ewes's 'Journal,' a good authority, it is reduced to one hundred and seventy-seven.

Ridley speaking in Queen Mary's days said 'The nobles, the commonalty, the prelates, the clergy are quite changed. They never were persuaded in their hearts but for the king's sake.'

† Four bishops seem to have held their sees under Henry, Edward, and Mary,—Kitchin of Llandaff, 1545-67; Chambers of Peterborough, 1541-59; Tunstall of Durham, 1530-61; Saloot, alias Capon, of Salisbury, 1539-59.

CHAP. II.

—William Barlow, John Scory, John Hodgskins, and Miles Coverdale.* Matthew Parker was consecrated Archbishop of Canterbury. He immediately after proceeded to consecrate bishops for the other sees.† The new bishops were as thoroughly Protestant as the martyrs that had died in the last reign. A large number of them would gladly have dispensed with Episcopacy, while the ceremonies which the Queen imposed were barely tolerated. Parkhurst, who was made Bishop of Norwich, expressed his joy in a letter to Bullinger that henceforth the bishops were to have no palaces or country seats. Jewel, who was made Bishop of Salisbury, in a letter to Peter Martyr described the worship which the Queen was establishing, as scenic and such as they had often laughed at.‡ Grindal, who was made Bishop of London, disliked the ceremonies, but thought it better to conform than to leave the Church on account of

The new bishops oppose the ceremonies.

---

* There was also a suffragan bishop of Thetford, and John Bale, Bishop of Ossory.

† The new Bishops stood thus in 1559, excepting those which have dates affixed:—
Matthew Parker, Canterbury.
Richard Davies, St. Asaph's.
Rowland Merrick, Bangor.
Gilbert Berkley, Bath and Wells. 1560.
William Barlow, Chichester.
Thomas Young, St. David's.
Richard Cox, Ely.
William Alley, Exeter. 1560.
Richard Cheyney, Gloucester. 1562.
John Scory, Hereford.
Anthony Kitchin, Llandaff.
Nicholas Bullingham, Lincoln. 1560.
Thomas Bentham, Lichfield and Coventry. 1560.
Edmund Grindal, London.
John Parkhurst, Norwich. 1560.
Hugh Curwyn or Coren, Oxford. 1567.
Edward Scambler, Peterborough. 1561.
Edward Gheast, Rochester.
John Jewel, Salisbury.
Robert Horne, Winchester. 1561.
Edwin Sandys, Worcester.
Thomas Young, York (translated from St. David's). 1561.
John Best, Carlisle. 1561.
William Downham, Chester. 1561.
James Pilkington, Durham. 1561.
John Salisbury, Sodor and Man. 1571.

‡ In a letter of a still later date Jewel finds a reason for the dresses. The clergy were very ignorant, 'no better than mere logs of wood, without talent, learning or morality.' They were the same for the greater part that had been priests under Mary. What could the politic rulers of Church and State do with them? They were of no use as ministers of a Protestant Church, and to cast them out would have been to convert them into enemies. So they resolved, Jewel says, 'to commend them to the people by a comical dress' ... 'since they cannot obtain influence in a proper way they seek to occupy the eyes of the multitude with these ridiculous trifles.' —*Jewel's Letters.*

'The scenic apparatus of divine worship is now under agitation, and those very things which you and I have so often laughed at are now seriously and solemnly entertained by certain persons (for we are not consulted), as if the Christian religion could not exist without something tawdry.'—*Ibid.*

In another letter he says, 'The doctrine is everywhere most pure, but as to ceremonies and maskings there is a little too much foolery.'

them. This apparently was the position of most who conformed, while many remained in the Church without entire conformity. Cheyney, the Bishop of Gloucester, is said to have declared for the Lutheran view of the real presence; but all the others, as far as it is known, agreed with the Swiss Reformers.

Of the four bishops who consecrated Parker the best known is Coverdale, who had been bishop of Exeter under Edward, and who first published a complete translation of the Bible in the English language. The writings that are extant of Coverdale's are mostly translations from the foreign Reformers. 'The Old Faith,' translated from Bullinger, is remarkable for nothing but its defence of the ordinary doctrines which are known as Protestant. In a translation of Calvin's *De Cœna Domini*, we find the Reformer of Geneva less averse to the language of the Fathers concerning the presence of Christ in the Eucharist than some of the Reformers in England. Calvin thinks it right to call the bread the body of the Lord, because it is the sacrament and figure of that body. Yea the inward substance, he says, is annexed to the visible sign, and as the bread is distributed in the hand, so is the body of Christ communicated to us, to the intent we should be partakers thereof. It is not a sacrifice which the priest is to offer for the remission of sins, but a sacrifice on which the people are to feed. In 'The Hope of the Faithful,' translated from Otho Wermullerus, the author triumphantly quotes St. Jerome against John of Jerusalem on the resurrection of the flesh. It did not please St. Jerome merely that the body was to rise again, for there are different kinds of bodies. He could be satisfied with nothing less than the resurrection of the flesh, 'a substance of blood, sinews, bones and veins set together.' Coverdale's own language concerning the Eucharist is identical with Cranmer's and Calvin's,—that as truly as we eat bread and drink wine in the sacrament, 'so do our souls by faith receive Christ's body broken and His blood shed, yea even whole Christ, into whom worthy receivers are incorporated and made one with Him, flesh of His flesh and bone of His bone.' In the dedication of his translation of the Bible to King Henry, Coverdale sets forth the royal supremacy in much the same terms as the other Reformers had used. Aaron was obedient unto Moses, and Nathan fell down to the ground before King David. The Holy Scripture, says Coverdale, declares most abundantly that the office and authority given unto kings is above all powers, 'let them be Popes or Cardinals or whatsoever they will.' And that this had always been, tacitly at least, acknowledged in England, he adds, 'When your grace's subjects read your letters, or begin to talk or commune of your highness, they move their bonnets for a sign or token of reverence unto your grace, as to the most sovereign lord and head under God, which thing no man useth to do unto any bishop.' Coverdale lived through a great part of the reign of Elizabeth, but was not restored to his bishopric. It is said that he renounced his episcopal character, but there is no evidence of this. He conformed to the Church, though dissatisfied with many things which he thought should have been changed. He is usually claimed, along with Hooper, as a precursor of the Puritans, and though one of the consecrators of Parker, his history justifies the claim.

Among Elizabeth's first bishops the best known names are those of Parker, Barlow, Cox, Grindal, Parkhurst, Scambler, Jewel, Horne, Sandys, and Pilkington. Parker was a strict conformist, and a rigid enforcer of conformity. He was also a thorough Protestant, and in this respect a worthy successor of Cranmer. He renewed the correspondence with Calvin about uniting all the Reformed Churches into one communion. From this correspondence it appears that neither would the foreign Churches have objected to Episcopacy, nor would the English Bishops as a body have objected to such a modification of Episcopacy as would have satisfied the foreign Reformers. The death of Edward and the martyrdom of Cranmer put an end to the first negotiation. The second was frustrated by the death of Calvin.

Barlow was the oldest Protestant bishop. From him, through Parker, the succession of bishops is continued in the Church of England.* Cox was the leader against Knox's

* Barlow was made Bishop of St. Asaph's, 1535. It is a curious fact that there are no records to be found of his consecration. The registers of the

party at Frankfort, when they differed about the use of the English service-book. He was a valiant Protestant and a thorough conformist.* Scambler is said to have preached secretly to a congregation of Protestants in London during the whole of Mary's reign. Parkhurst, Horne, and Pilkington were afterwards famous as promoters of Puritanism. The last wrote several theological books, chiefly practical and expository. Grindal succeeded Parker in the Primacy, and was suspended by Elizabeth for refusing to enforce the laws against nonconformity. Sandys passed from Worcester to London, and thence to York. He objected to the vestments when promoted to Worcester; but was persuaded by his friends that it would be injurious to desert the Church at such a time, on account of rites not absolutely evil. He recommended that the ceremonies should be laid aside, not all at once, but by degrees, and as it could be done quietly.†

Of these bishops Jewel alone was a great writer. His 'Apology for the Church of England' led to an endless controversy with the Jesuit, Harding. It was written while the Council of Trent was sitting, and is the final plea against Rome that the Reformers are shut out from the Council unheard. The Pope would only admit Protestants on condition that they first recanted their errors. If he had taken us for men, said Jewel, he would, first 'have seen what might be said with us, and what against us, and not in his bull whereby he lately pretended a Council, so rashly have

Jewel's 'Apology for the Church of England.'

Archbishop have been searched in vain. As he was in law *the* consecrator of Parker, it has been maintained that the validity of all English consecrations depends on his. According to Barlow's own principles, consecration was not necessary. He said, in a sermon, 'If the king's grace, being supreme head of the Church of England, did choose, denominate, and elect any layman (being learned) to be a bishop, that he, so chosen (without mention being made of any orders), should be as good a bishop as he is, or the best in England.' In the same sermon, he said, that 'wheresoever two or three simple persons, as cobblers or weavers, are in company, and elected in the name of God, there is the true Church of God.'

* To Wolfgang Werdner, Cox wrote, 'We are thundering forth in our pulpits and especially before our Queen Elizabeth, that the Roman Pontiff is truly Antichrist, and that traditions are for the most part mere blasphemies. At length many of the nobility and vast numbers of the people begin by degrees to return to their senses, but of the clergy none at all.' —*Zurich Letters.*

† 'It is scarce wisdom,' he says, 'whereas in many years a beautiful and costly house is builded, if a window be set a little awry or some small like eyesore do appear in respect thereof, to disturb the whole house, or pull it down and lay it flat with the ground.' —*Sermons*, Par. Soc. Ed. p. 95.

condemned so great a part of the world, so many learned and godly men, so many commonwealths, so many kings, and so many princes, only upon his blind prejudice and foredetermination, and that without hearing of them speak or showing any reason why.' It was not thus, he says, that the old Fathers proceeded, who were 'Catholic men.' When they wished to convince heretics, they appealed to the Scriptures.

We may take Jewel's 'Apology' as fairly representing the mind of the Church of England at its re-establishment under Elizabeth. It defines 'Catholic' as not shut up to one nation like the Church of the Jewish dispensation. The '*Quod ubique semper et ab omnibus creditum est*' of Vincentius Lirinensis, is regarded as something which never existed. In this sense even the doctrine of Christ is not Catholic. Our enemies, says Jewel, taunt us with the divisions of Protestants; but unity is not a sign of truth. There was perfect unity among the Israelites when they worshipped the golden calf. Among the murderers of Christ there was the greatest consent. With one voice they cried 'Crucify Him, crucify Him.' In the early Christian Church the members, even the chief Apostles were not all agreed. Paul does not square with Barnabas, nor Barnabas with Paul. In later times, Theophilus, Epiphanius, Chrysostom, Augustine, Ruffinus and Jerome, all Christians, all Fathers, and all 'Catholics,' opposed each other with bitter and endless contentions. The 'Catholics,' who now boast of their being the only true Church, Jewel compares to the old Arians who used to boast themselves 'Catholics,' calling the Orthodox, Ambrosians and Athanasians. When 'these folks' speak of the Church they mean themselves alone, like those of old time who said, 'The temple of the Lord—the temple of the Lord,' or like the Scribes and Pharisees, 'which cracked that they were *Abraham's children*. Thus with a gay and jolly show deceive they the simple, and seek to choke us with the very name of the Church.' God's grace, he adds, is not promised to sees and successions, but to them that fear God.

The Reformed Church of England, according to Jewel, is not built on the Church of the Fathers, but on the Church of the Apostles. The Reformers sought to lay its foundation where at first the foundation of the Church was laid, on Jesus Christ. The Fathers were fallible, and therefore we must go beyond them. Yet the Church of England has never admitted that these Fathers are on the side of Rome. Augustine, Ambrose, Jerome, and Cyprian were 'learned men and vessels full of grace.' They are to be read and reverenced. They were witnesses unto the truth, pillars and ornaments of the Church, 'yet may they not be compared with the word of God. We may not build upon them, we may not make them the foundation and warrant of our conscience.' Augustine himself has said of those who were Fathers in his time that they were not to be weighed with the canonical Scriptures. We have departed, said Jewel, from the Church of Rome, but not from the Church of the Apostles. The modern citizens of Rome have come down from the seven hills, and now live in the Plain of Mars, where they find the water necessary for life which had failed them on the hilltops; so we have left the Church of Rome where the fountain has failed, in search of the waters of life.

On the sacraments Jewel was wholly Zwinglian. The true use of the sacrament of the Supper was, he said, a remembrance of Christ's death. All other uses are abuses.* The benefits of Christ's death are applied to us by faith, and not by the massing priest. When Harding spoke of Calvin as undervaluing the sacraments, Jewel at once and without reserve took up the cause of Calvin. He reproached Harding with 'misrepresenting so worthy an ornament of the Church of God,' and told him, if he had ever seen the order of the Church of Geneva, and 'four thousand people and more receiving the holy mysteries together at one communion,' he would have been ashamed to have published to the world that by Calvin's doctrine the sacraments were superfluous. In his letters to Peter Martyr, he more than once expressed his great satisfaction at the thoroughness of the Reformation as it was carried on in Scotland.†

After Jewel, the most voluminous writer of the Reformers

---

* Sermon at St. Paul's Cross.
† 'All the monasteries are everywhere levelled to the ground, the theatrical dresses, the sacrilegious chalices, the idols, the altars are consigned to the flames; not a vestige of the ancient superstition and idolatry is left.'—*Jewel's Letters*.

who had been in exile, in the time of Mary, was Thomas Becon.* His name was on the list of those marked out for high preferment; but the highest he ever received was a stall in Canterbury cathedral. The majority of Becon's writings are practical, and must at one time have been household books. The very titles of them have a Puritan quaintness, as 'The Sick Man's Salve,' 'A Potation for Lent,' and 'A Pleasant New Nosegay.' Their wisdom is simple and unadorned, recalling the homeliness of Latimer.† Becon was the author of the 'Homily on Whoredom' in the authorized book of Homilies, where it is evident that he was accustomed to plain speaking, and to the use of words that did not leave any doubt about his meaning. Another peculiarity in Becon, is his frequent quotation of the Apocryphal writings. He had a fondness for the lessons of wisdom, regarding the ordinary affairs of daily life, in which the Apocrypha is scarcely surpassed by any portion of the canonical Scriptures. He denied the distinction between bishop and presbyter, maintaining that there are but two orders in the Church, bishops or presbyters, and deacons. He advocated the restoration of what he called the old custom of electing ministers, when the names of some 'good and godly men' were submitted to the chief inhabitants of a town or parish, who after fasting, prayer, and hearing a sermon on the duties of pastor and people, proceeded to election. Then other ministers laid their hands on the head of him that was chosen, admitting him to the ministry 'without albe, vestments, or cope, and without docking, greasing, or shaving.' This was unlike the custom which, he said, prevailed in the Roman Church, where a man was made a priest by a bishop with

---

* Becon had been chaplain to Archbishop Cranmer.

† Here is advice to parents: 'If they be sons whom they intend to set forth in marriage, let them provide godly virtuous maids to be their wives, as may say with Sara, young Tobias' wife, 'Thou knowest, O Lord,' etc. Let them be no delicate minions, nor no white-fingered house-wives, which can do nothing else but trick up themselves like puppets, and prick upon a clout without any gain, swift to command, but ready to do nothing, except it be to eat and drink, to keep company with some he-saint, to play at the dice and cards, to dance and play upon a lute or pair of virginals, etc.; but let them be such as would lay their hands to work, help to get the penny, save such things as the man bringeth in, dress meat and drink, spin and card, look to her family, nurse her own children,' etc.—*Becon's Catechism*, Par. Soc. Ed. p. 356.

the help of another priest, or with the assistance of a bishop's scribe or secretary. The elect or invisible Church was the Church which could not err. In expounding the Apostles' Creed, he said that he believed *in* God, but he believed the Church, that is, he believed that there was such a thing as the Church, but he did not trust in it. Sacraments, he called signs and figures of God's grace. They preach to the eyes as the word of God preaches to the ear.* If the sacraments could give grace, salvation would be of works.

The scruples which many of the Reformed clergy had about the dresses and ceremonies, were overcome partly by the arguments of the Reformers abroad, who recommended conformity as to things indifferent, and partly by explanations that they were not connected with any superstitions. But there were some to whom the ceremonies were idolatry, and the dresses relics of Antichrist. Sampson, Dean of Christ Church, and Humphreys, President of Magdalen, corresponded with Bullinger and Peter Martyr without being convinced that it was not a mortal sin to wear a surplice or a square cap.† The number of the clergy who participated in the scruples of Sampson and Humphreys must have been considerable. When Parker summoned to Lambeth a hundred clergymen, and exhibited one Thomas Cole canonically robed, with 'a square cap, a scholar's gown priestlike, tippet, and in the church a linen surplice,' only sixty-one out of the

---

* 'Christ plainly and purely ministered the sacrament to His disciples without any ceremonies; the Papists must have censers, bells, candles, candlesticks, paxes, corporasses, super-altaries, altar cloths, cruets, napkins, besides their dowkings and loutings, their turnings, and returnings, their gaspings and gapings, their kneelings, and winkings, their mockings and mowings, their crossings and knockings, their kissings and lickings, their noddings and nosings, their washings and wipings, their bowings and bleatings, and as I may speak nothing of their prostrations and inclinations, of their commemorations, and histrionical gesticulations, more meet for madbrains and drunkards than for grave and sober honest men.'—*Works*, Par. Soc. Ed. p. 456.

† Bullinger wrote to Sampson and Humphreys concerning the habits: 'For the sake of decency and comeliness of appearance such a regulation may be made. If a cap and habit not unbecoming a minister and free from superstition are commanded to be used by the clergy, no one can reasonably assert that Judaism is revived; nor do I see why it should be unlawful to use, in common with Papists, a vestment not superstitious, but pertaining to civil regulation and good order.'—*Zurich Letters*.

Peter Martyr wrote to Sampson, 'You may therefore use those habits either in preaching or in the administration of the Lord's Supper, provided however you persist in speaking and teaching against the use of them.'—*Ibid.*

hundred were willing to be robed after the fashion of Thomas Cole.* They wrote their names with a *Nolo*, and preferred losing their benefices to wearing a surplice. Immediately after the XXXIX. Articles were subscribed in Convocation, petitions were presented in both Houses against private baptism, baptism by women, the sign of the cross, organs, copes, surplices, saints' days and kneeling at the communion. In the Lower House one of the most sweeping of these petitions was supported by fifty-eight members with only fifty-nine against it. Another petition of the same kind was subscribed by thirty-three members of Convocation, of whom five were Deans, one a Provost of Eton, twelve Archdeacons, and twelve Proctors. It is not now possible to ascertain the number of the clergy who had these scruples. In many dioceses conformity was not enforced, and many acted on Peter Martyr's advice to conform until the objectionable ceremonies were legally removed.

It is difficult to describe the party which about this time or soon after got the name of Puritans. The name was generic, and included men of widely different views. Tyndale, Hooper, and Coverdale might be called Puritans, and indeed many of Elizabeth's first bishops. Historically, the word came to mean those who never entirely conformed, or those who suffered for nonconformity. But these again might be divided and subdivided. The royal supremacy was not objected to by any of the earlier Reformers. Under King Henry it meant simply the rejection of the supremacy of the Pope. But under Elizabeth there was a vague belief, that the Church should be governed by its own officers and not by the civil ruler. To this undefined belief a partial concession was made, when the Queen rejected Henry's proud title of Head of the Church. She was to be the 'governor' of the Church, on the ground that the Church was one of the institutions within her realm. Christ was the Head, and the Queen the ruler under Him. This satisfied the scruples of the conforming prelates. But when the Queen enforced on the clergy practices and ceremonies against which their consciences

---

* Thomas Cole had just conformed. There was a spice of demonism in having the poor man robed out immediately after, as a terror to evil-doers. Thomas Becon was among those who wrote *Nolo*.

rebelled, her government seemed to them to conflict with what was due to the true Head of the Church. Among those who scrupled conformity, there grew up gradually a belief that the Church should be governed by Church officers. They began to ask if Christ had not given laws to His Church; if the New Testament did not lay down a scheme of Church government, and if so, were they to obey God or man? It was argued that if God's providence is over the Church, the Scriptures must contain such a scheme of government. God had prescribed the worship of the Jews, even to the minutest rites. Was it likely that He who thus provided for the people of Israel under the old law should leave the Church under the Gospel to the arbitrary will of princes?

Is Church government prescribed in the New Testament?

The leader of this party was Thomas Cartwright, a Cambridge Professor of Theology. He supposed that he found a system of government clearly prescribed for the Church in the New Testament, and that this system was identical with the discipline that had been established at Geneva. The Reformers who had been in exile had no special objections to this scheme of government. Even those who were unwilling to introduce it in England considered it good in itself, and suitable for the Churches of France and Geneva in the circumstances in which they had been placed. But a divine origin, except in a vague and limited sense, had not been claimed for it even by Calvin himself.

Thomas Cartwright.

Cartwright is for us a figure of considerable importance. He was the first who gave tangible form and expression to the Presbyterianism of the Church of England. He was the earliest complete incarnation of Puritanism, on its controversial and theological side. To him the Bible was an 'infallible book,' literally 'God's word,' not depending for its authority on the testimony of the Church, nor to be interpreted by the reason of man, but shining by its own light. It asks from human reason not an inquiry into its claims, but an humble submission to its laws. The proofs that the Bible is the word of God, are drawn from the matter and excellency of the Scriptures. Truth there preserves an equal level, 'unbroken by any untruth or contradiction.' It is assumed that the 'reasonable man' has a faculty by which he can be assured that the Bible is the word of God. Cartwright finds

Presbyterianism.

the Bible to carry its own miraculous evidence along with it. 'No pen of man,' he says, 'is able to lodge so much matter in so small room, and with such facility of speech.' And moreover, 'the word of God has such an effect and working in men, both in good and bad, as will easily sort it and single it from all men's words.' The Church in a sense is a witness, but in what sense is not very clear. The Fathers and Councils may have excluded books that are canonical; yet Cartwright says the Church being the pillar and ground of truth, it is impossible that it can err in its judgment of the whole canon. The Scriptures being received as the word of God, every letter infallibly inspired, and being moreover the only light which God has given to man, it follows that there is no morality or well-doing but among those who receive light from them. Tyndale and Latimer, as we have seen, denied the possibility of anything but an external morality among the heathen. Cartwright goes even beyond this, affirming that 'chastity in Papist women is not chastity, nor obedience in their children true obedience,' because they had not learned these things 'in the school of the word.'

In 1570 Cartwright wrote 'An Admonition to the Parliament holden in the thirteenth year of the reign of Queen Elizabeth.'* He spoke of the rigour of the bishops for the last six or seven years as unbearable. He called their reign wicked. All the best Reformed Churches were against them. Once, he said, these very bishops were of the same mind as

---

* There are two Admonitions to Parliament. Neal says that the first was written by Field and Wilcox, who presented it to the House, for which they were committed to Newgate. The second was written by Cartwright. The occasion of this 'Admonition' was the enforcing these three articles: (1) That the book commonly called the Book of Common Prayer for the Church of England authorized by Parliament, and all and every the contents therein, be such as are not repugnant to the word of God. (2) That the manner and order appointed by public authority about the administration of the sacraments and common prayers, and that the apparel by sufficient authority appointed for the ministers within the Church of England, be not wicked nor against the word of God, but tolerable and commanded for order and obedience to be used. (3) That the articles of religion which only concern the Christian faith and the doctrine of the sacraments, comprised in a book imprinted *Articles whereon it was agreed by both Archbishops*, etc. and every of them, contain true and godly doctrine. The mottoes of the 'Admonition' were—'Put yourselves in array against Babel round about, all ye that bend the bow, shoot at her, spare no arrows: for she hath sinned against the Lord.' (Jer. l. 14.) 'They shall not take of thee a stone for a corner, nor a stone for foundations, but thou shalt be desolate for ever, saith the Lord.' (Jer. li. 26.)

we are, but since their consecration they have become quite transmuted. The Parliament is exhorted not only to abandon 'Popish remnants and ceremonies,' but to bring in and to place in God's Church only those things which 'the Lord Himself in His word commandeth.' It was admitted that the doctrine preached by the conformable clergy was sound and good, but then, as Cartwright had said of 'the chastity of Papist women,' it did not come as it had been prescribed in the word. The ministers were not 'proved, elected, called, or ordained.' In the early Church the candidate for the ministry was examined as to his ability to teach, and inquiry was made of his godly conversation. But now by 'letters commendatory of some one man, noble or other, tag and rag, learned and unlearned, of the basest sort of the people, to the scandal of the gospel in the mouths of the adversaries, are freely received.' In the primitive times, idolatrous sacrificers or heathenish priests were not appointed preachers of the Gospel, but now the Church is full of the 'Popish massmongers, men for all seasons, King Henry's priests, Queen Mary's priests, who if the word of God were precisely followed should be utterly renounced.' In the old times the congregation had power to call ministers, now all is done by buying and selling of preferments. The bishop appoints the minister without consulting the people, and often a man is instituted whom the people 'justly dislike for his unhonest life and lack of learning.' The remedy was to remove advowsons, patronages, impropriations, and the authority to ordain claimed by bishops, and to return to the primitive custom of election by the people. Cartwright's arguments have most weight when he assails the manifest evils of the Church. His plea against reading Homilies was, that faith cometh not by hearing of Homilies but by the word of God; and he found a conclusive argument against keeping saints' days in the Fourth Commandment which said, 'Six days shalt thou labour.' The service of the Prayer Book, he regarded as interfering with the order of the word, as it is given us in the Bible. The Psalms were turned about 'like tennis balls.' Parts of Scripture were read in different places, without regard to the Apostolic rule of edification. The *Nunc Dimittis* was sung as if the

CHAP. II.

Church abuses.

The Prayer Book not in harmony with the 'Word.'

people were about to die, and the *Magnificat* as if they were celebrating the memory of the Virgin or of John the Baptist. It was considered out of place to pray for deliverance from thunder and tempest when no danger threatened, and to pray that *all men might be saved* was not merely out of place but out of reason, and contrary to the *word of God*. The liturgy was described as a profanation of the Scriptures.* The conformists pleaded that it had the sanction of the martyrs, and that they were following the footsteps of good Bishop Ridley. Cartwright answered that they ought rather to follow Bishop Hooper, who was a martyr as well as Ridley, but the martyrs did not die for the Prayer Book. They died for God's book. Even in King Edward's days they did not all conform to the orders of the liturgy.

'The Admonition to Parliament' was answered by John Whitgift, Master of Trinity College, Cambridge, who afterwards succeeded Grindal in the Primacy. Whitgift had always been known as zealous in the cause of Protestantism. He was not disposed to defend the evils and abuses in the government of the Church of which Cartwright had complained, but he earnestly defended the established order as becoming in itself, and preferable to the discipline of Geneva. Whitgift treated Cartwright not as a disciple of Calvin, but as a restless, perverse innovator on ancient laws and customs. Of Calvin he always spoke with respect, and appealed frequently to his judgment as to that of a truly great man to whom deference was due. Indeed throughout Whitgift's answer this appeal to Calvin, Zwingle, and the foreign Reformers on the duty of submission to a general order, is re-

---

* Here is Cartwright's description of Church worship in his day:—'The people, some standing, some talking, some praying by themselves, attend not to the minister. He again posteth over it as fast as he can gallop; for either he hath two places to serve, or else there are some games to be played in the afternoon, or lying on the whetstone, heathenish dancing for the ring, a bear or a bull to be baited, or else Jack-an-Apes to ride on horseback, or an interlude to be played, and if no place else can be gotten this interlude must be played in the church. Now the people sit, and now they stand up. When the Old Testament is read they make no reverence, but when the Gospel cometh then they all stand up, for why? They think that to be of greatest authority, and are ignorant that the Scriptures came from the one Spirit. When Jesus is named then off goes the cap, with such a scraping on the ground that they cannot hear a great while after, so that the word is hindered.'—*Admonition to Parliament*, p. 14.

markable, as coming from one who is known chiefly as the great enemy of the Elizabethan Puritans. Cartwright is classed with the men of whom St. Paul spoke, who knew nothing as they ought to know,—the contentious and vainglorious, who provoked one another and envied one another. It is denied that the Puritans were treated with severity. They had a custom, Whitgift said, of crying persecution when they did not get all they wanted. Lack of severity is declared to be the principal cause of their licentious liberty.* As to popular elections in old times, Whitgift rejected the case of the choosing of Matthias as a precedent, on the ground that both the office and the calling were extraordinary. Against the election of the clergy by the people he advanced this notable argument, 'that the Church now being full of hypocrites, dissemblers, drunkards, and whoremongers, they would choose ministers like themselves.'

The favourite part of the Geneva discipline was the eldership, by which a body of elders or seniors were appointed for government in every congregation. Whitgift, though refusing to admit that this was the meaning of the eldership or presbyteries mentioned in the New Testament, yet allowed that in the primitive Church, before princes and magistrates were Christian, this was the kind of government that prevailed. It was not meant to be permanent, and he quoted St. Ambrose, who says that both the name and the office of these seniors were extinguished before his day, for diversity of time and place required diversity of government in the Church. As to external ceremonies and ecclesiastical polity, the Church was left free. There were things done in the Apostles' times which are not binding on the Church now. Then they lived under tyrants, baptism was performed in rivers, and the disciples had all things in common. If the Christian Church was left free to adapt its government to the circumstances of different times and countries, it followed that rites and customs were not necessarily

---

* Whitgift says, 'You are as gently entreated as may be, no kind of brotherly persuasion omitted towards you. Most of you as yet keep your livings, though some one or two be displaced. You are offered all kinds of friendliness if you could be content to conform yourselves, yea but to be quiet and hold your peace; you rail at those who show this humanity towards you.'

wrong because they were not enjoined in Scripture, or had not the example of the primitive Church. Things necessary to salvation must indeed be found in Scripture, but when we come to ceremonies, it is not even determined in the New Testament which day of the week is to be kept as the Sabbath.

Whitgift Erastian.

Whitgift was confessedly Erastian. In answering Cartwright he fell back upon broad principles of reason. To the definition of preaching as not reading homilies, but proclaiming the word, he answered by saying that to preach the gospel was to instruct the people in faith and good manners, which might be done either 'by writing or reading, or speaking without book.' He accused Cartwright of misrepresenting the doctrine of the Church, where he said that the conforming clergy attributed to the water in Baptism what is proper only to the work of God in the blood of Christ.

Denies sacraments confer grace.

'You know very well,' said Whitgift, 'that we teach far otherwise, and that it is a certain and true doctrine of all such as do profess the gospel, that the outward signs of the sacraments do not contain in them grace, neither yet that the grace of God is of necessity tied unto them.' He then describes them as 'seals,' 'testimonies,' and 'effectual signs,' by which God works, as by instruments in them that believe.

Whitgift maintains that some must have authority in the Church.

Cartwright's arguments for the equality of ministers were disposed of with the remark that there is equality nowhere. The celestial spirits are not equal. The stars are not equal. The Apostles themselves were not equal. In every body there must be members inferior as well as superior. Christ forbade His disciples to be called Rabbi, and He said that he who desired to be great was to humble himself, but nowhere has He forbidden that some should have authority in the Church. In rejecting every rite or custom that had prevailed before the Reformation because it had been in the Church of Rome, Whitgift likened Cartwright and his party to the Arians of old, who resolved to do the contrary of whatever the Church did. This, for us, was neither necessary nor desirable. 'We borrow,' he said, 'good laws from the Gentiles, and we use the church's bells, pulpits, and many other things used by the Papists.'

To Whitgift's 'Answer' Cartwright wrote a long 'Reply.' This evoked from Whitgift a 'Defence of the Answer.' The 'Defence,' in which Whitgift quoted for refutation the greater part of the 'Reply,' extended over 800 folio pages. Whitgift declares the essential difference between him and his opponent to consist of these 'two false principles and rotten pillars, (1) that we must have the same kind of government that was in the Apostles' times and is expressed in Scripture and no other; and (2) that we must not in anywise or upon any consideration retain in the Church anything that hath been abused under the Pope.' It did not require an immense volume to refute these two positions, but the controversialists wandered into every minute question that could possibly arise out of their discussion, even to the lawfulness of compelling the Catholics to receive the sacrament, which Whitgift defended; while Cartwright said they should only be compelled to hear 'the word,' and if that did not convert them they were to be punished. Cartwright wrote 'The first part of a second Reply,' and afterwards 'The rest of the second Reply.' This begins with a chapter 'Against Civil Offices in Ecclesiastical Persons.' Their business is to preach the kingdom of God. To them were addressed the words of Jesus, *Let the dead bury their dead.* Christ refused to perform the office of a judge, and so should His ministers. The keys delivered to Peter were spiritual; civil keys belong rightly to those who hold offices of state. Whitgift had already asked if the ruling eldership could not be filled by those who held the office of magistrate. As Cartwright had called the eldership an ecclesiastical office, he was compelled to admit that the elders might have the keys, both civil and spiritual. To the practical question if the minister of religion should also hold a civil office, he answered that one was enough for one man, while Whitgift said that by holding civil offices ecclesiastical persons found help to perform their spiritual.

The next chapter was intended to demonstrate 'that the Church government by an eldership in every congregation is by the ordinance of God, and perpetual.' For this was alleged the Presbyterian text concerning 'elders that rule well,' and another of less significance that 'Paul and Barnabas ordained elders in every church.' This eldership was declared to be the continuation of the Jewish Sanhedrim. For the existence of these elders in the early Church, Cartwright adduces the testimony of the Fathers. St. Cyprian describes their office as assisting the bishop ' by dividing the communion bread into equal portions, and carrying it in little baskets or trays.' In the African Church, Valerius, the Bishop of Hippo, committed the office of teaching to Augustine, an elder, which was remarked at the time as contrary to custom. Socrates mentions that in the Church of Alexandria there was a decree passed, ' that elders should no more teach.' The bishop only had right to preach and to administer the sacraments. Tertullian and Jerome both testify that the elders were not to baptize, but in cases of necessity and by licence of the bishop. Their office did not embrace the ministry of the word and sacraments. They had the government of the Church, from which it followed that the power of excommunication rested in them, and not solely in the bishops.

Deacons not preachers.

After establishing the divine origin of the eldership, Cartwright proceeds to prove that deacons were not preachers, but persons appointed to care for the poor. That this was their sole duty was difficult to establish in the face of what is recorded of Philip and Stephen: but Cartwright said that Philip's diaconate had ceased when he became an Evangelist; and that Stephen did not preach but only defended himself from the accusations of the Jews. Baptism by private persons was objected to, on the ground that the administration of sacraments belongs only to those who have the office of teaching. In the remaining chapters, Cartwright treats of several other subjects, as the faults of the Prayer Book, the 'Popish apparel' of the clergy, and the necessity that in our ceremonies we should not be Antichristian. He objects to the word priest, the sign of the cross in baptism, and the ring in marriage.

The Church and the Commonwealth.

The only chapter of what we may call doctrinal interest is on the authority of the civil magistrate in causes ecclesiastical. In this chapter, Cartwright undertakes to show the difference between the Church and the Commonwealth, even under a Christian magistrate. The arguments are chiefly drawn from the Old Testament, as 1 Chron. xix., where we find that certain priests and scribes had the government of things belonging to the Church, while those of the State were committed to other persons. To this Whitgift replied that in both cases the power was committed to them by Jehoshaphat the king. Cartwright also adduces many cases in the history of the Church where the bishops asserted their authority against that of the emperors, as when Ambrose refused to have a Church matter referred to Valentinian, and when Augustine reproached the Donatists with preferring the decision of the emperor to that of the bishop. This question had already been debated between the Reformers and the Roman Catholics. The Reformation had proceeded on the principle that our most certain remedy for deliverance from the evils of ecclesiastical government was in the protection of the civil ruler.

When Whitgift was promoted to the Archbishopric of Canterbury, the controversy with the Puritans devolved on Richard Hooker. This new apologist for conformity had been educated under Puritan influence,* and like Whitgift himself, though no lover of the Geneva discipline, had a profound reverence for Calvin. Hooker is on all sides admitted to have been the greatest intellect that had yet appeared in the Reformed Church of England, and all parties agree to receive him as the wisest exponent of her doctrines and the truest incarnation of her spirit. Therefore it is that every party claims Hooker as on their side. One of his modern editors, John Keble, has been at great pains to prove that he defended the divine origin of Episcopacy, in opposition to the claim of Cartwright for the divine origin of Presbytery. That Keble has succeeded none will admit but those who are of Keble's party.† Had this been

Marginal notes: CHAP. II. — Richard Hooker. — Does not defend the divine origin of Episcopacy.

---

* Hooker had for his tutor at Oxford, Dr. John Rainolds, the most learned of the Elizabethan Puritans.

† Such passages as the following, sufficiently declare Hooker's position:—'Which divisions and contentions might have easily been prevented, if the orders which each Church did think fit and convenient for itself had not so peremptorily been established under high commanding form, which tendered them unto the people as things everlastingly required by the law of that Lord of Hosts against whose statutes there is no exception to be taken. For by this it came to pass that one Church could not but condemn another of disobedience to the will of Christ.'—P. 161, Keble's Edition.

'If we did seek to maintain that which most advantageth our own cause, the very best way for us and

Hooker's belief, the longest and most elaborate arguments in the 'Ecclesiastical Polity' would have been unnecessary. This is the judgment that every impartial man must pronounce, previous to the inquiry concerning the genuineness of the last three books. And when he comes to these books and finds the undeniable evidence of interpolation either by Episcopalian or Presbyterian, there is no choice but to leave them out of the reckoning, for the divine origin of Episcopacy is there both affirmed and denied. Hooker, judged of by the five books that were published in his lifetime, is satisfied with refuting the claims of the 'Discipline' to be founded on Scripture, with maintaining the antiquity and conveniency of Episcopacy, and with resisting the Puritan innovations on rites and ceremonies established in the Church.

The last three books to be left out of the reckoning.

Hooker defends the divinity of order.

Order is divine. Therefore Hooker begins not with a defence of the divinity of any particular form of order, but with a general dissertation on the nature of law, setting forth the origin and object of different kinds of laws. It was admitted that Calvin had done well in establishing his discipline at Geneva. Deprived suddenly of the former government, the people were fickle. They had banished Calvin and recalled him again. He returned, but on the condition that they would accept a discipline which would bind them to order, and prevent any future expression of their mutability. So far Calvin did well, but he erred when he began to teach that the special form of government which he had established was of divine origin. His followers soon claimed for the ruling eldership the power of the keys, and divine authority to excommunicate even kings and princes. Hooker denies explicitly that in Scripture there must be of necessity a form of Church government. Discipline is needed everywhere, but there is no necessity that it be everywhere the same. Throughout the world there is need of speech, but from this, he says, does not follow the necessity that all

---

the strongest against them were to hold even as they do, that in Scripture there must needs be found some particular form of Church polity which God hath instituted, and which for that very cause belongeth to all churches and all times. But with any such eye to respect ourselves, and by cunning to make those things seem the truest which are the fittest to serve our purpose, is a thing which we neither like nor mean to follow.'—P. 494, *ibid.*

men should speak one language. 'Even so,' he concludes, 'the necessity of polity and regiment in all churches may be held without holding any one certain form to be necessary to them all.'

CHAP. II.

The Church, so far, is left in possession of a rational freedom. It is guided by a public reason. The Scriptures which contain the supernatural light, presuppose in man the existence of a natural light. There are many things which we may do for the glory of God which are not commanded in Scripture. In the use of this natural light, we should not despise the judgment of grave and learned men. Here we learn a reverence for antiquity, and the order established by those who have lived before us. That order was the expression of their sense of law, which, as Sophocles said, 'is no child of to-day or yesterday's birth.' For the private reason to depart from the decisions of the public reason is to engender confusion. We are not to be tied to authority when there is a reason to the contrary. This Hooker calls 'brutish,' yet we are not to think our *yea* as good as the *nay* of all the wise and learned men of the world. The disciples of Jesus did not despise the judgment even of the scribes. Elias they thought must first come, for the scribes had said it. The order and ceremonies of which the Puritans complained were good in themselves. They did not belong to any sect, but were the ancient rites and customs of the Church of Christ. That they have been abused to purposes of superstition by the Church of Rome is no reason for our rejecting them. To do so would be to imitate the unreasonableness of the old Romans, who because of the wickedness of Tarquinius Superbus, banished every ruler who bore the name of Tarquin. After establishing these principles, Hooker's argument culminates in the fifth book, with a special defence of all the rites and ceremonies to which Cartwright had objected in his controversy with Whitgift. The objection had been that there was no command for these things in Scripture, and the inference was that they were therefore not of faith, and not being of faith were of sin. It was further added that they were inseparably connected with superstition. The latter Hooker denied, and to the former he answered, as we have seen, from the natural

The Church free as to its polity.

Defence of the rites and ceremonies of the Church.

reason, which is to be our guide where Scripture has not spoken.

Hooker added nothing to the answers to the Puritans.

It cannot be said that Hooker added anything to the answers that were made to the Puritans. He carried the question up to a higher region, where the atmosphere was purer. The Puritan was not without a sense of that order of which Hooker discoursed. He believed, however, that it was not furthered but hindered by the retention of the order and ceremonies that had been in the Church of Rome. We had rejected many things that had been for ages in the Church. We had protested against the Papal supremacy, and much of the teaching of the Church of Rome. Why, it was asked, are we to conclude that what is retained is any more the expression of a divine order than what has been rejected? The Puritans could not see the force of the long disquisition about law as urged against them. They were agreed with Hooker as to the abstract divinity of order, but to him the order established in the Church was the expression of the divine order. The discipline of Geneva had a beginning. It was modern. It was local. The discipline of Episcopacy, on the other hand, was ancient. It could be traced to the times of the Apostles. It was universal. We know of no churches that were without bishops. In these matters of detail, Hooker only reasoned as others had done who advocated conformity. If he differed it was in this, that he was not guided by mere expediency or conservatism, but by a conviction that in being conservative he was faithful to the universal principle of order which is rational and divine.

Hooker a Rationalist.

In a general sense, with many qualifications, Hooker's position might be explained as that of the Rationalist against the Scripturalist. The Puritans, as represented by Cartwright, denied the natural light, that they might give greater glory to the supernatural. Hooker, on the other hand, vindicated the use of reason within certain limits. The supernatural light presupposed, he said, the natural. Scripture comes to help in the further enlightenment of reason. Tertullian even maintains that to allege reason, serves as well as to cite Scripture, for whatsoever is reasonable is also lawful. It is by reason we know the Scriptures to be the word of God. This is one of the things we cannot know by the Scriptures themselves, so that reason is the instrument of faith. When we speak to men of God, we suppose them in possession of a faculty to understand and to judge something of what we tell them. It was St. Augustine's judgment that there are rational principles, on which men are universally agreed, and out of which the greatest moral duties we owe to God and man may without difficulty be gathered. So far Hooker defended reason and the light of nature, but he denied that God had given to man such natural reason as could lead him to a knowledge of salvation. He endorses a saying of Lactantius, that God would not suffer men to find out truth except by supernatural revelation. Without faith, hope, and charity, there can be no salvation, and of these 'there is no mention but in the revealed gospel.' Nature teaches nothing of the resurrection of the flesh, and it is only the gospel which tells us that concupiscence is sin. Cartwright said that the heathen sent men to the light of reason for the difference between good and evil, but the Apostles to the school of Christ. His word *only* can give us assurance and resolution in our doings. Hooker objected to the word 'only.' From which we are to conclude that he held reason or the light of nature able to teach us our duty, but unable to lead us to the knowledge of salvation.

The occasion of Hooker's being involved in the Puritan controversy was the circumstance of a personal collision with one of the Puritan leaders. The Master of the Temple, John Alvey, had died. Alvey was a Puritan, and greatly esteemed by the benchers. It was his wish that he might be succeeded by Walter Travers, who was afternoon lecturer. But Whitgift, with whom the patronage rested, was not favourable to Travers, and gave the preferment to Hooker. Travers continued for some time in the lectureship, refuting in the afternoon what Hooker had preached in the morning, and Hooker again in the morning replying to the arguments of Travers. The Archbishop rudely silenced Travers, taking advantage of the circumstance that he had been ordained abroad by presbyters and not by a bishop. Whitgift did not plead the invalidity of Travers's ordination, but only that it did not authorize him to exercise his ministry in England.

CHAP. II.

Travers addressed 'A Supplication to the Council,' in which he argued that a man who had taken his degree as Doctor in any university was a Doctor throughout Christendom. In the Church of Rome, a priest ordained in one country was a priest in all countries, and moreover, by an express statute in the 13th of Elizabeth, it was decreed that those ordained otherwise than by bishops were to exercise their ministry in England. The case of Whittingham, the Dean of Durham, was adduced as proof of the position that Presbyterian ordination was a legal qualification for preferment.*

In the 'Supplication' Travers discoursed of the relation of faith to reason, and of the Church of Rome. On these subjects Hooker treated in his two sermons on 'The Certainty and Perpetuity of Faith in the Elect' and on 'Justification.' Hooker, as we have seen, differed from the Puritans in maintaining that it is by reason we know the Scripture to be the word of God, and in holding that the certainty of evidence concerning what we believe is less than concerning what we perceive by the senses. This followed from his position that reason is first and Scripture next. He could not believe the gospel without reason. The first outward motive which leads to belief in the Scriptures is, he says, the authority of the Church. Then we read them, and are assured that the Church has not misled us. Reason, as it were, confirms our belief. He distinguished between *a certainty of evidence and a certainty of adherence.* When a thing is manifest to us we have a certainty of evidence. This is the case with what is known by the senses, or by infallible demonstration. But matters of faith are only discerned spiritually by those in whose hearts God kindles the light of grace. This is the certainty of adherence. What is believed in this way is more certain than what sense reveals, but it is not so *evidently* certain. In one place Hooker calls it an inward beholding, an intuition which God gives to His elect, and he intimates that this intuition is a kind of reason, or at least does not exclude reason. We never doubt of what is evidenced by the senses or demonstrated by reasoning, but as to matters of

Scripture and reason.

---

* Travers was invited to Dublin by Archbishop Loftus, where he was made Master of Trinity, and had James Ussher, afterwards Archbishop, for his pupil.

faith, he asks who is there that does not sometimes doubt? It is said of Abraham that 'he did not doubt,' which is explained that he had not the doubts of infidelity though he was not without those of infirmity. God works in all that certainty which is sufficient for their salvation, but in none that which in this life reaches perfection. The faith of true believers has many downfalls, but it 'convinces invincibly' and is conqueror in the end. In the second book of the 'Ecclesiastical Polity' there is a remarkable definition of faith, which might legitimately include among believers ordained to eternal life, the earnest men of the pagan world. Hooker is refuting Cartwright's favourite doctrine that good can alone be done by those who have learnt it out of the Scriptures, a doctrine which was supposed to be established by the text 'that whatsoever is not of faith is sin.' Cartwright said it was impossible that there could be faith but in respect of the word of God. Hooker admitted that in the first and ordinary sense of faith, it meant belief of certain things on the testimony of witnesses. But the faith of which St. Paul speaks in the Epistle to the Hebrews does not come under this description. Hooker and Cartwright agreed that it was 'a full persuasion that that which we do is well done,' but, as in Cartwright's judgment well-doing can only be known by the Scriptures, this persuasion could only exist in the minds of those to whom the Scriptures were made known. Hooker, who did not set these limits to our knowledge of right, said there might be a certain belief grounded upon other assurance than Scripture. He quotes Cicero as expressing a doctrine of faith identical with St. Paul's, where he says, 'That nothing ought to be done whereof thou doubtest whether it be right or wrong.' From this we might infer that a heathen who had never heard of Christ might yet have faith. Hooker however refuses to allow the inference. He denies that the heathen could have held the foundation of Christianity. It was urged by some that they acknowledged the providence of God, His wisdom, goodness, and mercy; that they looked forward to a future judgment, when the righteous would be recompensed and the wicked punished. In these things, it was said that the substance of our faith concerning Christ is virtually contained, and therefore they held the foundation.

CHAP. II.

The certainty of faith differs from the certainty of evidence.

Can a pagan have saving faith?

To which Hooker answered that the first principles of knowledge do not constitute knowledge, and that an acorn is not an oak actually, whatever it may be virtually.

The other sermon, that on 'Justification,' relates to the teaching of the Church of Rome. To a Puritan like Travers the Church of Rome could only appear as the Church of Antichrist. Salvation, among the genuine disciples of Calvin, came to man only in virtue of election, which was necessarily followed by that faith which was the condition of acceptance; a condition not performed *by* the believer, but performed *in* the believer. To this extent Hooker was legitimately committed to the same kind of opposition to the Church of Rome as his opponent, for to this extent he too was a disciple of Calvin. But he was not committed to the 'Discipline.' He did not reckon it necessary to constitute a Church. The Church of Rome, then, might be a true though a corrupt Church. Our forefathers who lived in the times of superstition, and believed the errors of the Church of Rome, may have been saved. This was not denied by Travers, but Hooker gave as the reason their ignorance. This sounded as if ignorance was the instrumental cause of their being saved. Hooker explained that they were saved by knowledge of Christ, which might be learned in the Church of Rome. Their ignorance excused their errors. But no such excuse could be made for us who know better. He maintains that the Church of Rome perfectly agrees with us, in teaching that 'Christ hath merited to make us just,' and that without 'the application of His merits' there can be no justification. They join other things, but not to the work of redemption. They differ from us not as to the remedy that has been provided, but as to the mode of the application of that remedy. The Protestant doctrine is that we are reckoned just because of the righteousness of Christ. We are accounted righteous once for all. The Church of Rome makes justifying righteousness a quality inherent in us. It is a work that progresses. Grace is applied 'by holy water, Ave Marias, crossings, Papal salutations, and such like, which serve for reparations of grace decayed.' The error of the Church of Rome, Hooker says, consists not in requiring works, but 'in attributing unto works a power of satisfying God for sin, and a virtue to *merit* grace here and glory hereafter.' This, it is admitted, is not a direct denial of the faith, but it is indirect and tends to its overthrow. Hooker is conscious of an ambiguity in the word *merit*. He explains that there is a sense in which works may be called justifying and meritorious. He tells us that by *meriting*, the ancient Fathers meant *obtaining*. But after all this pleading for the Church of Rome, he says in this very sermon that since he began to understand this doctrine, he judged the Church of Rome an enemy to Christ's merits. And in another sermon, 'Of the Nature of Pride,' after quoting the words of the Rhemes Commentators that *works are the price of the joys of heaven, and heaven the very stipend of the hired labourer*, he pronounces such sentiments more full 'of Lucifer than of Christ.' Still the Church of Rome holds the foundation. If it denied this directly it could be no true Church, but while the denial is only indirect, we must hold it for a member of Christ.

Travers was the author of a Latin book on the 'Discipline.'* This book was translated into English by Cartwright, and was reckoned the standard authority on the subject. It laid down a system of Church government the same as what we now call Presbyterian. It was maintained that this system was directly educed from the Scriptures, and it denounced those who left Church government to the civil magistrate or the judgment of the people, as persons who robbed Christ of His offices as prophet, priest, and king.

<small>Travers on the 'Discipline.'</small>

The only reply to Hooker which manifested marked ability was called 'A Christian Letter of certain English Protestants to Master R. Hooker.' It has been ascribed to Cartwright, but without sufficient reason. There is nothing in it which is like Cartwright. It was said that Hooker was so sensible of its force that it hastened his death. It charged him with undermining the faith of the Church of England as set forth in the XXXIX. Articles. The writers collected a series of passages out of the 'Ecclesiastical Polity,' and placed alongside of them passages from the Articles where not only the tone and spirit, but the very words appeared to differ.

<small>The 'Christian Letter.'</small>

* 'De Disciplina Ecclesiastica,' 1574.

CHAP. II.

Hooker said to contradict Art. I.

Hooker says 'the Father alone is that Deity which Christ originally is not,'* and again, 'the co-eternity of the Son of God with His Father and the proceeding of the Spirit from the Father and the Son are in Scripture nowhere to be found by express literal mention.'† The authors of the 'Letter' call the first Arianism, comparing it to the Arian formula 'There was when the Son was not.' Hooker indeed says in the context that what Christ had was *given* but given *eternally*, which is not in agreement with Arianism, at least as expressed in this formula, which fixes a time in eternity when the Son was not existent. The authors of the 'Letter' said of the second quotation that this kind of speech was likely to raise scruples in weak minds. They thought moreover that the co-eternity of the Son with the Father was clearly contained in the words of Wisdom, 'The Lord possessed me in the beginning,' and when Jesus prays that He might be glorified with the glory which He had with His Father before the world was.

Hooker says, 'The insufficiency of the light of nature is by the light of Scripture fully and perfectly supplied.'‡ Again 'It sufficeth that nature and Scripture do serve in such full sort that they both jointly, and not severally either of them, be so complete that unto everlasting felicity we need not the knowledge of anything more than these two.'§ The authors of the 'Letter' consider this as opposed to Article VI., concerning the sufficiency of Scripture for salvation. They ask if there is any natural light, teaching knowledge necessary to salvation, which is not contained in Holy Scripture. If there is not, why is natural light joined to Scripture as necessary to salvation? If there is, then Art. VI. is at fault. They deny that human wisdom knows anything of God which is not expressed in Scripture, or that moral virtues are rightly taught except in the word of God, and they think this is established by the text that there is salvation in no other but in Jesus Christ.

Art. VI.

Hooker says, 'It is not the word of God which doeth or possibly can assure us that we do well to think it His word.'‖ Again, 'By experience we all know that the first

* B. v. 54.   † B. i. 14.   ‡ B. ii. 28.
§ B. i. 14.   ‖ B. ii. 4.

outward motive leading men so to esteem of the Scriptures CHAP. II.
is the authority of God's Church,' ... 'it presumeth us otherwise taught that itself is divine and sacred.'* The authors of the Letter ask that this be compared with the words of Jewel, 'In time of dissension it is most behoofefull for the people to have recourse unto the Scriptures.' The word of God, they maintain, is not to derive its authority from the Church, but from its own spiritual power. St. Paul sought his testimony in the conversion of the heart.

Hooker says, 'There is in the will of man naturally that freedom whereby it is apt to take or refuse any particular object whatsoever being presented unto it.'† And, again, 'There is not that good which concerneth us, but it hath evidence enough for itself, if reason were diligent to search it out.' Art. X. says that 'we have no power to do good Art. X. works pleasant and acceptable to God, without the grace of God by Christ preventing us, that we may have a good will, and working with us when we have that good will.'

Hooker says, 'I will not dispute whether truly it may not be said that penitent both weeping and fasting are means to blot out sins.'‡ Art. XI. says 'that we are justified by Art. XI. faith only.'

Hooker says, 'God's very commandments in some kind, as namely His precepts comprehended in the law of nature, may otherwise be known than only by Scripture, and that to do them, howsoever we know them, must needs be acceptable in His sight.'§ Art. XIII. says that 'Works done before the Art. XIII. grace of Christ, and the inspiration of His Spirit, are not pleasant to God,' that 'not being done as God hath willed and commanded them to be done, they have the nature of sin.'

Hooker says, 'God approveth much more than He doth command.'|| Art. XIV. says, 'Voluntary works besides, over Art. XIV. and above, God's commandments, which they call works of supererogation, cannot be taught without arrogancy and impiety.'

Hooker says, 'though we cannot be free from all sin collectively,' yet we may be 'distributively,'** 'so that in this

---

* B. iii. 8. † B. i. 71. ‡ B. v. 72. § B. ii. 8.
|| B. ii. 8. ** B. v. 48.

sense to be preserved from all sin, is not impossible.' Art. XV. says that though we be 'born again in Christ, yet we offend in many things; and if we say we have no sin, we deceive ourselves.'

In defending the prayer that all men might be saved Hooker says, 'If any man doubt how God should accept such prayers, ... our answer is, that such suits God accepteth, in that they are conformable to His *general inclination*, which is that all men might be saved.'* Art. XVII. speaks only of some men 'chosen in Christ out of mankind.' If the rest 'by His counsel secret to us' are passed by, the authors of the Letter ask how can He have a general inclination that all men might be saved?

Hooker says of the members of the Church of Rome, 'we gladly acknowledge them to be of the family of Jesus Christ,'† and again he calls the Church of Rome 'a limb of the visible Church of God.'‡ Art. XIX. says that 'The visible Church of Christ is a congregation of faithful men, in the which the pure word of God is preached, and the sacraments be duly administered according to Christ's ordinance in all those things that of necessity are requisite to the same,' and further that 'the Church of Rome hath erred in matters of faith.'

Hooker says, 'Touching our sermons, that which giveth them their very being is the will of man, and therefore they oftentimes accordingly taste too much of that over-corrupt fountain.'§ The authors of the Letter answer that preaching the pure word of God is the first mark of the visible Church as defined in Art. XIX., and they call preaching a supernatural gift of the Spirit.

Hooker, speaking of lay baptism, says, 'There is an error which beguileth many ... by not distinguishing services, offices, and orders ecclesiastical, the first of which three, and in part the second, may be executed by the laity.'‖ Art. XXIII. says 'It is not lawful for any man to take upon him the office of ministering the sacraments in the Congregation before he be lawfully called, and sent to execute the same.'

Hooker calls sacraments 'heavenly ceremonies.'** The au-

---

* B. v. 49.   † B. iii. 1.   ‡ B. v. 68.
§ B. v. 22.   ‖ B. v. 78.   ** B. v. 57 and 59.

thors of the Letter say that Art. XXV. does not contain this account of them, and they ask where it is found that God ordained sacraments to tell us when God giveth grace, and that they are means conditional and as necessary as faith?

Hooker says, 'Predestination bringeth not to life, without the grace of external vocation, wherein our baptism is implied.'* The authors of the Letter do not find this in Art. XXVII., and they find the contrary in Jewel and Babington. The first of these says that 'the children of the faithful are born holy,' and the other says that 'a man may stand in the state of salvation and out of all danger of damnation before he be baptized.'

Hooker says, 'Sith we all agree that by the sacrament Christ doth really and truly in us perform His promise, why do we vainly trouble ourselves with so fierce contentions, whether by consubstantiation or else by transubstantiation the sacrament itself be first possessed with Christ or no?' The authors of the Letter answer that Art. XXVIII. says of Transubstantiation that 'it is repugnant to the plain words of Scripture' and 'overthroweth the nature of a sacrament,' and they add that surely was not an indifferent matter against which the Reformers gave their lives as witnesses. They conclude with a condemnation of Hooker's 'prefaces,' 'digressions,' and 'amplifications.' They did not see the necessity of the long disquisition about law proving things which nobody denied, and establishing abstract principles where the question was one of facts. They commended Whitgift as a better controversialist than Hooker, because he came at once to the subject and pressed it to a definite issue, while Hooker only beguiled men 'with fair words and a melodious style.'

The 'Letter' was answered by Dr. William Covel in 'A Just and Temperate Defence of the Five Books of the Ecclesiastical Polity and against an uncharitable Letter of certain English Protestants.' There is nothing in this answer which is not in Hooker. Dr. Covel strongly advocated predestination, and showed great jealousy for the honour of Calvin. He repeated what Hooker had said about the 'Discipline,'

---

* B. v. 67.

that it was good for Geneva but not suitable for all places.*

The controversy begun by Cartwright and Whitgift did not end with Hooker and Travers. The 'Discourse of the Discipline' was answered by Dr. John Bridges, Dean of Sarum. Bridges' work was a quarto volume, consisting of 1400 closely-printed pages, besides a 'Preface to the Christian Reader.' It was called 'A Defence of the Government Established in the Church of England for Ecclesiastical Matters.'† The author was to refute Calvin, Beza, and Danæus. He was to overthrow the Puritan tetrarchy of doctors, pastors, elders, and deacons. If we except the tedious length of Dr. Bridges' book, there is nothing specially to be said either for it or against it. The arguments were those of Hooker and Whitgift. The spirit of it was neither better nor worse than the spirit of the books written on the other side. He calls the Puritans 'dear brethren,' and laments that there should be any difference between them. He says he would much rather be engaged against the enemies of God's truth, by which he means the doctors of the Church of Rome, and he expressed a hope that they who were of the household of faith might yet bend their forces against the great Antichrist. 'So long,' he says, 'as we jointly followed the quest of that uncouth beast and of the purple harlot on his back, God mightily

---

* In Keble's Hooker there is an appendix containing a fragment of an answer by Hooker to the 'Christian Letter,' chiefly on the points of Predestination and Free-Will. Mr. Keble tries to show that Hooker was not so strongly Calvinistic on these points as Whitgift, but the evidence does not bear out the conclusion. In the Sermon on 'Justification,' Hooker says, 'God knew us, God loved us, was kind towards us in Christ Jesus, in Him we were elected to be heirs of life. Thus far God, through Christ, has wrought in such sort alone that ourselves are mere patients, working no more than dead senseless matter, wood or stone or iron, doth in the artificer's hand, no more than the clay when the potter appointeth it to be framed for an honorable use, nay, not so much.' If this passage is not meant to express the simple truism that all man's capacity is from God, it has no meaning but that of the Lambeth Articles. In some respects, indeed, Hooker had mentally outgrown the theology of Calvin, but he would have trembled to reject it.

† Bridges' work was not only a reply to Travers on the 'Discipline,' but also to a multitude of Puritan tracts that had been lately published. Forty-two of them were collected into one volume and published by Waldegrave, the Puritan printer. Several of them are against the ceremonies, some are in defence of the 'Discipline,' but the majority are records of the trials and sufferings of Puritan ministers. This volume is called 'Parte of a Register.'

prospered us in all our affairs.' The Puritans compared their opponents to the Ammonites, and their opposition to the Discipline of Geneva to the contempt of Sanballat for the good laws of Nehemiah. They called the Papists Canaanites; and as the children of Canaan were driven out before the children of Israel, so, they said, should those who had conformed in Queen Mary's days be driven out of the Church. They prophesied of fire and tempest, earthquake and famine, if 'the Lord's Discipline' was not established in the land. Bridges answered that those who supported the Queen and the bishops were on the side of Nehemiah, that the old Canaanites were not expelled from Canaan when they conformed to the Jews' religion; and as for national calamities, 'God be praised,' he said, 'her majesty's reign have been the days of the halcyon's sitting in the nest most free from tempests of all other parts of God's Church, insomuch that it hath been a refuge and haven to harbour at anchor many other Churches that have indeed been tossed in the midst of many tempests.' The book, however, was not entirely free from the animosity of party. The author sneered at the frequency with which the Puritans called themselves the *godly* ministers. He charged them with coveting the dignity and maintenance of the bishops, and he questioned the sincerity of their affected gravity. 'God be praised,' he said, 'they are merry enough and in good liking, save that they put on a sour visour of mourning and terror.'

The publication of Dr. Bridges' work was the occasion of the famous Marprelate tracts.* The mysterious Martin

The prosperity of the Church in the days of Elizabeth.

Martin Marprelate.

---

* Mr. Maskell, in his book, 'Martin Marprelate,' arranges the tracts in this order:—(1) The Epistle; (2) the Epitome; (3) An Admonition to the people of England; (4) Hay any worke for Cooper; (5) The appelation of John Penri; (6) A Dialogue; (7) M. Some laid open in his coulers; (8) The Protestatyon of Martin Marprelat; (9) Theses Martinianæ; (10) The iust censure and reproofe of Martin Iunior; (11) Pappe with an hatchet; (12) A Countercuffe giuen to Martin Iunior; (13) An Almond for a Parrot; (14) The Returne of the renowned Caualero; (15) Martin's months minde; (16) Plaine Percevall the Peace-Maker of England; (17) A treatise on reformation, etc., by John Penry; (18) The First Parte of Pasquils Apologie. Of these, Mr. Maskell says, there are in the Bodleian Library, Nos. 1, 3, 4, and 9 to 17 inclusive; and, in the Museum Library, Nos. 1, 4, 11, 15, 16. This was in 1845, since then, 9 and 10 have been added to the Museum Library, from the library of Henry Francis Lyte; Nos. 2, 3, 4, 7, 11, 14, 16, and 18, are in Dr. Williams' Library.

Marprelate had a secret press, which he set up first at Kingston-on-Thames. It was afterwards traced to Northamptonshire, and finally seized at Manchester by the Earl of Derby. Martin's secret was never revealed. He boasted that he kept court with Queen Elizabeth, and that he was often with the bishops when his presence was not suspected, but to the world he was never more than 'dust and a shadow.' The first of Martin's tracts began, 'Oh read ouer Dr. John Bridges, for it is a worthy worke.'* The arguments are the ordinary Puritan arguments, but it is not these which make Martin's tracts remarkable. They expose the evils of the Church. They rail at the bishops. They publish strange stories about their doings. They are, or at least were, reckoned to be libels. Dean Bridges is asked where he got the money to purchase his deanery. In another place he gives Bridges credit for some other gifts besides honesty. 'Thou knowest not,' Martin says, 'how I love thee, brother John, for thy wit and learning, as for thy godliness, I might carry it in mine eie and see never a whit the worse for it.' There was not much in the 'Epistle' to excite public attention. It was not remarkably clever, and the arguments had been often repeated. The 'Epitome,'† which followed soon after, reveals the eagerness of the search made for the author. Martin, apparently safe in his hiding-place, banters the

---

* 1. 'Oh read ouer D. John Bridges, for it is a worthy worke: or an Epitome of the fyrste Booke, of that right worshipfull volume, written against the Puritanes, in the defence of the noble cleargie, by as worshipfull a prieste, John Bridges, Presbyter, Priest or elder, doctor of Diuillitie, and Deane of Sarum. Wherein the arguments of the puritans are wisely prevented, that when they come to answere M. Doctor, they must needes say something that hath bene spoken. Compiled for the behoofe and overthrow of the Parsons, Fyckers, and Currats, that have lernt their Catechismes, and are past grace; By the reverend and worthie Martin Marprelate gentleman, and dedicated to the Confocation house. The Epitome is not yet published, but it shall be when the Bishops are at conuenient leysure to view the same. In the meane time, let them be content with this learned Epistle. Printed oversea, in Europe, within two furlongs of a Bounsing Priest, at the cost and charges of M. Marprelate, gentleman.'

† 'By the reverend and worthie Martin Marprelat gentleman, and dedicated by a second Epistle to the Terrible Priests. In this Epitome, the foresaide Fickers, etc., are very insufficiently furnished, with notable inabilitie of most vincible reasons, to answere the cauill of the puritanes. And lest M. Doctor should thinke that no man can write without sence but his selfe, the senceles titles of the seueral pages, and the handling of the matter throughout the Epitome, shewe plainly, that beetleheaded ignoraunce, must not liue and die with him alone. Printed on the other hand of some of the Priests.'

bishops in this strain, 'Why my cleargie masters, is it even so with your terribleness, may not a pore gentleman signifie his good will vnto you by a letter, but presently you must put yourselves to the paines and charges of calling four bishops together,—John Canterburie, John London, Thomas Winchester, William of Lincolne and posting over cicie and countrie for poor Martin? Why his meaning in writing vnto you, was not that you should take the paines to feel for him. Did you think that he did not know where he was himself, or did you think him to have been cleane lost, that you sought so diligently for him? I thanke you, brethren, I am well enough though you do not send to know how I be. My mind towards you, you shall from time to time understand by my pistles. I have been entertayned at the Court. Euerye man talks of my worship. Many would gladly receive my books if they could tell where to find them.' *

The four bishops were John Whitgift, John Aylmer, Thomas Cooper, and William Wickham. Martin's hatred to Whitgift is without measure. He will not allow that the Archbishop had either ability or learning. Whitgift was a rigid disciplinarian, and exercised unnecessary severity towards the Puritans. Beyond this, and his holding the 'Antichristian' and 'Popish' office of Archbishop, Martin has nothing against him. He says that Whitgift was a poor scholar at Peterhouse, which in itself was nothing disgraceful, but which the Archbishop's friends denied. The best thing we know of Whitgift is, that he promoted Richard Hooker; the worst we know of him is, that he silenced Walter Travers.

Whitgift a poor scholar at Peterhouse.

John Aylmer, Bishop of London, had less favour at Martin's hands than even Whitgift. His severity against the Puritans was not less than the Archbishop's, while his zeal in searching for them, and his vigilance in watching for any breach of conformity, were even greater. Aylmer had been

John Aylmer.

---

* In the errata to the 'Epitome,' Martin says, 'There is nothing spoken here at all of that notable hypocrite Scambler, Bishop of Norwich, Take it for a great fault unless he leave his close dealing against the truth ile bestow a whole book upon him.' It is difficult to know what Martin had against Scambler, for though it is said he was a great dilapidator of his See, he was not an enemy to the Puritans.

tutor to Lady Jane Grey, and had gained a great reputation in his youth for learning. He had courageously defended the cause of the Reformation, when by it there was everything to lose and nothing to gain. He had borne the hardships of exile, and was highly esteemed by the Reformers abroad. Had he perished in the Marian persecution, he would have gone to heaven in a chariot of fire, but unfortunately he lived to be a bishop, and in his old age became earthly, covetous, and cantankerous. The snow is beautiful when it first falls from heaven, but when it has lain long on this sordid earth, its purity is not unsullied. Martin calls him 'Dumb John of London,' because he rarely preached. This, however, is denied by Strype. In his younger days it is certain that he was a frequent and zealous preacher. When Bishop of London, he had a custom of swearing by *his faith,* which he defended as being only equivalent to *certainly* or *in truth,* and no more an oath than *amen.* This we frequently meet in Martin as 'John of London's oath.' He played bowls on the lawn at Fulham Palace on Sunday afternoons, on the principle that the Sabbath was made for man, and that bodily exercise was as necessary as the Sunday's dinner. He used to be so excited by the game that it was dangerous to speak to him, lest his temper should break out with some more violent oath than *Amen.**

---

* Aylmer's covetousness is a matter of history. Strype records that when he was made Bishop of London he demanded of his predecessor, Sandys, the previous half-year's income of the see; and a year or two before his death he tried to arrange for a successor on terms that would enable him to escape the dilapidations, which were very heavy, and for which some years afterwards his eldest son was compelled to pay £4000. He bought estates, lent moneys on mortgage, let out leases of the episcopal lands, some of them for one hundred years. He cut down the elms at Fulham Palace; and, according to the testimony of Bancroft—one of his successors in the See—realized £6000 by the sale of them. This brought him into a great deal of trouble, and obtained for him the name of Mar-elme, an anagram of Aylmer, or, as it was sometimes spelt, Aelmer. He refused to pay a tradesman's bill after the tradesman was dead. When the executors called for the money, the Bishop denied that it was due, and ordered the executors to be gone, calling them 'rascals, thieves, villains, cozeners,' and telling them to 'take that for a bishop's blessing.' Strype maintains that this is one of Martin's vilest libels, for the Bishop paid the money, though he was out of temper about it at first, as he always paid tradesmen ready money. But Martin has a story against Aylmer which Strype does not succeed in explaining with any satisfaction. Some cloth, to the value of £30, had been stolen from some dyers in Thames Street. It was found on the Bishop's lands. The thieves were

In the days of his youthful ardour Aylmer had written 'An Harborowe for Faithful and True Subjectes,' in answer to John Knox's blast against the 'Monstrous Regiment of Women.' In this book there were strong words against the bishops, which did not escape the memory of Martin Marprelate. He called Aylmer 'a wicked bishop,' and 'a pattern of hypocrisie,' for taking upon him an office which he had declared to be unlawful. Aylmer had called the Communion Service 'a blistered masse,' and the bishops, because of their rochets, he called 'rachetters.' To the bishops and clergy he had said, 'Howl and wail, not for the danger you stand in of losing your bishoprics and benefices, your pomp and your pride, your riches and welth, but that hel hath opened his mouth wide, and gapeth to swallow

CHAP. II.

Wrote 'An Harborowe.'

executed, after having confessed that this was the cloth which they had stolen. The dyers applied for their property, but the Bishop refused to give it up till they had proved that it was theirs. Proof to satisfy the Bishop was never brought, and so he kept the cloth. 'The Bishop,' says Martin, 'knew as well as the owners to what good uses it could be put.' 'It is very good blew, and so would serve well for the liveries of his men; and it was very good green, fit to make quishions and couerings for tables.' 'Brother London,' continues Martin, 'you were best make restitution, it is playne theft, and horrible oppression. Bonner would have blushed to have been taken in the like of it.'

Aylmer had admitted his gatekeeper at Fulham to the holy order of priesthood, because he was blind, and unable otherwise to get his living. The porter was made Rector of Paddington, because the inhabitants of that parish were so few, that a blind man could do all that was required of a clergyman. Martin says that certainly he could not starve so many souls as the Bishop of London. The blindness of the porter was denied, and his ordination defended, because of the impoverished state of the parish of Paddington, through lay impropriation.

It appears that Aylmer had a fiery, ungovernable temper. It is said that Bishop Bonner used to apply his fists to the heads of heretics, to beat the Catholic faith into them. His successor, Aylmer, does not seem to have been less unwilling to use physical force. He had great courage, but as he was a man of small stature, he often found the contest unequal. There was in Essex a Lord Rich, with whom he had many strifes. This Lord Rich was a great favourer of the Puritan ministers. He had for his chaplain a Mr. Wright. Lord Rich and his uncle went to Fulham to demand that the Bishop should license Mr. Wright to preach without conformity. They came to words, and at last to blows. Lord Rich's uncle took the Bishop by the collar, and gave him a thrashing. The Bishop said he was never so abused at any man's hands since he was born.

One of Aylmer's daughters was married to a clergyman of the name of Squire. The Bishop loaded his son-in-law with preferments. His prosperity led him to a dissolute and profligate life. To cloak his own evil-doing, he feigned a story meant to reflect on his wife's fidelity. The Bishop found out the real facts, and, Martin Marprelate says, 'went to buffets with his son-in-law for a bloody nose.' The true story is, that the Bishop shut himself and Dr. Squire into a room in Fulham Palace (it would be interesting to know which room it was), and with a cudgel, probably cut from the Fulham elms, the Bishop belaboured the dissolute divine.

you.' He had also said, 'Come down, you bishops, from your thousands, and content you with your hundreds; let your diet be priest-like and not prince-like.' The memory of the 'Harborowe' could not have been agreeable to Bishop Aylmer. Martin concludes: 'Here, Brother London, I think you would have spent 3 of the best elms which you have cut down in Fulham, and 3 pence half penie besides that I had never met with your book.' Strype says that Aylmer wrote against 'the Popish bishops,' and not against those of the Reformation. His book was published in Strasburg immediately after the accession of Queen Elizabeth. He advocated, as, indeed, all the Reformers had done, that the immense property in the possession of the Church should be applied to civil uses, such as paying the expenses of the war, supporting the poor, and the education of youth.* But when he saw the Queen and the nobles taking lawless possession of the Church's lands, he contended that they should be retained for the use of the Church. 'When I was a child,' he used to say, in reference to his early zeal in the Reformation, 'I spoke as a child; but now, *by my faith*'————. The Church of England was delivered from the Pope, and, as the Litany expressed it, 'all his detestable enormities;' but there were other 'enormities' from which it was not delivered.'†

Aylmer advocated the secularization of Church property.

---

* The property of the Church, according to William Tyndale, was a third of the whole landed property of the country, and the tenth or tithe of the other two-thirds. The most zealous opponent of *sacrilege* must have seen that it was not for the good of the Commonwealth that so much property should be in the hands of the clergy. It used to be said, that 'if the Abbot of Malmesbury were to marry the Abbess of Shaftesbury, their heir would be richer than the King of England.'

† In the 'Harborowe,' to illustrate an argument, he tells a story which is almost blasphemous:—'This,' he says, 'riseth of wronge vnderstanding, as the Vicar of Trumpington vnderstoode Eli, Eli, lama Sabachthani, when he read the Lesson on Palme Sunday. When he came to that place he stopped, and, calling the churchwardens aside, 'Neighbours, this geare must be amended. Here is Eli twice in the book. I assure you if my Lord of Elie come thys veye to see it hee will have the booke. Therefore by mine advice we shall scrape it out, and put in our owne town's name of Trumpington, Trumpington, lama Sabachthani. They consented, and he did so.' The see of Ely was much richer than London, and Elizabeth kept it without a bishop for eighteen years, that she might have its revenue. During these years Aylmer had often applied for it, that he might have a larger income than he could get out of London. His failing to get the translation may have suggested to Martin a story which he puts in the mouth of a bishop who, being asked whether he should be Bishop of Ely, answered, 'That he had no great hope to be Bishop of Ely; and, therefore,'

THOMAS COOPER.

CHAP. II.

Thomas Cooper.

Of Thomas Cooper, Bishop of Winchester, we know almost nothing, except from his connection with Martin Marprelate.* Wood bears testimony to the evil reputation of his wife, which is really the only thing that Martin has against him. Cooper wrote an answer to 'The Epistle' and 'The Epitome,' which he called 'An Admonition to the People of England.' It did not bear his name, but only the initials T. C. He begins with a lamentation over 'the loathsome contempt, hatred, and disdain with which the bishops and clergy were generally treated by the public.' He believed the consequences of it would be something like what happened to quothe he, 'I may say well enough, Eli, Eli, Lama Sabacthani.'

For the condition of the Church in Elizabeth's reign we have the best possible evidence. Archbishop Sandys says:—'The disease spreadeth, for patrons gape for gain, and hungry fellows, utterly destitute of all good learning and godly zeal, yea, scarcely clothed with common honesty, having money, find ready entrance to the Church.' Bishop Jewel said:—'The masters of the work build benefice upon benefice, and deanery upon deanery, as though Rome were yet in England. The poor flock is given over to the wolf; the poor children cry out for bread, the bread of life, and here is no man to break it unto them. . . . The noblemen or gentlemen, the patrons of benefices, give presentations of benefices either to be farmers themselves or else with exemption of their own tenths, or with some other condition that is worse than this. The poor minister must keep his house, buy his books, relieve the poor, and live God knoweth how, and so do you too.' Jewel continues: 'View your universities, view your schools, which have ever been nurseries to this purpose. Alas! how many shall you find in both the universities, and in all the schools through England, not only that are already able, but also that are minded to the ministry? If they be not found there, alas! where think you to have them? Where think you they will be found? Think you they will spring out of the ground or drop down from the heavens? No, no, they be of you, and must be bred and reared amongst you. . . . I speak not of the curates, but of the parsonages and vicarages; that is, of the places which are the castles and towers of defence for the Lord's temple. They seldom pass now-a-days from a patron if he be no better than a gentleman but either for the lease or for present money. Such merchants are broken into the Church of God, a great deal more intolerable than were they whom Christ chased and whipped out of the Temple. Young men that are toward and learned see this. They see that he which feedeth the flock hath least part of the milk, he which goeth a warfare hath not half his wages. Therefore they are wearied and discouraged; they change their studies; some become prentices, some turn to physic, some to law; all shun and flee the ministry.'

If the bishops who had conformed deplored the sad state of the Church, what must have been the lamentations of those who, from the beginning, had scrupled about conformity? To vest the government of the Church in the civil ruler, and not in the bishops, had been the doctrine of all the Reformers, whether of those who were for the bishops or of those who were against them.

* He was the author of the Dictionary called 'Thesaurus Linguæ Romanæ et Britannicæ.' Mr. Maskell, quoting from Dr. Bliss, says, that this work was so highly esteemed by Queen Elizabeth, that ever after she endeavoured to promote the author as high in the Church as she could.

the Jews when they despised the prophets, and were carried into captivity, or that the earth would open and swallow up the people, as it did Corah, Dathan, and Abiram, when they called Aaron 'a proud prelate.' He does not claim perfection for the clergy, yet he asks that they be treated as Noah was by Shem and Japhet. He asks, too, that the whole body should not be held responsible for the sins of individuals. He speaks of Martin's tracts as odious libels, and proceeds to defend the bishops from the 'untruths, slanders, and reproaches cast upon them by Martin.'*

Bishop Cooper maintained that the Church never had so many able and godly men in her service as at that time, which, after all, is probably true. He even marvelled at their gifts. As for Simony, he laid the blame on the patrons. They were, he said, greedy of gain, and were ready to bargain with any disreputable minister who would deal with them. Martin had said a great deal about the covetousness of the clergy and their providing for their families out of the substance of the Church. To which Cooper replied that he did not think it right that bishops' wives should be 'ladies,' yet, as a clergyman's income ceased at his death, it was proper that he should make some provision for his family, and not leave them destitute on the world. Especially was this necessary in these uncertain times, when no man knew how long he was to hold his living. To the general charge in Martin's book, Cooper answered that in all ages the ministers of the Church had been calumniated by heretics, and it was not remarkable that what had always been should continue to be.

---

* As to Whitgift, Cooper denied that he had been a poor boy at Peterhouse. It was generous in Cooper to defend Aylmer, for when Aylmer was Archdeacon of Lincoln, and Cooper bishop, the archdeacon gained a lawsuit against the bishop, which arose out of a difference about the extent of their respective jurisdictions. As to the elms, it was urged that the Queen had for a time made Fulham Palace her lodging, and that she was pleased with the removal of the elms, which obstructed her view of the country. The dyers, Cooper says, were offered part of the cloth, and would have got it all had they made good their claim. The grocer's bill is affirmed to have been paid, the Sunday bowling on Fulham lawn is defended, and for the Rector of Paddington, it is maintained that when he held the porter's office at the gate of the palace, he 'was a godly man, well-read in the Scriptures,' and that he faithfully fulfilled the duties of his parish for eight or nine years, till his sight failed him through age. Martin does not seem to have divined that to make the old porter a clergyman, relieved the bishop from making him a pensioner.

The Bishop of Winchester's 'Admonition' did not lessen the zeal of Martin. He appeared almost immediately after its publication with another tract, which was called 'Hay any worke for Cooper?'* This was preceded by an 'Epistle to the terrible Priests,' which begins: 'A man of Worshipp to the men of Worshipp, that is, Martin Marprelate, gentleman, Primate and Metropolitane of all the Martins wheresoever. To the John of all the Sir Johns, and the rest of the terrible priests, saith haue among you once again my cleargie masters. O Brethren! there is such a deal of love growne of late, I perceive, between you and me, that although I would be negligent in sending my Pistles unto you, yet I see you cannot forget me. I thought you to be very kind when you sent your Perceivants about the countrie to seeke for me. But now that you yourselve have taken the paines to write it is out of all crie. Why, it passes to think what louing and careful brethren I have, who, although I cannot be gotten to tell them where I am, because I loue not the ayre of the Clinke or Gatehouse in the cold time of winter, and by reason of our business in Pistle making, will notwithstanding make it known vnto the world that they have a moneths mind towards me.' Martin relates some ludicrous things which a neighbouring priest is said to have uttered when he heard the Morrice-dancers, and, suddenly finishing his sermon with 'John of London's amen,' rushed out to join his companions in the dance. He boasts that the Bishop had not confuted, but rather confirmed what he had written, so that now Martin was known to be 'truepenie' indeed. He repeats his former stories concerning John of Fulham, and he asks Bishop Cooper to deny, if he dare, that the Bishop of St. David's had two wives.†

*4. 'Hay any worke for Cooper? or a briefe Pistle directed by Waye of an hublication to the reverende Byshopps, counselling them, if they will needs be barrelled vp, for feare of smelling in the nostrels of her Maiestie and the State, that they would vse the aduise of reuerend Martin, for the prouiding of their Cooper. Because the Reuerend T. C., (by which misticall letters is vnderstood eyther the bounsing Parson of Eastmeane, or Tom Coakes his Chaplaine,) to bee an vnskilfull and a beceytfull tubtrimmer. —Wherein worthy Martin quits himselfe like a man I warrant you, in the modest defence of his selfe and his learned Pistles and makes the Coopers hoopes to flye off, and the Bishops Tubs to leake out of all crye. Penned and compiled by Martin the Metropolitane. Printed in Europe, not farre from some of the Bounsing Priestes.'

† This was Marmaduke Middleton, who had been Bishop of Waterford, and was translated to St. David's.

CHAP. II.

Martin's arguments religious curiosities.

Martin's arguments for the tetrarchy of doctors, pastors, elders, and deacons, as of divine institution, are, in their

He was an illiterate man, without school or university learning, and was ultimately deprived for his evil life. The 'Admonition' had only the initials T. C., which left Martin room for speculation as to the authorship. It might be 'Tom Coakes or it might be Thomas Cooper.' He concluded that it must be the work of 'Mistress Cooper's husband.' 'The style and phrase,' he says, 'is very like her husband's, that was sometimes woont to write unto Dr. Day of Welles.'

The bishops had a formidable enemy in the person of Mistress Lawson, who is frequently mentioned in Martin's tracts. Cooper had spoken of some of her doings with disapprobation, to which Martin answered, 'Concerning Mistress Lawson, profane T. C., is it not lawful for her to go to Lambeth by water, to accompagnie a preacher's wife going also (as commonly godly matrons in London do) with her man? "No," saith T. C., "I do not like this in women." Tushe, man, Thomas Lawson is not Thomas Cooper, he has no such cause to doubt of Dame Lawson's going without her husband, as the Bishop of Winchester had of Dame Cooper's gadding.'

Martin says they are shameless who deny what all the world knows, that John Whitgift was 'a poore schollere' at Peterhouse, under Dr. Perne, and that he carried Perne's clothes-bag. He often confessed that he was unable to buy a dinner-napkin, the want of which led to sad consequences. The point at which Martin aims, is not Whitgift's poverty, but his connection with Dr. Perne. This Perne was the man who had caused Bucer's bones to be dug up and burned, and for which he has obtained an undesirable immortality in Foxe's 'Book of Martyrs.' He had shown kindness to Whitgift in his youth, and Whitgift rewarded him in his old age with a friendly home in the Palace of Lambeth, where he died. Perne had subscribed to everything in every reign, so that he kept his preferments undisturbed under Edward, Mary, and Elizabeth. He was known among the Puritans as 'old Andrewe Turne Coate.' Fuller records a jest which makes Perne to be remembered nearly as much as his burning the bones of Bucer. One rainy day Queen Elizabeth was determined on her daily ride, and though not in good health, she could not be easily persuaded from her purpose. The Archbishop, who happened to be at hand, was appealed to. He used his best arguments to persuade the Queen not to go abroad that day. After he had spoken, Clod, the Queen's fool, exclaimed, 'Madam, heaven dissuades you not only by its weeping aspect, but by the eloquence of the Archbishop; earth dissuades you by your poor fool Clod; and if neither heaven nor earth can succeed, at least listen to Dr. Perne, whose religious doubts suspend him between both.'

John Bullingham, Bishop of Gloucester, seems to have been a kindred spirit to Dr. Perne; Martin calls him 'an old steale counter masse priest.' 'It is no shame,' he says, 'to be a L. Bishop, if a man could, though he was as unlearned as John of Gloucester or William of Litchfield. And I tell you our brother of Winchester had as liue play twentie nobles a night at Premiero on the cards, as trouble himself with any pulpit labour, yet he thinks himself a sufficient bishop.' It is insinuated that Bishop Westfaling was not always sober, and 'Parson Grauat of Sir John Pulchres of London,' is described as one of 'dumb John's bousing mates.'

Westfaling, Bishop of Hereford, William Overton of Lichfield, and William Wickham of Lincoln, are three of the five bishops who married the five daughters of Bishop Barlow. Another of the five was the wife of Day of Winchester, and the fifth was married to Toby Matthews, Archbishop of York, having been previously the wife of Matthew Parker, son of the Archbishop of Canterbury. The epitaph on the mother of these five episcopal ladies is worth recording.

'Hic Agathæ Tumulus Barloi præsulis inde,
  Exulis, inde iterum præsulis, uxor erat,
Prole beata fuit, plena amnis, quinque suarum,
  Præsulibus vidit, præsulis ipsa, datas.'

way, religious curiosities. The Church, he says, is the body of Christ, its officers are members of the body, and when these are wanting, the body is maimed. Bishops are unlawful, because not prescribed in the New Testament as part of the body. The civil ruler cannot make members for the body different from those that already belong to it. If the bishops are created by the State, and if their office may be abolished by the State, then it is no lawful office, for no magistrate can abolish out of the Church any lawful office. In the 'Hay any worke,' Martin says, 'Do you think, T. C., that the Maiestrat may make an eie for the visible body of the Church? ... Would you have the natural eies put out— and unnatural squint gogled eies put in their stead? ... Whereas the keeping out of eyther of the former offices of pastors, doctors, elders, and deacons, is a maiming of the Church, the placing of other in their stead a deforming. Now, ... reverend Martin hath sufficiently prouued it to be unlawful for the civil magistrate to abolish any lawfull churche officer out of the Churche. ... Every Christian magistrate is bound to receive the government by pastors, doctors, elders, and deacons, into the Church within his dominions, whatsoever inconvenience may be likely to follow the receiving of it.' Martin goes on to say, that the Queen and State are in great danger from Almighty God for deforming His Church. After which he calls T. C. 'a sodden headed asse' and a 'bishop of the Diuell.'

In the 'Epitome' there are passages which might suit a modern Sacerdotalist without a word of alteration. 'The sacrifices,' says Martin, 'of the old lawe after the building of the temple, were to be offered only in Jerusalem by a Levite of the line of Aaron only, vnlesse a prophet extraordinary ordained it otherwise, as Elias did. And the said sacrifices were to be consumed and burned only by a fire proceeding from the Lord. Briefly, none were to meddle with the tabernacle or anything belonging to the service of God but the sonnes of Levi, whome the Lord appointed for His oune service. So that if anye sacrifice were offered out of Jerusalem by any other than a sonne of Aaron, consumed by strange fire, or any service about the tabernacle performed by a stranger not appointed by the

CHAP. II.

The sacerdotalism of Presbyterianism.

CHAP. II. Lord, then an horrible breach of God's ordinance was committed and punished very memorably by the Lord in Uzza, Corah, Dathan, Abiram, and fiftee captaines of the congregation, who, not being of the sonnes of Aaron, would needs offer incense before the Lord.' After this passage follows an account of the Presbyterian government, which is introduced with the words, 'In this way Jesus Christ.' It was really maintained that the doctors, pastors, elders, and deacons, were as literally appointed to their offices by the command of God, as the Jewish priests to the Levitical priesthood, and that departure from the New Testament order, that is the Geneva discipline, would be visited by such punishments as befell Uzza, Corah, Dathan, and Abiram. These arguments once did good service to Presbyterianism. When worn out, they were laid aside, but, in the strange transformations of religious thought, they have been taken up by others, who little know that they are only wearing the cast-off clothes of Thomas Cartwright, John Penry, and Martin Marprelate.

John Penry. The next in order of the Marprelate tracts is 'The Appellation of John Penry,'* etc. The seventeenth is also by John Penry. It is a treatise on Reformation.† The only reason for including Penry's tracts in the Marprelate series is the supposition that Penry was the real Martin Marprelate. He was imprisoned on the charge of being the writer of 'Hay any worke for Cooper?' but was released after a month's confinement, there being no evidence against him. Some time after, a warrant was again issued for his apprehension, when he fled to Scotland. After four years he returned to London, intending to plead with the Queen for the reformation of Church abuses. He was immediately apprehended on a charge of sedition, and soon after perished on the scaf-

---

* 5. 'Th' Appellation of John Penri, vnto the Highe court of Parliament, from the bad and injurious dealing of th' Archb. of Canterb. & other his colleagues of the high commission: Wherin the complainant, humbly submitting himselfe and his cause vnto the determination of this honorable assembly: craueth nothing els, but either release from trouble and persecution, or just tryall.'

† 17. 'A treatise wherein is manifestlie proved, that reformation and those that sincerely fauor the same, are vnjustly charged to be enemies, vnto hir Maiestie, and the state. Written both for the clearing of those that stande in that cause; and the stopping of the sclaunderous mouthes of all the enemies thereof.'

fold. The persistency with which the Marprelate tracts have been ascribed to Penry, is a notable instance of the recklessness with which men write history when they have a party to serve. The great object of John Penry's life was to provide preaching ministers for his native country. He did not think the Church as established in Wales was suited to accomplish the work that had to be done there. He wanted to dispense with bishops, as plants 'which the right hand of the Lord had not planted.' He pleaded that men who could preach in Welsh should be sent among the people. He called upon the State to make proper provision for the instruction of the Welsh population, which he said was the duty of the civil magistrate, who was to provide, not bishops and non-preaching ministers, but a 'government according to God's own laws.' The evils which vexed the souls of righteous men in England, were tenfold in Wales. The population were sunk in superstition and ignorance, unable to understand English, and yet the remedy was English bishops and ministers, who could not preach in Welsh and were not concerned to teach the people English. 'Non-residences,' says Penry, 'have cut the throat of our church. Some that never preached have three Church livings. Many of our livings are possessed by students of either of the Universities, who never come amongst us, unless it be to fleece.' There is nothing in Penry's character or in his writings that gives any countenance to the conjecture that he was Martin Marprelate.

Out of the Penry controversy arose another of the Marprelate tracts. This was called, 'M. Some laid open in his coulers; wherein the indifferent Reader may easily see how wretchedly and loosely he hath handled the cause against M. Penri. Done by an Oxford man to his friend in Cambridge.' Both Universities were strongholds of Puritanism; but of the two, Oxford, up till this time, was the stronger. This was due to the influence of Sampson and Humphreys. 'M. Some laid open in his coulers' was as ordinary a tract as could have been written. It was a reply to 'A Godly Treatise, etc., written by Robert Some, Doctor of Divinity.' There are, Some said, two sorts of recusants which deny that we have a visible Church or a proper ministry, the Papists and the Anabaptists. Under the latter name, he evidently included the Brownists and the extreme Presbyterians represented by Martin Marprelate. These denied that the Episcopal Church was a true Church. Cartwright, however, did not maintain this, which caused Robert Brown to censure him for continuing in the Church of England. But Some writes against those who say the Church of England is no true Church. He likens them to the old Donatists, who had been refuted by Augustine and Calvin. He says that a godly prince may and ought to compel his subjects to the external service of God. For this we have the example of Jehoshaphat and Artaxerxes. Asa commanded Judah to seek the Lord God of their fathers. Josias compelled his subjects to seek the Lord their God. Augustine at first said that heretics should be reasoned with, but, after more experience with that kind of people, he found that it was best for the civil magistrate to compel them to follow the Catholic faith. Men are invited in the gospel to the supper of a great householder, and if they will not come in of their own accord, we have a command to compel them. So far Conformists and Puritans, both Presbyterians and Independents, were disciples of Augustine, but as they were not agreed as to what is the right faith, they were not agreed as to what faith the civil ruler should compel his subjects to adopt. Whitgift said that the Papists should be compelled both to hear the word and to receive the sacraments. Cartwright said they should only be compelled to hear the word, and if that did not convert them, then they should be punished. John Penry and Martin Marprelate said, it was the duty of the civil ruler to establish discipline according to the word of God, and not government by bishops. Dr. Some said that the godly prince should allow none but the true religion, and therefore neither Penry's religion nor the Pope's should be allowed. Nebuchadnezzar made a decree that all peoples, nations, and languages should worship the God of Shadrach, Meshach, and Abednego. Constantine did not suffer idolatry in his dominions. Theodosius and Gratian suppressed the Arians. The pious Edward VI. would not suffer the Lady Mary to have her 'Popish Mass.' Cranmer and Ridley interceded for her, and the king at last consented, 'his tender heart bursting out into bitter weeping and sobbing.' The teachers of religion should be maintained, for Nehemiah showed kindness to the house of the Lord. Some wanted to vindicate Elizabeth and her government of the Church, but unwittingly he asks, 'Where then is their kindness, who sell Church livings as Judas did Christ,' and he adds, 'The abominable sale and merchandise of Church livings is cried out against in Court, city, and university; *propter abundantiam*, as one said of late, *non potest, et propter impudentiam non vult celari*, that is, the polling and sale of church livings is so common, that it cannot, and so shameless that it will not, be hid.' Then came the question, if what had been dedicated to the maintenance of idolatry in 'Popish times' should now be converted to the service of God, which Some said ought to be, as Eleazar the priest took the brazen censers which they that were burnt had offered, and made broad plates of them for a covering of the altar. Gideon also offered unto the Lord a bullock that had been fed for Baal's service. The baptism of Roman Catholic priests was true baptism, for though they have not a lawful calling, yet they have a calling. He maintained, too, that sacraments administered by ministers who did not preach were valid sacraments, which Penry had denied, and they were not affected either by the ignorance or the evil life of the minister. God's ordinances are the same whatever be the character of the minister. To affirm the contrary is, said Some, the error of the Donatists.

What has been dedicated to idolatry may be used for the service of God.

Martin's next piece after 'Hay any worke,' was 'A Dialogue,' etc. The speakers are *Puritane, Papiste, Jacke of both sides*, and *Idoll minister*. Bishop Aylmer comes in for his usual share, but Martin has nothing more to say against him than has already been said. 'Master Vicker,' says Puritane to Idoll Minister, 'will you swear? I think you learned that of your Lord Bishop of London, for he useth it when he is at bowles.' The vicar is called a 'Vicker of the Diuell,' and Whitgift 'Beelzebub of Canterburye, the cheefe of the diuels.' Archbishop Parker, in dealing severely with the Puritans, was mainly but the instrument in Queen Elizabeth's hands. Grindal, as we have seen, resisted 'the nursing mother' of the Church, and was suspended from

Martin's 'Dialogue.'

his office. Whitgift was dutiful to the Queen, but how far his own judgment went in enforcing conformity on the Puritans we do not know. Martin declares that Whitgift himself was the persecutor. 'Of all the bishops,' he says, 'that ever were in that place, I meane in the see of Canterbury, none did neuer so much hurt vnto the Church of God as he hath done since his coming.'*

Richard Bancroft.

In February, 1588, Richard Bancroft, chaplain to Archbishop Whitgift, preached against the Puritans, or, as he called them, the Martinists, at St. Paul's Cross. It was felt even by Hooker that the Puritans had an advantage with the popular mind in the very claim that their 'Discipline' was prescribed in the New Testament. He wished that he could have made the same claim for Episcopacy, but he could not do it sincerely, and he scorned to do it for the sake of victory. Bancroft had not Hooker's scruples.

Proclaims the divine right of Episcopacy.

He proclaimed the divine right of government by bishops. The Conformists were amazed at the novelty of the doctrine. The Puritans were confounded with the boldness of the claim. Whitgift said he did not believe the doctrine to be true, but he wished that it were. The text of Bancroft's sermon was, 'Beloved, believe not every spirit.' The false spirits that had gone out into the world were heretics, such as the Arians, Donatists, Papists, and Anabaptists. Outwardly their deportment was humble and lowly, but inwardly they were full of contention. Heretics and schismatics have always had the same marks by which they could be distinguished from those of the true faith. The first of these marks is contempt of bishops. St. Jerome says that bishops were placed in the Church that the seeds of heresy might be taken away. It is no marvel, then, that heretics hate bishops. But for their authority, there would be as many schisms in the Church as there are priests. Another mark of heretics is the desire of pre-eminence. Arius coveted a bishopric, though he said that there was no difference between bishops and presbyters; 'an assertion,' says Epiphanius, 'full of folly, and one of the heresies enumerated by St. Augustine.' A third mark of heretics is self-love.

Four marks of heretics.

---

* For the full history of the Marprelate tracts, see Appendix to this Chapter.

As Pygmalion worshipped his own workmanship, so did they worship their own opinions. The fourth mark of heretics is covetousness. Those who are not heretics or schismatics follow the guidance of the Church, which is directed in her chief officers, especially when assembled in council, by the Spirit of God. Bancroft does not say that the Church is infallible, but he transfers to the visible Church the marks which the Reformers ascribed only to the invisible.*

Besides this sermon at St. Paul's Cross, we have two other tracts written by Bancroft. The one is called 'Dangerous Positions.' It consists chiefly of extracts from the writings of Knox and Goodman, to show the inherent spirit of rebellion which is natural to Presbyterians. Jewel, Horne, and other bishops that had been in exile for the Reformation, commended the work of Knox in Scotland, but Bancroft saw in it nothing but rebellion against their rulers, and destruction of sacred places.† The other tract was, 'A Survey of the Pretended Holy Discipline.' When the Bishop of Geneva was banished, Calvin thought it best to put the government of the parishes under the Consistory, which consisted of twelve senators and six ministers. This was a temporary arrangement to suit the circumstances in which they were suddenly placed. Out of this union of senators and ministers grew the doctrine of elders, who were to rule, but not to teach. What at first was a temporary arrangement at Geneva, became at length in England a scheme of government claiming divine authority. Bancroft was at war with the 'Discipline,' not only because it opposed bishops, but because it denied the authority of princes which had been established by the Reformers. So far it was against the Reformation, and, like the Church of Rome, the enemy of national churches.

Bancroft proclaimed the divine right of Episcopacy, but

Origin of Presbyterianism.

---

* Two years later, 1590, Saravia advocated the divine origin of bishops in 'De diversis Ministrorum Evangelii Gradibus;' and Matthew Sutcliffe, in 'A Treatise of Ecclesiastical Discipline.'

† In Bancroft's time the ministers of the Church of Scotland preached in the parish churches in England. This was first stopped by Bishop Aylmer, not on the plea of want of proper ordination, but because a Mr. Davison had preached against King James just before he came to England, in the church of St. Lawrence in the Old Jewry.

CHAP. II.

Royal supremacy incompatible with ecclesiastical independence.

he did not renounce the divine right of the civil ruler. His theory of bishops was an invention to meet an emergency, but there was no emergency to call for a renunciation of the divine authority of the Sovereign. At the Reformation all the Reformers were agreed as to the right of the King to make laws for the Church, and to settle its polity. The Puritans first learned that practically it was impossible to combine the regal supremacy with a free church life. In England the Queen was opposed to them as rebels against her government. They never abandoned the theory that she was the nursing mother, but they supposed that she was to learn from them what principles she was to nurse, and how she was to nurse them. In Scotland the Church and the Sovereign were in collision from the beginning of the Reformation. To resist the Sovereign was therefore a necessity implied in the very act of Reformation. Bancroft, in his 'Dangerous Positions,' quoted passages out of Knox, where it was declared to be the duty of the nobility and commonalty to seek the reformation of religion even when the King was opposed to it; and that if kings were tyrants, then subjects were free from the oath of allegiance. Bancroft commended the Scotch king for taking to himself his lawful authority in ecclesiastical causes. He had tried to change the Church government that had been set up in Scotland, on the principle that it was the duty of a king to establish the true Church in his kingdom.

Bancroft's writings have nothing more than a historical interest. He was a noisy polemic, with no remarkable endowments either in learning or intellect. It is a melancholy memorial of the times, that such a man should have risen to the primacy. The bishopric of London was given him because of his zeal in the Marprelate controversy, and his only title to the Archbishopric was his capacity to harass the Puritans.

Thomas Bilson.

About three years after Bancroft's sermon at St. Paul's Cross, Thomas Bilson, Warden of Winchester College, and afterwards bishop of Winchester, published his treatise on 'The Perpetual Government of Christ's Church.' Bilson was a man of higher intellect than Bancroft, and his book must even now be regarded as one of the best defences of the divine right of Episcopacy. Its object was on the one hand to refute the claim of the Puritans to be the lineal descendants of the Jewish Church, and on the other hand to establish this claim for Episcopacy. The Catholic Church, from Adam to Moses, and from Moses to Christ, was governed, he says, by 'an inequality and superiority of pastors and teachers.' In the Patriarchal Church the Patriarchs were the divinely appointed rulers. Adam governed the Church nine hundred years, and Seth five hundred. The father governed the family, and the first-born was ruler over his brethren. The government of the household was transferred to the Church, which was the household of the saints. Under the dispensation of Moses there were priests above Levites, and priests above priests, and some Levites above other Levites. Bilson distinctly renounced the doctrine which had prevailed in the Church of England since the Reformation, that we are to establish in the Church that form of government which is most convenient for the time and country in which we live. 'We must rather,' he says, 'observe what kind of external government the Lord established in His Church.' The Puritans said that without their discipline the body of Christ was maimed, and that bishops were 'gogled eyes' put in the place where the natural eyes had been thrust out. Now Bilson turns on the Puritans, and maintains that bishops are the natural eyes of the Church, 'primitive members for the guiding and directing the whole body, which without them is maimed and unable to provide for the safety and security of itself.' He professed, however, to be afraid to claim for the bishops all that the Puritans claimed for their discipline. Their exaltation of the power of the presbyteries seemed to be conferring on Church rulers that sceptre which belonged only to Christ. To avoid this, he tells us that he is careful to distinguish between the visible Church and the kingdom of God. The visible Church was not the kingdom of God. This consisted only of the true members of the mystical body of Christ, which is the Church invisible. This distinction tells us that Bilson did not see all that his own theory implied. The confounding of the Church visible with the Church invisible, followed as certainly on the divine right of Episcopacy as on the divine

Uses the Puritan arguments in defence of Episcopacy.

right of Presbytery. In either case the Church officers professed to be Christ's vicars. The Church visible is the body of which Christ was the Head, and was therefore not distinguishable from the kingdom of God. The Puritans claimed for the eldership a descent from the Jewish Sanhedrim. Bilson answered that that was a judicial part of the Mosaic law, and, like the ceremonies and the priesthood, was abolished by the death of Christ. The Puritans said that *Tell the Church* was Tell the Sanhedrim. To the Christian this was the eldership, to the Jew it was the magistracy appointed in every city. As the members of the Sanhedrim had the government called the power of the keys, the eldership or Christian Sanhedrim had the same keys, and were to bind and to loose in the government of the Church. The answer to this was, that the Sanhedrim were civil magistrates, with the power of life and death, and that to give this to the eldership would be to interfere with the magistracy. Bilson's arguments for Episcopacy are those with which we are now familiar. 'Philip,' he says, 'baptized and preached, but he could not confer on believers the gifts of the Holy Ghost.' That was reserved for an apostle. St. Paul laid his hands on the disciples at Ephesus, and straightway they spoke with tongues and prophesied. Christ established an inequality of ministers when he sent out the twelve Apostles and seventy disciples. St. Jerome found a prophetical announcement of this distinction in the twelve fountains and seventy palm-trees at Elim. The Apostles had authority. They were as infallible in their doctrines when they spoke as they now are in their writings. Their decisions were binding on the Church. They were not guided by the number of voices in the congregation, or by the consent of the presbytery. St. Paul said peremptorily that what he preached was to be believed, and every doctrine opposed to it was to be refused, even if preached by an angel from heaven. The power of the keys was first settled in the Apostles. They did not derive it from the Church, but the Church has it through them. This power was given to their successors, without whose presence no presbyteries could exercise the 'laying on of hands.' Cranmer said the King might make a priest or the people might make a priest, but Bilson says that 'princes cannot authorize pastors to preach the word or to administer the sacraments. The King of Heaven has appointed messengers of His word and stewards of His mysteries.' It is their business also to redress disorders in the Church, to remove abuses, and to displace them that do evil. But, he adds, in a Christian State the officers of the Church are not to do these things without the consent and assistance of the civil magistrate.

The public life of Whitgift consisted of two great battles, one against the discipline of Calvin, and another for the doctrine of Calvin. The Puritans and the Conformists differed mainly about discipline. They were both satisfied with the doctrines of the XXXIX. Articles. Our Reformers, like Luther, Calvin, and Melancthon, were Augustinians. They expressed themselves differently on predestination; that is to say, instead of pressing it to its logical consequences, as Calvin did, they simply stated the doctrine itself. They spoke of a predestination of some men to eternal life. Of the others, who were not predestinated, they said nothing. That Calvinism, or at least the Augustinianism of Calvin, really differed from the Augustinianism of the Church of England, was never disputed. For this we have the unbroken testimony of the Church for seventy years after the Reformation. In Strype's 'Ecclesiastical Memorials' mention is made of free-willers being in the prisons in 1554. They are described as men who held free-will, tending to the derogation of God's grace, and who had refused the doctrine of absolute predestination and original sin. They are only mentioned to be condemned. Ridley and Bradford wrote treatises on election and predestination to refute them. Philpot, the martyr, told his Roman Catholic examiners that the doctrine of Calvin on predestination was the doctrine of the Fathers of the Church, and that it agreed with the Scriptures. Election and reprobation, in the most strict sense of Calvin, are distinctly taught in the notes and preface of the Bishops' Bible, which was published by the sanction of Elizabeth's first bishops. The same doctrines are again found in the 'Questions and Answers concerning Predestination,' and some other authorized documents in the time of Elizabeth. The first commentary

CHAP. II.

Whitgift's Calvinism.

Calvinism of the Church of England.

CHAP. II. on the XXXIX. Articles was that of Thomas Rogers, who refuted the Papists, and the Family of Love, defended the divine right of Episcopacy, and the doctrines of Calvin. Art. XVII. is explained in these propositions :—that there is a predestination of men unto eternal life; that predestination has been everlasting; that they which are predestinated unto salvation cannot perish; that not all men, but certain men, are predestinated to be saved; that in Christ Jesus, of the mere will and purpose of God, some are elected unto salvation, and not others; that they who are elected unto salvation, if they come to years of discretion, are called outwardly by the word, and inwardly by the Spirit of God; that the predestinate are both justified by faith, sanctified by the Holy Spirit, and shall be glorified in the life to come. The texts which Rogers quotes, and his manner of quoting them, show a determined opposition to the belief of an election merely conditional. He claims the ancient Catholic and Orthodox Church for his doctrine, saying it was condemned only by Carpocrations, Valentinians, Cerdonites, Manichees, Hieracites, and the Family of Love.

Strype gives some account of one Thomas Talbot, parson of Mary Magdalene Street, who, about the year 1562, got into great trouble from teaching that God did not predestinate evil, but that He only foreknew it. But it was not till 1595 that any one in a high position in the Church of England ventured to contradict the doctrine of Calvin concerning the decrees. It was first done by Peter Baro, a Frenchman, a professor at Cambridge, who, in a Latin sermon, addressed to the Clergy, maintained these four propositions:—

Peter Baro.

(1.) God created all and every individual, with a real will to save him.

(2.) The will of God is twofold, antecedent and consequent. God reprobates no man by His will of antecedence.

(3.) Christ died for all and every individual of the human race.

(4.) God's promises respecting eternal life are universal, and were made equally to Cain and Abel, to Esau, to Jacob, to Judas and Peter; nor till Cain excluded himself, was he any more rejected of God than was Abel.

THE LAMBETH ARTICLES.

In the same year William Barrett, a Fellow of Caius College, preached against predestination, and was forced to read a retractation in St. Mary's.* He was afterwards sent to Lambeth, where he was examined and admonished by the Archbishop. This assault upon the received doctrines of the Church, at a public university, was of so grave a charater that the Archbishop immediately assembled a Conference at Lambeth, consisting of the Bishop of London, the Bishop of Bangor, Tindal, the Dean of Ely, Dr. Whitaker, the Queen's Divinity Professor, and other learned men from Cambridge, who framed the Articles in opposition to Barrett's teaching, which are known as the Articles of Lambeth. They consist of these nine propositions:—

(1.) God hath from eternity predestinated certain persons to life, and hath reprobated certain persons unto death.

(2.) The moving or efficient cause of predestination unto life is not the foresight of faith or of perseverance, or of good works, or of anything that is in the persons predestinated, but the alone will of God's good pleasure.

(3.) The predestinate are a predetermined and certain number, which can neither be lessened nor increased.

---

* We have no knowledge of Barrett's doctrines, except from the Retractation which he was compelled to read, where it is put down in these propositions:—

(1.) That no man in this transitory life is so strongly underpropped, at least, by the certainty of faith, that is to say (as afterwards he explained it himself), by revelation, that he ought to be assured of his own salvation.

(2.) That the faith of Peter could not fail, but that the faith of other men might fail, our Lord not praying for the faith of any particular man.

(3.) That the certainty of perseverance for the time to come is a presumptuous and proud security, forasmuch as it is in its own nature contingent, and that it was not only a presumptuous, but a wicked doctrine.

(4.) There was no distinction in the faith, but in the persons believing.

(5.) That the forgiveness of sins is an article of the faith, but not the forgiveness of the sins particularly of this man or that; and therefore that no true believer either can or ought believe for certain that his sins are forgiven him.

(6.) That he maintained against Calvin, Peter Martyr, and the rest, (concerning those that are not saved), that sin is the true, proper, and first cause of reprobation.

(7.) That he had taxed Calvin for lifting up himself above the high and Almighty God; and

(8.) That he had uttered many bitter words against Peter Martyr, Jerome Zanchius, and Francis Junius, calling them by the odious name of Calvinists, and branding them with a most grievous mark of reproach, they being the lights and ornaments of our Church, as is suggested in the Articles that were exhibited against him.

As the recantation is not found among the registers of the University of Cambridge, Peter Heylin casts doubts on its accuracy. We must, however, remember that Heylin was a partisan on the Arminian side.

(4.) Such as are not predestinated to salvation, shall inevitably be condemned on account of their sins.

(5.) The true, lively, and justifying faith, and the Spirit of God justifying, is not extinguished, doth not utterly fail, doth not vanish away in the elect, either finally or totally.

(6.) A true believer, that is, one endued with justifying faith, is certified, by the full assurance of faith that his sins are forgiven, and that he shall be everlastingly saved by Christ.

(7.) Saving grace is not allowed, is not imparted, is not granted to all men, by which they may be saved if they will.

(8.) No man is able to come to Christ unless it be given him, and unless the Father draw him, and all men are not drawn by the Father that they may come to His Son.

(9.) It is not in the will and power of every man to be saved.

Whitgift said that these Articles were agreeable to the XXXIX., established by authority. They were approved by the Archbishop of York, Dr. Hutton, who was unable to attend the Conference, but who added, 'These positions may be collected from the Holy Scriptures, either expressly or by necessary consequence, and also from the writings of St. Augustine.'

Lord Bacon. Amidst these Elizabethan strifes Lord Bacon was laying the foundation of the philosophy of experience, but he was not an indifferent spectator of what was going on in the religious world. He stood on the platform on which the Reformed Church of England was established, that Episcopacy is not opposed to the Scriptures, but that the Scriptures do not prescribe for the Church any perpetual unchangeable polity. He refused to condemn the Reformed Churches that had adopted Presbyterian government, but *Blames the Puritans.* he blamed the Puritans for trying to thrust their discipline on the Church of England. It was not better than Episcopacy, but, even if it had been, there were reasons why it should not be adopted in England. Bacon strongly condemned the Marprelate tracts, but he said that those written on the side of the bishops were as meet to be suppressed as those written against them. Two causes he gives as the origin of atheism, curious controversies and profane scoffing. He praised Bishop Cooper for answering Martin not according to his folly, and he hoped the clergy had nothing to do with the interlibelling. When the controversy was with the Romanists, and such questions as the adoration of the sacrament were discussed, the issue, Bacon said, was important, but now the question is about ceremonies and government, which are indifferent. The unity of the Church should not depend on these, but on the *one faith* and the *one baptism*. We should distinguish between the things of religion which belong to eternity, and those which merely belong to time. We should distinguish between essentials and things non-essential. When the Apostles differed about subordinate matters, they did not lay down positions and assertions. They gave their counsel and advice. They said, 'I, not the Lord;' but now every one is crying, 'The Lord, and not I.'

But while Bacon approved of Episcopacy, and blamed what he thought blamable in the Puritans, he was not blind to the manifold evils for which the Church was responsible, nor did he think that the Episcopal treatment of the Puritans was capable of any defence. He spoke with astonishment of 'some indiscreet persons who have been so bold in open preaching to use derogatory and open censure of the Churches abroad, and that so far as some of our men, as I have heard, ordained in foreign parts, have been pronounced to be no lawful ministers.' He blamed the bishops for their stiffness in refusing to alter anything, and he asks why the ecclesiastical state should continue upon the dregs of time, when the civil state is purged continually as disorders arise. He told the bishops that their wrongs against the Puritans could not be dissembled nor excused. They had been too ready to hear accusations against ministers, often from those who had quarrelled with them, only for being reproved on account of their evil lives. The Puritans were usually classed with the Family of Love, and represented as refusing tribute and as withholding obedience from the civil magistrate.

Bacon was not satisfied with some things in the Church. He objected to the bishops having so great a superiority

Blames the bishops.

over the rest of the clergy. He did not think it right for them to give orders, to excommunicate and to govern the Church by their own authority. They ought to have a Presbytery always associated with them, so that their judgment might not be merely that of an individual. He wished also that the word 'priest' might be laid aside. He knew that it was only an abbreviation of the word presbyter, yet, as we have no word to designate the sacrificing priest of the old law, for the sake of avoiding confusion we should use the word minister or presbyter, as under the gospel dispensation we have no priest in the Levitical sense. He thought that we had put Confirmation out of its place, in connecting it with Baptism. In the primitive Church it was a preparation for the first communion. He objected to lay baptism, because the rite was not of such importance that any person might perform it lest the child die unbaptized. In the early church Baptism was celebrated once a year. The minister did not hasten to baptize sick children, nor did the laymen think of doing it if the minister was not at hand. As a means of training up good preachers, Bacon recommended the restoration of the Puritan custom of 'prophesying.'

It is interesting to know what Lord Bacon thought of the controversies which divided the Conformists and the Puritans, but what we may call his theological writings have a higher interest than even this. Did the author of the inductive philosophy say anything new in theology? Did his philosophy affect his theology? Did he lay down any rules for the guidance of the theologian as he did for the philosopher? It was impossible that in any new method of studying the works of God theology could be untouched. But the first thing remarkable in Bacon is his desire to progress in philosophy, but to be conservative in theology. He is orthodox beyond most philosophers. He described the character of a 'believing Christian' by a number of paradoxes, in which the Christian faith seemed such a series of contradictions that a German historian of philosophy thinks it doubtful if Bacon really believed in the Christian religion. Ritter's conjecture is groundless. The paradoxes are simply expressions of the most orthodox forms of Christian belief. They are such as these: a Christian is one who believes against reason, believes that a Father is not older than His Son, and that the God of all grace was angry with one who never offended.* Bacon says that for philosophy we must go to God's works, but for divinity we must go to His word. The heavens declare God's glory, but the Scriptures reveal His will. In nature we only see second causes, but in the Scripture we come to the head of the fountain. It is unsafe to seek articles of belief in the works of nature. We must give to faith the things that belong to faith. It is here, he says, that we find the reason why so many great men are heretics. They seek to fly up to the secrets of the Deity on the waxen wings of sense. It was once said by one of Philo's school that the sense of man resembles the sun. It reveals the terrestrial globe, but it obscures the stars and the celestial world. So sense discovers things natural, but it darkens and shuts up things divine. Human knowledge is likened to the waters, some descending from above and some springing from beneath. The one is from the light of nature, the other by divine revelation. By that which springs from beneath we have enough 'to convince atheism, but not to inform religion.' And so God never wrought a miracle to convince atheists, but miracles have been wrought to convince the idolatrous and the superstitious.

It is often said that Bacon refused to admit the Theistic argument drawn from final causes. It is true that he has spoken of the search for final causes as prejudicial to the true investigation of nature. But he is not speaking of religion. His complaint is that many—for instance, Plato, Aristotle, and Galen—often seek for the final cause, and this being found, they are blinded as to the physical. But the investigation of nature has to do with the physical. When the natural philosopher proceeds to the final, he becomes a theologian. That the hairs of the eyelids are a quickset to defend the sight may be true, but the question for the physical inquirer is to find what is the cause of hairs growing over the eyelids. The answer is that 'pilosity is incident to

---

* It is doubtful if Bacon wrote 'The Christian Paradoxes.' See 'Lord Bacon not the Author, etc. Memorials of Herbert Palmer,' by Rev. A. B. Grosart.

CHAP. II.

Faith and reason.

Revelation to be received, not examined.

orifices of moisture.' To seek the physical cause is not to deny the final cause. Nor is it to call in question the divine wisdom, but rather to exalt it: as he is the greater politician who can make men the instruments of his will, and yet never acquaint them with his own purpose, so is the Divine wisdom magnified in using the result of the physical cause to execute the final.

The distinction which Bacon made between the word and works of God implied another distinction, which was its counterpart,—that between faith and reason. What is revealed in His word is to be implicitly believed, however it may contradict our reason. To assent to the matter revealed because it is agreeable to reason is no more than we should do when the witness was discredited or his testimony doubtful. We are to give our consent to the author, whatever may be the agreement or disagreement of our reason with what is revealed. This is true faith. This is the faith of Abraham, which was accounted for righteousness. He believed when Sarah laughed. Abraham was the pattern of faith, Sarah was the image of natural reason. We are to go to the law and the testimony, not only to learn the great mysteries of creation and redemption, but even the duties of the moral law. Bacon felt at this point that an objection might be raised from the sense of the moral law which men have by nature. He anticipates it by answering that in one sense the light of nature means an inward instinct, and that the law of conscience is a sparkle of the purity of our first estate. But this is sufficient only to check vice, not to teach duty. The use of reason in religion is limited to two kinds. The one gives us an apprehension of the mysteries revealed. The other derives doctrines and directions from what is revealed. In the one case reason does not teach the mysteries by way of argument, but by way of illustration. In the other, reason has but a secondary, not an absolute use. We are not permitted to reason on what is revealed. It is exempted from examination, but when received, we may make inferences from it. This is illustrated by games of wit, such as chess, where there are *posita* or *placita* which are not established by absolute reason, but which, being agreed on, are first laws of the game. The doctrines of revealed religion are the *placets* of God, on which the secondary reason may be exercised. Bacon said that the principles of nature were examinable by induction, but it was not the same with those of revelation. There God speaks. It has been observed, he said, of Jesus, that when questions were propounded to Him, He answered rather according to the thoughts than the words of those who put the questions. So it is with the Scriptures, which, being written for all ages, are infinite springs and streams of doctrine, intended to water the Church not only when they were written, but in all ages. The literal sense is the main stream, but the moral chiefly, and sometimes the allegorical or typical, is that which the Church uses most. The Bible is not therefore to be interpreted as we would interpret any other book.

In Bacon's 'Confession of Faith,' he seems to express a belief that a Mediator was always necessary, as neither man nor angel could stand for a moment in God's sight. Therefore the Lamb was not only slain to redeem men from the Fall, but He was slain before all worlds. It is not surprising that Bacon believed in election. The doctrines of Calvin were as yet the orthodox faith of the Church of England. Among the generations of men, he says, God elected a small flock in whom, by the participation of Himself, He proposed to express the rays of His glory. For this end the angels are ministering servants. Devils and reprobates are condemned that God may be glorified in His chosen saints. The Catholic Church is described as consisting of holy persons throughout all ages and dispensations. It is the spouse of Christ. It is Christ's body, and is not to be confounded with the Church visible. In nature God works by law, but redemption is a miracle, and to it all miracles refer. The explanation of original sin is that the fall of Adam resulted from knowledge,—not the natural knowledge of creatures, but the knowledge of good and evil. Man did not believe that right and wrong had their beginnings by God's positive laws. He expected to find other beginnings. He believed that God did not make right, but that it was co-eternal with God. Had Adam been content with the inductive philosophy of Bacon, he would never have fallen into the sin of speculating about the origin of right.

Bacon a Calvinist.

APPENDIX TO CHAP. II.

'Hay any More Worke for a Cooper.'

Martin Marprelate's printing-press was taken at Manchester while printing a tract called 'Hay any more worke for a Cooper.' There is, it is supposed, no copy of this tract extant. Soon after the seizure of the press Martin appeared again with a paper, called 'The Protestatyon of Martin Marprelat.'* It opens thus: 'Thou canst not lightly bee ignorant, good reader, of that wich hath lately fallen vnto some things of mine, which were to be printed, or in printing; the presse, leteres, workman and all apprehended and carried as malefactors before the magistrate, whose authoritie I reverence, and whose sword I would fear were I as wicked as our Bb. are.' Martin proceeds to say that he is not dismayed at what has befallen him:—'Good reader, I would not have thee discouraged at this that is latlie fallen out. As to the present action let them be well assured it was not undertaken to be intermitted at every blaste of euill successe. Nay, let them knowe by the grace of God the last day of *Martinisme* that is, of the discrying and displaying of L. Bb. shall not be till full 2 years after the last year of *Lambethisme*. Be it known vnto them that *Martinisme* stands vpon an other manner of foundation than this prelacy doth or can stand. Therefore yf they will needs overthrowe me, let them goe in hand with the exdloyte (exploit?) rather in prooving the lawfullness of their place, than by exercising the force of their vnlawfull tyranny.' The 'Protestation' gives an account of what Martin had said in the 'Hay any more worke':—'To tell the truth, good reader, I sigh to remember the loss of it, it was so prettie and so witty. First, there was set down the true, proper, natural definition or rather description of Martinisme to this effect. That to be a right Martiniste indeede, is to be neither Brownist, Cooperist, Lambethist, Schismatike, Papist, Atheist, traytor, nor yet L. byshop, but one that as at defyaunce with all men, so far forth as he is an enimy

---

* '8. The Protestatyon of Martin Marprelat wherein notwithstanding the surprizing of the printer, he maketh it known vnto the world that he feareth, neither proud priest, Antichristian pope, tiranous prellate, nor godlesse catercap: but defiethe all the race of them by these presents and offereth conditionally, as is farthere expressed hearein by open disputation to appear in the defence of his cause against them and theirs—Which chaleng if they dare not maintaine aginst him: then doth he alsoe publishe that he never meaneth, by the assitance of god to leaue the assayling of them and theire generation vntill they be vterly extinguised out of our church. Published by the worthie gentleman D. martin marprelat, D. in all the faculties primat and metropolitan.'

to God and her maiestie. Whereupon I remember, I did then aske the reader whether it were not good being a Martiniste. Nexte to this followed a pre-amble to an Eblitaph upon the death of olde Andrewe Turne-Coate, to be sung antephonically in his grace's chappell on Wednesdays and Frydayes, to the lamentable tune of *Orawhynemeg*. The next prettie thing to this, was to my remembrance. Chaplain Some confuted with the blade sheath of his own dagger. Then there was recorded a brave agreement which Martin of his courtesie is contended to make with the bishops.'

After the taking of the printing-press Martin, as if dead or lost, was to be succeeded by his sons, who were to carry on the 'Pistling' instead of the father. Martin Junior published 'Theses Martinianæ.' The 'Theses,' in number 110, were said to have been found among old Martin's papers. In themselves they were trite enough. It was argued that the doctrine of the Church of England did not admit different degrees of ministers. The proof was that this was the doctrine of Tyndale, Frith, and Barnes, which Fox had been allowed to publish by royal privilege. At the end of the 'Theses' Martin Junior speaks in his own person. He wonders what has become of his father, who was said to be hiding himself, and by some supposed to be dead. It appears that by this time Martin had other enemies besides the bishops. He had been ridiculed on the stage by what his son called 'poore seelie hunger starred wretches,' and pamphlets had been written against him. This tract was followed by 'The iust censure and reproofe of Martin Iunior.'* This is the last of Martin's tracts, that is, of those which are extant. It is here repeated that it is due to Whitgift, and not to the Queen, that the Puritans were treated with severity. Martin recommends that if 'John of Canterburie will needs have a foole in his house wearing a wooden dagger and a cookes combe, that none is so fit for that place as his brother John Bridges, Deane of Sarum.' Martin says it is Bridges' right 'to displace those who now play the asse at Lambeth, and to be invested in that office in the solemn manner appointed for ordaining Bishops and Priests. His daily attendants are to be Dr. Robert Some, who is to be his confessor, and

---

* 10. 'The iust censure and reproofe of Martin Iunior.—Wherein the rash and vndiscreete headines of the foolish youth is sharply mette with, and the boy hath this lesson taught him, I warrant you, by his reuerend and elder brother, Martin Senior, sonne and heire vnto the renowmed Martin Marprelate the Great. Where also, least the springall shold be vtterly discouraged in his good meaning, you shall find that hee is not bereaued of his due commendations.'

when absent to read for him 'the Staruc-us booke in his chapel at Lambeth.' Dr. Underbul was to be his almoner, Bancroft and 'drunken Gravate' to be 'yeoman of his cellars.' Anderson, 'parson of Stepney, was to make room before him with his staff as he used to do in the morrice dance, and his supporters, who were to lead by the arms, Sir Gerrard Wright and Sir Tom Bland Bedford.' In this tract the name of the vicar of Stepney turns up as it were by accident. It was through his instrumentality that John Penry was apprehended. The parish of Stepney was then full of Puritans. It is described as being a short distance from London, surrounded by fields and groves of trees, which made it a convenient resort for those who sought a place of refreshment from their persecutors. Some who have been interested in tracing the history of Penry have tried in vain to find the name of the vicar by whose help he was apprehended. Of the pamphlets written against Martin, Disraeli says that they crushed him more effectually than the hanging of him. This is said in the belief that Penry was Martin. Some of them were supposed to have been written by Thomas Nash, and, as Nash was witty, it was assumed that they must be full of wit. Without bestowing very great praise on the literary merits of Martin, we may safely pronounce the answers to be slender imitations of the originals.

The first in order is called 'Pappe with an hatchet; Alias a figge for my Godsonne or Cracke me this nut, or a countrie cuffe that is a sound boxe of the eare for the idiot Martin.' To give pap with a hatchet was a proverbial expression for doing a kind thing in an unkind way. In Lyly's 'Court Comedies' is this passage:—'They gave us pap with a spoone before we can speake, and when we speake for that we have pap with a hatchet.' As a specimen of the wit we may quote this passage:—'He saith he is a cavalier. It may be he is some jester about the court, and of that I marvaile, because I know all the fools there, and yet cannot guess at him.' Again, the writer says, 'there is small difference between a swallow and a martin, save only that the Martin hath a more beetle head.'

There is no argument in the tract, except that those who now assault bishops will ere long aim at the throne. It is dedicated 'To the Father and two Sonnes, Huffe, Ruffe, and Snuffe, the three tame ruffians of the Church; which take pepper in the nose beccausse they cannot marre Prelates, grating.' About the same time appeared 'A Countercuffe given to Martin Iunior.' It was 'by the venturous, hardie, and renowned Pasquill of England Caualiero.' The next is called 'An almond for a Parrot, or Cuthbert Curry Knaves.' To give an almond to a parrot is the same as to give a sop to Cerberus. This tract is supposed to have been by the same author as 'Pappe with an hatchet.' They are both ascribed to Nash, and are reckoned among the cleverest of those against Martin. The writer of the 'Countercuffe' appears again, pretending that he has been out of England. This time he writes 'The Returne of the renooned Caualiero Pasquill of England from the other side of the seas and his meeting with Marforius at London upon the Royall Exchange.' The author promised to write a 'Golden Legend,' to consist of the lives of the Puritan Saints. It was to be a collection of stories about the Puritans, like what Martin had told of the bishops and Dr. John Bridges. It appears, however, that the materials were not plentiful, for Pasquill in the end asks for help against Martin. He makes this 'Protestation upon London Stone:'—'I Caualiero Pasquill, the writer of this simple hand, a young man of the age of some few hundred years, lately knighted in Englande with a beetle and bucking tub, to beat a little reason about Martin's head, doe make my protestation vnto the world that if any man, woman, or childe haue any thing to say against Martin the great or any of his abettors, of what state or calling soever they be, noble or ignoble, from the very court gates to the cobbler's stall, If it please them these dark winter nyghts to sticke up the papers upon London stone I will there give my attendance to receive them from the day of the date hereof to the full terme and revolution of seven years next ensuing.'

APPENDIX TO CHAP. II.

The report that old Martin was dead, suggested the idea of mourning for him, writing his epitaph, and even dissecting him. This was done in 'Martin's Months Minde, that is, a Certaine Report and True Description of the Death and Funerall of Olde Martin Marreprelate, the great Makebate of England.' The author of the 'Months Minde' says that Martin had some wit, though it was knavish, that he could make women and pot companions laugh over the ale-benches, but his sons were 'dull asses.' It is announced as good news to England that old Martin is dead. How he died left a wide field for conjecture; some say he was taken by the Spaniards, others that he was hanged by his own company at Lisbon, and some report that he died after drinking too much wine. But the true account is, that having troubled the State, and sought to overthrow the Church, and being made a maygame on the stage, he was afraid that he should be made a bishop and compelled to wear a tippit, and so his

Martin dead.

APPENDIX TO CHAP. II.

Martin's Epitaphs.

radical moisture failed him. In his will his house was given to the Martinists and his work to Machiavelli. When his body was opened by the anatomists, it was not marvellous that his heart was hollow, his lungs made to prate, his gall-bladder full of choler, his tongue swollen with blasphemy, and his head without a crumb of brain. His epitaphs were,—

> 'Sic pereant omnes,
> Martinæ et Martinistæ.

By his friends—

> 'Art dead, old Martin? farewell then our schooles;
> Martin, thy sonnes are but two paltrie fooles.'

The Marprelate Tracts were distributed by a cobbler, which may be the cause of an epitaph by 'Clippe,' the godly cobbler,—

> 'Adieu, both naule and bristles, now for ever,
> The shoe and soale (woe is me) must sever,
> Besides mine Aule, thy sharpest point is gone,
> My bristles broke, and I am left alone.
> Farewell old shoes, thombe stall, and clouting leather,
> Martin is done, and we undone together.'

One epitaph more—

> 'London, lament, the East that sticks on sand,
>   The West that stands before the statelie hall,
> The North, the boure, that bounds with trible band,
>   The South, where some at Watering catch a fall.
> Newgate and Bedlem, Clinke and Bridewell, bray,
> And ye crowes crie, for ye have lost your praye.'

This last reminds us of Byron's satire:—

> 'The Tolbooth felt defrauded of her charms
>   If Jeffrey died, except within her arms.'

The Author's own epitaph on Martin should not be omitted:—

> 'Hic iacet, ut pinus,
> Nec Cæsar, nec Ninus,
> Nec magnus Godwinus,
> Nec Petrus, nec Linus,
> Nec plus, nec minus,
> Quam clandestinus,
> Miser ille Martinus,
>   Videte singuli.

> 'O vos Martinistæ,
> Et vos Brounistæ,
> Et Famililouistæ,
> Et Anabaptistæ,

> Et omnes sectistæ,
> Et Machiuelistæ,
> Et Atheistæ,
> Quorum dux fuit iste,
>   Lugete singuli.

> 'At gens Anglorum,
> Præsertim verorum,
> Nec non, qui morum,
> Estis bonorum,
> Inimici horum,
> Ut est decorum,
> Per omne forum,
> In sæcula sæculorum,
>   Gaudete singuli.'

There are yet two more tracts to be noticed, but as Martin is dead, dissected, buried, and epitaphed, we need not say much more. The first is, 'Plaine Percevall the Peace-Maker of England. Sweetly indevoring with his blunt persuasions to botch vp a Reconciliation between Marton and Mar-tother.' The other is, 'The First parte of Pasquils Apologie. Wherein he renders a reason to his friendes of his long silence: and gallops the field with the Treatise of Reformation lately written by a fugitiue, Iohn Penrie.' Mr. Maskell says that 'Plaine Percevall' was written by a Puritan, under pretence of opposing Martin, but in reality favouring him. This, however, is an invention of Mr. Maskell's, who evidently loved the Puritans with the same love that Martin loved the bishops. We are not willing to accuse Mr. Maskell, as he does Neal, the careful historian of the Puritans, of 'lamentable ignorance or wilful lying.' Neal was a partisan, and so is Mr. Maskell; the species is different, but the genus is the same.

There are some pieces in verse which ought fairly to be included in any list of Marprelate tracts; one is, 'A Whip for an Ape, or Martin Displaied.' It begins,—

> 'Since reason (Martin) cannot stay thy pen,
> We'll see what rime will do, haue at it then.'

The argument is the solitary one that was always urged against Martin,—

> 'And think you not he will pull down at length,
>   As well the top from tower as Cocke from Steeple,
> And when his head hath gotten some more strength,
>   To play with prince as now he doth with people;
> Yes, he that now saith, Why should Bishops be?
> Shall next crie out, Why Kings? The saints are free.'

Another piece was called 'Marre-Martin.' A few lines will show the tenor of it:—

> 'Martins, what kind of creature mought they be?
> Birds, beasts, men, angels, feends? nay, worse say we;
> What favor would these Martins, shall I say?
> As other birds wherewith young children play;
> Let them be caged, and hempseed be their food,
> Hempseed the only meat to feed their brood.
> Dis-claim the monsters, take them not for thine;
> Hell was their womb, and hell must be their shryne.
>
> Many would know the holy asse,
> And who mought Martin been,
> Plucke but the footcloth from his backe,
> The asse will soon be seene.'

To this there was an answer from the peace-making party, called 'Marre Mar-Martin, or Marre Martin's meddling in a manner misliked.' One verse is enough:—

> 'While England falls a Martining and a marring,
> Religion fears an utter overthrow;
> Whilst we at home among ourselves are jarring,
> The seedes take root which foreign seedesmen sow;
> If this be true, as true it is for certaine,
> Woe worth Martin Marprelate and Mar Martin.'

It is a question which some have raised, how far the Puritans as a body were responsible for the publications of Martin Marprelate. We should be glad to conclude that, on both sides, the tracts were the work of individuals who did not represent either party; Martin repeatedly disclaims any co-partnership, declaring that he alone is responsible for what he writes. In a tract called 'The Plea of the Innocent,' by Jonas Nichols, published in 1602, we have a distinct repudiation, on the part of the Puritans, of any sympathy with Martin Marprelate. The writer says that 'when they had made their petition to the reverend fathers, and were expecting them to join in ending the strifes, there arose grievous accidents which darkened the righteousness of their cause.' The first of them,' he says, 'was a foolish jester who termed himself *Martin Marprelate*, and his sons, which under counterfeit and apish scoffing did play the sycophant, and slanderously abused many persons of reverend place and note, and such was the wisdom of the time, that many filthy and lewd pamphlets came forth.' Nichols described it as the work of the devil in disguise, and he complains that the blame fell on the Puritans. 'We,' he says, 'obtained a new name in many pulpits (how justly, God knoweth),—we are called Martinists.' It is recorded in Strype's 'Life of Whitgift' that the answers were written by the advice of Bancroft, and there is reason to believe that he had to do with the writing of some of them. Whitgift recommended Bancroft for the bishopric of London, and this was one of the deeds which entitled him to that high preferment. Another was, that by his vigilance the books and press of Martin were discovered. It is said that the plays against Martin were performed in St. Paul's Cathedral. In the margin of 'Pappe with an hatchet,' over against the mention of a play, it is written, 'If it be shewed at Paules, it wul cost you foure pence; at the theatre, two pence; at Sainct Thomas a Watering, nothing.'

APPENDIX TO CHAP. II.

Plays against Martin in St. Paul's Cathedral.

CHAPTER III.

HAMPTON COURT CONFERENCE.—FIELD ON THE CHURCH.—WORKS OF KING JAMES.—OVERALL'S CONVOCATION BOOK.—BISHOP ANDREWES.—BILSON AND BROUGHTON ON THE 'DESCENT INTO HELL.'—ARCHBISHOP ABBOT.—THE SABBATH CONTROVERSY.—TITHES.—THE FIVE POINTS OF ARMINIUS.—RICHARD MONTAGU.—THE VICAR OF GRANTHAM AND HIS 'ALTAR.'—BISHOP WILLIAMS.—ARCHBISHOP LAUD.—USSHER.—BISHOP HALL AND THE SMECTYMNIANS.—PRYNNE ON TIMOTHY AND TITUS.—JOHN MILTON.—CONFERENCE AGAINST INNOVATIONS AT THE DEAN OF WESTMINSTER'S.

Hampton Court Conference.

WHEN King James came to England, a petition was presented to him, signed by a thousand* of the Puritan ministers, asking the removal from the Prayer-Book of certain things to which they objected. The King immediately called a Conference at Hampton Court, to consider their objections. In the imperfect account of that Conference, given by Dean Barlow, there is mention of almost every subject relating to doctrines or ceremonies, on which there was then any difference of opinion. There were nine bishops, seven deans,† Dr. King, Archdeacon of Notting-

---

* Signed by seven hundred, but generally called the millenary petition, as representing the wishes of a thousand ministers.

† The bishops were—Canterbury, John Whitgift; London, Richard Bancroft; Durham, Toby Matthews; Winchester, Thomas Bilson; Worcester, Gervase Babington; St. David's, Anthony Rudd; Chichester, Anthony Watson; Carlisle, Henry Robinson; Peterborough, Thomas Dove.

The deans were—The Chapel Royal and Worcester, James Montague; Christ's Church, Thomas Ravis; Windsor, Giles Thompson; Sarum, John Bridges; St. Paul's, John Overall; Chester, William Barlow; Westminster, Launcelot Andrews. These deans became bishops respectively of Winchester, London, Gloucester, Oxford, Norwich, Lincoln, and Winchester. Patrick Galloway, sometime minister of Perth, in Scotland, was also admitted to this Conference.

ham, and Dr. Field, afterwards Dean of Gloucester, to represent the side of the Conformists, with Dr. Rainolds, Dr. Sparks, Mr. Knewstubs, and Mr. Chatterton as representatives of the thousand ministers. The Conference contributed nothing towards the object for which it was assembled. The bishops, it is generally said, had made up their minds not to yield anything, and James's instincts were keen enough to discern that he was safer with the bishops than with the Puritans. The King, however, had studied theology, and had a judgment of his own on all disputed questions. He first asked for information concerning confirmation. He had been told that it was a part of baptism, without which baptism was not valid. This the King pronounced blasphemy. The Archbishop explained that it was simply an ancient ceremony of the Church, which had been wisely retained at the Reformation, but it was in no way necessary to the validity of baptism. Bancroft, Bishop of London, said that it was something more than a mere custom derived from the primitive Church. It was an apostolical institution. To confirm this view, he quoted Calvin's interpretation of Heb. vi. 2, where Calvin identifies the laying on of hands with the rite of confirmation. The King approved of Calvin's exposition. Toby Matthews, Bishop of Durham, read from St. Matthew's Gospel about the imposition of hands on children, and suggested that the ceremony should be called 'An Examination with a Confirmation.' The King gave his judgment upon absolution, which he described as being of two kinds, general and particular. All prayers and preaching imply absolution. It is particular when applied to special persons, who have done penance for their sins. Whitgift read to the King the Confession and Absolution from the Prayer-Book, which 'his Majesty highly approved.' Bancroft said they must deal fairly with the King. In the service for the Communion of the Sick, there was another form of absolution. He showed that a similar form was retained in several of the German Confessions, and he quoted Calvin as approving not merely general, but also particular and private absolution. The King expressed himself strongly opposed to baptism by lay people, especially by women. The Archbishop said it was

CHAP. III.

Discussion on confirmation.

CHAP. III.

not allowed in the Church of England. Babington, the Bishop of Worcester, said that the compilers of the Prayer-Book had designedly left an ambiguity in the words. If this had not been done, there might have been difficulty in getting the book through Parliament. Bancroft repudiated the idea of the venerable men who framed the Book of Common Prayer, trying to deceive by ambiguous words. He maintained the necessity of sometimes having recourse to lay baptism. We read in the Acts of the Apostles that three thousand were baptized in one day; and as there were no bishops or priests there, except the Apostles, they must have been assisted by laymen. For the antiquity of the custom, he quoted Tertullian and Ambrose, and then he reminded the Conference of the great importance of baptism.

Baptism by laymen.

A child might be dying when no clergyman was at hand. If it dies unbaptized, we know nothing of its future state, but if sprinkled with the water of baptism, we have certainty of its salvation. Bilson, the Bishop of Winchester, took the same view as Bancroft. He pleaded that it was an ancient custom of the Church of Christ, that the minister was not of the essence of the sacrament, and therefore it should be done by a lay person when a minister could not be found. The King answered that if the minister was not of the essence of the sacrament, he was nevertheless of the essence of its right and lawful ministration. It was only to the Apostles that the words were addressed, *Go ye and baptize.*

Falling from grace.

On the second day of the Conference, Dr. Rainolds moved that after the words 'depart from grace,' in Art. XVI., there should be added some explanation, such as 'neither totally nor finally.' He thought this necessary to remove an apparent discrepancy between this Article and the one on Predestination. He suggested, also, that the Calvinistic Articles known as the Lambeth Articles, should be added to the XXXIX. He mentioned some other changes, as in Article XXIII., where 'in the congregation' might be interpreted as meaning that one *out* of the congregation might take upon himself the office of ministering sacraments; and Art. XXV., where confirmation is classed with some things that have their origin in the 'corrupt following of the Apostles,' which seemed to be in collision with what was elsewhere said of confirmation, where it was grounded on the practice of the Apostles. Here Bancroft begged that an ancient canon might be observed which forbids schismatics against bishops to be heard. Moreover, he said there was a decree of an ancient Council which did not permit any one to speak against that which he had already subscribed. Now, if any of the four Puritans present were among those who had petitioned the king for a reformation, they were evidently schismatics, and therefore not to be heard. This was the voice of antiquity, which, next to that of King James, was to Bancroft the voice of God.* The King suggested that some such word as 'often' might be inserted after 'grace given.' He then entered upon a discourse of God's eternal predestination, setting forth the necessity of always keeping this doctrine untouched. He objected, however, to the insertion of the Lambeth Articles; not that he did not approve of them, or that he thought they expressed any doctrine different from that of the XXXIX. The King only objected to the addition of more Articles than we already have. He did not want, as he expressed it, 'to stuff the book with all conclusions theological.'†

* It has been said that Bancroft was an Arminian. It is certainly strange that Whitgift should have had an Arminian for his chaplain. The Bishop of Ely, following Dr. Cardwell, says, that Bancroft, at the Hampton Court Conference, replied to Dr. Rainolds on this question. So far this is true, but the substance of Bancroft's answer was, that we should not trust to predestination, saying, 'If I shall be saved I shall be saved.' He did not speak against predestination, but only against the abuse of that doctrine. Toplady says he was at the Lambeth Conference, but this is probably incorrect, as he was only made Bishop of London that year. Fletcher was probably the bishop at the Conference. The Bishop of Ely, who goes in for the non-Calvinism of the Reformers, following Archbishop Laurence, says that even Bradford's Calvinism was of the most moderate kind. He might as well have said that John Calvin's Calvinism, or Jerome Zanchy's Calvinism, was of the most moderate kind. Archbishop Laurence was an excellent special pleader, but he must be very cautiously received as an authority.

† The character of James was charmingly manifested at the Hampton Court Conference. He instructed the bishops in theology, like a true 'Head' of the Church. He discoursed on predestination, the wickedness and presumption of the ministers of the kirk in the country from which he had come, and other profound subjects. He was at once theological and playful. When Dr. Rainolds objected to the words in the marriage service, 'With my body I thee worship,' the King said, 'I am thinking if you had a gude wife yoursel', doctor, you wouldna think any worship or reverrance too much for her. Many a man speaks of Robin Hood who never shot in his bow.'

Dr. Rainolds suggested that in large dioceses confirmation might be administered by presbyters. Bancroft quoted Jerome and other Fathers as opposed to confirmation by any except bishops. The King reminded Bancroft that Jerome did not believe in the divine institution of bishops. To which Bancroft replied, that if he could not prove his ordination lawful from the Scriptures, he would not remain a bishop for four hours. Bilson spoke of the inefficiency, or as it was then called, the 'insufficiency' of the clergy. He blamed the lay patrons for presenting incompetent men to the livings. Since he had been Bishop of Winchester very few masters of arts had been instituted. He knew that the men were inefficient, but he dare not refuse to institute, or he might be served with a *Quare impedit*. Bancroft fell on his knees and begged the King that they might have a 'praying ministry;' 'priests that could bless the people,' 'administer Sacraments,' 'absolve penitents,' and such like offices. He complained of the hypocrisy of the times which placed religion in hearing sermons instead of receiving priestly benedictions. The King, however, had some sympathy with preaching. He said that a preaching ministry was best. He recommended more frequent reading of homilies, until more preachers could be found for the parishes. Dr. Rainolds asked for the revival of the 'prophesyings' that had been suppressed in the time of Elizabeth.*

The members of the Hampton Court Conference were all men of some reputation in the Church, and several of them are still known as writers. Of Whitgift, Bancroft, and Bilson, we have already spoken. Matthews, the Bishop of Durham, afterwards Archbishop of York, wrote a reply to Campion, the Jesuit. Babington's works are chiefly practical and expository. He was a favourer of the Puritans. So also was Rudd, the Bishop of St. David's. Dr. Rainolds, the chief speaker on the Puritan side, was a learned man and a great writer, chiefly on the Romanist Contro-

* The 'prophesyings' were preachings and religious exercises which the ministers held among themselves. Neal says that in Elizabeth's time they were patronized by the bishops, but in 1574 Archbishop Parker told her that they were nurseries of Puritanism. The Archbishop died next year, and his successor, Grindal, was sequestrated, and suspended because he refused to put them down.

versy.* He is said to have been well read in the Councils and Fathers. But the name to which we turn as best representing the spirit of the Church of England is that of Richard Field, the friend of Richard Hooker. His 'Book of the Church' was to the Church of Rome what Hooker's 'Polity' was to the Puritans. Field treated his subject with the utmost moderation, and never sought an unfair advantage over his opponents. In the 'Epistle Dedicatory,' which was addressed to the Archbishop of Canterbury, he declared his object to be to search out which was the *household of faith,* which the *spouse of Christ,* which the *pillar and ground of truth.* This announcement might lead us to expect that he looked for the 'spouse of Christ' to be one of the communities into which the Church universal was divided, and that he was to prove it to be the Church of England as opposed to the Church of Rome and all other Churches. But this was not his thesis. It was enough to prove first, that the Church of Rome was not *the spouse of Christ,* not the *pillar and ground of truth.* He compared the Church of Rome to the Donatists of Africa. These poor Donatists, who were really the Puritans of the North African Church, have always been a bugbear to all who claimed the name of Catholic. They of course called themselves Catholics, but Augustine called them heretics, and Augustine is a great authority. They said that all who adhered to them throughout the world, were the Catholic Church, the true Church, undefiled, uncorrupt, pure as a 'gathered church' of Brownists, or Barrowists. Against all who were out of their communion,

---

* Merely to call Dr. Rainolds a Puritan is to describe him very imperfectly. His reputation for learning was so great that Conformists have objected to calling him a Puritan at all. It has even been said that he did not willingly undertake to be the leader of the Puritans at this Conference. He does not always appear to advantage in Dean Barlow's account, and it is evident that he was frequently interrupted and treated rudely both by the King and by Bancroft. Yet he spoke at this Conference, as Aristotle said of Anaxagoras, compared to the other philosophers, 'like a sober man.' He was a Puritan who did not scruple about the ceremonies. He wore his square cap and surplice, and conformed in everything. But though, like all the more moderate and rational men of the Puritans, he conformed himself, he yet wished that conformity should not be enforced on those who made it a matter of conscience. Among the things which Dr. Rainolds recommended at the Conference was a new translation of the Bible. To this recommendation we owe our present translation. Among the names of the translators are Andrewes, Overall, Rainolds, Ravis, and Barlow.

they pronounced an anathema as from the Lord Jesus. Augustine said they were not the Catholic Church, because they were a small body. They did not number in their ranks the multitudes of Christians throughout the world. They were the most numerous party in Africa, but not in other countries. Therefore they were not universal. So far it was a question of numbers; and if it were still a question of numbers, Field could scarcely have doubted which of the two Churches, that of Rome or that of England, represented the Donatists. But he was not, like St. Augustine, a mere rhetorician. He would not rest his argument for Catholicity on the fluctuating basis of numbers. His point of comparison was that the Church of Rome, like the ancient Donatists, claimed to be the only true Church, to embrace Catholicism within itself, to exclude from the Catholic Church, and consequently from salvation, all who were not of that communion. This Donatism of the Church of Rome was supported by what Field calls 'glorious pretences of antiquity, unity, universality, and succession.' The simple were made to believe that everything is ancient which the Church of Rome professes, that it has the consent of all ages, and that the bishops, succeeding each other in the various sees throughout the world, never taught anything different from what the Church of Rome now teaches. This pretence, in Field's judgment, is unfounded. These bishops, he said, taken as a whole, agreed with the Church of England rather than the Church of Rome. At the Reformation we separated from a part which claimed to be the whole, that we might hold with the Church Catholic against the pretensions of the Church of Rome.

To defend this position, it was necessary to make some careful definitions. Field begins with the Church, in its first and most abstract conception, as consisting of unfallen men and angels. They felt themselves imperfect, and longed for fulness of being. This craving did not belong to the inferior creation. They were satisfied, while men and angels feeling in themselves a capacity for blessedness, formed the Church of God. But this was abstract. The next conception of the Church is as it consisted of unfallen angels and redeemed men. This is properly the Church. The schoolmen gave as the reason of redemption, that men having fallen in Adam, God would have been deprived of a race of His most excellent creatures, if He had not redeemed them. Angels were on a different footing,—each was created by himself, and stood or fell by himself. The Church was in Adam, but, as Abel first offered sacrifice, we usually say that the Church began in Abel. The Jewish Church was called the synagogue. The Christian assembly, which was first formed on the day of Pentecost, was called the Church as distinguished from the synagogue. Heretics and schismatics are of the Church in some sort. They are not out of it or separated from it in the same sense as unbelievers are separated from it. The Church is a Church as opposed to infidels. It is Christian as opposed to Judaism, Orthodox in regard to heretics, and Catholic in regard to schismatics. But this universal Christian Church is only the Church visible, and is not to be considered as commensurate with the Church invisible, which is truly 'the body of Christ, the Church of the elect.' There may be many who are members of the visible Church, and yet not of the Christian Church, such as Jews. Some may be of the visible Church, but not of the Orthodox as heretics. Some may be orthodox, but not Catholic, as schismatics. Some may be of the visible, and not of the invisible, which consists only of the elect. The visible Church is always visible; that is, there always have been and will be Christian men holding the true doctrines of Christianity. It had been charged against Luther and other Reformers that they held the Church to have been sometimes invisible. Field says that this is not to be found in their writings. There is a sense in which the visible Church is sometimes invisible, not that there are no orthodox Christians, but in that company which is the true Church, many, yea, the greatest number and the most influential, may be in error. This was the case in the time of St. Athanasius, when the Church denied the Divinity of Jesus Christ; when the bishops, assembled in the Councils of Seleucia and Ariminum, condemned the Nicene faith. Athanasius alone, of all the bishops of the universal Church, raised a standard for the truth, when Jerome noted that 'the world poureth forth sighs marvelling how it had become Arian.'

CHAP. III.

The Church in its relation to those who are outside of it.

If the Church visible is liable to err, and if it has among its members many who are merely professors and not true Christians, how is it then the *spouse of Christ*, the *bride of the Lamb*, and *His mystical body?* Field answers that it is only under certain limitations that we can apply these terms to the Church visible. The Church is to be distinguished from Pagans, Jews, and schismatics, by two kinds of notes. Some are not perpetual, as numbers, largeness of extent, and the name Catholic. Others are perpetual, as the profession of all revealed truth, the use of the appointed sacraments, and union under lawful pastors. He goes on to say that there may be true Churches without the entire and sincere profession of the truth approved by God. Such were the Churches of Corinth and Galatia, whom St. Paul charged with departing from the faith, and yet acknowledged for true Churches. Schismatics may have right faith and the due use of the sacraments, and may be schismatics still. There is required in addition 'orderly communion,' which is another expression for *lawful pastors*.

The Church of Rome claims to be a true Church. The notes are,—(1.) Antiquity. Field answers that the Church of Ephesus and many Churches of Ethiopia have this note. (2.) Succession. Field says that a lawful and holy ministry is an inseparable and perpetual note of a true Church, for no Church can be without it. But there may be a continued succession and yet no true Church, as among the Greeks, Armenians, and Ethiopians, which, in the judgment of Roman Catholics, are not true Churches. It is not enough that there be succession. It must be true and lawful, with no new or strange doctrines. (3.) Unity. This, too, Field says, the Armenian and Ethiopian Churches possess, and so it is not enough in itself. He assents to this description of the true Church as given by the Roman Catholics:—'Wheresoever any company and society of Christians is found in orderly subjection to their lawful pastors, not erring from the rule of faith, nor schismatically rent from the other parts of the Christian world by factious, causeless, and impious divisions, that society of men is undoubtedly the true and not offending Church of God.' (4.) Universality. St. Augustine says that this does not mean that all the world be of the Church, but only some of all provinces. And even this need not be all at once. It constitutes Catholicity, that some in different ages in all countries be of *one* Church. Field says that he admits this note when thus understood:— 'What Church soever can prove itself to hold the faith once delivered to the saints, and generally published to the world without heretical innovations or schismatical violations, is undoubtedly the true Church of God.' With this one Church Field identifies the Reformed Churches, such as those of England, Germany, and Geneva. They are called Churches as belonging to different nations, but they are connected with that one Catholic Church which was established at Pentecost. They did not begin with the Reformers, but God used the Reformers as His servants to put away some evils that had grown up in them. The inclusion of non-Episcopal Churches determines what is meant by a *lawful* ministry. (5.) The name *Catholic*. Field says that the Roman Catholics boast of the 'bare and empty name' *Catholic*. There may, he admits, have been something in it in the days of our fathers, but it is now common to schismatics and heretics, and therefore not a mark of the true Church. When there was but one main body of Christians, the word Catholic meant something. But when the East was divided from the West, the name remained common to both parties. The Greek Church, not less than the Latin, is the Catholic Church. As this name has ceased to be a note of the true Church, so the names derived from men have ceased to be marks of heresy. Those who followed the form of administration left by Ambrose were called Ambrosians, those who followed Gregory, Gregorians; so Lutheran, Calvinist, and Zwinglians are called from Luther, Calvin, and Zwingle, 'worthy servants of God.'

The Latin Church, Field says, was the true Church until our time. We condemn the errors, not the doctrines of that Church. The chief of these errors were a different canon of Scripture, uncertainty of grace, seven sacraments, and local presence, or transubstantiation, in the Eucharist. Yet the whole Latin Church did not fall into these errors. They were only the errors of some men. Luther did not begin a new Church. It is therefore a frivolous question to

Marginalia: CHAP. III. Non-Episcopal Churches included in the Catholic Church. Errors of the Church of Rome.

ask where was our Church before Luther. It was where it is now. In saying that the errors were only received by some men in the Latin Church, Field's meaning seems to be that this was the case at the time of the Reformation. By the Council of Trent they were adopted by the whole Roman Catholic Church. It is not so difficult to know what he means as to express his meaning. He is speaking of Churches, and the thing to be settled is, what constitutes a Church? His argument evidently is that the Reformed Churches are the same which they were before the Reformation. It was but a faction that embraced the errors which were afterwards ratified by the Council of Trent. Calvin is quoted as having proved that the doctrines of the old Fathers were the doctrines of the Réformation. It is, however, admitted that the Fathers did not speak with great precision, and that some of their sayings require a latitude of construction to make them harmonize with the Reformed faith.

In what light Field regarded the foreign Churches that did not adopt the same polity as the Church of England appears from what he has said of the Church. But he is even more explicit. He defines principles, and explains them by examples. Orders, he reduces to the necessity of order. He dare not, he says, condemn those worthy men who were ordained by presbyters when the bishops were opposed to the truth of God. In their circumstances ordination by presbyters was order, and therefore valid orders. He finds that from the earliest times there have been bishops in the Church, but they were not really distinct from presbyters. The office arose from the custom of placing a chief pastor in every city. This pastor had other ministers under him as his assistants. It was an orderly superiority of presbyters placed over other presbyters. Field directly contradicts what was said by Bilson and Bancroft at the Conference of Hampton Court, that there were especial offices which were not performed by presbyters. In the primitive Church presbyters performed the offices of ordination and confirmation, and also dedicated churches. The Romanists, he says, freely confess that a bishop does not excel a presbyter by a distinct or higher order, but by dignity of office. St. Jerome is quoted as saying that some things were generally done by bishops only, and this not by the necessity of any law, but rather for the honour of their ministry. The old canonists, some old bishops and writers are cited as teaching that the Pope may give authority to a presbyter to confer orders. It is also maintained that the suffragans in the Roman Church are not bishops, and yet they do the work of a bishop. The Lutheran and Presbyterian Churches are therefore reckoned as one with the Church of England, and as members of the Church Catholic. Unity under one head is declared unnecessary for Catholicity. It is to be regretted that there are diversities among the Reformed Churches, yet it is to the Church of Rome that we owe even these. When the abuses of the Church were great, there was no remedy provided. The prevailing factions of the Pope's flatterers prevented the calling of a General Council. There was no universal remedy, and therefore every nation had to set about the reformation of its own Church.

The Church Catholic.

Among the members of the Hampton Court Conference who were authors, we should not omit the King himself. His works are not of much intrinsic value, yet they reflect the spirit of a time when theological learning formed part of the intellectual armoury even of a king. The Sovereign of England was defender of the faith; it was, therefore, right that he should understand what he had to defend.

James Montague, Bishop of Winchester, introduced the works of the King to the public with a preface, in which he showed that many kings had written books, beginning even with the King of kings. This was to refute an objection which he said was in the mouths of many people, 'that it ill befits his majesty to spend the powers of his so exquisite understanding on paper, which, had they been spent on powder, could not but have prevailed ere this to the conquest of a kingdom.' It is said that James lived in great dread of actual warfare, but he evidently delighted in the strife of tongues. Besides writing a commentary on the Revelation, meditations on the Lord's Prayer, 'Basilicon Doron,' or instructions for his son in the science of kingcraft, and 'A Treatise on Witches,' he assailed tobacco-smoking with a

The works of King James.

'Counterblast,' defended Protestantism against Cardinal Perron, and Calvinism against Vorstius, the successor of Arminius at Leyden. There is nothing remarkable in James's theology. The bishops said that he was a king by divine right, and he, in return, told them that they were bishops by divine right. Like the ministers among whom he had been educated, and the clergy of the kingdom to which he had come, the King was a strict Calvinist. Man, he said, was at the creation made in the image of God, but he lost that image by his fall. By grace it was in part restored to the elect only. The rest were given over 'to the hands of the devil, henceforth to bear his image.' James called Vorstius 'a monster,' 'a blasphemer,' and sundry other names of the same import. He regretted that he had not heard of Arminius till that arch-heretic was dead. By his death only did Arminius escape the vengeance of the 'Most High and Mighty Prince.' Bertius, another disciple of Arminius, published a book, 'De Apostasia Sanctorum.' He sent a copy of it to the Archbishop of Canterbury, accompanied by a letter, in which, says the King, he was 'so shameless as to maintain that the doctrines of it were agreeable to the doctrines of the Church of England.'

The most eminent of the Hampton Court deans was John Overall, Dean of St. Paul's, afterwards Bishop of Lichfield, and finally of Norwich. Overall is now chiefly known by his 'Convocation Book,' which was first published by Archbishop Sancroft, with a view to helping the cause of the last of the Stuarts. This work is of great historical interest, not merely because of the object for which it was published by Sancroft, but from its partly official character. The first book was read and approved by the Convocations of both provinces. It is signed by Richard Bancroft for Canterbury, and by John Thornborough, Bishop of Bristol, for York.* The rest of it passed the Lower House of Canterbury, and was in progress at York when the Convocation was prorogued. Overall's object was to establish the divine right of kings and bishops in opposition to the divine right of any bishop or bishops to be above kings, and in opposition to the divine right of the Presbyterian discipline. He

* The see was vacant; the Bishop of Bristol was Dean of York.

begins with the Biblical account of the creation of the world. CHAP. III. It was made by Christ, who was, so to speak, the instrument of the Father in its creation. It had a beginning and that beginning was divine. We are not, he says, to suppose that the first men were without education and civilization; that they ran about in woods and fields, or, like wild creatures, rested in caves and dens. Adam's posterity could not please God by their natural powers. It was necessary that God should reveal to them the mystery of salvation. He ordained that there should be some with civic authority, and others with ecclesiastical authority. The former were to rule men, and the latter to instruct them in mysteries hid from nature. At first these offices were vested in heads of families, who were both rulers and priests of their own households. After the Flood the heads of the three families of the earth are Shem, Ham, and Japhet. But before they exercised their sovereignty Noah was the chief ruler. He was made king by God. His right to rule was not determined by the Deluge, nor was it bestowed upon him through the suffrages of his sons and nephews. It proceeded from God, and descended by divine appointment to his sons. As with kings so with priests. Abraham, Isaac, and Jacob, were not chosen by the people to be priests, but were called by God. The tyranny of Nimrod led to confusion and barbarism; the people making priests for themselves led to idolatry. After the death of Joshua, God raised up judges. The consent of the people was not necessary to their election. The civil ruler was also above the priests. Aaron and the Levites were under the direction of Moses. The kings of Israel had authority, not only in things civil but in things ecclesiastical. They were commanded by God to instruct the people in righteousness. The kings, however, were not in ecclesiastical matters to command whatever they listed. There were civil duties with which the priest was not to interfere, and so the priest had duties which were not within the province of the civil ruler. Urijah did wrong when he obeyed Ahaz in building an altar like to the one in Damascus, and Uzziah was properly resisted when he sought to burn incense before the Lord. These are examples for priests to guard their own offices, but not examples

The civil ruler above the bishops.

for them, under pretence of warrants from God, to dethrone kings, or to use violence against them. Solomon deposed Abiathar from the priesthood. A king may depose a priest, but a priest may not dethrone a king. Samuel and Elisha anointed successors to kings that had been deposed. But they were expressly commanded of God, and so are not examples for others without a similar command. A subject ought not to take up arms against the king, unless he has been himself made a king by express command of God. Overall follows the Jews throughout their history, and finds that they always acknowledged the duty of obedience to their civil rulers, whoever these rulers might be. At one time they were under the kings of Persia, and had Zerubbabel and Nehemiah for their lawful princes, who were placed over them by God without the election of the people. At another time they were the subjects of Alexander the Great, and when his government was settled over them, obedience was still their duty. When they were delivered from the kings of Syria, they were the lawful subjects of Mattathias and his posterity. It is difficult to believe that Overall and the Convocation really supposed that these cases made anything for the divine right of kings.* The people simply obeyed whatever government was actually settled among them. The kings, in many cases, were usurpers, but so far as they represented the principles of order and government, they were ordained of God. Christ, Overall says, from the beginning was the chief governor of the world. Adam represented Him, and so did Noah, but since the days of Noah there has been no visible king over the whole world. The kingdom of Christ is made up of particular kingdoms. Christ's secular government of the world has its parallel in the government of the Church. The Catholic Church in the Jewish times was not one visible communion. It did not consist merely of Jews and proselytes to the Jews' religion. It embraced devout men of all nations. The uncircumcised worshippers of God as well as the circumcised. Such were Job, Jethro, Rahab, the Ninevites, the woman of Sarepta,

---

* James commanded the Archbishop of Canterbury not to bring the Convocation Book for his assent. The royal prerogative was not declared sufficiently divine to satisfy the King.

Naaman, Cornelius, and many others. Christ Himself was still King of the world, with the kings of the earth under Him. He was also the sole Head of the Church Catholic, which Church, says the Convocation Book of the Church of England, consisted of all devout men, whether Jews or Pagans, throughout the world.

In the second book Overall shows that we have no warrant from the Old Testament writings for any priest or bishop to claim jurisdiction over all the Churches of the world. The duty of obedience to order, whether civil or ecclesiastical, remained under the Christian dispensation unchanged. Such obedience is part of the moral law. Grace does not destroy nature; the law, therefore, is binding under all dispensations. Christ was obedient to the temporal governors; His example should be followed by His disciples. He kept the festival of the Dedication of the Temple, which was established by Judas Maccabæus. From His example Christians ought to keep the festivals established by Christian kings. He rejected the glosses and false interpretations of the Scriptures made by Scribes and Pharisees, and therefore learned men are justified in rejecting the false glosses and interpretations of the governors of the Church. He did not change the secular government which he established before His incarnation. His followers, therefore, are to obey their rulers, even when these rulers are infidels or Pagans. He did not materially alter the ecclesiastical government that had existed among the Jews. The essential parts of the priesthood under the law were instituted by God, not for a time only, but for all times. To this Overall makes one exception, which is, that the priesthood, so far as it was typical, was changed—an exception which to most people will seem excepting more than is left unexcepted, the essence of the Jewish priesthood being its typical character. Overall's object is to make the Jewish hierarchy correspond to that established in England. Rome, he said, makes the Pope to resemble Aaron, head over all the Churches. The Presbyterians make every parish pastor an Aaron. But the Church of England has the exact counterpart of the divine order established among the Jews. The king is first, and under

CHAP. III.

Christ and His Apostles obeyed their temporal governors.

Orders of the Jewish and Christian Churches compared.

him, as under Moses, the ecclesiastical power is delegated to archbishops and bishops. The Jewish division is—(1) Priests with Levites; (2) Twenty-four *Principes Sacerdotium*; (3) Aaron with Moses. The order under the Christian dispensation is—(1) Ministers of an inferior degree; (2) Bishops of a superior degree; (3) Archbishops, and in some places Patriarchs.* It is curious that this is not the division of the Church of England, and not the division generally made by those who advocate the divine institution of Episcopal government. The probable explanation is that Overall and the Convocation were mainly on the defensive. They had to prove against the doctors of the Church of Rome that kings were above bishops; and against the Presbyterians, that all the ministers of the Church were not of one degree. They had to prove that a bishop was a lawful officer in the Church, and that the power of the keys was vested in bishops, and not in presbyteries. Overall maintains the antiquity and apostolicity of Episcopal government, and the Convocation declares in a canon that till of late years no man was considered a lawful minister in the Church who had not been ordained by a bishop. They prove from subscriptions appended to the Epistles, that Timothy and Titus were bishops respectively of Ephesus and Crete, and they declare that to doubt the authority of these subscriptions is 'prejudicial to the writings of the Holy Spirit.'

Bishop Andrewes.

The works of Launcelot Andrewes consist chiefly of sermons, and some controversies with the doctors of the Church of Rome.† He is said to have been a great preacher, and a

---

* When the Church became more *Catholic* and more *Orthodox*, another parallel was formed.

Jewish Church.	*Christian Church.*
(1.) High Priest.	(1.) Bishops, successors of the Apostles.
(2.) Priests.	(2.) Presbyters, succeeding the Seventy disciples.
(3.) Levites.	(3.) Deacons.

—From Bishop Cosin's sermon at the consecration of Dr. Francis White.

The Presbyterian parallel was.—

Jewish Church.	*Christian Church.*
(1.) Priests.	(1.) Pastors.
(2.) Teaching Levites.	(2.) Doctors.
(3.) Rulers of the Synagogue.	(3.) Elders.
(4.) Levitical lookers on of the Treasury.	(4.) Deacons.

—From the 'Counterpoyson' by D. Fenner, in 'Parte of a Register.'

† 'Tortura Torti,' against a book attributed to Bellarmine, but under the name of his almoner, Matthew Tortus; and 'Responsio ad Apologiam Cardinalis Bellarmini.'

very learned man. It is difficult to read his sermons now, and more difficult still to conjecture what interest could possibly have been in them. They must have repelled every hearer who had not an inveterate love of pedantry and punning. In the days of King James, Andrewes was the favourite Court preacher. For nearly twenty years he preached before the king every fifth of August and every fifth of November, the anniversaries of the Gowrie Conspiracy and the Gunpowder Plot. On these occasions he never failed to tell James that he was a king by the special appointment of the King of kings. To fight against King James, Andrewes said, was to fight against God. He illustrates this sublime thesis by playing on the words ordinance and ordnance, saying that a man might as well put himself in the face of all the 'ordnance in the Tower of London,' as against the will of the king, which was 'God's ordinance.' Preaching on the text 'By me kings reign,' *Per me reges regnant*, Andrewes says, 'So many *per me's*. Per me Clement, Castell, Catesby;* and then again so many *pers*. Per knives, pistols, poisons, powder, all against this *per* by continuance.' Then he applies it thus, 'If *per me reges* be from Christ, from whom is the other *per me*? If by me kings reign be Christ's, by me *kings slain*, whose *per* is that *per* of any but Christ's opposite?'

To Andrewes as a theologian, it is not easy to assign a fixed place. He was thoroughly Protestant in his doctrines, but his love of ecclesiastical or patristic language makes him often appear out of harmony with the principles of the Reformation. He maintained a sacrifice in the Eucharist, indeed, a real objective presence, but then he explained that presence not as the presence of Christ's natural body, but of the members of His body, the elect or mystical Church.†

A curious explanation of the Real Presence.

---

* Conspirators against the life of King James.

† This extraordinary conceit was evidently a sort of last refuge, when the Roman doctors urged that without transubstantiation the Church of England had no proper sacrifice to offer. Andrewes explained the power of the keys as given to the clergy only. It consisted in the commission, 'Preach the gospel,' 'Do this,' and 'absolve.' In Prynne's 'Canterbury's Doom,' there is a description of Bishop Andrewes' private chapel. It had all the sacerdotal utensils of a Roman Catholic church,—an 'altar' and candlesticks, a basin for oblations, a silver canister for the wafers, an aire, a tricanale for the water and wine and the holy water, a ewer for the polluted priests to wipe their unhallowed fingers, a credentia, a censer for in-

In words he agreed with the doctrines of the Church of Rome, in meaning he was a whole world separated from them. He made the Church of England to resemble the Church of Rome, but it was only as a shadow, without the substance. He received the theory of Episcopacy set forth by Bancroft and Bilson, but he did not exclude from the Church Catholic the non-Episcopal Churches. He was clear on justification by faith, and he advocated the perpetual obligation of the Sabbath. He said that the Pope was Antichrist; and if he preferred—as he seems to have done—a milder form of the doctrines of Calvin, there is yet no evidence that he entirely renounced them. There is occasionally in his sermons strong language about the efficacy of baptism and the renovating power of grace in the other sacrament. He illustrates also by curious figures from the ark and the propitiatory, that a man must be in the Church to receive grace at all, for by it only, as by 'conduit pipes,' does grace flow to man. But Andrewes must not be judged by his figures nor by the sound of his words. He is only adopting the indefinite, and, indeed, often meaningless language of the Fathers and the Schoolmen.

Christ's 'descent into hell.'

At the last revision of the XXXIX. Articles, under Archbishop Parker, the conclusion of the third, concerning Christ's 'ghost' departing from Him, and being with the 'ghosts that were in person,' was omitted. It was given originally as an interpretation of St. Peter's words about Christ preaching to the spirits in prison. If we are to interpret it by what is said on the same subject in 'The Institution of a Christian Man,' it meant that Christ went to deliver from Hades the just and righteous souls that had lived before Christ's advent. This was an old belief, which some would call the Catholic belief of the ancient Fathers; it was and is the doctrine of the Church of Rome. But St. Augustine, whose authority was equal to all the other Fathers combined, did not understand the meaning of the word Hades. That renowned Father, being ignorant both of

cense, etc. Dr. Hook, in his 'Ecclesiastical Biography,' takes this for a proof that many things were retained in the Church service till this time, which were lost during the reign of the Sectaries, and which we never since regained. Prynne, who lived at the time, takes notice of them, just because they were innovations on the Reformed worship.

Greek and Hebrew, supposed Hades to be the place of the damned, and concluded that Christ went and preached to the lost souls suffering the torments of hell fire. Calvin had interpreted the descent into hell as being no real descent, but only as meaning that Christ suffered on the Cross all the torments which the damned suffer in the place of punishment. It is not said for what reason the conclusion of Art. III. was omitted, whether out of deference to the opinion of Calvin, or because of agreement with the doctrine of Augustine. It is certain, however, that in Elizabeth's time the views of Augustine on this subject were generally adopted by the clergy of the Church of England. Whitgift had openly avowed them. He was supported by Bancroft and Barlow, but more especially by Bilson, who wrote 'A Survey of the Sufferings of Christ for Man's Redemption.' Bilson was to refute Calvin's opinion, which he said was novel. He was to defend Whitgift's, as the ancient opinion of the Catholic Church. Christ went down into hell, that is, the place of the damned, that He might possess the keys of hell and of death.

Whitgift, and especially Bilson, were answered by Hugh Broughton, 'the great Albionean divine,' as Dr. Lightfoot calls him. Broughton wrote on this subject: 'An Explanation of the Article Κατῆλθεν εἰς ᾅδου of our Lord's Soul going from His Body to Paradise,' and 'An Oration to the Geneveans,' in Greek and English. The latter referred to Calvin's doctrine. The former was a reply to Bilson. Christ said on His cross that that day He would be in Paradise. How then, Broughton asks, could He have descended to the place of torment? He did not descend. He ascended to His Father. He went to blessedness, as the souls of all righteous men had done before Him. The Hebrew word for the place of torment is Gehenna. Christ did not go there, but to Sheol, 'that which requireth all men to come to it.' Sheol is hell, or 'that which haileth all hence.' In Greek it is Hades, the unseen world. In Latin, to go to Hades is to go *ad inferos*, to those below. These three words all mean nearly the same. They express the negative of the present existence, rather than anything definite either of happiness or misery in another life. The Psalmist says, 'My life is come near to Sheol'—that is, hell or the grave. Job, speaking of the prosperous wicked, says, 'In a moment they go down to Sheol.' He desired that he might be laid in Sheol till his change came; that is, till the resurrection. In the Old Testament it is generally translated the grave or the pit. The corresponding Greek word is used by all Greek writers in the same sense. For happiness they were sent to Elysium, for misery to Tartarus; but all went to Hades. 'Bury me quickly,' said Patroclus to Achilles, in his dream, 'that I may pass the gates of Hades. The souls, the forms of the dead, keep me aloof, and suffer me not to pass over the ocean; but I wander fondly by the house of broad-gated Hades.' It is the grave, or a vague world of dim shadows which all men associate with the grave. Broughton concludes that the 'descent into hell' means nothing more than that Christ died, and, like all other men, His soul went to the world of spirits. The souls of the righteous have been in Paradise ever since they left the world. Whitgift said that Christ descended into hell, or Gehenna, when He yielded up His spirit. Bilson, in defending Whitgift, said that Christ's soul first went into Paradise, and, after His body was buried, He 'descended' into Gehenna. Broughton said that Christ went, not to Gehenna, but to Sheol or Hades; and to speak of going there from Paradise was like speaking of going from England to Britain, from that which is included to that which includes.

Christ descended not to hell but to Sheol.

Bancroft died in 1611. He was succeeded in the Primacy by George Abbot, who held that office till 1633. During these years the Puritans had rest, and under Abbot's indulgent reign they gathered strength for the conflict which followed in the days of Archbishop Laud. Abbot had been distinguished at Oxford for his opposition to the rising party, who were generally known as Arminians, but who called themselves Catholics; and as they imitated Roman Catholic ritual, were supposed to be restorers of the Pope's dominion in England. In 1600, when Abbot was Vice-chancellor of the University of Oxford, the citizens of London asked his advice about re-erecting the cross in Cheapside, which had fallen to decay. Abbot recommended that a 'Pyramis,' or

Archbishop Abbot.

some object 'of mere beauty,' should be set up in place of it. He said that crosses and crucifixes helped to keep the people in superstition. He commended, however, their prudence in seeking the advice of other persons, instead of following their own judgment. Reformations in religion made deliberately were most likely to be permanent. He recommended them, further, to seek the advice of the Archbishop of Canterbury and the Bishop of London. This, it appears, was done by the citizens, and with the approbation of Whitgift and Bancroft,—the latter of whom was then Bishop of London,—the cross in Cheapside was re-erected.

Abbot did not write much, and the few tracts which he did publish were mostly without his name.* The most important of them, at least the one which most concerns us here, is called 'A Treatise of the Perpetual Visibility and Succession of the True Church in all Ages.' It is a defence of the existence of a visible Church, independent of the Church of Rome. God has always had His own faithful people in every age. There never was a time when it could be said that there is no visible Church. It might be dispersed. Its members might not be able to meet for worship. It might be concealed for a time, but non-existent it has never been and never will be. It is true of the visible Church, that it shall never fail, and the gates of hell shall not prevail against it. Before the Incarnation the Church was sometimes like a city set on a hill, at other times scarcely visible. And so it has been with the Church under the new dispensation. All Protestants, Abbot says, hold that there ever has been, infallibly and without exception, at all times some men professing the true faith. The Church of Rome says that there has always been an apparent hierarchy, but, according to Abbot, it is not that which constitutes a Church. Going back to the Old Testament, he finds that sometimes the saints were very few, and so difficult to be found, that the Psalmist said, 'there is not one godly man left.' Micah cried out, 'Woe is me, I am as the summer gatherings, and as the grape gleanings of the vintage.' In the time of Ahaz, both king and priest conspired to bring in idolatry. The priesthood defaced the

* His largest work was 'An Exposition of the Prophet Jonah.'

CHAP. III. visible Church. But there were faithful souls who did not bow the knee to Baal. So it was at the birth of Christ. The priests and Pharisees had all the show. They boasted themselves to be the Church visible. They had the succession from Aaron and Moses. They were Abraham's children, the authorized teachers of the law; but Jesus called them 'blind guides.' The true Church consisted of those who looked for redemption in Israel; old Simeon, 'just and devout;' Anna, 'the prophetess;' Zacharias and Elizabeth, 'walking blameless in the commandments of the Lord;' Joseph, 'the just man,' and Mary, his espoused wife, with the humble shepherds that watched their flocks in the fields, to whom the angels first announced the 'glad tidings of great joy.'

When Christ established His Church, it was indeed visible, yet often it would have been difficult to know where to find it. The Apostles and the first Christians were scattered and persecuted, while the whole Jewish priesthood were against them. In later times they were forbidden to meet for worship, and the Roman emperors sought to extirpate them from the earth; but they continued to exist, a visible Church indeed, and yet almost invisible. The Catholic Church,—that is, the Church represented by the hierarchy in the time of St. Athanasius,—became Arian, but the true Church still existed. Tertullian said, 'Where three are, there is a Church, although they be lay persons.' St. Paul predicted a great apostasy. Even the Rheims commentators interpret this of the Church of Rome, as referring to a great falling away from the Catholic faith. St. Ambrose compared the Church to the moon, saying, that in that apostasy it would be hidden by the darkness of night. Augustine uses the same comparison, saying that, like the moon, the Church waxes and wanes. Sometimes it is partially and, to appearance, almost totally eclipsed. Such a period of partial darkness, Abbot says, preceded the Reformation for some hundreds of years. But in the darkest times God always had a Church, not consisting of bishops and priests, sees and successions, but of men holding the faith of Christ.*

The Church consists of those who hold the faith of Christ.

---

* Abbot wrote 'An Historical Narration of some Most Learned and Godly English Bishops, Holy Martyrs, and others.' This consisted of

THE SABBATH CONTROVERSY.

CHAP. III.

The Sabbath controversy.

Dr. Rainolds recommended at the Hampton Court Conference 'that some order be taken for the better observance of the Lord's Day;' which, says Dean Barlow, was 'unanimously agreed to.' Notwithstanding this agreement, we may date from this time the beginning of a long controversy about the Sabbath. The Puritans had practised more rigid Sabbath observance than had been taught by any of the Reformers, either English or foreign. The more rigid they became, the more the other party endeavoured to reduce the Sabbath to the level of other days, or at least to make it of a class with the saint and festival days of the Church. It was the custom in England, as it is now in Continental countries, for the people, after the services of the Church, to spend the rest of the day in sports and pastimes.

extracts from the writings of Hooper, Latimer, and Cranmer, on predestination. It was suppressed by Laud, but printed again in 1644, 'for the comfort of all God's people.' The copy in the British Museum has this account of its history prefixed in MS., and dated the same year as the book was printed; the year, the writer says, in which the Parliament then sitting passed sentence on Laud. There are no extracts in the book from the writings of the Reformers, which we have not already met. They do not prove that Hooper, Latimer, and Cranmer ever spoke of predestination in the strong and decided language used by Whitgift and in the Westminster Confession of Faith. This, however, is true, that they only spoke of predestination incidentally, or in popular sermons addressed to the multitude. It is evident to every unbiassed person, that all the Reformers were Calvinists in doctrine. The denial of this is the most daring thing in all ecclesiastical history. The continual appeals which the Reformers made to the people in their sermons, not to build on predestination, everywhere assume that there is such a predestination as that in which Calvinists believe. They ask the people not to look to the decree, but to see that they themselves are believers; not to be curious whether or not their names are in the book of life, but to strive to enter in by the strait gate.

There is a quotation from Cranmer, in which he says, that Jesus Christ came 'to preach and give pardon and full remission of sins to all His elected,' and to do this, it is added, 'He made a full redemption, satisfaction, and propitiation for the sins of the whole world.' This universality of atonement may seem to conflict with Calvinism, but it is only some Calvinists that limit the atonement. The Synod of Dort declared it to be universal.

It is to the lasting honour of Archbishop Abbot that he refused to read King James's 'Book of Sports.' We look back with a peculiar pleasure to the fact, that Grindal did what he thought right, in spite of Elizabeth, and that there was an Archbishop who had the courage to resist King James. Dr. Hook says, that by this refusal Abbot 'helped on the rebellion.' In the amusing and almost ludicrous account which Hook gives of Archbishop Abbot in his 'Ecclesiastical Biography,' there is this passage,—'Under the lax rule of a man who united, with an austere and repulsive temper, the most latitudinarian principles, the way was prepared for that rebellion which levelled to the earth the altar and the throne.' It is curious how that old party venom which should have been buried with the seventeenth century, should have descended to us in such writers as Dr. Hook.

This was offensive to the Puritans. The other party must have seen that a better observance of Sunday would be favourable to religion, but they feared the spirit of Puritanism, and the mere love of opposition was not a vice of the Puritans only. At the Hampton Court Conference the agreement for the order was unanimous; yet before King James's reign was ended, he published a declaration, which he commanded to be read in all the churches, that the people were to have their wonted recreations. This declaration was called the *Book of Sports*. The history of the Sabbath controversy is curious, and often instructive. The opposing parties appear sometimes to change sides. The Jews were commanded to keep the sabbaths, and to reverence the sanctuary. Both commands seem precisely of the same kind, and to stand or fall with each other; yet in England the Puritans kept the Sabbath, and the Conformists reverenced the sanctuary.

Dr. Bownd.

The best defence of the Puritan view of the Sabbath is the work of Dr. Bownd, first published in 1595, but suppressed until 1606. It was called '*Sabbathum Veteris et Novi Testamenti*; or, The True Doctrine of the Sabbath.' It was dedicated to John Jegon, Bishop of Norwich, in whose diocese Dr. Bownd was beneficed. The arguments are those which we find in every orthodox treatise on the Sabbath. It is declared to be not a bare ordinance of man, nor a mere civil and ecclesiastical constitution appointed for the sake of polity, but an immortal commandment of Almighty God, and therefore binding on the consciences of all men. It was given to our first parents, and observed by them, and by the patriarchs both before and under the law. It was revived on Mount Sinai, by the command of God to the Israelites. There was then prefixed to it an especial *Remember*, and after it were added reasons for its observance addressed to all kinds of men. It is moral in its nature, and therefore perpetual, remaining after the merely ceremonial was abolished. By the direction of the Spirit of God the Apostles changed the seventh day for the eighth, the memory of creation giving place to the memory of redemption. We are bound to keep the seventh, that is, one day in the seven, not one in every six or every eight. And we are to keep it by resting from our usual calling, to attend on the service of God. If we are to abstain from our daily labour, much more from all pastimes, or such recreations as may withdraw our minds from the service of God. Great liberty is left for cases of necessity, especially to rulers, both in the Church and Commonwealth. But the day should be spent entirely in God's service, either in public worship or in private devotion, or in giving instruction to our children, servants, or neighbours. There is an obligation resting on all masters of families, magistrates, and princes, to provide for the proper observance of the duties of the Sabbath, and to compel all who are under them to observe at least an *outward rest*.

The seventh day, says Bownd, was sanctified as soon as it was made. It would have been kept by Adam and Eve, as a day sacred above the others, even had they never sinned. Peter Martyr is quoted as saying that God blessed and sanctified the seventh day, to teach us that it was not first given on Sinai, any more than the other moral commandments were first given on Sinai. Bullinger is quoted as saying that the Sabbath came in with the first man, and it must go out only with the last man. It was in the beginning of the world, and must continue till the world's end. Bownd says that in Exodus xvi. Moses speaks of the Sabbath as known to the people before the giving of the law from Sinai. He classes it with the traditional knowledge that had descended from Adam and Noah. As the Patriarchs worshipped the true God by a public service, it is concluded that they must have observed the seventh day. Their religious exercises, which we find on record, might indeed have been performed on any day, yet they are of such a kind as are generally referred to the seventh. Beza was of opinion that Job kept a weekly Sabbath. There were many things inculcated by Moses which were known before his time, such as the distinction between beasts clean and unclean, which was handed down from Adam and Noah. The Gentiles kept a day holy, which, though not the seventh, yet shows that the Fourth Commandment is inscribed on the heart of man. Thomas Aquinas said it was partly moral and partly ceremonial. The Gospel did not take away the

CHAP. III.

The Apostles observed the first day of the week.

Sabbath. Christ and His Apostles generally went into the synagogues on the Sabbath day. St. John declares the continuance of the Sabbath in the Church under the new and more honourable name of *the Lord's day*. It is commended in the first book of the Scriptures, and it is not without due praise in the last. If Adam stood in need of that day to preserve him from falling, how much more do we require it to help us in rising again! Bownd notices a difference in the mode of giving the ceremonial and the moral law. The former was given to the people through the ministry of Moses, the latter was given immediately to the people by the Lord Himself; and Irenæus declares that no part of the decalogue is taken away by the coming of Christ. St. Cyprian says that from the creation of the world the number seven was a sacred number. This was known to the Greek philosophers. The Romans, indeed, lost the seventh day and kept the ninth in its place. From the Greeks, too, Satan took away altogether the memory of the seventh day. They kept the eighth as a holiday by wicked and superstitious rites. Perkins says it is probable, and Bownd adds, most sure and certain, 'that the Sabbath of the New Testament was limited and determined by Christ Himself to be the Lord's day.' The Apostles observed the first day of the week, and they had the command of Jesus to observe and do whatever they had seen Him do. Chemnitius explains how the change of the day is not the taking away of the Sabbath. The general law remains. It is still the seventh. The particular only is changed; it is not that seventh which was kept by the Jews. Faustus, the Manichee, objected to Augustine that he must either renounce Moses or Christ, for their doctrine was different. To which Augustine answered, that their doctrine was not diverse, but the day or time which Christ appointed was not the same which Moses taught. In Acts xx. 7 we find the day changed, Paul preached on 'the first day of the week, ready to depart on the morrow.' Ignatius says, 'Let every one that loveth Christ keep holy the Lord's day, renowned by His resurrection, which is the Queen of all days, in which death is overcome, and life is sprung up in Christ.' Dionysius, Bishop of Corinth in the second century, is recorded by Eusebius as saying, 'To-day we have celebrated the Lord's Holyday.' Justin Martyr testifies how it was observed in his time; the Christians ' met in one place to hear the writings of the prophets.' Augustine says, ' the Apostles and men of apostolical authority have thought that the Lord's day ought religiously to be kept, because on it our Saviour did rise from the dead;' and again he says, ' Let us take heed that our rest be not turned into idleness and vanity, but being sequestered from all rural works and from all business, let us wholly attend upon the worship of God.' Dr. Bownd advocated such an observance of the day of rest as was enforced by Nehemiah, when he put down the treading of the winepresses, the bearing of burdens, and the selling of victuals on the Sabbath day.

The changing of the day was the most formidable difficulty in the Puritan argument. The Jewish Sabbath was never expressly set aside, nor the first day of the week put in its place. If it was merely ceremonial, it doubtless ended with the ceremonial law. The Puritan said it was not ceremonial but moral, and therefore it was to continue always. But if the command to keep holy the seventh day in memory of the creation was moral, to keep *that* day sacred must have remained the essence of the Commandment to the end of time. There were men who felt that this argument had weight, and there were some who did not fear to accept the conclusion, that the seventh day, or Jewish Sabbath, was binding on all men in all ages. This was maintained by Theophilus Brabourne, who wrote ' A Defence of that most ancient ordinance of God's, the Sabbath day.' Brabourne adopted all the Puritan arguments, except those that related to the change of the day. The Fourth Commandment, he said, was simply and entirely moral. The seventh day, that is Saturday, ought to be an everlasting holiday. It obligeth all Christians as well as Jews. Sunday he called an ordinary working day, to convert which into a Sabbath was ' superstition and will-worship.' All the Commandments were given at the same time, by the immediate voice of God, and engraven with His finger on the tables of stone. Christ did not come to destroy the law and the prophets, but to fulfil them. He kept the Sabbath day, frequented the synagogue on that day, and instructed His disciples to do the same. For three hundred years, Brabourne says, the Church followed His example, and kept holy the Jewish Sabbath. The change to Sunday was one of 'the corruptions of Popery.' It began at the Council of Laodicea, which condemned the observance of the Saturday Sabbath. Ignatius called Sunday the Queen of days, implying that there was another day higher, which is 'the King of days.' Socrates is quoted as saying, that the first Christians kept two days in the week, which Brabourne explains, that one was kept for the Sabbath, the other was kept partially, as it were, a light holiday or lecture day. The seventh being the memory of the creation, should be kept by all men, because all men were benefited by the creation. To substitute another than the day appointed is to sin against God. We are not commanded to keep holy the first day of the week. Its observance, therefore, cannot be a matter of faith, and whatsoever is not of faith, the Scripture says, is sin.

Brabourne was specially answered by Francis White, Bishop of Ely, who at the same time examined the arguments of Dr. Bownd. White called his book 'A Treatise of the Sabbath Day, containing a Defence of the Church of England against Sabbatarian Novelty.' It was written at the request of Archbishop Laud, to whom it was dedicated. The dedication is chiefly occupied with the subject which had now become the life of the Church,—the *jus divinum* of bishops. The Church of England, says White, is part of the Catholic Church. Her doctrine of the Sabbath is the Catholic doctrine. The Church of Rome errs in claiming to be the only spouse of Christ. The Presbyterians fall into a similar error in supposing their sect the only kingdom of Christ. White speaks of the Sabbatarian controversy as having disquieted both Church and State ever since Thomas Cartwright's 'unlucky days.' He hoped his book might be the means of settling the long-vexed question. Brabourne's doctrine he shows to be opposed to that of the Church of England, and of the divines who lived at the beginning of the Reformation; that it was condemned by ancient Councils; and that the Church of England has on her side the consentient testimony of the ancient Catholic Church. This ancient Catholic

Church is declared to be the pillar and ground of truth,— the conduit-pipe through which true doctrine comes down to us. White denies that any command was given to Adam to keep the Sabbath, or that we have any historical record that the Sabbath was observed by the Patriarchs. In such a case, the rule of Athanasius is to be followed:—'Because the Holy Scripture is altogether silent in this matter, we may be assured there was no such thing done.' It is the judgment of the ancient Fathers that God imposed upon Adam but one positive precept, and that was abstinence from the fruit of the tree of knowledge of good and evil. The nature of the things required in the Fourth Commandment is such as could not have been required in Paradise. What need was there, in a state of innocency, that man should rest from toilsome labour? Were the ox and the ass, the man-servant and the maid-servant, to be in want of a seventh day's rest in the blessedness of Eden? We have many testimonies, from the ancient Fathers, that the Sabbath was not observed before Moses. Justin Martyr says, 'In the days of Enoch, people observed not circumcision nor the Sabbath.' Again, he says, 'Before Abraham there was no use of circumcision, nor before Moses of keeping holy the Sabbath.' Tertullian says, 'Enoch, Noah, Melchisedec, Abel, and others observed not the old Sabbath.' Irenæus says, 'Abraham believed God, and it was imputed to him for righteousness, before he was circumcised, and without observance of the Sabbath.' Brabourne and Dr. Bownd had noted that the mode of giving the moral law is as different from the mode of giving the ceremonial. The one, they said, was given immediately by God; the other, immediately by angels. White refuses to admit the distinction, for often where God is said to have spoken to men with His own voice, it only means that He spoke by angels or by the prophets. St. Augustine, he says, is resolute that Almighty God, in the time of the Old Testament, did not speak to the Jews with His own voice, but only by means of His ministers, either angels or men. But even if it were granted that God had spoken immediately, White argues that this would not prove the precept to be moral. As to Jesus and His Apostles keeping the Sabbath, the answer is, that Jesus was under the law, and the Apostles went

CHAP. III.

The Sabbath not from the beginning.

138   RELIGIOUS THOUGHT IN ENGLAND.

CHAP. III. into the synagogue on the Sabbath days, that they might embrace every opportunity of preaching the Gospel. There were reasons why the first Christians should sometimes observe the Jewish ceremonies. Augustine says, it was right they should be observed for a time, to give them, as it were, a decent burial. Ignatius, in calling Sunday the Queen of days, did not imply that there was a day higher than Sunday. He meant only to designate the transcendent honour of that day. Gregory of Nyssa says, that the two days were equal, as it were, *brothers german*, but the Sabbath was not preferred to the Sunday. The mere fact of all men having benefited by the creation makes nothing for the seventh day, as all men are benefited by redemption as well as by creation. The sacrifice of the cross was for the whole family of man. The first day may not be commanded in the Scriptures, but it is appointed by the Church, and we are commanded to *hear the Church*, and to obey those that have the *rule over us*. There are many things which we receive solely on the authority of the Church, as the interpretation of certain portions of the Scriptures, the baptism of infants, the perpetual virginity of Mary, and the superiority of bishops over priests and deacons. Brabourne, like Dr. Bownd, claimed for the Sabbath a rigid observance. They differed only about the day to be observed. Christ told His disciples not to profane the Sabbath by working or travelling, and in view of the destruction of Jerusalem, they were to pray that their flight might not be in the winter nor on the Sabbath day. White answers that this was not on account of the sanctity of the day, but that it had respect to the remaining Jewish reverence for the day of rest. He then shows that the Catholic Church has always had power to give licence for working on the Lord's day. In St. Jerome's time the most devoted Christians did ordinary work on the Lord's day. Jerome, in his funeral oration for the Lady Paula, says that she 'repaired duly to the Church or house of God, which was nigh her cell, and after her return from thence to her own lodging, she herself and all her company fell to work, and every one performed their tasks, which was the making of clothes and garments for themselves and for others as they were appointed.' White agreed

The first Christians kept two days holy.

The Church to be obeyed.

It gives licence for work and sports on Sunday.

THE SABBATH CONTROVERSY. 139

with Brabourne, that the Sunday was a day on which ordinary work might be done. It was a kind of light holiday or lecture-day, appointed by the Church. He advocated, in the spirit of the king's declaration, that after the Church service was ended, it was a proper time for sports and recreations, such as music, dancing, playing at games, especially those conducive to bodily strength; and he quoted from the Talmud that the same things were allowed by the Jews on their day of rest, 'Young people were to disport themselves on some part of the Sabbath with running, leaping, or dancing, provided that they were done in honour of the Sabbath.'*

CHAP. III.

It might have been thought, beforehand, from their traditional principles, that White's party would have been the most rigid Sabbatarians. The idea of a traditional Sabbath from the beginning of the world to the end of time, ought to have been congenial to them. Sacred days must ever claim kindred with sacred places. The advantages to religion of reserving certain days, exclusively for the cultivation of devout feelings, must have been as obvious as the advantages of keeping sacred certain places for the performance of religious duties. The Puritan, freed from the influence of controversy, has felt the sacredness of the place where he was accustomed to worship God and the devout High Church-

Sacred days and sacred places.

---

* In 1633 complaints were made to the chief justices about 'revels,' 'church ales,' etc. Dr. Pierce, Bishop of Bath and Wells, gives an account of them, and the great good they did by promoting benevolence and good feeling. After church the people went to their sports and pastimes in the churchyard, or in some public-house, where they drank and made merry. Under the influence of beer their liberality expanded, and they collected money for such objects as re-casting the church bells, called 'church ales;' maintaining the parish clerk, called 'clerk ales;' setting up a poor parishioner, which was called 'a bidale.' Of the bishops' advocacy of Sunday desecration, Milton said, 'I am sure they took the ready way to despoil us both of manhood and grace at once, and that in the shamefullest and ungodliest manner, upon that day which God's law, and even our own reason, hath consecrated, that we might have one day, at least, of seven set apart wherein to examine and increase our knowledge of God, to meditate and commune of our faith, our hope, our eternal city in heaven, and to quicken withal the study and exercise of charity; at such a time, that men should be plucked from their soberest and saddest thoughts, and by bishops, the pretended fathers of the Church, instigated by public edict, and with earnest endeavour pushed forward to gaming, jigging, wassailing, and mixed dancing, is a horror to think. Thus did the reprobate hireling priest, Balaam, seek to subdue the Israelites to Moab, if not by force, then by this devilish policy, to draw them from the sanctuary of God to the luxurious and ribald feasts of Baal-peor.'

man has not been insensible to the sacredness of the Sabbath feeling and the Sabbath day. If Milton could sing,—

> 'And let my due feet never fail
> To walk the studious cloister's pale;
> And love the high embowèd roof,
> With antique pillars massy proof;
> And storied windows, richly dight,
> Casting a dim religious light,'—

George Herbert could burst out in raptures on the return of the day,—

> 'Most calm, most bright.'

Dr. Heylin on the Sabbath.

Peter Heylin wrote 'A History of the Sabbath.' His hatred of the Puritans is a sure pledge that he will maintain the opposite of whatever they maintained. Heylin declared in the preface that the Puritan notions of the Sabbath were so entirely new that no Church whatever had entertained them. Their advocates were of Calvin's platform, but in this they had no countenance from Calvin. They forsook their master 'to give themselves up to the glory of a new invention.'

Heylin argues that the Sabbath was not established in Paradise, that it is not naturally imprinted on the soul of man, and that it was not kept by the Patriarchs before Moses. It was never reckoned a moral precept, but was always disregarded when business or necessity required; and it was abrogated for ever with the other ceremonies at the destruction of the temple. The Lord's day was not instituted by Christ nor commanded by His Apostles. It was ordained by no authority but that of the Church. By the Church it was voluntarily consecrated to religious uses. It advanced to its present state slowly and by degrees. It owed its present advancement partly, says Heylin, to the edicts of princes, the canons of particular councils, the decretals of several Popes, and the orders of inferior prelates. In many Protestant countries it is still subject to the laws of the Church. In no Church in the world was the day of rest ever esteemed akin to the old Jewish Sabbath. At all times not appointed for public worship, men might apply themselves either to business or pleasure. The Church of England, he says, of all Churches in the world, has kept the

The Lord's day not an Apostolic institution.

safest medium between superstition and profaneness. The old Fathers ranked the Sabbath with circumcision. Eusebius, showing that the religion of the patriarchs before the law did not differ from that of Christians, says, 'They were not circumcised, no more are we; they kept not any Sabbath, no more do we. They were not bound to abstinence from sundry kinds of meats which are prohibited by Moses, no more are we.' Irenæus indeed says, that 'the Decalogue is in full force, enlarged rather than dissolved by Christ.' Heylin explains this, that Irenæus must refer to that part of the Fourth Commandment which is moral, if he did not altogether exclude this commandment from the moral code. The Jews, according to Heylin, were not strict in their observance of the Sabbath, if we except some points of superstition. They did not work, but they employed others to do work for them. They would not milk a cow, but would hire another person to milk it. Buxtorf mentions some of the minute laws of the Jews, illustrating their superstitious observance of the Sabbath. A horse might have a bridle or a halter but not a saddle. A tailor might not wear his needle in his sleeve. People were not to wear clogs or pattens. They were not to wipe their hands with a towel, but with the tail of a cow or a horse, and, to do despite to what Jesus said about works of mercy on the Sabbath day, they are forbidden to take an ox or an ass out of a ditch. Jesus, continues Heylin, set Himself against the Sabbatical observance of the Jews, and, from His day, reverence for the Sabbath began to decline. Tostatus says that the festivals under the Old Testament were appointed by God, but under the New they are left to the prelates of the Church. For the first thousand years after Christ, the word Sabbath meant Saturday. In 791, Paulinus, Patriarch of Aquilegia, at the Synod of Friuli, decreed that on Saturday evening the people should prepare themselves for keeping Sunday. In the middle ages sports and games were as lawful on Sundays as on other days. The general voice of the schoolmen on the Fourth Commandment is, that it is ceremonial and, unlike the other nine, not moral. Heylin says, that before the Reformation, the Church had become Sabbatical. It was a mortal sin for a cook to dress a dinner, for a man to travel

CHAP. III.

Jewish Sabbatical superstitions.

The Church before the Reformation Sabbatarian.

on business, for a ferryman to transport passengers, except when going to Mass. Against these things the Reformers protested. Calvin speaks of carnal superstitions about the Sabbath which existed in his time. Peter Martyr says the day was left to the liberty of the Church, when the memory of the resurrection was preferred to that of creation. Zanchy says that, as the Apostles did not command a day, it was left to the judgment of the Church. In 1571, dancing on Sunday was forbidden by the Reformed Church of France at the Synod of Rochelle. This prohibition, in Heylin's judgment, was detrimental to the progress of the Reformed religion, for the French are greatly addicted to the exercise of dancing. In Scotland, by a Parliament held at Scone, under Alexander II., it was forbidden to fish in any waters from Saturday after evening prayers until sunrise on the Monday. Such was the power of the Pope in Scotland that this enactment was again enforced under James I. The Pope's power was never so great in England. In a synod, held at Lambeth, under Archbishop Peckham, it was decreed that all obligations from the old law were ended, and that the Lord's day was kept solely because of the institution of the Church. Buying and selling on Sunday were not forbidden by this synod. The prohibition of Sunday markets is of a later date. But it was this synod which determined what is now the Church of England doctrine concerning the Sabbath.*

* There are two volumes on the literature of the Sabbath, by R. Cox. Dr. Hessey treats of it largely in his Bampton Lectures. Among the curiosities of the controversy in the seventeenth century, was a treatise called 'The Seventh Day Sabbath, or a Tract on the IV. Commandment, wherein is discovered the cause of the controversies about the Sabbath day, and the means of reconciling them: more particularly is showed, (1.) That the seventh day, from the creation, which was the day of God's rest, was not the seventh day which God commanded His people to keep holy; neither was it such a kind of day as was the Jews' Sabbath day. (2.) That the seventh day in the law commanded to be kept holy is the seventh day of the week, viz. the day following the six days of labour with all people. (3.) That Sunday is, with Christians, as truly the Sabbath day as was Saturday with the Jews. By Thomas Chafie, Parson of Nutshelling,' 1652. The argument is that it is only a conventional arrangement which makes Sunday the first day of the week. It might just as well be called the seventh, for it really is the seventh day, following the six days of labour.

In 1634, Christopher Dow wrote a 'Discourse of the Sabbath and the Lord's Day.' It was a plea for making merry on Sunday, because it was the festival of the resurrection. It was to be kept according to Nehemiah viii. 9, 10, where the people are told, after the reading of the law, to go their way, 'to eat the fat and drink the sweet, and send portions to them for whom nothing is prepared.'

It would be a profitable discovery if we could determine how far men's interests have an influence on their belief. The clergy lost nothing by denying the divine origin of the Lord's day, but there was another subject discussed about the same time, by which they were likely to lose something, if they could not show a divine origin. This was the question of tithes. Were they instituted at the beginning of the world? Is the tradition of their payment universal? Was a tithe always a tenth, neither more nor less? and was it a tenth of all a man's possessions or only of a part of his possessions? There had been several books written on the subject, but the first which excited any great interest was the work of John Selden, called 'The History of Tithes,' published in 1618. Selden said, in his preface, that his object was not to prove that tithes were not due by the law of God. He did not wish to prove that the laity may not pay them. He was not against the maintenance of the clergy. He wished only to write a history, and to state such facts as he could find concerning the payment of them. The first mention of tithe is in the history of Abraham. Returning from the slaughter of the kings, he met Melchisedec, to whom he paid tithes of all. But of what all? His substance or his spoils? The old Jews understood of his spoils only. Josephus is of the same opinion. The Septuagint expressly says that he paid tithes of the spoils, and the writer of the Epistle to the Hebrews follows the reading of the Septuagint. The next mention of tithing is in Genesis xxviii. 22, where Jacob says, 'And the stone, which I have set up for a pillar, shall be God's house, and of all that thou wilt give me I will tithe, and give the tenth unto thee.' Josephus says that upon his return, twenty years after, he performed his vow by giving the tithe of all that he had gotten. We read in the beginning of Genesis that Cain and Abel made offerings to the Lord, but there is no mention of quantity. There is notice only of the mind that offered and the quality of the oblation that was made.

These are the only cases of tithes before the Levitical law. The Jews say that the law was instituted before the creation. We, however, know nothing of it till Moses and Aaron. By the Levitical law, the first fruits of the ground

CHAP. III.

John Selden on tithes.

CHAP. III.

Tithes among the Jews.

were to be offered. The first of the forwardest of wheat, barley, figs, grapes, olives, pomegranates, and dates were to be given to the priest, and, of these, the owner was to pay what quantity he chose. Then came the *thereumah*, or heave-offering,—first fruits of corn, wine, oil, and fleece. The quantity not being determined by Moses, the old Jews assessed it at the fiftieth part. Some paid only a sixtieth, but richer people a fortieth. In the Book of Tobit, there is mention of a *third tithe*, or tithe of a third year; for the Levite, the fatherless, and the widow. It is so explained by Josephus, and was called by the Rabbins the poor man's tithe. The first-born of the cattle were the Lord's. They were paid to the priest, of clean beasts, in kind; of unclean, in money. The tithing of herbs was not in Scripture. It rested solely on tradition. The whole of these tithes were paid irregularly, some of them were omitted, and sometimes there was more, sometimes less than was fixed by law. The herb-tithe was paid with the greatest exactness, and though not commanded, yet Christ said it was among the things which ought not to be left undone.

Tithes among the Gentiles.

Among the Gentiles, there is at least the use of the word tithe. The Greeks tithed their estates to Hercules. They spent the tenth in sacrifices, gifts to his temple, and feasts to his honour. Selden says that this was merely a thanksgiving, and not commanded by any law, pontifical or civil. Similar arbitrary vows and thanksgivings were practised among the Romans. The old Pelasgi gave to Apollo, at Delphi, by command of the oracle, a tenth of the gains by the merchandise of the sea. Postumius, the dictator, on his victory over the Latins, tithed the spoils for the service of Ceres, Bacchus, and Proserpine. It had been concluded from a passage out of Festus that the ancients generally paid tithes for the service of religion, but Selden says there are many things to disprove this. Their custom was, as Harpocrates testifies, ' to tithe the spoils of war to the gods.' Even this was but a custom, depending on the choice of individuals, and not obligatory upon any one.

No tithes among the first Christians.

Under the Christian dispensation, for the first four hundred years, no tithes were paid. The devotion of the first Christians was so great that their liberality was unbounded.

They even sold all their possessions and laid the money at the Apostles' feet. We read of tithes in the third and fourth centuries as being paid to emperors and lords of the soil. The free gifts of the faithful had made the clergy so rich, that they were envied for their riches. In the fifth century tithes were paid to abbots, to the poor, and to the clergy. By tithes is meant 'free-will offerings to the amount of tithes or the tenth part of their possessions.' In the eighth and ninth centuries some were endowed with the perpetual right of collecting tithes. In some cases this right was granted voluntarily by the owners of the lands. In the time of Charles Martel tithes were not of sufficient value to tempt him to seek possession of them. The wealth of the Church did not consist in tithes. There are some canons professing to be of this date, enforcing tithes, but Selden says they are not general. The Fathers asked the faithful to pay tithes as a duty. A tenth was not enforced by law, but recommended as what ought to be given; and while some gave less than a tenth, others gave more. In the tenth and eleventh centuries we find more frequent consecrations of tithes made voluntarily by the owners of land. We find also frequent canons enforcing the right of collecting them. The Church claimed them as inalienable property, and the secular power helped the Church to possess them.*

Sir James Sempil wrote a treatise on the sacredness of Church property, which he called 'Sacrilege Sacredly Handled.' The occasion of this treatise was the munificence of the King towards the Church, and the argument is, that what is once consecrated to religion can never be alienated without sacrilege. He devoted an 'Appendix' to Selden's work, in which he denied that Abraham gave tithes only of the spoils. He pleaded that the institution of tithes was moral and not ceremonial, that the tithes paid to Melchisedec and the Levitical priests were still due to the clergy, and he thought that St. Paul inculcated the payment of them, when he said, 'No man goeth a warfare at his own charges.'

Divine right of tithes defended.

---

* Selden was compelled to read a recantation of what he had written on tithes, and King James ordered him, at his peril, not to answer those who had replied to him.

Richard Tillesley, Archdeacon of Rochester, wrote 'Animadversions on Mr. Selden's History of Tithes.' He dedicated his work to King Charles, 'the advocate and nursing father of God's portion, the Church, that is, tithes.' He said 'the number tenth or tithe was certainly very mystical.' It belonged only to sacred and consecrated persons, such as kings and priests, who 'stand in God's place to receive their portion as God's upon earth.' Tillesley says that Selden is wrong in confounding tithes with arbitrary gifts consecrated to the Church. The tenth is by divine law due to the clergy. A gift of land is a gift which may be either given or withheld. As Sir James Sempil replied to Selden's arguments from Scripture, and proved by Scripture that tithes are divinely instituted, Tillesley was to take up the subject where Sempil left it, and to demonstrate from the Fathers, the great interpreters of Scripture, that they understood the institution of tithes to be divine. Vincentius Lirinensis had laid it down as a rule that the constant and unanimous consent of antiquity was the best evidence of the meaning of Scripture; and Tillesley, in this belief, adduced a long catalogue of ancient authors, who testified that tithes, that is, the exact tenth part of all property, belonged to the Church by divine right.*

Arminianism in the Church of England.

Towards the end of the reign of King James the doctrines of Arminius began to find favour among the clergy of the Church of England. Hitherto Calvin was the idol theologian. Those who say that the Church of England is not Calvinistic in doctrine have but two arguments that have even the appearance of being plausible. The first is, that our Reformers followed Melancthon and the Augsburg Confession, rather than Calvin. This, however, was a difference not in the doctrine itself, but only in adopting a milder form of expressing it. The other is, that the Lambeth Articles were rejected at the Hampton Court Conference. To this it is justly answered that the archbishop and bishops who were at the Hampton Court Conference held the same sentiments

---

* Richard Montagu, afterwards Bishop of Chichester, wrote, in 1621, 'Diatribes upon the First Part of the late History of Tithes.' In 1685, Thomas Comber, Precentor of York, wrote 'An Historical Vindication of the Divine Right of Tithes.' The latter is of considerable value, from its containing the substance of all that had been written against Selden.

as the framers of the Lambeth Articles; that James himself was a high Calvinist; and, moreover, that the doctrine of the Lambeth Articles was not rejected. The king refused to incorporate them with the authorized standards, giving a distinct reason that he would not 'stuff the book with all conclusions theological.'

James, as we have seen from his own writings, was no friend to the Anti-Calvinistic divines that had risen up in the States of Holland. He wrote against Vorstius; and when the Synod of Dort assembled in 1618, to condemn the doctrines of Arminius, James sent commissioners* to represent the Church of England. The five points condemned were:—

(1.) 'That God, from all eternity, determined to bestow salvation on whom He foresaw would persevere unto the end in their faith in Christ, and to inflict everlasting punishment on those who should continue in their unbelief, and resist unto the end the divine succours.

(2.) 'That Jesus Christ, by His death and sufferings, made an atonement for the sins of all mankind in general, and of every individual in particular; that, however, none but those who believe in Him can be partakers of this divine benefit.

(3.) 'That true faith cannot proceed from the exercise of our natural faculties and powers, nor from the force and operation of free-will, since man, in consequence of his natural corruption, is incapable of thinking or doing any good thing; and that therefore it is necessary to his conversion and salvation that he be regenerated by the operation of the Holy Spirit, which is the gift of God through Jesus Christ.

(4.) 'That this divine grace or energy of the Holy Ghost, which heals the disorders of a corrupt nature, begins, advances, and brings to perfection everything that can be called good in man, and that consequently all good works, without exception, are to be attributed to God alone and the operation of His grace; that, nevertheless, His grace does not force a man to act against his inclination, but may

---

* Dr. Carleton, Bishop of Llandaff; Dr. Hall, Dean of Worcester; Drs. Ward and Davenant, heads of colleges at Cambridge. Mr. Walter Balcanqual, Fellow of Pembroke Hall, represented the Church of Scotland.

be resisted and rendered ineffectual by the perverse will of the impenitent sinner.

(5.) 'That they who are united to Christ by faith are thereby furnished with abundant strength, and with succours sufficient to enable them to triumph over the seductions of Satan, and the allurements of sin and temptation; but that the question whether such may fall from this faith, and forfeit finally this state of grace, has not yet been resolved with sufficient perspicuity, and must therefore be yet more carefully examined by an attentive study of what the Holy Scriptures have declared on this important point.' The later Arminians determined that a man may fall from a state of grace totally and finally.

The Church Calvinistic in the beginning of James's reign.

At the beginning of the reign of King James the Lambeth Articles were generally received by the clergy. By the end of his reign, or at least in the reign of his son, Arminianism was taught openly even by dignitaries of the Church. It is said that some one at the court of King James once asked what the Arminians held, and was answered that they held all the best bishoprics and deaneries in the kingdom. This change did not take place without a struggle. It gave rise to many controversies. William Prynne, afterwards celebrated for his sufferings, wrote a defence of the Calvinism of the Church. Prynne was a Churchman of the old Elizabethan type,—a Calvinist and a Conformist, yet not a believer in the Divine right of Episcopacy. He called his book 'Anti-Arminianism,' and he urged the bishops to extirpate these 'Arminian thieves and robbers.' He quoted the words of Abbot, the Bishop of Salisbury, who said he did 'not know by what force of the winds the unclean breath (of Arminianism) had also blown upon our regions and infatuated some of our divines,' and he denied a rumour then current that King James himself had renounced Calvinism. After calling upon the bishops to extirpate the new heresy, he appealed for the same object to the High Court of Parliament. He told them that the Arminian novelties had almost overturned the ancient doctrines of the Church. He explained to the Parliament that it was properly within their province to exercise jurisdiction over the rites and tenets of religion, and he found in the progress of Arminianism the cause of all the disasters that had of late overtaken the nation.* 'God's heavy wrath and curse,' he said, 'had been upon us ever since this heresy had reached our shores.' Prynne applied the test of Vincentius Lirinensis, that what all the Fathers of the Church declare to be heresy must be received for heresy. The universal consent of all the Fathers and Doctors of the Church since the Reformation was against Arminianism. It must therefore be a heresy. He quoted various writers of Elizabeth's time who had guarded the expression 'fall from grace' with the explanation 'but not totally or finally.' He gave the history of the Lambeth Articles, and their incorporation into the Articles of the Church in Ireland, which were approved by King James, and printed here as by authority. He reasoned also that the two Churches being one, there was an argument that their doctrines did not contradict each other. He quoted such passages from the Prayer Book as speak of the elect, the chosen, and the necessity of special grace to change the heart. He explained the universality ascribed to the Atonement as being *sufficient* for all, but efficient only for the predestinated. He quoted from the Homilies such passages as traced to God's Spirit the origin of any good in man; and, as to perseverance, he found it written that 'the Spirit of God doth always dwell in the hearts of the regenerate, and that David, Solomon, Noah, Lot, and Peter, though they fell into gross and scandalous sins, yet they did not fall finally nor totally from the state of grace.'†

The theologians whom James had sent to the Synod of Dort were still living, and ready to join with Prynne in declaring Arminianism a novelty in the Church of England. Davenant, now Bishop of Salisbury, denied the universality of the Divine love. An anonymous author wrote an Arminian treatise, which he called 'God's Love to Mankind.'‡ Davenant wrote an answer, in which he admitted that God

---

* Cromwell complained in Parliament that Dr. Neile, Bishop of Winchester, gave countenance to divines who preached Arminianism and Popery. Mr. Rouse followed, saying, among other wild things, 'An Arminian is the spawn of a Papist, and if the warmth of favour come upon him, you shall see him turn into one of those frogs that rose out of the bottomless pit.'

† This was collected out of several Homilies.

‡ This was written by Samuel Hoard.

had a general love to mankind, but he showed the danger of magnifying this common love. It might obscure that special love which God had from all eternity for His chosen. Davenant made no scruple about reprobation. He despised to take shelter under the mere absence of the word from the seventeenth Article. He saw and admitted that predestination, if it means anything, carries reprobation with it. It may be called preterition, non-election, or the decree negative, but, whatever be its name, it is as absolute as the other, and as independent of the foreseen difference of men's actions. Reprobation, he says, is not a denial of sufficient grace, but a denial of such special grace as God knows to be necessary to bring man to salvation. The doctrine of Arminius, that men are chosen for faith and perseverance foreseen, and reprobated for the lack of them, Davenant pronounces 'false, vain, and disagreeing with the notion of predestination rooted in the hearts of all Catholic and orthodox Churchmen.' He explains Supralapsarianism so as to annihilate the difference between it and Sublapsarianism, the Deity not being subject to that order of time which regulates the works of men. Priority and posteriority in the eternal, immanent decrees of God are but the imaginations of the weak reason of man. The elect were created for this end, solely that they might be glorified with Christ Jesus. From the general reasoning, it might have been fairly inferred that the non-elect were created that they might not be glorified with Jesus Christ, but tormented with the devil and his angels. Davenant says that this does not follow, which leaves the alternative either that there was no end in their creation, or that they defeated the end for which they were created.

The opposition to Calvinism connected itself with the growth of the party which began with Bancroft. The tone of the Thirty-nine Articles had more affinity with the doctrine of Geneva than with that of the Prayer Book and Episcopacy. This was manifest in the Hooker controversy, and did not escape the notice of the author of the 'Christian Letter.' It was more manifest now, when Churchmen were disposed to make the most of their affinity with the primitive Church while opposing the Church of Rome. Richard

Montagu, afterwards Bishop of Chichester, wrote a defence of the Church of England in reply to a tract called 'A Gagg for the new Gospel.'* Among the charges brought against Protestants, the 'Gagger' said they teach that, by the fall of Adam, man lost his free-will, and that faith, once possessed, can never be lost. Montagu denied that these were doctrines of the Church of England. The latter he admitted to be the private opinion of many Churchmen, but not the doctrine of the Church. The former, he said, was a question more befitting the schools than the popular ear. This was denied, not merely by Montagu's Roman Catholic adversaries, but by members of the Church of England. He was called an Arminian. He protested that he knew nothing of Arminius. 'I am not,' he said, 'nor would be accounted willingly Arminian, Calvinist, or Lutheran (names of division), but a Christian. For my faith was never taught by the doctrine of men.' Words like these are easily said. They only serve to evade what should at once be admitted. Montagu held the doctrines of Arminius. Whether or not these were in harmony with the Scriptures, the opinions, practices, traditions, and consent of the ancient Church, was a further question. Montagu believed that they were. He called his next book 'Appello Cæsarem, or a just Appeal from two unjust Informers.' It was dedicated to King Charles, who was to decide whether the new Arminianism or the old Calvinism was the doctrine of the Church of England. The divines who flourished under Elizabeth would have scouted the heresy, and burned the heretic. Montagu argued concerning the fall of Peter that, if it really was a *fall*, he fell totally and finally. A fall can only mean that a man has lost that footing by which he can hold himself fast. We must either, he says, allow that Peter fell, or take the Roman Catholic view, that Peter's faith did not fail. But evidently Peter's faith did fail, and so Peter fell. Now, if the faith which justifies be lost, justification, which is an act consequent on faith, may also be lost. And this agrees with Article XVI., which says that the regenerate 'may depart from grace given, and that they may rise

---

* The answer was called, 'A Gagg for the New Gospel? No: a New Gagg for an Old Goose.'

again;' but it does not say that they certainly will rise again. He quoted from the Homily 'Of falling away from God,' where it is distinctly said that those who fall away shall no longer be governed by God's Holy Spirit. He proved it, moreover, from experience. Children, he says, are by baptism put into a state of grace and salvation. Now, we all see that many baptized children lead a wicked life, and so fall away from God.

Bishop Carleton opposes Arminianism.

Carleton, whom King James had sent to the Synod of Dort, was now Bishop of Chichester. It grieved the old man to see the triumph of the heresies which it had been the work of his life to oppose, and for opposing which he had risen to be a ruler in the Church. He wrote 'An Examination' of the 'Appello Cæsarem,' which he also dedicated to King Charles. He told the King that there were two dangers which had of late assailed the kingdom. These were the plague and the Pelagian heresy; the one a destroyer of bodies, the other of souls. He says that Montagu had troubled the Church with strange doctrines concerning predestination. He had tried to bring in a *respective decree*, and he had taught that a man may fall away from grace totally and finally. The latter was contrary to the express words of Augustine, who says, 'They that are called and justified according to God's purpose cannot fall away.' Montagu maintained his doctrines to be those of the Church of England. This Carleton denied, asserting that the English Reformers, in compiling the Articles, were assisted by Peter Martyr and Martin Bucer, with whose doctrines they agreed. He noticed that, though the Puritans were disquieted about the discipline of the Church, they had no quarrel about the doctrines. He gave an account of Baro, Barrett, and others who had broached Arminianism in England, showing that what Montagu now advocated had been systematically condemned, and had against it the universal consent of the Fathers of the English Church. Montagu called the framers of the Lambeth Articles, Puritans. The application of this name* to such men as Archbishop Whitgift and the other framers of the Lambeth Articles was itself an evidence of the change

All doctrinal Calvinists are now called Puritans.

---

* This name was now applied to all the Calvinistic clergy as a term of reproach. Bishop Sanderson, whose churchmanship was never questioned,

that was coming upon the Church. Davenant, as we have seen, merged Supralapsarianism into Sublapsarianism, maintaining that with God no opposition between them was possible. Carleton retained the old distinction. Augustine he called a Sublapsarian. God saw the human race as a mass of corruption. He predestinated that some should be saved, and the others left in their misery. This decree was irrespective of any good foreseen in the predestined. The rest were passed by. It did not please God to have mercy upon them. This, Carleton says, is not only the doctrine of Augustine, but the ancient Catholic doctrine of the Church. Before Augustine's time, it had not come into dispute. Montagu said that St. Peter was not called, saved, and glorified, without regard to his faith, obedience, and repentance. Carleton answered that Peter was *called* without respect to these things, but not saved and glorified without regard to them. If a man were *called* in respect of his faith, obedience, and repentance, then grace would be given according to merit. Pelagius, Carleton says, taught that there was somewhat in nature which caused God to confer grace. Montagu corrected this, saying that God gave grace in respect of grace, which, as Augustine said of the Pelagians, was enforcing grace in words, but in reality denying it. The heresy is traced from the Pelagians to the Schoolmen, John Scotus expressly teaching that charity and repentance may be had *ex puris naturalibus*. Carleton discusses at length the question of falling from grace. He says it is possible to lose such grace as ordinarily comes by hearing the Gospel, which is called the word of grace. But the grace which proceeds from predestination can never be lost. Peter fell into great sin, but that does not involve a failure of faith. The Homily which Montagu quoted, Carleton explains as referring only to the wicked that go from God in the sense of never having come to Him. Article XVI. refers to the Pharisaic pride of the Cathari, or Perfectionists. It declares that we may fall into sin, may depart from grace; yet the benefit of repentance is not to be denied

The doctrine of Calvin the ancient Catholic doctrine.

said, 'Could that blessed Archbishop Whitgift, or the modest and learned Hooker, have ever thought, so much as by dream, that men concurring with them in opinion should, for some of these very opinions, be called Puritans?'

CHAP. III.

<small>Augustine on sacramental justification.</small>

to those who thus fall. This article was not, as Montagu said, challenged at the Hampton Court Conference. Both sides were agreed that the doctrine it taught was true. Dr. Overall denied expressly that a man could fall totally or finally.* To Montagu's explanation of grace from regeneration in baptism, Carleton answers that if he had been pleased to observe the judgment of the ancients, he would not have been troubled with such novelties. St. Augustine might easily have satisfied him. Augustine makes a great difference between those that are regenerate and justified only *sacramento tenus* (sacramentally), and those that are regenerated and justified according to God's election. Abraham received the sacrament of circumcision, as a seal of the righteousness of faith. The sacrament is good to them to whom it is a seal of the righteousness of faith, but it is not a seal in all that receive it. For many receive the sign which have not the thing signified. Ishmael and Isaac were both circumcised, but Ishmael was born according to the flesh, and Isaac according to the Spirit. He that was born according to the flesh was justified only *sacramento tenus*; but he that was born according to the Spirit was justified freely. St. Augustine says, 'Though the sacraments are common to all, yet grace is not common to all that are baptized in the name of the Father, the Son, and the Holy Ghost. Yea that grace whereof these are sacraments, whereby the members of the body of Christ are regenerate with their Head, is not common to all.' Carleton, following Augustine, explains that, though we call all that receive baptism the children of God, regenerate and justified, yet it is 'only a speech of the Church's charity.' They are regenerated sacramentally, but it is only by their lives that we can know if they are regenerate and justified according to God's eternal election.

* Bishop Carleton here refers to what was said by Overall at the Hampton Court Conference about falling from grace. He did not say that a justified man might fall finally from grace. No one at the Conference maintained that. He only said that, if such a man fell into sin, while in sin he was subject to God's wrath. Those who deny the Calvinism of the Church of England have tried to make out that there were Arminians at the Hampton Court Conference, and that Overall was one. A full account of Overall's opinions on this question will be found in Dean Goode's careful and judicious work on the 'Effects of Infant Baptism.' Overall was certainly a Calvinist, but, like Richard Baxter, he tried to soften and modify his belief in such a way as to have made Calvin ashamed of him.

In 1625 a Conference was held at York House, by the Duke of Buckingham, concerning Montagu's books. This Conference was called at the solicitation of Lord Warwick and Lord Say. They were moved to solicit it by the representations of Thomas Morton, Bishop of Lichfield, who charged Montagu with contradicting the plain teaching of the XXXIX. Articles. The account which we have of this Conference was written by Bishop Cosin, who was a partisan on Montagu's side, and who represents the Duke of Buckingham as rebuking Bishop Morton for making charges that had no real foundation. Buckeridge, Bishop of Rochester, and Dr. White, then Dean of Carlisle, with Dr. Cosin, were also members of the Conference.

CHAP. III.

Conference on Montagu's books.

The substance of the charges was, that Montagu had maintained (1) that the Turk and not the Pope was Antichrist, (2) that General Councils neither have erred nor can err, (3) that justification consists in forgiveness of sins previously, and grace infused secondarily, (4) that we get heaven through our own deservings, (5) that the King is not the head of the Church, (6) and that the Church of Rome has not erred in matters of faith. To the first of these it was easily answered that the Church of England has never taught in any authoritative formulary that the Bishop of Rome is Antichrist. The second was more difficult to explain, for Art. XXI. says that General Councils 'may err, and sometimes have erred.' Montagu's doctrine was that the first four General Councils were infallible, and that all Councils lawfully called and qualified as they were, would also be infallible. They did not err, because they decreed truth, which Bishop Morton reckoned to be a paralogism, equivalent to saying that Councils do not err when they do not err.* Montagu's words were that such Councils could not err 'in matters fundamental.' The words of the Article are 'in things pertaining to God,' which embraces more than 'matters fundamental.' Bishop Buckeridge added in expla-

Charges against Montagu.

---

* Peter Heylin maintained, in an academical exercise at Oxford, that the Catholic Church was infallible, but not the Church of Rome. The test is that it has always declared truth. It has, therefore, never erred. In the last analysis the argument comes back to what John Bradford said, when he defined the Catholic Church as consisting of all people in all nations who agreed with him in the doctrines of faith.

nation of this, that the Council of Trent could scarcely be said to have erred in 'fundamentals,' though it erred in many 'things pertaining to God.' As to justification, Montagu satisfied Bishop Morton by saying that it was by faith alone as the instrument, and by God as the cause. Considering our controversies with the Church of Rome on the value of good works, it was admitted that 'deservings' was an offensive word, but Montagu said that this referred to justification at the last day, when all men would be rewarded according to their works. The explanation of denying the royal supremacy was, that though the King have the supreme power under God 'over all persons in all causes,' yet he has not the 'power of the keys.' He cannot excommunicate. The Church of Rome, Montagu's friends said, had erred in 'matters of faith,' but not in 'the foundation of faith,' which was really the expression which Montagu had used.

Under James and Charles the great controversy with the Church of Rome about transubstantiation still remained. That party whose origin dates from Bancroft had occupied new ground, and had therefore to meet objections from the Roman doctors directed against their new claims. The Reformers were content that the Church should rest on the simple maintenance of the doctrines clearly taught in the Scriptures. Now, it was said that a succession of bishops was necessary to constitute a Church. Those who maintained this position for the Church of England as against the Church of Rome, had also to maintain, in consistence with this idea of a Church, that we have a proper sacrifice, proper altars, and a proper priesthood. These were understood to be the furniture of a divinely-appointed visible Church. How we can have these without transubstantiation was the problem to be solved. If we have a sacrifice proper, what is it that we have to offer? When Bishop Buckeridge preached Bishop Andrewes' funeral sermon, he maintained that, in the Christian Church, we have an external altar on which we offer Christ. The statement to this extent was an answer to the question. But the explanations which followed deprived the answer of its substance. He said that the offering which Christ made on the cross once for all was the only true sacrifice among Christians; and he explained the 'altar' mentioned in the Epistle to the Hebrews as the cross of Christ. But we have an altar on which we commemorate this sacrifice of Christ, and on it we offer Christ in His members,—that is ourselves. We offer, not the material, but the mystical, body of Christ. The doctors of the Church of Rome regarded this as trifling with the argument. Buckeridge did not maintain a real presence of Christ's body in any proper sense. He called the Eucharist a commemoration of the true sacrifice, and he quoted Augustine and Aquinas as saying that only in this sense could the Eucharist be called a sacrifice at all.

CHAP. III.

The stone altars were taken down in all the churches in England at the Reformation, and tables made of wood substituted for them. The word 'altar' was dropped from the Prayer Book in 1552. These things implied that a sacrifice, as the Church of Rome understood a sacrifice, was no longer to be offered in the Church of England. This was an argument against altars not easily answered; yet it was maintained that we have an altar, a sacrifice, and a priesthood, though different from those of the Church of Rome.

The altars taken down at the Reformation.

In 1637, about four years after Laud had been elevated to the primacy, the Vicar of Grantham, following probably the example of some other vicars, removed the communion table from the place where it had previously stood, in the choir, to what he called the altar-place. The vicar was new; he had just come from college, and was eager to introduce the teaching and the practices of his party. He 'turned out the two *painful* ministers that were salaried by the town,' and made changes in the church which alarmed the parishioners. The churchwarden, who was also an alderman of the town, caused the communion table to be put back into its place. This was the beginning of a warfare between the vicar and the people. He told them that he did not care what they did with 'the old tresle;' he would build an altar of stone at his own charge, and fix it in the altar-place. Grantham was in the diocese of Lincoln. The bishop was the Lord Keeper Williams. He immediately forbad this moving and removing of the communion table, and soon after, in a letter to the vicar, gave his judgment about altars in churches. He told the vicar that if he should erect

The Vicar of Grantham.

such an altar as he intended, his own discretion would prove 'the only holocaust to be sacrificed thereon.' The vicar had subscribed to the Articles of the Church of England, which declare the oblation offered by the Church of Rome to be a *blasphemous fable* and a *dangerous deceit*. The bishop also reminded the vicar of the words of the Homily, ' that we, in the Church of England, ought to take heed lest our communion be made a sacrifice.' The Canons of 1571 appoint that the churchwardens, not the vicar, are to provide for the communion; and they are not to provide an altar, but a 'fair joined table.' According to the Queen's Injunctions of 1559, the altars were removed by law, and tables placed in their stead in most, if not all, the churches in England. Vicars were never charged to set up altars, but, in the first years of Elizabeth, they were allowed with others to pull them down. The vicar asked that he might place the table altar-wise. The bishop said that if by this he meant in the chancel, where in former times the altar stood, there could be no objection, provided that the choir is open, and mounted up by steps; which at Grantham church was not the case. If by altar-wise the vicar meant that the table should stand along close by the wall, as it did in great men's chapels, then the bishop said that tables were never so placed in country churches. Queen Elizabeth's Commissioners, by their orders in 1561, directed that the table should stand, not where the altar stood, but where the steps of the altar formerly stood. The bishop further gave it as his opinion, that it was intended by the Reformers that the table should stand with one end towards the east window, so that the minister might stand at the north side. This was grounded on the principle that a table has not four sides, but, being oblong, has two sides and two ends. When the table stands altar-wise, as it does now, the minister officiates at the north end, while the rubric prescribes the north side.

It was only as to the parish churches that there was any difference about the placing of the communion table. In cathedrals and private chapels it stood altar-wise.* Bishop

---

* Not always; the table in Durham Cathedral stood table-wise until about this time. So did that in Gloucester Cathedral, and others that might be named.

Williams did not admit that these were precedents for parish churches. He explained how it may have been that there were no changes at the Reformation in cathedrals and private chapels. He thought it possible that even the altars in some of these may have remained, or, at least, that tables corresponding to the altars in size and shape had been substituted, that the coverings and ornaments of the old altars might still be used. The altars stood a year or two in King Edward's time, and the Queen's Commissioners of 1559 were content that those still standing should remain as they were, but the sacrifice being abolished, they were no more altars. In 1552 the name 'altar' in the Liturgy was changed for 'the Lord's Board.' Christ, as Archbishop Cranmer remarked, instituted the Sacrament upon a table, not upon an altar. The name table was in the Church, Williams said, two hundred years before the name altar. To see this proved out of St. Paul, Origen, and Arnobius, he recommended the vicar to read Jewel against Harding. The name altar, he conjectured, might have crept into the Christian Church by a kind of complying with the Jews, or because of the oblations laid on the table for the clergy or the poor. The bishop directed that at Grantham church the table was to stand *table-wise*. He also directed that, though it may stand in the higher part of the church, it is not to be fixed there. The Rubric says it 'shall stand in the body of the church or chancel, where morning prayer and evening prayer is appointed to be read.' If, therefore, these are read in the body of the church, as in most country churches, then the body of the church is the canonical place for the table. It should be moved, when the communion is celebrated, to such place as the minister may be most distinctly heard by the communicants, and of this the people, not the minister, are to be the judges. How long communion tables stood in the middle of the churches, the vicar is directed also to find in Jewel, who shows it out of Eusebius, Augustine, and Durandus.

An answer to Bishop Williams's Letter to the Vicar of Grantham, was written by Peter Heylin. This was called 'A Coal from the Altar.' It had for a motto the text in the Epistle to the Hebrews, 'We have an altar;' a text

CHAP. III.

which, used in this sense, seemed a satire on the Church of England for having the altars removed. But Dr. Heylin did not advocate either sacrifices or altars, as these are understood in the Church of Rome. The vicar, he said, did not wish an altar of that kind which is 'raised by the Papists who offer the sacrifice of masses for the remission of sin.' In that case the vicar would not only have offered the holocaust of his own discretion, but would have ceased to be a worthy son of the Church of England. But though Article XXXI. condemns the sacrifice of the Mass in the Church of Rome, it does not, says Heylin, condemn the commemorative sacrifice which we of the Church of England offer as a perpetual memory of Christ's precious death. Where the Homily warns us of the memory of the Lord's Supper, not to make a sacrifice, the meaning is such a sacrifice as Art. XXXI. condemns. There is no reason, Heylin says, for suspecting that the Vicar of Grantham intended the revival of the Mass. But as the Lord's Supper is called a sacrifice, so may the communion table be called an altar. John Frith, John Lambert, Archbishop Cranmer, and Bishop Ridley, with other martyrs and Reformers, are quoted as calling the Lord's Supper 'the sacrament of the altar.' Heylin enters into an elaborate argument to prove that the table is to stand close to the wall, altar-wise. The ground of the argument is, that as the Queen's Injunctions ordered the table to stand where once the altar stood, the table must cover precisely the same area that was occupied by the altar. Putting these Injunctions alongside of the Articles of Advertisement of 1565, which direct that the Ten Commandments should be inscribed on the east wall over the Lord's Table, he concludes that the table was meant to stand above the steps, under the Commandments, and, therefore, along the wall. Table and altar he maintained to be the same thing. The table is an altar, not only in regard of the oblations, but also of the communion. In the Jewish temple there were altars not for sacrifice only, but also for the worshippers to eat of the sacrifice. For encouragement to the Vicar of Grantham, Heylin mentioned the case of the church of St. Gregory, near St. Paul's in London, where the table had lately been placed altar-wise, and with the consent of his

The Lord's Supper called 'the sacrament of the altar' by the Reformers.

Majesty, who, in 1633, had passed a decree in Council that the metropolitans, bishops, and their ordinaries should so place the tables in all churches committed to their care.

The Bishop of Lincoln replied to Heylin, but without giving his name. He called his treatise 'The Holy Table, Name and Thing, more anciently, properly, and literally used under the New Testament than that of an Altar.' He described the treatise as having been written long ago by a minister of Lincolnshire in answer to Dr. Coal, 'a judicious Divine of Q. Mary's days.' He refused to admit the royal chapel as a precedent for parish churches. That wise princess, Elizabeth, had for a time used her sister's seal, and on the same principle she kept her ceremonies till others should be provided. She had to make her worship appear to the foreign princes as if she was not 'so far esloigned from the Catholic religion as was bruited abroad.' Miles Huggard, a Roman Catholic writer, speaking of the table in King Edward's time, says, at first 'they placed it aloft where the altar stood, then must it be set free from the wall that one might go between, the ministers being in contention on which part to turn their faces either towards the west, the north, or south.' At last it was determined that the minister was to stand on the north side of the table. Now, the question to be settled is—north side or north end? The Latin for north side is *pars septentrionalis*, which may mean either north side or north end. The bishop maintained that altars as well as tables have two sides only. Among other authorities he quoted Gregory XIII., who speaks in his Pontifical of the two sides of the altar.

As to the King's decree in Council, the bishop showed that the placing of the tables was left to the decision of the ordinary; and as to the martyrs and Reformers who had spoken of 'the sacrament of the altar,' he answered that they used the current language of their time. Indeed, after the words 'sacrament of the altar,' they frequently added 'as they call it.' Bishop Ridley told the examiners that the Supper of the Lord was not at any time better administered, nor more duly received, than when the altars were taken down. When some in his diocese used the table altar-wise, he decreed that to use it as a table was more agreeable to the Scriptures. Heylin said that the Lord's Supper is a sacrifice because it is the memory of a sacrifice. To this Bishop Williams answered, 'we must take heed of quillets and distinctions that may bring us back again to old errors reformed in the Church.' A sacrifice *commemorative* cannot be a *proper* sacrifice, and therefore from it we cannot infer a proper altar. It is an established principle with the Roman Catholics that a stone altar is not needed for prayers or praise. These are sacrifices which do not require a proper altar. The holy table, according to the Bishop of Lincoln, was not copied from the square altar of the Jewish Temple, but from the long table of the shewbread; and in the Act of Council for changing the altars into tables, it was expressly mentioned that the form of a table would 'more move the simple from the superstitious opinions of the Popish Mass.' Heylin said that the order of Council for removing the altars was sent only to Bishop Ridley. And so the Act read as given in Fox's 'Book of Martyrs,' which was explained by Williams that Fox had access only to the copy sent to Ridley, which, by the substitution of a period for a comma, seemed as if the order had been sent only to Ridley. Heylin said that the word altar was omitted from the Prayer Book of 1552 to please Calvin. To which Williams answered that Calvin himself had used as a communion table a marble altar, which in former times had served for the sacrifice of the Mass. When the Fathers used the word altar they only used it metaphorically, meaning table. Irenæus says, 'that every sanctified man that makes a lively, holy, and well-pleasing sacrifice, offering alms and the calves of his lips to Almighty God is a priest serving at the altar.' He says also that David in this kind was a proper priest. St. Cyprian explains the altar as the offerings or contributions made for religious objects. Ignatius calls the Church an altar. This holy table, or altar as it was improperly called, was placed generally in the middle of the church. In St. Chrysostom's Liturgy it is said that 'the deacons perfume the holy table in all the compass thereof.' Synesius says that he will 'compass about the altar of God.' In the Eastern Church the tables were always placed so that they might be compassed by the priests or deacons. Walafridus Strabo says truly that Christians in the beginning placed their altars indifferently,—east, west, north, or south. To suppose God more propitious in one part of the world than in another was pronounced a relic of Paganism. It is well said by Minutius Felix that 'all things are full of God.'

Heylin wrote '*Antidotum Lincolniense,* or an Answer to a Book entitled the Holy Table, Name and Thing.' The admission made by Williams that some altars were allowed to remain at the Reformation was the ground on which Heylin rested his first argument. As to these altars, there could be no question, he said, but the north side meant the north end.* The altars, it is admitted, became tables. The Jewish sacrifices, Heylin said, were sacrifices in figure. They prefigured Christ. Our sacrifice is in memory of Christ. The Jewish sacrifices were taken away by Christ, but ours was established. Being a sacrifice, it implies that we have priests and altars. The difference between our sacrifice and that of the Jews is, that theirs was a bloody sacrifice, ours is unbloody. Their priesthood was of the order of Aaron, ours is after the order of Melchisedec. Speaking to His Apostles as laymen, Christ said, *Eat, drink;* but speaking to them as priests, He said, *Do this.* This interpretation of these words had been rejected hitherto in the Church of England. But Heylin did not understand by *Do this,* what the Roman doctors understood. To them it is a command to make out of bread the body of Christ. To Heylin it only meant 'consecrate.' This is the commission of priests, and this, he said, was the extent of the commission as understood by the old Fathers and the great divines of the Church of England. Irenæus tells us that there were sacrifices in the Jewish Church, and that there are now sacrifices in the Christian Church; but in the Christian Church they are only eucharistic; sacrifices of gratitude and thanksgiving. Eusebius says, 'Christ is the propitiatory sacrifice for all our sins,' and He appointed us to offer daily unto God the commemoration of His one offering. Of any expiatory sacrifice besides that which was made on the cross, Heylin says, the Fathers knew nothing. Bishop Andrews said to Bellarmine, 'Take away from your Mass

* The modern interpretation of north side being in front of the table, towards the north, does not seem to have been thought of.

transubstantiation, and we will have no difference with you about the sacrifice. The memory of a sacrifice we acknowledge willingly, and grant the name of sacrifice to have been frequent with the Fathers.' The same bishop says that as the Eucharist is fitly called a sacrifice, so the communion table is fitly called an altar.

Dr. Pocklington.

The cause of the Vicar of Grantham was taken up by John Pocklington, D.D. He wrote 'Altare Christianum, or The Dead Vicar's Plea, wherein the Vicar of Grantham being dead, yet speaketh and pleadeth out of antiquity against him that hath broken down his altar.' This was a second edition of a treatise which Dr. Pocklington had written some time before. It was now corrected and enlarged to refute the Bishop of Lincoln. The argument surpassed anything that had ever entered into the head of Peter Heylin. Dr. Pocklington settled the matter of altars at once, by saying that the Christian Church existed under the old dispensation, and who could deny that there were altars then? Does not Christ make mention of a Christian altar, when He says, 'If thou bring thy gift to the altar'? And does not St. Paul speak of altars, where he says, 'they that wait on the altar live by the altar'? Damasus, in the Decretals, mentions bishops and martyrs who spoke of altars. This was in the year one hundred and fifty-eight, when, as yet, there is no mention of communion tables. St. Martial says, 'The Supper of the Lord is offered on an altar.' Irenæus exhorts us to offer gifts at the altar of God. Tertullian and other Fathers do the same. We are one Church with the Apostles and the Fathers. 'Miserable,' says Pocklington, 'were we, if he that now sitteth Archbishop of Canterbury could not derive his succession from St. Augustine, St. Augustine from St. Gregory, and St. Gregory from St. Peter.' Unlearned either in the ways of the Church or the world, Dr. Pocklington did not go back for the succession to the British Church before Augustine. He was content to have his altar direct from the Church of Rome. The chancels were ordered 'to remain as they had been in times past.' The chancel, Pocklington wisely said, does not mean the chancel alone. It does not mean merely the walls and windows. It means also the furniture of the chancel. So

Pleads for altars.

that the Lord's table or altar was to stand as it had done in times past. The Article which condemns the Mass in the Church of Rome, does not, he says, condemn the sacrifice, 'representative, rememorative, and spiritual.' Bishop Montagu, reiterating the words of Bishop Morton, says, that he believes 'no such sacrifice of the altar as the Church of Rome doth.' The 'sacrifices of Masses' were 'blasphemous fables and dangerous deceits,' because it was commonly believed that they were 'propitiatory, external, visible, true, and proper sacrifices for the quick and the dead.'*

In 1641, four years after the troubles of the Vicar of Grantham, George Hakewill, Archdeacon of Surrey, wrote 'A Dissertation, with Dr. Heylin, touching the Pretended Sacrifice in the Holy Eucharist.' Hakewill said that Heylin was the first man, belonging to any of the Reformed Churches, that had taught this doctrine. It was contrary to the teaching of all the Reformers, both English and foreign. But it was possible, he said, that he had not quite understood what Heylin meant. He wished that Heylin had defined sacrifice, and then there might have been some hope of an agreement, or at least of both sides understanding each other. He wished also to know how that could be called a sacrifice which was only commemorative or representative of a sacrifice. Augustine says that the true sacrifice is inward in the heart, and that it is only improperly that any outward offering is called a sacrifice. Bellarmine says, that for a true sacrifice, it is necessary that that which is offered be manifestly destroyed. Dr. Field also agrees that to present anything to God as a proper sacrifice, it must be consumed. If this definition is to be admitted, then, in the Eucharist, either the bread and wine are consumed by the change of the substance, which is transubstantiation, or they are consumed by the communicants. In the one case we have the doctrine of the Church of Rome. In the other, the people are sacrificers as well as the priest, for they eat the bread and drink the wine. Bellarmine agrees with us so

* It is worthy of notice that Montagu, Buckeridge, Pocklington, Heylin, and all the High Church divines of this age, never dream of interpreting Art. XXXI. as Dr. Pusey does. It was understood as directed against the *propitiatory* sacrifice in the Mass, and not merely the abuses of private Masses.

far, that the Supper is a sacrifice commemorative. But he says this is not a sufficient reason for calling it a sacrifice proper. To be this, it must be more than commemorative. Hakewill says that we acknowledge the Jewish sacrifices to have been properly called sacrifices. They were not merely figurative of Christ, but they had in themselves the elements which made them properly sacrificial. Could the same be shown for the Eucharist, the controversy would be at an end. Aquinas and the Master of the Sentences both call the Eucharist commemorative, and an improper sacrifice.

The Eucharist an improper sacrifice.

The Roman doctors have endeavoured to prove that they have authority to make a proper sacrifice, from the words *Do this;* but Bishop Morton, Hakewill says, has well proved how sandy is the foundation. Bishop Jewel says, 'Neither did Christ, by the words *Do this in remembrance of me,* erect any new succession of sacrificers to offer Him up really unto His Father, nor ever did any ancient learned Fathers so expound it. Christ's meaning is clear by the words that follow, for He saith not only *Do this,* but He addeth also, *in my remembrance;* which doing pertaineth not only to the Apostles and their successors, but to the whole congregation,—*As often as ye shall eat this bread and drink this cup, ye do show forth the Lord's death till He come.*' Yet Hakewill says, if we grant that Dr. Heylin's interpretation of *Do this* is the right one, we have still to see it proved that Christ Himself did then offer a sacrifice, properly so called. He consecrated bread and wine to a mystical use. He left the power of consecration to His Apostles and their successors, but He neither made a sacrifice Himself nor did He commission His followers to make a sacrifice in memory of Him. In the prayer before the Communion Service we ask God to 'accept our sacrifice.' But this prayer is said by the people as well as by the minister, so that either the sacrifice is only improperly so called, or both priest and people unitedly offer a sacrifice *proper.* The text, 'We have an altar,' is explained by Aquinas, that altar here means the cross of Christ. This interpretation, Hakewill says, is generally received by the Church of England. He quotes, for the improper sacrifice in the Eucharist, the words of several bishops, as White, Davenant, Hall, Abbot, Bilson,

Hoc facite.

'We have an altar,' that is, Christ's cross.

and of several doctors, as Hooker, Field, Crakanthorp, Perkins, and Nowell. Hooker says, 'The Fathers of the Church, with like security of speech, call usually the ministry of the Gospel, priesthood, in regard to that which the Gospel hath proportionable to ancient sacrifices, namely, the communion of the body and blood of Christ, *although it have properly now no sacrifice*. As for people when they hear the name, it draweth no more their minds to any cogitation of sacrifice than the name of senator or alderman causeth them to think of old age.'

The question of altars, priests, and sacrifices engaged the thoughts of the 'pious and profoundly learned Joseph Mede' in his retirement at Cambridge. He has left us a sermon on Mal. i. 11, 'My name shall be great among the Gentiles, and in every place incense shall be offered unto my name, and a pure offering.' Mede says that this is a prophecy of the sacrifice in the Christian Church, but in what that sacrifice consists 'is beyond belief obscure, intricate, and perplext.' In the ancient Fathers there is frequent mention of the *unbloody sacrifice of Christ in the Eucharist*. By sacrifice the ancient Church understood the whole action and solemn service of the assembled congregation, of which the Eucharist was the principal part. It was, as it were, the pearl or jewel of that ring. It had two objects, one of which was the offering of prayer and praise, the other, the commemoration of Christ's sacrifice, whereby prayer and praise were accepted. The incense spoken of in the text is the prayers of the saints. The pure offering is the bread, which is accompanied by the wine as the drink-offering. The Jews offered polluted bread, but this is pure, because of Him whom it commemorates. According to the usage of the ancient Fathers, this commemoration is called a sacrifice, but it is only commemorative. Christ's body was offered once for all. It is an oblation because it is something truly presented to God. It is not $\theta\upsilon\sigma\iota\alpha$, a slaughter-offering. We slay nothing, and therefore it is only a sacrifice metaphorically. It is one thing to say that the Lord's Supper is a sacrifice, and another thing to say that in that sacrifice we offer Christ. The latter was never taught by the ancient Fathers.

CHAP. III.

Joseph Mede on sacrifices and altars.

The Christian altar and the Pagan.

Mede explains sacrifice in another sense. He calls it a sign or seal of a covenant, a sacred feast, wherein God mystically entertains man at His own table. Tried by the meaning ascribed to sacrifices by the Jews, and the meaning which we ascribe to the sacrifice of Christ, it is only called a sacrifice improperly, but under this other description the Eucharist is properly a sacrifice. It is a commemoration of Christ's death, not only for ourselves, but 'a putting of God in mind of the sacrifice of His Son.'* In another place Mede explains the words used by the old Fathers. The Holy Table was generally called θυσιαστήριον. This is to be distinguished from another Greek word for altar, βωμὸς, which was a pedestal or altar of an idol. In Maccabees we read that the ministers of Antiochus Epiphanes sacrificed upon the βωμὸς, which was upon the θυσιαστήριον.† The θυσιαστήρια were altars for sacrifice to the true God; the βωμοὶ were the altars of the Gentiles. The Latin Fathers sometimes made a similar distinction, calling the Church altar *altare,* while the Pagan altar was *ara.* In the Vulgate *ara* is never used for the church altar. In a sermon, Mede makes some corresponding distinctions as to the names of ministers, whom he divides into two orders, but three degrees. *Sacerdos,* the Latin word for priest, is a word to which, he says, we have no equivalent in English. Our word priest is simply *presbyter.* In the old dispensation כהן was priest, but the word means nothing more than minister. Etymologically it is the same as deacon. 'We strive,' Mede says, ' to distinguish between the old and the new priests, and in avoiding Scylla we fall into Charybdis. We call the ministers of the Gospel by the name of those of the old law, *ministers;* and those of the old law by the name of the new, *priests,* or presbyters.'

Archbishop Laud.

Archbishop Laud further developed Bancroft's theory of Episcopacy, uniting with it the doctrines of Arminius and the new form of the real presence in the Eucharist. There is not much in Laud's writings on the points of Cal-

---

* Joseph Mede was reckoned a Puritan. Brook gives his biography in the 'Lives of the Puritans.' The sentence quoted in the text is the same as the 'Times' three years ago made famous as 'pernicious nonsense.'

† Θυσιάζοντες ἦσαν ἐπὶ τὸν βωμὸν ὃς ἦν ἐπὶ τοῦ θυσιαστηρίου.—Mac. i. 59.

vinism. He promoted his cause by favouring those who were anti-Calvinistic, and by passing injunctions forbidding the clergy to preach on subjects connected with predestination. Calvinism was the doctrine of the Church, and Laud forbade the preaching of it. The works of the martyr Archbishop are chiefly of value to us as marking out his position in relation to the Church of Rome. The Church of England hitherto had made common cause with the other Reformed Churches against Rome; but now the Church of England was defended on principles not applicable to the other Reformed Churches. Laud had not retrograded in the doctrine of king-worship. He had not progressed, because it was impossible to surpass his Calvinistic predecessors. In spite of his lofty views of the calling of the Church's officers, the King was to him, as to Bishop Andrewes, 'a little god.' In the Psalms, the old divines, whether Puritan or Conformist, saw both Christ and David portrayed under the same words. Laud, improving on this acknowledged principle of psalteric exegesis, found God and the King under the same actions. And the reason of this is, that the King is God's lieutenant upon earth, and what is his act by execution is God's by a divine decree. The power of the King is, he said, God's power, *in* him as well as over him.

Laud had to justify the separation of the Church of England from the Church of Rome. A schism had been caused, and one of the parties must be schismatics. Which side is chargeable with the sin of schism? Laud answers, the Church of Rome, in virtue of its claim to infallibility. In the 'Conference with Fisher the Jesuit,' the only work of Laud's which really does justice to his learning and ability, he refutes the Papal claims, and justifies the English Reformation. He examines the supposed testimonies of Cyprian, Jerome, Gregory Nazianzen, Cyril, and other Fathers, to the infallibility of Rome, and finds them wanting in validity. He does not claim infallibility for the universal or Catholic Church, any more than he admits it for the Church of Rome. The Church, he says, cannot add to the faith; its sole office is to declare it. This distinction is not fully explained. Laud leaves it to be inferred that, though the Church cannot add to the faith, it can yet declare it infal-

Marginal notes: CHAP. III. — Laud against Fisher the Jesuit.

libly. This seems to be the same as what Montagu said, that when General Councils do not err, they are infallible.

The ordinary principle of Protestantism was to rest solely on the Scriptures. The Roman Catholic asked by what authority we know the Scriptures to be divine. He answered his own question, that it was only through the Church, for without an infallible authority we do not know that the Scriptures are divine. Laud agreed in this, that we must have a sufficient, infallible, divine proof that the Scriptures are divine. He agreed, also, that such proof might be properly called the word of God, and that it might be either written or unwritten. He endorsed the words of Bellarmine, that it is God uttering or revealing truth to His Church which makes the word of God. Before Scripture was written,—that is, before it was Scripture,—it was God's word. But this does not, Laud says, authorize us to regard all the unwritten traditions of the Church of Rome as God's word. There were words unwritten, but never delivered over to the Church, as the words of Jesus during the forty days preceding the Ascension. How we are to know the Scriptures to be the word of God is discussed at some length. Laud does not admit that this can be known sufficiently by the internal light of Scripture, nor by special revelations made to individuals. Such revelations from the Holy Spirit are not promised. Yet there is a sense in which the Holy Spirit assures us of the truth of Scripture. This is included in what is properly called faith, which is God's gift in man. It is described as an infused habit in respect whereof the soul is merely the recipient. Laud claims that reason should be allowed to come in and prove what it can. Without grace, reason can never see the way to heaven, nor believe the book in which God hath written the way. Yet God puts grace into reasonable men as a spiritual eyewater, to make reason see what by nature it cannot see. Men often ask why they should believe, but when we once believe, Laud says, faith grows stronger than either reason or knowledge. Something must be believed before much can be known. The Manichee would only believe so far as he knew. But all *savants* have certain postulates. There are four byeways by which the Scriptures may be proved to be the word of God, but they must be taken together. No one alone is sufficient. The first is the tradition of the present Church; but this is not absolutely divine. The second is the light which is in the Scripture; but this is not enough. It does not bear sufficient witness of itself. The third is the testimony of the Holy Ghost. This is infallible, but not of much value here, where the question is not how or by what means we believe, but how the Scriptures may be proposed as a credible object for belief. The fourth is reason, which no man expects should prove the Scriptures divine. It is enough if reason can disprove what other men conceive against it. All these ways being, Laud says, insufficient, we must find another, or see what can be wrought out of them.

He considers first the *tradition of the Church*. But what Church? As to the primitive Christian Church, and the Apostles who had immediate revelations from heaven, there can be no question but it is divine. This tradition the Church of England has always received, and its uniform testimony has been that the books of Scripture are the written word of God. It was this primitive inspired Church to which Augustine referred when he said, 'I would not believe the gospel, unless the authority of the Church moved me.' Tradition without and grace within are described as helps whereby the divine light of the Scriptures is made to shine. They help a man to see that light. The natural vision sees some light of moral counsel and instruction in the Scriptures, but it takes that glorious lustre for candlelight. But the tradition of the Church and God's grace clear the understanding, and then the soul hears plainly, in the Scriptures, the voice of God. This is truly faith. We never *know* the Scriptures to be the word of God, but we believe they are. That the Apostles were divinely inspired depends merely on their own testimony. Miracles do not prove much, for miracles are sometimes counterfeit, and even true ones are not always infallible marks of true doctrines. The entrance into divinity is inaccessible to those men who believe nothing but what is demonstrated from principles of reason. Christ asked men to deny the understanding by avoiding an unquiet search into the secrets of

Tradition of the Church.

Him who made it. If revelation can be proved to be necessary, Laud undertakes to prove that it has been given.

The difference concerning the Church, between Laud and Fisher, seems to be, that while Fisher claimed an abiding infallible inspiration in the Church, Laud held that this belonged only to the Apostles' times. Their successors, indeed, had inspiration and spiritual guidance, but not infallible. Both of them confined the inspiration to the officers of the Church. It only reached the laity by means of the clergy. Had the Church been infallible, the Reformation could not have been justified, for no Reformation would have been needed. But it was only too evident that Reformation was needed. And therefore the Church of England was justified in the Reformation.

Whitgift and Hooker had opposed the Puritans simply as enemies of order. But Laud was in everything a Puritan reversed. He could see nothing as they saw it. He could not even agree with them as to the shape of the human head. Martin Bucer used to say that he did not know why he should wear a 'square cap,' since nature had made his head round. Laud said it was a sin for people to make their heads round since God had made them square. Moreover, it was expressly commanded in Leviticus, 'Thou shalt not make round the corners of thy head.'

Besides Bishop Williams, Laud had another opponent in the Primate of the Irish Church. Archbishop Ussher did not regard the Presbyterian minister as unordained, but he thought it desirable to restore the Apostolic model of bishops, acting with their presbyteries. Ordination by presbyteries might be schismatical, but it was justified by circumstances. He asserted the divine morality of the Sabbath or seventh day's rest. It was not only commanded in Scripture, but we have God's example for resting, and we are instructed in one of the Homilies,* that God has expressly charged all men to rest on the Sabbath day and devote that day to His service.

---

* The Homily 'Of the Time and Place of Prayer,' is clearly on Ussher's side. It says, 'God hath given express charge to all men that upon the Sabbath Day, which is now Sunday, they should cease from all weekly and work-day labour.'

Ussher was a Calvinist. He denied the universality of redemption. A price was paid to the Father by the Son sufficient to atone for the sins of all men, but it is available only for the elect, to whom saving grace is given. He noticed the progress of what he reckoned an essentially new doctrine in the Church of England,—the belief of a real presence in the Eucharist. It had crept in unconsciously under cover of the old words. Bishop Andrewes said to Bellarmine that we believe a real presence as much as the Church of Rome, but we determine nothing concerning the manner of it. Ussher said that the Church of England has determined the manner of it. It says, 'That Christ's body is received only after a spiritual and heavenly manner,' which is intended expressly to exclude the Roman Catholic doctrine of a presence of the actual body.

CHAP. III.

Ussher a Calvinist.

During the reign of Charles, the bishop question became more urgent than ever. The civil power was not merely, as in the days of Elizabeth, protecting itself; it protected also the divine claim of the episcopate. The bishops in return defended the arbitrary government of the king. Moderate men were alienated from the Episcopal side, and the more zealous Puritans were exasperated. They had frequently written with violence, and as frequently had severe chastisement been administered to them. But violence in writing and severity in punishing reached their climax now. Dr. Leighton, a Scotch minister, wrote 'An appeal to Parliament,' which he called 'Sion's Plea against Prelacy.' This was an intemperate book. Its arguments were those of the Presbyterian party, not strong in themselves, yet deriving strength from the manifold evils unreformed in the Church. Facing the title-page was a picture of an old castle in ruins. From the walls of this castle were bishops tumbling headlong towards the ground. Beneath were inscribed the words,—

The bishop question.

'Sion's Plea against Prelacy.'

> 'The tottering prelates, with their trumpery all,
> Shall moulder down like elder from the wall.'

Leighton was arrayed in the old Presbyterian armour. He professed to be continuing the fight for the *keys of Christ*. These keys had been given to the Church apart from the

State. But the State had taken possession of them at the Reformation, and now the bishops even dared to say that these keys had been committed to them, not by the State, but by Christ Himself. Leighton wondered at the audacity of their claim, after Episcopacy had been so long tolerated in the Church as something derived from the prerogative of the king. This new pretension involved, he said, want of loyalty to the sovereign, and was opposed to the laws of the country. Christ had, indeed, established a government in His Church. This he proved by the usual arguments, the chief of which were derived from the Old Testament. If God remembered the bars of the ark, was it likely, Leighton argued, that 'He should forget the pillars of His Church? that He would appoint the least pins of the House, and forget the master-builders,—mention the snuffers, and pass by the great lights?' But the Church is complete without the bishops; they are but 'knobs and wens in the body.' To continue them in the Church is to 'jostle Christ out of His government.' The true polity is the *Discipline of Geneva*. To establish it the hierarchy must be renounced. The Lord has a controversy with the land, because the prelates have usurped the place of Christ. Parliament is asked to remove Ashtaroth, that God's judgments against us may cease, that the honour of the State may be redeemed, and that there may be 'a dashing of Babel's brats against the wall.'

Bishop Hall and the Smectymnians.

The great controversy on Episcopacy, before the overthrow of both Church and King, was that between Bishop Hall and Smectymnuus. Hall was a Calvinist, yet a supporter of Laud, and an advocate for the *jus divinum* of bishops. He was blind to the changes which were going on before his eyes. He denied the prevalence of Arminianism after the Church in many of her dignitaries had parted with Calvinism. He upheld Laud's party, and yet he spoke of those who introduced worshipping towards the East, and bowing to the altar as 'addleheads' and 'Popish fools.' Between Laud and Hall there could have been nothing in common, if we except their agreement on the question of Episcopacy. They both stood apart from Rome on clear and definite grounds. They both claimed to belong to the

Catholic Church, while protesting against the Church of Rome; that is, belonging to the Catholic Church in virtue of Episcopacy in another sense than the non-Episcopal Churches belonged to it. Hall, in his tract, 'Roma Irreconciliabilis,' 'No Peace with Rome,' maintains that the guilt of separation lay at the door of the Roman Catholics. The Church of Rome was a church 'miserably corrupted.' Without an entire reform of these corruptions, there could be no hope for the union of Christendom. They are in the pit, we are on high. They must ascend to our truth, we cannot descend to their errors. The Roman claim to infallibility annihilates, he said, every hope of reformation. We cannot be 'so foolish as to bolster up the great bridge-maker of the Tiber. His infallibility is written nowhere, unless, as Luther said, perhaps in Rome, at St. Peter's, upon some chimney with a coal.' They must come to us, for it is impossible that we can go to them. But the claim to infallibility is 'a fetter which binds them to their errors.'

The occasion of writing the treatise on the divine right of Episcopacy was when Graham, Bishop of Orkney, renounced his office, and claimed pardon from the General Assembly of the Church of Scotland for having ever accepted it. Hall calls this 'a foul deed,' and declares the penance such as the world never heard of. 'How weary,' he says, 'would I be of this rochet, if you can show me that Episcopacy is of any less than divine institution.' In another tract he defines what he means by *divine institution*: 'We mean not an express law of God requiring it upon the absolute necessity of the being of a Church, what hindrances soever may interfere, but a divine institution warranting it and requiring it when it may be had.' The largeness of this definition might seem to neutralize the high claim for divinity. Its object is to leave a defence for the foreign Churches, but to take away every plea for the Church of Scotland. The latter obstinately refuses Episcopacy, the former are without it by circumstances which they did not create. The argument is general, but the pleading is special. If the last Bishop of Geneva had become a Protestant, and agreed in doctrine with Calvin, Farel, and Viret, there is no reason, Hall says, for believing but that Geneva would have

Jus divinum, what it means.

retained its Episcopacy. Calvin used to say that he would yield even to Popish bishops as much authority as was necessary for the due ordering of the Church's government. Beza, Zanchy, and other Reformers, as well as Bozermannus at the Synod of Dort, spoke of the happy condition of the Church of England in having retained its bishops. The Scotch cannot plead that they have conformed themselves to the pattern of the foreign Churches. Their acts were done in a case of extremity, and are not, therefore, precedents for others. The mariner casts out his goods in a storm. The roof of a house is taken off when the next house is on fire. The physician cuts off a limb to save the life of a patient. These Churches were in danger of wreck. They were in danger of being consumed by Roman persecution. But for the amputation, they would have died of the gangrene of superstition. The necessity of defending these Churches was a serious difficulty to Bishop Hall. If the Church could exist at all without bishops, can bishops be divinely instituted? Did not such an institution imply that they were necessary to the very essence and existence of a church?

We must gather Hall's meaning from his own explanations. He undertakes to prove—(1.) That Episcopacy is not only holy and lawful, but of divine appointment. (2.) That the Presbyterian government has no footing either in Scripture or the practice of the Church in all ages, from Christ's time to the present. The process by which the divine institution of Episcopacy is proved is, by showing that its foundation was laid by Christ, and its superstructure reared by the Apostles. What the Apostles practised and recommended must be apostolic, and the further inference is that what is apostolic is divine.

Apostolic practice.

For a commentary upon apostolic practice, we have the practice of the universal Church in the times immediately succeeding those of the Apostles. It is not, Hall thinks, for a moment to be supposed that the primitive Saints and Fathers would set up a new form of government. But even were this possible, it is altogether impossible that in so short a time they should have diffused it throughout the Christian world. It would be necessary, too, that the Scripture, on which this new form of government was founded, should be more evident and unquestionable than that alleged for the form which was rejected. As for the Presbyterian claim, it is simple impiety to say that the Son of God should erect a form of government upon earth which was to lie hid for sixteen hundred years, and even then not be fully known. The Presbyterians, Hall says, are not agreed as to what officers and rulers are necessary for the polity of the Church. Cartwright proposed that every parish should be a Presbytery by itself. It was a question not determined whether the Church officers were to be three or four orders. Some denied the necessity of 'doctors,' leaving only pastors, lay elders, and deacons. Others objected altogether to presbyteries and synods, making every congregation a complete Church in itself. The last class were the Independents, who, as yet, were little more than discernible from the Presbyterians. Hall's hatred of this sect was unmeasured. For them, he said, 'no answer was fit but dark lodgings and hellebore.'

Hall's hatred of the Independents.

It greatly weakened Hall's argument for Episcopacy that he was compelled to admit the promiscuous use of the names bishop, presbyter, and deacon in the New Testament writings. An evangelist was called an apostle, an apostle a bishop, and a bishop a presbyter, deacon, or minister. He had to lean on an antiquity which was younger than the apostolic age. Still it was antiquity, and for the persons with whom he was pleading it was something to be able to show what was the judgment of the foreign Reformers on the age succeeding that of the Apostles. Calvin's account of those times is, that the presbyters in every city chose one of their number for their bishop. He was, as it were, the consul in the senate. This illustration was not fortunate, as a consul was but an annual president. The negative position, that there was not equality among the ministers of the Church, was proved by the fact that Christ had sent forth two classes of preachers, the twelve Apostles and the seventy Disciples. The former were the patriarchs of the Church. Other labourers were at work, but these were the twelve master builders. Others could do works of healing by a touch, but the shadow of the Apostles was sufficient to heal.

The age after the Apostles.

Difference between the Apostles and other ministers.

Others had the Holy Ghost, but the twelve could *give* the Holy Ghost. Philip was an Evangelist. He preached and wrought miracles. He converted and baptized the Samaritans; but it was not till Peter and John prayed and laid hands on them that they received the Holy Ghost. The place from which Judas fell was filled up by an election of one out of the seventy. Hall argues, that if the apostleship had not been a higher office, there would have been no necessity for a new election by the direction of the Spirit. The twelve Apostles were to sit on twelve thrones. What are these but, as Augustine says, the thrones of the bishops when they sit in judgment, with the power of the keys to bind and to loose? Jerome's account of the origin of the distinction between bishop and presbyter is, that the Apostles, to avoid schism and division, found it necessary to place some eminent persons over the rest of the presbyters. These they ordained as their own successors, and gave them authority to govern the Church. This suggestion of Jerome's Hall confirms by the cases of Timothy and Titus. Timothy is charged by St. Paul to instruct the preachers what doctrine they are to teach. He is to *charge* them to teach sound doctrine. If he was only their equal, how could he exercise such authority over them? It is for superiors to charge, and for inferiors to obey. Timothy was to check the doctrines of the false teachers of Ephesus. He was to exercise and prove the deacons, and promote those who were deserving to a higher degree. If St. Paul was to be long absent, Timothy was to learn how to behave himself in the house of God, which is the pillar and ground of the truth. This, Hall said, could not be a private congregation. It must have been a diocesan church. He was to put the brethren, that is, the presbyters, in remembrance of the dangers foretold to be in the last times. He was charged with censures, and was not to rebuke the elders roughly. He was to see that the presbyters be liberally maintained. He was not to receive an accusation but in the presence of witnesses; to do nothing with partiality; and in his ordinations to lay hands suddenly on no man. Titus was left in Crete to put in order the things that were left undone. Crete, or Candia, was an island with a hundred cities. Titus was to ordain presbyters in every city. The diocese was large, the clergy many. To the cases of Timothy and Titus is added that of the seven angels who presided over the seven Churches of Asia.

We have next the testimonies of the ancient Fathers. Clement of Rome, in his Epistle to the Corinthians, shows how the Apostles, foreseeing the contentions that would arise about the name of Episcopacy, 'appointed the degrees, and gave a list of the offices.' Ignatius, in his Epistle to the Trallians, tells them 'to do nothing without their bishops, and to be subject also to the authority of their priests.' Again, he says that the bishop bears the resemblance of God, the Father of all things; that without the bishop it is not lawful to baptize or to offer sacrifice. The canons 'of the most holy and venerable Apostles forbid a presbyter or deacon to leave his division or parish without permission from his bishop.' Irenæus says, 'We can number up those who by the Apostles were made bishops in the Churches and their successors even to our time.' This same Irenæus testifies that he had seen Polycarp, who was made a bishop by the Apostles. Tertullian says, 'Let them set forth the originals of their Churches; let them reckon up the order of their bishops so running down from their successors from the beginning, so that the first bishop had one of the Apostles, or apostolic man, for his author and predecessor.' All antiquity, Hall says, makes bishops the successors of the Apostles. By Ignatius they are called 'rulers;' by Ambrose, 'chiefs of the priests;' by Dionysius, 'hierarchs.' In many passages, both of the Fathers and Councils, presbyters are called 'the bishop's presbyters.' The power of ordination belonged to bishops alone. Jerome and Chrysostom testify that, in laying on of hands, bishops go beyond presbyters. Colluthus, a presbyter of Alexandria, took upon himself to ordain presbyters. He was summoned before Hosius and other bishops at a General Council, where he was reprimanded, and the orders of those whom he had ordained were pronounced invalid. A blind bishop, who employed a presbyter to read the words of ordination and blessing while he laid on hands, was condemned by the Council of Seville. Episcopal government, Hall says, was everywhere in the whole Christian Church in all times. It was retained by the sects not in communion with Rome, as the Waldenses and Albigenses. A Church or sect without a bishop was unheard of till the invention of the Geneva 'Discipline.' As to the lay elders, antiquity knew nothing of presbyters which were not of the clergy. The Ambrose usually quoted is not the true Ambrose; but even what the pretended Ambrose says of elders is nothing for the Presbyterians. They were aged men, whose experience might give them knowledge, and whose gravity might procure them reverence. The same Ambrose interprets the text concerning the elders that rule well, as preachers who were also Christ's vicars because of their fidelity in administering their office. Soon after this defence of Episcopacy, Bishop Hall published 'An Humble Remonstrance for Liturgy and Episcopacy,' addressed to the High Court of Parliament. This was a tract of not more than ten pages. It contained no arguments which had not been already advanced.

Both the 'Humble Remonstrance' and the 'Divine Right of Episcopacy' were answered by 'Smectymnuus.' This was a word formed from the initial letters of the names of the authors,—Stephen Marshal, Edmund Calamy, Thomas Young, Matthew Newcomen, and William Spurstow. These five divines are generally classed as Presbyterians. They were moderate men, willing to tolerate both the liturgy and Episcopacy for the sake of peace and unity, though preferring what they called 'conceived prayer,' and the Presbyterian government. They represented the party of the Puritans who had always been the most numerous and the most deserving of respect; that party which would have remained in the same Church with Bishop Hall, if Hall had not allied himself with Laud and joined the advocates of Episcopacy by divine right. They were satisfied with the negative position, that liturgy and Episcopacy had not their origin in the times of the Apostles. An inference was charged upon Hall, from some words in his preface, which, however, he afterwards explained. He had made a comparison between civil and sacred government. With us the one is monarchy, the other, in Hall's judgment, Episcopacy. The one, he said, is variable and arbitrary, the other divine and unalterable. From which it was inferred, that the guilt of altering the monarchy was less than the guilt of altering the Episcopacy. Hall calls this a 'dangerous slander,' and says his words were, 'If antiquity be the rule, the civil polity hath sometimes varied, the sacred never. And if original authority may carry it, that came from arbitrary imposers, this from men inspired.' The Smectymnians had to vindicate themselves from the charge of being disturbers of the Church. Hall urged, that if those who were trying to introduce another form of administration upon a neighbour Church were branded as incendiaries, we could not suffer those to escape who were trying to change the polity of the Church of England. This referred to attempts made to enforce Episcopacy on the Church of Scotland. The Smectymnians answered, that the Episcopal faction in Scotland were strangers, endeavouring violently to obtrude innovations upon *a settled Church and State;* but multitudes who were not satisfied in the Church of England, complained less of the liturgy and Episcopacy in themselves, than of the claims which were now made for Episcopacy, and of recent innovations which were changing the character of the Church.

The Smectymnians were ready to dispute with him concerning the antiquity of liturgies and the divinity of Episcopacy. They quoted Tertullian, who says that in his day the public assemblies prayed without any prompter but their own hearts; and Augustine, who says that we are free to ask the things desired in the Lord's Prayer in other words. Justin Martyr also bears the same testimony, where he says, 'He who instructed the people prayed according to his ability.' Settled forms of worship were not introduced till the Arians and Pelagians propagated their heresies in their prayers and hymns. And even then the form of prayer was composed by the minister. It is enjoined by the Council of Carthage that no minister is to use a new form of prayer without first conferring with his brethren. Bishop Hall had said that the Lord's Prayer itself was in part borrowed from the Jewish liturgies. To the Smectymnians this was blasphemy. 'The Lord Christ, *the Wisdom of the Father, borrow* from the wisdom of the Rabbins! impossible!' they cried. Bishop Hall maintained that there was a liturgy used by God's people since the days of Moses, which the Smectymnians could only deny, for proof was wanting on both sides. Hall said that the compilers of our liturgy were holy martyrs and reformers. The Smectymnians answered that of 'the tribe for which he pleads, not a few have called them *traitors* rather than martyrs, and *deformers* rather than reformers.' One or two objections are made to the liturgy in the form of queries. The first is this very weighty one, that whereas, by the Scriptures, the minister is the mouth of the people to God, yet responses are appointed in the service to be said by the people. It is urged that in King Edward's book, there was a rubric which left it to the discretion of the minister what and how much was to be read when there was a sermon. The ground, they said, of the first binding of the liturgy upon all ministers was not to hinder them exercising their right in prayer, but to prevent the old Popish priests from returning to the Mass. Bishop Wren was the first to condemn 'conceived prayer' in the Church.

In replying to Hall on Episcopacy, the Smectymnians had nothing which was really new, yet their book contains all that can well be said on their side. Hall had admitted that a bishop, as distinct from a presbyter, was not clearly discernible in the New Testament. How then, said they, can it be shown that there were bishops in the Apostles' time? And, if bishops, there could be no dioceses, for there were no parishes till two hundred years after Christ; and if no dioceses, the bishops could not be diocesan. The Smectymnians said that, if Hall had been learned in antiquity, he would have found learned authors affirming that there was a time when the Church was not governed by bishops, but by priests. In the New Testament bishops and presbyters are the same, both in name and in office. Titus was left in Crete to ordain presbyters. A description is given of the character required of the persons to be ordained, and the reason is added that a bishop must be blameless. The elders to be ordained were to be also bishops. In Acts xx. 17, the Apostle calls the elders of the Church of Ephesus by the name of 'bishops.' Chrysostom says that, while the Apostles lived, the names were not distinguished. Cyprian was styled 'brother' by his presbyters. Paul exhorts Timothy not to neglect the gift that was given him by the laying on of the hands of the presbytery. Jerome says that, previous to the divisions in the Church, it was governed by a common council. To prove this, he appeals to the Scriptures, when Paul, writing to the Philippians, says, 'Paul and Timotheus to the bishops and deacons.' The commentaries that go by the name of Ambrose say that rectors or governors were ordained in every city when the Church began to increase. The presbyters themselves, St. Jerome says, brought in this uniformity concerning the line of succession; and the Smectymnians urge the difficulty in which Protestant bishops are placed by having to trace their pedigree through the loins of Antichrist. They then argue that the bishops of the present day are not like those of the days of the Apostles; yea, those of the Apostles' days were unlike the bishops of four hundred years later. Episcopacy, like the ship Argo, has been so often repaired that there is now nothing left of the first materials. In former times the sole jurisdiction of a bishop was 'a stranger and a monster.' Ordination, admonition, and excommunication were not in the hands of any single man. Cyprian, in exile, writing to his charge, says that Aurelius was ordained by him and his colleagues who were present with him. In his day bishops did not ordain alone, but only in conjunction with the presbyters. Firmilianus says of them that rule in the Church, that they possess the power of laying on hands and of ordaining, and that these rulers are called *seniores et præpositi*, by which is understood presbyters as well as bishops. From these passages it is concluded that presbyters might ordain without bishops. The commentaries which go under the name of St. Ambrose say that, in Egypt, if the bishop is not present the presbyters ordain. Augustine affirms the same thing in almost the same words. The Chorepiscopos, who was but a presbyter, had power to lay on hands, if licensed to do it by the bishop. The Council of Carthage decreed that a bishop should not ordain a clergyman without the counsel of the presbyters. In his ordinations a bishop took the concurrent assistance of his clergy. The same Council appointed that all the presbyters

CHAP. III.

Presbyters can ordain without bishops.

present should lay on their hands with the hands of the bishop. Jerome and St. Chrysostom make bishops and presbyters to differ from each other only in having the power of ordination, but this was simply a difference *de facto*, not *de jure*. Leo I. says that bishops are beholden for this priority to the canon of the Church more than to the canon of God's word.

For the Scripture arguments, in favour of Episcopacy, the main cases are those of Timothy and Titus and the seven angels of the Asiatic Churches. As to Timothy and Titus, it is urged by the Smectymnians that they were evangelists, and not bishops or presbyters. Paul exhorted Timothy to abide at Ephesus for a time. He was not placed there permanently, as one who had the pastoral or episcopal charge at Ephesus. We read in the Acts of the Apostles that Paul sent him up and down on various services of the Church. When Paul fled from the tumults at Berea, he left behind him Silas and Timothy. From Athens Paul sends Timothy to Thessalonica to confirm the Thessalonians in the faith. He returned again to Paul at Athens, whence he and Silas were sent into Macedonia. They returned to Corinth and then went to Ephesus. At Miletus, Paul assembled the elders of the Church, and charged them to feed the flock of Christ,—a charge which would surely have been given to Timothy had he been Bishop of Ephesus. Moreover, St. Paul calls these elders 'bishops,' which certainly he would not have done in the presence of Timothy, if Timothy had been their bishop. Yet St. Paul says nothing of any superiority of Timothy over them, nor of any duty which they owed to him as their bishop. The clear inference which the Smectymnians make from the passage is, that St. Paul did not leave Timothy at this time as Bishop of Ephesus. It is rather evident that he took Timothy with him to Jerusalem and thence to Rome, for the Epistles written from thence, either in the text or the inscriptions, bear the name of Timothy as St. Paul's companion and fellow-labourer. Timothy is called a minister, an evangelist, an apostle, a messenger of the Church, and many other names, but never once is he called a bishop. The history of Titus, in the same way, is incompatible with the supposition of his being a bishop settled in any particular Church or diocese. We read of him as Paul's companion in his journey through Antioch to Jerusalem, returning again to Antioch, and thence proceeding into Syria and Cilicia, confirming the Churches. From Cilicia he goes to Crete, where he is left *for a while* to put in order the things that remain. He was called Bishop of Crete by the ancients, as Dr. Rainolds explains it, because he did for a time the things which were afterwards done by the bishop. But Titus and Timothy, say the Smectymnians, were never delegated to ordain alone or to govern alone, or to rebuke an elder, but to entreat him as a father. Here follows a curious explanation of St. John's angels. The angel of Thyatira is addressed as plural, *I say unto you*, whence it is argued that the angel was not an individual, but the whole presbytery of the Church collectively. The Smectymnians reminded Hall of the conditions on which bishops were retained in the Church of England at the Reformation. The laws of the land* proclaim that not only *bishoprics, but bishops and all the jurisdiction they have is from the King*. The divine right of Episcopacy cannot, therefore, be advocated without prejudice to the sovereignty. Hall answered that the place and exercise of a bishop's jurisdiction are of regal donation, but the function itself is divine. A few passages for the lay eldership were quoted by the Smectymnians from the Fathers. Augustine writes 'to the beloved brethren, the clergy, the *seniors*, and all the people of the Church of Hippo.' Albaspineus, in his edition of Optatus, speaks of seniors in this passage, 'to the brethren, the sons, the clergy, and the *seniors*.'

Bishop Hall replied to Smectymnuus in 'A Defence of the Humble Remonstrance against the frivolous and false exceptions of Smectymnuus.' The question of the liturgy was easily dealt with. Augustine might say, we were at liberty to ask for the things prayed for in the Lord's Prayer, but surely this did not prove that there was no liturgy then used in the service of the Church. He illustrated the present custom of the Church of England where we have a liturgy, and yet the minister may use extempore prayer before the sermon. The Rubric of Edward's book was simply a licence to omit part of the service, which, says Hall, may

Marginalia: Jurisdiction of bishops from the king. Bishop Hall's defence.

* 37 Henry, cap. 17.

yet be given by the ordinary. Timothy was said to have had the ministerial gift by the laying on of the hands of the presbytery. Hall, quoting Calvin, explains presbytery to mean the office of a presbyter, and not the men composing a presbytery. Timothy was ordained by the laying on of St. Paul's hands. As to Jerome, he, indeed, says, that there is no difference between a bishop and a presbyter, yet he contradicts himself when he shows that bishops were first made to prevent schisms in the Church; and, as schisms began in the Apostles' days, so also must the office of bishop. The true Ambrose, and not the commentator who bears his name, tells us that 'God requires one thing of a bishop, another of a presbyter, and another of a deacon.' And as for the necessity of a presbytery to join the bishop in his ordination, Hall asks who ever heard of a bishop ordaining a presbyter alone, without the concurrent imposition of many hands? The elders from Ephesus might not all have been from Ephesus. They were probably from divers parts. Timothy might have been Bishop of Ephesus, and yet have gone with Paul to Jerusalem. In the judgment of antiquity, Titus was ordained, by Paul, after the journeys mentioned in the Acts. As to Augustine's *seniores*, they were old, grave men of Hippo, magistrates and men in authority, such as we call aldermen. The Church, doubtless, had the advice of these men, but it was not governed by *elders*, *pastors*, and *deacons*.

The Smectymnians vindicated their answer to the 'Humble Remonstrance,' and Hall answered the Vindication, but the arguments on both sides were exhausted.

The question of the bishoprics of Ephesus and Crete was handled with rare ability by William Prynne. In 1636 he published a treatise called 'The Unbishopping of Timothy and Titus.' He does not find that Timothy is ever once called a bishop in the New Testament. He was St. Paul's associate and fellow-worker, always accompanying the Apostle in his travels. He was properly his 'minister' or helper in the Gospel. When St. Paul wrote the Epistle, Timothy was a very young man; and was charged not to rebuke an elder. He was to honour those elders that ruled well. His 'gift' was given him by the 'laying on of the hands of the presbytery,' which surely could not confer on him the function of a bishop. The inscription at the end of the Second Epistle, where he is called the first bishop of the Ephesians, is a mistake. He went about with St. Paul, or was sent by him to different places, as the Apostle found work for him to do. If he had been a bishop, it is not likely, Prynne says, that St. Paul would have asked him 'to carry his clothes-bag, his books, and parchments after him.' When he was left at Ephesus, he had just entered on his ministry. As soon as Paul returned from Macedonia, Timothy was sent to Achaia. He joins Paul in the salutations in the Epistles to the Corinthians, Philippians, and Thessalonians. In the Epistle to the Ephesians, where we should have expected to read something of him had he been then bishop, he is not even mentioned. St. Paul himself, and not Timothy 'the bishop,' excommunicated Hymenæus and Philetus. In the words which St. Paul addressed to the elders of Ephesus, Timothy is not spoken of as if he had any episcopal pre-eminence among them. Tychicus was sent to Ephesus to do the same things which Timothy was commissioned to do. This Tychicus, according to Dorotheus, was one of the seventy disciples, and afterwards Bishop of Chalcedon. It is therefore more likely, Prynne says, that Tychicus was Bishop of Ephesus, if there was such a person; but Paul expressly calls the 'elders' or presbyters 'bishops.' When he went to Ephesus, long after Timothy was *left* there, he laid hands on those who had only been baptized with John's baptism, that they might receive the Holy Ghost.

Titus was another of Paul's fellow-labourers. Long after he had been left at Crete, he was sent by the Apostle to Dalmatia. He is charged, as Paul's vicar, to come to him diligently to Nicopolis. He was to bring with him 'Zenas the lawyer.' Paul tells Timothy that he is to ordain elders, overseers, or bishops in every city. These bishops, Prynne concludes, must have been of the same order to which Titus himself belonged. Homer says that Crete had ninety walled cities. Is it likely, Prynne asks, that an archbishop over so many great cities would stoop so humbly as to wait on a lawyer?*

The Archbishopric of Crete.

* Prynne here beat himself with his own flail. An English bishop always has his 'lawyer' with him. A friend of Archbishop Laud's said that Zenas may have required fees when Titus gave 'Letters of Orders.'

CHAP. III.

Bishop Hall and John Milton.

Bishop Hall met a more formidable opponent in some respects than Smectymnuus. This was John Milton. We say in some respects, for, whatever may have been Milton's ability as a writer, he had not that knowledge of the subject which was possessed either by Hall or the Smectymnians. His treatise 'Of Prelatical Episcopacy' was a reply to the 'Humble Remonstrance' and Ussher's 'Apostolic Institution of Episcopacy.' He dealt more with general principles than special arguments. He concluded from the New Testament accounts of Timothy and Titus that they were not bishops, but rather vicegerents of the Apostles. The ascribing of bishoprics to them had its origin with what Milton calls 'that undigested heap and fry of authors which they call antiquity.' In these ancient writers we find nothing worthy of trust. The history of Councils is corrupt, and the Councils themselves were corrupted by an ungodly prelatism.

Milton's contempt of the Fathers.

'Whatever,' he says, 'time or the heedless hand of blind chance hath drawn down of old to this present in her huge drag net, whether fish or seaweed, shells or shrimps, unpicked, unchosen, these are the Fathers.' What value, he asks, can we place on the judgment of Councils as to the distinction between presbyters and bishops when they were such blind judges of things before their eyes? The Council of Chalcedon acknowledges Rome for an apostolic throne, and Peter in that see for the rock. Eusebius says it was difficult to tell who were appointed bishops by the Apostles. Yet Leontius, an obscure bishop of Magnesia, out of the history of the Council of Chalcedon, reckoned twenty-seven successors to Timothy in Ephesus. What could he know beyond his own diocese; and how could he determine what kind of bishops these were? Many of the bishoprics ascribed to these bishops were merely apocryphal, being raised out of misunderstood places of Scripture. A dozen epistles are ascribed to Ignatius, five of which are admitted to be spurious, full both of trifles and heresies. This Ignatius is called Bishop of Antioch Theopolis, which betrays an anachronism, for Antioch was not called Theopolis till the time of Justinian. In the Epistle to those of Tarsus, Ignatius calls them ministers of Satan, who say that 'Christ is God.' In that to the Trallians, he says that 'a bishop has power over all and beyond all government and authority whatever.' In his Epistle to the Ephesians, Milton says there is a line which casts an ill hue upon all the epistle. It is this:—'Let no man err; unless a man be within the rays or enclosure of the altar, he is deprived of the bread of life.' In the Epistle to the Church of Smyrna, Ignatius tells them 'to follow their bishop as Christ did His Father, and the presbyters as the Apostles.' Then follows the sentence, 'It is not lawful without a bishop to baptize, nor to offer, nor to do sacrifice.' Again, 'My son, says Solomon, honour God and the king; but I say honour God and the bishop or high priest, bearing the image of God according to his ruling, and of Christ acording to his priesting, and after him honour the king.'

Irenæus says that Polycarp was made Bishop of Smyrna by the Apostles. When Irenæus was a boy he saw Polycarp. A distinct and supreme order, says Milton, is concluded from the young observation of Irenæus. We might as well say that Calvin, and after him Beza, were bishops of Geneva in the unsettled state of that Church. Irenæus, according to Eusebius, was a disciple of Papias, the weak and superstitious Chiliast. This patron of Episcopacy is also the patron of some of the heresies of the Papists. He says that 'the obedience of Mary was the cause of salvation to herself and all mankind.' Again, that 'Eve was seduced to fly God, that the Virgin Mary might be made the advocate of the Virgin Eve.' Tertullian is quoted by the advocates of Episcopacy, as saying that Polycarp was placed at Smyrna by St. John, and Clement was ordained at Rome by St. Peter; but this same Tertullian denies the equality of God the Son with God the Father. Of the worthlessness of what is called Catholic antiquity, Milton produces a notable instance in the case of the disputes about keeping Easter. Could Polycarp have erred in what St. John did, or could Anicetus at Rome have erred as to what Peter and Paul did? Yet these men, who themselves conversed with Apostles, or with those who had been the companions of the Apostles, could not agree in so simple a matter of Church order as the time when Easter should be kept.

In another tract, called 'The Reason of Church Government urged against Prelaty,' Milton explains more in detail his views of Church polity. He takes up the ground which was now occupied both by the Presbyterian and Episcopalian, that there is a definite scheme of ecclesiastical government prescribed in the New Testament. He cannot conjecture it as even possible that God should leave His 'frail and feeble Church in this dark voyage without the aid and compass of discipline.' If He had so left it, who is there, he asks, that will dare ' to guide the living ark of the Holy Ghost, though he should find it wandering in the field of Bethshemesh, without a high calling?' The profane prelates may well tremble lest the fate of Uzza be theirs. Milton argues his point from such figures as those which compare the Church to the wife or bride of Christ, and reasons from such relations as these, that Christ must yield her the protection of a perfect discipline. Again, there is the often-repeated argument from the minute care which Jehovah had over the smallest matters in the ceremonial of the Jews, and the inference that if He cared so much for the inferior building, is it likely that such glorious architecture as the Christian Church should be varnished over by the devices and embellishments of man's imagination? Milton, however, differs both from the Episcopal and the Presbyterian advocates of Divine right, in refusing to find the pattern of the Christian offices and officers in the law of Moses. He is willing to let the prelates go to Adam for their first bishop, and recommends them to go even higher, and begin Episcopacy from Lucifer. The gospel, he says, was a fulfilling of the law, and not an imitation of it. There is no parallel between Episcopacy and the priesthood of Aaron; and, as for the plea that bishops were raised up to prevent schisms, Milton answers that they have promoted more schisms than they have prevented. He also wrote 'An Apology for Smectymnuus' and 'Animadversions upon the Remonstrant's Defence against Smectymnuus.' The one is put in the form of objections and answers. It is remarkable for its want of argument, and the prevalence of passion. The other piece is commended by one of Milton's editors as having 'shattered to atoms the feeble logic opposed to him,'—commendation which it scarcely deserved.

The writings of Milton which relate to the Church question were published about 1640-1, when he was still comparatively a young man. He had been destined for the service of the Church by his parents, but the progress of the Laudensian innovations made him despair of the Church's future. But for the success of Laud's party, John Milton's name might have been in the roll of the great divines, probably among the most revered prelates of the Church of England. At this time his views seem to have been Presbyterian, but of that moderate kind which would have conformed while conformity was practicable, and while there was hope of reformation. But, with the Smectymnians and the great body of the moderate and conformable Puritans, he was converted into an open enemy of the Church as it then existed.

Milton left behind him an unpublished work on Christian doctrine, from which it is evident that he had departed widely, in his later years, from the doctrines and the polity of the Presbyterians. This is called 'A Posthumous Treatise on Christian Doctrine, Completed from the Scriptures alone.' Milton's reliance on the Scriptures is characteristic of that age. It is surprising that to one so impatient of tradition or authority, the question of demarcating between the provinces of reason and Scripture does not seem to have presented itself. 'Let us,' he says in one place, 'discard reason in sacred matters, and follow the doctrines of the Scriptures exclusively.' What would be the value of the Scriptures after reason has been discarded, we do not at present care to inquire. Had Milton kept his own rule, he would not have written a treatise of Christian doctrine. He could not have compared Scripture with Scripture if he had discarded reason. He could make no inferences from the words of Scripture but those which reason made. Milton meant that he was to receive as Christian doctrine only that which was evident to his reason from Scripture. But even to this principle he was not faithful. He said, 'Let us discard reason,' yet soon after he is reasoning about the deep questions of the Trinity, denying the equality of the Son with the Father, and again speculating on the essence of being, affirming that that which *is* could never have begun to be, and because it *is*, it can never have an end of being. The Scripturalist will be pleased with Milton's proud boast that he follows no heresy nor sect, but the Holy Scriptures alone. Yet Milton begins this very treatise with a regret, that though the Reformed religion is so well justified against Papists, it is not completely strengthened by works of defence. He asks for champions who will be fearless of truth, who will recognize the conditions on which religious knowledge is given; that, as in other things, the offers of God are all directed, not to an indolent credulity, but to a constant diligence and unwearied search after the truth. Religious knowledge, he says, is grounded not upon an easy faith, but on a full and earnest exercise of the faculties with which men are endowed. As Milton left reason and its province undefined, so did he omit to determine in what sense Scripture is Scripture. The result is, that in this treatise things, which to some are most plainly taught in the Scripture, are explained away by reason; and other things, which have no great accordance with reason, are received because they seem to be sanctioned by the letter of Scripture.

Milton begins with the doctrine *of God*. When it is said we can know God, this is explained, that it is to be understood with reference to the imperfect comprehension of man. We cannot know God as He really is. To speculate on the nature of an essence so much beyond us is dangerous. It is to think of God after the manner of men. Our safety, therefore, is in conceiving of God as He is represented in the Scripture. We may be sure, Milton says, care has been taken that there be no unworthy representation of the Divine Being in the sacred writings. It may be objected, that the conceptions there are human, just such as men would form who had not read the Scriptures. To which Milton answers, that the similitude between things in heaven and things on earth is probably greater than we imagine. But even if they are not, there is still more truth to us in these imperfect conceptions, which are adapted to our capacities, than in vague speculations as to the Divine Essence.

Milton an Arminian.

Milton renounced the doctrines of Calvin, and embraced the tenets of Arminius. God, he says, has not decreed all things absolutely. He maintains that the theory of contingent decrees is not unworthy of God, and that it may be defended on human principles as most wise. There is a special decree called predestination. It means that God, before the foundation of the world, predestinated to eternal life those who should believe and continue in the faith. Predestination means election. It does not include reprobation. This is an error of the schools. There is a book of the living, but we never read of a book of death. God is long-suffering to usward, that is, to all men. He hates nothing that He has made. He has omitted nothing that was necessary for universal salvation. The schoolmen distinguish between the revealed will and the hidden will of God. But this is to make two wills in God, the one of which is contrary to the other. The decree of reprobation, if one may speak of such a decree, is conditional, like that of predestination. As election is confirmed by faith, so reprobation is rescinded by repentance. All men have given to them grace sufficient to enable them to attain a knowledge of the truth, and the final salvation to which it will lead them.

Against the doctrine of the Trinity, as commonly received, Milton openly protests. The Church of Rome, he says, declares that it cannot be proved by any passage of Scripture. The eternal generation of the Son is a doctrine invented since the Apostles' days. As the *Logos*, or Word, He existed in the beginning, and was the first-born of the whole creation. He was the *first-born*, but not generated from eternity. God imparted to Him a measure of the divine nature, —we may say of the divine substance, but the Son did not receive the entire of the divine essence. The orthodox, says Milton, had a great opinion of their own acuteness, and so they started an hypothesis that the Son was numerically and personally distinct from the Father, and yet one. In this way they preserved the divine unity. But Jesus disowns co-essentiality with His Father, where He says, ' My Father is greater than I.' He is the first-born among many brethren, the beginning of the creation of God,—the first of those beings which God created, but not Himself God. The Holy Spirit was produced of the divine substance, probably before the foundations of the world were laid, but

marginalia: CHAP. III.

marginalia: An Arian.

later than the Son, and we may say much inferior to Him.

The Son and the Holy Ghost are thus created or formed out of the Divine substance, so far they are kindred to God, but this relationship, in a less degree, Milton maintains to exist between God and all creation. All things flowed from the Divine substance, not of necessity, but by the will of God. He produced all things from Himself. This, with Milton, was no speculative doctrine of reason, but the plain teaching of the Bible. The Hebrew, Greek, and Latin words which are translated 'create,' do not mean, he says, to form out of nothing, but out of a previously existing matter. The things which are seen were not made out of things which do appear. They were made out of things invisible, or of things not visible as they now are. From this follows the impossibility of annihilation. God neither can nor will annihilate anything. He works for an end, and that end can never be nothing.

We read of two institutions in Paradise,—the Sabbath and marriage. Milton is doubtful if the law of the Sabbath was ever revealed to Adam, or, indeed, if there was any such commandment given previous to the law on Mount Sinai. Scripture is silent on the subject. He conjectures that Moses, who seems to have written the Book of Genesis much later than the promulgation of the law, inserted this sentence about the Sabbath into a place which seemed suitable for it. When the people gathered twice as much on the sixth day, the ruler of the congregation wondered, which seems to show that they were ignorant of the law of the Sabbath. On marriage, Milton's views are peculiar. He advocated divorce, not merely because of fornication, but whenever the persons married were dissatisfied with each other. To meet this, he explained the word fornication in a wide sense, so as to make it embrace everything on which a man and a woman might not agree. Marriage was instituted for the happiness of the persons married, and if this object was not obtained, a marriage might be dissolved, on the principle that no covenant can be obligatory when it ceases to secure the end for which it was made. Marriage was made for man, and not man for marriage. Nor does Milton advocate that marriage should only be of one woman to one man. The Scriptures nowhere forbid polygamy. Abraham and other patriarchs and pillars of our faith had more wives than one. 'Kings' daughters' were among Solomon's 'honourable women,' and 'the virgins' were the queen's companions. Milton's imperfect sense of the province of Scripture, as a teacher of men, is the only reason that can be assigned for this advocacy of polygamy. It is the result of interpreting the Bible after we have discarded reason. *[Advocates polygamy.]*

In the same way Milton finds that the death of the body is a punishment for sin, that even beasts are not excluded from the penalty. He finds, too, that the whole man dies,—body, soul, and spirit. This he proves by such passages as 'Man giveth up the ghost, and where is he?' 'Before I go hence and be no more;' 'I am not yet ascended;' and 'I go to prepare a place for you,' which plainly declares that as yet there was no place for the glorified spirits of men. Christ's death was a satisfaction made to God,—a fulfilment of the law, a payment of a price for the whole race of man. Infants are not to be baptized, and baptism is to be performed by immersion in running water. There are no clergy as distinct from laity. All believers are God's heritage, and to them is committed the power of the keys. Christians are to meet together for worship and mutual edification until Christ comes. He will reign personally on earth for a thousand years, and at the end of the thousand years, those saints who have fallen asleep before His coming shall awake to a never-ending life. *[The soul sleeps till the resurrection. Milton a Baptist. A millenarian.]*

Milton, as a theologian, will disappoint none more than those who wish to draw a system of Christian doctrine from the Scriptures alone. He shows the worthlessness of antiquity, for 'our fathers have transgressed.' He rejects the authority of the Church, applying to it the words of the prophet, 'Plead with your mother, plead, for she is not my wife.' He admits that the Scriptures have various readings, that we have no original manuscripts, and that the Bible has been committed to 'uncertain and variable guardianship.' Antiquity, the Church, the Bible, have each their offices, but the Great Teacher of man is the Holy Spirit, which Milton calls 'a more certain Guide than the Scripture.'

CHAP. III.

Conference on innovations at the Dean of Westminster's.

In 1641 the Lords appointed several of the leaders of the Church who were opposed to the doctrines and practices of Laud and his party, to meet at the Bishop of Lincoln's house, in Westminster.* There were present, Archbishop Ussher, Dr. Prideaux, afterwards Bishop of Worcester, Dr. Ward, Dr. Brownrigg, afterwards Bishop of Exeter, Dr. Featly, Rector of Lambeth, and Dr. Hacket, afterwards Bishop of Lichfield and Coventry. They were to report 'Touching Innovations in the Doctrine and Discipline of the Church of England.' The account of their proceedings contained also 'Conversations upon the Book of Common Prayer.' Under the first head—'Innovations in Doctrines'—they expressed a doubt about the genuineness of the clause in Art. XX., which says, 'The Church has authority in controversies of faith.' They gave a catalogue of doctrines which they regarded as not in harmony with the teaching of the Church of England. Some of these were, that in justification good works 'are concauses with the act of faith,'† that works of penance are satisfactory before God, that private confession is necessary to salvation, that absolution is not merely declaratory, that the Lord's Supper is a proper sacrifice,‡ that prayers for the dead are lawful,§ that the Lord's day is only of ecclesiastical institution, that subjects are to pay whatever sums of money are imposed on them,‖ that election is because of faith foreseen, and that grace is imparted to reprobates as much as to the elect. Among the innovations in discipline were some with which we are familiar. The communion table was turned altar-wise and called an altar. Then the people were taught to bow towards the 'altar' or towards the East. This was done 'many times with three congees, but usually in every motion, access, or recess in the church.' Upon the 'altar,' in many churches, there was an array of candlesticks, and over the 'altar' a canopy, and before it, upon the parafront or 'altar-cloth,' crucifixes and images. The minister read the prayers with his back to the people and his face towards the East.

Novelties in worship.

---

* Bishop Williams was also Dean of Westminster.
† Dr. Dove.
‡ Dr. Heylin.
§ Done by a Mr. Brown at Cambridge.
‖ Dr. Sibthorp and Dr. Manwaring, Bishop of St. David's.

Besides the 'altar,' there was erected a *Credentia* or side table. When a child was baptized, the minister carried it to the 'altar' and made an offering of it to God. Some other things are marked as novelties, which in our day no one would wish to change. At the administration of the Lord's Supper all the communicants were required to come up to the rails to receive the elements. This, it appears, was not the ancient custom of the Church of England. Among the other extraordinary innovations was the taking down of galleries in churches, singing the *Te Deum* in prose, and causing the people to stand at the hymns and the *Gloria Patri*. The changes recommended in the Prayer Book were considerable. The names of some saints were to be dropped from the calendar. The Rubric about vestments, according to the second year of the reign of King Edward, was to be mended. The lessons from the Apocrypha were to be omitted, and in the Burial Service, for the 'sure and certain hope,' was to be substituted, 'knowing assuredly that the dead shall rise again.'*

CHAP. III.

Proposed changes in the Prayer Book.

---

* Neal remarks that in 1641 Charles made good appointments of bishops. Williams was translated to York, Winiffe to Lincoln, Duppa to Salisbury, King to Chichester, Hall to Norwich, Skinner to Oxford, while Brownrigg was promoted to Exeter, Westfield to Bristol, Prideaux to Worcester, Ussher to Carlisle *in commendam;* soon afterwards, Frewen to Lichfield and Coventry, and Howel to Bristol. These were all more or less liberal Churchmen, but it was too late, the Church was to fall with Laud.

CHAPTER IV.

WESTMINSTER ASSEMBLY OF DIVINES. — TWISSE. — BURGES.— CAWDRY. — CHEYNELL. — THE 'DISSENTING BRETHREN.'— THOMAS GOODWIN ON INDEPENDENCY.—THE SAVOY DECLARATION. — RISE OF THE BAPTISTS. — CONTROVERSY BETWEEN TOMBES AND MARSHALL. — FAMILY OF LOVE. — QUAKERS.— BEHMENISTS.—ROSICRUCIANS.—MUGGLETONIANS.—FIFTH MONARCHY MEN.—JOHN BIDLE.—ANTINOMIAN CONTROVERSY.— PETER STERRY.—JOHN HOWE.—JOHN OWEN.—JOHN GOODWIN. —RICHARD BAXTER.

Westminster Assembly of Divines.

IN 1643 the Lords and Commons passed an ordinance in Parliament 'for the calling of an assembly of learned and godly divines and others, to be consulted with by the Parliament for the settling of the government and liturgy of the Church of England, and for vindicating and clearing of the doctrines of the said Church from false aspersions and interpretations.' To this Assembly a hundred and twenty-one clergymen were invited. They were nominated by Members of Parliament, and all parties were in some measure represented. The great body of them were men who had hitherto been conformable ministers of the Church of England. Among them were Archbishops Ussher and Williams, Bishops Morton, Prideaux, Brownrigg, and Westfield, with Drs. Hammond, Sanderson, and Hacket. The King pronounced the Assembly illegal. After this, the Bishops with their supporters, to the number of twenty-one, refused to attend. There were in the Assembly four ministers from the Church of Scotland, and several laymen, mostly Members of the Houses of Parliament. The Assembly began with a revision of the XXXIX. Articles, but they ended by rejecting Episcopacy, and substituting for the Articles and the Prayer Book a Confession of Faith and a Directory of Worship.

It would be difficult to fix upon any point of doctrine in which the Confession of Faith materially differs from the Articles. It has more system. What is taught is reduced to a logical form. There is not only a statement of certain doctrines, but an open recognition of the consequences which necessarily follow from these doctrines. The majority of the ministers of the Assembly were willing to set aside Episcopacy, though there were some who wished to retain it.* The majority were also willing to set up Presbytery in its place, though there were a few who preferred the Independent or Congregational government. On one subject they were all united, and that was in their adherence to the doctrines of Calvin. Arminianism had found its way into the high places of the Church. It had defied all the traditions of the Reformation. It had even claimed as on its side the Augustinian Articles written by the Calvinistic Reformers, who hated 'freewillers' as they hated the Pope and the other great enemy of man. It is, then, to be expected that the Confession of Faith will express an undoubted Calvinism, and express it so as neither an old Arminian nor a modern Rationalist can raise a doubt about 'the literal and grammatical sense.'

The first chapter of the Confession treats of the Holy Scriptures. We are told that the light of nature is just sufficient to leave men 'inexcusable,' but not enough to give them 'that knowledge of God, and of His will, which is necessary to salvation.' In other words, the light of nature may do men great harm; for this end it is given; but it can do them no good whatever. The anxiety of the Calvinist to condemn man always ends in leaving God without excuse. Job wished to order his cause before God, and he felt confident that he could do it righteously; but the Westminster Assembly of Divines made it impossible for God to order His cause righteously before man. The next

CHAP. IV.

The Confession of Faith not materially different from the XXXIX. Articles.

Light of nature.

---

* It is impossible to speak with any accuracy on this subject. What the Assembly really opposed was the Episcopacy by divine right, which had offended the nation under the administration of Laud. The cause of the Assembly's opposing Episcopacy altogether is said to have been the influence of Scotland. The Parliament required help from the Scotch army.

subject is revelation. God in old times spoke to the people in divers manners, but this mode of revealing His will is now laid aside, and what He wishes us to know 'is wholly committed to writing.' The canonical Scriptures are given by inspiration to be 'the rule of faith and life.' The apocryphal books are in the same category with other human writings. The Holy Scripture does not come to us on the testimony of any man or church, but depends wholly upon God, and must be received as the word of God. Our assurance of its infallible truth and divine authority 'is from the inward work of the Holy Spirit, bearing witness by and with the word in our hearts.' We are to have no new revelations of the Spirit. The work of the Spirit is now limited to giving a saving understanding of what is 'revealed in the word.' The Scriptures, in the original Hebrew and Greek, were immediately inspired by God, and by His 'singular care and providence kept pure in all ages.' In all controversies the final appeal must be to them. The Holy Spirit, speaking in Scripture, is the supreme judge; and the infallible rule of interpretation is to interpret Scripture by Scripture.

The second chapter treats of God and the Trinity in words resembling those of the first Article of the thirty-nine. In the third chapter we are hurried on to what the Assembly regarded as the great subject of revelation,—the existence and evolution of 'God's eternal decree.' It has just been said that the compilers of the Confession were willing to admit the logical consequences of their doctrines. But to this there were some exceptions. We read in this chapter, that God did, from all eternity, 'unchangeably ordain whatsoever comes to pass;' but it is added that He is not thereby the 'author of sin:' so that either sin was not ordained from all eternity, or it was one of those things which never 'came to pass.' God did not decree anything because He foresaw it. But to manifest His glory, He predestinated some 'men and angels' unto everlasting life, and 'others, He foreordained to everlasting death.' The number of these men and angels is so certain and definite that it cannot be increased nor diminished. The predestinate to life are appointed to be saved through Christ, and for this end all the means are ordained, and they are effectually made righteous.' Though God ordained from eternity whatever has happened, yet the Assembly said that God did not ordain the Fall, for the elect were elected, being 'fallen in Adam.' The rest of mankind God was 'pleased to pass by,' 'to withhold mercy' and to ordain them to despair and wrath *for their sin,* ' to the praise of His glorious justice.' Their sin consists in their having fallen in Adam before they had done good or evil, and, to make them 'inexcusable,' God withheld His mercy. In Chapter VI., it is said, through Adam's fall all men are corrupt. The guilt of Adam's sin is imputed to them, and, through this corruption, we are 'utterly indisposed, disabled, and made opposite to all good, and wholly inclined to all evil.' The predestinated are effectually called, faith is wrought in them, and God accounts them righteous. They are not righteous in themselves, but Christ's righteousness is imputed to them. They are justified, and the work of inherent righteousness or sanctification is carried on during their life on earth. Chapter XVI., 'Of Good Works,' follows Art. XIII., in limiting good works to such things as are commanded in the Scriptures. The object of the limitation is evidently, in the first place, to oppose the superstitious ceremonies of the Church of Rome; but the question is so broadly stated as to exclude all good works not expressly commanded in Scripture, yea, and all good works commanded in Scripture, if done by unregenerate men. They are said, in this case, 'to be sinful,' such as 'cannot please God or make men meet to receive grace.' But, sinful as the 'good works' of unregenerate men are, 'the neglect of them is still more sinful and displeasing to God.' Chapters XVII. and XVIII. establish the certainty of perseverance for the elect, and the impossibility of their ever being destitute of the life of faith.

In Chapter XX. there is an effort made to reconcile liberty of conscience with obedience to 'the powers which God hath ordained.' Those who publicly maintain opinions or practices contrary to the light of nature or to the known principles of Christianity are 'to be proceeded against by the censures of the Church and by the power of the civil magistrate.' The Church, as represented by the Westminster As-

CHAP. IV.

The Civil Magistrate.

CHAP. IV.

The Sabbath day to be kept holy.

sembly and the civil magistrate, were, it appears, to be the final judges as to 'the light of nature and the known principles of Christianity.' Chapter XXI. treats of religious worship and the Sabbath day. Prayer is declared to be equally acceptable to God in all places. The Sabbath is founded in a law of nature, that a due proportion of time be set apart for the worship of God. This law is ratified by 'a positive moral and perpetual commandment.' The word of God appointed the seventh day to be kept holy in memory of creation, and, since the advent of Christ, the first in memory of redemption. It is to be kept by a holy resting all the day from our 'own works, words, and thoughts about worldly emploments and recreations.' Chapter XXIII. returns to the duty of the civil magistrate, which is explained in nearly the same words as in Art. XXXVII., with, however, this difference, that the civil magistrate is not to have 'the power of the keys.'* He is to preserve peace in the Church, to keep the truth of God pure and entire, to suppress heresies, and to reform abuses in worship and discipline. He is to do all this, and yet he is not to have 'the power of the keys,' for he is to do it by calling synods, being present at them, and providing that 'whatsoever is transacted

---

* This of course depends on what is meant by 'the power of the keys.' The Confession seems to make it Church government, or the exercise of discipline. The English Reformers, Cranmer, Barlow, and probably all of them, vested in the king the power to make bishops or priests without consecration or ordination; but Art. XXXVII. denies him the right of administering the word or sacraments. The title also of 'head of the Church,' was taken away. For the word 'head' was substituted the word 'governor,' and the Article declares the civil magistrate to have the 'chief government.' The article and the chapter in the Confession of Faith may be made to agree or to differ, according to the interpretation put on the words 'keys' and 'government.' If we take the actual fact of the exercise of Church government in the Church of England, it has ever been virtually in the hands of the State. The Church cannot excommunicate the civil ruler; indeed, it cannot excommunicate any one without the authority of the State. It has no proper disciplinary power. It is said that Augustus veiled his absolute monarchy by giving the people the semblance of a constitution. A like semblance has the Church of England. The amount of its power is purely imaged in the fact that the State makes the bishops, while the Cathedral chapters pretend to elect them. The Church of Scotland has always had more ecclesiastical independence than the Church of England, but even this independence has never been complete. Its measure was that only which the State allowed. Mr. Innes, in his valuable work on 'The Law of Creeds in Scotland,' has clearly shown that the Kirk believed in its independence till 1843, when the Act which led to the Disruption, demonstrated that the ultimate source of government was not in the ecclesiastical officers, but in the State.

in them be according to the mind of God.' There is no remedy prescribed in case the civil magistrate and the synod should not agree as to what is heresy, which is the Church, and what is 'according to the mind of God.'

Chapter XXV. defines the Catholic Church as the Church invisible, consisting only of the elect, who are the spouse, the body, the fulness of Him that filleth all in all. The visible Church is also Catholic. It is not confined to one nation, as under the Jews. It consists of all who profess the true religion. It is the kingdom of Christ,—the house and family of God, 'out of which there is no ordinary possibility of salvation.' The Catholic Church has been sometimes more, sometimes less visible. The purest churches are subject to error. Some that were once true churches, are now synagogues of Satan. Nevertheless, there will always be a Church on earth to worship God according to His will. The Pope is Antichrist.

Chapter XXVII. calls sacraments 'holy signs and seals of the covenant of grace.' They represent Christ and His benefits. They are usually said to confer grace, because there is a sacramental union between the sign and the thing signified, whence it comes to pass that 'the names and effects of the one are attributed to the other.' In reality they confer grace only on those who receive them worthily; and this not through any power in them, nor because of the piety or intention of him that administers them, but because of the work of the Spirit and the promise of benefit to worthy receivers.

In Chapter XXVIII. baptism is called a 'sign and seal of regeneration.' It is to be performed by a minister of the Gospel, 'rightly called thereunto.' Dipping is not necessary. Infants are to be baptized when one or both of the parents are believers. 'Grace and salvation are not so inseparably annexed unto it (baptism), as that no person can be regenerated or saved without it, or that all that are baptized are undoubtedly regenerated.' This chapter, however, speaks of 'the efficacy of baptism,' saying, that by the right use of the ordinance grace is 'really exhibited and conferred by the Holy Ghost.' But as grace, with Calvin's disciples, was indefectible, it was necessary not to limit the grace to the moment of administration, nor to give it to any but the elect, to whom it belongs. Those who are ordained to life, whether infants or adults, have the grace of baptism conferred when it pleases God to confer it. Chapter XXIX., on the Lord's Supper, is simply an amplification of Art. XXVIII. Transubstantiation and consubstantiation are renounced, but the body and blood of Christ are 'as *really*, but spiritually, *present* to the faith of believers in that ordinance, as the elements themselves are to their outward senses.'

To the Confession was added a form of Church government, which was called Presbyterial. The ordinary officers of the Church are,—(1.) The pastors, who are to preach the Gospel, read the Scriptures, administer sacraments, instruct, pray for and bless the people. The pastor has also a ruling power over the flock. (2.) Teachers or doctors whose place is in schools and universities, as of old in the schools of the prophets and at Jerusalem, where Gamaliel and others taught as doctors. (3.) Other Church governors, such as elders who have gifts of government. (4.) Deacons, whose office is not to preach or administer sacraments, but to have a special care in distributing to the necessities of the poor. Particular Churches form one Church, which is to be governed by several kinds of assemblies. These assemblies have power to hear and determine differences, and to dispense Church censures. (1.) Congregational assemblies of the ruling officers of a particular congregation. Their business is to manage the affairs of that congregation, to admit to fellowship, or to cast out offending ministers. (2.) Classical assemblies: a presbytery, with many particular congregations under it. The lawfulness of this assembly is proved from the state of the Churches of Jerusalem and Ephesus. (3.) Synodical assemblies. These are general, and may be either provincial, national, or œcumenical. All pastors, teachers, elders, and other fit persons, when it shall be deemed expedient, may be members of them. No man is to take upon himself the office of the ministry, but is to be ordained to it by the presbytery. Every minister is to be examined before ordination, and no man is to be appointed over a congregation, 'if that congregation can show just cause of exception against him.'

The members of the Westminster Assembly were all probably men of some eminence in their day. They have been highly extolled by their friends, and loudly decried by their enemies.* Both the praise and the censure are equally undeserved. When we put their names alongside of those who stood by the King and the bishops, they are indeed insignificant. The most eminent of them were Edward Reynolds and John Lightfoot, who conformed at the Restoration. When these two are excepted, there is scarcely another that could be put in any list of the great theologians of England. It is, however, certain that they were nearly all men of some mark. They were either popular preachers, or they had distinguished themselves as scholars, or they had written books. It is probably a fair estimate to say that they were the average good men of the Church in their time.†

* Clarendon says (the Episcopal divines being excepted) 'the rest were all declared enemies to the doctrine and discipline of the Church of England; some of them infamous in their lives and conversation, most of them of very mean parts in learning, if not of scandalous ignorance, and of no other reputation than of malice to the Church of England.'

Richard Baxter's account is different. 'Being not worthy to be one of them myself, I may the more freely speak the truth, even in the face of malice and envy; that, so far as I am able to judge by the information of all history of that kind, and by any other evidence left us, the Christian world, since the days of the Apostles, had never a synod of more excellent divines than this and the Synod of Dort.'

† We have searched the Puritan Hagiologies for all that could be found of the ninety-eight divines who constituted this Assembly. Of twenty there is no trace. After the names of fourteen, we have written nothing remarkable. The rest had some celebrity, either as scholars or as preachers. John White, of Dorchester, and Robert Harris, of Hanwell, were eminent preachers. Thomas Gataker, of Rotherhithe, was a Fellow of Sydney College, and an eminent Hebrew scholar. Oliver Bowles was a Fellow of Queen's, and a celebrated tutor. Jeremiah Whitaker was a celebrated preacher. Fuller includes him among the learned writers of Sydney College. Anthony Tuckney was a Fellow of Emanuel, and John Arrowsmith of Catherine Hall. Simeon Ashe had 'a good estate, and was liberal with it.' Of Jeremiah Burroughs, Richard Baxter said, 'If all the Episcopalians had been like Archbishop Ussher, all the Presbyterians like Stephen Marshall, and all the Independents like Jeremiah Burroughs, the breaches of the Church would soon have been healed.' Dr. Temple was a Fellow of Trinity, Dublin, and brother of Sir John Temple, Master of the Rolls. Richard Baxter recommended him to Hyde for the bishopric of Hereford. George Walker was chaplain to Dr. Felton, Bishop of Ely. Wood calls Lazarus Seaman 'a learned man.' Joshua Hoyle was a Fellow of Trinity, Dublin. Francis Taylor had some reputation as a Hebrew scholar, sufficient to secure the patronage of Archbishop Laud, who gave him a living. Thomas Valentine was 'a very popular preacher.' Andrew Perne was a Fellow of Catherine Hall. John Langley was Master of St. Paul's School. He had been Master of the College School at Gloucester, and Prebendary of the Cathedral. Here he joined the Bishop of Gloucester, Miles Smith,

CHAP. IV.

William Twisse.

The first Prolocutor was William Twisse, whom, from his being chosen to this office, we may suppose to have been one of the best, if not the best man, in the Assembly. He had been a Fellow of New College, Oxford, and had earned a great reputation in the University by his public lectures and disputations, but especially by assisting Sir Henry Savile in correcting the works of Bradwardine. King James made him chaplain to the Lady Elizabeth, whom he accompanied to the Palatine. When he returned to England, he became curate of Newbury. He declined several offers of high preferment, the provostship of Winchester College, a prebend's stall in the cathedral, a professorship at Oxford, and a more valuable living than Newbury. He was also offered by the States of Friesland a professor's chair in the University of Franeker. Dr. Twisse refused to read the 'Book of Sports,' which marked him out at Court for a Puritan. He wrote on the Sabbath question judiciously and moderately, on the side advocated by Dr. Bownd. But Twisse's great subject was 'the eternal decrees.' His largest books are refutations of Arminianism. His adversaries were Thomas Jackson, Dean of Peterborough; Christopher Potter, Canon of Windsor; John Goodwin, of Coleman Street; and Samuel Hoard.* The first he answered in 'A Discovery of Dr. Jackson's Vanities,' and the last in 'The Riches of God's Love unto the Vessels of Mercy, consistent

in resisting the efforts of Laud, who was then Dean of Gloucester, in placing the communion table altar-wise. Laud, however, defied both bishop and prebend. The titles of the books and pamphlets of John Ley fill a page in Brook's 'Lives.' Charles Herle, the Prolocutor after the death of Twisse, in 1646, was a considerable writer. Henry Scudder is placed by Fuller among the learned men of Christ's College, Cambridge. John Conant was Master of Exeter at the Restoration. He was ejected, but conformed seven years after. Henry Wilkinson, jun., was made Principal of Magdalen Hall, Oxford. Edward Corbet was a Fellow of Merton. Thomas Coleman was reputed a good Hebrew scholar. Thomas Ford was a tutor of Magdalen Hall. Dr. Frewen, the President, put the table altar-wise, the first that had been so placed since the Reformation; and Ford preached against the innovation, which brought him into trouble. Joseph Caryl was preacher at Lincoln's Inn. He wrote a 'Commentary on the Book of Job,' in eleven quarto volumes, afterwards published in two immense folios. Herbert Palmer is acknowledged to have been a worthy man. Laud presented him to the vicarage of Ashwell, in Hertfordshire. Cawdry and Palmer together wrote one of the ablest books on the Sabbath, defending the Puritan side.

* Jackson was not a controversial writer, and Potter was scarcely an Arminian. Samuel Hoard was one of Laud's divines.

with His absolute Hatred and Reprobation of the Vessels of Wrath.' Twisse did not shrink from advocating the doctrine of reprobation in all its naked and unadorned deformity. The 'vessels of wrath,' he said, were hated from all eternity, not only before they fell in Adam, but before Adam was created. And from this he drew an argument for the marvellous love of God in ordaining to life the vessels of mercy from the same eternity. The reprobate were not reprobated for any evil that they did, either in themselves or in Adam; and the counterpart of this is that the elect were not elected because of faith or repentance. In both cases the decree was absolute, eternal, and immanent, depending merely on the will of God.

The second name on the list is that of Cornelius Burges. He was preacher at St. Paul's in the time of the Commonwealth, when there was no dean. Burges was made chaplain to Charles I. in 1627, but he had been greatly harassed by the High Commission, because of his determined opposition to the doctrines and practices that were sanctioned and encouraged by Archbishop Laud.* In 1629 he published a treatise on the 'Baptismal Regeneration of Elect Infants.' This is a little book of singular interest. It helps us to understand how the highest form of Calvinistic doctrine may be compatible with the belief of an actual regeneration in baptism. It is sometimes convenient to forget that the whole Church of England followed Calvin in doctrine for seventy years after the Reformation. In the Baptismal Service we thank God that every baptized child has been regenerated by the Holy Spirit. To a Calvinist who believes that one who is once made a child of God cannot fall finally from grace, these words cannot have the same meaning as to an Arminian, who does not believe that grace is indefectible. At first sight we would declare the words of the Baptismal Service to be opposed to Calvinism, and subversive indeed of its first and essential principles. But the fact with which we have to deal is, that we receive these services from men who held the doctrines of Calvin. And

---

* Burges had a clear and solid intellect. He must have been a tower of strength to his party. All High Church writers have borne him a peculiar hatred. He had valuable preferments in the Church when Laud came into power.

then we have another fact, which is, that the same language which is used in the Baptismal Service concerning regeneration, is common to all the Calvinistic writers of the time of the Reformation, both English and foreign. They did not scruple about using it, but seemed rather to glory in its use. The interest of Dr. Burges's explanation of baptismal regeneration is, that it may fairly be taken as the view generally received in the Church of England in his time, and probably by the majority of Churchmen since the Reformation.

The regeneration which he defends is real. It is not merely outward, ritual, or sacramental, but internal, actual, and spiritual. Baptism he calls the sacred laver in which 'the Holy Spirit seizes' on the baptized 'for Christ.' It is the fountain open for sin and for uncleanness to all the inhabitants of the spiritual Jerusalem. Some persons, Burges says, make it a bare sign to distinguish the members of the visible Church from the rest of the world. Others, again, admit the efficacy of baptism for the remission of sins, but deny that the Spirit then works an actual regeneration. Burges says, that the baptized child is regenerated. A spiritual life is begun in it at the moment of baptism. It is thereby transplanted out of the first Adam into the second Adam. The Holy Spirit takes up His dwelling in the baptized child.

On Baptismal Regeneration.

The words of the Service are universal. Every child after baptism is declared to be regenerated, because, Burges says, the Church teaches us, in the language of charity, to regard every child as among the elect. Art. XXVII. says, 'they that receive the sacrament of baptism rightly are grafted into the Church, etc., by the Holy Ghost.' The Catechism explains who they are that 'receive baptism rightly,' where the child is taught to say, 'the Holy Ghost sanctifies me and all the *elect* people of God.' Before the act of baptism there is a prayer in the Service, that the child 'now to be baptized' may be received into the number 'of the faithful and *elect* children of God.' If they belong to the covenant which God made with His chosen, then, in baptism, they are *made members of Christ, children of God, and inheritors of the kingdom of heaven.* This language of charity was illustrated from the Burial Service, where a hope is expressed of the eternal well-being of every person who is buried. Yet in that very prayer we are taught that eternal felicity belongs only to the chosen. We give thanks to God *with whom do live the spirits of them that depart hence in the Lord, and in whom the souls of them that be elected* are in joy and felicity.

Dr. Burges fortifies his arguments by quotations from Calvin, Peter Martyr, Bucer, and Zanchy. All these writers are clear on the efficacy of baptism when administered to elect children, and all of them use that general language of charity, which regards all baptized persons as among the elect. There are also many quotations to the same effect from great writers of the Church of England. Of these the most important are the passages from Hooker. As Hooker was a Calvinist, and at the same time a believer in baptismal grace, it was impossible for his doctrine on this subject to have been different from that of Dr. Burges. Hooker says, 'Predestination bringeth not to life, without the grace of external vocation, wherein our baptism is implied. For as we are not naturally men without birth, so neither are we Christian men in the eye of the Church of God but by new birth, nor according to the ordinary manifest course of divine dispensation new born but by that baptism which both declareth and maketh us Christians. In which respect we justly hold it to be the door of our actual entrance into God's house, the first apparent beginning of life, a seal perhaps to the grace of election, but to our sanctification here a step that hath not any before it.' This passage is quoted to show that Hooker believed an actual regeneration in baptism. The next question is, if Hooker believed that this regeneration happened to every person baptized? That he did not, Burges quotes 'judicious Hooker' saying, 'All receive not the grace of the sacrament that receive the sacrament of His grace.' Dr. Burges also brings forward an abundance of evidence that his view of baptism was that of all the Reformed Confessions, and that the language of these Confessions is precisely that of the Church of England. The grace is actual. It is said, in the language of charity, to be given to all; but in reality it is given only to the elect. The

The foreign Reformers on Baptismal Regeneration.

Hooker on Baptismal Regeneration.

Helvetian Confession says that in baptism 'we are inwardly regenerated, purified, and renewed, through the Holy Ghost.' The Confession of the Reformed Church of France says, 'We believe, as is aforesaid, that, as well in the Lord's Supper as in baptism, God doth bestow upon us in very deed, that is to say, truly, whatsoever He therein sacramentally doth represent unto us.' Equally strong are the words of the old Confession of the Church of Scotland: 'We do certainly believe that by baptism we are ingraffed into Jesus Christ, and made partakers of His righteousness, whereby all our sins are done away.' The difference between the Protestant view of baptism and the Roman Catholic is explained to be, that the efficacy is not *ex opere operato* to all who receive baptism, that God is not tied to His ordinance though ordinarily it is in and by His ordinance that He works. Another difference is that, while the Church of Rome believes a complete sanctification in baptism, 'we say that it is then only begun, and is daily perfected by degrees.'

Daniel Cawdry, another member of the Assembly, had some reputation as a controversialist. He wrote on the Sabbath question, and 'A Diatribe against Dr. Hammond on Superstition and Festivals.' But his chief controversies were with the Independents. Against them he wrote 'Vindiciæ Clavium,' and afterwards 'The Inconsistency of Indepency with Scripture and Itself,' which contained, among other things, a defence of the 'Vindiciæ.' The main questions to be settled were those which concerned the Church and its government, or, as it was called, 'the power of the keys.' Christ gave to Peter, and then to the other Apostles, 'the keys of the kingdom of heaven.' The kingdom of heaven is understood to be the Church. But is it the Church invisible, or the whole Catholic Church visible, or is it a particular congregation? Christ said, 'Upon this rock will I build my Church.' This could not surely mean a particular congregation. It must mean the Church universal. And this is the Church both visible and invisible, for these are but different characters of the same Church. It must have been of this Church that Christ spoke, when He said it should never fail. Particular congregations may fail, but not the whole Catholic Church. The next question is, to whom were the keys given?—to the Church itself or to its officers?—to Peter as an Apostle and elder, or to Peter as a believer? Cawdry, of course, as a Presbyterian, answers that they were given to the officers of the Church, that they might exercise government. An offended brother was to 'tell the Church'—that is, the Church in its officers; and the offender was to 'hear the Church'—that is, he was to submit to the censures of the Church rulers, who had power to bind and loose.

There is but one other member of this assembly who requires special notice. It is Francis Cheynell. Dr. Johnson says* that he was 'considered the most learned and acute of his party.' He had a living of great value near Banbury. About the year 1632 he had a dispute with Laud; but of what was said on either side we have no record. Dr. Johnson describes both the disputants as 'to the last degree zealous, active, and pertinacious.' Our estimate of Cheynell can only be formed from a few tracts, which in themselves are of no particular value. One is called 'The Rise, Growth, and Danger of Socinianism.' It is not so much a refutation of the errors of Socinus as a protest against the exercise of reason in religion. Churchmen of Laud's school extolled the Fathers, and, under pretence of exalting the Catholic reason of antiquity, they checked the exercise of the individual reason. The Puritans decried reason, and lightly esteemed the Fathers, that they might exalt the Scriptures. But the Socinians, according to Cheynell, exalt their own private judgment above Scriptures, Fathers, and Councils. They make every man a Pope. The Reformers made the final appeal always to the Scriptures. The Puritans went a shade further, and made the Scriptures a *judge* of controversies; that is to say, they supposed the Holy Spirit so to speak in the Scriptures as to exclude the necessity of the use of reason. Socinianism asserted the unlimited right of private judgment. If we are not to bow submissively to the decrees of Councils and Fathers, and if the Spirit does not speak in the Scriptures with such clearness as to leave no ground for differences,

* 'Gentleman's Magazine,' March, 1775.

CHAP. IV.

An appeal to Scripture is an appeal to reason.

the only remaining alternative is that the principle of an appeal to the Scriptures involved in it an appeal to reason.

Cheynell found this principle of Socinianism in the writings of Chillingworth. 'The Scripture,' Chillingworth says, 'is not to be believed finally for itself, but for the matter contained in it. So that if men did believe the doctrines contained in the Scriptures, it should no way hinder their salvation not to know whether there were any Scripture or no.' Cheynell, as a sound Puritan, believing that nothing good can be learned except it come through the Scriptures, found these sentiments full of Deism and Socinianism. The Scriptures, he said, are to be acknowledged as divine, not because of the doctrine, but because of the authority of God speaking in them. Chillingworth said that God would not impute errors to those who had done their best to discover the truth. He even maintained that 'a Papist might be saved.'*

The 'Dissenting Brethren.'

There were seven members of the Westminster Assembly known as the 'Dissenting Brethren.' These were, Philip Nye, Thomas Goodwin, Jeremiah Burroughs, Sydrach Sympson, William Bridges, William Greenhill, and William Carter. They agreed to the Confession of Faith and the

---

* Another treatise of Cheynell's is called *Chillingworthi Novissima;* or, The Sickness, Heresy, Death, and Burial of William Chillingworth.' To this was added 'A Prophane Catechism, collected out of Mr. Chillingworth's Works.' The object of the Catechism was to set forth Chillingworth's Socinianism, and to prove Cheynell's favourite thesis, that faith was founded on authority, and not on reason. Chillingworth died at Chichester. He begged, before he died, that he might be buried according to the rites of the Church of England. But Cheynell refused to bury him as a Christian, or to express, concerning him, any hope 'of the resurrection to eternal life.' He met the funeral procession at the grave, with Chillingworth's great work in his hands. He made an oration to the mourners on the heresies of the 'grand seducer.' He pronounced him 'happy, thrice happy, if his works do not follow him;' and casting the book into the grave, he said, 'Get thee gone, then, thou accursed book, which has seduced so many precious souls; get thee gone, thou corrupt, rotten book. Earth to earth and dust to dust; get thee gone into the place of rottenness, that thou mayst rot with thy author, and see corruption. Touching the burial of his corpse, I need say no more than this,—It will be most proper for the men of his persuasion to commit the body of their deceased friend, brother, master to the dust; and it will be most proper for me to hearken to that counsel of my Saviour, *Let the dead bury their dead, but go thou and preach the kingdom of God*. And so I went from the grave to the pulpit, and preached on that text to the congregation.' Many of the names of the members of the Westminster Assembly are but little known. Of some of them no record can be found. If their spirit was that of Francis Cheynell, we may be thankful that the memory of them is 'clean gone for ever.'

Catechism, but objected to the Presbyterian government. Their objections, with the answers of the Assembly, were published by order of the House of Commons.* The argument is, that as a pastor is made an overseer of a flock, his governing power should not exceed the limits of his teaching power. The 'Dissenting Brethren' said that this was Christ's order, but that the Presbyterian destroyed it by making a preaching elder rule over congregations where he did not preach. In the presbytery all members were ruling elders, but they were only preaching elders to their own flocks. This was supposed to set aside the distinction between the elder that rules and the preaching elder. It was also objected, that the Presbyterian polity made an 'incongruous disproportion' between the eldership and the diaconate. If there was a presbytership over all churches, why, it was asked, should there not be a deaconship over all churches? The Presbyterian argument was drawn from the circumstance of many elders being in one town, as in Jerusalem. It was concluded that as there were many elders, there must have been many congregations, and the elders must have formed a presbytery, for they had the government of the Church. The 'Dissenting Brethren' answered, that the believers of Jerusalem were but one congregation. Peter stood up in the midst of them. They were all with one accord in one place. These and many similar passages seemed to show that there was really but one congregation, though many elders, and, consequently, that no elder had jurisdiction, except over the people to whom he ministered.

The presence of these 'Dissenting Brethren' in the Westminster Assembly is the first manifestation of the existence of Independent or Congregational principles within the Church. The earlier Independents were distinguished from the Presbyterians mainly in this, that they regarded separation from the Church as a duty. We meet them as early

---

* This is a curious document. The first part is called 'The Reasons of the Dissenting Brethren against the Third Proposition concerning Presbyterial Government, Humbly Presented.' 1645. The second is called, 'The Answer of the Assembly of Divines unto the Reasons of the Seven Dissenting Brethren.' 1644. The differences of dates must be a mistake, for the two pieces are not only bound together, but the first ends with page 45, and the second begins with page 46. The printer is enjoined, at his peril, not to print more than three hundred of them.

as Cartwright, when Browne and Harrison advocated separation from the Church of England on the ground that it is not a Church. From Browne they were called Brownists, and from one Barrow, Barrowists. It was not till the Westminster Assembly that the difference between the Presbyterian and the Independent was clearly marked out. Even then they both held that 'the discipline' of doctors, pastors, elders, and deacons was necessary to constitute a true Church. The Independent only differed from the Presbyterian in rejecting the government by presbyteries and synods. Every congregation was in itself a Church, and independent of all other Churches. It is probable that many of those who were called Presbyterians in the time of Elizabeth were Independents. It is not evident that government by presbyteries was a necessary part of 'the Discipline.' In Travers's treatise, which was the authorized exposition, presbyteries are not even mentioned.

Thomas Goodwin on Independency.

Thomas Goodwin, one of the seven 'Dissenting Brethren,' wrote an elaborate work in defence of the principles of the Independents.* The visible Church, which consists of those who walk as saints, have, he says, Christ for their Head, and under Him officers which He has appointed. These officers have the power to bind and loose, to forgive sins, and to deliver over to Satan. So far this is Presbyterian, but Goodwin adds, that every congregation has this jurisdiction within itself without reference to other Churches. Long arguments are used to establish the position that Christ must have given to the Church a definite polity. Some of these are the same in kind that were urged by the advocates of Episcopacy and of Presbyterianism. Some of them are original. It cannot be supposed, according to Goodwin, that the Church should be governed 'by the laws of nature or by the maxims of human prudence.' Then, we have a demonstration from the fact that the Church has the power of excommunication. It can deliver over to Satan, which is 'a supernatural work.' The Church is Christ's house; He lives in it, presides over it, and governs it, not as the Author of nature but of grace. His Spirit was in the

* 'Of the Constitution, Right Order, and Government of the Church of Christ.'

Apostles when they established the Church, and whatever they did are examples amounting to commands for us to follow. Moses was faithful over his house, much more is Christ faithful. Every house is builded by some man. The Church is a house specially built. It has nothing in it of the natural. It is all outside of nature and human reason. It is a special institution. Everything in the Church is to be done according to what we find in the Scriptures, and in no matter of discipline or worship is human reason to be followed. By adhering to the letter of the discipline laid down in the Scriptures we get a special or supernatural blessing. The bread and wine convey to us the body and blood of Christ when we celebrate the Supper as Christ commanded it. The preaching of the Gospel has a special efficacy when it is done by the officers of the Church regularly appointed for the office of preaching.* To give alms is a natural or common law, but to give alms in worship is a sacrifice. The officers of the Church are bishops and deacons. The bishops are of three kinds, pastors, teachers, and ruling elders. To each, in the exercise of his vocation and ministry, belongs a special blessing. By this channel does grace flow to the members of the Church. Discipline, therefore, Goodwin says, is no less important than doctrine. By discipline is meant a certain order in the Church. This, Goodwin in many ways proves to be divine,—by precepts, by examples, and by Old Testament prophecies concerning the discipline that was to be under the Gospel. Did not the Psalmist say 'This is the day the Lord hath made'? And again, 'To-day if ye will hear my voice.' And in both these passages, did he not prophesy of the Christian Sabbath? Again, did not God say, 'I will take of thee for priests and Levites'? and was not this fulfilled when Christ appointed two chief orders in the Church,—bishops and deacons? Man's reason is wholly excluded from this region. It must never be exercised except in finding out what God has laid down as parts of the government of His Church. As Goodwin exercised his reason, the

Independent ministers channels of grace.

---

* The late Mr. J. I. Tayler, in his 'Retrospect of Religious Life in England,' says that some of the Puritan ministers professed to be able to cast out devils in virtue of their ordination.

result was to find in the Old Testament a deep and mystical meaning about the polity of the Christian Church. The Acts of the Apostles were written, he says, to teach us how the Church is to be governed. No one who reads that book can doubt that Church everywhere means a congregation of Independents, with its pastor, teacher, ruling elders, and deacons.

Independency goes further from Presbyterianism.

Independency, in its later history, made a further departure from Presbyterianism. The doctors and ruling elders ceased to be reckoned a necessary part of the divinely appointed polity. The minister, with the deacons and the congregation, were sufficient to constitute a Church. The beginning of this change was first discernible in the congregation at Amsterdam. Francis Johnson, one of the five hundred Puritans who had subscribed the 'Book of Discipline,' written by Travers, retired to Amsterdam, where he gathered a Church. Ainsworth, the Hebrew scholar, was doctor or teacher to this congregation. The pastor and the teacher differed about the government of the Church, and their difference led to a schism. Johnson, like the older Independents, who were almost Presbyterians, placed the government of the Church in the elders' hands, but Ainsworth placed it in the congregation, of which the elders were but a part.

The Savoy 'Declaration.'

In 1657 Cromwell gave his 'consent' to a petition from Parliament that the polity of the Independents might become the Church polity of the nation. Toleration, however, was to be granted to those who differed from them in worship and discipline, but who agreed in doctrine. All others were to be without 'protection,' disqualified for holding any 'civil' office, and 'incapable of receiving the public maintenance appointed for the ministry.' Two hundred delegates met at the Savoy, under the presidency of 'the Dissenting Brethren,' and made a 'Declaration' of their 'Faith and Order.' They adopted without change the Westminster Confession, excepting only what related to discipline. The Presbyterians had never been able to establish Presbytery, except in London, and in some parts of Lancashire. They were thwarted by the Independents, who rose suddenly into power and importance. The conference at the Savoy was

RISE OF THE BAPTISTS.

sanctioned by Cromwell; but before they met, Cromwell had passed away, and with him all hopes of Independency becoming the established religion of England.

Out of the Independents sprang another sect, as the Independents had sprung from the Presbyterians. This was the Baptists, who at the Westminster Assembly do not appear to have had even one representative. Yet throughout the interregnum between the first and second Charles, they were the only party, besides the Presbyterians and Independents, that had complete toleration. There were Baptists, or, as they were called Anabaptists, in Germany long before this, but the genealogy of the English Baptists is not fairly traceable to them. It is true, there had been Baptists in England since the Reformation. Henry VIII. issued a proclamation against all the false opinions of 'Anabaptists and Sacramentarians.' Joan of Kent is said to have been of this sect, and in the judgment of the martyr Philpot, 'well worthy to be burnt.' Cecil begged of the King that the bishopric of Rochester should be given to John Knox, that he might be 'a whetstone to quicken and sharpen the Bishop of Canterbury,' and that he might be 'a great confounder of the Anabaptists lately springing up in Kent.' These Anabaptists were 'free-willers' and Pelagians. They denied predestination and original sin. They refused to baptize children because children had no sin, and therefore did not need regeneration. Strype mentions Henry Hart as the chief of these free-willers. John Bradford wrote against them as 'enemies of God's grace.' These Anabaptists had their doctrines from Germany, and were probably extinct before the beginning of the seventeenth century.

The English Baptists originated among the Brownists of Amsterdam. The first was John Smyth,* who, being con-

CHAP. IV.

Rise of the Baptists.

John Smyth baptizes himself.

---

* There is a curious tract in Sion College, called 'The Differences of the Churches of the Separation, contayning a Description of the Leitourgie and Ministerie of the Visible Church, etc. By John Smyth.' 1608. In the preface Smyth says that he differs from 'the ancient Brethren of the Separation in the Leitourgie Presbyterie and Treasurie of the Church.' He does not approve of reading the Bible in churches. Spiritual worship is from the heart, and not from printed books. He applies this also to singing psalms, which should not be done with the book before our eyes. He denounces the 'triformed presbyterie' of pastors, teachers, and rulers; lay elders, he says, are Antcihristian. He denies that the Apostles read the Old Testament when they worshipped. He calls the Septuagint

vinced of the necessity of adult baptism, and having no one to baptize him, baptized himself. This was the climax of all that is absurd, but Smyth was logically right upon the principles of the Brownists. They rejected the ministry of the Church of England. They denied it to be a true Church. From this it followed that all the ordinances of that Church were invalid. They re-ordained their pastors, why should they not re-baptize? The first Independent Church in England had a schism similar to that in Amsterdam. Henry Jacob was succeeded in his pastorate by John Lathrop, and in his time the congregation divided, a part of whom formed the first of the Baptist denomination in London.*

The Baptist controversy.

Though the Baptists do not appear to have had a representative in the Westminster Assembly, yet that Assembly appointed a special committee to consider the arguments that might be urged against the baptizing of children. To this committee John Tombes, who held the Rectory of 'Gabriel's Fanchurch,' addressed 'An Exercitation about Infant Baptism.' The Exercitation was not answered by the Assembly, but it was the beginning of a long controversy, which embraced the many questions that are involved in the denial of infant baptism. Tombes and his first opponents were all Calvinists. This kept the controversy within certain limits, and gave it some peculiarities which it could not otherwise have had. The first general argument for infant baptism is drawn from the fact, that children, as well as people of mature years, are or may be members of the kingdom of God. The Arminian who made the divine family co-extensive with the human family, did not hesitate

---

translation 'a grievous sin,' because it revealed the covenant of grace to the Gentiles before the fulness of time. He puts all translations of the Bible in the same category with apocryphal books. He thinks the division of chapter and verse wicked. It is quite unapostolic. The Apostles never gave chapter and verse when they quoted the Scriptures. There was a John Smyth, Vicar of Mitcham, in Surrey, who was a member of the Presbytery set up at Wandsworth. It is supposed by Brook, in his 'Lives of the Puritans,' that this was the same as John Smyth of Amsterdam. He became an Arminian in doctrine. Dr. Evans makes him probably the first of the General Baptists; but his principles were ultimately more like the Quakers.

* Dr. Evans's 'History of English Baptists.'

to admit all children to baptism, for all being redeemed, they might receive the seal of the covenant of redemption. If they did not keep the conditions of the covenant, the blame rested with themselves. So far they came short of what God intended for them. The Calvinist, believing in a family elected or chosen out of the human race, must set a limit to the persons who receive the sign of the covenant, in consequence of the limit already set to the persons in the covenant. It was one of the vices of Calvinism that it could never distinguish between the conditional and the unconditional. A covenant must be limited to a fixed number of persons, and the promises of its fulfilment on God's part must be absolute. Baptism was to be administered to those in the covenant. But how are they to be known? Believers or persons professing to believe is the nearest approach that we can make. But some children must also be in the covenant. We cannot divide them into believers and unbelievers. The only distinction we can make here is between the children of those who believe and of those who do not believe. Hence the conclusion, that the children of believers are universally to be baptized. To this Tombes answered, that there was no command in Scripture for baptizing any children whatever, that the children of believers were not more holy than the children of unbelievers, that the Gospel covenant was not the same as the covenant with Abraham, and that even in that covenant all the children of Abraham, as his sons by Keturah and his descendants by Ishmael, did not receive the inheritance, even though some, as the sons of Ishmael, received the sign. Baptism, said Tombes, is not to be confounded with any Old Testament rite, nor the Gospel covenant to be interpreted by the terms of any other covenant.

The arguments in detail for baptizing infants were, that baptism is to us what circumcision was to the Jews; that if the sign of the covenant is not given to children, the grace is more restricted under the New Testament than under the old; but the words of the promise are, 'to you and to your seed,' from which promise it is said to follow that infants may be signed with the seal of the covenant. Moreover, St. Paul tells the Corinthians that if one of the parents is a

CHAP. IV.

Arguments for and against Infant Baptism.

believer, then the children are holy. Tombes answers, that baptism did not in all things take the place of circumcision, that if denying the sign of the covenant to children was a restriction of grace under the New Testament, then denying the Lord's Supper was a restriction of grace also, for the Jews gave the passover to children. As to the promise being not only to believers but to their seed, Tombes says that it is their children's on the same conditions that it is theirs. These conditions, as we may learn from the context, are faith and repentance. To be *holy* by covenant was not a sufficient reason for baptism. The *elect* Israelites, Tombes said, who are not yet called to the profession of Christianity, are holy by covenant, but they are not on that account to be baptized. As to St. Paul's argument about the children of believers, he is not speaking of federal holiness, but of what Tombes calls 'matrimonial holiness.' If one parent was an unbeliever and the other a Christian, they were not on that account to dissolve the marriage union, for the children were 'holy,' that is, they were not bastards. The baptism of infants, Tombes said, did not agree with Christ's institution, nor with the practice of John the Baptist and the Apostles of Jesus. Christ's command was to preach the Gospel and then baptize. John the Baptist and the disciples of Jesus preached repentance and baptized believers. Lodovico Vives and Walafridus Strabo are quoted as having proved that infant baptism was not practised in the age succeeding the Apostles. In after times there is some mention of it as resting on an unwritten tradition, or in imitation of Jewish circumcision. It is classed with giving infants the Lord's Supper and other 'human inventions that went under the name of Apostolic traditions.' It has given rise to many other human devices, as sureties, confirmation, confession of faith before receiving the Eucharist, and 'Church covenants,' as they are practised in New England. It has occasioned many errors of doctrine, leading men to believe that it confers grace, that it is regeneration, that only baptized infants are saved, and that the regenerate may fall from grace. It has caused many abuses in discipline, as private baptism, baptism by women, baptism of children before they are born, and of children

Evils arising from Infant Baptism.

whose parentage is uncertain. It occasions many unnecessary disputes, such as those concerning the children of persons excommunicated, apostates, persons who are not members of a gathered Church, or whose ancestors were believers, though their parents were unbelievers. In the dark times of the Papacy, the same men who opposed invoking the saints and other superstitions of Rome, opposed also the baptizing of infants. Those who practise it cannot agree upon the grounds on which they do it, while it defeats the end for which baptism was instituted, which is, that the person baptized thereby declares himself a disciple of Christ.

During the Session of the Westminster Assembly, some of the most eminent members preached every morning at the Abbey Church. They mostly took for their subjects the principal doctrines of Christianity. Stephen Marshall preached a series of sermons on the sacraments. The last was on baptizing children. The preacher began by affirming that this was the practice of the primitive Church. Justin Martyr, who lived in the second century, disputes concerning the different conditions of children, the baptized and the unbaptized. Irenæus, who was contemporary with Justin, says, 'Christ came to save all through Himself, I say, all who through Him are born again unto God,—infants and little children and boys.' By the words 'born again,' the old commentators show that Irenæus, after the example of Christ and His Apostles, meant baptism. Origen, who lived in the beginning of the third century, says, 'The Church received this tradition of baptizing infants from the Apostles.' In his Homily on Leviticus, that same Father says, that, 'according to the custom of the Church,' he grants baptism to be administered to little children,' and again, on Luke xiv., 'Little children are baptized for the remission of their sins.' Gregory Nazianzen calls baptism 'a sign for those entering on the career of life;' afterwards, indeed, he seems to limit it to cases of necessity. Cyprian, in his epistle to Fidus, who denied that infants should be baptized before the eighth day, answers him, that, by the unanimous consent of sixty-six bishops, baptism was to be administered to infants without distinction as to age. This testimony is cited by

Augustine and approved. The same judgment is expressed by Ambrose. The first strenuous opponent of infant baptism, Marshall says, was Baltazar Paccominitanus, in Luther's time. To him succeeded the German Anabaptists, who, like all sectaries after they have departed from the Church, divide again into new sects. This way of speaking of the sects and of the Church was common with the Presbyterians, who did not then expect that there was a time coming when they, too, would be numbered with the sects. But the Baptists were a peculiar thorn to the Presbyterians. They were carrying out, in their way, the old Puritan principle of 'rooting up every plant which the right hand of the Lord had not planted.' They persuaded the people to leave the regular ministry, and not to receive the sacraments at the churches, denouncing all who had not been baptized as they had been, for 'limbs of Antichrist.'

Marshall said much against the Baptists for putting the children of believers in the same condition with the children of Turks and Indians. Either, he argued, they are lost, or they are without original sin and saved in the Pelagian way of universal grace; or, what seemed to be worse still, some of them may be saved that die in infancy, even if children of Turks or Indians. In this last case there is salvation outside of the covenant, where God has not promised it should be found. Such were the alternatives to which, as a Calvinist, he reduced the Calvinistic Baptists. His own position is, that infants of believers are within the covenant of grace. They belong to Christ's body, they are of His kingdom, His family, and they should be signed with the seal of the covenant. It was objected that, under the old law, women did not receive the seal. To this it was answered, that they were circumcised in the males. The covenant of grace has been the same under all dispensations and in all ages. It was the will of God that infants should be admitted to all the external benefits of that covenant before Christ came, and why should their privileges be less now that He is come? The children of believers have the inward grace, why should we deny them the outward sign? The disciples forbade children to be brought to Jesus, just because they were children, too young to receive instruction, but Jesus said, 'Suffer them, for of such is the kingdom of heaven.' The mere want of an express command is not reckoned a sufficient reason for not baptizing children. We have no express command for many things the propriety and moral right of which we never doubt. In the New Testament there is no law concerning the forbidden degrees of marriage, no law against polygamy, no law for keeping the first day of the week as the weekly Sabbath, no law for admitting women to the Lord's Supper, nor for baptizing the children of believers after they have come to mature years. Christ's command to go and 'teach all nations, baptizing them,' was not, Marshall says, the first institution of baptism. It was but the enlargement of the Apostles' commission, which hitherto was confined to the Jews, but is now extended to the Gentiles. Teach first, and then baptize, is the law in the conversion of the heathen; but why should we apply it to the children that are born in the Church, who, as members of a corporation, have the birth privileges of the family of God? The Baptists' argument is that they are unbelievers, and, therefore, they are not to be baptized. Marshall's answer is, that if they are to be classed with unbelievers, they cannot be saved. Let the Baptists admit that infants may be saved, and he will prove, by their own arguments, that they may be baptized.

Tombes took Marshall's sermon for the Assembly's answer to his 'Exercitation.' He replied to it immediately in 'An Examen of the Sermon of Mr. Stephen Marshall.' Supposing, he said, it were true that the baptizing of infants had been in the Church for 1500 years, could not the same be said of Episcopacy, keeping Easter, the religious use of the cross, and some other things,—all of which the Assembly had just laid aside? He reviews the testimonies of the Fathers that had been quoted by Marshall. It was urged, indeed Marshall had admitted, that the treatise quoted as Justin Martyr's was not his. It was not to be denied that it testified to the fact of infant baptism. But then children were not baptized because they were children of believers. They were baptized on account of the faith of those who brought them, and the writer of the treatise, whoever he was, believed that by this baptism they obtained salvation.

As to Irenæus, he wrote in Greek, but we have his works only in a Latin translation. How, then, can we have any certainty of his meaning? After the very passage quoted by Marshall, these words follow: 'Openly affirming the tradition of the Apostles concerning the baptism of infants against Anabaptistical impiety.' Could Irenæus have written this? It is the addition of Feverdentius, 'that impudent monk,' as Rivet calls him, who corrupted the writings of Irenæus. But even if the passage quoted by Marshall is genuine, its reference to baptism depends upon the gloss that it was the custom of the Apostles to call baptism the new birth. Tombes denies that this was a custom of the Apostles; and, moreover, he says that in this place the text and scope of Irenæus show that he was not speaking of baptism. We are in the same condition as to the works of Origen. They were written in Greek, but we have to depend on the Latin version of Ruffinus. Concerning this version, Erasmus said that no man could know whether he was reading Origen or Ruffinus. There are passages against the Pelagians which could only have been put there after the great Pelagian controversy in the time of Augustine. Gregory Nazianzen, indeed, recommended children to be baptized lest they should miss the grace of the sacrament; but he gave it as the opinion of others that they should wait till they were capable of instruction. Cyprian, Tombes admits, is clear for infant baptism. 'He says enough upon it, and more than enough, unless he had spoken to better purpose.' His testimony of sixty-six bishops is called the fountain-head of infant baptism. On him Augustine and Jerome relied for what they called Apostolic tradition. They baptized infants that they might give them saving grace; such was the 'darkness of those that were counted the greatest lights of the world.' Judaism had not yet been weeded out of the Church. Infant baptism was established by the great authority of Augustine. Yet Walafridus Strabo proves, from Augustine's own writings and his own long continuance as a catechumen, that the baptizing of infants was not then the custom of the Church. Petrus Cluniacensis says of Augustine that 'he rejected the authority of the Latin doctors, himself a Latin, ignorant of Greek.' His plea for baptizing children was to wash away their original sin; and in this he found an argument against the Pelagians, who denied original sin. Tombes doubts, however, if Augustine really baptized children, except they were dying, or with a view to cure them of bodily sicknesses. It was certainly, he said, not because they were the children of believers that Augustine baptized them. Nothing of this can be found in the ancient Fathers. It was objected against Augustine, in his own day, that faith should precede baptism as a condition. He proved by the most certain logic that children had faith, for by the sacrament they were made believers.

Tombes expressed his surprise that there should be nothing for infant baptism in Eusebius, Ignatius, Clemens Alexandrinus, Athanasius, or Epiphanius. The questions put to baptized persons proved, he said, that in the Greek Church infant baptism was not common. Then we have some strange facts, which are matters of history. Constantine the Great, though the son of Helena, a Christian queen, was not baptized till he was an old man. Gregory Nazianzen, the son of a Christian bishop, was not baptized till he had reached manhood. Chrysostom, though born of Christian parents, and educated under Miletus, a bishop, was not baptized till he was twenty-one years of age. In 315, the Council of Neocæsarea determined that a pregnant woman might be baptized, because the baptism did not reach the child. From this canon, Balsamon and Zonaras infer that an infant could not be baptized. The Greek Church, says Tombes, rejected the baptism of infants for many hundreds of years. And even in the Latin Church there were opposers of infant baptism before Paccominitanus. In 1030 the great Berengarius, who opposed the corporal presence of Christ in the Eucharist, rejected also the baptizing of young children. In the next century, according to Bernard, it was denied by the Cathari, Albigenses, and other witnesses for truth against the Papacy. It was also reckoned among the heresies of Petrus Cluniacensis.

Marshall and Tombes were both conscious of the value of the testimony of antiquity, yet neither of them rested on this. They were both willing to make it finally a question of Scripture. Marshall's main argument was that the chil-

CHAP. IV.

Baptism delayed in the early Church.

dren were in the covenant, as explained in the promise 'to thee and thy seed.' Tombes said the covenant of grace was not made with the seed of believers. St. Paul's interpretation of the Abrahamic covenant is that God did not justify the seed of Abraham merely because they were his seed. All are not Israel that are of Israel, neither because they are the seed of Abraham are they children.* We have no more certainty concerning God's election of a believer's infant than of a Pagan's infant. That all children are in the same condition would have been admitted by Cyprian's sixty-six bishops, who would have given grace and baptism to them all. God may take children into His covenant without requiring them to be baptized. There is no necessity that all who are in the covenant of grace have the seal of the covenant. They may be in the condition of women under the old law, who were not circumcised actually, nor even, as Marshall says, virtually. But if they were sealed virtually in the males, may not children also have the seal of the covenant virtually in the parents without actual baptism? It is as much will-worship to baptize children under the gospel as to have given women the seal of the covenant under the dispensation of Moses. As a Calvinist to Calvinists, Tombes pressed upon his opponents for applying to all children the promises of the covenant of grace, which are applicable only to the elect. This was done by the Assembly of Divines in the very words which Marshall had used. It was done by them in words still more express when, as conformists of the Church of England, they had subscribed to the service for baptism in the Prayer Book. Their answer was, as they could not distinguish between the elect and the non-elect children, they used charity in their judgment, taking them all for the elect. Tombes asked them how, as believers in the indefectibility of grace, they could speak of children who were not elect as being under the covenant. Could they fall from it? or are we to conclude that they were put there without faith or works, which is pure Antinomianism? The Church of God, Tombes says, is not a corporation into which men are born with birth privileges. It is a kingdom into which its members are chosen by the election of grace.

* Rom. ix. 6, 7.

Marshall replied to Tombes in 'A Defence of Infant Baptism.' The arguments from Scripture were exhausted on both sides. Antiquity alone remained. Infant baptism, Marshall said, had been in the Church for 1500 years, but Episcopacy, in the sense of bishops as a distinct order from presbyters, had not been in the Church for 1500 years. The religious use of the cross is of still later origin. That there was a doubt about the genuineness of the treatise ascribed to Justin Maryr was not denied, but it was certainly very ancient. Tombes did not dispute its testimony to the facts. He only said the reason of baptizing children was not their being in the covenant in virtue of their being children of believers. Irenæus may have been corrupted by Feverdentius, but there are no grounds for believing that the passage in question is not the genuine text. Marshall says he is convinced that it is, because the Greeks usually called baptism a new birth. Vossius, in reference to this very passage, says, that to call baptism regeneration was a form of speech common to the ancients. The doubts which Tombes had raised concerning the testimonies from Origen were equally without foundation. He had no tangible evidence that they were not Origen's. There were, indeed, passages in that treatise against the Pelagian heresy, but that heresy may have existed before Pelagius. Justin Martyr refuted the heresy of the Arians long before Arius was known. All that we can conclude from Gregory Nazianzen is, that infants were baptized in his time, but that he himself recommended delay except when the child was dying. Tertullian persuaded people to delay baptism, yet he intimates that in his time it was the custom to baptize children. Moreover, he speaks of the children of believers as appointed to holiness, though not made *holy* till they were born of water and of the Spirit. The testimonies of Cyprian and Augustine were not questioned.

Tombes had expressed his surprise that, if infant baptism were of such antiquity, there should be nothing of it in Eusebius, Ignatius, Clemens Alexandrinus, Athanasius, and Epiphanius. To this the answer is, that these writers speak of the questions which were agitated in their day. It is no glory to the Baptist that the error of refusing baptism to children was not of such antiquity as to be refuted by these authors. As to Ignatius, if anything were quoted from him, Tombes would certainly dispute it, because of the uncertainty of the text. Clemens Alexandrinus had to deal with heathen. What he has to say about baptism concerns the baptizing of adults converted from Paganism. In Athanasius we have the testimonies which Tombes could not find. He says, 'the dipping of the infant quite under water thrice, and raising of it up again, doth signify the death of Christ and His resurrection on the third day.' Athanasius asks Antiochus how it is to be known that he was truly baptized and received the Holy Ghost when *he was a child*. Again, he says, 'Now your children are holy, it is manifest that the infants of believers which are baptized as unspotted and faithful enter into the kingdom.' Epiphanius says, 'Circumcision had its time until the great circumcision came, that is, the washing of the new birth, as is manifest to every one.' It appears from Balsamon that the same questions which were put to adult believers were also put to children. Marshall will not say that this was done wisely, but he thinks the fact is evident. Tombes mentioned the case of several distinguished men in the early Church who were not baptized in infancy, though their parents were Christians. Marshall answers that baptism was often deferred, and for causes which called forth severe invectives from the Greek Fathers. Sometimes it was done in imitation of Christ, who was not baptized till He was thirty years of age. Sometimes it was deferred that it might be administered by an eminent bishop or in some particular place. More frequently, however, baptism was deferred in the belief that it washed away all sins, but that forgiveness of sins committed after baptism was not so easily obtained. It was common to say, even of a notorious sinner, 'Let him do what he likes; he is not baptized.' Constantine deferred his baptism that he might be baptized in the Jordan. It is not proved that his mother was a Christian when he was born. Gregory Nazianzen was sent to Athens to be educated in the schools of the Pagans, which does not look as if his parents were Christians. The ecclesiastical historian says that they were of a high family of Antioch; he calls them 'Hellenes,' but does not say a word of their religion. The case of baptizing the woman with child mentioned by Balsamon, and the decision of the Neocæsarean Council, Marshall explains as the case of a woman converted from Paganism, whose child was not yet born. Our case is that of the children of women who are believers. Balsamon makes a distinction between infants unborn for whom no man can be surety in baptism, and infants after they are born. In his gloss on that canon, he relates a story of children coming from a Christian country who were taken by Scythians and sold to the Romans. The question was raised if these children had been baptized. Some argued that they must have been, as they came from a Christian country. Others recommended baptizing them, because of the want of positive evidence that they had been baptized. On both sides the custom of infant baptism is evidently implied. The Council of Carthage pronounced an anathema against those who refused baptism to new-born infants, and Photius quotes an Imperial constitution, in which it is appointed that all baptized Samaritans and Greeks should be punished if they did not bring their wives and their children to holy baptism. As to the Berengarians, Waldenses, Poor Men of Lyons, Albigenses, Catharists, and Peter Brusians, Marshall denies that they opposed the baptism of infants. This was a charge made by their enemies, the foundation of which was that they opposed the notion of grace coming through the sacraments *ex opere operato* as taught in the Church of Rome.

Tombes was removed from London to Bewdley, in Herefordshire. In 1649 he had a public disputation on infant baptism with Richard Baxter, who was then at Kidderminster. The substance of what Baxter said was afterwards published in his 'Plain Scripture Proof of Infant Church Membership and Baptism.' Baxter quoted all the Fathers that had been quoted by Marshall, adding the case of Hyginus, Bishop of Rome, who lived about the year 137. He was the fourth bishop before Irenæus, and must have been contemporary with Polycarp, who was a disciple of St. John. Hyginus first ordained godfathers and godmothers at the baptizing of infants. It is impossible, Baxter says, that these men, who lived so near the time of the Apostles, could have been ignorant of what was the custom in the Apostles' days. All antiquity, he says, firmly held that believers' infants received remission of sins by Christian baptism.

Baxter challenges Tombes to name one man who was against infant church-membership, from the creation till about five hundred years ago. It was the law of the old dispensation, and if Christ changed the law, it is surely strange that there is not a word in the Scriptures about the change. There was no necessity for a command to baptize infants. The right of infants to church-membership stood unrepealed. The point of baptizing infants, Baxter says, is in itself of comparatively little moment, but not so the grounds on which it rests. It is to deny them any part in the covenant of grace, unless, like the Antinomians, we confound that covenant with God's election. It is to deny the interest which parents have in their children to make a covenant in their behalf. It is to call that common which God has made holy. The Baptists, according to Baxter, set up a new model for the visible Church. They forbid little children to be brought to Christ, and as they deny them entrance into the visible Church, they leave but little hope of their being admitted to the invisible. Infants are Christ's disciples *de jure*, as a king is a king before he is crowned. Christ's command was that persons should be baptized as soon as they were disciples. It is therefore sinful to defer the baptism of young children. Baxter said that the Baptists broke the sixth commandment when they baptized in cold weather, and the seventh when the subjects of baptism were without clothing. Anabaptistry he regarded as the opening of the flood-gates of licentiousness. He never knew the meaning of 'heresy and schism till the rise of the Anabaptists. With them originate all horrid opinions, and from them begin all manner of Separatists, Antinomians, Arminians, Socinians, Libertines, Seekers, and Familists.'

To the 'Plain Proof for Infant Church-membership,' Baxter added an Appendix, which regarded another controversy inseparably connected with infant baptism. It was always a question but vaguely answered, what is the real benefit which children receive from baptism? The Calvinists said that as children of believers they were already in the covenant; to give them the seal could not benefit those who were not elect; and, strictly speaking, it could add nothing to the security of those who were elect. The usual answer was, that to elect infants baptism conveyed grace, but as to the non-elect, we used the language of charity. This was the general answer, but it took various forms. Thomas Bedford, a friend of Baxter's, and a neighbouring minister, had come to the conclusion that in every case baptism conveyed saving grace to infants. At first he had taken up the belief that a sacrament was a visible sign, a word to the eye, as preaching was a word to the ear. He read Dr. Burges on regeneration, and was convinced that in baptism grace was actually conferred on elect infants. Meeting afterwards with what Davenant and Ward said on that subject, he found no necessity for restraining the efficacy of grace to the elect. A man not predetermined to salvation may have ordination to eternal life for a time. Falling away from this grace is not the apostasy of saints. According to Davenant, the first grace given was the remission of original sin. Out of this proceeded regeneration, justification, and adoption. During the condition of infancy it was a state of salvation. But this regeneration, justification, and adoption were not the same as the regeneration, justification, and adoption that afterwards came by faith. Bedford did not see the necessity of having two regenerations, one for those who died in infancy, and one for the children who lived and believed. He thought it better to settle the matter at once in the ordinance, and say that every child was really regenerated, that is, made actually holy, and endowed with the new heart which God promises His elect. Baxter answered, that if the new heart was given to all, then all must be saved. Bedford, as a Calvinist, would be compelled to admit this, but he preferred saying that the *new heart* or actual holiness is given to many who are never actually saved. Baxter said that baptism did not confer the grace of the absolute covenant. Its benefits are, that it is the seal of the covenant whereby God engages,

CHAP. IV.

Regeneration in Baptism.

CHAP. IV.

Dr. Featly's 'Dippers Dipt.'

Jeremy Taylor on Infant Baptism.

on the fulfilment of certain conditions, to give men forgiveness of sins. It is a moral instrument, rather than a physical, and conveys the means of obtaining the grace of salvation, rather than the actual grace itself.

The year preceding the controversy between Tombes and Marshall, Dr. Featly, who had been Rector of Lambeth, published 'The Dippers Dipt; or, the Anabaptists Ducked and Plunged over Head and Ears.' Dr. Featly was one of the divines appointed to meet in the Assembly of Westminster. He had been chaplain to Archbishop Abbot, and was willing to promote the reforms suggested by Archbishop Ussher. After the bishops and their supporters withdrew from the Assembly, Featly remained, but soon after he was imprisoned for reporting their proceedings. He was a Calvinist in doctrine, and retained the old Church of England veneration for Calvin, whom he called 'the bright burning taper of Geneva.' His book contained an account of a disputation which he had with some Baptists in Southwark, and a history of the various sects of Anabaptists in Germany. The arguments for infant baptism are the same as Marshall's. He denied the necessity of dipping, arguing from the meaning of the word *baptize*.*

In 1651, when the Baptists had become a sect of some importance, Jeremy Taylor, in his retreat in Wales, published 'A Discourse of Baptism,' to help, as he said, the solution of the question 'by which the ark of the Church was violently shaken.' The first part treated of the institution and efficacy of baptism. The second was 'A consideration of the practice of the Church in Baptizing Infants of Believing Parents, and the Practice justified.' Taylor, as an Arminian, was not under any necessity to limit baptism to the children of believing parents. Yet he is content to carry the argument no further than this. They are the children of the Church,

---

* Featly's book has some curious pictures of men *in puris naturalibus*, and 'virgins of Sion' undergoing the process of dipping, with representations of fifteen kinds of Anabaptists. It was written in Peter's House prison. Such was his zeal against the Anabaptists, that though himself in prison, he pleaded that these wicked sectaries should be put down by the civil magistrate. He says that the German Anabaptists had *spiritual marriages* of many wives, with whom they committed adultery and incest. This expression *spiritual marriages* is also in Sleidan's 'Commentaries,' where he speaks of German Anabaptists.

and, therefore, not less capable of being in covenant with God than the children of the Jews. He dwells chiefly on the great importance of baptism, untouched by the difficulty which perplexed the Calvinist about the non-elect children. If they are baptized they are saved, for the new birth comes by the descent of the Holy Ghost in baptism. It is not broadly stated that the unbaptized are lost, yet the argument points to this inference. Nature, says Taylor, cannot bring us to heaven. Grace alone can do that, and this grace we have in baptism. Infants have the punishment of sin, and, therefore, sin is imputed to them. By baptism comes sanctification. 'Except a man be born of water and of the Spirit, he cannot enter into the kingdom of heaven,' is true also, Taylor says, of young children. Baptism is the means which God has appointed for the salvation of infants, and for us to neglect to baptize them is to neglect their salvation.*

CHAP. IV.

Children saved by Baptism.

* The Baptist controversy, dating it from 1642 and ending it in 1674, consists of a very large number of tracts and sermons on both sides. 'A Treatise of the Vanity of Childish-Baptizing, by A. R., 1642,' was answered by Dr. Featly in the 'Dippers Dipt.' The argument was addressed to the clergy of the Church of England, asking how, as Calvinists, they could pronounce children regenerated in baptism, and then, perhaps, twenty years after, beseech them to be converted, as if those once-made 'members of Christ' could afterwards become 'limbs of the devil.' The author said that the clergy had to make strange shifts to maintain this, and yet defend themselves against the charge of Arminianism. Samuel Richardson and Henry Denne replied to Featly. Denne was in prison in 'Lord Peter's house' at the same time as Featly. He asks if Dr. Featly could say of his parishioners in Lambeth, or Mr. Marshall of his in Finchingfield, that they were believers, and so their children entitled to believers' baptism. He spoke of the Church, in Luther's day, as having travailed to bring forth the doctrine of justification, and now he said it was in birth of the doctrine of water-baptism. Nathanael Homes and John Geree wrote against Tombes. John Spilsberie and Christopher Blackwood wrote on Tombes' side, and were answered by Thomas Blake and others. In 1674, Henry Danvers wrote a treatise in defence of the Baptist doctrines, which was chiefly collected out of Tombes. He said that infant baptism was not practised for the three first centuries, and was not enjoined till four hundred years after Christ. It was first decreed by the Melevitan Council in the fifth century. Danvers also said that Adrian, Bishop of Corinth, in the seventh century, was accused by a Bishop of Rome of refusing to baptize infants; that Cresconius opposed Augustine on this question, that the Donatists did not practise infant baptism, and that it was not approved of by Hincmar, Bishop of Laudau, and Peter Abelard the Schoolman. Danvers was answered by Obadiah Wills, who found him not too correct in matters of history.

Many of the Baptists in the seventeenth century took up wild doctrines, and several of them were Fifth Monarchy men. Dr. Evans speaks of some who argued from Heb. v. 12, 13, that laying on of hands was a part of baptism, and that, unless the minister put his hands on the head of the persons baptized at the time of the ceremony, they were not babes in Christ. Even this led to a division; those who had been baptized with the laying on of hands refused to hold

CHAP. IV.

The sects not tolerated.

The Presbyterians, Independents, and Baptists were the three tolerated sects during the Long Parliament and the Protectorate of Cromwell. But there were other sects which were not tolerated. Some of these had just sprung into being, and others that had been carefully suppressed, rose again with renewed strength. We set aside at once the exaggerated accounts of these sects given by such Presbyterian writers as Edwards, in his 'Gangræna,' and Ephraim Pagitt in his 'Heresiography.' We also set aside Richard Baxter's classification, which makes a sect of the disciples of Harry Vane, and another of the followers of Peter Sterry.* Ranters and Seekers† must also be struck out from the list of sects. Either they never existed, or these were names applied to parties otherwise named.

The Family of Love.

Of these sects, the least known, the most remarkable, and the most maligned was the Family of Love. In 1580, Queen Elizabeth issued a proclamation against them, commanding the clergy to give all assistance to the archbishops and bishops for their suppression. Search was to be made for their books that they might be burnt, and all persons found possessing these books after this proclamation were to be imprisoned. They are described as a dangerous sect, because it is one of their principles, that before a magistrate they will deny anything when the denial is an advantage to them.

---

communion with those who had merely been dipped. Vavasour Powell, 'the apostle of Wales,' one of the *Tryers*, always laid on his hands when he baptized, and when he visited the sick he anointed them with oil. Henry Denne is mentioned by Edwards in the 'Gangræna.' He was an Arminian, and therefore not a *tolerated* Baptist. He said that Christ died for all, Judas as well as Peter, which, in those days, was a fearful heresy. He often preached in the isle of Ely, 'an island,' Edwards says, 'full of errors and seditions.' He was to preach one day at St. Ives, but 'the Committee gave order against it, and being not suffered, he went to a churchyard not far off that place, and, under an ewe-tree, he preached, many following him, and shook off the dust of his feet against St. Ives.'

* On the Vanites and Sterryites Baxter made the poor pun of *Vanity and Sterility.*

† John Goodwin describes the Seekers as 'A generation who think they do God a most choice service in overlooking all that is written, upon pretence of looking after somewhat higher, more mysterious, and sacred, —as if God, who hath spoken by His Son, were yet to reveal something of greater import.'—*Cata-Baptism.*

Richard Baxter says, 'They taught that our Scripture was uncertain; that present miracles are necessary to faith; that our ministry is null and without authority, and our worship and ordinances unnecessary or vain, the true Church, ministry, Scripture, and ordinance being lost; for which they are now seeking.'

The Family of Love was not indigenous to England. They were properly a species of Anabaptists, originally imported from Holland. They began with Henry Nicholas, of Amsterdam. The name of the sect always suggested the transition from heavenly love to earthly, and it was generally said that the leaders of the sect were more under the influence of the latter than the former. But this is not the account which is given in their books. After the death of Henry Nicholas, Tobias, 'a Fellow Elder in the Household of Love,' wrote 'Mirabilia Opera Dei; Certain Wonderful Works of God which happened to H. N., even from his youth, and how the God of Heaven hath united Himself with him, and raised up His gracious word in him, and how He hath chosen and sent him to be a minister of His gracious word.' The story in this book is simple, yet full of strange religious interest. Henry Nicholas was the child of devout Roman Catholic parents. In the eighth year of his age, the same year in which Maximilian was made Roman Emperor, the father of Henry Nicholas was one evening exhorting his family to give thanks to God for His wonderful grace. 'What grace?' the son asked. He was answered, 'The sufferings of Christ as set forth daily in the service of the Mass.' The son answered that he knew that, but if Christ had died to make us righteous, why were we not righteous? If Christ died to restore us, why is there no evidence of restoration? His father told him that he must not dig deep into the works of God. The next time that the elder Nicholas went to confession he took his son Henry with him, who told the priest what he had said to his father about the need of a righteousness within us. The priest said that the boy had 'strange whimsies in his head.' He recommended the father to chastise him, and drive away such madness. Henry begged of the priest not to speak such words. He was anxious to learn, anxious to understand the meaning of what he was taught. The priest was pleased with his quiet manner, and allowed a further conversation, when Henry told him that we had not understood the necessity of being righteous; 'we had not yet followed Christ in His Passover to His Father,' and until this were done, sin and death should have dominion over us.

CHAP. IV.

Henry Nicholas.

The priest did not know what to answer. He consulted another priest, who spoke of the child's foolishness. This priest told Henry that he had committed wellnigh one of the greatest sins. He had searched and digged into the secrets of God, and he feared the punishment would be hellfire. The child cried, 'Oh that I and all men might be forgiven our sins!' He never again spoke of the subject till he had reached years of maturity. He kept his thoughts to himself, but devoutly attended the Mass, and became an intense lover of the services and ceremonies of the Roman Catholic Church.

Henry Nicholas made one with the Deity.

Soon after this Henry had a strange dream. He saw a great mountain, which surrounded him on every side. The mountain was covered with resplendent light, and he was illuminated with its glory. Then it dissolved its being into his being. This was the completion of righteousness within him. He was made one with God. It was then revealed to him that he had many fellow-servants upon the earth. In the thirty-ninth year of his age he had further and more open revelations. God's love was revealed to him as he had never felt it before. He was called to the service of a minister or preacher of this love, and it was told him that 'the Lord had prepared and ordained for his assistance Daniel Eldad and Tobias.' These continued always with him. Soon after this revelation they were warned to leave that place, that they might escape from bloodthirsty men. They went into the land of the East, and dwelt in a city called Pietas. This seems a mystical journey, in which they lose Henry Nicholas. The disciples are called to a pilgrimage, which also seems to be an allegory. They travelled forty-nine days, eating no kind of food or creature that had life, and drinking no wine or strong drink, but endeavouring to fulfil the will of the Lord in all righteousness. For the first six days they travelled with joyful minds, and on the sixth they came 'to the view of the land of uprightness, in which they saw, as in a glass, the righteousness in which man was created.' In the same glass they saw the hatefulness of sin, and continually hungering and thirsting after righteousness, they were more and more conformed to it day by day. They were tempted with all manner of things that the flesh lusted after, but they lived in fasting and self-denial. In the celebration of the Lord's Supper the bread became the very body of Christ. They were united to Christ and made one with Him, as a bride is united to the bridegroom. One day in their journey, there came a still soft voice by which they were enlightened in Christ. They participated in the living Godhead of the Son. God gave them ordinances, as He gave to Moses in Horeb. They were made members and priests of the Family of Love.

Henry Nicholas and his disciples professed that they were specially called by God to introduce a new era in the Church. They did not form a sect but a society. They conformed to the established religion wherever they sojourned. Their business was to teach the love of God to man, and that all men should love each other. Now was to begin the reign of the Spirit of love, when men were to be in actual possession of that righteousness which in other ages was spoken of but not realized. It is said that the Familists were a sect of Anabaptists, but it is uncertain if they observed sacraments at all, or if they attached any importance to external ordinances. The baptism for which they looked was a baptism of the Spirit, and the Supper they commemorated was a communion of the Holy Ghost. The letter was of no value to them compared with the Spirit. The literal is so little noticed, or so frequently turned into a spiritual meaning, that it has been supposed they even denied the historical statements of the New Testament. The crucifixion of Christ was the crucifying of the old man; the resurrection, our rising to newness of life; and Christ returning to judgment, our governing the natural man with righteousness and equity. Angels and devils are explained as good and bad men with their virtues and vices. The seven devils which possessed Mary Magdalene were the seven deadly sins.*

---

* The books of Henry Nicholas, translated from Base-Almagne, are in the British Museum. They are called 'Terra Pacis, a True Testimony of the Spiritual Law of Peace;' 'Comœdia, a work in Ryme;' 'The Prophecy of the Spirit of Love;' 'Evangelium Regni, a Joyful Message of the Kingdom of God;' 'The Proverbs of H. N.' There is no doubt that Nicholas claimed to be sent from God in the same sense as Moses and Jesus, but there is no ground for believing the charges of impiety and immorality that were brought against the sect.

CHAP. IV.

Rise of the Quakers.

During this period another sect arose, whose principles have some affinity with those of the Family of Love. This was and is a purely English sect, yet its origin was due to causes similar to those which produced the doctrines of the Familists. Henry Nicholas and his disciples were led to the rejection of external ordinances by the undue importance attached to their literal observance. George Fox and his disciples sprang from a similar recoil against mere ceremonial, which had reached its climax in the Baptist disputes about the necessity of baptism. The Quakers are logically descended from the Baptists. They protested against the old leaven of literalism which was manifested in John Smyth when he re-baptized himself. The steeple-houses, against which George Fox cried out as temples of idol worshippers, were the churches of England when in possession of Presbyterians, Independents, and Baptists, and the doctrines of these sects were the doctrines which he opposed with all the vehemence of an old Hebrew prophet raising his trumpet voice against the servants of Baal. They had cast down Laud and his priests. They had rejected them and their pretensions to be channels of grace and conduit pipes of the Divine favour, but these sects were still clinging to the dead letter of a book. They were still trusting in ordinances, to some extent unconscious how much they were retaining of what they really supposed they had rejected when they put down the bishops. The church was their idol temple, and the Bible the idol which they worshipped. 'We have a *sure word* of prophecy,' said the minister of the church at Nottingham: 'it is the Scriptures by which all doctrines, religion, and opinions are to be tried.' George Fox was present. The spirit within him could not be restrained. He cried out, 'It was not the Scriptures, but the Holy Spirit by which holy men of God gave forth the Scriptures, whereby opinions, religion, and judgments are to be tried.' That Spirit, he said, leads into all truth. The Jews had the Scriptures, and yet resisted the Holy Ghost. They rejected the 'bright and morning Star,' and persecuted Him and His disciples. They professed to try their doctrines by the Scriptures, but they did not try them aright, because they did it without the Spirit of God.

This error of trusting to the mere letter of the Bible, Fox CHAP. IV. detected in every detail of belief and practice. There might be external worship in the Church; there might be preaching, sacraments, sacrifices, but what are these if there is no Spirit in them? God dwells not in temples made with hands. It is not the water baptism which saves, but the answer of a good conscience. It is not ceremonies which justify, nor even belief in an external Christ. It is Christ within, who is to us both justification and sanctification. The Quakers may have erred in refusing to worship in a church, or to celebrate the sacraments of the gospel, but their error was generated by an error in another direction. Theirs was a battle for the reality against the shadow, for the substance at the expense of the form, for the law in its spirit even at the risk of sacrificing the law in the letter. The Quaker was the only thorough opponent of the Churchman of Laud's school. The principle of that school was to take care of the external body or form of the Church, for in so doing we take care of the life of the Church. The Quaker said, let us make sure of the life or spirit, and the body or form will take care of itself.*

From the translations made at this time of Jacob Böhme's writings we may conclude that he had many readers, probably, disciples, in England. But it is difficult to determine with certainty if his followers in England could be definitely marked off from some other sects which resembled

---

* It is not to be denied that the Quakers at their beginning were extravagant. Richard Baxter says, 'The Quakers, when I go along London streets, say, Alas! poor man, thou art yet in darkness. They have oft come into the congregation, when I had liberty to preach Christ's Gospel, and cried out against me as a deceiver of the people. They have followed me home, crying out in the streets, The day of the Lord is coming, when thou shalt perish as a deceiver. They have stood in the market-place, and under my window, year after year, crying out to the people "Take heed of your priests, they deceive your souls!" and if they saw any one wear a lace or a neat clothing, they cried out to me, "These are the fruits of thy ministry!" If they spoke to me with the greatest ignorance or nonsense, it was with as much fury and rage as if a bloody heart had opened in their faces. So that though I never hurt, or occasioned the hurt of one of them, that I knew of, their tremulent countenances told me what they would have done had I been in their power.' Those who know the peaceful Quaker of the present day, would say that Horace was wrong when he wrote:—

'Neque imbellem feroces
Progenerant aquilæ columbam.'
Baxter says that the Quakers were but the old Ranters 'turned from horrid profanity and blasphemy to a life of extreme austerity on the other side.'

them. Under the vague names of Ranters, Seekers, Familists, and Behmenists were included many persons who did not form distinct sects.* Among these we may include the Rosicrucians, whose doctrines were expounded by Robert Fludd, Doctor of Medicine. In his 'Mosaical Philosophy' Fludd enters upon a long argument to prove that the Bible explains the philosophy of the universe. This philosophy is properly theology, and therefore to be distinguished from that philosophy which begins from a knowledge of the material world. In other words, theology is *à priori*, and philosophy *à posteriori*. They meet finally and bear to each other a mutual testimony. But without the Scriptures, which are inspired by God, and are to us, so to speak, the finger of God, we could never penetrate into the centre and essence of being. The old poetical image found in Plato is received as probably true, that nature is a chain, the highest and last link of which is fastened to the foot of Jupiter's throne in heaven, while the lowest is fixed on earth. If such is the labyrinth of being, how could we, whose souls tabernacle in clay, penetrate to the resplendent essence of that Being whose centre is everywhere, His circumference nowhere? It is only because God has revealed Himself that we can explain the mysteries of the Creator or the creature.

There is but one universe, and with this universe God is one; but we must speak of God and the world, for they are yet distinct, and though but one world or universe we must speak of the world which is aerial and that which is temporal. The first has neither beginning nor end. The last has both a beginning and an end. But the aerial or angelical, which is the dwelling of the angels and blessed spirits, had a beginning, but will have no end. The angelical world is the intermediary between the eternal and the tem-

---

* The Behmenists, or disciples of Jacob Böhme, were chiefly represented in England by Dr. Pordage, Rector of Bradfield. He was charged before the Ministers' Committee with teaching many wild things which had no proper connection with the doctrines of Böhme. The whole of the proceedings against him, with his defence, were written by Christopher Fowler, the minister of Reading. Pordage said that he had communion with angels, and that he could know good or bad spirits by sight or smell. Richard Baxter says that he and his family, by which he seems to mean those of the same belief, lived together in communion.

poral. It is imaged by Jacob's ladder, which unites earth and heaven. From the eternal these angels pass to the temporal. Then these worlds, being one universe, are, as it were, a wheel within a wheel. The central mover, or eternal Spirit, is in the aerial. By it the temporal is quickened, so that, as the Scriptures say, God is all in all. This, Fludd maintains, is the true Christian philosophy. He is to demonstrate it, not only by the Bible, but by natural reason and by ocular demonstration. He is ' to confound infidelity, and turn men from Ethnic philosophy to the wisdom of God.' It is not easy to understand the ' ocular demonstration,' which seems to be simply that, as a weather-glass is full of air, and is rarified or condensed by the presence or absence of the sun, so the universe is full of spirit differently modified in different places and at different times. God, or Christ, who is the wisdom of God, is said to fill all. This had been explained by some as filling all virtually but not essentially. To which Fludd answered, that where Christ is virtually he must be essentially. All the passages of Scripture which are capable of what we may call a Pantheistic meaning are quoted and interpreted as teaching the immediate presence of God in all nature. Spirit is the catholic element of the universe. It is invoked by the prophet to come from the four winds, and vivify the dead bones. It is the breath which makes frost and snow; as it is said in Job, when God bloweth from the north the ice is made. It is God that thundereth,—that rolleth the thick clouds, and maketh the cedars of Libanus to bend. The philosophy of the Bible is put in opposition to the philosophy of the Heathen. But by Ethnic philosophy Fludd means the doctrine that God only works in the world by second causes, which at last he declares to have been the doctrine of Aristotle and his followers, but not of Plato, Empedocles, and Heraclitus.

Another sect which attained some notoriety in the middle of the seventeenth century was the Muggletonians. The story of Lodowick Muggleton has some resemblance to that of Henry Nicholas. He was born in Bishopsgate, of poor parents. His mother died when he was a child. At an early age he was apprenticed to a tailor. This man was not religious, but some pious Puritans frequented the shop, and when young Lodowick heard them reproached with scoffs and sneers he felt in himself that these men were better than those who reproached them. He was sober, honest, and had a very tender conscience. He sacrificed fair prospects in life because he refused to sanction the lawfulness of lending money on pawns.* His religious feelings became deeper after this early sacrifice, and, meeting with John Reeve, a man of like spirit with himself, they believed that God had commissioned them to be the 'Two Witnesses' of the Apocalypse. They addressed their books to Oliver Cromwell as messages from the 'Lord Protector of Heaven' to the Lord Protector of England.† There had been, they said, three commissions,—one by Moses and the Prophets, one by Christ and His Apostles, and one by John Reeve and Lodowick Muggleton. The giving of one commission implied the taking away of the one preceding it, so the law and the gospel gave place to the dispensation of the Spirit. All worship was to cease except spiritual worship, and the sum of all knowledge was to be the knowledge of 'the true God and the right Devil.'

The 'Two Witnesses' were zealous in advocating the personality of God, in opposition to the Behmenists. They denied that God was an impersonal, formless spirit. They called those utterly dark who said that God's essence was pure reason. They identified body with person, affirming that if God had not a body He could not be a person. It was the one personal God who took flesh, and was known on earth as God the Son. The addition of the two persons to the one personal Deity was the work of Antichrist. With Jacob Böhme's speculations on the being of God before them, the 'Two Witnesses' were careful to distinguish between the essence of the creature and that of the creation;

---

* The story is, that Lodowick lodged with a woman in Houndsditch who, in addition to tailoring, did a small business as a pawnbroker. The woman had a daughter to whom Lodowick was to be married, but one condition of the marriage was that he should continue the mother's business. The refusal from conscience to do this led to a separation.

† The collected works of Reeve and Muggleton were published by subscription in 1836, in three volumes. There were forty-seven subscribers, who were probably all Muggletonians. The editor presented a copy to the British Museum.

THE FIFTH MONARCHY MEN. 243

Yet there were points on which they agreed with the mystics. The substance of earth and water was, they said, eternally in the presence of God. Darkness, death, and hell lay secretly hid in the earth. They had learned that the word *create* did not signify to make out of nothing. Dead matter must be eternal, for it could never proceed from the mouth of Him who is life and light. The 'Witnesses,' like the Quakers, did not fail to make their solemn protest against the idolatry of the Bible. It was a proof, they said, that they who worshipped the records instead of the Spirit which gave the records, had not the Spirit. These were, indeed, able to make men wise unto salvation, but only those men who had the light of the Spirit to understand the mind of God. Unfortunately for their own credit of being taught by the Spirit, the 'Witnesses' declared that they received it from heaven that the sun and moon were not much larger than they appeared to our eyes. The knowledge of the 'right devil,' which was an important part of true knowledge, was to know that there is no other devil but the evil that is in men's hearts. The 'Witnesses' believed in election in the Calvinistic sense, but they charitably excepted children from the number of the reprobates.*

The Fifth Monarchy Men formed another sect, of whom we often read, especially in Cromwell's time. It does not appear, however, that they were more than a party of Millenarians, who interpreted the prophecies concerning the personal reign of Christ in a way that was not flattering to the Lord Protector. They took their name from designating the Messianic reign as the fifth monarchy. The last of the four monarchies of Daniel was the Roman. It was represented by the fourth beast, which had ten horns, and among these horns came up *a little horn* previous to the final destruction of the empire, and just before the introduction of the millennial reign. Was not Oliver this 'little horn'?

---

* In 1695, the Rev. H. Maurice wrote to the Archbishop of York (Sharp) an account of John Mason, Minister of Water Stratford, who had been under some hallucination even wilder than Muggleton's. He gave out that he was Elias. He had 'two witnesses' to bear testimony. He said that Christ had appeared to him and told him that he would not die till the second advent, which would take place at Water Stratford.

CHAP. IV.

John Tillinghast.

The Fifth Monarchy Men did not hesitate to call him a usurper, and to pronounce him the last of Christ's enemies, whose usurpation of government was the only hindrance to the reign of Christ. The most prominent of the Fifth Monarchy Men seem to have been of the Baptist sects, especially those of the Baptists whose views were kindred with the views of the Anabaptists of Germany. But Millenarianism took many forms. It was part of the creed of John Milton, and it was the subject of the learned dissertations of Joseph Mede. It embraced those who said King Charles I. was 'the little horn,' and those who expected Christ to reign in the person of Charles II. There is a 'Narrative of the Sufferings of Fifth Monarchy Men,' who were apprehended at a meeting in Coleman Street, 'while old John Canne was preaching.' In the writings of John Tillinghast it is said that in Cromwell's time the prisons were full of them. Tillinghast was the minister of Trunch, in Norfolk. He had embraced the Millenarian doctrines with some ardour, and had gained considerable notoriety in London as a preacher of them. He left his living in Norfolk partly that he might have more time to proclaim the nearness of the advent, and partly that he might visit and comfort those who were in prison for the faith which he was to preach. His death followed soon after his arrival in London. His sermons, which are in no way remarkable,* were published after his death, with a preface by Charles Feake, from 'his watch-tower in Windsor Castle.' This was the second time that Feake had been imprisoned by Cromwell. On the day when Cromwell was proclaimed, Feake preached on 'the little horn.' He did not apply the prophecy to the Protector, but it was supposed that he intimated this without saying it. Cromwell examined Feake about his sermon. Feake denied that he had made that application of the little horn. He did not

---

* A book with the following title is advertised at the end of the contents, as if written by Tillinghast :—

'Romæ Ruina Finalis, Anno Dom. 1666. Or a treatise wherein is clearly demonstrated that the Pope is Antichrist, and that Babylon the City, or Rome, shall be utterly destroyed and laid in ashes in the year 1666. And that the Turk shall shortly afterwards be destroyed by fire from heaven; presently after which will be the second coming of Christ, and general resurrection. (Sold by Sherley, at the Pellican, in Little Britain.)'

then know to whom it was applicable; but now that Cromwell had become 'a persecutor of the saints,' the meaning of the prophecy was plain. Cromwell was 'the little horn,' who was to oppress the saints. Feake was confident that the kingdoms of this world were near their end. The sand-glass was almost run. 'Our David' was about to appear, and day by day the hosts would run to Him, and take the kingdom from Saul, giving it to Him whose right is is. 'With what consternation of mind,' says Feake, 'will the proud Nimrods of the world flee before the Lamb and His followers, when the mighty hunters themselves shall be hunted from mountain to hill by the little handful of those who are redeemed from the earth! And whither will ye run for shelter, O ye tyrants? Who shall be your *Lord Protector* in the day when Jehovah's fury shall be poured out like fire? And if the rocks are thrown down by Him, what shall become of the reeds? If the sons of ancient kings be hurried out of the world to their own place for their oppression and persecution, for their contempt of God's word and His works, what shall be the portion of the *new monarchical tyrants* who are but of yesterday, and have not had time to take root on the earth, neither shall ever be able to confirm or establish their dominion?'

Among the men who at this time singly represented some special doctrines, we may include John Bidle. He may fairly be regarded as the first of the English Unitarians, though as a sect they can scarcely be said to have existed till towards the end of the next century. Bidle had the misfortune to be imprisoned for his opinions, under the Long Parliament, under Cromwell, and again under Charles II. In 1644 he was master of Crisp's Grammar School, in the city of Gloucester. He had been led, he said, 'by diligently reading the Scriptures,' after 'imploring divine illumination,' to doubt the received doctrines concerning the divinity of the third person in the Trinity. He allowed his doubts to be known, and was charged before the magistrates with heresy. His views were not yet matured. He made a confession of his faith, in which he maintained the unity of God, and the divinity of Jesus Christ not as a distinct person, but as united to 'the only person of the Infinite

Almighty Essence.' This 'confession' did not satisfy the magistrates. When Bidle had further considered the different senses of the word 'person,' he acknowledged three persons in the Trinity. But while he admitted this, he wrote against the divinity of the third person. Parliament appointed a committee to examine him. He appeared before the Assembly of Divines, who censured his books, and procured from Parliament an ordinance that all persons who were unsound as to the doctrine of the Trinity, be put to death. This was in 1648. Before any sentence was executed on Bidle, the power both of the Assembly and of that Parliament had passed away.

Bidle's tracts are collected into one volume, under the title of 'The Apostolical and True Opinion concerning the Holy Trinity Revived and Asserted.' This is done by 'XII. Arguments,' 'A Confession of Faith,' and 'Testimonies of the Fathers and Others.' There is prefixed 'A Letter written to Sir H. V., a Member of the Honourable House of Commons.' Sir H. V. was probably Sir Harry Vane. Bidle beseeches him either to procure his discharge, or to have his cause determined. He had been urged to declare his judgment concerning the Divinity of Jesus Christ, but that, he said, was a question which he had not yet sufficiently studied. He states his belief concerning the Holy Spirit, offering to bring for his opinions many solid proofs out of the Holy Scriptures. He calls the Holy Spirit the chief of all the ministering spirits, in the same way that Satan is the chief spirit among the devils. Along with the other passages from the Scriptures, he quotes one from the Septuagint version of the Psalms: 'Uphold me with thy principal spirit.' He describes the orthodox Trinitarians as deluding themselves with personalities, moods, subsistences, and such like brain-sick notions, which are without 'sap or sense.' These notions, he says, were 'first hatched by the subtlety of Satan in the heads of Platonists to prevent the worship of the true God.' The 'XII. Arguments' are made up of those passages in the Scriptures which speak of the Holy Spirit as a being distinct from God. Jehovah gave the Holy Spirit to the Israelites. The Holy Spirit speaketh not of himself, but heareth from another what he shall speak. He is sent by another. He is the gift of God. Men who have not believed in the Holy Spirit have yet been believers in God. The Holy Spirit changes place, and is therefore not present in all places. He has understanding and will distinct from God. He maketh intercession according to the Divine will. In the 'Confession of Faith' Bidle declares his doctrine concerning the Deity of the Son, as well as concerning the personality of the Spirit. He lays down a view of the Trinity which, he says, is the same as St. Peter's. There is first God, who alone is God. Then there is one 'chief Son, or spiritual, heavenly, and perpetual Lord and King set over the Church of God.' The third person is the Holy Spirit, the gift of God. Jesus Christ was born of the Virgin Mary by a miraculous birth. Had he been the eternal God, it could not have been said that that which was conceived in Mary was *of the Holy Ghost*. He was a 'man approved of God by miracles,' and exalted to be both 'Lord and Christ.' His name is 'Wonderful' by reason of His exaltation. He is 'Counsellor,' because He reveals the counsels of God. He is 'the Mighty God,' because the Father has conferred upon Him dominion over all things. The 'Testimonies' from the Fathers were not of much service to Bidle's cause. He found many passages which declared that there was only one God, and that He created all things by His word. Irenæus said that neither 'the Apostles nor the Lord Christ confessed any other to be of His own person Lord or God.' Justin Martyr acknowledged that there were Christians in his day who said that Christ 'was a man born of men.' Tertullian says, 'there is but God, and He produced the universe out of nothing by His Word,' who was in the fulness of time 'made flesh.' It is surprising that Bidle should have gone to the Fathers at all. The very passages he quotes are full of that Platonism which he reckoned the first beginnings of the doctrine of the Trinity in Unity.

The Fathers Platonists.

After the controversies with the Independents and Baptists, the most exciting, though certainly the least profitable, was that with the Antinomians. When Luther opposed the doctrine of justification by faith to the Roman doctrine of justification by works, there were two things to be explained

The Antinomian controversy.

CHAP. IV.
—what was meant by faith, and what was meant by works? By faith the theologians of the Church of Rome frequently understood simply receiving the creed of the Church; and by works they sometimes meant the ceremonial works enjoined by the Church. All Protestants were agreed that neither of these was a condition of justification. By faith Luther meant reliance on the divine forgiveness, and by works the commands of the moral law. When he said that men are justified by faith, and not by works, did he mean that faith alone was the condition, without the works prescribed by the Church of Rome, or without the works of the moral law? If he meant the latter, the inference was that he made void the law through faith. But the word *condition* has also to be explained. Did it mean something which man was to do in order to justification, or did it mean something which God was to do for him to fit him for justification? In the one case it is equivalent to a work wrought by man. In the other case the law may be either fulfilled in him or for him. If fulfilled in him, he is sanctified; if only for him, he is not holy in himself, but in another. It is not to be denied that the Scriptures distinctly declare the impossibility of salvation to any that are not sanctified in themselves. But it is also true that they speak of Christ as 'made of God unto us wisdom, sanctification, and complete redemption.'

Danger of the Lutheran doctrine of Justification by Faith.

In the warfare which the Reformers had with the Church of Rome, it was natural for them to cling, perhaps with an undue tenacity, to the passages which seemed to make Christ alone active, and to leave man entirely passive in the work of salvation. In none of them was this tendency stronger than in Luther, as we may see in his commentary on the Galatians. After his death it gave rise to a great controversy which took this form—whether man is justified by the passive righteousness of Christ only, or if also by the active righteousness. The meaning of this was, whether men are justified because of the satisfaction for sin which Christ made by His death, or whether also His actual obedience is imputed to them as their obedience. The one side wished to avoid any appearance of our obedience being in any sense the ground of our justification. The other wished to avoid the inference which some might make, that they might live in violation of all law, because Christ had kept the law for them. Those who said that man had nothing to do in order to justification were called Antinomians; but the word had a double meaning, for it included those who made this inference and those who held the doctrine but denied that the inference was just.

Of the latter class was Dr. Tobias Crisp, a conformable clergyman, who died in the year 1642. Crisp's sermons have really but one subject—Christ and His elect. There is only one doctrine running through them all, which is that Christ stands in the place of His elect. Every expression in the Bible concerning atonement, satisfaction, or redemption, is taken in its literal meaning. Man's sin was a debt. He could not pay it, but Christ paid it. This is not understood as merely illustrating the doctrine of redemption. It really is the doctrine of redemption. If the price is paid, the man who owed it is out of debt. His believing or not believing has nothing to do with the question. Christ came to take away the sins of His people, therefore they have no sin. They may 'walk in excess of riot,' and 'commit all the abominations that can be committed,' yet 'the Lord has no more to lay to their charge than to the charge of a believer.' If it be objected that in this life the elect suffer as well as the non-elect, and that suffering implies the presence of sin, Crisp answers that they do not suffer *for*, but *from* sin. The punishment of all sin was laid on Christ. The object of punishment is not to make men better, but to satisfy offended justice. Christ is a gift. There can be no conditions as to a gift. It would then become a bargain. Christ is given, and in consequence of the gift the elect are holy and righteous. God has made a covenant of grace absolutely. In this covenant man is tied to no conditions. If he were, and failed to keep them, the covenant would be void, which is not possible. It depends not on conditions, but on unfailing promises. God has said, *I will put my law into their hearts. They shall all be taught of God. I will sprinkle clean water upon you.* The covenant is made sure to the chosen before they are capable of doing good or evil. Jacob was loved when *the children were not yet born.* Faith is necessary to salvation, but it is not a condition. It is the result of justification. A justified man believes. Faith comes to him through Christ, as passively as sin came to him through Adam. For as all men were literally one in the loins of Adam, so are all the elect one in Christ.

We are likened to men who have no tongues to ask and no hands to receive. God provides us with raiment. He puts Christ upon us. Crisp indeed makes an active as well as a passive receiving, but the latter comes first. Salvation, he says, is forced upon the elect in spite of themselves. They are made to receive grace as a froward patient is made to take bitter medicine. The passive receiving prepares the way for the active. What at first is forced is afterwards received willingly. Unbelief is no bar to salvation. God's covenant is absolute. The elect are sealed and saved before grace begins to work in their hearts, or to show itself in their lives. Esau was rejected before he had done evil. God says of His chosen, *I am found of them that sought me not.*

In the literal transfer of sin to Christ, Crisp does not hesitate to use the extravagant language which has been ascribed to Luther. He calls Christ 'the greatest of all transgressors,' because He bore the transgression of all. Nor is imputation understood to mean merely that there is charged to one that which belongs to another, but it means that sin is imputed to Christ, because it really belongs to Him in virtue of His being one with the elect. For our sins He was separated from God when in the hour of the darkness of His soul he cried, *Eloi, Eloi, lama sabachthani.* David was wrong when he said that his sins were a burden to him. A justified person has no sins. God has transferred them to Christ. God has done it, for it is impossible that it could have been done by man. Some good people, Crisp says, imagine that they can lay their sins on Jesus, but that is something which they cannot do.

The Antinomianism of Crisp was an exaggerated form of the doctrines of Calvin. Its tendency was to make men indifferent as to their lives, for if they were elect they would certainly be saved. This was the danger of Calvinism.

But the ordinary Calvinist had the answer ready, that God in His own time would effectually call, justify, and sanctify those who were ordained to eternal life. Crisp also reckoned on faith and works as being manifested in the lifetime of the chosen; yet, as they were chosen from eternity, they were from eternity the children of God. They were not justified in time but in eternity; not only before they were baptized but before they were born.

The chief of the Antinomian teachers after Crisp was John Saltmarsh, minister of Brasteed, in Kent. Saltmarsh provoked the other ministers by maintaining that there was no real difference between him and them. They were all zealous for free grace. Each party looked at the danger to which the other was exposed; the one fearing lest sanctification should appear as the ground of justification, and the other lest the necessity of sanctification should be denied. The fears on both sides, Saltmarsh said, were without foundation. For his part he preferred crying down man, that he might exalt Christ. To do this he had only to follow Crisp in denying that the new covenant had any conditions. Christ is not ours by any act of our own, but by an act of God's. He is ours without faith, by a power more glorious and infinite, but it is by believing that we know Him to be ours. Saltmarsh called one of his books, 'Free Grace; or, the Flowings of Christ's Blood Freely to Sinners.' The whole meaning of 'freely' was, that man is passive, even in the receiving of gifts from God. Legal teachers say, 'Believe and obey;' but where God works, faith and obedience follow as results. At the end of his book Saltmarsh quoted passages from Calvin, Dr. Preston, Sibbs, Perkins, Gataker, Thomas Goodwin, and others, to show that these writers, as well as himself, were all advocates of free grace. The only quotation which was of real value to him was from Perkins, who said that faith, though 'mentioned after the form and manner of a condition, is, in truth, the free gift of God, as well as eternal life.'

When Richard Baxter was chaplain to the army he found Antinomianism one of the prevailing heresies. It was the subject of the first book which he wrote, 'Aphorisms of Justification.' Baxter admitted that the promises of the covenant were absolute, and that faith is not a condition of the covenant, but one of the things promised. Yet the covenant has conditions which are to be performed by man. We need both a legal and an evangelical righteousness. The first we have through the satisfaction which Christ made by His death to the broken law of the covenant of works. The second we can only have by fulfilling the conditions of the covenant of grace. It is the will of God that man have 'some ground in himself of personal and particular right and claim.' God, Baxter says, has made it as possible for us to fulfil the conditions of the covenant of grace, as it was for Adam to keep the covenant of works. The conditions of the covenant of grace are faith and repentance. How these are at the same time promised by God, and yet required of us, Baxter explained by distinctions which ordinary people cannot easily follow. The absolute promises were to the elect, but as no man knows he is among the elect till he is sanctified, the promises of the covenant are to us conditional. From this doctrine of an absolute covenant with the elect, the teaching of Dr. Crisp was a fair and logical inference. But Baxter neutralized his own admissions by the introduction of other and opposing principles. He thought it a sufficient answer to Antinomianism to separate between election from eternity and justification from eternity. Logical Calvinists, like the Supralapsarians, would admit no *before* or *after* in the divine decrees. What God does has been done from eternity. His acts are transient to us, but immanent with Him. Baxter saw that this was the main pillar of Antinomianism, and, to oppose it, he virtually renounced election from eternity. He made faith and works the conditions of the covenant, and the ground of our proper and complete justification at the day of judgment. We work, he said, from life, but we have also to work for life.

Censured by Calvinists.

Baxter's 'Aphorisms' were censured not only by Antinomians proper, but by many Calvinists, whose views were not Antinomian. He withdrew his book from circulation, and acknowledged that there were in it several expressions which required amendment. In 1655 he published his 'Confession of Faith,' which was a defence of the 'Aphorisms.' There was nothing remarkable in the 'Confession' beyond the effort to show his agreement with the doctrines of the Assembly's Catechism. In 1676 he answered objectors in his 'Treatise of Justifying Righteousness,' and again, in 1690, he published 'The Scripture Gospel defended, and Christ, Grace, and Free Justification Vindicated against the Libertines.' This consisted of two pieces, one of which was called 'A Breviate of fifty Controversies about Justification.' It had been written thirteen years before, and was now published along with 'A Defence of Christ and Free Grace against the Subverters, commonly called Antinomians or Libertines, who ignorantly blaspheme Christ under pretence of extolling Him.' This book was published in the midst of a great excitement, which had been raised by the republication of Dr. Crisp's 'Sermons.' These sermons were edited by Crisp's son, and recommended by twelve of the Nonconforming ministers of London. Among these ministers were John Howe, the two Mathers, and some others who were not supposed to have any sympathies with the peculiar opinions of Dr. Crisp. The republication of the 'Sermons' was the occasion of renewing the controversies about grace and justification. Dr. Daniel Williams, a Presbyterian minister of London, undertook a special refutation of Dr. Crisp's heresies. He answered from the stand-point of moderate Calvinism, and his answers come down to us recommended by some of the men who had allowed their names to be prefixed to the republished sermons of Dr. Crisp.*

CHAP. IV.

Baxter's 'The Scripture Gospel Defended.'

---

* The controversy which we have connected with the name of Crisp, might be dated earlier than his time. It was not properly one controversy. A difference of views on justification led to the publication of many books on both sides, some of which were controversial and some not. In 1642, John Goodwin, not yet an Arminian, but evidently on the high-road, wrote a 'Treatise of Justification,' in which the question was made easy by maintaining that not Christ's active righteousness was imputed to us, but our own faith was imputed for righteousness. We are not in justification made righteous before God, but only accounted righteous. By Christ's obedience unto death, we have the forgiveness of sins. Goodwin, with a singular freedom from all the scholastic subtleties about nature and grace, at once declares that the *natural* man can believe. 'Unless,' he says, 'it be possible that *natural* men believe, it is impossible that they should ever become spiritual. And if it be possible that they may believe, then may they do such things whereunto God hath, by way of promise, annexed grace and acceptation.'— *The Divine Authority of the Scriptures Asserted.*

Thomas Gataker wrote 'Antinomianism Discovered and Refuted' in reply to Saltmarsh. Anthony Burges, minister of St. Lawrence, Old Jewry, preached thirty discourses against the Antinomians, to check the progress of

When we have excepted the members of the Westminster Assembly, and the divines who adhered to the cause of the bishops, the only men of note belonging to this era are the leaders of the Independents. These are Lord Brook, Peter Sterry, John Howe, John Owen, and John Goodwin. Lord Brook had been in the Long Parliament a zealous opponent of Episcopacy. He is reckoned an Independent, but he would have been better described as a Platonical or mystical Christian. In 1640 he wrote a book on 'The Nature of Truth,' in which he was to prove that truth is one with the soul, which, again, is one in its essence, faculties, and acts. The understanding of man, he says, is a ray of the divine nature, conforming it to the likeness of the Creator. Betwixt Christ and the human soul there is a union, as it were, of hypostases. All beings are but one, and all things are more or less excellent in the measure in which they partake of the first Being. Time and space are not existent, and sin is but the privation of good. Since all things are one, Lord Brook maintains that reason and faith can differ only in degree. Faith knows more of God than reason, because faith has its seat in the affections, and he that loves most has most of the image of God, and, therefore, the higher knowledge of God.

Peter Sterry was, under Cromwell, one of the *royal* chaplains. He was of the same mystical spirit as Lord Brook. His sermons on 'The Rise, Race, and Royalty of the Kingdom of God in the Soul of Man,' are full of the Platonic theology, teaching that God is all things and everything,—as 'was said by Euthydemus and, after him, by St. Paul, God is the fulness that filleth all in all.' But Sterry adds, by way of explanation, all things mean each according to the manner of that in which they are. God is as truly in the froward as in the gentle, but with the pure, says David, God is pure, and with the froward He is froward. He is on Mount

the heresy in the city of London. In 1677, John Troughton, 'minister of the Gospel,' wrote 'Luther Redivivus,' and William Eyre, 'pastor of a church in the city of New Sarum,' published, in 1654, 'Vindiciæ Justificationis Gratuitæ, Justification without Conditions.' Both these were in reply to Richard Baxter. A multitude of other writers appeared for and against Baxter. Their names will be found in the 'Treatise of Justifying Righteousness,' and 'The Scripture Gospel Defended.'

Sinai as well as on Mount Sion; but on Sion He is a calm, clear light, on Sinai He is a consuming fire. He is in Himself and in the creature. In Himself He is the Eternal Essence, in the creature He is but the shadow of Himself. We are in a world of images, yet this world is a type of God. The heathen in this sense rightly called the world 'the Great God.' Solomon said that Wisdom lifts up its voice, and cries in the corners of every street. Wisdom is the Brightness of Eternal Beauties. The streets are the outward form in which all the creatures walk forth. In them Wisdom cries aloud, and her voice has gone forth, as St. Paul says, unto the world's end. We are in this life as in a show. It is a reflection of holy images, a reverberation of blessed sounds. Desire is awakened within us. A sweet sense of high joys is infused into the soul. We spread our spirits through the world, to take the world into our spirits, as 'the noise of harmony sounding from afar.' If we slide downward, it is a waste desert. If we ascend with the holy images of the Eternal, they shall continue to become brighter and fuller, till we and they shall reach the fountain, and be received into an immortal Fulness. Every man is exhorted to ask himself if he is changed, or if he still stands in the circle of vanity, darkness, and woe? If the latter, then, Sterry says, he has gone forth from his centre outward into a waste wilderness. From this he must return. It is death, and from it he must rise again. Our resurrection is the same with Christ's resurrection. As the sun draws forth the plants, so does the Father disclose Jesus Christ in the soul.*

---

* Sterry's sermons only pursue the beaten tract of mystical theology, but he is sometimes very happy in his analogies. Speaking of John and Peter he says, 'God made John the Evangelist of a gentle heart, seasoned with a *still* but strong affection; like a river that runs quiet, but swift and deep. This John Jesus Christ takes into His bosom, makes him His lute, on which He sends forth His softest, sweetest loves, beauty, delights. So he lives, and so he dies. . . . St. Peter was more of the rock and flint, sharp, hard, and fiery, and so Jesus brings the wheel over him, and breaks him sorely.'

'The woman said to Saul, "I saw gods ascending out of the earth." But the soul in the divine principle sees God Himself with the whole host of the sons of God, *God-like forms* ascending out of every point of the earth, and the lowest parts of things.'

Again: 'The devil would be all *alone*. God is alone, but so as that He is *one* with *all* things. The devil would be alone, but on a precipice broken off from all things.'

John Howe. John Howe was of Independent or Congregationalist principles, but he does not seem to have thought them of divine institution. He refused to conform at the Restoration, on the ground that to conform would be to abandon the liberal views which he entertained as to the government of the Christian Church. His biographer says that he was for the union and communion of all visible Churches, and that he made nothing necessary for church-membership but to be a Christian. It is said that his chief objection to conformity was re-ordination. He had been ordained by presbyters. That he called the beginning of his ministry, and to be ordained again would be beginning a second time. The majority of the men who held Howe's views conformed both under the Presbyterians and under Episcopacy. They regarded receiving ordination as submitting to the order of the Church,—acknowledging an order in both cases. To Howe it appeared, that to receive the second ordination was to dishonour the first. He was, however, an occasional conformist, and long after the Restoration was permitted by the Archbishop of Armagh and the Bishop of Antrim to have full liberty to preach in their dioceses. Howe enjoyed the friendship of Tillotson, and is said to have been partially within the circle of the Cambridge Platonists. Traces of this influence may be found in his 'Living Temple,' but they are not many. On the ordinary doctrines of Christianity he is orthodox, as orthodoxy was then understood. His explication of the Trinity is Platonic, but sufficiently guarded to prevent any insinuation of heresy.

John Owen. John Owen believed that the principles of Congregational Church polity were prescribed in the New Testament. His first appearance as a writer was in the Calvinist controversy. He wrote a 'Display of Arminianism,' which secured for him the patronage of the Committee for the Ejection of Scandalous Ministers. The theology of the 'Display of Arminianism' is Calvinism of the darkest kind. The Deity which John Owen worshipped was a Being who had no attributes of goodness, as men judge of goodness. His character transcended human capacity as much as His essence. He had made decrees, and as these decrees were divine, they must be eternal; and if eternal, they could in no way be contingent on the doings of men. But proud carnal reason, says Owen, rebels against the *word of God.* It maintains that the events of this world take place according to man's doings, and not according as God has ordered them. Men reason, and presumptuously exclaim that if God ordains evil and punishes them for it, 'He is unjust; His ways are not equal.' Blinded by their own self-sufficiency, they reply against God. They deny the divine foreknowledge, because they cannot reconcile God's decrees with their favourite idol—the freedom of the human will. They suppose the Almighty to desire things to be done in the world otherwise than they are done. They make final impenitence the cause of reprobation, and they reprobate none but the finally impenitent. As if God had not settled it from all eternity that they were to be reprobates, without regard either to their unbelief or their impenitence. They say that Christ died for all, which means in reality that He died for none. An atonement as a price for all, and yet effectually applied to none, is a price not paid. In making this objection to Arminianism, Owen saw, what not many men have seen, that satisfaction with the Arminian cannot consistently mean the same thing as satisfaction with the Calvinist. They may use the same language, but there is a difference as to the very nature of the satisfaction. The 'Arminian heresies' were awful. But the worst of them was the belief that even Pagans who had never heard the Gospel might be saved. How, Owen asked, could God save those to whom the Gospel had never been preached? The Pagans, who had made endeavours after an upright life, had their reward here in outward prosperity or internal peace of mind. They may also have a reward hereafter in a diminution of the degrees of their torments. But out of torments they cannot be, for by nature they were corrupt, and from all eternity children of wrath.

CHAP. IV.

Against the Arminians.

The main pillars of Owen's theology were—that the Bible is a book written immediately by God, therefore whatever it seems to say, should be received, however it may be opposed to the reason of man or the light of conscience. This involves two things—one, a belief that the Bible everywhere and in everything is infallible, and another, that the only

Pillars of Owen's theology.

use of reason is to find out what the Bible contains; a limitation of reason which, from the very nature of the contents of the Bible, most men have found to be impossible.

When John Owen was great in power at the University of Oxford, Brian Walton published his Polyglott Bible. Martin Luther was not a more formidable enemy to the Pope than Brian Walton, with his different versions and various reading, to the Biblical belief of John Owen. The Quakers had told him not to trust the Bible, but the Spirit; and Owen called them 'poor deluded fanatical souls.' Walton had no intentions of heresy. He came to his work simply as a scholar. He compared the various readings that he might, if possible, determine the true reading. But the mere mention of various readings made Owen tremble for the Ark of God. He said that the Bible was inspired, infallible, and preserved from corruption by the providence of God in all ages of the Church. Some theologians of the Church of Rome had already collected various readings, and had made some progress in the criticism of the Bible. Owen said he could understand their position. The Vulgate was their authorized version. The Hebrew text was not their Bible, and in any case they trusted to the Church, placing it above the word written. But to make the Hebrew text uncertain was to undermine the foundations of Protestantism and of Christianity. It was, Owen said, the subtle work of the great enemy of man. God had promised that His Spirit and His words should abide for ever. This promise was found in Isaiah lix. 21, which, on the principle of not applying reason to the Bible, was understood to apply to the canon of the Old and New Testaments. By the Spirit, which was a 'Spirit of verifying,' the true Church knew what books were canonical. This Spirit the Church of Rome had lost. It added to the canon books that were not inspired.

The result of Walton's criticism was that the Hebrew writings had been subject to the same accidents as the works of profane authors. He ascribed a late origin to the Hebrew points. By comparing the old translations, which were made before the invention of the points, he thought to get a better text. Owen said that if we had no certainty of the correct reading of the Bible, we could have no certainty of the doctrines it contained. He thought it inconsistent with the providence of God over His own word that He should suffer it to be corrupted even in the smallest matters. He said that Walton's going to translations was exalting translations above the original. Unfortunately for the credit of his own scholarship, Owen maintained that the Hebrew was faultless. The points, he said, were completed under Ezra and his companions, the men of the great synagogue; and in this work they were guided by the infallible direction of God's Spirit. We do not receive these books as we do other books. Here we have nothing to do with probable arguments about genuineness and authenticity. These are not the ground of our belief in the Scriptures. We receive the Bible with a divine supernatural faith. The authority of God is manifest in it. As the voice which spoke in the writers of the Bible was to them evidence of inspiration, so the voice speaking to us in the Scriptures is evidence that they are the word of God.

John Goodwin,* vicar of St. Stephen's, Coleman Street, was also an Independent. It is a reflection which must often be made how little we know of a man when we merely know the sect to which he belonged. John Goodwin and John Owen had nothing in common. They were types of two classes of men entirely distinct from each other. Goodwin was an Independent in principle, but among the Independents he was rather as an outcast from them than one that was of them. He stood isolated, and no party has had an interest in doing justice to his memory. But no man of that age had more advanced views, both in religion and what concerned civil government. No man brought a clearer head and a sounder judgment to the many questions that had helped to bring confusion on the Church and the nation. He alone, of all the sectaries of any eminence, openly and decidedly renounced the dogmas of Calvin. It is hard for us to conceive how great a thing this was for

---

* John Goodwin is generally called a Fifth Monarchy Man. This statement is made by Bishop Burnet, Bishop Kennett, Dr. Eachard, and after them by Toplady. The sole foundation of it is that, in Cromwell's time, a meeting of the Monarchy Men was surprised in Coleman Street one Sunday morning by Cromwell's officers, and, as John Goodwin's church was in Coleman Street, it has been concluded that they were under his protection. Alas for history!

CHAP. IV.

An Arminian.

a man in Goodwin's position. Arminianism had been identified with the ecclesiastical extravagances of Laud. Calvinism was regarded as the strength of Puritanism. Arminianism was another name for tyranny, and for all that was slavish and obsequious to the 'powers that be.' Calvinism was identified with liberty, manliness, uprightness, and all that formed the character of a good citizen. Goodwin was an ardent republican, but he failed to see that the doctrines of Arminius were less favourable to liberty than those of Calvin. On all these subjects men were surrounded by a thick mist. The mist was a kind of influence under which they had been educated. They were guided by historical sequences rather than by the reason of things. John Goodwin saw through the mist. Civil government was a matter to be settled so as to secure the greatest good for the governed; but what men are to believe concerning Christian doctrine was to be learned from the Scriptures. Conscious of the greatness of the interval which lay between the doctrines of Calvin and those which he reckoned Scriptural, he called one of his books 'Redemption Redeemed.' He was to clear away the false glosses which had gathered round the doctrine of redemption. He was to refute the things most surely believed by all Puritans, whether Presbyterian, Independent, or Baptist, and, we may add, by all Churchmen except those of the school of Laud.

A thorough life of John Goodwin would be a history of all the controversies and of all the changes, both in Church and State, which were witnessed between the first assembling of the Long Parliament and the restoration of Charles. In his almost forgotten tracts there is scarcely a subject, either in politics or theology, on which he has not written. With the Presbyterians he had a continual warfare. He ridiculed them as 'the saints,' and 'displayed' them in a 'Hagio-Mastix.' The Divine right of Presbyterianism was with the Presbyterians as much a mental madness as the Divine right of Episcopacy with the followers of Laud. They succeeded, to some extent, in making Presbyterianism the State religion; but, not satisfied with this, they were unceasingly preaching that it had Divine authority and power to invoke the magistrates to punish heretics even with death. Goodwin

The Presbyterians punish heretics with death.

did not find fault with the Presbyterianism set up by the Government. That, he said, was peaceable, and might be borne by men whose views were congregational. But 'the presbytery of the ministers' was like the fourth beast in Daniel, which devoured and broke the residue to pieces. The residue were those who would not consent to what Goodwin calls the *High* and Anti-Parliamentary Presbytery, the spirit of which was manifested in the 'Ordinance' for punishing heretics with death, and in the 'Gangræna' of Thomas Edwards. The ministers defended death for heresy by the example of Ananias and Sapphira. They reserved to themselves the power of determining what was or was not heresy. Goodwin said that the House of Commons had judged that the denial of the Trinity was not a 'damnable heresy, and not contrary to the manifest word of God.' It was not that Goodwin himself was a denier of the Trinity, but, as the Scriptures had nowhere expressly said that God is one in three persons, he thought it unreasonable to sentence men to death for the denial of what was not expressly in the Scriptures. The Trinity is an inference depending on fallible reason, as all inferences do. Men dispute about the persons in the Godhead, and yet the word *person* is never applied to God in the Scriptures. He is neither said to be one person nor three persons; and if the ministers were asked what they meant by person, they would probably answer no better than the Apocryphal elders in the Story of Susannah. The 'Ordinance' condemned some opinions which, in the judgment of the Presbyterians, subverted the foundations of the Christian religion. Among these was denying the Scriptures to be the word of God. To which Goodwin answers that the word of God is a part of the Scriptures. We surely, he says, do not ask men to believe that the English translation of the Scriptures is the word of God; and if this can be said only of the Greek and Hebrew copies, how many there are who know nothing of the word of God!*

God never called a Person in the Scriptures.

---

* In another tract, called 'The Divine Authority of the Scriptures Asserted,' Goodwin says, 'The true and proper foundation of the Christian religion is not ink and paper, not any book or books, not any writing or writings whatsoever, whether translations or originals, but that substance of matter, those glorious counsels of God concerning the salvation of the

CHAP. IV.

The civil magistrate has no right to punish heretics.

But Goodwin disputed the whole claim of the Presbyterians, or of any sect, to punish men for heresy. He questioned altogether the right of the civil magistrate to interfere in matters of religion. The ministers pleaded that, under the old law, blasphemers and idolaters were put to death. Goodwin answered, that the Sadducees denied the resurrection, the existence of angels or spirits, rejected all the books of the prophets, excepting only those of Moses, and yet the Sadducees were not put to death. The Pharisees made void the commandments of God, yet Christ gave no charge to His disciples that they should be put to death; and Christ was zealous, for the zeal of His Father's house did eat him up. They who put men to death for heresy should have an infallible certainty what is heresy. For the right of the civil magistrate to interfere in religion, the ministers said that 'He was the keeper of both tables.' Goodwin answered, that if this were an Apostolic saying, he would inquire more deeply into its meaning. As it stands, it may mean either that the civil magistrate should be an example to the people by keeping the whole law, or it may mean that he should provide for the performance by those under his jurisdiction of all duties authorized by God. But it was a question regarded as open for further consideration, if the office of the civil magistrate be not entire in itself, without reference to his religious creed. Till the days of Constantine, he had no jurisdiction in the Christian religion. The ecclesiastical elder has his within the Church, and why should not the civil ruler have his within the State?

The London ministers assembled at Sion College, and subscribed 'A Testimony to the Divinity of Jesus Christ, and to a Solemn League and Covenant.' Goodwin says that he alone was aimed at in this assembly. He answered in 'Sion College Visited,' protesting against the 'Solemn

'Sion College Visited.'

world by Jesus Christ, which are indeed represented and declared both in the translations and the originals, but are distinct from both.' Again he says, 'The Word of God had a being, and was extant in the world, nay, in the hearts and consciences of men, before there was any copy of the word extant in writing, either in the one language or the other. Moses was the first penman of the Scriptures, but the *word* was from the beginning 2000 years before Moses.' He goes on to say that Matthew, the first penman of the New Testament, did not write till eight years after the Ascension, but the foundation of the Christian religion was long before that.

League and Covenant,' and telling them that Jesus Christ, and not the Scriptures, was the foundation of the Christian religion. At a later date he had the opportunity of meeting them again, when the 'Triers' were sent out to examine the incumbents of all livings, as to their learning and conversion. It is true that among these 'Triers' there were Independents and Baptists, as well as Presbyterians. But they all hated Arminianism, and John Goodwin was a notorious Arminian. He wrote 'The Triers (Tormentors) Tried, and Cast by the Laws both of God and Man.' He represented them as mounted on thrones far above the level of their predecessors, the bishops. As Leviathan esteemed iron and brass as straw, hay, and rotten wood, so did they esteem all law.

As a disciple of Arminius, the question of the possibility of salvation to those who had never heard the Gospel, was forced upon Goodwin by the Calvinists. He considered it in a paper called 'The Pagan's Debt and Dowry.' There was first the question, what is the Gospel? The writer of the Epistle to the Hebrews says the Gospel was preached to the ancient Jews. Yet Christ by name was not preached among them. The rock in the desert is said to have been Christ, that is, a type representative of Christ. In the same way we call God's goodness to the heathen Christ. The Apostle says that the goodness of God leads men to repentance. Now, if it leads to repentance, it must lead to faith in Christ, whether the name of Christ be known or not. The substance of the Gospel was preached both to Jews and Pagans. The Scriptures, Goodwin says, intimate that there is a capacity in all men, by the light of nature, to know that some atonement has been made for sin. St. Paul declares that they have heard the Gospel who have heard that sound which goes out day and night from the heavens unto the end of the world. In all ages there have been grains or seeds of piety in men's hearts. What men have actually known by the light of nature is considerable, but not to be measured with what they might know.

In three different pamphlets* Goodwin defended the civil

---

* 'Right and Might well met.' 'Os Ossorianum, or a Bone for a Bishop to Pick.' 'Ὑβριστοδίκαι· A Defence of the Honourable Sentence passed upon the late King by the High Court of Justice.'

war, the doings of the army under Fairfax, and the sentence of death passed and executed upon King Charles. For subjects to defend themselves against a bad king was but, he said, to take the sword out of the hands of a madman, or to take charge of a vessel, that under the guidance of an inebriate captain, was drifting on to the rocks and the quicksands. After the King was executed, the London ministers sent forth 'a Faithful Representation,' vindicating themselves from being in any way concerned in the King's death. Goodwin sought no vindication of himself, but published a pamphlet in defence of the execution. It was justified, he said, by Scripture, reason, law authorities, and precedents. The law of the land punishes all murderers with death. It does not ask whether they be tailors or shoemakers, why then should it ask if they are kings? It is enough that they are murderers. The thing made is not above the maker of it. Kings are the workmanship of the people. This is so plain from Scripture, that even in the case of David, who was chosen by God, the appointment rested with the people. St. Peter calls the civil magistrate the ordinance of man, because kings and magistrates receive their very being from the people. From this spring, originally, all authority and all power of government. The House of Commons, without consent of either King or Lords, may determine whatever they judge conducive to the safety and well-being of the commonwealth. From past experience, he argues that it is not desirable to advance kings to the government of States. So universally had kingly government become tyranny in ancient times, that St. Jerome expressed a doubt if it is possible for any king to be saved.

It was not likely that the Baptists, then a new sect, should escape the keen controversialist of Coleman Street. He named them 'The Brethren of the Dip.' He traced the logical origin of the sect to the belief that men were exposed to the wrath of God, if not baptized by the way of immersion. This was the belief of the Anabaptists in Germany, but it was checked and modified by circumstances in England. The Baptists promised to be a numerous and powerful sect in Goodwin's time, but they were kept in check by the Quakers, among whom, Goodwin says, 'there is little question but the devil dwelleth bodily.'

There is no name that we meet more frequently in all that concerns the religious history of the seventeenth century than that of Richard Baxter. It is difficult to put Baxter under any classification, for he at some points comes near to all parties, and yet he stands apart from all. Baxter represented the spirit of his century more than any other man that could be named. He had its weakness as well as its strength. Though deeply influenced by the prevailing theology of his time, yet his intellect struggled against it in almost every form.

Baxter began his career as a Calvinist and a Conformist. He scrupled about conformity as soon as he understood it, and he rejected the more rigid form of Calvinism as soon as he had examined it. The prevalence of Antinomianism, which was the logical consequence of Calvinism, led, as we have seen, to the publication of his first book, 'Aphorisms of Justification.' To the end of his life he professed to be a Calvinist, but he explained Calvinism so as to make it appear Arminianism without being it. He rejected the Supralapsarianism of Dr. Twisse, but approved the decisions of the synod of Dort and the doctrine of the Assembly's Catechism. That is to say, he approved them in a sense in which he thought they could be reconciled with moderate Arminianism. He threw back on the high Calvinists the consequences of their doctrine, that they made God the author of sin, denied man free-will, and in this way overthrew the foundations both of natural and revealed religion. Baxter would have parted entirely with Calvinism but for one decision of the synod of Dort, which was that Christ had died for all men. He thought that by believing this he escaped the difficulty of charging reprobation on the mere will of God. Christ, he said, died for all men, but not equally. He died for the good of all, and, as Bishop Davenant said, He ordained the elect to faith, perseverance, and glory. The non-elect were not ordained to unbelief, but, because of unbelief and impenitence foreseen, they were ordained to everlasting reprobation. It was the merest vestige of Calvinism that Baxter retained, and even that vestige would have disappeared had he applied to it the same reasoning which he urged against the conclusions of Dr. Twisse.

CHAP. IV.

Whatever he might yield to Calvinism, he always maintained that a condition was to be performed by man, which, if it meant anything at all, was a subversion of the first principle of Calvinism. With the keenness of a genuine scholastic, he pursued the Calvinists to their last hiding-places among the subtle labyrinths of metaphysical reasoning. He denied, without qualification, the assumption, which is really the foundation of all false theology, that we can know nothing of the being of God. To know Him, said Baxter, is eternal life. A merely negative knowledge of God would not be sufficient for positive love. The glass in which we are to know God is our own soul, where we may see His image. Our conceptions of Him may be inadequate, still they are true. It may be that His will, His being, and His decree are all one. It may be that knowledge with God is not always the same as knowledge with man. We do not know the all of God. Our knowledge of Him is that which we have on the human side, and by this we must reason. He is God to us, just so far as we know Him. Questions, then, about the order of the divine decrees, or the influence of the divine foreknowledge on futurity, are beyond us, except so far as we can see God mirrored after the image of man.

Can we know God?

Baxter and Conformity.

As to Conformity Baxter was always on its very borders. In his first diocese the enforcement of ceremonial could not have been rigid, for he says that he never wore the surplice on any occasion. He did not object to Episcopacy, but he refused to take the oath known as the *et cetera*, in which he was to promise that he would never endeavour to change the government of the Church as then administered by archbishops, bishops, archdeacons, chancellors, and some others, indefinitely included under ' *et cetera.*' Baxter was reckoned the leader of the Presbyterians, but he was never a Presbyterian in any proper sense. He denies that either the Long Parliament or the Westminster Assembly were composed of Presbyterians. They were conformable members and ministers of the Church of England who sought in the first instance to protect the Church from the novelties, both of doctrine and ceremonial, that were introduced by Laud and his party. The work which this Parliament began fell into other hands, and ended in acts and measures which Baxter deplored. He showed then no inconsistency when he appeared among the first to bring back the king, and when he was ready to accept a bishopric, on condition of some moderate but desirable changes in the discipline of the Church.

On Episcopacy.

In 1680 Baxter published 'A Treatise of Episcopacy,' which he began in 1640, but which was not really written till 1671. It was not, he said, the Episcopacy of the Church of England which he opposed, but Episcopacy as understood by Cousins, Zouch, and Dodwell. He would have preferred more bishops, and the interval between bishops and presbyters greatly lessened. His ideal was a bishop in every city, with the clergy of the district and country churches under him. Yet, he said, if it pleased the king to give a bishop charge of a larger diocese, he would submit. Twenty-six bishops over all England seemed to him an Episcopacy in name, without the reality. The parishes, at that time, were 9725 in number. In Lincoln diocese, in which Baxter then lived, there were nearly 1100 churches. The diocese was 120 miles in length. Some other dioceses were equally large. London had parishes with populations from 20,000 to 50,000. It was impossible, Baxter said, for any man to do the work of a bishop among such vast populations, or over so wide a district of country. Yet not one of the six-and-twenty bishops had so much as a suffragan. Neither Scripture, the example of the early Church, nor the requirements of the Church of England, authorized such an Episcopacy as this.*

Rise of Episcopacy.

The rise of this 'Diocesan Prelaty' was accounted for in several ways. The Apostles planted churches, and ruled over them for a time. They appointed fixed bishops, one over each congregation; but while the Apostles lived, the fixed bishops were under them. Hence the historians frequently call the Apostles or evangelists the bishops of these churches. Another reason may have been in the natural disparity of age and gifts, which made disparity of rank. When a man gathered a church, it was probably thought

---

* It is 200 years since this was written, and only a few weeks ago has the Government agreed to appoint a suffragan for Lincoln.

CHAP. IV.

Primitive episcopacy a bishop for every market town.

right that those who came as his helpers should come with his consent, and be under his control. The unfixed Apostles gathered churches, and thus it fell to them to ordain fixed pastors or bishops. The fixed bishops afterwards took the ordinary duties of the Apostles, appropriating to themselves ordination and some other offices. But these bishops at first were nothing more than chief ministers. Every church had its bishop, and, when it was necessary, its presbyters to assist him. They generally lived together in one house, and were not distinct orders, but two different ranks of one order. Every market town had its bishop. One council decreed that villages should not have bishops. At the Council of Carthage there were bishops whose sees were so insignificant that the names of four or five of them have never been found in geographical books or tables. The change from the primitive Episcopacy was after Christianity became the religion of the empire, when the government of the Church was fashioned after the model of the government of the State. Baxter said that the primitive Episcopacy was properly the Episcopacy of the Church of England. It was that which Cranmer taught, who said that the difference between bishops and presbyters was a device of the Fathers. This, too, was the Episcopacy which the Westminster Assembly did not wish to oppose. Their object was to give the bishops such dioceses as they could govern, and not to take away from the presbyters all power of government, for they also were bishops in the primitive sense.* At the Restoration, Baxter says, the Nonconformists asked the king for Episcopacy after the model of the primitive Church, as laid down by Archbishop Ussher. And if the king had kept his promise about appointing suffragan bishops, and some other needful reformations, they would not have scrupled to conform.

* It is difficult to believe that Baxter is right here. Had the Assembly been satisfied with a modified Episcopacy, Archbps. Ussher and Williams, and, indeed, all the moderate bishops, with the great body of the clergy who were deprived, would have gone with them. In the 'Reliquiæ Baxterianæ' it is said that the Presbyterians rejected the changes which Ussher's party proposed. In the same book, however, it is said, that when the Covenant was proposed, they objected, being for a moderate Episcopacy, and they did not subscribe the covenant till the word *prelacy* was explained to mean government by archbishops, bishops, chancellors, etc.

In 1691, the last year of Baxter's life, he published a book, 'Of National Churches.' It was in this work, more than in any other, that he showed how thoroughly he entered into the spirit of the old Conformists of the Church of England.* Here he must stand with Cranmer, Hooker, Field, and the great defenders of the Protestant principle of nationality, on which the Reformed Church of England was established under Henry, Edward, and Elizabeth. Papacy, he said, is built on the ruins of national Churches. It profanes the sacred offices of kings and magistrates, 'feigning them to be but a sort of secular animals, who have the care only of men's bodies, and trading and worldly affairs, and not of souls and men's everlasting safety.' These things are made to appear as if they belonged only to priests, and so kings are made as much baser than priests as the body is viler than the soul. This mistake, Baxter says, has of late corrupted the innovating prelates of the Church of England, who think that a national Church should be unified, not by the sovereign head, but by a collective sacerdotal head, as if the prince were not sufficiently sacred to be the head of the Church in his own dominions. Baxter calls this a 'novel opinion.' He pronounces it contrary to the law, to the judgment of the lawyers, and to the doctrine of the Church of England. By this error, the clergy had taught princes that it is not necessary for them to be studious about the Scriptures, but to follow luxury, sports, and debauchery. National Churches are Christ's institutions. Baxter objects to the distinction civil and ecclesiastical, as if the government of the magistrates were not ecclesiastical government. In a national Church, the prince is the chief officer under Christ. He does not preach the word or administer sacraments. He has not the power of the keys, but he rules them that have the power. Pastors are the prime matter of a national Church, but it is by the prince that it has its 'unifying form.' Baxter had once said that the Scotch Church Confederation was a saddling of the horse for Papal usurpation. He retracted this when he thought of that confederation as na-

---

* Baxter was a Nonconformist because of some reforms which he wanted. He was a Conformist so far, that he worshipped and took the sacrament at church kneeling.

tional. He ascribes to it the success which Presbyterianism in Scotland has had in keeping down sectaries.

In the treatise on Episcopacy, Baxter was not certain if the Apostles had any proper successors. He was of the opinion that, as the Church ceased to be missionary, the migratory evangelists ceased as an order, and the government of the Church devolved on the fixed bishops or pastors. In this book on National Churches, he says he once doubted if the Apostles' superiority was a settled superiority of office; now he is convinced that it was, and that Apostles appointed a superior order of ministers to succeed them in their general work. He takes the Episcopal view of the 'bishopping of Timothy and Titus.' They were overseers or bishops over inferior bishops. There were three ranks of bishops,—the ordinary presbyters; the presiding bishops, as it were incumbents of large parishes with curates under them; and the successors of the Apostles. It might seem that here Baxter has really come to the most orthodox theory of bishops, but the change is less than at first we might suppose. His complaint still is, that the last sort of bishops have not only got the name exclusively appropriated to them, but also the offices which belong also to the presbyters or inferior bishops. The inferior bishops are unbishopped: the diocesan bishops have unlawfully taken away their Episcopal character. At the time of the Reformation, the ordinary parish clergy were in such ignorance and error that it was necessary to restrain them; but now, Baxter said, the diocesan bishops should share the government of the Church with the inferior bishops, and not make them, as it were, a sort of half-pastors. The Church of England, as it now stands, is, says Baxter, a national Church according to Christ's institution. It is under one superior governor, as the unifying head. It consists of baptized Christians and baptized churches. It has national laws subservient to Christ. It makes none magistrates who are not professed Christians. It has diocesan or general overseers, successors of the Apostles, and it justly makes bishops members of Parliament. But there are some things which need reformation. It is wrong for a national Church to make its doors so narrow as to exclude those who differ from it only on things that are not essentials. It is wrong to make needless laws to silence or eject any true or tolerable ministers. The dioceses and parishes are too large. The patrons have too much power in choosing the ministers, and the people too little. Bishops should not be chosen without the consent of synods. Ordinations should not be made without the assistance of presbyters, not merely for the sake of form, as it is now, but they ought to be the acts of the bishop and *his presbytery.* Not only should the gates of a national Church be as wide as possible, but all Dissenters should have full toleration, except those *that are heretics.* The Protestant Nonconformists, according to Baxter, are members of the Church of England as truly as the Conformists.

In the history of religious thought in England, Richard Baxter claims a special place as the first English writer on the evidences of Christianity. Even in 1649, when he published the 'Saints' Everlasting Rest,' he speaks of the prevalence of unbelief, not in any open form, but as involved in the doctrines of the 'Libertines, Familists, Seekers, and Anti-scripturalists.'* It was not that these sects refused to be called Christians, but they took up positions which seemed to Baxter subversive of the foundations on which Christianity rests. In the second part of the 'Saints' Rest,' he turned aside from the immediate subject of his work to discourse of the grounds on which men ought to receive the religion of Christ. He complained of a custom which had arisen among the Puritans of resolving all into the testimony of the Spirit. It is in things of this kind that we discover how honestly Baxter used his intellect, and how little he feared to state the truth precisely as it appeared to him. To resolve all into the Spirit was to lay our minds open to any extravagance, and to be ready to receive any doctrine, however absurd and unintelligible. The illumination of the Spirit

---

* All these names mean nearly the same class of people. The Familists are the only well-defined party. Baxter had specially before him one whom he calls Clement Writer, though this was not his proper name. Writer defended himself against Baxter in a little book, of which a copy is preserved in the British Museum. His doctrine simply was that we could not believe in Christianity without miracles; but so far was he from being a sceptic, that he believed the power of working miracles had never ceased in the Church, but would always continue as a necessary sign to convince unbelievers.

was not to be denied, and the better men were in their lives, the more of the Spirit they would have. But the Spirit did not give men eyes. It only opened the eyes which men already possess. The gift of reason, said Baxter, is God's gift, as well as the gift of the Spirit. The reason has to be rectified, purified, illuminated, and then the evidence of the truth of Christianity is invincible. The Spirit may be called the efficient cause of our belief; but the question to be examined is the evidence itself, the objective cause. The evidence exists independently of the Spirit's testimony. But for this, men who had not the Spirit would be excusable in their unbelief.

The definitions which Baxter was led to make both of faith and reason, and the offices he assigned them, were not approved by all who in his time were reckoned orthodox. He rejected from his view of faith* the idea of implicit trust without proper evidence. Faith was rather to be regarded as the rational act of a rational creature. It proceeded from an exercise of the understanding, and the stronger the ground which faith had for the validity of the testimony, the stronger itself became. A great part of sanctification consists in the rectifying of reason, and he who has the highest reason has most grace. The meaning which such statements as these would now have, was, however, modified by Baxter's views of Scripture. He has no sooner said that reason is the proper foundation for faith, but he tells us, that for the rectifying of reason there is need, not only of the Spirit's illumination, but also of the Scriptures. Not that God ties Himself not to give revelations by His Spirit, but that He has ceased to give them. He has perfected the Scripture revelations, and now He reveals by His Spirit what is revealed in the word, not independently of the word, but by giving His Spirit to illumi-

---

* The explanation of 'above reason' would not be reckoned orthodox even now. 'Those knowing divines that tell the Socinians that the matters of faith are *above* reason, can reasonably mean no more but that mere reason by natural light could not have known them without Gospel supernatural revelation.'—*End of Doctrinal Controversies.*

Baxter, like all the old orthodox divines, generally put grace in opposition even to what was good by nature; but in one place he says, 'I afterwards perceived that education is God's ordinary way for the conveyance of His grace, and ought no more to be set in opposition to the Spirit, than the preaching of the word.'—*Reliquiæ Baxterianæ*, p. 7.

nate our reason, to understand what is already revealed in the Scriptures.

Part of Baxter's argument necessarily is to prove that the Scriptures are a revelation from God. He does not hold that this belief is necessary to salvation; yet it is a true belief. A man may be saved who only believes one book, if it contains the doctrine of salvation, or a man may be saved who takes the Scriptures for the writings of honest, worthy men, and believes in Christ, not because of the testimony of the Scriptures, but because of the doctrine and miracles which he finds in the Scriptures. Nevertheless, the Scriptures *are* the word of God. This is proved by the miracles. That doctrine and those writings which are confirmed by miracles must be of God. It may be objected that Antichrist was to work wonders. The answer is, that Antichrist would perform lying wonders, such as the feigned miracles of sorcerers and witches, but not true miracles. It cannot be supposed that God would ever give such power to any but those that are commissioned by Him. It may still be asked, who is to distinguish between the false and the true? Baxter tries to lay down a criterion, which is, that true miracles are not done by natural means, but he finally resolves it into this, that God's faithfulness will not suffer men to be deceived. We have the testimony of Scripture that miracles were wrought. This testimony, of course, cannot be taken at once as decisive, for it is by the miracles that the truth of Scripture is to be established. Baxter is prepared for all this, and asks simply that we receive the testimony of Scripture as mere human testimony, and, this granted, he will prove that we have certainty of the miracles recorded in Scripture. The process of the argument is from the certainty of human testimony in general. We never doubt that there are such places as London or Paris, even though we may never have seen them, or that there were such persons as King James, Queen Elizabeth, or Queen Mary, though we know nothing of their existence but what we read in history. There is no ground for doubting the testimony of those on whose word we believe that such persons once existed. There are still better grounds for believing a testimony, when those who are witnesses not only had no advantage from their testimony, but made it at the risk of losing all they had,—their property, their good name, yea, their lives. It was so with those who witnessed Christ's miracles. They knew the truth of what they testified. They had no object in deceiving the world. Moreover, their testimony has come down to us by a way so infallible that there can be no doubt about the authority of the records. Thousands of persons saw the miracles of Jesus. Many cities and countries were witnesses to those of the Apostles. It was impossible that the records could be corrupted. The books were scattered among the Christians all over the world. They never had an opportunity of meeting to consult about defacing the Scriptures. 'Even the more learned and honest among the Papists,' says Baxter, 'maintain the perfection of the Hebrew text.' The argument from the improbability of miracles had not the force in Baxter's time which it acquired in the next century. The miraculous still existed. Baxter could express amazement at the incredulity of men who doubted that it rained manna in the wilderness, when he had seen showers of manna in England.* Human testimony is really divine. Ordinary testimony to any ordinary fact, Baxter calls *revelation*. On the certainty of this testimony all belief is founded. We begin in everything by taking something on trust from man.

Had Baxter stopped here, we might have praised his ingenuity, without supposing that any one was ever convinced by his arguments. But what always amazes the reader of Baxter is, that he says so many things well, and then many things, perhaps immediately after, that are neither well said nor good in themselves. He goes on to a further

---

* 'They think the Scripture miracles incredible; and yet every age still hath such wonders as the next age will not believe. Why is not raining of manna or quails from heaven as credible as the raining of that grain about ten years ago in England? It fell in many parts of the kingdom. It was like a withered wheat corn, but not so long, with a stem of a dark colour, which being pulled off, the grain had a taste somewhat sharp and hot. I tasted it, and kept some of it which fell on the leads of the church and of the minister's house in Bridgnorth, where I preached the Gospel.'—*Saints' Everlasting Rest*, p. 223, note.

Baxter mentions another public miracle which happened in his lifetime. November 2, 1660, there were three tides in the Thames in twelve hours.

argument to prove that the Scriptures are the word of God. The argument is, that they must either be the invention of men or devils, or they are from God. But they are too good for devils to invent. They must have been supernatural, because, though without human learning, they are such as the philosophers could not reach. Some of the old Puritans argued for the divinity of the Scriptures, from their manifest superiority to all human writings. Yet Baxter found their divinity in this, that they had so little in them of what was properly human excellence. They were full of David, not of Goliath. A third argument was from the fulfilment of prophecy, and the extraordinary providence of God over His Church. Christ, by His Apostles, after He had risen, wrought faith in multitudes of people. The success of the Gospel by such feeble agency was evidence to the fact of His resurrection. Great miracles have been wrought in answer to the prayers of the saints. The story of the 'thundering legion' is well known and well authenticated. The first enemies of the Gospel were visibly punished. Antiochus, Herod, Pilate, and Julian were public examples of divine retribution. Even so late as the silencing of the Nonconformists, it was manifest that divine justice did not sleep. Soon after the Act of Uniformity many of the churches of England were torn to pieces by lightning in the time of the service, and some persons killed as they sat in their pews. The fourth argument is, that if the Scriptures be not the written word of God, then there is no written word of God, but there *is* a written law, and this is it. It could not agree with the wisdom and goodness of God to leave men without a written law, and there is no book in the world whose claims can be placed beside those of the Bible. If all this fails, Baxter has yet in reserve proofs of what the Scriptures reveal concerning a future state. Can we deny that there is a devil, and that he has often appeared to men; and can we deny that there are witches, and that men make covenants with them? As to the certainty of witches, and their evil doings, Baxter not only gave some *authentic* cases, but he published a whole book about them. It was well known that the devil had appeared to Luther more than once, sometimes as a black boar, and sometimes as burning torches; so that the great soul of Luther almost quailed in the presence of the arch-fiend. But Baxter's undeniable proof was the appearance of the devil at Mascon, in France, where he went out and in for the space of three months, conversing with people of both persuasions, Catholic and Protestant, and holding a public disputation with a Roman Catholic priest. Peter du Moulin had established all this on irrefragable evidence. But miracles are soon forgotten. Fifty years after, when some persons went from England to inquire concerning this visitation of the devil, the people of Mascon knew nothing about it.*

In 1655 Baxter published, as a further discourse on the evidences, a book called 'The Unreasonableness of Infidelity.' He had as yet no infidels before him, except the Anabaptists, who, on the Pelagian side, became Socinians, or, on the Antinomian side, Libertines, Familists, Seekers, and, of late, Ranters or Quakers. He maintained that it was evident, from the light of nature and the common principles of mankind, that there is a God, a life to come, with rewards and punishments. He drew an argument also for the truth of Christianity from the fact that Christians are the most rational of men, while unbelievers are the most like to brutes. The Spirit in the Church in the first ages, sanctifying men and working miracles, was an evidence of the truth of the Christian religion. The arguments used in the 'Saints' Rest' are brought forward again, without any material change. Baxter professes to determine the question, whether the miraculous works of Christ and His disciples oblige those who never saw them to believe? But though he treats of this question, he does not seem to have seen the real difficulties that accompany it, such as the à priori improbability of miracles, and the fact that the Gospel miracles come to us on the testimony of men who lived many centuries ago. He argues that the Spirit in the

---

* This is the visit referred to by Ralpho in 'Hudibras':—

'Did not the devil appear to *Martin Luther* in *Germany*, for certain,
And would have gulled him with a trick?
But *Mart.* was too, too politic!
Did not he help the Dutch to purge,
At *Antwerp*, their Cathedral Church?
Sing catches to the saints at Mascon,
And tell them all they came to ask him?'

Christian obliges him to believe works which he never saw. CHAP. IV.
The meaning of this seems to be that the fact of sanctification
proves that all which the Christian records say is true. The
certainty of miracles in the general argument is resolved into
the certainty of human testimony, but that which really Power of
produces belief in Christianity is the Spirit of God purifying Christianity.
men's hearts, so that they feel it to be true. 'The melody of
music,' Baxter says, 'is better known by hearing it than by
reports of it; and the sweetness of meat is better known
by tasting than by hearsay, though upon report we may be
drawn to taste. So is there a spiritual sense in us of the
effects of the Gospel in our own hearts, which will ever cause
men to love it, and hold it fast.'*

---

* Baxter says that when at Kidderminster, he was 'terriby assaulted with unbelief, and tempted to doubt if the Scriptures were the word of God. Then,' he says, 'I perceived that all other religions leave the people in their worldly, sensual, and ungodly state, even their zeal and devotion being commonly servants of their fleshly interests; and the nations where Christianity is not, being drowned in ignorance and earthly mindedness, so as to be the shame of nature.'—*Rel. Bax.*, p. 23.

In the *Reliquiæ Baxterianæ* there are many things worth remembering. Baxter never used a surplice, and only sometimes read the service in the Prayer Book before the sermon. It appears that Bridgnorth, where he was curate before he went to Kidderminster, was not under episcopal jurisdiction. Six parishes, including Bridgnorth, had the minister of Bridgnorth for their ordinary. When the Scots army was about to enter England, the minister refused to pray against them, because there was no command from the king, but only from the bishops. At Kidderminster images of the Trinity, and of the Virgin Mary, with some crucifixes, were still standing; Parliament ordered their removal, in the execution of which, the mob at Kidderminster sought to kill Baxter and his churchwardens. Baxter had generally to cure the bodies as well as the souls of his parishioners. Some of the prescriptions would edify the medical men of the present day. When a tumour rose on the tonsils of his throat, he swallowed a gold bullet, 'between 20s. and 30s. weight.' This was prescribed in some book as a cure for tumours of this kind. For £8 or £10 a year, Baxter was able to maintain youths at the universities. A minister named Farringdon preached in a theatre, a *desecration* which gave great offence to King Charles II. Baxter laments that the writings of the ancient heretics and schismatics are destroyed. He suspects that the Fathers have not told us the honest truth about these men. He says, 'Freeholders and tradesmen are the strength of religion in the land, and gentlemen and beggars and servile tenants are the strength of iniquity.'

CHAPTER V.

THE RESTORATION.—THE KING'S DECLARATION.—THE SAVOY CONFERENCE.—EXCEPTIONS OF THE MINISTERS AGAINST THE PRAYER BOOK.—THE BISHOPS' ANSWER.—BAXTER AND GUNNING.—BISHOP MORTON.—BISHOP COSIN.—BISHOP WALTON.—BISHOP PEARSON.—BISHOP SANDERSON.—DR. HAMMOND.—HERBERT THORNDIKE.—ARCHBISHOP BRAMHALL.—BISHOP HOPKINS.—JEREMY TAYLOR.—JOHN GAULE AND HENRY JEANES.—SAMUEL RUTHERFORD.—LIBERTY OF CONSCIENCE.—SIR THOMAS BROWNE.—SIR MATTHEW HALE.

Restoration of Charles II.

AT the restoration of Charles II. only nine bishops survived out of the twenty-seven that had been deprived at the beginning of the Long Parliament. These were Juxon, Pierce, Wren, Duppa, Skinner, Warner, Frewen, King, and Roberts.* Archbishop Laud had perished on the scaffold. John Williams died in poverty in his native country, after all his high preferments in Church and State. Archbishop Ussher was for some years Chaplain to the Honourable Society of Lincoln's Inn. This office he resigned

---

* The bishops stood thus in 1641:—

William Laud, Canterbury.
John Owen, St. Asaph's.
William Roberts, Bangor.
William Pierce, Bath and Wells.
Thomas Howell, Bristol.
Henry King, Chichester.
Roger Manwaring, St. David's.
Matthew Wren, Ely.
Ralph Brownrigg, Exeter.
Godfrey Goodman, Gloucester.
George Coke, Hereford.
Morgan Owen, Llandaff.
Thomas Winniffe, Lincoln.
Accepted Frewen, Lichfield and Coventry.
William Juxon, London.
Joseph Hall, Norwich.
Robert Skinner, Oxford.
John Towers, Peterborough.
John Warner, Rochester.
Brian Duppa, Salisbury.
Walter Curle, Winchester.
John Prideaux, Worcester.
John Williams, York.
James Ussher, Carlisle.
John Bridgman, Chester.
Thomas Morton, Durham.
Richard Parr, Sodor and Man.

as he became enfeebled by age. He died soon after, at the house of the Duchess of Peterborough, and was honoured by Cromwell with a public funeral at Westminster Abbey. Bishop Hall, too, had passed away, and so had John Prideaux, the learned Bishop of Worcester, and Ralph Brownrigg, 'the Puritanically affected' Bishop of Exeter, with Thomas Morton, Bishop of Durham, who, through a lifetime of almost a hundred years, had been a steadfast supporter of the old Protestant doctrines of the Church of England.

With the restoration of the King, there were some hopes that such changes would be made in the services of the Church as would enable all earnest men to conform with a good conscience. The king found the Presbyterian ministers among the best upholders of his cause. Encouraged by his promises, they laid their case before him, stating the things to which they objected, and suggesting the changes which were likely to be the means of including all parties within the national Church. They took it for granted, they said, that on doctrine all parties were agreed. Their only difference concerned Church government, and some particulars about the service and ceremonies. They asked the king that care might be taken to provide for every parish a learned, orthodox, and godly minister, who might instruct the people by diligent preaching and frequent administration of the sacraments. They asked that none might be admitted to the sacrament of the Supper till they had understood the principles of the Christian religion; and further, that the king might take some effectual course to secure 'the sanctification of the Lord's day.'

The Presbyterian ministers, as they were called, protested that though in taking the Covenant they had disclaimed 'hierarchy' and 'prelacy,' yet they had never renounced 'the true, ancient, primitive Episcopacy' of the Church. They had only maintained that, to secure just and impartial government, the bishop should always act in conjunction with a presbytery. In the Episcopacy which existed before 1640 there were evils which urgently required a remedy, four of which were specially mentioned. The dioceses were too large. In consequence of this, the bishops had to depute much of their work to officials, some of whom were secular persons. Those bishops who supposed a bishop and a presbyter belonged to two distinct orders, assumed to themselves the sole power of ordination and jurisdiction. The fourth evil was, that bishops had been arbitrary in the exercise of this power, and that they had imposed innovations and ceremonies not required by law, both upon ministers and people. To prevent the return of these evils, the ministers suggested the adoption of the scheme of Episcopacy laid down by Archbishop Ussher. Part of this scheme was the appointment of suffragan bishops in large dioceses. They asked that no oaths or promises of obedience to the bishops, nor unnecessary subscriptions or engagements be made necessary for ordination or institution, and that the bishops may not have the power to exercise arbitrary government at their own will and pleasure, but be made subject to canons and constitutions ratified by Act of Parliament.

The Presbyterians are satisfied that there should be a liturgy.

Concerning the service of the Church, the ministers said they were satisfied that there should be a liturgy. They only asked the matter of it to be agreeable to the word of God, and suited to the necessities of the Church; that it should not be dissonant from the liturgies of other Reformed Churches, nor too rigorously imposed. The object of the last request was that the minister might have an opportunity of exercising those gifts of prayer which Christ has given for the edification of His Church. As the Book of Common Prayer had been long laid aside, and as it contained many things which were 'justly offensive,' the ministers asked that a commission might be granted to compile a new Prayer Book, or effectually to reform the old one. It was objected to the ceremonies that they had been a matter of contention and endless dispute. Being things indifferent, it was the duty, they said, of the Christian magistrate not to give offence to weak brethren by their imposition. Kneeling at the sacrament, saints' days, the surplice, the cross in baptism, and bowing at the name of Jesus, were mentioned as ceremonies the abolition of which might help 'to heal our sad breaches.' Then there were divers ceremonies which had 'no foundation in the law of the land.' These were 'erecting altars, bowing towards them, and such like,' which had grieved many 'reverend and learned bishops,' and 'divers ministers of the gospel,' though conformable to the 'established ceremonies.'

Charles sent forth a 'Declaration' to his 'loving subjects, concerning ecclesiastical affairs.' He told them of the experience which he had acquired among the Reformed Churches abroad. He said that the learned men of these Churches regarded the Church of England as 'the best fence God had yet raised against Popery in the world.' He would restore the Church of England to its old dignity and power. He had been attended, he said, by Presbyterian ministers in Holland, whom he had found to be no enemies either to Episcopacy or the liturgy, and well affected towards himself. He would repeat what he had said in his 'Declaration' from Breda, that 'no man would be called in question for differrence of opinion in matters of religion.' In his own chapel he had used the liturgy without imposing it on the nation. But owing to seditious pamphlets and jealousies that had been stirred up in the hearts of the people, he was compelled to give some decision as to religious differences until a synod should be called for that object. He would not enforce some ceremonies which, though introduced by the piety, devotion, and order of former times, were not so agreeable to the present. He would take care that 'the Lord's day' be kept holy. He would promote to the office of bishops none but men of learning, piety, and virtue, and he would see that they were frequent preachers. Suffragan bishops were to be appointed in all dioceses. No bishop was to ordain without his presbyters. And that the bishops might always have judicious and pious presbyters to help them, deaneries and all cathedral preferments were to be given to the most learned and pious men in the Church. The king promised that care would be taken as to the admission of persons to the Lord's Supper, in accordance with the request of the ministers. He promised also that no bishops should be allowed to exercise arbitrary power; and to promote peace and uniformity, he was to appoint 'an equal number of learned divines of both persuasions' to review the Book of Common Prayer, and to make such alterations as might be thought necessary.

282 RELIGIOUS THOUGHT IN ENGLAND.

CHAP. V.

Presbyterians offered bishoprics and deaneries.

In the meantime some of the Presbyterians were made chaplains to the king. Baxter, Calamy, and Reynolds were offered bishoprics. Manton, Bates, and some others were offered deaneries. Baxter was willing to accept a bishopric, provided the king's 'Declaration' became law. He wished to wait till he saw some certainty of the changes which were promised. Hyde pressed him for an immediate answer, and that answer was a refusal. It had been agreed between Baxter, Calamy, and Reynolds that they should act together, either in accepting the bishoprics or in refusing them. Calamy complained that Baxter had acted singly. Reynolds had done the same, but he pleaded that his friends had taken out a *congé d'élire* unknown to him. Calamy was committed to Presbyterianism more than either Baxter or Reynolds, and all his friends felt that if he became a bishop he would lose his good name. Manton at first accepted the deanery which was offered to him, but it was afterwards refused.

The Savoy Conference.

Next year the king issued a warrant for a conference on the Prayer Book.* The bishops and Presbyterians were to meet 'to advise, consult, and determine' upon the changes to be made. Their place of meeting was to be at the lodgings of the Master of the Savoy, who was also Bishop of London. The Presbyterians understood that they were 'to advise and consult' with the bishops. The bishops understood that they were to sit as judges. On the first day of their meeting, the Bishop of London told the ministers that they had sought the conference, and therefore it rested with them to bring forward their exceptions, with their additional alterations. In this demand there was nothing particularly unfair. It was clever dealing, and the spirit of it was not conciliatory. Bishop Sheldon, who managed for the bishops, was a shrewd man of business. Richard Baxter, who was the ruling spirit on the other side, was not made

---

* On the Bishops' side:—Archbishop Frewen, Bishops Sheldon, Cosin, Warner, King, Henchman, Morley, Sanderson, Laney, Walton, Sterne, and Gauden. Assistants, Doctors Earle, Heylin, Hacket, Barwick, Gunning, Pearson, Pierce, Sparrow, and Mr. Thorndike.

On the Presbyterian side:—Bishop Reynolds, Doctors Tuckney, Conant, Spurstow, Wallis, and Manton; with Calamy, Baxter, Jackson, Case, Clark, and Newcomen. Assistants, Doctors Horton, Jacomb, Bates, Lightfoot, Collins, Drake, Mr. Rawlinson, Mr. Cooper, and Mr. Woodbridge.

for this world. The Presbyterians at first objected, on the ground that it was an open conference, according to the king's warrant. At last they consented to the plan which Bishop Sheldon had proposed. Bishop Burnet conjectures that Sheldon foresaw that the multitude and minuteness of the Presbyterian objections would raise an outcry against them as men who could never be satisfied.

The paper of exceptions against the Book of Common Prayer was indeed formidable, if we look only to its length and the number of changes proposed. The ministers expressed their 'honourable esteem' of 'the first compilers of the public liturgy.' They called the liturgy itself 'an excellent and a worthy work.' They said it was no disparagement, either to the liturgy or to its compilers, if, after a hundred years had passed, some further emendations required to be made. After this preamble, the ministers suggested some general changes. They wished that the liturgy might not be charged with more than was necessary, that it might not contain any matters of mere private opinion, or what concerned Church pomp, garments, or prescribed gestures. When the liturgy was composed, there was a good reason for departing as little as possible from the forms in use among the Roman Catholics. That reason had now ceased, and it was thought desirable that the liturgy be made so as to gain the affections of all Protestants who agree with the Church of England in the substantials of religion. The responses by the people were to cease: except only at the close they were to signify their consent by saying *Amen*. This was an old and curious objection against the liturgy, grounded on the Puritan principle, that 'the minister was the mouth of the people to God in prayer.' The ministers objected to keeping Lent as a fast, and especially in imitation of Christ's fasting forty days. They objected also to saints'-days and their vigils. They asked that the liturgy might not be so imposed as to prevent the minister 'exercising his gift' in prayer; a liberty which was allowed even in the first Prayer Book of Edward VI. They pointed out defects in the translations of the Scriptures used in the Prayer Book, which at this time followed the old versions. They objected to the Apocryphal

CHAP. V.

lessons, the use of the words *priest* or curate, and calling portions of the Scriptures 'Epistles,' which were not epistles. They asked an improved version of the psalms to be sung in the churches, the laying aside of obsolete words; and that, considering the want of discipline, the offices of the Church should not assume all persons to be regenerated, converted, and in an actual state of grace. The collects were said to be too short, and the parts not in harmony with each other. It was suggested that they should be formed into one long, methodical prayer. The Confession was reckoned defective, because it did not clearly speak of original sin, nor sufficiently enumerate actual sins and their aggravations. The matter of the prayers was considered too general, not descending to special petitions; and the Catechism was declared defective, even as to the essentials of Christianity. Complaint was also made of the impositions in the litany, that the minister must wear a surplice, use the sign of the cross in baptism, and administer the Lord's Supper only to the people kneeling. As these things were by some reckoned 'sinful,' the imposers, it was said, should not give occasion of offence to a weak brother.

Special objections.

Under the general were added some special objections. The ministers asked that the rubric, which prescribes the prayers to be said 'in the accustomed place,' be changed for the old rubric of the second book of Edward VI., that they be said 'in such place of the church, chapel, or chancel, and the minister shall so turn, as the people may best hear.' The rubric about the vestments in the second year of King Edward was to be left out, as it seemed to bring back the cope, albe, and other vestments, forbidden by the Book of Common Prayer. The last clause of the Lord's Prayer was always to be added whenever that prayer occurs, and the *Gloria Patri* to be used but once in the morning and once in the evening service, the lessons were never *to be sung*, and the Apocryphal *Benedicite* was to be omitted. In the litany fornication is included among deadly sins, as if, the ministers said, all sins were not deadly. For the petition to be delivered from sudden death, it was suggested to substitute 'from dying suddenly and unprepared.' There was an incomprehensible objection to the word 'all' in the petition for 'all that travel by land or water.' It was to be written, 'those that travel by land or water.' Several of the collects were to be altered, and especially the words 'this day' to be struck out both in the collects for Christmas Day and Whitsunday.

CHAP. V.

The chief changes were to be made in the offices of the Church. It was asked that before the communion a longer notice be given to the curate by intending communicants, and that he might have greater power in repelling improper persons from the sacrament; that the preface might be restored to the Ten Commandments; that the people be not enjoined to kneel when they are read, and that instead of the responses, the minister conclude with a suitable prayer. It was asked that preaching might not be left indifferent, as it seemed to be in the rubric, which enjoins the reading of a homily if there is no sermon. The rubric said that the homily was to be one of those already set forth, or hereafter to be set forth. The ministers thought they should not be bound to things not yet in being. Of the sentences in the offertory, some, they said, were Apocryphal, and others 'more proper to draw out the people's bounty to their ministers than their charity to the poor.' The collection for the poor, they thought, would be better made a little before the departing of the communicants than at the beginning of the service. In the 'exhortation' to be read when the people are 'negligent to come,' there were some things 'unseasonable' if it were meant to be read at the communion. It was thought that the rubric, which forbids any to come who have not 'a full trust in God, and a quiet conscience,' might discourage persons whose conscience is troubled. The confession was to be said by the minister alone. The rubric following the confession, directs that he shall stand up to say the absolution, 'turning himself to the people.' The ministers note here that 'this is most convenient throughout the whole service.' The words 'this day,' again occur in the collects for Christmas Day and Whitsunday. It was thought incongruous that these words should be repeated for seven or eight days together. The words in the prayer preceding the consecration, seemed to give more efficacy to the blood than to the body of Christ.

Objections to the offices.

The Communion.

The prayer at the consecration was not reckoned sufficiently explicit, because it said nothing of the minister's breaking the bread. It was asked that the minister might use Christ's words as nearly as possible, that he might not be required to deliver the bread and wine into every communicant's hand, nor to repeat the words to each, addressing them singly; that the parishioners be not enjoined to communicate thrice in the year; that kneeling may be left to the choice of the people, as it was in the time of King Edward; and that the long rubric in King Edward's Prayer Book, explaining that kneeling did not imply any natural presence of Christ's body in the elements, might be restored.

Baptism.

On baptism, the ministers mentioned the scruples which many learned and pious men had about baptizing the children of unbelievers. It was asked that they might not be obliged to baptize such children till their parents had made a profession of their faith and repentance. A longer notice than 'over night or in the morning,' was thought necessary. It was requested that parents might always stand sponsors for their children, or at least that it might be left free for them either to have sureties or not. The font should be placed so as all the congregation might see and hear the whole administration. A doubt was expressed if 'the flood, Jordan, and all other waters' were sanctified to a 'mystical washing away of sin.' The interrogatories were not to be addressed to the children, but to the parents, who were to be asked if they would have the child baptized in the Christian faith. The second prayer before baptism was supposed not to be well expressed. It asked *remission of sins by* spiritual *regeneration*. For this it was proposed to substitute the prayer that the child 'may be regenerated, and receive remission of sins.' In the prayer after baptism, an objection was made to giving thanks that the child 'had been regenerated by God's Spirit.' This was not true of every child, at least it was a question open to doubt. Private baptism was never to be admitted, except by a lawful minister; and where the child had been once baptized, there was no need, it was said, for reiterating in public any part of the administration. The office for private baptism was therefore unnecessary.

The ministers proceeded next to the Catechism. They asked that the first three questions be altered, as the multitude of children baptized during the last twenty years had no godfathers nor godmothers. For 'made a child of God, a member of Christ, and an inheritor of the kingdom of heaven,' they proposed to substitute 'visibly admitted into the number of the members of Christ, the children of God, and the heirs of the kingdom of heaven.' The answer concerning the number of sacraments was to be 'two only,' omitting the words 'as generally necessary to salvation.' After some more objections against promises made by sureties, grounded on the Presbyterian doctrine that the covenant is only made with the children of believers, the ministers suggested some additions to the Catechism, in the form of expositions of the Lord's Prayer, the Creed, the Commandments, and something about the essential doctrines of Christianity, such as faith, repentance, the two covenants, justification, sanctification, adoption, and regeneration.

CHAP. V.

The Catechism.

The remaining offices are, Confirmation, Solemnization of Matrimony, Visitation and Communion of the Sick, and the Burial of the Dead. A rubric, which said that the baptized had all things necessary to salvation without Confirmation, was allowed to be well meant, yet it was supposed dangerous, as likely to mislead ignorant people. The requirements for confirmation were thought insufficient, and that instead of the capacity to say certain articles of belief, it should be required of those to be confirmed, that they be of perfect age and instructed in the Christian religion. There was a rubric at the end of the Catechism which prescribed that the person to be confirmed 'shall be brought to the bishop by one that shall be his godfather or godmother.' The ministers thought this seemed to bring in other sureties besides those in baptism, and they could not see the 'need either of the one or the other.' The prayer before the imposition of the bishop's hands supposes the persons to be confirmed, regenerated and their sins forgiven, which certainly, the ministers said, is not the case, for many show no evidence of serious repentance or of 'saving grace.' Another prayer cites the example of the Apostles for laying on of hands, saying, that it is a 'sign' of God's favour and

Confirmation.

goodness. The ministers referred to Art. XXV., which says, that confirmation is a 'corrupt following of the Apostles.' They thought, also, that making it a 'sign,' seemed raising it to the dignity of a sacrament, while Art. XXV. says that 'confirmation hath no visible sign appointed by God.' It was also desired that confirmation might not be made so necessary to communion as that none might be communicants without it. The objections to the Marriage service were the use of the ring, because of its connection with Roman Catholic superstitions; the expression, 'with my body I thee worship,' because of the obsolete use of the word 'worship;' the performing of the ceremony in the name of the Trinity, lest it should be supposed a sacrament; the words, 'till death us *depart;*' the minister going to the table to read the psalms, and then turning to the people; the words, that matrimony is consecrated to 'an excellent mystery,' which also seemed to countenance the opinion that it was a sacrament; and, lastly, the rubric, since changed, that 'the new married persons the same day must receive the holy communion.' In the Visitation of the Sick it was recommended that the minister should have more liberty to vary his ministrations according to the different necessities and conditions of sick persons. It was also asked that the absolution be declarative and conditional, and that in the Communion of the Sick the minister might have a discretionary power of administering or refusing the sacrament. In the Burial of the Dead a rubric was required which might explain that the service was not read for the benefit of the deceased, but for the instruction and comfort of the living. Instead of meeting the corpse at the church stile, it was proposed that the minister might use his own judgment, and that when the weather was inclement he might be allowed to read the whole service in the church. The words 'in sure and certain hope' were not to be said over 'persons living and dying in open and notorious sins.' Even the largest charity does not allow us to assume that these have departed in the true faith, and to thank God that they are delivered out of the miseries of this life. In the old liturgy there was a rubric which enjoined, that in the churching of women, the woman was to kneel nigh unto some place where the table stands. The ministers said, that in some churches this was not convenient. A change in the psalm read at this service was recommended, and a rubric concerning the churching of unmarried women. The rubric enjoining that the woman must offer accustomed offerings, 'seemed to sound like a Jewish purification;' and another rubric that she must receive the Holy Communion, could not be well enforced, for 'a scandalous sinner may come to make this thanksgiving.'

To the exceptions of the ministers the bishops made a minute and full answer. They thought the best way to preserve peace was to keep to the liturgy, so that they might all speak the same thing. The alterations required to please the ministers would give offence to others. To the first general proposal, they answered that there was no private opinion in the liturgy; everything there was either evidently according to the word of God, or what has been generally received in the Catholic Church. The private conceptions of prayers before and after sermons were declared more likely to be the means of introducing private opinions into public worship. They denied that the liturgy was burdened with matters of church pomp, garments, and prescribed gestures. It was compiled in such a way as neither Romanist nor Protestant could justly find fault with it. The first never charged it with positive errors, but only with the want of something supposed to be necessary. It was acceptable to those to whom the name of Protestant most properly belongs,—that is, those who profess the Augustan Confession. The responses were defended for the very reason that the ministers sought to remove them. They served to quicken devotion, and were said to be certainly more edifying than a long and tedious prayer. The custom of keeping Lent as a religious fast was a custom received from the earliest times, and was always observed by the Catholic Church. This is also true of saints' days. They are not, indeed, of divine institution, but Christ Himself kept the feast of dedication, which was a festival of human origin. As to leaving the minister to omit parts of the liturgy for the sake of exercising his gift of prayer, the bishops answered that the spirit of prayer consisted in the inward graces of the Spirit, and not in extempore expressions, which were at the command of any man of natural parts, having a voluble tongue and audacity. If there was any such gift as that which the ministers called the gift of prayer, it was to be subject to the prophets and the order of the Church. The Council of Carthage knew how to prevent the mischiefs that come of extempore prayers, when they forbade any prayers in public except those prescribed by public authority. The reason given why the Books of the Apocrypha should not be read in Church was, that all things necessary to be believed were in the Holy Scriptures. To this the bishops answered, that the same argument would make sermons unnecessary. They wished that all sermons might be as profitable as the discourses contained in the Apocrypha. The communion service had always been read at the communion table, and there was no sound reason for changing this custom. The word minister was not always convenient, as sometimes there were offices performed by a deacon, and others by a priest. No sober person, it was said, could be offended with the word curate, which properly signifies one to whom the bishops commit the care of souls. The use of the words regenerated and converted, as applied to all professed members of the Church, was defended from the example of St. Paul to the Corinthians and the Galatians, where he called them Churches of God, sanctified in Christ Jesus, though many members of these Churches were known to be very far from being sanctified. In charity he applied to them all that character which belonged only to the greater part. The construction and order of the Collects were defended, and their general character, as meeting the necessities of Christian worship. There was no need, it was said, for the confession of original sin. That had been washed away in baptism. Then came 'the three nocent ceremonies,' which had from the beginning been a sore burden to the Puritans,—the surplice, the sign of the cross in baptism, and kneeling at the communion. The reasons against them were, that they were not prescribed in the Scriptures; that their use was an unwarranted addition to the service of God, who had commanded His people neither to take from His commandments nor to add to them; that they were a stumbling-block to the weak brethren; and that they had been the fountain of many evils to the Church and nation. The bishops said that the Church had always the power of imposing whatever was conducive to the decency and propriety of public service; that of this the superiors, and not the inferiors, were to be the judges. If persons are offended with these ceremonies, it is not the imposers who lay the stumbling-block in the way. By 'vain scrupulocity' they offend themselves. If their consciences are tender, the most easy way to have them satisfied is to obey their superiors. Much had already been written of the lawfulness of these ceremonies; the bishops would therefore only add, that decent ornaments and habits preserve reverence. They are held necessary to the solemnity of royal acts and acts of justice, and may as well be necessary to the solemnity of religious worship. No habit, they said, can be more suitable than the white linen, which resembles purity and beauty. The cross was always used in baptism in the earliest times. By its use, we testify our communion with the Christians of the first ages, and declare that we are not ashamed of the cross of Christ. The posture of kneeling was thought to be most convenient for the communion. When it was the custom to stand at the prayers of the Church, then the sacrament was received by the people standing. Now that we kneel when we pray, it surely would not be becoming to adopt a less reverent posture at the communion. Against sitting, the bishops offered this memorable argument, that if any one in this posture were to ask a prince to give his seal, it is not likely that he would give it.

When they came to the particular objections to the services, the bishops had as little to change as in the ceremonies. The place in the church for reading the prayers was best left to the judgment of the ordinary. It was thought best that the rubric about the vestments should continue as it is. The last clause of the Lord's Prayer is not in St. Luke, nor in the old copies of St. Matthew, nor used in the Latin Church; it was, therefore, a question, the bishops said, if it is a part of the Gospel at all. The Lord's Prayer is only used twice in the morning, and twice in the evening service, except when it occurs in the litany, the communion,

The particular objections answered.

or baptism, which are distinct services. The doxology being so short, and yet so solemn a confession of the blessed Trinity, should not be considered a burden to any Christian liturgy. The singing of the lessons was explained as meaning only distinct reading, and the *Benedicite* was defended on the same ground as the *Te Deum* or the *Veni Creator*, to which the ministers had not made any objections. The alterations suggested in the litany were described as so 'nice,' that they could only be proposed by men that were 'given to change.' In the Communion Service the first objection was against kneeling when the Commandments were read. The bishops could not see why the people should not on their knees ask pardon for having broken the divine laws, and grace to be enabled to keep them for the time to come. The homilies were defended on the ground that many livings were so small that they could not maintain a preacher. Moreover, to read a homily, it was said, was as much preaching the word as a man reading a sermon. The sentences, the exhortations, the minister's turning, and all the other parts of the service to which the ministers had objected, were defended by the bishops. The restoration of the rubric from King Edward's Prayer Book was refused, because the danger now was not idolatry but profanation.

All children to be baptized. The first request as to the service of baptism was, that the children of unbelieving parents should not be baptized. The bishops thought it too hard to punish the 'poor infants for the parents' sake.' The Church charitably concludes that Christ will accept every infant. It was declared an erroneous doctrine, and the ground of many other errors, that children have no right to baptism unless their parents are believers. It is found in St. Augustine that it was forbidden to leave it to the choice of the parents whether or not they should have sureties. The font, in primitive times, stood at the church door, to signify that baptism was the entrance into the Church mystical. Jordan and all other waters are declared to have been so far sanctified by Christ as to be the matter of baptism. The ministers thought the words, 'remission of sins by spiritual regeneration,' not well expressed. Their meaning was not to object to the doctrine itself, but to guard against confounding regeneration with remission of sins. The bishops do not seem to have understood the nature of the objection. They answer by defending the position that baptism is regeneration, and that in baptism we have remission of sins. Every child is regenerated in baptism. God's sacraments always have their effects, when the receiver does not 'place a bar' against them, which children cannot do. This benefit, conferred always in baptism, was the ground of defence for private baptism. It was thought better that a child should be privately baptized than not at all.

Coming to the Catechism, the bishops objected to removing the interrogatories because during the last twenty years many children had no godfathers or godmothers. Rules were not to be altered for other men's irregularities. 'Inheritors' was explained to mean the same as 'heirs.' The words, 'generally necessary to salvation,' were said to be a reason of the answer why there are only two sacraments. To the objections against sureties it was answered, that the effect of the sacrament depends neither on the faith of the parents nor the sponsors, and as for the proposed additions to the Catechism, the answer was, that it was not intended for a body of divinity, but for articles of faith suited to children and common people. As to the rubric before Confirmation, which says that those who are baptized have already all things necessary to salvation, the bishops said they could see no reason to fear misleading the vulgar by teaching them truth. St. Augustine says he is an infidel who teaches the contrary to be true. The requirements of the candidate for confirmation were regarded rather as what is necessary than as what is sufficient. It is charitably presumed that all baptized persons have not totally lost the grace conferred in baptism, and, therefore, in confirmation there is a prayer for the increase in them of the gifts of grace. That this rite should be administered only by the bishop, was defended as the ancient custom of the Church, and from this custom an argument was drawn for the superior dignity of bishops over presbyters. It was denied that the words of Art. XXV. are meant of confirmation. This rite is not included among those sacraments which have their origin in the 'corrupt following of the Apostles.' The imposition

In the Catechism 'inheritors' means 'heirs.'

Confirmation not a 'corrupt following of the Apostles.'

of hands is not a sacrament, but it is declared to be a very fit sign to certify 'the persons of what is then done to them.' This is explained by the language in the Acts, 'they laid their hands on them, and they received the Holy Ghost.' The ring in marriage was allowed to be a human institution. It is given as a pledge of fidelity and constant love. We have no such reasons for its use as are given by the Roman Catholic ritualists. Blessing in the name of the Trinity does not make a sacrament, and surely, the bishops said, the words of Scripture, that marriage is a representation of the union between Christ and His Church, need not have given offence to the ministers. Marriage being a solemn covenant, it was thought more becoming that it should be followed by the communion than by licentious festivities. The absolution in the Service for the Sick was said to be more agreeable to the Scriptures than one merely declaratory, and it was not thought proper that the minister should deny the 'viation' to any sick person humbly desiring it. As to the Burial of the Dead, the bishops said, that as the changes were not meant for tender consciences, but for tender heads, a cap would do better than a rubric. The words of hope and charity may be pronounced over the graves of all of whom we dare not say that they are lost. It is better to hope for the best than rashly to condemn. In the Churching of Women it was thought best that the woman should kneel near to the holy table, because of the offering she was to make. The bishops said, that in this the ministers need not fear Popery, for in the Church of Rome the woman has to kneel at the church door. If the woman is unmarried, she is to do her penance before she is churched. Offerings are required under the Gospel as well as under the law, and a time of thanksgiving is thought a fit time for an oblation. The bishops made some concessions, but they were not many, and consisted chiefly in verbal alterations. All of them, however, were not admitted when the Prayer Book was revised,* and some were then admitted which the bishops at the Conference refused.†

---

* Two especially, 'With my body I thee worship,' was to be changed into 'With my body I thee honour,' and in the Burial Service, 'sure and certain' were to be left out.

† One important concession was the restoration of the rubric which denied the presence of Christ's body in the Eucharist.

The Commission was limited to four months. By the time the exceptions and answers were made, only ten days remained. The Presbyterians begged a personal conference, in which they might discuss the questions at issue. This was granted. Dr. Pearson, Dr. Gunning, and Dr. Sparrow were on the episcopal side. Dr. Bates, Dr. Jacomb, and Richard Baxter represented the ministers. Gunning was a man of war. He had been in the arena with Roman Catholics, Baptists, Socinians, and almost every sect that had risen during the time of the Commonwealth. Theological controversy was the breath by which he lived. Baxter's life, too, had been a warfare against heresy. Agreement was hopeless when two such veterans were pitched against each other. Baxter made long speeches, and the bishops interrupted him. At last Bishop Cosin offered a paper as if from 'some considerable person,' proposing a way of reconciliation. This was, that the ministers should put down what they thought sinful in the doctrine or discipline of the Book of Common Prayer; or, if they thought nothing sinful, to propose what they desired as expedient. To this the ministers agreed. They had no fault to find with the doctrine of the Church. But they thought it contrary to the word of God that ministers should not be allowed to baptize without using the sign of the cross, to pray without the surplice, to administer the communion except to those that knelt, and to be obliged to say of every baptized infant, whether or not its parents are believers, that it is regenerated by the Holy Ghost. It was declared contrary to the word of God that a minister should be compelled to give the sacrament to unworthy persons; to pronounce absolution on all those who desired it; to give thanks for all who were buried, as brethren whom God in mercy had taken to Himself; and to be compelled to declare that there was nothing contrary to the word of God in the Prayer Book, the Book of Ordination, or the XXXIX. Articles of Religion. These subjects furnished matter for the disputants during the few remaining days of the Commission. They broke off at an *ergo*; and the conclusion was that they were further from agreement than when the King issued the warrant for the Conference. And thus was lost the best opportunity that

CHAP. V.

The public disputation.

Things 'sinful' in the Prayer Book.

296   RELIGIOUS THOUGHT IN ENGLAND.

CHAP. V.

was ever offered of uniting into one Church the two great parties that represented between them the religion of the nation. Every impartial man will owe the bishops a grudge that they were not more anxious for reconciliation than for victory; and, at the same time, every impartial man will utter a regret that the Presbyterian ministers, as they were called, were not wiser in their generation.

The Prayer Book revised by Convocation.

While the Commission was still sitting, a Convocation had begun to meet. In the first session after the close of the Savoy Conference, the Convocation entered upon the consideration of the Prayer Book. Many additions were made, and alterations to the number, it has been reckoned, of six hundred. But scarcely one of these alterations was of a kind likely to conciliate the Puritans. On the contrary, some things were made more offensive. The word 'priest' was substituted in several places where formerly it was 'minister.' 'Bishops, pastors, and ministers of the Church,' was changed into 'bishops, priests, and deacons;' and not content with the Apocryphal lessons already in the calendar, they added the extraordinary story of Bel and the Dragon. The revised book passed the Commons by a majority of six, and with it some rigid laws, which the Lords tried to mitigate. The Commons showed great jealousy lest any of Laud's peculiar doctrines might be introduced into the new book.* But the doomsday of the Puritans had come. The bishops had doubtless received 'hard measure' when they were ejected from their sees. Now by the revengeful Act of Uniformity they lead a triumph over a fallen enemy, and in the spirit of those to whom it is said—*Reward her even as she rewarded you, and in the cup which she hath filled fill to her double.*†

---

* Dr. Cardwell says that this fear was not without grounds. There is still in existence a corrected book in MS., prepared for this Convocation, and carrying so much the appearance of authority, as to contain minute instructions for the printer. The corrections are in the handwriting of Sancroft, who was then chaplain to Bishop Cosin. It is supposed to have been drawn up under the directions of Cosin and Wren. 'These corrections,' says Dr. Cardwell, 'contain strong indications of such sentiments respecting the real presence in the Eucharist, and prayers for the dead, as were entertained by these bishops, and became afterwards the distinguishing creed of the non-juring clergy.'

† The bishops stood thus in 1660:—
William Juxon, Canterbury.
George Griffith, St. Asaph.
William Roberts, Bangor.
William Pierce, Bath and Wells.
Gilbert Ironside, Bristol. (1661.)

THOMAS MORTON.

Of the bishops who died between the death of Charles I. and the restoration of Charles II., besides those already mentioned as writers, there is only one who requires special notice. This is Thomas Morton, Bishop of Durham. His works belong to the early part of that century. As he lived to a great age, he had seen the Church in all the vicissitudes of its history back almost to the days of Archbishop Parker. Morton was a true descendant of the old Elizabethan Churchmen. In his youth he had defended the ceremonies against the Puritans.* In his mature age he had battled against the innovations of Laud. He was promoted to the bishopric of Chester in 1616. When King James was in the northern counties the people gave expression to their feelings of loyalty by an increase of Sunday revelling. It is said that Morton remonstrated with James, and to this difference between the king and the bishop some have traced the origin of the 'Book of Sports.'† But Morton's chief controversies were with the Church of Rome. He wrote 'A Catholic Appeal for Protestants,' and a treatise on the 'Institution of the Sacrament.' He said that the word 'mass' was more applicable to the Communion in the Church of England than to the Eucharist as it is celebrated in the Church of Rome. The settling of this depends on the meaning of the word. Some trace it to *Missah*, the Hebrew word for an

CHAP. V.

Bishop Morton.

Origin of the 'Book of Sports.'

Henry King, Chichester.
William Lucy, St. David's.
Matthew Wren, Ely.
John Gauden, Exeter.
William Nicholson, Gloucester.
Nicholas Monk, Hereford.
Hugh Lloyd, Llandaff.
Robert Sanderson, Lincoln.
John Hackett, Lichfield and Coventry. (1661.)
Gilbert Sheldon, London.
Edward Reynolds, Norwich.
Robert Skinner, Oxford.
Benjamin Laney, Peterborough.
John Warner, Rochester.
Humphrey Henchman, Salisbury.
Brian Duppa, Winchester.
George Morley, Worcester.
Accepted Frewen, York.
Richard Sterne, Carlisle.
Brian Walton, Chester.
John Cosin, Durham.
Samuel Rutter, Sodor and Man.

* His early controversies were with William Ames, generally called Amesius.

† There are other accounts of the origin of the 'Book of Sports' not so creditable to Morton. Some say that he was really the author of the book, others make it a compromise between him and the king. Here is the account given by Mr. Perry in his History of the Church of England,—'In his progress through Lancashire last year, the king had been offended at a Puritanical strictness in the observation of the Lord's day, which he found prevalent. It was represented to him that the Papists were gaining much influence through the rigours insisted on by the Puritan clergy, and Morton, Bishop of Chester, who was with the king, recommended him to publish an edict, authorizing certain sports and games on the afternoons of Sundays.'

offering. Morton prefers the other derivation from *Missa est*, the words at the end of the service dismissing those who are not to communicate. In Roman Catholic churches all that choose may remain, though they be not communicants; but in the Church of England the non-communicants are dismissed. In this sense the word 'mass' was retained in the Augustan Confession. The Fathers, Bishop Morton says, call bread and wine a sacrifice, but improperly. They never reckoned the body and blood of Christ to be the subject matter. They speak of a bloody sacrifice in the Eucharist in the same way that they call baptism a sacrifice, because it was a representation of Christ's death. And in agreement with this, they called the communion tables more frequently by their proper name of tables than by the figurative name of altars, which they would not have done had they been proper altars.

Morton was succeeded in the diocese of Durham by John Cosin, who was one of the chief speakers at the Savoy Conference.* He had come into some repute in the time of Charles I., and was reckoned among the supporters of Archbishop Laud. He had published a book of devotions, which might have passed for Laud's. It was severely handled by William Prynne, who had always a keen sense of the presence of the new heresy. Cosin had been made a Prebendary of Durham Cathedral by Bishop Neyle, one of the earliest promoters of what was called Arminianism. He was impeached by the Commons at the instance of Peter Smart, another prebendary. The charges against him were that he had placed the table in Durham Cathedral *altarwise*; that he had officiated in front of it with his back to the people; and that he had worn some unusual vestments in the performance of the service. He appeared, as we have seen, at the conference concerning Richard Mon-

---

* Richard Baxter says:—'Bishop Cosin was there constantly, and had a great deal of talk with so little logic, natural or artificial, that I perceived no one moved by anything he said. But two virtues he showed (though none took him for a magician); one was, that he was excellently well versed in Canons, Councils, and Fathers, which he remembered, when by citing of any passages we tried him. The other was that, as he was of a rustic wit and carriage, so he would endure more freedom of our discourse with him, and was more affable and familiar than the rest.'—*Reliquiæ Baxterianæ*.

tagu's books in company with the leaders of that party. Again, in 1626, we find him in the same company when he preached the sermon at the consecration of Francis White.*

This sermon bears the marks of a period when the two parties were both powerful, and both determined to have the victory. Cosin exalts the bishops collectively to that place in the Church which, in the Church of Rome, belongs only to the Pope. Through the bishops comes that 'ghostly power' which is the strength of the Church for ever. The clergy derive this grace from the bishops, and together they are the salt of the earth, without which nothing can be savoured. The sermon is not controversial; but at such a time, and on such an occasion, it would have been impossible to let pass the opportunity of setting forth the errors of those who did not take this view of the bishops and the clergy. The Puritans—by this term we mean those earnest Churchmen who were not of Cosin's party—had always believed that 'a minister's first duty was to preach the Gospel.' So far King James was on their side at the Hampton Court Conference. It was by preaching that they had acquired their influence in England. The other party could not say that preaching was not an important part of a clergyman's duty, but they tried to lessen its importance. They wished to exalt the priest above the preacher. Cosin said that he had not come there to preach down preaching, but he did wonder that some ministers should think preaching an independent office, 'as if we were all bishops when we preach.' He said that orders did not confer authority to preach the Gospel. In virtue of our ordination we may offer up the prayers and sacrifices of the Church, administer sacraments, bind and loose, but the 'book says we are not to preach unless we be thereunto appointed.' It is the office primarily of a bishop to preach, but of a presbyter only when 'thereto licensed by the bishop himself.'†

Cosin does not seem to have taken the side of his friends on the question of the Sabbath. He said that it was

---

* The consecrators were, Neyle, of Durham; Buckeridge, of Rochester; Field, of St. David's; Murray, of Llandaff.

† The words which Cosin here quotes are now to be found only in the service for 'The Ordering of Deacons.'

morally binding on us to keep holy one day in seven. He thinks Calvin wrong in supposing the day might be changed at our pleasure, or not kept so frequently as one in seven. And he thinks that by Scripture and the judgment of the Fathers, the day must be the first, because we rest in memory of the Resurrection. So far Cosin was a Puritan, but no further. He says nothing of the 'Sports.' When he explains the Fourth Commandment, he says, that all the Jews' Sabbaths being gone, it can only mean to us 'Remember to keep the festivals.' The Sunday is holy in the same way as all consecrated things or persons. It is set apart from a common use, as priests and magistrates are set apart. It is holy as the water in baptism, or the bread and wine in the communion. No Sabbatarian could well object to this explanation of the holiness of the Lord's day. But it is incompatible, surely, with the morrice-dance and the 'church ales,' or the Sunday may-pole on the village green.

Cosin on the History of the Canon of Scripture.

Bishop Cosin's chief works were connected with the Roman Catholic controversy. He wrote a 'Scholastical History of the Canon of Holy Scripture.' In this work he gave the history of all the books that were held canonical till the Council of Trent made a new canon. He showed that the universal testimony of the Church was for the books which we have, without the Apocryphal writings. Their number, he said, was fixed, and there is no doubt which books they were. Individuals may have objected to some of them. At different times doubts may have been raised about their genuineness, but none of them have ever been rejected by entire Churches. Cosin does not overlook the internal testimonies which the Scriptures give that they are divine, but he does not raise this internal evidence to the same certainty as the external. He depends on the constant testimony of the Catholic and universal Church. On this subject we cannot draw a distinct line between the views of the Puritan and those of the High Churchman. Neither of them denied the internal light or the external testimony. But some of the Puritans made internal evidence amount to a proof of the canonicity, as well as divinity of the books, and some High Churchmen rested solely on the testimony of the Church. Cosin is, in a great measure, free from the faults of both sides. His argument, as directed against the Church of Rome, is, that the Council of Trent had no right to add to the canon that had been hitherto received by the whole Catholic Church since the Apostles' days. The Jewish canon was fixed. Josephus testifies that it consisted of twenty books. This testimony is repeated by Eusebius. There are passages in the New Testament which show that Jesus and His apostles were familiar with the Apocryphal writings, yet never once do they allege a passage from them to prove a doctrine. Origen says that the Apocryphal books were not received as of equal authority with the Scriptures. To the same effect are the testimonies of all ecclesiastical writers in all centuries, as Cosin quotes them down to the Council of Trent. At that council Rome dared to defy the traditions and the authority of the universal Church.

Cosin wrote also 'The History of Popish Transubstantiation,' to which he opposed 'The Catholic Doctrine of the Holy Scriptures, the Ancient Fathers, and the Reformed Churches, about the Sacred Elements and the presence of Christ in the Blessed Sacrament of the Eucharist.' When we say Cosin taught that there was a *real presence* of Christ's body and blood in the Supper, we only affirm what was true of all orthodox Protestant divines. Even the Westminster Assembly had maintained a real though *spiritual* presence of the body and the blood. Cosin said that between his doctrine of the 'real presence' and the transubstantiation of the Church of Rome, there was 'a great gulf fixed.' He explained, as the Reformers had done, that when the Fathers call the bread and wine the body and blood of Christ, we are not to understand them according to the letter. It was the usual manner of speaking of sacraments, to give to the sign the name of the thing signified. The Fathers therein, Cosin says, explain in other places how their words are to be taken. They frequently call the sacramental bread and wine types, symbols, figures, and signs of the body and blood of Christ.

Archbishop Cranmer had seen all this, and expressed it. He had seen, too, that transubstantiation was the natural fruit of speaking of this sacrament in the high figures of rhetoric. The metaphors of the Fathers were taken for literal speeches by the men of later ages. Though Cranmer saw this, he persisted in using the old figures. Bishop Cosin does the same. He denies that the body of Christ is present, but he affirms at the same time that it is present as a spirit. How it can be a body when divested of all the attributes by which it is a body, is *to be received by faith, and not inquired into by reason.* We eat the body, Cosin says, mystically. This word he uses as equivalent to sacramentally. This again is equivalent to spiritually; and though the body is only eaten spiritually, it is eaten as truly as if it were a corporal eating. He quotes Bishop Ponet's 'Diallactic,' where it is said 'the holy Eucharist contains in itself the truth, nature, and substance of the body of our blessed Saviour,' and that these words *nature* and *substance* are not to be rejected 'because they are used by the Fathers.' The difference is, that we have not Christ's body in its natural form. In the sacrament we have the mystical body. The subject is the same, but the manner of the presence is different. Cosin quotes also from Antonio De Dominis, whom he claims as 'a sound Church of England man.'* De Dominis, he says, has proved that for a thousand years the Church knew of no presence of the body of Christ but the spiritual presence as it is received by the Reformed Churches. Cosin again quotes from the Gallican and Helvetian Confessions, which contain the doctrines of the Churches of Geneva and Scotland. In these confessions we have the same distinction continually asserted. The eating of Christ's body is called 'spiritual' and 'sacramental.' It is said to be the substance of His body which is eaten, yea, 'the very substance which He took of the blessed Virgin.' How that body can be in heaven and also in the Eucharist, is explained in these Confessions by the power of the Spirit, which 'exceeds our sense and apprehension.' The body is present, and yet not as a body; for, though received by the communicants, it cannot be carried about in the consecrated bread. This mode of speaking becomes in-

The foreign Confessions on the 'real presence.'

---

* Cosin vindicates Spalatensis, denies that he ever renounced the Church of England, and blames the 'rigid sort' of clergy for causing him to leave England.

telligible only when it is accompanied by such explanations as were given by Cranmer, Ridley, and Latimer, when they said that the body of Christ was eaten not in the Eucharist only, but in all acts of worship. This is not stated explicitly by Cosin; and it is perhaps here that we have the first marked difference on this subject between Laud's Churchmen and the Reformers. The latter said that the faithful eat the body of Christ and drink His blood always in their life of faith. The former limited the spiritual eating and drinking to the Eucharistic feast. The Church of Rome professes to offer Christ in the Supper. Andrewes and Buckeridge said that in the sacrament we offered Christ in His members. Cosin expressly denies that Christ is sacrificed in the Eucharist.

The exact measure of the civil ruler's authority in the Church does not seem ever to have been well defined. Charles II. said that he had the power to excommunicate as well as the clergy. This was told to Bishop Cosin, who answered, that the King had no such power. That was a power derived from Christ 'in virtue of holy orders.' We have classed Bishop Cosin with the High Churchmen of his day, but in many things he was not a man of a party. He believed in bishops, and he believed that to bishops properly belonged the power of ordination. He thought this could be fairly inferred from the practice of the Apostles, but he could not say more for it. 'I would be loath,' he says 'to determine that those ordained by presbyters are no ministers.' It is not desirable that presbyters should make presbyters, yet their ordination is good and valid. 'It is,' he says, 'the judgment of learned and eminent men, both Catholics and Protestants, that presbyters have the intrinsic power of ordination *in actu primo*.' And that this was the doctrine of the Church of England, he brings forward the case of a French minister coming to incorporate himself with us. In such a case we do not re-ordain, and never did. Cosin says that if we are to consider the ministers of the Presbyterian Churches as unordained, we must excommunicate the Lutheran Churches as well, for their bishops or superintendents have no other ordination but that of presbyters. And then, he asks, what shall become of the Protestant party?

Bishop Walton.

Brian Walton, who was made Bishop of Chester, belonged to the same class of Churchmen as Bishop Cosin. He was deprived, in 1643, as one of 'the scandalous ministers.' He had been incumbent of St. Martin's Orgar, in Cannon Street. The parishioners petitioned against him, making nearly the same charges as were made against all the ministers who held his views of the Church and its government. He had ordered the churchwardens to place the table *altarwise* alongside of the wall. They refused. With the help of the Bishop of Rochester and some other friends Walton removed it himself. When this was done, he read part of the service in the reading pew and another part at the 'altar.' He refused to preach in the afternoon, or to allow another to preach for him, though the parishioners offered to provide a preacher at their own charge. They complained also that he was non-resident all the summer, and left the souls of the people in ' the care of an ignorant curate, with a salary *catched out of the revenue of the parish lands.*' He had made lawsuits to recover his tithes, and he had spoken not too reverently of some of the men who had got into power in the beginning of the Long Parliament. The tithe question was the occasion of Walton's first appearance as a writer. The London clergy, since the time of Henry VIII., derived their incomes from the oblations of the parishioners. It had been fixed by Henry at two-and-ninepence in the pound. But the clergy could not always get the exact sum, as they had no means of knowing the precise amount of the rents. They had sought redress in the time of James, but nothing had been done. They had petitioned Charles, who arbitrated in their favour. Walton's appearing as the advocate of the clergy against the citizens was not in his favour when the time came for Parliament to receive petitions against *scandalous ministers.* Like the High Churchmen of his day, he was equally opposed to the Church of Rome and the Church of Geneva. He was probably the first who used that comparison which has often been repeated, that the Church of England has been crucified between two thieves, the Papist and the Puritan.

A scandalous minister.

Driven from his parish, Walton spent many years in the

preparation of his 'Biblia Polyglotta.' It was a vast work, and the execution of it at such a time, and under such circumstances, bespoke a patient and a faithful soul. But the enemies that harassed the Church of England did not spare, he says, the labours of her sons. His object had been to assert the purity, integrity, and supreme authority of the original texts against those of Rome, and to reject the Jewish opinions received by the Puritans. But his was the lot of every man who has laboured to know the real truth concerning the Scriptures. Origen and Jerome had both been censured in their day for seeking to correct the current versions of the Bible, and Erasmus was denounced by the monks as a profane subverter of *the word of God*. John Owen said of the Bible critics, when speaking of Walton's Polyglott, 'they print the original and defame it; gathering up translations of all sorts, and setting them up in competition with it.' He said that Walton 'had taken away all certainty about sacred truth, and that now men had no choice but to turn Atheists or Papists.' It had really come to pass that 'men take upon them to correct the Scriptures, which are the *word of God*.'

Walton defended himself against Owen's objections. The vindication has a special value, as giving us the position which the better class of High Churchmen in that day took up in regard to the Bible. The inferences that Walton made truth uncertain, and subverted the foundations, not only of the Protestant religion but of Christianity, are, of course, denied. Walton had only rejected the authority of the Masoretic points, and he had compared the various readings that he might, if possible, determine the correct reading. These various readings, he said, were of no moment. They were but the casual mistakes of transcribers, and do not touch any doctrine. With the exception of these two things, the Hebrew points and the various readings, Walton was as much a Scripturalist as Owen. He maintained that the original texts had not been corrupted either by Jews, Christians, or heretics. He said that their authority was supreme in all matters of doctrine, and that they were the rule by which translations were to be tried. The copies which we now have are the true transcripts of the first autographs. The special providence of God, Walton said, had watched over these writings to preserve them pure and uncorrupt, and they will be so preserved to the end of the world, in spite of all sectaries and heretics. The various readings are all such as may be rectified and emended by collation of other copies. To correct an error crept into the original is not, Walton said, to correct the original, for no error can be a part of the original text. This, of course, was true only where the error could be demonstrated. That there were no errors in the text beyond the reach of our criticism to discover was proved by the previous argument, that it was against the providence of God and the fidelity of His Church, to whom the sacred oracles were committed, that they should be corrupted. Walton did not then take up the ground which is generally taken by the doctors of the Church of Rome, that the Hebrew text is not to be trusted. He maintained rather that it was possible for us to get a correct Hebrew text, and that this was to be our guide. He could not conclude without a fling at the sectaries. The Church was the keeper of Holy Writ, but heretics and sectaries have ever tried to corrupt it. And this not only in old times, but even now they 'boldly endeavour to deprave it either in the letter or sense, or both.'*

When Walton left London for his bishopric, his journey to Chester was like the triumphal march of a conquering monarch. His reception in the city was a great ovation. Saluted by the train bands, amid the rejoicings of the multitude, he hastened to the cathedral to give thanks to God that at length peace and victory had come. We always

---

* Walton had twenty-eight assistants in his work. The greater part of them were among the deprived clergymen, as Ussher, Thorndike, Pocock, Hammond, Fuller, and Casaubon. Two at least were Presbyterians, John Lightfoot and Patrick Young. Some of them were not deprived, as Sanderson and Wheelock. Some were laymen, as John Selden. Of some of the others nothing is known.

Walton's hatred to the Puritans was intense. We must forget this when we try to make a true estimate of the man. But what we excuse in him is not to be excused in those who endeavour to perpetuate the party spirit of the times in which he lived. During the last thirty years we have had biographies of Walton, Laud, and some other Churchmen of this era, written in the *spirit which now worketh in the children of disobedience.*

think of Walton as a stately Churchman. He loved pomp and splendour, but he loved work too. No man could have enjoyed the hour of triumph more than he, but the sand-glass of life was nearly run. He was consecrated in December, 1660. He went to Chester in September, 1661. Two months later he returned to London to attend the Convocation, where he was seized with a fatal sickness, and died.*

Walton's consecration and death.

Some years later John Pearson, the author of the 'Exposition of the Creed,' was made Bishop of Chester.† All we know of Pearson's theology is from this work. It consisted originally of sermons to his parishioners when he was Rector of St. Clement's, Eastcheap. The 'Exposition of the Creed' is ponderously orthodox, but destitute of originality. It is a curious fact that this work was intended originally as a check to infidelity. But this was characteristic of Pearson's mind. He was a believing theologian, who never in any way understood the doubts which seem to be part of the nature of some men. He says in the preface that 'the principles of Christianity are now as freely questioned as the most controverted points; the grounds of faith are as safely denied as the most unnecessary superstructures.' To establish Christianity against the unbelievers of his day, he goes to the Creed, because the Creed leads to the Scriptures. Pearson divides revelation into two kinds—immediate and mediate, or that which is made to a man directly, and that which depends on the testimony of another. Those to whom God spoke immediately, knew and perceived the truth of what was revealed. They had it on the immediate testi-

Bishop Pearson.

---

* From all that can be learned of Walton's early history, he seems to have been of very humble origin. He had begun as a sizar at Cambridge, and before he was forty years of age, he had worked his way into three rectories—St. Martin's Orgar in the City, St. Giles's in the Fields, and Sandon in Kent, with a prebend's stall in St. Paul's. He was also one of King Charles's chaplains.

† 'Dr. Pearson was their true logician and disputant, without whom, as far as I could discern, we should have had nothing from them but Dr. Gunning's passionate invectives, mixed with some argumentations. He disputed accurately, soberly, and calmly (being but once in any passion), breeding in us a great respect for him, and a persuasion that if he had been independent, he would have been for peace, and that if all were in his power, it would have gone well. He was the strength and honour of that cause, which we doubted whether he heartily maintained.'—*Reliq. Bax.*

mony of God. Other men have the same truth, not by manifestation, but by attestation. And this is properly faith. The people believed because of the miracles of Moses and of the Apostles. We give our assent to what is revealed, not as apparent or as probable, but only as credible. In the exercise of this kind of faith Pearson saw something divine. He called it 'a spiritual act, imminent, internal, and known to no man but him who believeth.' The excellence of what was taught was not denied. The purity of the doctrines of the Gospel, and their tendency to produce righteousness of life, were acknowledged, but they do not form any essential part of the foundation of belief. That rests solely on testimony. Pearson denies that man has any 'connate, inbred notion of a God.' That knowledge comes to the naked soul by sensation, instruction, and rational reflection. This reflection, however, is grounded upon a universal reason. The same distinction was made by Locke and his followers. But it is doubtful if the universal reason does not in the end mean the same thing as was meant by connate notion.

Bishop Pearson was decidedly a Scripturalist, not, indeed, of the Puritan class, who looked to the Scriptures alone, but of that class who regarded the Fathers in some vague sense as infallible interpreters of the Scriptures. All the passages in the Psalms called Messianic are quoted to prove that Jesus was the Messiah. Jeremiah xxxi. 22 is supposed to be a prophecy that He was to be born of a virgin. In Proverbs xxx. 4, the words 'Who hath established all the ends of the earth? What is his name? What is his son's name?' are thought to be a proof that God always had a son.

Pearson's definition of the Catholic Church includes all Christians. He quotes what the Fathers say of the Church Catholic, and of the impossibility of being saved out of it. But by the Catholic Church we can scarcely suppose that they meant the same as Bishop Pearson means. The word *Catholic*, as he shows, was a later addition to the Creed, and doubtless had its origin in one sect claiming to be the whole or universal Church, to the exclusion of those who differed from them.

Pearson entered into long and learned arguments to

prove that our material bodies would rise again. In the translation of the Creed in our Church service it is said that we believe in 'the resurrection of the body.' In the Greek and Latin the words are 'the resurrection of the flesh.' The Creed of the Church of Aquileia reads 'of this flesh.' In the translation of the Creed in the service for Baptism the words are rendered according to the Greek and Latin. St. Jerome gave his reason why we should say 'flesh' and not 'body.' The reason was virtually a refutation of St. Paul's argument about bodies natural and bodies spiritual, terrestrial and celestial. 'Thou fool,' said St. Paul, 'thou sowest not that body that shall be.' 'Fool again,' answered the profound St. Jerome and the orthodox Bishop Pearson, 'we do sow that body which shall be.' The very flesh which is buried shall rise again, they said, and therefore the Creed should be, 'I believe in the resurrection of *the flesh!*' St. Jerome argues the matter in detail. While the orthodox by 'body' meant 'flesh,' the heretics, he says, by body might mean a spiritual body. Bishop Pearson endorses St. Jerome's arguments against St. Paul. 'The bodies of men,' he says, 'however corrupted, wheresoever in their parts dispersed, how long soever dead, shall hereafter be re-collected in themselves, and united to their own souls.' The particles of matter which form our bodies have formed the bodies of men who lived before us, and will form the bodies of other men in generations to come. How each will possess the same particles which belonged to many different bodies may be beyond our comprehension, but nothing is impossible with God. Pearson says it is not only possible that every body at the Resurrection shall consist of the same particles by which it was constituted here, but it is highly probable, and on Christian principles infallibly certain. The parts of the body do not perish; and He who made man at first can make him what he was before.

CHAP. V.

On the resurrection of the body.

At the restoration of the King, Robert Sanderson was elevated to the see of Lincoln.* Sanderson had held the

Bishop Sanderson.

---

* Bishop Sanderson did not say much at the Savoy Conference. In the account which Baxter gives of the disputation between himself and Gunning, he says, 'When Dr. Gunning had read his insulting answer the

living of Boothby Pagnell during all the changes since the death of Charles I. He escaped by the simple device of not reading the Prayer Book, but using the prayers without reading them. He was of the moderate party, not a Puritan, but in doctrine a decided Calvinist.* His works consist chiefly of sermons, which have no theology peculiar to them. Among his smaller works there is a treatise on the Sabbath, in which he takes the side opposed to the Puritans. This name, he says, is altogether Jewish, and was never, till of late years, applied to our Sunday. The use of it is quite allowable, as its simple meaning is rest; but Sanderson recommends that it be only sparingly used. As we read the Fourth Commandment every Sunday in the Communion Service, and add a prayer that our hearts may be inclined to keep this law, there must be a sense in which we acknowledge it to be binding on us. Sanderson says that these laws do not bind us, because they were delivered to the Jews. They only bind us morally. The determination of the time of the seventh day was ceremonial, but the substance of it is moral, which is, that we devote a certain time to holy rest from secular occupations, that we may attend upon the public and solemn worship of God. Taking *jus divinum* in a wide sense, Sanderson says that keeping sacred one day in seven is of Divine positive right. The consequence of leaving it in the power of the Church to change the day at its pleasure would be evil. We deduce the obligation of keeping it from the Scriptures by the same kind of reasoning that we infer the *Divine right* of bishops,

---

day before, and made a great matter of my telling the respondent of '*begging the question*,' they put Dr. Sanderson, Bishop of Lincoln, into the chair, that his learning and gravity might put a reputation on his sentence (he being a very worthy man, but for that great peevishness which injuries, partiality, temperature, and age, had caused him). The bishop, in a few angry words, pronounced that Gunning had the better, and that the respondent could not beg the question, and that I was a man of contention if I offered to reply.' Baxter says in another place, 'Bishop Sanderson, of Lincoln, was sometimes there, but never spoke that I know of but what I have told you before. But his great learning and worth are known by his labours, and his aged peevishness not unknown. At his death he made it his request that the ejected ministers might be used again; but his request was rejected by them that had outwitted him, as being too late.'

* This we have gathered from his works. It is said that through the instrumentality of Dr. Hammond, Sanderson was converted from Calvinism to 'Catholic views.'

or the distinction of orders in the Church. It is among those things which any particular Church may change, but, being long established and confirmed by ecclesiastical and imperial constitutions, it is not desirable that it should be changed. All this reasoning leaves it a very open question what kind of a Sunday we are to keep. We might have concluded that Sanderson meant to enforce a strict observance of one day sacred in seven. But he says that recreation is not to be condemned, such as walking and discoursing with men of liberal education. This is very good for scholars, but for the common sort of people Sanderson thinks that his Majesty's declaration has settled that. The common people prefer recreation which is loud and boisterous. They are to have shooting, leaping, pitching the bar, and stool-ball. These are said to be better for them than dicing or carding, but in all these games the bishop recommends *moderation*. They are to be so used as that the people may be more fitted for the service of God on the rest of the day.

In another treatise, called 'Episcopacy not Prejudicial to Royal Power,' Sanderson tries to explain the relations between the civil ruler and the rulers of the Church. When the Divine right of Episcopacy was first taught in England, the Puritans said that this was an infringement of the royal prerogative. Had the king and the bishops been on different sides, this might have been proved; but as they were on one side, each acknowledging the divinity of the other, they easily settled between them their respective rights. Charles published a 'Proclamation,' in which he pronounced the Ecclesiastical Courts and ministers to be according to the laws of the realm. He gave them greater licence than they had before. Summonses, citations, and other processes ecclesiastical in their Courts were henceforth to be issued without the King's seal. In the time of Edward all this was forbidden. The laws of Edward's reign were repealed, so that bishops might hold their visitations without the great seal of England. Sanderson explained the *jus divinum* of bishops as meaning a great deal less than it was generally understood to mean. At the most, it only meant apostolical institution. It need not in any way interfere with the royal prerogative. The regal and episcopal powers were of two different kinds, and had no dependence on each other.

Henry Hammond was appointed to the bishopric of Worcester, but he died before he was consecrated. Hammond was a voluminous writer, and was engaged in all the controversies of his time that affected the Church of England. He wrote in Latin some Dissertations on Episcopacy, which were answered by the Provincial Assembly of London, in a book called *Jus Divinum Ministerii Evangelici*. In reply to this book, Hammond wrote 'A Vindication' of his Dissertations. There were peculiarities in Hammond's defence of Episcopacy which require to be specially noticed. He stated the question between the Presbyterians and the Prelatists to be simply whether the Apostles of Christ, when they planted Churches, left them to be governed by a common council, or whether in every Church there was one with superior power and authority. This was undoubtedly the clearest statement of the case that had ever been made. It left the course of the argument to be an inquiry into the facts as they could be determined from Scripture, and the writings of the age succeeding that of the Apostles. In accordance with this, Hammond, instead of deriving his argument from the names applied to the officers of the Church, tried to determine from the facts what the offices were which they held. The first root of authority in the Church was Christ's commission to His Apostles. Were the Apostles constituted a common council of social rulers, or were they sent forth each with individual power as a planter and governor of the Church? The latter, Hammond thinks, is evident. The first bishops which the Apostles made are also called apostles, as James the Bishop of Jerusalem. Each of the Churches of Asia had a bishop or individual governor, called the 'Angel of the Church.' The testimonies from antiquity are chiefly those of Ignatius, but to them are added testimonies from many other ancient writers.

If the angels of the Asiatic Churches were bishops, and Christ addressed to each of them an epistle, it follows that Christ approved of this superiority of bishops in the Churches. That the 'angels' were presidents over the Church is admitted by both sides. The Presbyterians said that by 'angel' was here meant a college of presbyters. Hammond was to prove that 'angel' was a single person, and therefore a bishop. Each Church had its 'angel,' as Andreas Cæsariensis, the first commentator on the Revelation, said, 'the number of bishops is equal to the number of churches.' Among the Jews the chief priest was called an 'angel.' For this Hammond refers to Malachi, and he quotes from Photius these words, out of Diodorus Siculus:—'Him they call the high-priest, and deem him to be an angel or messenger of the commands of God.' The Council of Chalcedon reckoned up twenty-seven bishops in the see of Ephesus to their time, Timothy being the first. Polycrates, who affirms himself to have been the eighth Bishop of Ephesus, bears testimony to the fact of Timothy being the first bishop. So that either Timothy, or one of his successors, was the angel to whom the Epistle was addressed. The testimony of Irenæus, that Polycarp was Bishop of Smyrna, is often quoted. It is affirmed by Tertullian, who says, 'As the Church of Smyrna relates Polycarp to have been constituted there by John, as the Church of Rome affirms Clement to have been ordained by Peter, so in like manner the rest of the churches exhibit the records of those whom they have had for their bishops constituted by the Apostles and conveyors of the Apostolical seed to them.' By whatever name the 'angel' or bishop may be called, Hammond concludes that he was certainly a bishop in our modern sense of the word, 'a single overseer in the church.'

It was objected by the Presbyterians that, in the Revelation, St. John never uses the name bishop. He frequently speaks of presbyters. He calls himself a presbyter, and that when he is describing the office of those who are nearest the throne of Christ in His Church. If Polycarp had been made a bishop by St. John, it is strange that the word bishop never occurs in his writings, though he lived so long after the time when it is said the Church was governed by bishops. Hammond answers that we are not to conclude negatively that there were no bishops because they are not mentioned by St. John. The objection only concerns the bare name of bishop, which, had it been found

St. John calls himself a 'presbyter.'

in St. John's writings, the Presbyterians would have explained as only meaning presbyter. So that the absence of the word affects the argument as little as if it had been present. Moreover, Hammond in the Dissertations had explained the four-and-twenty presbyters around the throne, as the four-and-twenty bishops of Judea sitting in council at Jerusalem, encompassing James the Metropolitan, with the four beasts as the four Apostles that were joined with them in the Council, and the seven lamps as the emblems of the seven deacons. Presbyter did not mean in the early Church what it means with us. It was then equivalent to bishop, or one set over others with authority. John in this very Revelation calls himself 'the presbyter,' and yet he was an Apostle, or superior governor of the whole Jewish Church in Asia. The Greek scholiast, speaking of this passage, said of St. John, 'By the word presbyter, he calls himself bishop.' The Presbyterians said that there was not the least intimation in all St. John's writings of the superiority of one presbyter over another, except the case of Diotrephes, whom he chides for affecting such a primacy. Hammond answers, that granting this, his argument is still good. He has maintained that bishops and presbyters are the same order, and above deacons; but presbyters in the modern sense of the word did not exist within the compass of the time in which the books of the New Testament were written. This Diotrephes contended for superiority, not only over his equals, but over St. John himself. 'He receiveth us not,' says St. John. This is not the primacy of bishops. They always acknowledged the superiority of Apostles.

The Presbyterians said that those very writers who affirm that St. John made Polycarp Bishop of Smyrna, and that St. Peter made Ignatius Bishop of Antioch, say also that John himself was for many years Bishop of Ephesus and Metropolitan of all Asia. From this it is inferred that they did not use the word bishop in the modern sense. St. John was an Apostle, which was an office above that of a bishop. Hammond admits that the statement is correct, but he refuses the inference. The office from which Judas fell is called a bishopric. Cyprian says that Christ 'chose Apostles, that is, bishops and governors of the Church.' Epiphanius says 'the Apostles were bishops.' A bishop in the prelatical sense is a governor of the Church, which John was at Ephesus and Peter at Rome. As planters of the Church they were apostles, as governors they were bishops. In later times canons were made, that no man should be a bishop without a title or particular see; but before these canons there were bishops that had no fixed dioceses. Such were the Apostles, who were bishops wherever they went. The Presbyterians again objected that the words 'angel' and 'star' were common to all ministers, and did not import any peculiar jurisdiction. Hammond denies that angel is ever applied in the Scriptures to any officer of the Church except to prophets, as in Haggai, to John the Baptist as in St. Matthew, and to the chief priests, as in Malachi. The stars are the same in number as the churches, which seems to limit the use of stars to bishops, or governors of the Church. Hammond admits that there is some force in the objection that a system of Church government is not to be built on such metaphorical words as we find in the Revelation. Yet he says that, though 'star' is allegorical, the word 'angel' is not. It is given rather as the explication of the mystery.

The point in the case of the seven angels of the Churches, on which the Presbyterians specially dwelt, was the use of the plural in the epistle to the Church of Thyatira. This, they said, was a proof that by 'angel' was not meant the bishop, but the presbytery, or council of ministers. Hammond's explanation is, that in an epistle addressed to a particular person, others under his care and charge may be occasionally mentioned. In the Epistle to Titus, Paul says in the end, 'Grace be with you all.' When the people of Israel or Judea fell into sins, God sent a prophet to the King to admonish him. The people were admonished in the King. Another way of solving this difficulty is a different reading. Some manuscripts read, 'But to you I say, the rest which are in Thyatira.' The Presbyterians said that the Church of Ephesus was a collective body. There were in it many presbyters, to whom St. Paul committed the charge of the Church. Hammond answered that though the Church of Ephesus was a collective body, it did not fol-

The 'angel' addressed as a plurality of persons.

low that the Church was the angel. The argument depended on the plurality of elders. Hammond had already given an exposition of these elders, which was an answer to this argument. The elders of Ephesus were the bishops of the other cities of Asia. Irenæus says St. Paul was 'as careful to take his leave of them, as many as could conveniently come to Miletus, as of the Bishop of Ephesus.' The Presbyterians said that it was usual in the Scriptures, especially in mysterious writings like the Revelation, to express a number of things or persons in singulars. A thousand members making one Church is a candlestick. The seven angels standing before God represent the host of angels. So the whole presbytery of ministers is one angel. The letters are addressed to the angels. Yet the very words show that the singular means a plural: 'I know thy works'—'This thou hast'—'Repent, and do thy first works.' In these words it is the whole Church that is addressed. Hammond answered that the Church is one; that he does not deny the whole collective body of the Church to have been addressed in the Epistle. Yet it is not necessary to infer that the word angel means the whole Church.

The seven 'angels' the metropolitans of Asia.

Dr. Hammond supposed the seven cities of Asia to be chief cities, and the bishops metropolitans. The Presbyterians said that this was improbable. The cities lay near to each other, and most of them were on the seaside. Hammond had an answer out of antiquity. Canons, councils, and Fathers had owned them for primitive and apostolical sees. According to Pliny, five of them were cities in which the Roman proconsuls held their courts or seats of judicature, and administered justice to the neighbouring cities. It was this which made a city metropolitan. Ulpian mentions Ephesus as the chief of these metropolitan cities. Ignatius mentions Trallis and Magnesia as episcopal sees, and these seem to have been under the metropolis of Ephesus. Clemens says that in every city where the Apostles had converts, they appointed a bishop over them, who was to be the governor 'of those that should afterwards believe.' The custom which the Apostles followed in their work as Apostles was to go first to the chief cities. When a whole nation was converted, the principal sees would therefore be the chief cities according to the priority in the Roman State. We need not suppose that in forming the Church, the Apostles copied the model of the Roman government. Yet it was natural that in every country to which they went, the polity of the Church would in some measure take its form from the civil polity. But we have not to go even to the Roman State for the ecclesiastical division of cities into metropolitan and inferior cities. It was the order instituted among the Jews. God commanded Moses to appoint judges and officers in every city, but in matters of weight they were to resort to the Sanhedrim at Jerusalem, which was the chief city. The metropolitan sees did not begin, as the Presbyterians affirmed, when Constantine made Christianity the religion of the State. They began with the Apostles themselves, and the first founders of Christianity. At the Council of Nice, not many years after the conversion of Constantine, there was a canon made which began thus:— 'Let the ancient customs continue in force.' One of the customs mentioned is, that 'if any man be made a bishop without the judgment of the metropolitan, he ought not to be a bishop.' A canon of the Council of Antioch began with the words, 'The bishop which presides in the metropolis ought to know the bishops of every province.'

The commonly received theory of Episcopacy is, that the Apostles appointed in the churches presbyters and deacons, the Apostles themselves, while they lived, being bishops. After the death of the Apostles they were succeeded in their office of bishops by some of the presbyters who were elevated over the others. Hammond's theory is, that the Apostles appointed bishops and deacons, but the presbyters, in the modern sense of presbyters, came in later. He agrees with the Presbyterians that bishop and presbyter in the New Testament always mean the same office, but he differs from them as to what that office is. The Presbyterians said that a New Testament bishop or presbyter was simply a minister of religion, who had a governing power only as a member of the presbyterial body. Dr. Hammond said that he had a governing power singly in himself. The word bishop he explains in such a way as it could never be applied to a presbyter in the modern sense. Its first

CHAP. V.

Christian polity copied from Jewish polity.

Bishops and deacons only in the early Church.

meaning is an overseer. Aristides uses it for governor, and Justinian for the ruler of provinces and metropolitan cities. Cicero translates it keeper or guard, which Hammond says is fitly 'angel,' who in Scripture is called an eye, and commonly a guardian. In the Septuagint it is generally used to translate the Hebrew El, which means God, lord, or angel, always bearing the idea of dominion, dignity, power, and superiority. In every place in the New Testament where it is used, it is capable, Hammond says, of this sense, and answers to our idea of a bishop or prefect in the church, and not a colleague in a presbytery. A few of these places are examined. The Epistle to the Philippians begins with a salutation to the bishops and deacons. This is one of the passages most likely to be of service to the Presbyterians. The Greek commentators, even those who are asserters of Episcopacy, understand that in this place bishop means presbyter, because there were not many bishops in one city. This is confirmed by several Fathers, who say that Epaphroditus, who was the bearer of this letter, was the bishop of the church at Philippi. Yet Epiphanius affirms that the 'bishops' saluted in the Epistle were properly bishops as we understand that word. Hammond follows Epiphanius, and explains the passage by his theory of metropolitans. Philippi was the chief city of Macedonia. The 'bishops' may have been the suffragans under Epaphroditus, and the Epistle, though addressed to the saints at Philippi, may have been intended for all the churches of Macedonia. Epiphanius explains that the deacons are mentioned next, because as yet the order of presbyters had not begun. Again, in the first Epistle to Timothy it is said 'a bishop must be blameless.' Here Hammond says there is no reason for doubting that bishop means a prefect or governor of the Church. The only appearance of the contrary is the immediate subjoining of the deacons as in the Epistle to the Philippians, but the Roman Clement and Epiphanius both testify that before the government of the Church was complete in all its offices, the Apostles created no more than a bishop and deacon in each church. Hammond admits that the word presbyter may sometimes have the meaning in the New Testament which

CHAP. V.

Meaning of the word bishop.

Of the word presbyter.

it now has with us, but this is rare and exceptional. In all languages the corresponding word means a ruler or governor. Wherever it is used in the New Testament, it must either of necessity be so understood, or it is at least capable of this meaning. The passage which the Presbyterians quoted was in the Epistle of James, where it is said, 'Is any sick? let him call for the elders of the Church.' It was objected that to visit the sick was not the proper work of a bishop. Hammond answered that it must have been in the primitive times, when there was only one bishop and one deacon in each church. Testimonies were added from Polycarp and Justin Martyr that this was the office of a bishop.

CHAP. V.

The third chapter of this treatise is devoted entirely to the testimony of antiquity, in confirmation of the view of Episcopacy which Hammond advocates. The sum of these testimonies is, that there were but two orders in the early Church, and the point in controversy is, what these two orders really were. The Epistles of St. Ignatius are decisive for Dr. Hammond's side, but in the judgment of the best critics, only a few of these Epistles are genuine; and those that are genuine are evidently so full of corruptions that no reliance can be placed on them. Hammond vindicates the Epistles, and even after criticism has done its best, he finds in the residue sufficient to establish his cause. For the other Fathers, Hammond begins with Irenæus. Eusebius testifies that he was Bishop of Lyons. He was not a presbyter in the modern sense of presbyter, yet he is called an 'elder' in the Epistle of the Martyrs of Lyons to Eleutherius, the Bishop of Rome. The Alexandrian Clement, speaking of St. John meeting the bishops of Asia, calls these bishops presbyters. Again, in his Epistle to Victor, Bishop of Rome, he speaks of Victor's predecessors as presbyters. To the same effect are many testimonies from the Fathers, the meaning of which is that a bishop, that is, one who had a governing power, was frequently called the presbyter or 'elder' of the Church.

Testimony of antiquity to Episcopacy.

Dr. Hammond was also engaged in the controversy about infant baptism. He had written a treatise on this subject, which was answered by John Tombes, the great champion

Hammond on infant baptism.

of the Baptist cause. Hammond replied in 'A Defence of Infant Baptism.' On this subject, as well as on Episcopacy, there are things which were not noticed by the other defenders of infant baptism. He does not deny the validity of the arguments which had been adduced by others, such, for instance, as the example of circumcision, the baptizing of households, and Jesus receiving little children. But while admitting that all these had some weight, he thought the foundation of the practice was more properly laid in the Jewish baptism, which was administered to all Jewish children, as well as to proselytes and their children. It was usually supposed that the Jews only baptized proselytes, but Hammond says they baptized all whom they received into the covenant, and the baptizing of Jews was the origin of their baptizing proselytes. The baptism or washing of the whole body was a Jewish solemnity, by which the native Jews were entered into the covenant of God made with them by Moses. To prove this, Dr. Hammond quotes from the Talmud, the Gemara, and Maimonides. Some of the Fathers said that the heathen borrowed the custom of baptizing from the Jews. Hammond admits this as possible, yet he thinks it probable that both Jews and Gentiles derived it from the sons of Noah, with whom it was a remembrance of the Deluge. The Greeks had a proverbial saying that 'the sea sweeps away all the evils of men.' To this St. Peter probably alludes when he makes baptism the antitype of Noah's flood. Athanasius, too, says, 'the first baptism is that of the Deluge for the excision of sins;' and Optatus says, 'the Deluge was the image of baptism, that the polluted world, by the drowning of sinners, might be cleansed into the ancient form.' The Fathers generally lay the foundation of baptism in Moses, or the baptism of the Jews. Gregory Nazianzen says, 'Moses baptized, but in water, and after this in the cloud and the Red Sea.' He makes this a type of Christian baptism, adding, 'John also baptized, but not Judaically.' Athanasius speaks of several baptisms—that of the Flood for the cutting off of sin, Moses' passing through the Red Sea, the legal baptism of the Jews, the baptisms of John and of Jesus.

The Baptists rested mainly on the commission which

Jesus gave to His disciples, 'Go ye and teach all nations, baptizing them.' The teaching preceded the baptizing. From this the Baptists inferred that none were to be baptized but those who are first instructed. Hammond translates this text as 'Go ye and disciple all nations;' and he interpreted the meaning of it to be, that the Apostles were to make disciples of all nations by baptizing them, that is to say, the baptizing is another word for the same thing as the discipling. He illustrated this by what is said of baptism by St. Peter, that it is 'the answer of a good conscience.' The Greek word here translated 'answer,' Hammond translates 'seeking,' so that baptism is a 'seeking to God,' inquiring, as it were, at an oracle for instruction as to future life. Previous actual instruction was not necessary. Persons were to be made disciples by baptism, and then instruction was to follow. Parents take their children to school that they may learn. The children are made disciples by the act of their parents, and that on the very day they are brought to school. So children are brought to Christ in baptism, to begin their discipleship. That children were to be baptized, Dr. Hammond adduces St. Paul to the Corinthians, that 'the children are holy' if one or both of the parents are believers. The interpretation which the ancient Fathers put on this passage is reckoned to be certain evidence that it referred to baptizing children. Tertullian says, 'when either the father or mother is sanctified, the children are holy.' The context shows that by sanctified he means baptized. Athanasius argues for infant baptism from these two texts, 'Suffer little children to come unto me,' and 'now are your children holy,' explaining the last text as meaning 'the baptized children of believers.' Cyprian and the twenty-six bishops that were in council with him, in the letter to Fidus, speaking of the baptism of infants, give as the reason why they should be baptized that they are holy. This, Dr. Hammond says, is true of believers' children. All the Fathers speak of the faith of the parents as profiting the children when they are brought to baptism. All baptized persons are spoken of as holy. This is the invariable language of the New Testament when addressing

Instruction not necessary before baptism.

Children of believers 'holy.'

those who profess Christianity. Dr. Hammond is not clear, neither are the Fathers, as he quotes them, whether the children of believers are holy because they are the children of believers, or in virtue of their baptism. Sometimes he puts it one way, and sometimes the other, evidently concluding that it is the same thing. The children of believers as such are entitled to baptism, and therefore they are called holy. Marshall clearly made the baptizing of children depend on their being already in the covenant. Hammond distinctly says that by baptism they are admitted to the covenant. St. Paul calls the children holy because the parents are believers. Dr. Hammond says that they are made holy by baptism. This is, probably, but a different mode of saying the same thing. The holiness which is brought by baptism is explained as merely of a relative kind. It is no actual regeneration, but simply an outward admission into the visible Church, and the gain of it is, that the child is put in the way of instruction. It is, so to speak, being brought to school.

There is but one other member of the Savoy Conference on the bishops' side, who was a voluminous writer. This is Herbert Thorndike. His works all concern the Church, and especially those questions which were agitated in his time. When the Presbyterians came into power, Thorndike wrote in defence of Episcopacy, adducing the usual arguments from what he supposed to be the primitive government of the Church. When the 'Directory' was confirmed by Parliament, and an ordinance passed for the ordination of ministers by the presbyteries, Thorndike wrote a treatise on 'The Right of the Church in a Christian State.' This was directed against the Presbyterians, but its special point was the Erastianism which was connected with the Presbyterianism then established. The 'Directory' had been framed by the Assembly of Divines, but it was 'sent in parts *to the Parliament*, where the same had been debated and confirmed, with such small variations as *they thought necessary*.' The 'Ordinance' also said that all the presbyters who should ordain other presbyters, according to the 'Directory,' should have 'the protection of both Houses of Parliament for their indemnity.' To the elderships within their respective provinces was given power to suspend from the sacrament of the Lord's Supper. But any dissatisfied person might appeal to the presbytery, from thence to the provincial assembly, from thence to the national, and from thence *to the Parliament.* Robert Baillie, one of the Commissioners from the Kirk, wrote to Scotland, ' that the power of jurisdiction in all things we require, excepting appeals from the General Assembly to the Parliament, is not put in ordinances long ago, *it is by the cunning of the Independents and Erastians in the House of Commons.*' There was, Thorndike says, some tincture of Erastian doctrine, which dissolves all ecclesiastical power into the secular. He was to bring forward reasons to establish what he had maintained in other books, that the society of the Church was to rest upon the power of the keys. He was to declare the persons to whom the power of the keys was given, the terms on which it was to be exercised, and the right or interest of the secular powers in establishing or reforming the Church of any State.

CHAP. V.

Erastianism of the Long Parliament.

The Church is sometimes unconnected with the State. It was so before it was allowed and protected by the Roman laws. Since that time there has been a State connection, the terms of which have never been well defined. Either the Church has interfered with the secular government, or the State has disturbed the government of the Church. Thorndike starts with the principle that the Church has no temporal power. It is a kingdom not of this world. It does not use the sword. All secular power, on the other hand, is finally a question of might. All secular disputes are resolved into the power of the sword. The Church's right is to hold assemblies for divine worship. It has this right previous to any grant from the powers of this world, and against any interdict forbidding assemblies. The Church is not in this respect a civil society. It is a society established by God, and without Christian assemblies Christianity cannot be professed. The first Christians obeyed the laws of the State under which they lived, as far as they could, but never to the violation of the command that they were not to forget the assembling of themselves together. But the more difficult question is to determine the ground of the right

Church and State connection.

CHAP. V. of the State to share in the government of the Church. Thorndike refuses to argue from the precedent of the Jewish kings. There is a difference between the law and the Gospel. The law was confined to one people, to whom it was the condition on which God was to give them the Land of Promise. The Gospel is the new covenant by which God promises to all men everlasting life. The Church of England has always given kings that power in the Church which was possessed by Jewish kings. It served a good end, for it preserved unity. But there was no proper reason for doing this merely in imitation of the Jewish kings. The Christian Church being for all nations, was not under any necessity of following the old law. Moreover, it was not by any divine command that the kings of Judah were governors of the Church. The law commanded them not to have a king at all. But they wished to be like other nations, and were allowed a king on sufferance. If the law did not allow them a king, it was impossible that the king could be the head of the Church. But though there is no express command, there is the fact that the kings of Judah had power in matters of religion. This arose naturally, and, indeed, necessarily. The Jews were commanded to destroy idolaters. This and some other commands were addressed to them as a community. When they had a king over them, the common power of the people fell to the king.

The origin of the civil ruler's authority in matters ecclesiastical.
In the same way, with the changes which require to be made for the difference of the cases, the civil ruler in a Christian country comes to have authority in the Church. He is to maintain Christianity by the sword of his power, yet only in subjection to the power which God has ordained in His Church.

Thorndike's theory of Church and State that of the Presbyterians.
Thorndike's doctrine of Church and State seems to be precisely that of the Westminster Confession. The independence of the Church is to be preserved. The civil ruler is to be nominally supreme, and his government of the Church is to consist in putting into execution the decrees of the governing body in the Church. This body, with the Presbyterians, was the presbyteries and synods. With Thorndike it was the council of bishops and presbyters. The Erastians, who denied that the Church had this govern-

ing power independent of the civil ruler, maintained that excommunication was a secular punishment. Thorndike argues on the other side that it was a punishment inflicted by the Church officers. They had the power of admitting to the Church,—not simply the power of baptizing, but of determining who were the persons to be baptized. Now, a power to admit implies a power to refuse. But there is yet a stronger argument that excommunication was a spiritual penalty. It is derived from the practice of penance. In the early ages of the Church, according to the most ancient church writers, such sinners as apostates, murderers, and adulterers were wholly excluded from penance. Erastus tried to prove that there was no excommunication commanded by the law. Thorndike admitted this, but he added that the synagogue had the power of life and death, and this was equivalent to the power of excommunication in the Christian Church. And though excommunication was not commanded in the law, it was evidently practised, as we read in Ezra. The power of the keys was an expression borrowed from Jewish customs. Its meaning was that those to whom it was given were the stewards of the house. The society of the Church is founded upon the sword of excommunication, which it cannot forfeit to the civil ruler.

The Church is thus independent and self-governed. No secular person as such can have any ecclesiastical power in it. But there is a distinction to be made between ecclesiastical power and power in ecclesiastical matters. The first can belong only to those who are appointed to be officers of the Church by its original constitution. But that kings may have power in ecclesiastical matters is proved both from Scripture and from their duty, not merely as secular powers, but as Christians. Thorndike's proof from Scripture is something not very intelligible about the fulfilment of some Old Testament prophecy. The other argument is established by St. Augustine's interpretation of the words of the psalm, 'Understand now, O ye kings.' The duty of a Christian king cannot be to destroy or injure the government of the Church, but rather to make laws that will tend to establish it. In all these arguments Thorndike assumes that the Church and the civil ruler are agreed on all

Distinction between ecclesiastical power and power in ecclesiastical matters.

CHAP. V.

the subjects on which they are to legislate, but he comes at last to discuss the great question, if the officers of the Church can excommunicate the sovereign. On the principles of Erastus this was impossible. Hooker in his later books specially refuted the Puritan doctrine that the Church could excommunicate the King. He admitted, however, a less excommunication, consisting simply of refusing admission to the Lord's Supper. Thorndike says there is but one excommunication, and the Church may excommunicate the sovereign.

The Conformist followed the Puritan in declaring the independence of the Church.

This theory of Church and State is, as we have already said, that of the Presbyterians. The Conformist gradually followed the Puritan in declaring the independence of the Church. This result was the necessary consequence of claiming that the Church had divinely appointed officers independent of the civil power. Thorndike's long and somewhat tedious works consist of the repetition of this doctrine in various forms, with occasional refutations of Presbyterians, Independents, and Erastians. He was the first complete specimen of the old-fashioned High-Churchman,—a species now almost extinct. He was to reform the Church of Rome by taking it back to the decrees and canons of the first six General Councils. When these Councils sat, there was a Catholic Church and a Catholic consent of the meaning of Scripture, which, in some way incomprehensible to ordinary people, were to be the judges of what we are to believe. He denied that the Roman Catholics are idolaters, though they use idols in their worship. He makes a distinction between worshipping God by means of images, and worshipping the images as gods. He professes to refute transubstantiation, and he openly denies the doctrine of the real presence, as explained by the Reformers of the Church of England. They all said that the faithful eat and drink Christ's body and blood in the Supper, in the same way as in all exercises of religion. Thorndike calls this the 'Calvinistic theory,' and conclusively asks, what necessity there is for celebrating the Sacrament, if the body and blood of Christ can be received without it?*

* Of the other members of the Savoy Conference we know but little, except from history. Frewen, the Archbishop of York, was the son of

ARCHBISHOP BRAMHALL.

CHAP. V.
Archbishop Bramhall.

Among the Irish bishops at the restoration of King Charles, there were three of some eminence as theological writers. These were Bramhall, Hopkins, and Taylor. Though bishops of the Church in Ireland, they were all na-

a Puritan minister, and bore the Christian name of 'Accepted.' He seems to have been a worthy man.

Of Gauden, Richard Baxter says, 'Bishop Gauden was our most constant helper. He and Bishop Cosin seldom were absent, and how bitter soever his pen be, he was the only moderator of all the bishops (except our Bishop Reynolds). He showed no logic, nor meddled in any dispute or point of learning, but a calm, fluent, rhetorical tongue, and if all had been of his mind, we had been reconciled. But when, by many days' conference in the beginning, we had got some moderating concessions from him (and from Bishop Cosin, by his means), the rest came in the end, and broke them all.' Gauden wrote a folio of many pages, called 'The Tears of the Church of England.' It is a book of no value, being merely a long lamentation over the fallen estate of the Church, while Presbyterians and Independents—'plants which the right hand of the Lord had not planted'—were flourishing on its ruins. Gauden was what is now called a *good* Churchman, but Dr. Hook calls him 'this unprincipled man.' The ground of Dr. Hook's wrath is, that Gauden allowed it to be published that he was the author of 'Eikon Basilike,' which had been long ascribed to King Charles I.

Morley was the most noisy bishop at the Conference. Dr. Hook calls him 'a High Church Calvinist.' It was Morley who, when one at the court of King James asked what the Arminians held, answered, 'the best bishoprics and deaneries in the kingdom.' He had great influence at court, under both the first and the second Charles. It was due to Morley that Richard Baxter could not obtain the curacy of Kidderminster after he had refused the bishopric of Hereford. Baxter at last begged that he might be allowed to preach in his diocese occasionally when he could get the use of a church, and Morley asked him, *if he really thought his preaching of so much importance that he could not be silent?* Morley and Sheldon had the practical management of the Savoy Conference, though Sheldon only came twice. Of Morley, Baxter says that he 'was oft there, but not constantly, and with free and fluent words, with much earnestness, was the chief speaker of all the bishops, and a great interrupter of us, vehemently going on with what he thought serviceable to his ends, and bearing down answers by the said fervour and interruptions.'

'Among all the bishops there was none who had so promising a face as Dr. Sterne, the Bishop of Carlisle. He looked so honestly, and gravely, and soberly, that I scarce thought such a face could have deceived me, and when I was entreating them not to cast out so many of their brethren through the nation which scrupled a ceremony which they confessed indifferent, he turned to the rest of the Reverend Bishops, and noted me for saying "in the nation." *He will not say* "in the kingdom," saith he, "*lest he desire a king*." This was all that I ever heard that worthy prelate say.'—*Reliq. Bax.*

'Dr. Gunning was their forwardest and greatest speaker, understanding well what belonged to a disputant, a man of greater study and industry than any of them, well read in Fathers and Councils, and of a ready tongue (and I hear, and believe, of a very temperate life, as to all carnal excesses whatsoever), but so vehement for his high, imposing principles, and so over-zealous for Arminianism, and formality and Church pomp, and so very eager and fervent in his discourse, that I conceive his prejudice and passion much perverted his judgment, and I am sure they made him lamentably overrun himself in his discourses.'—*Reliq. Bax.* In another place Baxter says, 'Dr. Bates urged Dr. Gunning that on the same reasons that they so imposed the cross and surplice, they might bring in holy water and lights,

328   RELIGIOUS THOUGHT IN ENGLAND.

CHAP. V.

tives of England. John Bramhall, formerly Bishop of Derry and now promoted to the Archbishopric of Armagh, was a zealous Churchman in the days of Laud. He had gained great applause for a disputation which he had conducted, when as yet a young man, with a Jesuit in the town of Northallerton. Toby Matthews, the Bishop of Durham, made him his chaplain, and soon afterwards a Prebendary of York Cathedral. This put him on the high-road to preferment. When Viscount Wentworth was made Lord Lieutenant of Ireland, he promoted Bramhall to the bishopric of Derry. The Protestant Church of Ireland had pledged itself to a strict form of Calvinism, by incorporating into its articles the 'Articles of Lambeth.' It retained, too, from the beginning of the Reformation a greater simplicity of worship and ritual than had been used in the Church of England. Bramhall entered on his work with a boundless energy. He was himself an anti-Calvinist, but no one could dare to deny the Calvinism of the Church of Ireland. He had to plead for toleration. As soon as he was able he appealed to Convocation to adopt the Articles of the Church of England, which embraced both Calvinists and Arminians. He was assured that the difference was only in the form of the words. This he did not deny, yet he felt that under the

Calvinism of the Church of Ireland.

and abundance of such ceremonies of Rome, which we have cast out. He answered, "Yea, and so I think, we ought to have more, and not fewer, if we do well."'

Of the other members of the Conference Baxter says, 'Bishop Lucy, of St. David's, spoke once or twice a few words calmly, and so did Bishop Nicholson, of Gloucester. Bishop King, of Chichester, I never saw there; Bishop Warner, of Rochester, was there once or twice, but meddled not that I heard of; Bishop Reynolds spoke much the first day for bringing them to abatements and moderation, and afterwards he sat with them, and spoke now and then a word for moderation. He was a solid honest man, but, through mildness and excess of timorous reverence to great men, altogether unfit to contend with them. Mr. Thorndike spake once a few impertinent, passionate words, confuting the opinion which we had conceived of him from his first writings, and confirming that which his second and last writings had given us of him. Dr. Earle, Dr. Heylin, and Dr. Barwick never came. Dr. Hacket, since Bishop of Coventry and Lichfield, said nothing to make us know anything of him. Dr. Sparrow said but little, but that little was with a spirit enough for the imposing, dividing cause.'

Of the bishops who lived through the period of the Commonwealth, Juxon, Wren, and Pierce were the best known. Juxon was a peaceable man, of whom little could be said, either for good or evil. He owed his promotions to the friendship of Laud, and not to any merits of his own. Wren was the most rigid disciplinarian and the most unpopular of Laud's bishops. The fame of Bishop Pierce rests on his labours to further the observance of the 'Book of Sports.'

XXXIX. Articles the Arminians might have a freedom which they could not have under the Articles of the Irish Church. He at last succeeded in passing his measure, under pretence of manifesting the agreement of the Church of Ireland with the Church of England. It was a clever device. The Convocation was outwitted. It has ever since been a question, if the subscribing to the Articles of the Church of England did not imply the repeal of the old Articles of the Church of Ireland. Bramhall's next work was to regain the lost revenues of the Irish Church. In this his success was so great that the property which he retrieved was the foundation of the greatest part of what is now the wealth of the Church in Ireland. In all these things Bramhall was helped by the Lord Lieutenant, encouraged by Archbishop Laud, and protected by King Charles. Like most of the Churchmen who came within Laud's circle, Bramhall was active, zealous, a good man of business, as well as a scholar, and if not profound was yet dexterously clever.

Bramhall succeeds in getting the Irish Convocation to adopt the XXXIX. Articles.

Bramhall's works may be arranged under three heads: his controversies with Hobbes, his defences of the Church of England against the Church of Rome, and against the sectaries. The first we shall have occasion to speak of again, and the last are of no interest. We notice the second only to learn what was the argument which Churchmen of Bramhall's day adopted against the Church of Rome. This series is divided into 'Discourses.' The second of these is called ' A Just Vindication of the Church of England.' The charge against the Church of England was schism. At first sight, Bramhall admits, there seems to be some ground for the charge. We did withhold obedience from him who professes to be the Vicar of Christ. But schism is unjustly charged upon us. For the first six hundred years or more after we embraced Christianity, we had no foreign patriarch over us. The obtrusion upon us after that time of such foreign jurisdiction was a violation of the canons of the Catholic Church. The Bishops of Rome did not exercise jurisdiction in Britain until they quitted the lawful patriarchate wherewith they were invested by the Church, and had assumed an unlawful monarchy over all

Defences of the Church of England.

Churches. The power which they gained in after ages was, Bramhall says, mere tyranny and usurpation. The kings of England, with their synods and parliaments, had always the right to limit and restrain the exercise of Papal authority. Henry VIII., in resisting the Pope, was only treading in the steps of his most renowned ancestors. The Bishops of Rome never had any quiet or settled possession of that power which was finally cast out at the Reformation. We separated from the Pope because of his innovations. From the Catholic Church we were never separated. Bramhall threw back upon the Church of Rome the charge of schism. By novelties of doctrine and worship it had departed from the Church Catholic.

Before it could be determined that the Church of England was chargeable with schism, it was necessary to define schism. It cannot, Bramhall says, be such dissensions as we read of between Paul and Barnabas, Jerome and Ruffinus, Chrysostom and Epiphanius. We cannot suppose Apostles and Catholic Fathers to have been schismatics. Jerome and Ruffinus, indeed, call each other heretics. Chrysostom and Epiphanius refused to worship together. Chrysostom wished that Epiphanius might not return home alive, and Epiphanius wished that Chrysostom might not die a bishop. The African Church was long in contention with the Roman Church about rebaptizing and appeals to Rome, but surely Augustine, Cyprian, and the African bishops who took their side, did not live and die schismatics. Two parts may be separated from each other, and yet both may remain in communion with the universal Church. The Roman Catholic argument was that, if Protestants separate themselves from the Church of Rome and yet acknowledge it to be a member of the Church Catholic, they separate themselves from the Catholic Church. Bramhall's answer is, that we have not separated from the Church of Rome, as it is a member of the Catholic Church. We have only separated from it as to that in which it had first separated from the whole Church; that is, abuses and innovations. We are willing to stand to the judgment of a free general council of the universal Church. The guilt of separation does not always fall upon those that are separated. It may be due to those who have caused the separation. St. Paul commands Timothy to 'separate' himself from those that 'consented not to wholesome words.' It is no schism to forsake those who have first themselves forsaken the common faith. When Eunomius, the Arian, was made a bishop, all his flock refused to communicate with him. To be of the Catholic Church it is not necessary that we be all in one communion, or united by an external unity. Schism is a culpable separation without sufficient grounds, or it is the causing of a separation by limiting the Catholic Church to a sect or party, as the Donatists did in old times, or as those of the Church of Rome are doing in the present day.

Schism a culpable separation.

The Church of England was the same garden after the Reformation that it had been before it, with only this difference, that the weeds were taken out of it. The external separation from Rome was not made by Protestants, but by Roman Catholics. It was determined openly in both universities, 'That the Roman bishop had no greater jurisdiction within the kingdom of England conferred upon him by God in Holy Scripture than any other foreign bishop.' This was received and established in full Parliament, by the free consent of all the orders in the kingdom. It had the sanction and approval of four-and-twenty bishops and nine-and-twenty abbots, all present in that Parliament. It was Roman Catholics who decreed that King Henry should be 'Head of the Church.' Even so late as the Council of Trent, Cardinal Pole wrote, 'The Emperor doth execute the office of Christ as a kingly head.' The many Acts which were passed in the reign of Henry VIII., declaring the independence of the Church of England, were passed by Roman Catholics when there were no thoughts of any Reformation. If it was this separation from Rome which constituted a schism, then the authors of it,—Heath and Bonner, Tonstall and Gardiner, Stokesley and Thirlby,—were the schismatics. The separation was made to our hands. It was not till Edward's days that the Church of England embraced the doctrines of the Reformation. We never, in any sense, even then separated from the Church of Rome. The English nation was excommunicated, Protestants and Roman Catholics alike. We were all thrust out of doors by the Bull of Pope Paul III. How, then, could we be the schismatics?

Roman Catholic bishops decreed Henry VIII. 'head of the Church.'

CHAP. V.

CHAP. V.

The Reformation a vindication of our ancient rights.

In maintaining our independence of Rome at the Reformation, we made no new laws, but only vindicated our ancient liberties. Pope Boniface, after the year six hundred, assumed the title of universal bishop. His successors, by degrees, extended their jurisdiction over other churches beyond the Roman see. The intrusion of the Papal power in England was a usurpation. Unjust in its beginning, it could be justified by no subsequent custom or prescription. No Saxon, English, or British king ever made any formal acknowledgment of submission to the Bishop of Rome. On the contrary, when Augustine, the monk, arrived in England, he stayed in the Isle of Thanet, and did not offer to preach in Kent till he had the King's licence. The most famous appellant from England to Rome before the Conquest was Wilfrid, Archbishop of York. He gained sentence upon sentence in his favour at Rome. The Pope even sent his nuncio to England to see the sentence put into execution; but Alfred told him that it was against reason 'that a person twice condemned by the whole Council of the English, could be restored upon the Pope's letter.' So rare were appeals to Rome, that we read of no other till after the Norman Conquest. The next was that of Anselm in the reign of Henry I., when Pascalis II. devised a new oath for archbishops. The oath touched this very question of appeals to Rome. The King pleaded the fundamental laws and customs of the land, that 'no Pope be appealed unto without the King's licence.' These laws, established by Henry's father, William the Conqueror, were no other than the laws of Edward the Confessor—the old Saxon laws. Henry yielded at the request of his barons, and Anselm took the oath. William of Malmesbury adds, 'In the execution of these things, all the bishops of England did deny their suffrage to their primate.' Legations from Rome were as rare as appeals to the Pope. A law was passed that 'if any one be found bringing in the Pope's letter or mandate, let him be apprehended, and let justice pass upon him without delay as a traitor to the King and kingdom.' Henry VIII. did nothing that had not been done by Kings of England before him. He governed the Church in his own dominions with the same title as belonged to Edward the Confessor, 'the

Kings of England before Henry VIII. ruled the Church in England.

vicar of God in his own kingdom.' Bramhall concludes, as he had begun, with charging the guilt of separation on the Church of Rome, which had introduced innovations and claimed a universal jurisdiction over the Christian world. No such jurisdiction was given to the Church of Rome by Christ or His Apostles, and centuries had passed away before it was thought of by the Bishops of Rome.

Ezekiel Hopkins succeeded Bramhall in the bishopric of Derry. His works are practical, consisting mostly of sermons. They are what in the present day would be called evangelical. They are Calvinistic, though the doctrinal element is not prominent. Hopkins, speaking of the death of Christ, says that by it all men are put in a 'salvable' state. That all men are not saved, he reckons a conclusive argument that God did not intend to save all men. But it was His will that men should be put in a state of salvation. Everything is precisely as God wills it, that is to say, there is nothing contingent. There is only one other point of doctrine specially to be noticed in Hopkins's sermons. It is his explanation of Baptismal Regeneration. We have seen under Dr. Burges how Calvinists generally understood an actual regeneration to take place in the baptized if they were among the elect. Under Dr. Hammond we found regeneration in baptism interpreted as simply a relative or outward change. The use of the words was reckoned only an adaptation of old Jewish phraseology. Hopkins' explanation is much the same as that of Dr. Hammond. Infants are already members of the Church, disciples of Christ, and therefore they are to be baptized. All who are admitted into the visible Church 'are dignified with the title of saints. They are called children of God and members of Christ.' The regeneration in baptism is 'ecclesiastical.' Infants are incorporated into the Church of Christ by this sacrament. Bishop Hopkins, as well as Dr. Hammond, says that they are members of the Church and of Christ before baptism, but baptism is the public or formal declaration of their membershp. Our services say that the regeneration of a child in baptism is by 'the Holy Spirit.' Hopkins explains this, that the Holy Spirit appoints this ordinance for the receiving of children into the visible

Church, which is the regenerate part of the world. That baptism is absolutely necessary to eternal life, he calls 'a grievous mistake in doctrine.'

Jeremy Taylor.

Among all the Churchmen of the Restoration none have achieved a more lasting reputation than Jeremy Taylor. His fame doubtless rests chiefly on his sermons and his devotional works, yet as a theologian he was great, and had many sides. He began his public life with unusual prospects, under the patronage of Laud, whose highest claim to the gratitude of posterity was his readiness to seek out men of ability, that he might raise them to positions where they were likely to be useful to the Church. Taylor's prospects were early clouded by the troubles which overwhelmed the bishops. Throughout his life he maintained the high views of Episcopacy that were held by Laud and his supporters, but with this exception, there is scarcely another point on which Taylor was a High Churchman. In fact there are but few doctrines on which Taylor's views would not exclude him from the common pale of the orthodox in the judgment of the majority of Christians, of whatever sect or party.

The men who had carried persecution for religious opinions to its utmost bounds, were now in adversity. Some of them learned wisdom, and pleaded for that toleration which they had denied to those who differed from them in the time of their prosperity. This might be an explanation of the origin of Jeremy Taylor's 'Liberty of Prophesying,' but the principles laid down are so comprehensive in their application that they embrace toleration for all sects and schisms. The argument, indeed, is directed against the Presbyterians, who were then in power, but it falls with even greater weight against such claims of exclusive Catholicity as are made by the Church of Rome, and by some in the Church of England.

'Liberty of Prophesying.'

The Church of Rome proposes a visible guide to re-unite in one all minds with all varieties of opinions, but who this guide is to be, Taylor says is part of the fire that is to be quenched. Protestants set up the Bible as a rule; but what is the interpretation of the rule, is part of the disease for which the rule was intended. So long as there are such varieties of principles, constitutions, educations, tempers, intents, and degrees of understanding, it is impossible that all men should be of one mind. From this follows the very rational conclusion that surely that which cannot be done is not necessary to be done. There is room in heaven for men of different opinions. There may be unity of faith where men's opinions are not the same. The first duty of all is unity of charity. The distractions of Christendom proceed from forgetfulness of this first duty. Men put opinions before charity. They convert opinions into articles of faith, impose them upon other men, and thereby raise quarrels and factions. The Christian faith is summed up in the Apostles' Creed. Yea, it is even less than the articles of that Creed. It is expressed in this one sentence,—that Jesus is the Christ. Every spirit that confesseth that Jesus is the Christ, is born of God. On this confession Christ built His Church. If this simple faith could bring men to heaven in the time of the Apostles, it is surely difficult to prove that more is needed now. The Church has no authority to enlarge the Creed. Christ did not promise a spirit of infallibility. Whatever the Church may add as a superstructure, cannot be of the same necessity with the foundation.

There is room in heaven for men of different opinions.

Taylor says that we never read in the New Testament of persons condemned for their errors, except as these errors implied corrupt motives in holding them. In the early Church multitudes violently retained circumcision, and yet went to heaven. Their error was not heresy so long as it stood with charity. That which is merely an error of the understanding is not heresy. There must be also an error of the will, as with those who taught circumcision for the sake of gain. They may both believe their errors to be true. Yet the difference is great between those who are in error through simplicity, and those who by a judicial punishment believe a lie. If a man's life is good, his error is not a heresy. No man can be a heretic against his will. In the early Church millenarianism was a Catholic doctrine. The further we go from the Apostles' times the more forward men become to magnify opinions into heresies. In many cases heresy is merely supposed. Some bishop who had the good fortune to be reckoned Catholic, condemned a

Heresy an error of the will, not of the intellect.

certain man or opinion, and so he was called a heretic, and the doctrine a heresy. Taylor cites the case of Nicholas of Antioch, who taught mortification of the flesh. His enemies said he taught that the flesh should be abused by filthy pollution. In St. Jerome's time it was beyond question that Nicholas was one of the vilest of men. But while the good man lived, no one ever thought of such accusations. He had lived in holy wedlock, his sons were celibate, and his daughters virgins, but he had the misfortune to get a black mark in the catalogue of heretics. Virgilius was condemned for heresy, because he said there were antipodes. In the same manner the friars of late suspected Greek and Hebrew of heresy, and had almost put Terence and Demosthenes into the 'Index.' Epiphanius put Montanus into the catalogue of heretics, because he taught abstinence from certain meats as unclean. Aerius was reckoned a heretic because he denied the necessity of prayer for the dead; Eustathius, because he would not pray to the saints, and the Osseni, because they refused to worship towards the east. Taylor adds many more cases, as the Parermeneutæ, who interpreted the Scriptures for themselves, instead of following other men's judgments; the Pauliciani, who were offended at crosses; and the Proclians, who said that in regenerate men all sin was not dead but only under a check.

'Heretic' only a name to frighten people.

The name heretic he calls a *terriculamentum*, to frighten people from their belief. But the curse causeless shall return empty. No man is damned because his enemies pronounce anathema. They that judge are as likely to be in error as they that are accused. Every good man is acceptable to God, whose belief is determined honestly, and who lives according to his light.

The development of opinions into heresies.

The process of the conversion of certain differences of opinion into heresies, Taylor discovers in the history of the Church. A party, which called themselves Catholic, took upon them to determine what was heresy and what was not. They did not do this at once. It grew upon them. Much as we read of the Pelagian heresy, and violent as St. Augustine was in suppressing it, we do not read that it was condemned by any General Council, though many Councils sat while it was in the world. The Nicene Council determined what doctrines they considered true, but they only declared what was their belief, without imposing it upon others. They enlarged the Articles of the Apostles' Creed, and expressed a wish that all the world might rest satisfied with the Creed as they left it. The Council of Constantinople added, 'I believe in baptism for the remission of sins.' The Fathers of the Council of Ephesus passed an anathema against all who would add to the Creed of Constantinople. The Church of Rome added the *Filioque,* and since that all the world knows how much. In the Creed of St. Athanasius there is nothing but damnation and perishing everlastingly, unless every article of the Trinity is believed, as it is there curiously and minutely explained. Certainly it may only mean that heresy is damnable, though the persons holding it may go to heaven. Yet how different is their language from that of the Scriptures, where no opinions are condemned but those which lead to an evil life! Thomas Aquinas says that Athanasius only meant this Creed for a declaration of his own belief. Since his time the Church of Rome has prescribed it to others on pain of everlasting fire.

Those who set up the Bible for a rule, Taylor says, have as many reasons for being tolerant towards those who do not agree with them, as they have who take the Church for a living judge. When we look at the many senses and interpretations of which the Scriptures are 'capable,' we must conclude either that our differences are not faults at all, or, if they are faults, they are excusable. The mind which is prepared to assent to God's truth as soon as it is with certainty discovered, has an implicit faith in God, which is of as great excellency as an implicit faith in any man or company of men. No man, whatever his sincerity and industry, can be sure that he understands the true sense of the Scriptures. First of all, there are many thousands of copies with a great variety of readings. Jews and Christians mutually accuse each other of corrupting the writings of the Old Testament. But even if we had perfect copies, much of the Scripture has various meanings. When we have understood the grammatical sense, we have made but little progress. The sense may be literal, and then it may be

Uncertainty of the meaning of the Scriptures should make men tolerant.

either natural or figurative. The sense may be spiritual, and then it may be allegorical or anagogical. Augustine has shown how frequently there may be different latent senses in one sentence. From the words in the Song of Solomon, 'Tell me, O thou whom my soul loveth, where thou feedest, where thou makest thy flock to rest at noon' (*in meridie*), the Donatists proved that the Church was only in the south part of the world,—in Africa. For re-baptizing heretics they had the agreement of almost all the Churches of Asia and Africa, of divers Councils, saints, martyrs, and confessors. Their arguments were drawn from such Scriptures as these: 'The oil of the sinner shall not break my head;'* 'He that washeth himself after the touching a dead body, if he touch it again, what availeth his washing?' 'Drink waters out of thine own cistern;' 'We know that God heareth not sinners;' 'He that is not with me is against me.' St. Augustine laughed at these arguments, but Taylor doubted if the other side had any arguments as good. If the words, 'unless a man be born again,' are conclusive against the Anabaptists, why should not 'unless ye eat,' be conclusive for bringing infants to the holy communion? Christ said to Peter, '*Feed* my lambs.' The Church of Rome understands 'feed' as 'teach,' 'command,' and, when desirable, 'put to death.'

We have no certain rule for interpreting the Scriptures. Some refer us to the context; others say we should compare Scripture with Scripture. Some speak of the analogy of reason, and others of the analogy of faith; and some place all certainty in reading the originals. All these are good helps in themselves; yet they may all be made the means of finding in the Scriptures only what we wish to find in them. Some propose as the guide to Scripture interpretation the traditions of the Church; but these again are all involved in uncertainty. Augustine says that those things held by the universal Church which have not been determined by Councils, are to be believed as having descended from the Apostles. The worth of this rule may be easily tested.

* Ps. cxli. 5. The Vulgate reading is 'Oleum peccatoris non impinget caput meum.' The LXX. reads, Ἔλαιον δὲ ἁμαρτωλοῦ μὴ διπανάτω τὴν κεφαλήν μου. The Hebrew gives quite a different sense.

Papias, a scholar of the Apostles, taught the doctrine of the millenarians. Justin Martyr says that millenarianism was the belief of all orthodox Christians. Yet what was the origin and what was the sum of this tradition? It was simply an error of Papias, a weak-headed man. If a doctrine so ancient and so generally received has no better foundation, what is to be said of some doctrine that two or three hundred years later was called by some Father, Catholic and Apostolic? The Nicene Fathers objected against the Arians a universal tradition of the three first centuries. Arius was willing to be tried by this alleged tradition; but, Taylor says, the orthodox would have failed, if they had not had arguments from Scripture better than their arguments from tradition. St. Augustine's rule was that we were to believe everything of which we did not know the beginning to be apostolic. The rule which we are now disposed to follow is the opposite of this,—not to receive any doctrine as apostolical unless we know that it had its beginning with the Apostles. The uncertainty of tradition in the earliest ages of the Church was manifest in the controversies concerning the time of keeping Easter. The Churches, both of the East and the West, alleged for their different customs a tradition from the Apostles. Clement of Alexandria said there was a secret tradition from the Apostles that Christ preached only one year. Irenæus, on the other hand, said that this was a tradition which came from heretics. He had it from St. John and other disciples that Christ was almost fifty years old when He died, and so he must have preached for nearly twenty years. When tried by the history of the Evangelists, both these traditions are wrong, for there the time of Christ's ministry is limited to three years. The Assumption of the blessed Virgin rests solely on the arguments and authority of St. Augustine. The baptizing of infants rests on the authority of Origen. The other Fathers, following Origen, call it a Catholic custom. The procession of the Holy Ghost from the Father *and the Son* pretends a tradition from the Apostles; but it was unheard of till the time of St. Augustine. On the other hand, there are some traditions that are now disregarded, which certainly did come from the Apostles. Such were abstinence from blood

CHAP. V.

Even tradition of customs is contradictory.

Apostolic traditions now disregarded.

and things strangled, the cœnobitic life of secular persons, the college of widows, standing during divine worship on the Lord's day, and giving milk and honey to the newly baptized. Again, there is the tradition, or rather the injunction, that a bishop should be the husband of one wife. The Church of Rome does not allow even one. Other Churches allow more than one.

If tradition leaves us in uncertainty, we are not much helped by Councils and Fathers. We may, indeed, reasonably expect that, as the Spirit is promised to private men, so will it be given to such assemblies as the Councils of the Church. But there is no promise of any infallible guidance. Before the days of St. Augustine, there was some appearance of unanimity among the Fathers. But the great reputation of the Bishop of Hippo made many opinions popular which were unheard of till his day. No Church Father before Augustine preached predestination, yet, through the influence of his name, predestination became a Catholic doctrine. But even if the Fathers did not contradict each other, what certainty have we that we really know what they taught? Their works have been corrupted by heretics. Many books that were never written by them bear their names. Many of their books are lost, some of which were necessary to shed light on those that remain. The Fathers have been made to speak, not what they thought, but what other men thought. In their writings there is, indeed, some truth preserved; and we thank God that it is not so clean gone as their great authority and reputation. Taylor cites some cases of the corruptions of the Fathers. In the fifth Decretal Epistle, ascribed to St. Clement, that Father is made to say that the Apostles had a community of wives, because St. Luke says that they had all things in common. Justin Martyr, who lived before Origen, cites Origen along with Irenæus for the baptizing of infants. And then, as to the writings of Origen, they have been so interpolated by heretics, that it is impossible to say what is his and what is not.

Taylor concludes this rational treatise in the same spirit in which he began it. He sets a higher value on a good life than on an orthodox creed. He estimates every doctrine by its capacity to do men good. Religion was meant to make us more just and more merciful, and it is a sufficient reason for the rejection of any doctrine if it does not serve that object. We may then conclude that it is not sound. All sects were to be tolerated, even the Anabaptists, so long as their doctrines were not injurious to the well-being of the State. If it were a mere matter of religious opinion, unlimited toleration might be extended to Roman Catholics. It is difficult to acquit them of the charge of idolatry, and this, Taylor says, no government can tolerate while it regards the well-being of the community. Many reasons are given why Christians should be forbearing and charitable towards those who differ from them. It is recommended that members of churches that have different doctrines should communicate with each other. God is not angry with men because they are in error when they have done their best to find out the truth. And if for this God is not angry with men, why should they be angry with each other?

CHAP. V.

Bishop Taylor is generally called a semi-Pelagian. All men who are familiar with theological writings know that names of this kind mean very little. We know nothing of the doctrines of Pelagius but from his opponent, St. Augustine, whose authority in matters of heresy is of the smallest imaginable value. Taylor denied that he was in any way a Pelagian. It is, certain, however, that on grace, good works, original sin, and some kindred subjects, he was very far from agreeing either with Augustine or Calvin. We should certainly decline the task of attempting to reconcile the doctrines of Jeremy Taylor with those of the Articles of the Church of England. In a treatise on the 'Doctrine and Practice of Repentance,' he says that under the new law it is possible to keep the commandments of God. Some African bishops said that there were Christians who from the day of their conversion to the day of their death, lived without sin. Augustine did not think this a great error, because these bishops said it was done solely by the grace of God. The Pelagians, on the other hand, according to St. Augustine, professed to be able to keep the commandments of God by nature, without grace. Taylor's argument is, that we are commanded to keep God's laws, and that God

A semi-Pelagian.

Nature and grace.

does not require of us what we cannot perform. Our duty under the Gospel is summed up in loving God with all our soul. This Taylor explains to be loving Him as much as we can love Him, which, by the very terms in which it is expressed, is possible for us. From this explanation it is evident that he did not mean keeping the Commandments of God perfectly. He says that this we cannot do, because of our weakness and our temptations. But after we have done our best there is an allowance made for our infirmities. Christ has died for us, and therefore God will not lay these to our charge. Since the Redeemer was promised, that is, since the fall of Adam, the covenant of exact obedience has never been the rule of life and death. The regenerate state is perfection, though it be imperfect in its degrees. The old law was a schoolmaster, to bring the synagogue to Christ, and not, as most theologians understand this passage, to bring us to Christ. We are done with the old law. We are under grace. The Apostle's argument about the old law is addressed to Jews only. In the experience of a Christian there is no such stage as being under the law. Some people suppose the law to have been nothing but terror, while the Gospel is nothing but grace. Taylor says there was grace under the law, and to the impenitent there are terrors under the Gospel more fearful than those which were under the law. But the Gospel is a covenant of more mercy. It is also a covenant of more holiness. Good works are as necessary now as they ever were. The only antithesis between the old law and the new, is that the one is better than the other. They are not properly opposed to each other. Faith is not placed in opposition to works. Both are necessary to salvation. They are so much of the same nature that the one cannot be separated from the other. From the necessity of works, Taylor inferred the invalidity of death-bed repentance. God, he admits, may save a man who does not repent till he finds that he is dying. But this is not the ordinary rule of the divine dealing. Repentance is not enough. Mere faith, however sincere, is not enough. There must be fruit following faith.

But Jeremy Taylor's heresies were not limited to his

teaching that men are saved by works under the covenant of grace, as well as under the first covenant with Adam, nor to his doubting the possibility of salvation without a miracle to a death-bed penitent. He denied what by some theologians is reckoned the first doctrine of the Gospel,—the imputation of Adam's sin to his posterity. St. Paul says, that death passed upon all men, for that all have sinned. Taylor explains this, that Adam first sinned. All his sons and daughters sinned after him, and so all have died, not because of Adam's sin, but because of their own sins. We are not made sinners in Adam. We did not die in Adam. For our own sins we suffer that death which passed on him for his sin. There are many passages in Scripture which seem to declare the opposite of what Taylor here teaches. It was necessary for him to explain these. The meaning he puts upon them is, that but for Adam's disobedience men would not have been punished so severely for their own sins. The consequence of Adam's disobedience is upon them. They are accounted sinners in the sense of having to bear the penalty of that sin. Their disobedience was not like his, not so great as his. They had not sinned after the similitude of Adam's transgression. His sin brought infirmity on all men. In this sense Christ as one of the sons of Adam was a sinner. The writer of the Epistle to the Hebrews says that *He offered first for His own sins.* Adam lost paradise and the tree of life. He was driven out into a less favourable region. In this region his children were born. When Anthony seized upon the lands of Cicero, his son was a loser, but he only lost what he never had. So was it with the children of Adam. They lost what they never had, but they were not by Adam's transgression made heirs of damnation, nor did they become naturally and necessarily vicious. An act committed thousands of years before we were born could not have been our act, nor could it, in any kind of justice, be imputed to us. It was not our choice that we were born at all, much less that we should be born guilty of Adam's sin, of which we should never have heard but by revelation. After saying all these things, and many more of the same kind, Taylor goes on to reason against the injustice implied in the suppo-

Men do not suffer death for Adam's sin.

sition that God would condemn any man to never-ending punishment for the sin of another. He dealt more equitably with the angels who kept not their first estate. They were to stand or fall by their own doings. We are by nature miserable and imperfect, but not criminal. There are many passages of Scripture continually quoted in evidence of the doctrine of original sin. David said, 'In sin did my mother conceive me.' Bishop Taylor adds, that David might have said this more truly of the conception of the eldest son of Bathsheba. St. Paul says that we are by nature children of wrath. Bishop Taylor says 'by nature,' not by birth. This was the actual condition of those to whom St. Paul referred, before their conversion. It is said that God threatens to visit the sins of the fathers upon the children. Bishop Taylor explains this, that God once tried this mode of dealing with men, but it was afterwards changed for another, which was, 'the soul that sinneth, it shall die.'

The doctrine of original sin, usually ascribed to the Pelagians, is that it consists in our sinning as Adam sinned, and not in our being affected by what he did. This plainly is not Taylor's doctrine. He does admit that men are partakers of infirmity because of Adam's guilt. He tries to harmonize his doctrine with the ninth of the XXXIX. Articles. It is there said that original sin is 'the fault and corruption of the nature of every man.' It is not said that sin is imputed, but only that we are born imperfect, and that ere we can reign with God we must be renewed. 'Corruption,' Taylor says, is exegetical of 'fault,' and as infirmity is connected with the body, the meaning of 'fault' is manifest. The body is subject to death. It is therefore said to be sown in corruption. This 'fault' or 'corruption' is predicated 'of the nature of every man,' which proves, according to Bishop Taylor, that 'it does not mean sin in us, for sin is not an affection of the whole nature, but of persons.' There is in the Article a limitation by the words, 'every man that is naturally engendered of the offspring of Adam.' This is generally taken for a limitation which excludes Christ from the participation of Adam's sin. But Christ was not without sin in the sense of original sin in this Article. He had the infirmities or natural desires common to all men. Without these He could not have been under the law. The Article says that we are 'very far gone from original righteousness,' which means that we are born in the greatest imperfection,—born under a law which we break before we have understanding. It is said also that man 'of his own nature is inclined to evil,' which is true of all men, but of some men more than others. It is an effect or condition of nature, but not properly sin. The Article goes on to affirm that 'the flesh lusteth contrary to the spirit,' which is taken as conclusive that concupiscence is the only effect of Adam's sin. This 'infection' is an imperfection, an inclination to what is forbidden. Other Protestant Confessions say that it is sin. The Council of Trent says it is not sin. This Article simply says it has 'the nature of sin.' It is not sin to those who do not consent, but it is the root whence sin may spring. The regenerate man is born into liberty. He has the victory over sin. The Gospel gives him power to conquer it. This is the excellency of the Gospel. In this it surpasses all other covenants and institutions.

Jeremy Taylor's arguments for Episcopacy are not so original as those against the imputation of Adam's sin, but they are more orthodox. The tract on this subject is called 'Episcopacy Asserted.' In the overthrow of the bishops by the Presbyterians, he saw the prelude to the great apostasy of the latter day. There must, said the Apostle, be a falling away first; and was not this falling away from the government that had been in the Church for sixteen centuries the greatest and most significant sign of Antichrist that had yet appeared? The argument which never was omitted by Episcopalian, Presbyterian, or Independent, was the corner-stone of Taylor's fabric. Has not God prescribed a government for His Church? To sit down in the calm spirit of philosophers, and examine whether or not there is such a government prescribed, was too humble a proceeding for the theologians of the seventeenth century. It was assumed to be abundantly manifest, previous to all examination, that God must have given a scheme of Church government; and every sect saw in the New Testament their own scheme. The Scriptures, Taylor said, prescribe private duties. It cannot, therefore, be supposed that they should not prescribe public duties. The ark of God could not be left to human prudence. After being as well satisfied that Episcopacy must be in the Bible as the Puritans were that the Geneva discipline was in the Bible, Taylor brings forth his strong arguments. Christ delegated to His Apostles power which they were to delegate to their successors. The ordinary offices of the Apostles were to continue and the extraordinary to cease. Priests and deacons, in a limited sense, are the successors of the Apostles; but the bishops are their full successors, truly and properly. The office of Judas was called a bishopric. St. James, Bishop of Jerusalem, though not of the twelve, was called to be an Apostle. St. Augustine testifies that, though Peter was the first of the Apostles, yet in James's diocese he yields his pre-eminence. Epaphroditus was the Apostle of the Philippians, which is explained by Theodoret to mean their bishop. Those Apostles who received their apostleship immediately from Christ were called Apostles of Christ. The others were called Apostles of the Churches. But all of them were bishops. Christ Himself first made the distinction between bishops and presbyters, when He sent forth the twelve Apostles and the seventy disciples. Epiphanius says that the seven deacons were chosen from the seventy presbyters.

Bishops in the Church of Antioch. In the Church of Antioch, the prophets laid their hands on Paul and Barnabas. These prophets were more than ordinary presbyters. Mark was of the Church of Antioch, but only as a minister of the Apostles. He had no part in the laying on of hands. Confirmation was performed only by the Apostles. This disparity of ministers in the Church is sanctioned by the Holy Ghost in the Epistles to the angels of the seven Churches in Asia. All antiquity bears witness to the apostolic succession of bishops. It calls all bishops successors of St. Peter. Cyprian says that the Church is founded on the bishops as the successors of St. Peter. St. Timothy was Bishop of Ephesus, St. Titus of Crete, St. Mark of Alexandria, St. Linus and St. Clement of Rome, and St. Polycarp of Smyrna. The primitive Church called the bishop 'pontifex,' and the Episcopacy 'pontificatum.' Eusebius says that when St. John was in his 'pontificals,' he wore on his forehead a πέταλον, a gold plate or medal, as a sign of his apostleship. One bishop could make a priest or a deacon, but a bishop must be ordained by two, or at least three, other bishops.

In 'A Discourse of Confirmation,' Taylor took a view of that rite which has been but rarely, if ever, advanced in the Church of England. He not only made it the complement of baptism, but he made it of more importance than baptism. Following the mystical St. Dionysius, he called it 'the perfection of the divine birth.' Until we are confirmed, we are but babes in Christ, in the meanest sense infants that cannot speak. By confirmation we become in reality the children of God. When the bishop blesses the baptized Christians, then a guardian angel is appointed over each one, to shield them from the assaults of the spirits of darkness. Taylor says that the Jesuits in England made confirmation of little importance, because they had then no bishops to confirm. It is not, indeed, a sacrament, as baptism and the Lord's Supper are sacraments; yet we are nevertheless bound to receive it. Repentance is not a sacrament, and yet repentance is a duty. Christ was confirmed immediately after He was baptized. John's baptism did not give the Holy Ghost. The effect of baptism is the washing away of sin; the effect of confirmation is the gift of the Holy Ghost. Confirmation sanctifies the soul, and represses the carnal desires. He that is only baptized, receives not the Holy Ghost. He that has not the Spirit of God is none of His. St. Clement and St. Cyprian understand 'water and the Holy Ghost' to mean *water and fire.* We must pass through fire and water; that is, baptism and confirmation. In baptism we make vows. In confirmation we get strength to keep them. Taylor leaves no doubt about his meaning, when he connects grace and the gift of the Holy Ghost with the rites of baptism and confirmation. All that is needed to make them valid is that they be performed by the regular ministers, who are the appointed channels of grace. The sacerdotalism so abundant in his later writings was almost unknown in the 'Liberty of Prophesying.' In that book Taylor advocated toleration for the Baptists, on the ground that no great harm was done if people were suffered to die

CHAP. V.

On Confirmation.

Baptism does not give the Holy Ghost.

unbaptized. Now he makes baptism necessary to salvation, the only exception being when it cannot be had. Grace comes to the Church through the bishops and priests. It is conferred by the simple performance of the regular offices of the Church. This is confirmed, as all profound questions in theology generally were, by the great authority St. Augustine. That saint testifies that he knew men who had resolved to marry and lead secular lives, but, being taken by violence and carried against their will to the bishops to be ordained priests, they received the gift of continency in the very act of ordination.

On 'The Real Presence.'

In a treatise on 'The Real Presence' in the Eucharist, Bishop Taylor returns to more rational theology. The old dread of transubstantiation, inherited from the Reformers, still existed even in the minds of the most advanced High Churchmen. The writers who most zealously advocated priests, altars, and sacrifices, always made a great difference between these things as they understood them, and as they were understood in the Church of Rome. Any doctrine of the 'real presence' that was in any way kindred to transubstantiation, was unknown among Laud's Churchmen. Taylor begins his treatise by quoting Erasmus, who says that 'it was late before the Church defined transubstantiation; for a long time together it did suffice to believe that the true body of Christ was present, whether under the consecrated bread, or any other way.' To the same effect Durandus, 'We hear the words, we perceive the motion, we know not the manner, but we believe the presence.' Taylor thinks that Erasmus and Durandus would have agreed with him that the presence of Christ is real and spiritual. The word 'spiritual,' he says, is particular in nothing but that it excludes the corporal and natural. A spiritual presence means a presence by effect and blessing. It is in reality not a formal presence, but a presence by His Spirit. The bread and wine become the body and blood of Christ. They are not changed as to their nature, but they are changed by grace as to their use. And this spiritual presence, Taylor says, is more real than a bodily presence. The earthly tabernacle was the visible, but the true tabernacle was the heavenly, the invisible. In this sense Christ is present *substantialiter*. The Council of Trent says that Christ is sacramentally present to us *in His own substance*. Here is at least an agreement in words between Protestants and the Church of Rome. Taylor thinks this might be the basis of an entire agreement between them both, if by the same words they meant the same thing. St. Bernard and Bellarmine are quoted as saying that Christ's body is not there corporally, but truly and substantially, that is, spiritually. But Taylor finds that Bellarmine does not understand by 'spiritually' what Protestants understand by that word. He means that the body is present not as a body, but as a spirit,—with the nature of a body naturally, and yet with that manner of being by which a spirit is distinguished from a body. This Taylor calls 'cozening the world,' for it is ' a direct folly and contradiction.' 'We,' he adds, 'by the real spiritual presence of Christ do understand Christ to be present, as the Spirit of God is present in the hearts of the faithful, by blessing and grace, and this is all that we mean besides the tropical and figurative presence.' We may say that Christ's body is present, meaning that a 'corporal sign' of that body is present. Taylor rejects John vi. as having any reference to the Lord's Supper, and he quotes Eusebius as interpreting the *flesh and blood* in that chapter as the words which Christ spake, and not of any eating of His body in the Eucharist.

The doctrine of Jeremy Taylor on original sin did not meet the approbation of the orthodox theologians of his day. To Dr. Sanderson it was a matter of great grief. To the Presbyterians a greater heresy could scarcely have been propounded. Two of their ministers undertook to refute it. John Gaule, 'Preacher of the Word at Great Staughton in Huntingdonshire,'* and Henry Jeanes, 'Minister of God's

---

* Gaule's book is very scarce. It is not in the British Museum nor in any London library to which the writer of this has access. There is a copy in the Bodleian, according to the catalogue. Bishop Heber, in his 'Life of Taylor,' speaks of it contemptuously, though he confesses that he never saw it, and knew nothing whatever of the author. But John Gaule is worthy of a note. He was Vicar of Great Staughton in the time of Cromwell, and an ardent Presbyterian, but he conformed at the Restoration, and recommended conformity to others. From the connection of Cromwell's family with the parish of Great Staughton, it is probable that Gaule owed this preferment to the Protector. He dedicated to Cromwell a book called 'Πῦς-μαντία, The Mag-Astro-mancer, or the Magical-

Word at Chedzoy.' These were not great men, but they both had some reputation in their day as authors and preachers. Henry Jeanes was one of the two thousand ejected by the Act of Uniformity. Wood gives him the character of 'a most excellent philosopher,' and 'a noted metaphysician.' He wrote against Taylor a treatise 'Of Original Righteousness and its Contrary Concupiscence.'

Astrological-Diviner posed and puzzled.' This was a book against astrology. In the dedication Gaule speaks of having received from Cromwell 'super-abounding favours for these sundry years past.' Gaule's fame rested chiefly on the part which he took in the great question of witchcraft. There was a witch-committee appointed by Government to hunt up all the witches in the country. The small towns and villages of the eastern counties were specially searched, being supposed to abound with these servants of the great enemy. Gaule said that there were no witches in his parish, and he protested in the pulpit against the government officers coming among his parishioners on that business. Matthew Hopkins, the witch commissioner, wrote to him from London that he was coming in a few days to Kimbolton, and he intended to begin his search at Great Staughton. He told Gaule that many ministers preached against the discovery of witches, saying that there were none in their parishes, but they were soon forced to recant. The commissioner had ways of finding out witches unknown to the ministers. This was the occasion of Gaule's writing a book called 'Select Cases of Conscience, touching Witches and Witchcraft.' It bears the date of 1646. It was dedicated 'To his ever honoured Valentine Wauton, Esquire, Colonel, and one of the Honourable House of Commons. As also to the other worthy Gentlemen, together with all the good people of the Parish of Great Staughton in the County of Huntingdonshire.' It is a scientific treatise on the science of witchcraft. Gaule did not deny the existence of witches. The man, he says, who refuses to admit this, will soon say that there is no devil, and after that it will not be long when he will say that there is no God. Then follows a learned discourse of the different kinds of witches,—the diviner, the observer of seasons, the enchanter, the poison-witch, the charmer, the familiar (this kind of witch is described as one that carries the spirit in a bottle, bag, or pitcher), the sciential witch, the necromancer. These are the learned divisions. The vulgar only spoke of white and black witches, or good and bad witches, the arted witch and the pacted witch, the active witch and the passive witch. Gaule said that the good witch was more to be feared than the bad one; the devil being most dangerous when he comes as an angel of light. Witches are all made, they are not born witches. The causes of witchcraft, in scholastic form, are God, the deficient cause; the devil, the efficient cause; divers sins, the moving cause; a covenant with the devil, the formal cause. The covenant is sometimes explicit, but most frequently implicit. Vulgar signs or tests of witches are,—long eyes, not weeping, ill-favoured face, and mumbling, burning the thing bewitched, burning the thatch of the witch's house, heating of the horseshoe, scalding water, casting the witch into water with her thumbs and toes tied across. But these signs are improbable. The probable are, strong and long suspicion, suspected ancestors, bare confession, a corpse bleeding upon the witch's touch, unusual bloody marks, cursing and banning, lewd and naughty life, declining judicature, haunting the houses of notorious witches, or keeping company with them, being impeached by other witches, forsaking public worship and sacrament, or maligning the word or worship of God. The object of Gaule's discourse was to check the custom of condemning people for witchcraft without sufficient evidence.

It is divided into two heads. These are, if there be such a thing as original righteousness, and what it is. Taylor and the Socinians, Jeanes says, deny the first. They explain original righteousness as simply being innocent of actual sin. Jeanes brings forward Scripture to prove that it was something positive. The proofs are, that man was made in God's image, which is righteousness and holiness; that God, after the creation, pronounced everything very good—this, applied to man, must be moral goodness. God made man upright, and St. Paul speaks of putting on the new man which is created after the image of God. These passages, Jeanes says, speak of an actual righteousness, and not a mere freedom from actual sin. Taylor had spoken of Adam's knowledge as limited. This was a secondary point, but connected with the main question. Jeanes could not say that Adam was omniscient, but he maintained that being made in the image of God, this image was a likeness in understanding. Knowledge in Scripture generally means practical knowledge. It is not merely agnition but cognition,—knowledge with an acknowledgment. It could not be inferior to that knowledge which is in the new man, for it is in this that man is said to be renewed. In the Epistle to the Colossians knowledge is put for the whole new man, by the figure synecdoche. Scripture ascribes to Adam actions which imply a high degree of knowledge, as his naming all the beasts of the field, and exercising dominion over them.

What the original righteousness was, is the next question. It is called original for several reasons. It was the first righteousness in the world. It was seated in our first parents. They had it as soon as they were created. Jeanes considers it after the Puritan fashion of divisions and subdivisions, till the subject seems to evaporate among the terms and distinctions. He tells us what it is materially, formally, subjectively, causatively, and in its effects. It is under the last head that we get the idea of something definite. It was a subordination of the body to the soul, of the lower faculties of the soul to the higher, and of all to God. That was original righteousness in its effects. The contrary is concupiscence, which in all the logical relations above mentioned is sin. It is the law in the members which warreth against the law of the mind. In its effects it is the contrary of original righteousness.

After this treatise follows a series of letters that were written by Taylor and Jeanes in a further discussion of this question. A passage out of one of Taylor's books was the text. He said 'that every man is inclined to evil, some more, some less, but all in some instances, is very true, and it is an effect or condition of nature, but no sin properly. (1.) Because that which is unavoidable is not a sin; and (2.) Because it is accidental to nature, and not intrusive and essential. (3.) It is superadded to nature, and is after it.' The meaning of some of the words here used were to some extent the main subject of the controversy. Taylor denies that infirmity, or that which is a state or condition of nature, being merely accidental to nature, is sin. Jeanes reduced Taylor's position to this premise, 'Sin properly is not accidental to the nature of man,' which of course he denied. Porphyry defines an accident as 'that which may be affirmed or denied of its subject, without contradiction to the essence or definition thereof.' To deny sin of man is not to contradict the definition of him as a being that reasons, and therefore sin is accidental. If it were natural and not accidental, then God, who is the author of nature, would be the author of sin. Christ was made like unto His brethren in all that is essential to the being of men, yet He was without sin. The saints at the resurrection shall be sinless, and yet men in all that is necessary to the being of men. It is evident that Taylor did not mean by nature what Jeanes understood him to mean. If he had, he would have been refuting himself. It would have been saying that all sin is natural in the sense of unavoidable. Taylor answered that by 'natural,' he meant 'regular,' 'uniform.' He was speaking of the Article on 'Original Sin,' where he understands the inclination to evil as not universal, but accidental. Christ had all natural desires, and yet He had no sin. If He had not natural human desires, He was not a perfect man. Mere capacity for evil, or mere inclination to evil, is not sin. The ordinary doctrine of original sin is that it is natural, necessary, unavoidable. It was just this which Taylor denied.

This controversy began with letters between Taylor and Jeanes through a mutual friend. It ended with their upbraiding each other mutually for want of discernment; Jeanes telling Taylor that he could not express himself properly, and Taylor recommending Jeanes to find some more profitable way of employing his ingenuity than by cavilling at other people's books.

CHAP. V.

Hallam calls Jeremy Taylor's 'Liberty of Prophesying,' the first famous plea in this country for toleration in religion. It was not the first plea, but it was the first treatise on the subject that had any special interest. The principles had been advocated by John Goodwin, Leonard Busher, John Baptist, and one or two other obscure or anonymous writers. Some have traced them to John Smyth, of Amsterdam, who was probably their first English advocate. The plea for liberty of conscience has always come most ardently from those to whom it was denied. Men begged to be tolerated long before they learned to tolerate. The most zealous advocate of liberty of conscience in the seventeenth century was Lodowick Muggleton. The 'prophet' could not understand why the Lord Protector suffered him to be so often put in the stocks and pelted by the populace. The 'Liberty of Prophesying' was written when Taylor's party were in adversity. The Presbyterians were in power. It was their turn to assert the right of the State to punish heretics. It was for those who were not tolerated to plead for toleration.

Liberty of conscience.

Samuel Rutherford, one of the leaders of the Presbyterians in Scotland, wrote, in answer to Taylor, 'A Free Disputation against Pretended Liberty of Conscience.' Rutherford was Professor of Divinity in the University of St. Andrew's, and one of the Commissioners from the Church of Scotland to the 'Assembly of Divines.' Jeremy Taylor, the friend of Archbishop Laud, pleads for toleration to all sects and sectaries. One of the leaders of the Church of Scotland answers that ecclesiastical authorities have a divine commission to punish heretics, even with death. This strange phenomenon is not fully explained by the mere circumstance that the one is in power and the other is not. The reason is deeper than this. It is connected, at least on Rutherford's side, with the essence of his creed. He de-

Samuel Rutherford against Liberty of Prophesying.

clares in the very first page of his book, that to give liberty of conscience is to suppose conscience to be a man's guide. It is to give it a royal prerogative, and to make it the rule of what we believe and of what we do. It is to put conscience in the place of God and the Bible. In other words, it is to deny infallibility and certainty as to what a man believes. How could Samuel Rutherford, as a minister of the Gospel, rebuke those who differed from him, if there was no guide for men but conscience? He will not deny that the saints have errors, and that there is need for indulgence and forbearance, but there must be 'a taking of the foxes which destroy the vines.'

Rutherford begins with a consideration of conscience, what it is, and what are its functions. It is a servant to be guided and directed by the word of God, or by what God reveals to us. This supposes an infallible certainty, independent of the conscience, of what God says to us in the Bible. We might suppose that Rutherford had simply transferred the Bible to that place which is supplied in the Roman Catholic system by the supposition of an infallible Church. But this would be a mistake. Rutherford, like all the thorough Presbyterians, believed in a divinely appointed Church, and, consistently with this, he believed that God speaks to us by that Church. So that the Church, speaking in its lawful assemblies, is to be the ruler and guide of conscience. He does not say in so many words that the Church is infallible, but when he explains why we should submit to the decisions of a synod, it is on the supposition that they are agreeable to the Scriptures. Christ has said, 'He that heareth you, heareth me.' The Dutch Arminians had objected to this reliance on the decisions of synods. They asked how the Church could determine anything with certainty when, in everything it determines, it may err, and is therefore fallible. Rutherford answered that the Scripture had determined all controversies. There was nothing in the Bible unexplained or controversial, except in regard of our dulness and sinfulness. The Church, though fallible, may determine infallible points of doctrine. The Apostles and prophets erred when deserted by the Spirit, but though liable to err, they yet declared infallible truth, and so it is now with the

Church and its pastors. Rutherford, like Laud, Montagu, and the High Churchmen of the Church of England, denied that because the Church was fallible, it was therefore to be inferred that it could not determine anything infallibly. The ministers of the Church have an official, authoritative judgment, in virtue of which they are 'to command, rebuke, and exhort.' The people are 'to obey those that are over them.' It is said of the ministers of the Gospel, not of the people, 'He that heareth you heareth me.' The officers of the Church declare the mind of Christ, as the judges, in interpreting the law, declare the mind and will of the king. The Arminians said that if anything was already determined in the Scriptures, there was no need for a synod to determine it. The answer is, that without the ministerial determination of the synod, people are left to interpret Scripture by their own private judgment; so that not the Scripture but their private interpretation of Scripture is their guide.

The Church, then, declares truth. It has a ministerial power. It is the duty of the ministers of the Church to instruct the civil magistrate in his duty. The Church cannot use the sword against heresy, but it can complain of heretics to the civil magistrate. It can give them over to him who has the power of the sword. The objection was raised that the civil magistrate has to do with manners, and not with religious opinions,—with what men do, and not with what they teach. Rutherford answers that heretics do fail against manners. His argument is not clear, but it seems to be that as heretics are murderers of souls, it is the duty of the magistrate not to suffer them to escape. And if the magistrate is remiss in his duty, the ministers or synods ought to admonish him that he must coerce with the sword seditious wolves and *Jezebels*. It is granted, indeed, that no external compulsion can change men's beliefs. The sword of the magistrate should not, therefore, be used positively to compel men to adopt externally a worship of which they do not approve. The magistrate is only to use his power negatively by punishing acts of false worship, in so far as these acts are public, and likely to be destructive to the souls of others. He may also punish omissions of hearing the doctrine of the Gospel, or of other external acts of worship. He does

The Church has power to determine what is heresy.

not, however, do this as a service to God, but only as false worship, or as the omission of true worship, may be injurious to men as individuals, or destructive to the commonwealth over which he presides. John Goodwin said that the magistrate cannot in justice punish errors of the mind, for they are unavoidable. They depend on conviction, not on free-will. Rutherford answers that this might as well have been objected against the Mosaic command that a seducer who tempted the people to worship false gods, was to be stoned to death. The magistrate has to protect the people whom he governs; and as to the injustice from the fact that heresies or mental errors do not depend on the freedom of the will, Rutherford says that the same might be urged for adultery and murder.

John Goodwin argued for a universal toleration, from the difficulty of arriving at truth. That required some degree of reason and understanding,—often, indeed, a supernatural illumination of the Holy Spirit. It had been proposed to extend toleration to all who held fundamentals, and to leave freedom in things that were not fundamental. But Goodwin showed that the difficulty of arriving at certainty was not less in the one case than in the other, and that heretics were to be pitied rather than punished. The distinction thus ceased to be of any service in the question of toleration. Rutherford asks if the false prophet mentioned in Deuteronomy, or Elymas the sorcerer, were men to be pitied, rather than punished for their errors. This mental blindness, which Goodwin said was excusable, was punished by command of God. Goodwin's principle was evidently grounded on the Arminian doctrine that God could only punish men according to the measure of light that had been given them. In Rutherford's judgment, this was to arraign the divine justice at the bar of human reason. It was, he said, the old plea of the Donatists, who argued from liberty of free-will to liberty of conscience, and who unquestionably would have opposed the decrees of Nebuchadnezzar and Artaxerxes. Rutherford preferred following the Book of Deuteronomy. There the idolaters and seducers were to be punished. The same laws warrant us to put to death those that 'seduce souls.' There are, indeed, some things left indifferent, such as opinions and practices about meats and drinks, or different expositions of the same text. But the point at which toleration is to cease, is when the difference makes a schism. St. Paul could not endure the divisions at Corinth. Christ was not divided. There were not two Churches, but only one. Christians are to strive to walk by the same rule, and not to divide themselves into sects, every one following his own private judgment. Heresy is not a mere innocent error of the mind. St. Paul classes it with the works of the flesh, making it one of the greatest of sins.

Heresy not an innocent error.

After explaining what is to be the rule of our belief, Rutherford brings forward many arguments against toleration. It is without authority either in the Old or the New Testament. It implies a sceptical spirit as to the certainty of what is revealed. There is but one way. It is the old way, the 'one Lord, one faith, one baptism.' God has not left it to men to serve Him as conscience dictates. He has given laws how He is to be served. It was in the days when there was no King in Israel, that Micah consecrated one of his sons, and made him his priest. The magistrate is to take care that such as Micah do not serve God according to their erroneous conscience. If he neglect his duty, the people will soon multiply groves and 'altars, according to the number of their cities.' The Arminians said that under the Old Testament the prophets were infallible, but no such infallibility belongs to the ministers or magistrates under the Gospel. Rutherford answered that we must have a 'full persuasion,' and though the Church be fallible, we are not to be carried about with every wind of doctrine. Toleration of heresy destroys our hope and comfort in the Scriptures. It takes away from the ministers of the word authority to rebuke and silence gainsayers. It takes away from magistrates the authority expressly given to them in the Fourth Commandment, and, as it has been already shown, it is contrary to all the laws of the Old Testament for restraining teachers of lies. Rutherford adds many passages from the New Testament, proving that the magistrate is to punish heretics. He is 'a terror to evil doers.' He is so to govern the State, as that men may 'lead

Toleration implies a sceptical spirit as to revelation.

The magistrate to punish heretics.

quiet and peaceful lives.' Moreover we read in the Revelation that the 'ten kings' as kings punished the idolatrous woman, and burnt her with fire. The old emperors made laws against heretics. Jeremy Taylor had quoted from some of the Fathers passages advocating toleration. But he also said that all sorts of Christians dissent from the doctrines of some of the most celebrated Fathers. Therefore, said Rutherford, they are not authorities for liberty of conscience.

Bishop Taylor's plea for toleration, strange as it may appear when coming from a High Churchman, really was the same as Goodwin's,—the uncertainty of the meaning of all that is revealed in the Scriptures. He pointed to the various readings, the different punctuations, the many senses in which a passage might be understood, the meaning often depending on a letter or an accent. Rutherford answered from the providence of God, which must have watched over His word so as to deliver it clear and infallible to the Church. Translators, copyists, or printers might err, but God could not suffer their errors to affect the infallibility of what is revealed.

The 'Liberty of Conscience literature,' before the publication of Jeremy Taylor's book, consisted chiefly of some tracts and pamphlets.* The oldest of them was that of Leonard Busher already mentioned. It was written in 1614, and presented to King James and the Parliament. Busher does not seem to have been a preacher. He is simply called 'a citizen of London.' His principles apparently were Presbyterian. The tract was republished in 1646, with an epistle prefixed by a Presbyterian, addressed 'To the Presbyterian Reader.' The epistle was an exhortation to the Presbyterians now in power to practise that toleration which Busher had begged from the King and the bishops. The arguments of the tract were solid. Busher told the King that true religion was not inherited by birth, and that it could not be propagated by fire or sword. The laws which compelled all subjects to be of the same religion as the King he called cruel and antichristian. Christianity can be received only by those who are convinced of its truth. It

* A good collection of these tracts, in Dr. Williams' library, catalogued bound in one volume, will be found under Leonard Busher.

rests on the command to 'go and teach all nations.' Its Apostles were not to compel, but to persuade men. Christ came not to destroy men's lives, but to save them. Kings must receive their faith in the same way as subjects receive theirs; that is, not as kings, but as men. Christ's kingdom is not of this world. It is not defended by the sword, but by the word and Spirit of God. Christ said, 'He that will not hear the Church, let him be to thee as a heathen and a publican.' He did not say, 'Let him be burned, banished, or imprisoned.' Christians may be persecuted, but they should never be persecutors. Abel did not kill Cain; Isaac and Jacob did not persecute Ishmael and Esau. We are the children of the patriarchs who suffered, not of those by whom they were oppressed. Believers do not live for the destruction of unbelievers, but for their conversion, edification, and salvation. It is the duty of kings and magistrates to attend upon temporal affairs, and of bishops and ministers to attend upon spiritual. They are not to interfere with each other's authority, office, or function. Constantine understood this when he wrote to the Bishop of Rome that he would force no man to receive the Christian faith.

To this address Busher added 'Certain Reasons against Persecution.' He did not find that Christ had commanded any king, bishop, or minister to persecute people because of differences in religion. He rather found the liberty of the gospel to consist in being free to receive or reject, according as a man was persuaded in his own mind. To force all men to one religion is to fill the Church with dissemblers, to make it a Babel where all is confusion, and out of which the people of God are to come and be separate. It was the true Church that was represented by the woman that fled into the wilderness. The prosperous, persecuting Babylon was the great Antichrist. Busher told the King and the Parliament that no harm could come to the State by free discussion of all religious questions. It was necessary to make laws to guard against treason, and, though Jews or Roman Catholics might be allowed freely to advocate their doctrines, it was thought desirable that they should only be permitted to argue from the Scriptures. All false ministers,

'Reasons against Persecution.'

Busher says, have little else to build their doctrine on but the Fathers. And if not allowed to reason from them, they will have very little to say. This was certainly a curious limitation in a plea for universal liberty of conscience and freedom of discussion.

A treatise which Samuel Rutherford had before him, besides those of John Goodwin and Jeremy Taylor, was called 'The Ancient Bounds; or, Liberty of Conscience, Tenderly Stated, Modestly Asserted, and Mildly Vindicated.' This was published in 1645, and does not bear any author's name. A preface says that the 'object was first to institute every Christian in his right to free judging, and accepting what he holds, and secondly to vindicate a necessary advantage to the truth which would result from this freedom.' The argument of the book is built on the supremacy of conscience. It is God's throne. As every man is a microcosm, or epitome of the world of nature, so every believer is said to be an epitome of Christ mystical. All vice is contrary to the light of nature. It does not proceed from conscience, but from an evil will.

The author of 'The Ancient Bounds' does not deny to the Christian magistrate the power and right to protect true religion, and to repress heresy. A man who is a Christian cannot merge his Christianity in his civil office. His duty as a Christian is enlarged by his magistracy. It is not changed. Morality must be within his cognizance. Christian ministers being teachers of the moral virtues, the magistrate is to protect them, so that they may teach the people in safety. Here the second table of the law is committed to the magistrate. He is not to see God dishonoured by a manifest breach of morality. As for the first table, it is his duty to keep it, so far at least as the light of nature teaches. He must put down all idolatry; image worship, the worship of 'the *breaden god*, the grossest idolatry of all.' He is also to put down blasphemy as a common nuisance to mankind, and he is not to tolerate the profanation of the Lord's day. All these things are by the light of nature manifestly good for society. It is reckoned evident, too, that he must take cognizance of external worship. He must punish disorder. He must also be an example by his own life and conduct.

He may do anything for the truth, so long as men of a different mind are left to their own conscience. It is the duty of the magistrate to do all he can for truth. He is to recommend, profess, persuade, and even teach what is true, but he is not to use force to make men believe. 'The Ancient Bounds' seems to be the work of an Independent. Its plea for liberty is simply an argument against coercion. It is directed especially against the 'Covenant.' The author is opposed to persecution, but it would be difficult for the civil magistrate to interfere in religion to the extent here recommended, without interfering also with the liberty of the individual conscience.

CHAP. V.

It is sometimes outside of ecclesiastical circles that we get the best insight into the theological spirit of any given age. Men who are in daily contact with the naked realities of life, are often indifferent to abstractions which, in the judgment of the clergy, are of the highest moment. The religious life of a nation may always be tested by its influence among the intelligent laity. It too often happens that the people submit their judgments to the clergy, in which case the result is only evil. It is worse still when the national thought is opposed to the ecclesiastical. The normal condition is when they mutually influence each other. In the seventeenth century books on religion were mostly written by the clergy. The exceptions are some theological writings by members of other professions. The two men whom we select as representatives of this class, at the era of the Restoration, are Sir Thomas Browne and Sir Matthew Hale, the one a physician and the other a lawyer. A physician, in the prosecution of the physical studies which belong to his profession, is necessarily in immediate contact with theology. If his spirit is secular and merely utilitarian, it may never rise above the study of the material and observation of the phenomena of nature. If his spirit is really scientific, it must be theological. His theology will probably be a heresy in the eyes of the Church, but a theology it must be, and for this simple reason, that the study of nature is the study of causes. If to the scientific spirit there is added a religious bias, then the religion of the physician will either become the ordinary theology of his time, or it will be a devout re-

Sir Thomas Browne.

verence of the all-pervading spirit of nature. The 'Religio Medici' of Sir Thomas Browne was of the former kind, but not without a mixture of the latter.

A half-reasoning, half-believing Christian.

In the beginning of the treatise the author takes notice of the general suspicion that physicians have no religion at all, or if they have, that it is a very indifferent one. There was a proverbial saying that where three physicians are, two of them are atheists. Sir Thomas Browne vindicates the profession from the charge of irreligion. He speaks in the first person, but placing himself, we apprehend, so as to speak for all physicians. He is a Christian, but there are points of his faith which he will not ardently defend, and there are errors which he will not violently oppose. The very nature of these questions teaches him moderation. He is a Protestant because he adheres to the Reformed Church. He confesses in himself a tendency to superstition, which he finds it necessary to check. He might reverence the holy water and the crucifix. The Ave Maria bell has a solemn sound. He respects the sincerity of the Roman Catholic, but pities his misplaced devotion. He believes in the Articles of the Church of England. Where Scripture is silent, the Church is his text, and where both are silent, he follows the dictates of his own reason. It is, he says, an unjust scandal of our enemies to reckon the nativity of our religion from Henry VIII. That monarch did what his predecessors had tried to do in times past. The Pope calls us heretics, but charity should teach us not to call him Antichrist, or the man of sin. The physician has no genius for disputes in religion. An inconsiderate zeal for truth may injure it. Every man is not a proper champion to stand up against error. When difficulties come in the way, it is best to forget them, or at least to defer them till more manly reason is able to solve them. 'In divinity,' Sir Thomas Browne says, 'I love to keep one road, and though not in an implicit yet an humble faith, follow the great wheel of the Church.'

He does not explain what he means by an humble faith, which is not 'implicit.' He wants to retain fidelity to the Church. To do this, he seemed to think submission to some extent necessary. But to what extent he does not very well know. His religion is to be, 'if possible,' something rational, at the same time it must be sufficiently orthodox to harmonize with that of the Church of England. He tells us of heresies which he had once entertained, but which he has now rejected. One was, that the souls of men perished with their bodies, and did not live again till the resurrection. Another was, that God would not persist in His vengeance for ever, but would at last relieve the souls of the wicked from the torments of hell; a third, which, however, he never practised, but wished that it had been agreeable to truth, was prayer for the dead. The physician fell into heresies, but he was restored by returning to the faith of the Church. He learned to answer all objections by the saying of Tertullian, 'it is certain because it is impossible.' He blessed himself that he did not live in the days of those who saw miracles, for then he could not have had the happiness of believing without evidence. Since he was of understanding to know that we know nothing, his reason was more pliable to faith. He believed that there was a tree in Paradise of whose fruit Adam and Eve partook, although the plants of the field were not yet grown, for God had not caused it to rain upon the earth. He believed the serpent crawled upon its belly before the curse was, and as a physician he knew that some women escaped the curse connected with childbirth. Faith taught him to believe many things which reason tried to persuade him were false.

<small>CHAP. V.

Does not allow himself to be a heretic.</small>

Sir Thomas Browne was one of those philosophers who reasoned or believed at the dictate of fancy. He followed reason when it suited him, and faith when he preferred faith. He vindicated the doctrine of predestination, on the ground that there was no distinction of past, present, or future with God. The *I AM* was ever the same in His doings and His designs. Predestination in this sense is obviously beyond the reach either of man's defending or denying. But the physician for a time becomes mystical. Pythagoras helps him to understand the Trinity. Hermes convinces him that the visible world is but an image of the invisible. The Divine Being is wise, because He comprehends all that He has made, but His great knowledge is in comprehending Himself, which is something that He did not make. After saying this, Sir Thomas leaves the mys-

<small>Followed faith or reason just as he fancied.

On predestination.</small>

tical. Knowledge of this kind, he says, is too high for us. We only see a reflex of the Deity. Our understanding is dimmer than the eye of Moses. We must be content to trace the footprints which God has left in nature. This is the debt which reason owes to God. This world directs us to a cause. So beauteous a structure can only be the production of divine art. Everything is made for an end. Nature has no 'grotesques.' The works of nature were the teachers of the Pagans. The natural motion of the sun taught them more than the Israelites learned by its standing still in the valley of Gibeon. The heathen read more in the book of nature than we do, because we are accustomed to another book.

The book of nature.

By not reading the book of nature aright, many have had their devotion perverted into atheism. Passion and reason have conspired against faith. The physician has endeavoured to compose these feuds. The propositions of faith seem absurd to reason, and those of reason, to passion. But the commonwealth of the soul should be so regulated that all the three should be kings, and yet but one monarchy. The doubts in divinity 'the physician conquered, not in a martial position,' but 'on his knees.' It is, he says, the devil with whom in this conflict we have to contend. The devil wished to resolve the miracle of the brazen serpent into the power of sympathy, and to explain by bitumen or naphtha the miracle of Elijah when he entrenched the altar round with water. But these temptations were resisted. Faith in the Divine Omnipotence solved all difficulties in the way of believing miracles. And not only miracles, but all things supernatural, in which men at that time believed. 'For my part,' Sir Thomas says, 'I have ever believed, and do now know, that there are witches.' He rejects, indeed, some of the more vulgar forms of the faith in witchcraft, but he does believe that devils possess men's bodies. He believes also that every man has a guardian angel, that the world is full of spirits, and that there may be, as Plato and the old philosophers said, a universal spirit common to the whole world. 'I am sure,' he says, 'that there is a common spirit that plays within us, yet makes no part of us, and that is the Spirit of God, the fire and scintillation of that noble and mighty essence, which is the life and radical heat of spirits.' The Platonic scale of creation was too fascinating a conception not to commend itself to the imagination of Sir Thomas Browne, even had it been less supported than it is by the facts of the physical world. That man was the microcosm of nature, seemed but a trope of rhetoric till his second thoughts told him that there was some truth in it.

CHAP. V.

On the nature of faith and the resurrection of the body, Sir Thomas Browne expresses himself almost in the words of Bishop Pearson. Only to believe possibilities, he says, is not faith, it is mere philosophy. Among the matters of faith impossible to reason, was the belief that the very particles of the body would all be restored at the resurrection. But though this is pronounced possible only to faith, Sir Thomas immediately explains, by analogies from nature, how it is possible to reason. Hell is explained rationally as something in the heart of man. There are many hells. There were more than one hell in Mary Magdalene; every devil was a hell. It is not reckoned within the province of reason to pronounce judgment concerning the final state of the good men among the heathen who lived before the incarnation of Christ. Sir Thomas says it seems hard that they should not be saved. There ought at least to be a limbo for them in hell, where their sufferings may not be extreme. Yet he dare not question the justice of God, if they should awake to torments, because of the sin of Adam. Then he explains by reason how these good works were only the result of living according to the rule of nature. They followed that rule as beasts follow the rule of their lives. It is, then, no merit in them that they were good men. These examples show that salvation is only through Christ, and that the most perfect actions of men have no title or claim to heaven. Sir Thomas Browne was only a philosopher by fits. He did not believe that virtue was its own reward. He looked for a reward superadded as necessary to encourage men to practise it; and when he gave alms it was not, he tells us, to satisfy the wants of his brother, but to fulfil the commands of God.

Sir Thomas Browne, after all, a believer.

And only a philosopher by fits.

Members of the profession of law are generally more orthodox than those of the profession of medicine. Having less to do either with nature or speculative philosophy, they seek in religion rather a rule of life than a subject for disquisition. We owe to lawyers many valuable theological writings, but there is scarcely one who has been a leader of a sect, or a great teacher of heresy. Bacon and Prynne, the two of whom we have already had occasion to speak, were rigidly orthodox. Sir Matthew Hale is no exception to the rule of legal orthodoxy. He was educated among the Puritans, and though a Conformist at the Restoration, he retained through life the religious strictness which he had learned and practised in his youth. Besides several small works on practical religion, Sir Matthew Hale wrote a treatise of some length on 'The Primitive Origination of Mankind.' He examined the subject simply in the light of nature. After comparing the various hypotheses of the Pagan philosophers with the account in the Book of Genesis, he came to the conclusion that the latter, apart from the question of inspiration, was the most agreeable to reason.

This work may be classed among those on the evidences of religion. Its immediate object is not to defend either Theism or Christianity, yet the author says that he does not know any better preservative against atheism than the consideration of the origination of mankind. He refutes, by the usual metaphysical arguments, the theories that suppose the world eternal. If the world had a beginning, of course it follows that man must have had a beginning. But the positive evidence is derived from facts. We have not, indeed, as to any events of past times, that evidence which is infallible. We have only moral evidence that such men as Augustus, William the Conqueror, or Henry VIII. ever lived. We have only moral evidence that there is such a city as Venice or Rome. The question, then, is one of history, even of the earliest history, where the alleged facts themselves must be measured by their congruity with other things. Another argument is from the late invention of arts, an argument common with the theological writers of this century. Kindred to this was an argument from the late origin of the Pagan deities, and the beginning of the cities and kingdoms of antiquity. The questions on which these arguments were based, were supposed to be settled in Sir Matthew Hale's day, but modern inquiries have placed them all in a different light. This work was intended, the author says, as but a discourse in the outward court of the temple. It proceeds no further than to show that the Mosaic account of creation is supported by facts of history, so far as we can learn them. The theology is, that all was made for man, that man was made for God, and that this life is a probation in which God has endowed us with free-will. It is preparatory to final and everlasting blessedness. God has made us for Himself, and in seeking His glory we seek our own happiness.*

---

* The great blot on Sir Matthew Hale's reputation is the burning of the witches at Bury St. Edmund's. Amy Duny and Rose Callender, two wrinkled old women, were charged with laying spells on several children, particularly William Durent, Elizabeth Pacy, and Deborah Pacy. The bewitching of William Durent rested on the testimony of his mother, who said that seven years ago, when he was a child, she had given Amy Duny a penny to take care of him for the day, charging her not to give the child suck. That night the child fell into fits, and was therefore supposed to have been bewitched. Dr. Jacob, a physician at Yarmouth, who knew something of witchcraft, told the mother to put the child into a blanket, and if there was anything in the blanket, she was to throw it into the fire. That same night a toad fell out of the blanket, which being cast into the fire, caused a great explosion like gunpowder, and vanished up the chimney. Next day Amy Duny was found to be in a deplorable condition, her face and legs being all scorched. The father of the two girls Pacy said that he had refused to give Amy Duny and Rose Callender some herrings, and they were on that account very angry. Soon after this his two girls were taken ill, and large quantities of pins and twopenny nails came out of their throats. The girls declared that Amy Duny and Rose Callender visited them in the shape of a bee and a mouse. It was also shown that Amy Duny had bewitched a cart which had wrenched the window of her cottage. The cart that day was overthrown several times. Amy Duny had also predicted that some geese which a neighbour had bought would all be destroyed, which prediction was duly fulfilled. The Jury returned a verdict of *Guilty*, though it is specially recorded, and even as evidence against the accused, that 'as soon as the witnesses came into Court they were struck dumb, and could utter nothing but inarticulate sounds, nor did they regain the use of their speech till the verdict was given.' It is strange that lawyers, ministers, and even physicians, should have had such faith in witchcraft as to burn old women on such evidence as this. It is not fair, however, to make this belief in witchcraft the test of the rational progress of an age. This special belief remained long after every foundation on which it rested had been overturned. In the estimate of progress it must certainly be allowed to have its weight, but it ought not to be taken as the sole measure.

CHAPTER VI.

RATIONAL THEOLOGIANS. — JOHN HALES, OF ETON. — WILLIAM CHILLINGWORTH.—THOMAS HOBBES, OF MALMESBURY.—REPLIES TO HOBBES.—LORD CLARENDON.—ARCHBISHOP TENISON. —ARCHBISHOP BRAMHALL.—SAMUEL CLARKE.—BISHOP PARKER. —THE CAMBRIDGE PLATONISTS. — DR. CUDWORTH. — HENRY MORE.—JOHN SMITH.—BENJAMIN WHICHCOT.—BISHOP CUMBERLAND.—LORD HERBERT OF CHERBURY.—REPLIES TO LORD HERBERT.—JOHN LOCKE.—THOMAS HALYBURTON.—DANIEL WHITBY. —RICHARD BAXTER.

WE have reserved for this Chapter the names of some writers who were properly outside of the Conformist and Puritan strifes. To Episcopacy and the ceremonies of the Church they had no special attachment, and at the same time no special objection. In their judgment, these were matters that belonged to the necessarily changing outward form. In the same way they regarded some doctrines, which others held to be essential, as mere opinions or mere forms of a doctrine which might sometimes be more wisely put in another form. These writers have been called Latitudinarians, Rationalists, Platonists, and some other like names, none of which are very appropriate, and all of which fail to describe the men when put into one class. In words, in modes of speech, and generally in their mode of thinking, they are all in some respects at variance with the words, and frequently with the tone of the Articles and formularies of the Church of England. It is not that they teach what might be called new truth, but they look at the old truth in new ways. They were men of progress,

Rational theologians.

who did not think it a sin to differ either from the Fathers or the Reformers. Other parties did this, and denied that they did it. The Latitudinarians, on the other hand, recognized such differences in different ages, as the necessary conditions of mental and spiritual development.

The Church of England's transition from Calvinism to Arminianism in the time of James and Charles, was one of those inevitable changes which come over every progressive community. Calvinism was the embodiment of Christian doctrine that grew out of the necessities of the Reformation. A milder form of the doctrines of grace might have been ineffectual to check the errors of the Church of Rome as to the merit of ceremonial works, and the virtue of the sacramental *opus operatum*. Luther and Calvin found the strength of their cause in the conviction that salvation was from Christ only, and without the mediation of any church or priest. The Arminian form of the doctrine is sufficiently distinct, but the doctrine was fortified, so to speak, in the system of Calvin, by being connected with an unconditional election of some men to eternal life. If the elect were chosen before they had done good or evil, there was no place left for the necessity of good works, and consequently no ground on which the Church of Rome could erect its doctrine of priestly mediation.

But the hypothesis of an unconditional election was not absolutely necessary to the argument. The Protestant principle was found to be clear without it. At the first wave of fresh thought after the Reformation, it struggled for existence. It was cast aside by the Churches of Holland and Geneva. The Church of England hastened to uphold it at the Synod of Dort, but there were changes going on in the Church of England, and there, too, it was convenient to drop the theology of Calvin and Augustine, and to fall back on what was called the 'Catholic' doctrine of universal love.

Among the Englishmen present at the Synod of Dort was 'the ever-memorable John Hales, of Eton.' He had gone with Hall, Davenant, Carleton, and Ward, to uphold the old faith of the Reformers on predestination and reprobation, but he came back a convert to Arminianism. At the Synod of Dort, to use his own words, he 'bade good night to John Calvin.' In giving up Calvinism, Hales parted with the old orthodox Churchmen, who soon after had to defend the Church of England against the new Arminians. As he was not a High Churchman, he could not take part with those in the Church of England who embraced Arminianism. These went back in search of authority for something which they called 'Catholic.' Hales preferred reason to authority. One of his tracts, in manuscript, had come under the notice of Archbishop Laud, who sent for him, and, as Heylin records the story, they had an excited debate over it, which ended in Laud procuring for Hales a prebend's stall at Windsor.

We can only judge of Hales from his tracts and his 'Golden Remains,' which consist chiefly of sermons written at different periods of his life. He was a reserved man, and standing almost alone with wide theological sympathies, he was exposed on all sides to suspicions of heresy. Arminian and Socinian were names freely applied to him, and it was even said that he took pleasure in reading the writings of the Familists. He buried himself in books; he read more than he wrote; he thought more than he said; he patiently waited God's time; like a true believer, he did not make haste. Firm faith and calm hope are always necessary to dispel the melancholy which threatens to gather round the soul of a great man who in religion has taken a step in advance of the world around him. He is not anxious to make mere converts to his opinions, nor to refute those who differ from him. He is content to say what he feels to be true. He knows that others will agree with him when they have the light which he has. He knows, too, that he will himself believe differently should he get more light than he has now.

One of Hales' tracts is on the Sacrament of the Lord's Supper. Here the difference of language from that of the Reformers is marked. The substance of what the Reformers taught when they spoke plainly is retained, but all that they seemed to teach when they used the old ecclesiastical phrases is entirely rejected. Cranmer thought he was obliged to use what he called the language of the old Catholic Fathers when he spoke of the sacraments, though he had plainly rejected the doctrine which that language was supposed to teach. The High Churchman, in retaining the language, retained also the doctrine which Cranmer had rejected. Hales received Cranmer's doctrine, but refused Cranmer's speech. He denied that there was any virtue in consecration, or that it was necessary to the celebration of the Supper. In Jesus the action of blessing the bread and the wine was proper and natural to the circumstances. But He gave no command that His disciples, in continuing the memory of the last Supper, were to use any words. St. Ambrose made it necessary to a sacrament that something be said and something done. Hales says it is enough that one thing is done by which something else is signified. He thought that if the words of consecration could be omitted, a great part of the superstition which attends the action of consecration would be cut away. Some persons speak of the body and blood of Christ being present, but not carnally, which Hales compares to the 'nonsense' of the divines of the Church of Rome, who tell us that the blood of Christ is really sacrificed, but not as blood. To this manifest solecism of the presence of a body spiritually, Hales traces 'the crude speeches of the learned of the Reformed parts,' when they tell the divines of the Church of Rome that they acknowledge a presence, but are ignorant of the manner how it is. This conceit, as he calls it, is declared to be not only a 'falsehood,' but a 'mere novelty.' It is nowhere to be found among the ancients. It originated with Martin Bucer, who was unreasonably afraid of separating too far from the Church of Rome. From him it descended to Calvin and Beza, and through their influence it found its way into all the Reformed Churches. Hales' own doctrine is, that in the Lord's Supper there is nothing given except bread and wine, and these are signs not of something there exhibited, but of Christ's body and blood, which were given for us many centuries ago. Jesus Christ is not eaten by any, either spiritually or really. The eating of His body is a figure, and the benefit intended by that speech is not confined to the Eucharist, but is common to all acts of sincere worship, in whatever place they are performed. The true use of the Lord's Supper is the com-

Crude speeches of the Reformers about the Lord's Supper.

memoration of His death. It is also a witness to our union with Christ, and our communion one with another.

Hales explains the 'keys' as the doctrine of the Gospel, including the administration of sacraments, or whatever is a manifestation of the doctrine of the Gospel. The power of the keys is declarative. Every Christian now living has this power, not only for his own use, but for the benefit of others. To exercise it is to teach men Christian truth, to lead them into the way of life, or, to use Hales' expression, 'to save souls.' A Church as distinct from the congregation of believers is unknown to him. Men and women, clergymen and laymen, are all simply believers in relation to the Church. The pretensions of the Church of Rome are dealt with in a few pointed sentences. That general councils may not err, and yet the individual persons may, Hales pronounces 'a merry speech.' Christ has promised perpetual assistance to His Church, but he has nowhere prophesied that the Church should perpetually adhere to Him. To those that persevere to the end, Christ has promised the victory over death and hell. Against them the gates of hell, which is a Hebraism for hell, shall not prevail. The benefit of confession Hales illustrates by a quotation from Pliny. That author says that when one is bitten by a scorpion, if he go and whisper it in the ear of an ass, he shall be at once relieved. Hales says he doubts not but that sin is a scorpion, and that its bite is deadly. But as for the sovereign remedy of whispering it in the ear either of a priest, or, what is the same thing, the animal mentioned by Pliny, he believes the one as much as the other.

The tract on schism is the best known of the 'Golden Remains,' probably from the circumstance that it is the one of which Laud took notice. Hales calls heresy and schism two theological scarecrows. They are commonly used by those who uphold a party, to frighten sincere people from inquiry. Heresy is an act of the will. It is not a mere mistake. If it were, then all men would be heretics, for all men have some errors. It is a wilful mistake. This was the judgment of all the Fathers, and to this agrees the saying of Augustine, 'I may err, I am unwilling to be a heretic.' Manicheanism, Valentinianism, Marcionism, and

Mahometanism are heresies truly and properly. The authors from whom they were named, invented them, knowing that what they taught was false. But this cannot be said of Arius, Nestorius, and some others, who erred about the Trinity. Their errors were not wilful, and therefore not to be called heresies. To avoid schism, Hales recommends the expurgation from all liturgies of all that is offensive to any party, and leaving nothing but that on which all parties agree. Loading public forms with men's private fancies, is the sure way, he says, to perpetuate schism to the end of the world.

From the sermons we may learn more fully what were Hales' views of the Church and the Scriptures. One is on the text 'My kingdom is not of this world.' If the text be true, it is useless to look for the kingdom of Christ here. To write of 'notes' by which it may be known, is 'a learned impertinence.' The Church cannot be pointed out if it is not of this world. The devil could show Jesus all the kingdoms of the earth, and the glory of them, but Christ's kingdom was not any of these. It is the glory of His kingdom that it is invisible. When we call any company of professing Christians the Church, it is only a speech of courtesy. We hope in charity that they all are what they profess to be. To send men up and down the world to find the Church is but 'Popish madness.' It is like the children of the prophets seeking Elias, or the nobles of Jerusalem seeking Jeremy the prophet. They could not find him, because the Lord had hid him. The profession of the Gospel is like a city set on a hill. It is easy to know what true Christianity is, but the true kingdom of God, which consists only of the true believers, is, as Jesus said, like a treasure hid in a field. Saul was sent to seek his father's asses, and found a kingdom. If we go in search of our Father's kingdom, looking for it as a visible Church, the contrary of what befel Saul may befal us. Instead of the kingdom we may find 'asses.' Jesus directs us in the Gospel where to find His kingdom. It is in the soul. It is invisible. It cometh not with observation. 'Neither shall ye say lo here or lo there, for the kingdom of God is within you.' Let every man, therefore, Hales says, 'retire into himself,

CHAP. VI.

On the kingdom of Christ

Not the visible Church.

CHAP. VI.

On the Scriptures.

and see if he can find this kingdom in his heart, for if he find it not there, in vain shall he find it in all the world besides.'

We know the Scriptures to be the word of God by the testimony of the professing Church. This is a testimony which all people can understand. Learned men have further evidence from the records of antiquity, and different copies of the books bearing the same titles. If it is objected that this only proves the genuineness of the books, not that they are divine, Hales answers that the miracles proved to those who saw them that the doctrine is of God. The infallible record of these miracles is proof to us. The thing to be proved was the infallibility of the records. Hales was here got into a common circle. The only thing remarkable is to find him in it. He mentions two ways by which people wrest the Scriptures. One is by denying their plain meaning, and another is by extracting from them what neither God nor nature ever put in them. The Manichees said that the Old Testament had no reference to the Messiah. Isidore Pelusiota said that everything in the Old Testament referred to Christ. When it is said that Scripture is the word of God, it is the sense that is meant, and not the mere words of the book. The saints of old time had immediate converse with God. Now the truth is committed to writings. They had the Spirit, the same Spirit which is promised to us, but in a different manner. What was written by God in their hearts, was written by them in books for our instruction. The Spirit teaches us, by stirring up within us a desire to learn, not by giving us information. We have now no direct revelation but that which is written in the Scriptures.

William Chillingworth.

A kindred spirit to John Hales, of Eton, was William Chillingworth. He was unlike the men of his century in this one thing, that he recognized in reason the final judge and arbiter of religion. It might be imperfect. We might crave an authority to supersede its use. But what we crave is not given. The Scriptures are to the Christian the rule of faith, but we have no infallible external authority to tell us what the Scriptures mean. In all things essential their meaning is plain to those who honestly and sincerely try to understand them. Chillingworth saw that, logically, this was the certain result of the Protestant principle that Scripture alone was to be followed. High Churchmen added something about the primitive Church. We were to take the Scriptures as they had been interpreted by the Fathers. But, as the Fathers had interpreted them in all sorts of ways, it was difficult to make this rule of any practical service. The Puritans were equally bewildered when they spoke of the Scriptures as the judge of controversies, supposing the Spirit of God to be there giving decisions after the manner of a personal judge. Chillingworth saw that the final responsibility must rest with men as individuals. They were to use their faculties honestly to find out the truth. As all men have not the same advantages, and, as reason is not equally developed in all, it is certain that there will be differences of opinion, and that even the wisest will have many errors. But the divine favour will not be refused to those who have done their best, even if they have failed to discern many things which in other circumstances they might have known.

Chillingworth seems to have been a Rationalist from his youth. He hesitated for a long time to declare his 'assent and consent' to the Articles of Religion and the Book of Common Prayer. But his scruples lay in another direction from those of the Puritans. The mountains that troubled the Puritans were but sandhills to William Chillingworth. His exceptions were against the outrageous clauses of damnation in the creed of St. Athanasius, the inaccurate and generally misunderstood language of Art. XIII. about 'works' done before justification, and reading the fourth commandment in the communion service, as if the Sabbath were to be observed by Christians in the same sense as it was kept by Jews. Archbishop Laud, who was Chillingworth's godfather, managed so to explain all these things as to satisfy Chillingworth that it was lawful to subscribe. But the reasoning process went on until Chillingworth, dissatisfied that he could get so little certainty by it, put an end to his difficulties by taking refuge in the Church of Rome. But he could not flee from himself. He could not set aside that responsibility for his belief which God has connected with every man's being. It was impossible to escape the divine conditions. He must reason, but reason did not lead him to the abnegation of reason, and he soon returned to the Church of England.

Chillingworth, with such a mental history, was the very man to say the right word for Protestantism. With his arguments it must stand or fall. He came in, as it were, in the middle of a controversy between the Jesuit Knott and Dr. Potter. Knott started with the principle that men who held right doctrines could alone be saved. Those who held errors must be lost. So that Roman Catholics and Protestants cannot both be saved, for the doctrines of both cannot be true. This principle was generally admitted by Protestants, so that they each mutually believed in each other's damnation. Knott, as a Roman Catholic, said that his Church was the true one, his doctrine the right doctrine, and therefore Protestants cannot be saved. Chillingworth called his answer 'The Religion of Protestants, a Safe Way to Salvation.' He is under no necessity of denying the possibility of salvation to Roman Catholics. He has only to maintain the thesis set forth in the title of his book. This was not entirely new, for Hooker and the more rational Protestants had already said that Roman Catholics might be saved, not because of their errors, but because the ignorance and darkness of the times in which they lived were an excuse for their errors. But though Hooker and many Protestants had said this, it was Chillingworth who first made it an integral part of the main argument in the controversy with the Church of Rome. That which was culpable in ignorance, error, and unbelief, was the moral and not the mental part.

The Church and the Bible are the two subjects on which all controversy turns between Protestants and the Church of Rome. Knott said that Christ had always had, and would always have, a visible Church on the earth; that that Church was the Roman Catholic; that it could not err fundamentally, for such error destroys the essence of a Church. Chillingworth said that Christ had always had, in some place or other, a visible Church; that is, 'a company of men that professed at least so much truth as was absolutely necessary for their salvation.' He believed that there would always be, somewhere or other, such a Church to the end of the world. The Church of Rome is a part of the Catholic Church,—a very corrupt part, yet holding as much truth as is necessary for salvation. We do not totally renounce communion with it. We only leave communicating with Roman Catholics in the practice and profession of their errors. But what by the one side is called an error, is by the other supposed to be a fundamental truth. Knott assumed the existence of an infallible Church. Whatever that Church proposed was to him truth. Whoever doubted what that Church taught was opposed to truth, and therefore without the pale of salvation. Chillingworth denied an infallible Church, and only made that error culpable which a man knew in his conscience to be an error. And then there appeared in this controversy what often appears. Knott was drawing by processes of reasoning conclusions which he did not really believe. He neutralized his own positions by admissions at variance with his argument. Though Protestants, by his logic, could not be saved, yet he said he did not conclude that when a Protestant died he was necessarily lost. There might have been an insufficiency of means for his instruction, or a want of capacity to understand, or contrition may have atoned for his sins. That is to say, there may really be mitigating circumstances in the condition of a Protestant which excuse his errors; and so, notwithstanding his errors, a Protestant may be saved. This charitable admission overturned the argument as expressed in the title of the chapter, that 'among men of different religions, one side only can be saved.'

CHAP. VI.

The Church Catholic and the Church of Rome.

But the radical difference between Knott and Chillingworth lay in their views of the nature of the faith which God requires of man. Knott, assuming that all which the Church of Rome teaches must be true, measured man's acceptability by the degree of his belief in the Roman Catholic doctrines. Chillingworth admitted the thesis that whatever God reveals is true, but he did not admit that we had a rational certainty that all the doctrines which we believe are revealed by God. The certainty which we have for

On faith.

the truth of Christianity is a moral certainty. Men may be unreasonable in their requirements, but God is not. He will not ask a higher faith than the evidence warrants. Men, Chillingworth says, 'will not be pleased without a down-weight, but God is contented if the scale be turned. They pretend that heavenly things cannot be seen to any purpose but by the midday light. But God will be satisfied if we receive any degree of light which makes us leave the *works of darkness and walk as children of the light.*' We believe that Christianity is true, but we have not the evidence for its truth of sense or science. The river cannot rise higher than the fountain. The degree and kind of faith must be in proportion to the evidence. The whole of this reasoning has a sceptical sound. But the position which seems most advantageous is not always the true one. They are the best friends to truth who look courageously at facts as they are. Men persuaded themselves that the Church is infallible because they craved an infallible guide. But neither their persuasion nor their craving makes the Church infallible if it be not infallible. Are we, then, left in doubt as to the truth of Christianity? This does not follow, but we have to seek another kind of evidence than the external. One of the facts of Christianity is the Christian life. The Spirit of God gives to earnest men a certainty of adherence, besides the certainty of evidence. To those that believe and live according to their faith, 'God gives by degrees the spirit of obsignation and confirmation, which makes them know (though how they know not) what they did but believe.' God requires of all that their faith be proportionable to the motives and reasons enforcing to it, but 'He will accept the lowest degree of faith if it be living and effectual unto true obedience.'

But it is evident, previous to all reasoning, that there must be some means of conveying to the understanding of man what God reveals. There must be a teacher, a rule of faith, or judge of controversies. Knott says that the Scriptures being in writing, cannot on that very account be a judge. They may be a perfect rule so far as a writing can be a rule, but not so as to exclude either unwritten tradition or an external judge, to keep and interpret the Scripture in 'a true orthodox and Catholic sense.' Chillingworth answered that if the Scriptures be a 'perfect rule,' the very terms of the definition exclude both tradition and the 'external judge.' It is not necessary to abrogate laws in order to set them aside. It is enough to deal with them as the Church of Rome deals with the Scriptures, which is to add to them, and to claim the power of interpreting their meaning infallibly. But why should not the Scriptures be the sole judge of controversies, that is, as Chillingworth carefully explains it, 'the sole rule for men to judge them by'? If it is not, who is to determine concerning *the Church and the notes of it?* And if it be the sole judge of this question, why not of others, or why not of all? There need be no exception, but only 'wherein the Scripture itself is the subject of the question, which cannot be determined but by natural reason, the only principle besides Scripture which is common to Christianity.' When Protestants say that Scripture is a perfect rule of faith, Chillingworth explains they do not mean that by it all things necessary to be believed may be absolutely proved. It can never be proved by Scripture to a gainsayer that there is a God, or that the book called Scripture is the word of God. What Protestants mean is, that to those who receive Scripture as divine, it is a complete rule of faith. Our beginning is neither with Scripture nor the Church, but with reason. 'Every man is to judge for himself with the *judgment of discretion*, and to choose either his religion first, and then his church, as the Protestants say, or, as Roman Catholics say, his church first, and then his religion. But, by the consent of both sides, every man is to judge and choose, and the rule whereby he is to guide his choice, if he be a natural man, is reason; if he be already a Christian, Scripture, which we say is the rule to judge controversies by.'

CHAP. VI.

We must always begin with reason.

The arguments are addressed only to Roman Catholics, who believe the Scripture to be the word of God. Knott's plea was that Scripture, not being a person, cannot judge of controversies any more than a law can decide a case without a judge. Chillingworth agreed that the Scripture was not a judge. It was only a rule; but, he said, a rule 'fit to direct every one that will make the best use of it to

Scripture a rule, not a judge.

that end for which it was ordained.' A man on a journey does not require a guide, if he has a plain rule by which he can learn his way. If a law be plain and perfect, and men honest and anxious to understand it aright, it must be sufficient to end all controversies necessary to be ended. If Scripture is plain in all things essential, and obscure only in things not essential, there is no need whatever of an infallible interpreter. Knott argued for the supremacy and infallibility of the Church from the necessity that some watchful eye should be over the Scripture, that we might receive it in its purity and integrity. Questions concerning Scripture itself could not be, he said, determined by Scripture; and he quoted Hooker, that 'that whereon we must rest our assurance that the Scripture is God's word, is the Church.' Chillingworth said that the watchful eye was Divine Providence. Since God requires men to believe Scripture in its purity, He will take care that it be not corrupted. Had we no other assurance but the vigilance of the Church of Rome, our case would be a hard one. There were various readings in the ancient versions, and no one can give a good reason why the Church of Rome takes one version and rejects all the others. We receive the canonical books on the tradition of the universal Church. We believe that they are not corrupted, because we believe in God's providence. We have here a moral assurance; to more than this we do not pretend. Nor can the Church of Rome pretend to more. It is confessed by Popes that the only way to determine the true reading is by the collation of ancient copies. For the passages from Hooker, Chillingworth turns to the context. Hooker, indeed, tells us 'that ordinarily the first introduction and probable motive to the belief of the verity is the authority of the Church.' But he plainly denies that it is the last foundation whereon our belief is rationally grounded. His words are, 'Scripture teacheth us that saving truth which God hath discovered unto the world by revelation, and it presumeth us taught otherwise that itself is divine and sacred.' Then follows an account of the means by which we know this. The first is the authority of the Church, the value of which Hooker simply makes to be that, for those who are brought up in the Church, it is a rash thing to be of a contrary mind without cause. The more we read the Scripture, the more we find that it answers to what the Church declares it to be. When men question the grounds of our belief, we sift the question deeper to find reasons for it. We go back to see what were the arguments which the ancient Fathers addressed to the unbelievers of their time as reasonable arguments. At last Hooker finds that the Scripture may be defended by some position the denial of which would be to deny some apparent principle which all men acknowledge to be true. Hooker's meaning is explained by Chillingworth, 'that natural reason built on principles common to all men, is the last resolution unto which the Church's authority is but the first inducement.'

Hooker on reason and the Bible.

The Bible, then, is a certain rule without the Church. Whatever may be our difficulties in receiving the Scripture as our sole guide, they are not greater, but less than those which accompany the Roman Catholic hypothesis of an infallible Church. Knott said that the ignorant and unlearned could not understand the Scripture. Chillingworth answered that in one sense the learned did not understand the Scripture any more than the unlearned; that is, they did not understand *all* Scripture. But the unlearned do understand some Scripture. They can all understand the story, the precepts, the promises, and the threatenings of the Gospel. It is enough for salvation to understand one of the Gospels. The rest of Scripture may be profitable, but it is not necessary to salvation. The Gospel was to be preached to all men, which supposes the essential part of it to be within the reach of the most unlearned. But if the Roman Catholic will raise such questions, there are parallel questions on his own side which have the same difficulties. How is the unlearned man to know which is the true Church? If he does not understand the Scripture, how can he learn from it what are the notes of the true Church? But suppose he does know what are the notes, how is he to be a competent judge what society of Christians has these notes? He must have a great knowledge of antiquity before he can be satisfied that any Church has 'perpetual visibility, succession, and conformity with the ancient

The Bible a safe rule without the Church.

Church.' How can an unlearned man know what are the decrees of the Church? Many of these are lost and corrupted. How can he understand their meaning if he is unable to understand the plain texts of Scripture? Then how can he know that they are true decrees? How can he know that any pope is a true pope, or any priest a true priest, or any baptism a true baptism? Before a man believes the Church infallible, he must use his reason. Roman Catholics, as well as heretics, set up as many judges as there are men and women in the world. All must use their reason in choosing their religion. If not, they disobey the plain commands to try the spirits, to render a reason, and to prove all things. They that receive a religion without a reason, offer to God the 'sacrifice of fools.'

The remaining chapters of Chillingworth's book contain nothing particularly different from what we find on the same points in other Protestant writers. Knott, believing his Church infallible, denied the distinction between doctrines fundamental and not fundamental. It was, moreover, he said, not 'pertinent in the controversy between Protestants and Roman Catholics, for the Church of Rome was infallible in all its teaching.' Chillingworth said that the Catholic Church could not err in fundamentals. According to his previous definition, the Church Catholic consisted of all who held the fundamental doctrines of Christianity. But the Catholic Church might err in points not fundamental, and in these the Church of Rome had erred grievously. The sum of all necessary doctrine was contained in the Apostles' Creed. He vindicated Protestants from the charges of heresy and schism. Though the errors of the Church of Rome were not fundamental, and not damnable to those who did not know that they were errors, yet it was necessary for those who knew that they were, to protest against them. Protestants cannot be heretics so long as they receive the Scriptures for the infallible word of God. These contain all Christian truth, and are able to make men wise unto salvation.

Chillingworth fearlessly acknowledged that in any case a man who reasons must depend finally on reason for the choice of his religion. Yet this was only a secondary part of his argument. It cleared the ground for what was the great question, whether a man in choosing his religion is to take the Church or the Bible as his infallible teacher? There is a great variety of opinions among Roman Catholics, but they all agree in receiving the Church as their guide. There is great diversity of opinion among Protestants, but they all subscribe to the Bible, and to the Bible only, as the perfect rule of their faith and actions. In the Church of Rome there are Popes against Popes, Councils against Councils, Fathers against Fathers, and some Fathers against themselves. The traditional interpretations of Scripture of which so much is said are very few, if any at all can be found. Whatever may be said for the Church as a guide, much more can be said for the Scripture. It is ancient, it is universal, it is infallible. He that follows the Church of Rome must believe impossibilities. He must be prepared to believe that virtue is vice and vice is virtue, if the Pope shall so determine. But he who follows Scripture must refuse every doctrine which is contrary to the Gospel of Christ.

Another remarkable author of the time of the Commonwealth, who has had a great and complex influence on the theology of England, was Thomas Hobbes, of Malmesbury. To understand his position, we must try to find out his relations to those who were before, and to those who came after him.

For the last two hundred years the name of Thomas Hobbes has been a name of terror to the religious world. Sceptic, deist, atheist, infidel, monster, are the epithets that have been generally bestowed upon him. When a man familiar with Hobbes' evil reputation comes for the first time to his works, there is a feeling of perplexity and wonder how one who has so clearly and fully enunciated his faith in God and the Christian revelation, should ever have been accused of unbelief in any form. Not only is Hobbes a professed believer in Christianity, but in the most orthodox form of it,—an upholder of the royal supremacy, an Episcopalian of the most unblemished type, a Christian who received the *mysteries of the faith* as matters of faith, in no way within the province of reason; one who, if in any sense

CHAP. VI.

Thomas Hobbes, of Malmesbury.

A professed believer in Christianity.

CHAP. VI.

he can be called a rationalist or a free-thinker, certainly arrived at conclusions entirely opposed both to rationalism and free-thinking.

The first solution which offers itself is the supposition that Hobbes did not write sincerely,—that under pretence of defending revelation he took every opportunity of raising doubts concerning it. This supposition is untenable. We do not know what any man believed if we do not know what Thomas Hobbes believed. If we doubt *his* sincerity, we may as well doubt the sincerity of any man who ever professed to be a Christian. Hobbes may be extravagant or eccentric; he may even be irreconcilable with himself, or what is more probable, not always understood; but there is no reason for supposing him insincere. It is strange, indeed, that Hobbes should have ever been misunderstood. No writer is so careful of definition, and no author of that century has been so much praised for the elegance, vigour, and clearness of his language. There is, besides, in Hobbes a completeness of system. All his ideas depend on each other. His mathematics fit into his physics, his physics into his politics, his politics into his religion. Isolated, his sentences are startling, and sometimes contradictory, but taken in their proper relations they can all generally be reduced to one connected whole.

Were we to begin at the beginning, we should start with an account of Hobbes' doctrine of motion, to which he traced the origin of all life and existence. It will, however, suit our purpose better to go at once to his politics, for his religious doctrines are inseparably connected with his theory of civil government. Though he starts as a physical inquirer, and ends as an expounder of Christianity, his political creed is the centre around which all gathers—the pillar on which all rests. Hobbes lived in the age of experimentalists. He was contemporary with Bacon. Galileo had just discovered that the earth moves; Harvey that the blood circulates. The attention of all philosophers was turned to the external world. Hobbes also lived in an age of strifes. The people had executed the sovereign. A great part of these strifes were about religion. The bishops were driven from their sees, the clergy from their parishes. Those in

Was Hobbes sincere?

Traces the origin of all things to motion.

power were divided into a multitude of sects,—some of them wild and fanatical. To Hobbes, everything in Church and State was in confusion. He would teach a doctrine that was to cure all these evils, restore order to the kingdom, and bring all sects to uniformity of religion. Among the new sciences, he claimed to be the founder of Civil Philosophy. He first embodied his doctrines in 'De Cive; or, The Philosophical Elements of a True Citizen;' afterwards in a more matured form in the great work with which his name is always associated, 'Leviathan; or, The Matter, Form, and Power of a Commonwealth, Ecclesiastical and Civil.'

CHAP. VI.

The 'Leviathan' was published in 1651. It consisted of four parts:—*Of Man, Of a Commonwealth, Of a Christian Commonwealth, Of the Kingdom of Darkness*. Man by nature is regarded as a savage. His desires are to preserve himself and injure his neighbour. He lives in a state of war. Every man being equal to every other man, and all having an equal right to everything, the possession depends on the power of getting it. This view of human nature was very dark. In its relations and consequences it shocked even the most determined believers in the *total depravity* of the human race. But Hobbes derived his doctrine from actual observation. The men by whom he was surrounded were distrustful of each other. Anarchy, as he judged, had gained the ascendency. In the civil wars men had returned to the state of nature. Hobbes saw them as *children of wrath*, hateful and hating each other. There was wanted a power to hinder them from injuring each other; a power both to teach what is right, and to compel the performance of it. This power is the Commonwealth, represented by the 'Leviathan,' to which no power on earth can be compared. It restrains the natural passions of men, and of warlike savages it makes peaceable and benevolent citizens. It is ' the *mortal god* to whom, under the *immortal God*, we owe our protection and safety.'

The 'Leviathan.'

This description already anticipates the reverence and submission that are due to the Commonwealth. The sovereign has absolute authority. He is God's vicar on earth. The doctrine of the divine right of kings was in high favour

The King is God's Vicar.

VOL. I. 2 C

with the followers of the Stuarts. It had risen, as we have seen, with the national desire to be rid of the sovereignty of the Pope. Hobbes was sincerely attached to the royal cause. The Puritans, who expelled the reigning family, may have been lovers of order and government as well as the Royalists; and perhaps, with their apparent anarchy, better friends to a genuine commonwealth; but they had to fight for justice with bold words and sharp swords. Hobbes, who was by nature a coward, would have had them yield implicit obedience to the lawful sovereign, the representative of order, and, as he said, the divinely-appointed ruler. The sovereign being to the people in the place of God, must be absolute. He cannot injure his subjects, for his acts are their acts. He cannot act unjustly towards them, for they hold their property conjointly with him. It belongs to the King as well as to them. His laws constitute just and unjust. The people cannot change the form of government. As the sovereign *cannot* break faith with them, his royal power cannot be forfeited; nor can he be punished by his subjects. He is to make peace and war, to choose his own councillors, to decree what opinions and doctrines are to be taught, and to be the judge of all controversies. From the historical fact that Hobbes took the side of the Royalists, it has been generally concluded that he said all these things about the sovereign power to show the enormities of those who had executed the King and usurped the government. This is more than probably true; yet Hobbes' earliest adversaries were the Royalists, and his last and best friends are the liberal politicians of the present day.* In extravagant expression of his political creed he outdid the first, and yet they instinctively hated him. So far as words go, he has condemned, without an atom of reservation, all that is dear to the last; and yet they revere his memory as that of one who helped forward the cause of human progress, and did something for the science of right government. No one has yet tried to explain this singular fact. But do we not find the explanation in what has been already said, that Hobbes, taken in isolated parts or pas-

* The complete works of Hobbes were reprinted by Sir William Molesworth, at the suggestion of Mr. Grote.

sages, is not the same as Hobbes in his entire system? His Commonwealth was the assertion of principles wider and deeper than the vindication of the Stuarts. It was the assertion of the divinity of order, of the majesty of law, of the necessity that kings should rule in equity, and that subjects should obey righteous governors. It would be easy to quote many passages from the 'Leviathan' which seem to oppose this interpretation, but there are many things that confirm it. The Commonwealth of which Hobbes discoursed was avowedly *ideal*. It had nowhere been realized. The perfection was to be reached after many efforts and failures. To use his own illustration, it was not at once that men learned to build houses that would last as long as the materials; but after long experience they did succeed, and so would it be with the perfect Commonwealth. That Hobbes is not a mere Royalist, but a teacher of order, seems to be clear from what he says of the *generation* of the 'Leviathan.' The sovereign power may come by *acquisition*, but it may also come by institution; indeed, this is its more legitimate form. Men constitute themselves into a commonwealth for their mutual benefit; so that those who before were wolves to each other, become *gods* to each other. They unite for protection and defence. For the sake of this common good they surrender their individual wills, and deny themselves liberties which they had in the state of nature. They commit the government of themselves to the Commonwealth, and in virtue of the united strength given up by individuals, the 'Leviathan' becomes the terror of their adversaries. This power is personated, but not necessarily, by a monarch either hereditary or chosen. There are several kinds of commonwealths. The sovereign power may be lodged in one person, in which case we have a monarchy. It may be committed to some chosen leaders, then we have an aristocracy; or it may be retained by a popular assembly, and this is called government by democracy.

But the sovereign ruler is not only absolute in things temporal; the same jurisdiction extends to things spiritual. It is his duty to prescribe the religion of his subjects, to determine what books of Scripture are to be held canonical, and what is the meaning of these books. The Common-

CHAP. VI.

Hobbes' Commonwealth, ideal.

The King prescribes religion and determines canonical writings.

wealth and the Church of the nation are coextensive. They are so connected as sometimes to seem identical. The authority of the Church is derived from the State. The bishops, indeed, say, in the beginning of the mandates, by 'Divine Providence,' which is the same as by 'the grace of God;' and 'thus deny to have received their authority from the civil State, and slily slip off the collar of their civil subjection, contrary to the unity and defence of the Commonwealth.' Hobbes, however, finds it difficult to adjust between the authority of the civil ruler and that of the Church, and especially as he traces the origin of ecclesiastical power to the Apostles. It had descended from them by imposition of hands to all who had been properly ordained. He says, in one place, that the prince must leave the mysteries of the faith to be interpreted by the clergy; and he admits that in the primitive Church the people had liberty to interpret the Scriptures for themselves. There were pastors from the beginning, but their interpretations had no authority till either 'kings were pastors, or pastors kings.' In another place he puts the civil ruler midway between the clergy and the laity: 'without the ministerial priesthood, and yet not so merely laic as not to have sacerdotal jurisdiction.' But Hobbes is most consistent with his own doctrine, though not with himself, when he teaches that 'the king may baptize, preach, and consecrate, and do all other offices without the laying on of hands.' The king, he says, is king by *the grace of God*; but the bishop is bishop only by the grace of the king.

For the Presbyterians, Quakers, and other sectaries of the seventeenth century, who spoke about worshipping God according to their conscience, and not according to the forms of the State religion, Hobbes had ready the never-failing case of Korah, Dathan, and Abiram. They rebelled against Moses, their civil ruler; and if the sectaries followed their example, what could they expect but to 'perish in the gainsaying of Core'? Unfortunately, St. Peter had said something about *obeying God rather than man*. This, for Hobbes, was an awkward passage. He had no great reverence for martyrs, and was not likely to have become one himself for anything that he believed. He thinks that no one in this country would condemn Mahometans who denied Mahomet and worshipped in a Christian church in obedience to the civil ruler. A denial of Christ might be prejudicial to the Church. Yet a man may hold the faith of Christ in his heart, though he does not profess it before men when he knows that they will put him to death for the profession. If we are compelled to worship God by an image, though we may reckon image worship dishonourable to the Divine Being, yet we are to obey. An image, indeed, limits the *Infinite*, but the responsibility rests with the ruler, and not with us. This doctrine, however, has another side. It is possible that the sovereign may command his subjects to blaspheme God, or to abstain from Divine worship. In either case Hobbes declares at once that it is *not* their duty to obey. And even as to idol-worship, obedience is only due to the sovereign so long as we have no other authority than the dictates of reason, for the will of the sovereign power stands to us for reason. But since, both in the old and new covenants, worship by images is expressly forbidden, we are free to disobey the Commonwealth when it commands what is contrary to the express word of God. An unlearned man in the power of an idolatrous king may worship an idol, and 'he doth well, though in his heart he detests the idol; yet, if he has the fortitude to suffer death rather than worship it, he doeth better.' But Hobbes adds, 'If he be a pastor, who, as Christ's messenger, has undertaken to teach Christ's doctrine to all nations, should he do the same, it were not only a sinful scandal in respect of other men's consciences, but a perfidious forsaking of his charge.' In another place he makes it part of our civil duty to know what are the laws and commandments of God, that we may know when to give obedience to the civil authority, and when to the Divine Majesty. It was a vice in Hobbes' theory not to have made the sovereign infallible. It is admitted that though he cannot sin against his subjects, yet he can sin against God. He may ordain what is contrary to eternal equity, or to the revealed will of God. We must, however, obey the sovereign so long as it is possible. We must sacrifice many things for the sake of national uniformity. The Catholic, the Lutheran, the Calvinist, in fact all parties, should merge

CHAP. VI.

Cases in which the sovereign may not be obeyed.

CHAP. VI. their peculiarities for the sake of order; yet there are limits. We are not to give up the great essentials necessary to salvation. These, however, are reduced to the *minimum*; in fact, to this single article—the belief that *Jesus is the Christ*.

The Kingdom of Darkness. The fourth part of 'Leviathan' concerns the Kingdom of Darkness. This is the kingdom of Satan, from which the Church is not yet entirely free. The enemy still sows tares. We err by not understanding the Scriptures, and by following the heathen doctrines concerning demons, which are only idols or phantasies of the brain. But the greatest perversion of Scripture is that which makes the kingdom of God to be the visible Christian Church. And consequent on this is the claim of the Pope, or some ecclesiastical assembly, to be God's representatives in this kingdom—an office which is given only to civil sovereigns. And so the Pope claims that Christian kings must receive their crowns from him, and that if they do not purge their kingdoms of heresy, they may be deprived at his pleasure. From this, too, arises the error of supposing that the pastors are *clergy*, maintained, like the tribe of Levi, out of the revenues by Divine appointment; and this error of supposing that they have a supernatural office makes them confound *consecration* with *conjuration*, so that they pretend to convert bread and wine into the body and blood of a man—yea, of a God; while by charms and incantations over children they profess to exorcise evil spirits, as if infants were demoniacs. Of the ceremonies and dogmas of the Church of Rome, Hobbes finds the original and counterpart in the demonology and vain philosophy of the Pagan world. But the foundation of all is the confounding of the visible Church with the kingdom of God. Here the Bishop of Rome, under pretence of successor to St. Peter, rules over his kingdom of darkness, which Hobbes compares to the kingdom of the *fairies*,—that is, the old wives' *fables* in England concerning ghosts and spirits, and the feats they perform in the night. The Papacy is the ghost of the deceased Roman empire sitting crowned upon its grave. Its language is the *ghost* of the old Roman language. The *ghostly* fathers walk like the *fairies* in obscurity of doctrine, in monasteries, churches, and churchyards. They have cathedrals,

The Pope reigns over the Kingdom of Darkness.

where they practise their spells and exorcisms like the fairies in their enchanted castles. They take from young men the use of reason by certain charms, compounded of metaphysics and miracles, traditions and abused Scripture, just as the *fairies* take young children out of their cradles and change them into natural fools or *elves*, fit only for mischief. When the fairies are displeased with anybody they send the *elves* to pinch them; so do the ecclesiastics pinch princes by preaching sedition. Several parallels of this kind Hobbes draws between the Papacy and the kingdom of the *fairies*. The last is, that, like the kingdom of the fairies, the spiritual power of the Pope has no existence but in the fancies of ignorant people. 'It was not therefore,' he says, 'a very difficult matter for Henry VIII. by his exorcisms, nor for Queen Elizabeth by hers, to cast them out. But who knows that this spirit of Rome—now gone out, and walking by missions through the dry places of China, Japan, and the Indies, that yield him little fruit—may not return, or rather an assembly of spirits worse than he, enter and inhabit this clean-swept house, and make the end thereof worse than the beginning? *For it is not the Roman clergy only that pretend the kingdom of God to be of this world, and thereby to have a power therein, distinct from that of the Civil State.*'

We have already alluded to Hobbes' general agreement with what is considered orthodox theology. In stating the grounds of the Christian faith he gives full validity to the evidence from miracles and prophecy. He maintains the necessity of supernatural evidence for some things which he says are beyond the reach of reason; as, that Jesus is the Christ, that the soul is immortal, that there are rewards and punishments after this life. Not content with this, he declares the incapacity of reason to judge concerning the attributes of God. He believed, with the strictest of the Puritans, that God had only elected to eternal life a small number of the human race, and that the rest were reprobate. To an objector he answered that it was rash to speak of what consisted or did not consist with the Divine justice. God's right to reign over men is not derived from His having created them, but from His omnipotent power. He afflicts men, not merely because they sin, but because He wills to do

How far Hobbes is orthodox.

it. Job's friends connected his sufferings with his secret sins, but God refutes them by showing that He is the Almighty Ruler of the universe, asking, 'Where wast thou when I laid the foundations of the earth?' Hobbes made sometimes a sharp distinction between reason and faith, entirely excluding the first. The mysteries of religion were to be received with a blind faith. To use his own too expressive illustration, they should be taken without examination, *as a man takes bitter but wholesome pills*. This passage is certainly the most offensive of all that Hobbes has written. Professor Maurice says there is no doubt 'latent irony' in it. If there is, it must be very *latent*. There is nothing in the connection to lead to the supposition that Hobbes did not mean what he said. Quite in agreement with this is Hobbes' doctrine concerning faith, to which Mr. Maurice also objects. It is, that we believe a prophet speaks in the name of God, simply because he says so, and thus our faith is really faith in men. 'If,' says Mr. Maurice, 'our readers dissent from these last conclusions as much as we do, we are bound to say that they are not more the conclusions of Hobbes than those of his contemporary, Bishop Pearson, whom English divines are taught not only to revere for his piety and learning, but to accept as their theological guide.'

Notwithstanding Hobbes' denunciation of philosophy, and the sharp distinction which he made between reason and faith, he pronounces reason to be the undoubted word of God,—a talent which the Master has put into our hands till His coming again, and which we are not to fold up in the napkin of implicit faith. That our reason is to be exercised in matters belonging to religion he thinks evident from the command of Jesus to search the Scriptures. The appeal is made to our reason, which in itself implies that we have the capacity to understand and interpret the sacred books. There are, indeed, many things in the Scriptures above our reason, but none contrary to it. In one place, Hobbes excludes the worship of God from those things which are to be known by reason; but in another place he says that God declares His laws three ways: *by the dictates of natural reason, by revelation, by the voice of some man to whom He has given the power to work miracles.* Hence, a threefold word of God, *rational, sensible,* and *prophetic,* corresponding to right *reason, supernatural sense,* and *faith.* Revelation here means what is revealed immediately to oneself. But as this supernatural revelation is exceptional, the kingdom of God therefore consists mainly of the *natural* and the *prophetic,*—what we know by reason and what we know from the Scriptures. The Bible is the word of God as well as right reason, for God speaks to us in the sacred books. We do not *know* that they are the word, but all true Christians believe they are, and the ground of this belief is the authority of the *Commonwealth,* which is identical with the *Church.* The sovereign power has determined which are the canonical books. Hobbes devotes a chapter of the 'Leviathan' to the Holy Scriptures, which is interesting as one of the first English essays on the criticism of the Bible. He brings forward the usual arguments from 'the five Books of Moses' to show that they were not *written* by Moses. He reckons that the Book of Joshua was not written till long after the time of Joshua; the Books of Judge, Ruth, Samuel, Kings, and Chronicles, not till long after the Captivity. The writers of the New Testament lived all in less than an age after Christ's ascension, and had all seen Christ, and been His disciples, excepting only St. Paul and St. Luke. Some time had passed before the books were collected into one volume, and recommended to us by the governors of the Church as the writings of the persons whose names they bear. The great doctors of the Church did not scruple at such frauds as tended to make the people more pious, yet there is great reason to believe that they did not corrupt the Bible. Hobbes' view of inspiration might pass for orthodox, if it implied infallibility, which, however, it does not. 'All Scripture is given by inspiration of God,' he calls an evident metaphor to signify that 'God inclined the spirit or mind of the writers to write that which should be useful in teaching, reproving, correcting, and instructing men in the way of righteous living.' The holy men of old who were moved by the Holy Spirit had supernatural revelations. A prophet was a prolocutor—one who speaks from God to man. Prophecy was a temporary employment from God, most frequently of good men, but sometimes also of the wicked. It

CHAP. VI.

Criticism of the Old Testament.

was necessary to use natural reason to discern the true from the false prophets. In the Old Testament his doctrine was required to be conformable to what was taught by Moses, the sovereign prophet; in the New, it was to be accompanied with the confession that *Jesus is the Christ*. The truth of any prophet's utterance was always to be determined by the ruler of the people; that is, God's vicegerent on earth. Corresponding to these views of inspiration and prophecy, Hobbes said that when a man has wisdom and understanding or affections for what is good, he has God's Spirit within him. If the affections are evil, there is the presence of a bad spirit; those who are thus possessed are called *demoniacs*.

The doctrine of miracles taught in the 'Leviathan,' without being unorthodox, in some respects anticipates modern criticism. A miracle is a *sign*, a *wonder*, a *strange work*. When we know the cause, or when a wonderful work becomes familiar to us, it ceases to be a miracle. The ignorant take many things for supernatural, such as eclipses of the sun and moon. Yet there are genuine *miracles*, immediate works of God, besides or beyond the ordinary operations in the world of nature as known to us. These miracles God works for an end; that is, for the 'benefit of His *elect*.' They are not intended to convince the unbelieving, such as Pharaoh, or the men of Galilee, in whose presence Jesus *would not* work miracles. Their object was to add to the Church such as should be saved—such as God had elected to eternal life. Miracles made manifest to them the mercy of an extraordinary ministry *for their salvation*. Hobbes' doctrine of the Trinity is the most startling of his theological heresies. Person he explains by its original meaning as one who acts a part. God, who is always one and the same, was first represented by Moses, then by His incarnate Son, and last of all by the Apostles. As represented by the Apostles, the Holy Spirit by which they spoke is God; as represented by His Son, who is God and man, the Son is that God; as represented by Moses and the High Priests, the Father—that is to say, the Father of our Lord Jesus Christ—is that God. Hobbes afterwards recalled this illustration of the Trinity, explaining that he only meant to show to such scoffers as Lucian how God, who was one, could also be three persons. The explanation of the Atonement is more than usually rational. Man had sinned, and was liable to a penalty. God was pleased to accept a ransom, not, however, as a satisfaction for sin equivalent to the offence. In the Old Testament He gave pardon on the condition of offering sacrifices of bulls and goats. Under the new dispensation, the sacrifice of Christ has redeemed us; 'not that the death of one man, though without sin, could satisfy for the offence of all men in the matter of justice, but in the mercy of God, who has ordained such sacrifices for sin as He is pleased to accept.'

But in Hobbes' rationalism the most strange of all is his disbelief of an endless punishment of the wicked. After he has denied that we are judges of what is just with God, after he has maintained that God's right over us is His omnipotence alone, and that He has determined, irrespective of our wills and characters, who are to be saved and who are not to be saved, yet on the ground of its inconsistency with the mercy of God, he denies that the sufferings of the wicked can be never-ending. Eternal they may be in the sense of sufferings in the eternal world; but though the fire be unquenchable, and the torments everlasting, yet it cannot be inferred from Scripture that the persons cast into the torments shall suffer eternally. On the contrary, death and the grave shall be cast into the lake of fire, which is the second death. There will be a final restitution, and no more going to hades or the grave.

Endless punishment denied.

Hobbes had explained *angels* as images in the imagination, which signified the presence of God in the execution of a supernatural work. On the same principle he explains that Satan, the Devil, and Abaddon do not set forth any individual person. They are not proper names, but appellations, and ought not to have been left untranslated, as they are in the Latin and in our modern Bibles. What is said in the Scriptures concerning hell is metaphor. It is called Hades, or the place where men cannot see,—*infernus*, or *under ground*. The simple idea of the dark grave became, indefinitely, a bottomless pit. As the giants of the old world were destroyed by the Deluge, hell is called the *congregation of the giants*. Job says, 'The giants groan under water;' and

The Devil not a person.

Isaiah, concerning the King of Babylon, 'Hell is troubled to meet thee, and will displace *the giants for thee.*' In allusion to the destruction of the cities of the plain, it is called the lake of fire. The Egyptians were in darkness when the children of Israel had light in their dwellings: hence the *outer darkness* without the habitation of God's elect. Near Jerusalem was the valley of the children of *Hinnom,* a part of which is called Tophet, where the old Pagans sacrificed their children to Moloch, and where the Jews carried the 'filth and garbage' of Jerusalem to be burnt with fire. From thence they called the place of the damned *Gehenna,* or the Valley of Hinnom, the word now usually translated *hell.* Hobbes thinks that after the Resurrection, the *real* place for the punishment of God's enemies will be on this earth.

Deliverance from sin.

Salvation is deliverance from sin, which is all one with deliverance from misery. It is to be secured absolutely against all evils, including want, sickness, and death. The kingdom of God does not exist now. This is but the *regeneration,* or preparation for the coming of the Son of Man. When He comes He shall be King over all the earth, the true Lawgiver, the eternal Sovereign who shall give light and peace and joy to His people for ever and ever. We need no ascent to another region of the universe to realize the felicity of the redeemed. The tabernacle of God shall be with men. The New Jerusalem, with its glorious temple, shall come down from God out of heaven. Christ shall reign with His saints. There shall be a new heaven and a new earth, wherein dwelleth righteousness. The dreams, as we often say, of the millenarian were sound reasoning to the sober intellect of Thomas Hobbes.

Hobbes hung dead weights to the wings of reason, but he laid no restraint on his own. He was willing to submit to the State, or to retract what he had written, but not till he had completed the cycle of human thought. Had he kept within the limits he prescribed for others, he would never have been classed with deists and unbelievers. After admitting that in many things Hobbes is undoubtedly orthodox, the 'Leviathan' is still a great world of rational theology, by which we mean theology founded on reason.

Rational theology.

Hobbes hated metaphysics as he hated ghosts, devils, and darkness.* He drew up articles of natural theology, giving a secondary place to that knowledge of religion which we have on the authority of another person. That there is a God he holds to be an inevitable result of the exercise of reason. 'Curiosity,' he says, 'or love of the knowledge of causes, draws on man from the consideration of the effect to seek the cause, and again the cause of that cause, till of necessity he must come to this thought at last, that there is some cause whereof there is no former cause, but is eternal; which is it men call God. So that it is impossible to make any profound inquiry into natural causes without being inclined thereby to believe there is one God eternal, though they cannot have any idea of Him in their mind answerable to His nature. For as a man that is born blind, hearing men talk of warming themselves by the fire, and being brought to warm himself by the same, may easily conceive and assure himself that there is somewhat which men call fire, and is the cause of the heat he feels, but cannot imagine what it is like, nor have an idea of it in his mind, such as they have that see it; so also by the visible things in the world, and their admirable order, a man may conceive there is a cause of them, which men call God, yet not have any idea or image of Him in his mind.'

One of the chapters in the 'Leviathan' is on the Kingdom of the God of Nature. In this Hobbes describes the worship of God taught us by the light of nature. We must attribute to God *existence*. We must speak of Him as the cause of the world, not as identical with it. The world being caused, cannot be eternal. We must regard Him as caring for us and loving us. We must not say that He is finite; that He has form; or that we have an *image* of Him in our minds. We must not ascribe parts to Him, nor limit Him by place. We must not say He moves, or that He rests, nor ascribe to Him passions—as repentance, anger,

CHAP. VI.

The light of nature.

---

* Hobbes had a great terror of being in the dark. He ascribes his natural timidity to the circumstance of his mother being frightened by the rumour of the Spanish Armada. 'She gave birth,' he says, 'to twins, myself and fear.' Bishop Atterbury, in a passage in his sermon on 'The Terrors of Conscience,' a passage by no means creditable to the bishop, represents Hobbes' natural timidity as his conscience troubling him for his religious principles.

mercy. We should speak of Him as the Infinite, the Eternal, the Incomprehensible. There is but one name to signify our conception of his nature, and that is, *I Am*. We should pray to Him, and offer thanksgiving. We should always speak worthily of Him, and above all things *keep His laws, for this is the greatest worship of all.*

In denying God passions and affections, Hobbes annihilates that personality which, from the limitations of our minds, we are necessitated, in a greater or less degree, to ascribe to the Divine Being. He said that we could have no *idea* of God. By this he meant image. All our mental images are of things finite. God is being infinite, which is contrary, or the negative, of the finite. God, as we conceive Him, does not exist. It is better to acknowledge Him to be incomprehensible than to attempt to define His nature. Following this principle, Hobbes objected to all the terms by which we try to express our thoughts concerning God, and the world which lies beyond the sensuous or finite. '*Incorporeal* spirit,' '*immaterial* substance,' '*eternal now*,' and all such phrases, he pronounced meaningless. For the same reason he ought to have rejected *infinite, immortal, eternal,* and many other terms with which he could not so easily dispense. He was, however, entitled to use words according to his own definitions so long as he made himself intelligible. But if God is not spirit *incorporeal*, nor substance immaterial, He is the opposite of these, which is corporeal body or material substance. In other words, God is body, or matter, or substance, taking these three terms as synonymous; nor does Hobbes shrink from this conclusion. He reasons that God must be corporeal, for 'whatsoever is not body is nothing. The universe consists of body and accidents, but in accidents there is no reality.' The corporeal is the only real existence. Spirit is body under another form, 'thin, fluid, transparent, invisible.' God is a most pure, most simple 'corporeal spirit.' It was objected that in this Hobbes identified God and the universe. The inference was denied, on the ground that God was the *cause* of the universe.

Hobbes only intended to be a physical investigator, but he could not use his reason in the material world without danger of its trespassing on the domain of the spiritual. Every effort to confine the human mind to the phenomenal has been a failure, and every such effort must be a failure to the end of time. Hobbes set aside the Greek philosophers with a sneer. For the Schoolmen he had not even that. Their phraseology he pronounced as unintelligible as the subjects of which they discoursed were incomprehensible; and yet he is compelled to treat of the same subjects, and sometimes to adopt the terms which he pronounces meaningless. Honestly, if unconsciously, he followed where reason led him. He was confessedly a man of limited reading. He flung it in the face of one of his opponents, that if he had read as many books as some people, he would have been as stupid as they were. He fell back on the resources of his own mind, and reached conclusions which seemed original. It does not appear to have occurred to him, nor to any of those who replied to him, that in teaching this doctrine of the consubstantiality of mind and matter, body and spirit, he was simply reviving the theology of the ancient Stoics. The identity of body and spirit, the division of the all of being into God and the universe, was but an enunciation of the one substance of Spinoza, the 'nature producing' and 'nature produced.' Hobbes reached his conclusion by the same vigorous and independent reasoning as Spinoza did. Indeed, it is the only conclusion to which reason can legitimately come—the only conclusion to which any philosophy worthy of the name has come. We may distinguish between the Stoics, the Platonists, the Eleatics, the Ionics, and the Italics; but on the great question of *being*, which was primarily the subject of all their speculations, the difference is one of words—a question of the meaning of *matter, substance, idea, essence, corporeal spirit,* and *spiritual body.*

The consubstantiality of mind and matter.

Hobbes may not have had many followers—that is, not many who agreed with all he said—but he had many readers, and many who admired even when they did not follow. The poet Cowley wrote:

> 'Vast bodies of philosophy
> I oft have seen and read,
> But all are bodies dead,
> Or bodies by art fashioned.

Cowley's praise of Hobbes' philosophy.

> I never yet the living soul could see
>   But in thy books and thee.
>   'Tis only God can know
> Whether the fair ideal thou dost show
> Agree entirely with His own or no.
>   This I dare boldly tell,
> 'Tis so like truth 'twill serve our turn as well;
> Just as in nature thy proportions be
> As full of concord their variety.
> As firm their parts upon their centre rest,
> And all so solid as that they at least,
> As much as nature, emptiness detest.'

But Hobbes had opponents as well as admirers. The 'Leviathan,' says Bishop Warburton, made the philosopher of Malmesbury 'the terror of that age.' It would require a long list to mention even the names of those who undertook to destroy the monster. Among them there was an earl, two archbishops, five bishops, several masters and fellows of colleges, a Boyle lecturer, many doctors of divinity, and country parsons without number. 'I will put a hook into his nose, and cast an angle into his jaws,' cried one of the last, with the bravery characteristic of his class when about to slay a monster of heresy. The earl was Edward Hyde, the loyal and faithful, but unfortunate Clarendon. He wrote from his exile 'A Survey of the Leviathan,' which he dedicated to Charles II. In his dedication he assures the king of his unshaken fidelity, and his 'abhorrence of the false and evil doctrine of Mr. Hobbes, *that a banished subject during his banishment is not a subject.*' The 'Survey' had for a frontispiece Andromeda chained to the rock, with the sea monster about to devour her. Perseus, appearing on his winged Pegasus, with a Gorgon's head in one hand and a javelin in the other, destroys the monster, and liberates the virgin. So Clarendon, the destroyer of monsters, harpoons the 'Leviathan,' that religion, like a stately goddess, might walk in beauty freed from fetters and from fears. Clarendon was ready to admit that there were many good things well said in Hobbes' book. He recommended disregarding the definitions, which are really essential to understanding what the author means; but he said truly that Hobbes 'did not so much consider the nature of a definition, as that he may insert somewhat into it, to which he may resort to prove somewhat, which men do not think of when they read the definitions.' He protested against Hobbes' dark view of human nature, and the more rationalistic of his religious doctrines. He maintained his own orthodoxy by approving the mode of receiving the mysteries of faith illustrated by the *pills*. He charges Hobbes with ignorance of the English monarchy and its history; with a misapprehension of the nature of laws, as well as of the actual laws of this realm. It is only on this subject that Clarendon's opinion is worth knowing, for law was his profession. The chief interest attaching to the 'Survey' is the repeated charge that Hobbes was furthering the interests of Cromwell.* The passages which Clarendon quotes in proof of this are very obscure, if this was their object. Cromwell must have had keen eyes to see, in what Hobbes said of the right of the sovereign to name his successor, an intimation that he should arrange for the succession of his son Richard. He might have found himself described in a later work 'as the single tyrant who occupied England, Scotland, and Ireland, and turned to mockery the democratic wisdom as well of their laymen as of their ecclesiastics.' He might have read that in the civil war, 'not bishops only, but king, law, religion, honesty, having been cast down,—perfidy, murder, all the foulest wickedness (covered, however, with hypocrisy), held sway in the land.' Indeed, Hobbes never misses an opportunity of denouncing

CHAP. VI.

Charges Hobbes with writing in favour of Cromwell.

---

* Clarendon seems to have been the inventor of this. Bishop Burnet calls the 'Leviathan' 'a very wicked book with a strange title,' and says that Hobbes 'wrote it at first in favour of absolute monarchy, but turned it afterwards to gratify the republican party. These were his true principles, though he had disguised them for deceiving unwary readers.' Dr. Whewell says that the face of the figure in the frontispiece of the 'Leviathan' has a manifest reference to Cromwell, but in a copy belonging to Trinity College library, the face appears to be intended for Charles I. A gentleman connected with Trinity College writes:—'I have before me the two editions of the "Leviathan," with date 1651. The frontispiece of the one is surmounted by a handsome face resembling, though not strikingly, the portraits of Charles I. The other face has the same crown, but is broader and coarser featured, *like* Cromwell, but not strikingly so— about as like his portrait by Cooper, as the former is like Charles by Vandyke. But the faces are in different types, the former high featured, and what may be called Norman, the latter flattened, with broad nostrils, and more of the bourgeois or Saxon type. The Cromwell plate is much brighter and more distinct than the supposed Charles plate; it has many more lines in the principal and in the accessory figures, and might, I think, be a retouch of the former.'

all that was done in England in the days of Cromwell. In the 'Behemoth' the Parliament men are pictured as traitors, rebels, fanatics, and hypocrites; and yet Clarendon could see in Hobbes a concealed enemy of the Church and the king.

One of the earliest works of Thomas Tenison, afterwards Archbishop of Canterbury, was called 'The Creed of Mr. Hobbes examined in a feigned Conference between him and a Student in Divinity.' Tenison had just been presented by the Duke of Manchester to the rectory of Holywell, St. Ives, Hunts. This little book, dedicated to his patron, was the first fruits of his leisure. It is perhaps the most sensible reply that was made to Hobbes. It gave ample evidence that Tenison was worthy of the duke's patronage, and fair promise that one day he might be a bishop. Tenison had the same advantage over Hobbes in philosophy that Clarendon had over him in law. He was well read in Plato and the Greek philosophers. Whether or not they meant by 'incorporeal spirit' what Hobbes meant by 'corporeal spirit' may be an open question, but that they did speak of *incorporeal* existences, and attach a definite meaning to the term, is not to be disputed. Tenison showed that if Hobbes had been at all acquainted with the Platonic use of the word *idea*, he would never have confounded it with *image*. It is 'an argument of a thickness of mind' to say that we have no conception without an image. 'Plato has contended for a knowledge soaring above the ken of fancy, and has taught us that the greatest and most glorious objects have no image attending on their conception. And Clemens Alexandrinus told the Gentiles that the Christians had not any sensible image of sensible matter in their Divine worship, but that they had an intelligent *idea* of the only sovereign God.' Tenison, not seeing that the doctrine of the Stoics concerning substance could be reconciled with that of the Platonists, urged against Hobbes that if God was corporeal, then He would be identical with the world, and so the world might be worshipped as God. And he repeated the worn-out jests from St. Augustine and Peter Bayle, that such men as Cain and Pharaoh, Herod and Judas, 'not to say Mr. Hobbes himself,' might be parts of God. Hobbes quoted Tertullian and the Greek Fathers to show that by body they meant *essence*; and as neither Hobbes nor Tenison could explain it further, Hobbes said he knew *that God is,* but he did not know *what* He is. To this Tenison sagely replied, 'Ye worship ye know not what.' Hobbes, not content with saying we could not know the essence of the Deity, leaving spirit and body as names for quantity or quantities unknown, carried this doctrine of human incapacity into the domain of the moral attributes, denying that human reason can judge of God's doings, and maintaining that that may be just in God which is not just in us, for *a thing is made just by God's doing it.* To which Tenison triumphantly replied that the reason of mankind must be the eternal and universal standard, since God Himself had appealed to it as the judge of His justice and righteous dealing. 'Are not my ways equal, and yours unequal?' 'Judge between me and my vineyard, O house of Israel.' Tenison also combated Hobbes' favourite tenet of the absolute supremacy of the sovereign in religion. The doctrine, he said, was derived from the Pagans. The laws of their country determined what gods should be worshipped. In the 'twelve tables' it was forbidden that any man should have a personal religion. The Gospel, on the other hand, required men no longer to worship the national gods, but only the true God as revealed by Jesus Christ. Tenison said that Hobbes got the doctrine of the 'Leviathan' from the oration of Euphemus in Thucydides, where the orator says, 'Now, to a tyrant or city that reigneth, nothing can be thought absurd if profitable.' It is *possible* Hobbes may have found it here, but that was going a long way for it.

Denies that a thing is made just by God's doing it.

John Bramhall, Bishop of Derry, and afterwards Archbishop of Armagh, was one of Hobbes' most determined adversaries. He was an able man, though somewhat rude and vehement, a fervent advocate of Episcopacy and the Stuarts, especially King Charles II. of *blessed memory.* He had long discussions with Hobbes on necessity, which need not trouble any one. Neither of them on either side said anything which had not been said before, and which has not often been said since. Hobbes repeated the usual fallacy about the will being always necessitated by the motive, and

Archbishop Bramhall replies to Hobbes.

CHAP. VI. the bishop answered that every man feels and knows that he has power to will. When the 'Leviathan' appeared, the Bishop of Derry could not resist the temptation to throw his line into the sea that he might entangle the great fish. He wrote a treatise called 'The Catching of the Leviathan,' and with a great deal of pleasantry which is very amusing in a man of episcopal dignity, he threatened to put an end to its existence by three harping-irons: one for its heart, a second for its chin, and a third for its head,—the religious, the political, and the rational parts. Yet the bishop confessed that he was only fighting with a shadow. 'The "Leviathan" was a mere phantasm of Mr. Hobbes' own devising. It was neither flesh nor fish, but a confusion of a man and a whale engendered in his own brains, not unlike Dagon, the idol of the Philistines; a mixture of a god, and a man, and a fish.' In fact, the great marine brute, 'the mortal god,' was Thomas Hobbes himself.

Calls the 'Leviathan' atheistical.

The theology of the 'Leviathan,' according to the bishop, was 'atheistical.' By making God corporeal, it denied His existence; by saying that He is not *wholly* in every place, it deprived Him of ubiquity; and by making eternity equivalent to endless duration, it reduced Him to the condition of a finite existence, 'older to-day than He was yesterday.' Hobbes' answers were not much wiser than Bramhall's objections. He said that if God was *all* in one place, that would imply that He was excluded from other places; and he railed against the Schoolmen, who made eternity an *everlasting now*, and who, instead of saying God was just, true, and eternal, called him justice, truth, and eternity. The use of these terms is not *atheistical*, as Hobbes imagined, neither is there any necessary heresy in the rejection of them. Bramhall, who had considerable learning, and was a tolerable theologian, protested manfully against the depraved view of human nature set forth in the 'Leviathan.'

Recommends Hobbes to try his government among the savages in America.

He ended his treatise with a recommendation that Hobbes should try his form of government in America, and if it succeeded among the savages, he might transplant it to England. In America, Hobbes might have a chance of being chosen the sovereign, but Bramhall expressed fears that if his 'ruling was as magisterial as his writing, his subjects might tear their *mortal god* in pieces with their teeth, and entomb his sovereignty in their bowels.' Hobbes, who could be cool as well as severe, wrote an answer to the 'Catching' ten years after it was published, saying that he had only heard of it about three months since, *so little talk was there of his lordship's writings.*

The Boyle lecturer was Samuel Clarke, rector of St. James's, Westminster. He classed Hobbes with Spinoza. For this classification there were some grounds. Hobbes agreed with Spinoza as to the consubstantiality of body and spirit. Spinoza, indeed, denied that God was a body, but then he explained that by *body* he meant that which has figure and dimensions, as length and breadth—that is, he denied that God was anything finite. Hobbes agreed, too, with Spinoza on necessity, and that the right of every man by nature depends on his might. On such questions as the nature of eternity Spinoza agreed rather with the Schoolmen, or we may say the old philosophers. Clarke chiefly combated the doctrine of necessity. One lecture, however, is almost entirely devoted to the consideration of law, in which Clarke shows that Hobbes frequently contradicts himself; sometimes maintaining that there is right and wrong in the nature of things, and at other times declaring right and wrong to depend on the will of the sovereign.

Samuel Parker, Bishop of Oxford, wrote, as a sequel to a Latin work, an English one,* called 'A Demonstration of the Divine Authority of the Law of Nature, and of the Christian Religion.' The bishop gives a woeful picture of the viciousness and profanity, infidelity and atheism, of his age. Even the common people set up for sceptics, and defended their

---

* Bishop Burnet speaks of Parker as 'a man of little virtue, and, as to religion, rather impious. He was originally an Independent, but after his conversion to Episcopacy he for some years entertained the nation with several virulent books, till he was attacked by the liveliest droll of the age (Andrew Marvell), who wrote in a burlesque strain, but with so peculiar and so entertaining a conduct, that from the King down to the tradesman his books were read with great pleasure. This not only humbled Parker, but his whole party.' He was at one time so far on Hobbes' side that he said the King was not under God and Christ, but under God and above Christ. According to Burnet, the second James made him a bishop to help on the ruin of the Church. Macaulay says 'the bishopric of Oxford was given to Samuel Parker, whose religion, if he had any, was that of Rome, and who called himself a Protestant only because he was encumbered with a wife.'

sins as harmless actions. The bishop said that he was in pursuit of truth, and would not be jostled out of the way, 'not by Thomas Hobbes *nor an angel from heaven.*' The demonstration of the laws of nature was mostly taken from Bishop Cumberland. The second part, on the authority of the Christian religion, was original. By careful study, says the bishop, we may find out that there is a future life, and rewards and punishments. But revelation has now made these things evident. The grounds of the Christian faith he reckoned to be so convincing that they must enforce belief. He called the 'Leviathan' 'a foolish book, by the reading of which those who were by nature sufficient dunces, fancy themselves philosophers.' The 'poor village curate is sure to be a trophy to the arguments of the forward youth who has read the "Leviathan."' The bishop threatens 'to load their infidelity with such a heap of absurdities as shall for ever dash their confidence and disarm their impiety.' The Apostles, he goes on to say, laid down their lives in attestation of what they had seen. It was impossible that they should agree to deceive the world. The books of the New Testament were written by the persons whose names they bear. The writers were sincere and impartial. Profane history, too, agrees with sacred. Josephus has given an account of Jesus. Phlegon speaks of an eclipse about the time of the crucifixion. Tiberius, according to Tertullian, believed in the divinity of Jesus Christ, and wished the Senate of Rome publicly to acknowledge it. Pontius Pilate wrote 'The Acts of Pilate' for Tiberius. Justin Martyr appeals to them, and surely he knew better about their authenticity than Casaubon, and some other modern scholars, who have had the boldness to doubt that they were written by Pilate. Agbarus, the King of Edessa, wrote a letter to Jesus, inviting Him to come and cure him of some disease. To this letter Jesus wrote *a brief and pithy answer*. The *Therapeutæ* mentioned by Philo were Christians, whatever Scaliger may say to the contrary. Justin Martyr testifies that in the city of Rome devils were cast out daily by the name of Jesus, when the Roman exorcists could not cast them out. Irenæus proves against the heretics that the Catholic Church had the true apostolical succession, for the clergy could work the same miracles as the Apostles. They could cast out devils, foretell things to come, cure the sick by imposition of hands, and even raise the dead. The Roman Emperors confessed the supernatural power of the Christians. Marcus Aurelius was witness to the rain and thunder and lightning that came down on their enemies in answer to the prayers of the 'thundering legion;' and this is saying nothing of the multitude of miracles mentioned by Origen, St. Cyprian, St. Ignatius, and St. Augustine. If the 'poor village curate' fell a victim to those who read the 'Leviathan,' it was his own blame. He ought to have known the valuable evidence from Christian antiquity provided for him by Samuel, Lord Bishop of Oxford.

Some of the small writers who made sport with the 'Leviathan' have not even left their names to posterity, and of what they wrote the British Museum has only been able to treasure up a few fragments. 'The True Effigies of the Monster of Malmesbury in his Proper Colours,' has only the six pages 'To the reader.' Cowley's verses to Hobbes were vilely parodied after his death. 'The Last Sayings of Thomas Hobbes,' consisting of startling passages from the 'Leviathan,' were cried through the streets after the fashion of the dying words of Baxter and Bunyan. Wits wrote elegies and epitaphs,* while religious visionaries saw Hobbes writhing in hell like Dante's monsters, half suffocated in sulphur.† 'The "Leviathan" found out; or, An Answer

---

* One elegy gives what we may suppose to have been the general estimate of Hobbes:—

'He with such art deceived, that none can say,
If his be errors, where his errors lay;
If he mistakes, 'tis still with so much wit,
He errs more pleasingly than others hit.'

To this elegy is appended an epitaph which is too coarse to be quoted here. This is the last verse:—

'In fine, after a thousand shams and fobbs,
Ninety years eating and immortal jobbs,
Here *matter* lies, and there's an end of Hobbes.'

Aliud.

'Here lies Tom Hobbes, the bugbear of the nation,
Whose death has frightened atheism out of fashion.'

† The following is from 'Visions of Hell,' ascribed to John Bunyan:—

'*Epenetus.*—I had no sooner spoke, but one of the tormented wretches cries out, with a sad, mourning accent, Sure I should know that voice. It must be Epenetus. I was amazed to hear my name mentioned by one of the infernal crew; and therefore, being desirous to know who it was, I answered: "Yes, I am Epenetus; but who are you in that sad, lost condition, that knows me?"

'*Dam. Soul.*—To this the lost unto Mr. Hobbes' "Leviathan," in that which my Lord Clarendon hath passed over,' was written by John Whitehead, of the Inner Temple, barrister-at-law. But the barrister had nothing to say which had not already been better said by others. One of the best pieces against Hobbes is a little tract, the copy of which in the British Museum wants the title-page. The writer undertook to show from '*Mr. Hobbes' own principles*, that the notions of laws of right and wrong, just and unjust, good and evil, are independent upon, and naturally and rationally antecedent to, the constitution of any commonwealth.'

William Pike, Alexander Ross, and Dr. Eachard on the 'Leviathan.'

William Pike, a clergyman, wrote 'Examinations, Censures, and Confutations' of 'the Strange Man' and 'his Strange Book.' Alexander Ross* wrote 'Leviathan drawn out with a Hook.' He likened himself to young David encountering Goliath when the armies of Israel had been frightened by the vast bulk of his body, and the dimensions of his spear and armour, and his bragging and defying words. 'The learned had been afraid to bridle Mr. Hobbes his "Leviathan;" but the spiritual shepherd, the least of the tribe of Levi, *little* in his own eyes,' would show that the *brute* was not so terrible that people should be cast down even at the sight of him. John Eachard, D.D., wrote 'Dialogues between Philautus and Timothy;' that is, himself and Hobbes. They

known replied: I was once well acquainted with you upon earth, and had almost persuaded you to be of my opinion. I am the author of that celebrated book, so well known by the title of "Leviathan."

'*Epenetus.* — What, the great Hobbes! said I. Are you come hither? Your voice is so much changed, I did not know it.

'*Hobbes.*—Alas! replied he, I am that unhappy man indeed. But am so far from being great, that I am one of the most wretched persons in all these sooty territories. Nor is it any wonder that my voice is changed, for I am now changed in my principles, though changed too late to do me any good. For now I know there is a God; but oh! I wish there were not!—for I am sure He will have no mercy on me, nor is there any reason that He should. I do confess that I was His foe on earth, and now He is mine in hell. . . .

'*Hobbes.*—Oh, that I could but say, I feel no fire! How easy would my torments be to that which I now find them! But oh, alas! the fire that we endure ten thousand times exceeds all culinary fire in fierceness.'

* Immortalized in 'Hudibras:'—

'There was an ancient sage philosopher
That had read *Alexander Ross* over,
And swore the world, as he could prove,
Was made from fighting and from love.'

In another place—

'And he who made it had read *Goodwin*,
Or *Ross*, or *Cælius Rodigine*.'

were dedicated to Gilbert, Archbishop of Canterbury (Sheldon), and were intended to be clever. One of them begins by Philautus asking Timothy if he had not hanged himself yet. The archbishop and his chaplain saw only food for pastime in the great 'Leviathan;' but they could not play with him as with a bird, nor, as companions, make a banquet of him.*

Hobbes, we have already said, had not many disciples. The beneficial influence of the 'Leviathan' was in the opposition which it raised. The principle of authority was put so nakedly, as if its refutation had been intended by merely showing that it was impracticable and absurd. That religion and morality had no origin but in the civil ruler seemed a picture drawn to make the Pisos laugh. Could Hobbes really mean—

> 'Ut turpiter atrum,
> Desinat in piscem mulier formosa superne?'

In his theory of a commonwealth, it is easy to see that there was some meaning in the authority which he gave to the sovereign. The doctrine was not a new one in England. The Reformers clung to a form of it under Henry and Elizabeth. With the power of the Papacy ever threatening to disturb the civil government, it was not remarkable that men should have made high claims for the absolute sovereignty of the ruler of the State. Hobbes' doctrine, looked at politically, had a meaning. But looking at it as to the real foundation either of religion or of virtue, it is doubtful if he really meant what he seems to mean. It is difficult on this subject to reconcile Hobbes with himself. He acknow-

---

* Benjamin Laney, Bishop of Ely, also wrote against Hobbes on the question of necessity; and Seth Ward, Savilian Professor of Geometry at Oxford, afterwards Bishop of Exeter, wrote, 'In Thomæ Hobbes Philosophicam Exercitatio Epistolica,' in which he controverted all the doctrines of the 'Leviathan,' metaphysical and physical, political and theological. But the great controversy of Hobbes' life was with Dr. John Wallis, another professor of geometry. This was merely on questions of geometry, and need not detain us. Dr. Whewell says of Hobbes' writings on this subject, that they are full of the 'most extravagant arrogance, ignorance, and dogmatism which can be imagined.' To the list of Hobbes' adversaries we may add Sir Robert Filmer, Daniel Scargill, Dr. Sharrock, Dr. John Templar, Mr. Shafto, Robert Boyle, George Lawson, Richard Baxter, Bishop Lucy, and Herbert Thorndike. Mr. Tyrell, a friend of Bishop Cumberland's, translated and abridged the disquisition 'De Legibus Naturæ,' adding 'A New Method of Dealing with Mr. Hobbes.'

Hobbes contradicts his own doctrine by acknowledging laws natural, immutable, and eternal.

ledged that there were natural laws, unchangeable and eternal. He said expressly that what *they forbid can never be lawful*, nor what *they command be unlawful*. Before the establishment of the Commonwealth there existed no law, according to his definition of law; but he admits that what we generally understand by the laws of right and wrong existed before all, and independent of all, civil society. However this may be settled, it is certain that he did ascribe to his grotesque monster a power to make right and wrong, and to dictate both religion and laws to the people. This position, even as laid down by Hobbes himself, seemed to leave no other foundation for either religion or morality than the will of the sovereign.

The Cambridge Platonists.

We shall be better able to understand the position of the Cambridge Platonists,* the chief Rationalists of this age, if we remember that the occasion of many of their books was opposition to this doctrine. Their object was to establish religion and morality not on anything transient or arbitrary,

Dr. Cudworth. but on principles immutable and eternal. Dr. Cudworth's great work, the 'Intellectual System of the Universe,' was intended for a refutation of the supposed atheism of the 'Leviathan.' The doctrine of necessity or fatalism appeared to Cudworth not only atheistic in itself, but subversive of reli-

---

* Baxter divides the Conformists into three kinds, the Conformists proper, some of the old ministers formerly called Presbyterians, and the Latitudinarians. The conforming Presbyterians were mostly, according to Baxter's account, very able and worthy men, who conformed and subscribed upon this inducement, that the bishop bade them do it in their own sense. The Latitudinarians were mostly Cambridge men, Platonists, or Cartesians, and many of them Arminians, with some additions, having more charitable thoughts than others of the salvation of heathens and infidels, and some of them holding the opinions of Origen, about the pre-existence of souls, etc. These were ingenious men and scholars, and of universal principles and free, abhorring at first the imposition of these little things, but thinking them not great enough to stick at when imposed. Of these, some (with Dr. More their leader) lived privately in Colleges, and sought not any preferment in the world, and others set themselves to rise. These two (the old Presbyterians and Platonists) were laudable preachers, and were the honour of the Conformists, though not heartily theirs, and their profitable preaching is used, by God's providence, to keep up the public interest of religion, and refresh the discerning sort of auditors.'—*Reliq. Bax.*

Bishop Burnet, in the 'History of his own Times,' says that these men were called Latitudinarians by 'men of narrower thoughts and fiercer tempers.' He adds, that through the prevalence of Hobbes' opinions, they were led 'to assert and examine the principles of religion and morality on clear grounds, and in a philosophical method.'

gion and morality. The 'Intellectual System of the Universe' was left unfinished. Hobbes had been dealt with in common with the old philosophers of the school of Epicurus and Democritus, and only on the one point of fatalism. Many years after Cudworth's death there was found among his manuscripts 'A Treatise concerning Eternal and Immutable Morality.' Bishop Chandler, who edited this treatise, supposes that the substance of it was intended for the 'Intellectual System,' but that Cudworth, despairing of being able to complete his great work, hastened to treat of the most material points in small volumes. This treatise is regarded as a sequel to the first book of the 'Intellectual System' against 'material fate.' Chandler regrets it had not been published earlier, that it might have served as 'an antidote to the poison of the writings of Hobbes and some others who revived in that age the exploded opinions of Protagoras and other ancient Greeks, and took away the essential and eternal discrimination of moral good and evil, of just and unjust, and made them all *arbitrary productions of divine or human will.*'

On immutable and eternal morality.

Cudworth's treatise, being directed against some of the ancient as well as the modern deniers of eternal and immutable morality, is necessarily historical as well as controversial. Plato, in the tenth book of the 'Laws,' speaks of men who said that nothing was naturally just. A thing was made just by arts and laws, not by any nature of its own. In the 'Theætetus' he speaks of the Protagoreans, who held that just and unjust, holy and unholy, depended on the authority of the city. Aristotle, too, in his 'Ethics' speaks of things honest and just not by nature, but only by law. He divides that which is 'politically just' into the 'natural' and the 'legal,' the one having everywhere the same force, the other being indifferent till it is determined by positive law. He adds that some think there is 'no other just or unjust' but what is made by 'law and men,' for 'things right and just are everywhere different.' Diogenes Laertius says of Archelaus, that he held just and dishonest 'not to be so by nature, but by law;' and of Aristippus that he believed 'nothing was good or evil otherwise than by law or custom.' Plutarch records that when Alexander was repenting for the death of Clitus, whom he had rashly slain, Anaxarchus comforted him with the doctrine that kings could do no wrong, for 'whatever is done by the supreme power is just.' Pyrrho, the father of the Sceptics and the disciple of Anaxarchus, was certain only of this, 'that there is nothing good or shameful, just or unjust,' but 'that men do all things according to law or custom.' Epicurus made all justice to depend on the mutual contracts that were made in civil society. This, also, according to Lactantius, was the doctrine of Carneades, the founder of the new academy. Cudworth finds the doctrine of these philosophers to be identical with that of Hobbes. He includes under the same condemnation another doctrine allied to it, but set forth by theologians who pass for orthodox. Some, he says, contend, not only seriously but earnestly, that there is nothing good on earth, just or unjust, but by the arbitrary will and pleasure of God. This doctrine, Cudworth says, was abhorrent to the ancient Fathers, but it is found among the Scholastics. Ockham says that there is no act evil, but as it is prohibited by God, and which can be made good if it be commanded by God. Cudworth quotes, from the writings of many Calvinists, such sentiments as that God might command what is contrary to all the precepts of the decalogue, that holiness is not conformity with the nature of God, and that God can with justice condemn the innocent to everlasting torments. Against Epicureans, Hobbists, and Calvinists, Cudworth is to prove that there is 'something naturally and immutably good and just.'

Things are what they are, not by will but by nature. It does not depend on will, either divine or human, that white is white, or that round is round. Omnipotence itself cannot make white or round without the nature and qualities of whiteness or rotundity. The nature of a thing must be present to constitute a thing that which it is. The will of God may be the efficient cause, but the formal cause it cannot be. Everything must be immutably determined by its own nature. Even in positive commands, it is not mere will that makes the thing commanded just or obligatory. It is natural justice which gives one the right of authority, and begets the duty of obedience. In accordance with these principles, Cudworth observes that laws or commands do not take the form of making what they command just, but only of enforcing it as just. This is true of the commands of God, as well as of the laws made by men. The divine will, no more than the human, can make that obligatory which is not obligatory in itself. Descartes thought it necessary to the idea of Divine omnipotence that all essences and natures be regarded as being what they are by the will of God. It is by that will, he said, that good is good and evil is evil. It is by that will that two and two make four, and that the three angles of a triangle are equal to two right angles. Cudworth said that the will of God could not have made these things otherwise than they are. If this were possible, science and demonstration would be impossible, for then truth and falsehood would only be names, and not realities. Even God's knowledge would be uncertain if it depended on the mutability of a will essentially indifferent and undetermined. To speak correctly, God, according to this hypothesis, would not be wise by wisdom, but by will. It was objected to Cudworth that his doctrine supposed the existence of natures and essences independent of God. He denied that this consequence followed. It only supposed an eternal and immutable wisdom in the mind of God, and that independently of the divine will the whole rational creation participated in this wisdom. This wisdom is God; and from the very nature of wisdom, it must be the rule and measure of the divine will. It was the opinion of some of the wisest philosophers, Cudworth says, that there is also in the scale of being a nature of goodness above wisdom, which is the measure of wisdom, as wisdom is of will. The idea of God is by some restricted to will and power, but Cudworth prefers a mystical representation, which compares the divine nature to a circle. The circle is infinite. Its inmost centre is simple goodness. The rays and expanded area are the all-comprehending and immutable wisdom. The exterior periphery is the omnipotent will or activity by which everything without God is brought forth into existence. The sphere of the activity of the will is thus outside of God, and is regulated by the wisdom and goodness which are in no way controlled by the will.

Even the will of God cannot make anything contrary to what it is by reason.

CHAP. VI.

The sceptical moralists among the ancients were also sceptical as to being.

The old philosophers who denied the immutable distinctions of right and wrong, were generally those who also denied the reality of any essence. They were ontological sceptics. The principal of these was Protagoras. His doctrine, according to Plato, was that 'nothing is anything in itself absolutely, but is always made so to something else, and essence or being is to be removed from everything.' As all things were made by motion or mixing together, they were not properly said to *be*, because 'everything is always made,' and that not absolutely, but in relation to something else. Protagoras himself applied this principle to moral essences as well as to physical. In the 'Theætetus' he is asked if he thought that 'nothing *is* good and honest, but is only made so.' He answers that 'whatsoever things seem to be good and just to every city or commonwealth, the same are so to that city or commonwealth so long as they seem so.' Protagoras, according to Plato, laid the foundation of his philosophy in that of Heraclitus, who taught a 'floating and moveable essence,' maintaining 'that nothing stood, but that all things moved and flowed.' They were opposed by Parmenides and Melissus, who ran into the other extreme. Plato facetiously calls the one 'the flowing philosophers,' and the other 'the standers.' Protagoras went even beyond Heraclitus in denying the stability of existence. His scepticism reached not merely to morals. He even asserted that heat and cold, light and colour, sight and sound had no real existence, but were only passions or sensations occasioned within us by external objects. Protagoras' error lay in his making sense the criterion or judge of the external world. It is not by sense, but by reason, that we know there is anything existing outside of us. This was proved even by Democritus, whose philosophy Protagoras abused to scepticism. Democritus, according to Sextus Empiricus, said 'that there are two kinds of knowledge, the one by the senses, the other by the mind.' That by the mind he calls properly knowledge, for it is that which may be trusted for the judgment of truth.

Reason converses with realities.

Cudworth spends several chapters in proving the certainty of rational knowledge. The mind of man converses with realities, and not with mere shadows. These realities exist altogether independent of our minds. The essence of a triangle, a square, or a circle would remain the same though no created mind were to think of a triangle, a square, or a circle. These 'essences' or 'natures' are the 'thoughts' or 'reasons' of the divine mind. The truth of them is common to all rational beings, because all rational beings partake of the divine intellect. They cannot be altered by any will whatever. Plato accordingly distinguishes between a 'law' proper and a 'decree of the state.' A 'law' is the invention of that which *is*,—that which is absolutely just in its own nature. A 'decree of the state' may be unjust, but in a secondary sense it is also a law; for there is a natural and immutable justice which requires the observance of political order.

Cudworth wrote a discourse on the Lord's Supper, in which, as we might have expected from his other writings, there is nothing of that awful mystery which superstition has gathered round this simple ordinance. He avoids the unintelligible language retained by Archbishop Cranmer,—language which, if its real history were known, would probably be found connected with some incipient doctrine of transubstantiation. The Supper is supposed to have some analogy to the old sacrifices, but it is not considered in itself a sacrifice. The manner in which Cudworth treats this and some other subjects, indicates an entirely different mode of viewing Christianity from that which prevailed in the seventeenth century. It cannot be said that he does not teach distinctly all the doctrines of the Gospel as they are understood by the most orthodox. The peculiarity is in the treatment. Other preachers set a high estimate on the mere creed. Cudworth dwells more on the necessity of a Christian life. We know that we are Christians, not so much by our believing a creed, as by our keeping Christ's commandments. Christ was not a master of the school, but of the life. He did not come to give us dogmas about which we are to dispute and wrangle. He came to make our hearts beat towards heaven. True faith is not believing certain doctrines, but it is having Christ's law written in our hearts and following it in our lives.

The first place among the Cambridge Platonists properly

CHAP. VI.

Henry More.

Puts on reason as the 'sacerdotal breastplate.'

Christianity is the only religion which appeals to reason.

belongs to Cudworth, though Henry More is usually named as their leader. More was a disciple of Plotinus rather than of Plato. He was rational certainly, but he was also mystical; and, like Plotinus, he was deeply influenced by the superstitions of his age. He wrote more books than any of the men with whom he was associated, but his fame would have been greater had he written less. His works may be divided into three kinds—the philosophical, the theological, and the ethical. The last we may pass by, as of little interest. The chief of the 'philosophical' are an 'Antidote against Atheism,' and a treatise on the 'Immortality of the Soul.' The theological are fairly represented by the 'Mystery of Godliness.' With a theologian of More's school, the philosophical impinged on the theological. The distinction between them was but imperfectly marked, if it was really more than imaginary. This was also true of the ethical, which was but the practice of what was learned in the regions of philosophy and theology. The essential principle, in which philosophy, theology, and ethics are one, is reason. Cicero said, 'I will follow reason wherever it leads me.' More says that he adopted the same resolution, and among other 'priestly habiliments,' he put on the 'rational' as his 'sacerdotal breastplate.' It was to cover the heart, the sincerity of which is the 'the root or well-spring of the soundest and purest reason.' Aaron's robes, according to Philo, were a representation of the universe; which means, More says, that every priest should endeavour to be a rational man and a philosopher. This, indeed, was Philo's own interpretation. He said that the high priest, when looking upon his attire, was reminded that he was not to say or do anything contrary to the laws of 'Eternal Reason,' which is the 'everlasting High Priest.' This High Priest is the Divine Logos. And of the Logos, Plotinus and the Alexandrian Clement declare that the human intellect is the image, as the Logos is itself the image of God. To take away reason, More says, is to despoil the priest of his breastplate; and, worse still, it is 'to rob Christianity of that special prerogative which it has above all other religions in the world, namely that *it dares appeal unto reason.*' Again, he declares that to take away reason is to make all religions alike true, for, the light being renounced, all things are of one colour. But though reason be the oracle of God, it must be consulted in 'His holy temple.' That is to say, it must be reason sanctified, by which we are to be led. Aaron's breastplate included the Urim and the Thummim; that is, the purity and integrity of the will and the affections, as well as the light of the understanding. It is, as Plotinus said, the reason of 'a soul already purged' which is truly divine. This purification is necessary to have reason in its integrity. In itself, it is the voice of God; yea, it is God in us. The language of Aristotle was heavenly when he said, 'It is manifest that God is in the universe, and that all is in Him; for it is the same divinity which is in us that moves all things, and is the beginning of reason, but something which is better. What, then, can be better than knowledge, except God?'

More says in the beginning of the 'Antidote against Atheism,' that the reason why he undertakes to prove that there is a God is, because of the danger to which men were exposed in that transition period. Religion was more freely discussed than in former ages, and the recoil from superstition might lead men into the other extreme of Atheism. He explains that, though he uses the word demonstration, he does not mean that the existence of God can be so demonstrated as that a man's understanding will be forced to confess the truth of what he demonstrates. He does not believe that in this sense anything can be demonstrated. His arguments will only be such as deserve a full assent, and will win it from every unprejudiced mind. There are things altogether improbable, and yet we cannot prove that they are not true. But this improbability determines our belief, even when we cannot strictly prove. If any one were to say that Archimedes was now in the centre of the earth studying geometry, we could not disprove it, but it is so improbable that we would properly disbelieve it. And so with things which require assent. It is possible that the urns, coins, and anchors that have been found in the earth may never have been made by human hands. It is simply possible, but the probabilities to the contrary are such as determine our assent. So much for the nature of the evidence.

More next undertakes to prove that we have a settled idea of *what* God is. Some men deny that God is, because they say they have no idea of what He is. But More thinks that before they can deny His existence, they must have an idea of what they are denying. He will offer them an idea of God as proper to Him as the idea of anything in the world is proper to that thing. God is an Essence or Being fully and absolutely perfect. This idea of God is in the mind of man. It is as much a property of the human mind as the idea of any truth in geometry. To separate the mind from these necessary and essential ideas is to separate it from its own existence. Some deny the being of God, because they cannot form an idea of 'spirit,' 'eternal,' or 'infinite.' More answers that if men will deny the existence of spirit, because of the difficulty of conceiving an idea of it, they may also deny the existence of body. Who, he asks, can frame so safe a notion of a body as to free himself from the entanglements which the idea of extension brings along with it? The nature of a spirit is as conceivable and as easy of definition as any other nature. He is but a novice in philosophy who does not know that mere essence or substance, whether of bodies or of spirits, is utterly unknowable. But the essential or inseparable properties of a spirit are as intelligible as those of a body. And as for 'eternal' and 'infinite,' every man is compelled to admit their existence. If God is not eternal, the universe at least must be. And no man can divest himself of the idea of infinite space. It will cling to the soul as closely as the power of imagination. Some suppose that these ideas, which More reckons the essential properties of the mind, are created by objects of sense. He admits that the first occasion of thinking is derived from external objects. But these are rather the begetters than the implanters. There is innate in man what More calls 'an actual knowledge,' or 'an active sagacity.' The mind is awakened by the impulses of outward objects. This is illustrated by a musician asleep. A friend awakes him, and, desiring him to sing, begins the first words of a song, which the musician takes up and sings to the end. Some instances of 'actual knowledge' in the soul are the ideas of cause and effect,—proportion, angles, and symmetry. When we say that there exists a Being absolutely perfect, the proof is the same in kind as we have for the existence of those things the ideas of which are properties of the mind. The existence of these things is direct natural light. If they do not exist, the alternative is that man is a being most mistaken when he thinks he knows a thing to be most evidently true. After discoursing of this indelible stamp of the Divine existence in our minds, More goes on to the argument from design. In all this he is rational; but before he ends he has a multitude of proofs from the existence of witches, and the power which the devil exercises over the elements of nature, ruling the tempest and the whirlwind, and proving himself to be what the Scripture calls him,—the prince of the power of the air.*

The treatise on the 'Immortality of the Soul' is occupied chiefly with proving that we have the idea of a spirit apart from that of a body. Incorporeal substance is not, as Hobbes said, a contradiction. More wishes to prove that there must be an immaterial substance in man, because matter has not the properties which belong to mind. All the arguments assume that Hobbes denied the existence of the soul as distinct from the present body. But as Hobbes' doctrine did not necessarily imply the denial either of the existence or the immortality of the soul, so neither are these proved by More's arguments.

In the 'Mystery of Godliness' he treats of Christianity. The full title of the book is 'An Explanation of the Grand Mystery of Godliness; or, a True and Faithful Representation of the Everlasting Gospel of our Lord and Saviour Jesus Christ, the only begotten Son of God, and Sovereign over Men and Angels.' The book is written without method or plan, but in such a way as to allow the author to introduce any subject whatever. One or two chapters are spent in refuting the 'Family of Love.' More's own sympathies with mystical doctrines might have disposed him to a patient con-

---

* Henry More makes use of all Baxter's witch stories, with additions and variations. The devil of Mascon plays an important part. According to More's account his visit was only *invisible*. He conversed with the people, but was never seen, except once about midnight, when he appeared in the shape of an old woman spinning under a hedge by moonlight. He soon disappeared when those who saw him came nearer to him.

sideration of the merits of this sect. But instead of that, he manifests against them all the bitterness of theological hatred and misrepresentation. He supposes that they deny the truth of the letter of Scripture. It is not evident that they did this, but the moral meaning of Scripture history was more important to them than the history itself. More was always deep in the moral meaning, but he never questioned the truth of the literal record. The revelation in Christianity he reckoned distinct in kind from all other revelations. Henry Nicholas, on the other hand, believed that he was commissioned to introduce a new dispensation, which he called the dispensation of the Spirit.

Mystery defined.

More speaks of godliness as a 'mystery.' To understand this mystery a man requires initiation. This is only given to the pure in heart. The proper entrance to divine knowledge is by the gate of holiness. *Mystery* is explained in various ways. It is something completely hidden, or not so utterly concealed but that it may be in due measure intelligible. What the mystery indicates is not only intelligible but true. It is not an impertinent or idle speculation, but something which has a religious use. The Platonists called mysteries initiations, because by them fallen men were restored to happiness. The obscurity of a mystery cannot be removed by any natural knowledge. There is but one interpreter of the mysteries of the Gospel. That is the Spirit of God, the 'Great Mystagogue.' It is that Spirit which reveals truth to our understanding, and begets faith in our hearts. God has not spoken so plainly in the Scriptures as that men can understand them without the Spirit. He keeps the staff in His own hand, directing the humble and the single-hearted, but leaving the proud to lose themselves in the obscurity of night.

Plato's Trinity.

Contrary to what we should have expected, More denies the identity of the Trinity of Plato with that of the Scriptures. The three hypostases of the Platonic Trinity were 'The Good' or 'The First One;' 'Intellect' or 'The All One; and 'Soul,' or 'The One and All.' The first hypostasis was 'Essentially the Good' and 'Causally the Intellect.' The second hypostasis was 'Essentially Intellect,' 'Causally Soul,' and 'Participatively the Good.' The third hypostasis was 'Essentially Soul,' that is, 'love and operation,' 'Causally Matter and the World,' 'Participatively Good and Intellect.'*

This Trinity, More says, is Pagan, and not to be confounded with the Trinity of the Scriptures. But before he ends this chapter, he tells us that the Platonists borrowed their Trinity from the Jews. He explains the miracles of Apollonius and the other Pagans by the supposed agency of the devil. He enters into long disquisitions concerning the nature of souls, and the mode of their existence when separated from bodies. There are many good things in the 'Mystery of Godliness,' as well as in More's other works, but it is only with very great qualifications that he can be reckoned among the number of rational theologians.

John Wilkins, who preceded Bishop Pearson in the bishopric of Chester, is also to be included among the Cambridge Platonists. He was less mystical and considerably more practical than Henry More. His treatise on 'The Principles and Duties of Natural Religion' was published after his death by his friend John Tillotson, afterwards the famous Archbishop of Canterbury. The design of it, Tillotson said, was to establish the great principles of religion, the being of God, and a future state, by 'showing how firm and solid a foundation they have in the nature and reason of mankind.' Hobbes is the author whose doctrines it is designed to oppose. Religious and moral duties must have a higher source than mere authority, whether that of God or man. Tillotson says it is plain that mankind always were under a law, even before God had made any external or extraordinary revelation. If they were under no law they could not be judged, for where there is no law there is neither obedience nor transgression. In Christianity we have unspeakable advantages, both as to the de-

---

* In Greek—
Τ' ἀγαθὸν = Τὸ πρῶτον ἕν.
Νοῦς   = Ἕν πάντα.
Ψυχὴ   = Ἕν καὶ πάντα.
First Hypostasis.
  Κατ' οὐσίαν τ' ἀγαθὸν.
  Κατ' αἰτίαν νοῦν.

Second Hypostasis.
  Κατ' οὐσίαν νοῦς.
  Κατ' αἰτίαν ψυχὴ.
  Κατὰ μέθεξιν τ' ἀγαθὸν.
Third Hypostasis.
  Κατ' οὐσίαν ψυχὴ, that is ἔρως καὶ δημουργία.
  Κατ' αἰτίαν ὕλη καὶ κόσμος.
  Κατὰ μέθεξιν νοῦς καὶ τ'ἀγαθὸν.

grees of light and as to the motives that induce us to keep God's commandments. Yet it is profitable for us to consider the primary and natural obligation to piety and virtue which is imposed by the law of nature. This law, Tillotson says, is 'every whit as much the law of God as the revelation of His will in His word, and, consequently, nothing contained in the word of God, or in any pretended revelation from Him, can be interpreted to dissolve the obligation of moral duties plainly required by the law of nature.'

Bishop Wilkins begins his treatise with a discourse of the different kinds of evidence. What he says on this subject has often been said since his time. The chief point of it is, that different subjects have different kinds of evidence. Human nature is so framed as to acquiesce in a moral certainty when the subject is capable of that alone. Faith properly is an assent upon such evidence as would convince reasonable and unprejudiced men. The arguments for the existence of God are the ordinary practical arguments. Wilkins had not much taste for metaphysics or abstract disquisitions on the Infinite. His first argument is, the universal consent of nations in all times and places. To those who allow that human nature is rational, this is an argument from universal reason. The assent of all men is a good argument of its kind. It was observed by Ælian, that the existence and nature of God and a future state were more firmly believed by the vulgar, who were guided by the simple dictates of nature, than by the philosophers who were able to reason themselves into doubts and uncertainties. This universal consent was noticed by the ancient philosophers. Cicero often refers to it. 'No nation,' he says, 'is so savage, no man is so rude, that his mind is not influenced by the fear of the gods.' And Seneca says, 'There is nowhere any nation so utterly lost to all matters of law and morality, as not to believe that there are gods.' If any object the case of some savage tribes, Wilkins answers, that like men born blind, they are exceptional. To reason from them is to deny that there is such a thing as reason, because there are some men who are without reason. The unity of the Godhead is not indeed so evident as the existence of Deity. Hence the difference between the wise and the vulgar. The philosophers of antiquity believed only in one God, but the multitude believed in many. This universal belief was not the result of any agreement. It was an effect produced by a cause. And the effect being universal, the cause must be so too. It is in the very nature of our minds. All men are so constituted that they seek after God. And it is agreeable to reason that God should set such a mark upon His creatures as would lead them to the Author of their being, to whom worship and reverence are due. These general ideas the Greeks called 'common notices' and 'seminal principles.' The Latins called them the 'innate or written law,' to which corresponds the Apostle's phrase, 'the law written in their hearts.'

Universal belief the result of a universal cause.

Another argument for the existence of God is from the original of the world. Either the world had a beginning, or it is eternal. If it had a beginning, it must have been either by chance or by the will of a Creator. That it had a beginning, and that from the wisdom of a Supreme Being, is the more credible hypothesis. This is shown by testimony and by reason. Aristotle, though he believed that the world emanated from God, yet declares that the philosophers before him were of opinion that it had a beginning. To the same effect is the testimony of the Hebrew Scriptures and the traditions of the Egyptians, Chaldeans, Phœnicians, and Greeks. The want of any relics of antiquity before the Trojan war, convinced Lucretius that the world had a beginning. Other proofs are the late invention of arts, and the fact that this world is not everywhere inhabited and cultivated. Two other arguments for the existence of Deity are derived from 'the admirable contrivance of natural things,' and from 'the works of Providence in the government of the world.' Wilkins' proofs of the attributes of Deity are chiefly drawn from the testimonies of Pagan writers. On the fact of these attributes he builds an argument for adoration and worship. To serve and obey a Being so great, powerful, just, and good, is a natural dictate of reason.

The world had a beginning.

The second book of this treatise is on the 'Wisdom of Practising the Duties of Natural Religion.' A religious and virtuous life is both our happiness and our interest.

Duties of natural religion.

To fear God and to keep His commandments is the whole duty of man. It is that for which man was made. It is man's business, and that on which his well-being depends. Wilkins makes good these principles out of heathen writers. Cicero says that 'Among all the living creatures that are in the world, there is none but man that has any notion of a Deity; and among men there is no nation so wild and barbarous but pretends to some religion.' Juvenal says, 'It is this which distinguishes us from the brute creatures, that we have souls capable of divine impressions.' Plutarch says it is 'exceedingly improper to ascribe true reason to those who do not acknowledge and adore the Deity.' It is religion which makes a man. He might be defined as a being capable of religion. This is the highest meaning of the word rational. Wilkins descends to details to show how in all things the good of man is promoted by religion. It is the moral cause of health. They that follow it have length of days. It is also the natural cause, promoting temperance and sobriety, moderating the passions, such as anger, hatred, sorrow, envy, and preserving a cheerful mind, which 'does good like a medicine, and makes a healthy countenance.' It is not a rule without exception, yet it is a rule, that good men live long, while the wicked are cut off in the midst of their days. Religion makes men rich, and teaches them contentment, which is the greatest of all riches. It yields the most lasting pleasures. It brings a good name, honour, and reputation in the world. It is the strength of a nation. Cicero and Polybius, as well as Augustine and Lactantius, say that the Roman Empire was in its greatest prosperity when the people were most virtuous.

Religion profitable for the life that now is and for that which is to come.
Religion has the promise of the life which now is and of the life which is to come. Wilkins finds the reason of all these things in natural religion. Christianity gives more light concerning the certainty of them. We are under obligation to do all the duties which reason and nature point out to us. But we who have the brighter revelation in the Gospel have even higher motives than the law of nature.

Wilkins' book had a distinct controversial bearing in its relation to the foundations of religion and morality, yet its main object was practical. Discourses on the religion of nature were well meant. They were intended both to refute infidelity and to establish Christianity. In the last chapter of this book there is a discourse of the excellency and advantages of the Christian religion. Sooner or later the question was sure to present itself, that if the light of nature was so clear, what need for the Christian revelation? Again, if men can be saved by keeping the laws of nature, how is this compatible with the declaration of the Gospel, that salvation is by Jesus Christ alone? The latter question Bishop Wilkins partly answers. He saw clearly the temporal benefits which God had connected with keeping natural laws. But we cannot, he said, from these outward dispensations infer anything with certainty concerning the eternal condition of those who never heard Christ's gospel. He admitted that Justin Martyr, Clemens Alexandrinus, and Chrysostom had expressed their belief that the good men among the heathen would be saved. But this is not the opinion of the rest of the Fathers. We know that God's goodness and mercy as well as His judgments are a great deep. He has not told us how He will deal with the heathen; and it is not proper for us, Bishop Wilkins says, to tell Him how He should deal with them. Of this we are assured, that if God saves them, it will be for the merits of Jesus Christ; for there is no other name given among men whereby we can be saved. There is no escape for those who neglect this salvation. He that believeth shall be saved; he that believeth not shall be damned. The only way of salvation for us, to whom the Gospel is preached, is by faith in Christ. This is proved from the evidence of the divine authority of Christianity, and from the excellency of the things contained in the Gospel. Wilkins at last escapes the question he had raised by the orthodox solution, that we are not judges of what is right with God. It was the peculiar and distinguishing doctrine of the Platonists of Cambridge, that justice is common both to God and man; that it is antecedent to the divine will, and consequently that God must deal justly with the heathen according to our ideas of justice. But it takes some men a long time to admit the legitimate consequences of their own doctrines.

CHAP. VI.

Can men be saved by natural religion?

The most philosophical, and, in many respects, the most

interesting of the Cambridge men, was John Smith. He died before he had reached the meridian of life, and left behind him nothing more than a volume of 'Discourses.' These were not popular sermons, but rather lectures or discourses addressed to a college audience. Dr. Worthington speaks of Smith as a 'great scholar and a humble man.' His death was deeply lamented at Cambridge. He was already the acknowledged leader of the earnest men of the University, and gave great promise for the future. Simon Patrick, afterwards the learned Bishop of Ely, preached his funeral sermon, taking for his text the words, 'And Elisha saw it, and he cried, O my father, my father!' The preacher said, 'When I saw the blessed spirit of our *brother*, shall I say? or our father, making haste out of that body which lies before us, these words which I have now read came into my mind; and methought I saw the good *genius* of the place, which inspired us with so much sense of learning and goodness, taking its flight and leaving this lower world, at which my soul catched, as I fancied Elisha to have done Elijah, and I cried out, *O my father, my father! the chariot of Israel and the horsemen thereof.* Desirous I was that his Ἀποθέωσις might have been a little while deferred, that I might have stayed the wheels of that triumphant chariot; wherein he seemed to be carried, that we might have kept him a little longer in this world, till, by his holy breathings into our souls, and the grace of God, we had been meet to have some share in that inheritance of the saints in light; and so he might have gone to heaven with his train, taking all his friends along with him as attendants to that glory and honour wherewith I make no doubt he is crowned.'

The first of Smith's discourses is 'Concerning the True Way or Method of Attaining to Divine Knowledge.' Every art or science, he says, has some certain principles upon which the whole frame and body of it must depend. He that would fully acquaint himself with the mysteries, must come furnished with the *præcognita*. But divinity is a divine life rather than a divine science. It is sometimes to be understood by a spiritual sensation rather than by any verbal description. The Greek philosophers have well said that 'everything is known by that which bears a just resemblance and analogy with it.'* Things of sense and life are best known by sentient and vital faculties. And so Scripture sets forth a good life as the *prolepsis* and fundamental principle of divinity. Wisdom hath 'built her an house, and hewn out her seven pillars.' But the fear of the Lord is 'the beginning of wisdom.' The foundation of divine science must be laid here. It is true that divinity is an efflux from the eternal light. Like the sunbeams, it does not merely enlighten. It also gives heat and joy and gladness. And therefore it was that Christ connected purity of heart with the beatific vision. The pure in heart shall see God. As 'the eye cannot behold the sun unless it be sunlike,† and has the form and resemblance of the sun drawn in it, so neither can the soul of man behold God unless it be god-like.' ‡ They that seek divinity merely in books and writings, seek the living among the dead.§ In them truth is more frequently 'entombed' than 'enshrined.' He that would truly learn divinity must follow the old precept, 'seek for God within thine own soul.'‖ He is best discerned, as Plotinus says, by an 'intellectual touch.'** We cannot be true theologians till *we have seen with our eyes and heard with our ears, and our hands have handled the word of life.* The soul itself has its sense as well as the body.†† When David would teach us what the divine goodness is, he says 'taste and see.' Zoroaster's disciples once asked their master what they should do to get 'winged souls,' that they might soar aloft in the bright beams of divine truth. He answered that they were to bathe themselves in the waters of life, which he explained as the four cardinal virtues, which are the four rivers of Paradise. Plutarch tells us that the priests of Mercury, when eating of the holy things, used to cry out 'Sweet is truth.'‡‡ 'Sweet and delicious,' Smith says, 'is that truth which holy and

CHAP. VI.

Truth is known by a faculty within us.

---

* Γνῶσις ἑκάστων δι' ὁμοιότητος γίνεται.
† ἡλιοειδὴς μὴ γινόμενος.
‡ θεοειδὴς μὴ γινομένη.
§ The German scholar will remember Goethe's lines:—
'Wär' nicht das Auge sonnenhaft
 Wie könnten wir das Licht erblicken?
Lebt' nicht in uns des Gottes eigne Kraft
 Wie könnte uns das Göttliche entzücken?'
‖ 'Intra te quære Deum.'
** νοερᾷ ἐπαφῇ.
†† Ἔστι τῆς ψυχῆς αἴσθησίς τις.
‡‡ γλυκὺ ἡ ἀλήθεια.

heaven-born souls feed upon in their mysterious converse with the Deity, who can tell but they that taste it ?' Reason is elevated by the divine Spirit to a communion with Deity. It is turned into sense. What was formerly but faith, now becomes an open 'vision.'

Simplicius, in his commentaries on Epictetus, speaks of the Epicureans as a 'herd who have drowned their own sober reason in the deepest Lethe of sensuality.' Besides these he reckons four sorts of men. The first is the 'multifarious man.' He is made up of soul and body, as it were, 'by a just equality, and arithmetical proportion of parts and powers in each of them.' In these men knowledge consists of sense and reason so 'twisted up together that it cannot easily be unravelled and laid out into its first principles.' They never rise above the surface of the earth. These souls are described by Plato as 'heavy behind.'† The second class is more spiritual. It is represented by the man who looks to what he is by his soul rather than by his body. He has the 'communes notitiæ' more clear and steady. He is fit to be initiated into the 'mysteria minora,' the minor mysteries of religion. The third class is the men who are already purged, and are continually flying off from the body and bodily passions. They are such as have escaped the pollutions which are in the world through lust. To them belongs a lower degree of science. The fourth class is represented by the metaphysical and contemplative man, who, 'shooting above the logical or self-rational life, pierceth into the highest life.' Men of this class have a true divine wisdom. They have in their souls an infant Christ, who is manifesting in them the glory of the Father.

Superstition. Another of Smith's 'Discourses' is on 'Superstition.' All truly religious men who have wished to follow reason have ever found superstition to be their greatest enemy. It is the counterfeit of religion, and has a more ready currency than religion itself. Smith defines it as a false opinion of the Deity. It is to represent Him as 'austere,' 'angry,' 'sour,' and 'arbitrary.' This is done, Smith says, by some Christians, and then it is supposed that God being angry will be 'appeased by some flattering devotion.' Supersti-

---

† ὀπισθοβαρεῖς.

tion was distinguished from rational religion among the heathen in the same way and by the same marks as among Christians. Plutarch ascribed to it the origin of bloody sacrifices. Maximus Tyrius says that 'the pious man is God's friend; the superstitious man is a flatterer of God.' Simplicius has beautifully said 'that repentance, supplication, and prayers ought to draw us nearer to God, not God nearer to us, as in a ship, by fastening a cable to a firm rock, we intend not to draw the rock to the ship but the ship to the rock.' Smith describes superstition as insidiously mixing itself with a seeming faith in Christ. He specially notices the tendency of some people in his own time who made nothing of a good life, but who wished to lay all on the active and the passive righteousness of Christ. Some made the offering of Christ an excuse for their sins, putting the merits of Christ between them and a 'severe and rigid justice.' The natural religiousness of man requires to be guided by reason. If not, it will develop into superstition. In the least cultivated man there is a desire after God, a kind of natural instinct antecedent to any mature knowledge. The Stoics called it the 'movement towards God.'* When not properly directed, it is what Plutarch calls it, the 'divine disease.'† Superstition begets atheism. The superstitious man makes a god like himself, and the atheist says it is no god. Colotes, the Epicurean, wrote a book to prove that a man could only be happy by the philosophy of Epicurus. As if all good concerned 'the pores and passages of the body.' If it were so that the highest happiness of man were such as might be felt by a corporal touch, we might well 'sit down and bewail our unhappy fates that we should rather be born men than brute beasts, which enjoy more of the world's happiness than we do, without any sin or guilt.'

Among Smith's 'Discourses' there is one on the 'Immortality of the Soul.' The bane of religion is superstition, but its foundation is faith in God and the life eternal. The author of the Epistle to the Hebrews has well expressed this in the words 'He that cometh to God must believe that He is, and that He is the rewarder of them that diligently seek Him.' The latter statement supposes the immortality

marginal notes: CHAP. VI. — Defined as a perversion of the religious instinct. — Immortality of the Soul.

* ὁρμὴν πρὸς τὸν θεόν.   † θεοῦ νόησιν.

of the soul. The Pagans made the highest knowledge to be the knowledge of God and of ourselves.* To know ourselves is to know our dignity and immortality. That the soul is immortal, Smith supposes to be so evident that it might be assumed as a postulate. Cicero quotes in proof of it the 'consent of nations.' This law is not, indeed, to be always followed, for by it might be established many errors and superstitions. But the immortality of the soul is one of the first or most original ideas of the human mind. It is one of the 'uniform judgments' which convinced Averroes that there is a 'common intellect.' The soul is eternal because it is 'indivisible.' In its own nature it is an essence which endures. It can only cease to be eternal by a positive decree of Heaven depriving it of being. The fact of motion supposes a soul distinct from matter. The soul reasons about the things presented by the senses, but in so doing, it has to abstract itself from 'all corporal commerce.' Its acts are spontaneous. It has mathematical notions, independent of the body, and clear ideas of moral truth. These all testify that in its nature it is immortal as well as immaterial. But the highest of all evidence for the soul's immortality is that which is begotten within us by goodness and virtue. Every man has not sufficient skill in reasoning to prove his own immortality. But every good man feels it. A higher radiance breaks in upon his soul. The purification of the mind by a righteous life is the opening of the soul's windows to let in the light of heaven. Then the good man sees God, knows God, and is conscious of a union with Him. He is assured that that divine presence which surrounds him now will continue to surround him for ever. 'These breathings and gaspings after an eternal participation of Him are but the energy of His own breath within us.' If God intended to destroy the soul of man, He would not show it such things as He has done. 'He would not raise it up to such *mounts of vision*, to show it all the glory of that heavenly Canaan flowing with eternal and unbounded pleasures, and then humble it down again into deep and darkest abysses of death and nonentity. Divine goodness cannot, it will not be so cruel to holy souls

---

* ΕΙ, thou art, and ΓΝΩΘΙ ΣΕΑΥΤΟΝ, know thyself.

that are such ambitious suitors for His love. The more they contemplate the blissful effluxes of His divine love upon themselves, the more they find themselves strengthened by an undaunted confidence in Him.' In our souls God has engraven His own image. It is there we can learn *what* He is. It is there we can consult the divine oracles. We can ask counsel from God by the Urim and Thummim on the breastplate of the soul.

Smith explained the resurrection body as St. Paul had done. It was not the present complex body of flesh and blood, but a spiritual body. What the Platonists called the 'spiritual vehicle' of the soul, or what Zoroaster called the soul's 'aerial mantle.'* And this is the explanation of the words, 'they shall be equal unto the angels.' Prophecy is defined as an enthusiastical mode of communicating truth; a free influx of the divine mind into our minds. One chief object of it is to quicken our minds ' to a more lively converse with the eternal truths of reason.' When truth comes into this world, it is content to wear our mantles, to learn our language, and, as it were, to conform itself to our fashions. 'It speaks with the most idiotical sort of men in the most idiotical way.'

The greatest preacher of the Cambridge Platonists was Benjamin Whichcot. We notice him last for several reasons. His sermons were not published till some time after his death, and they were connected with the controversies of the next century more than the writings of any of the others. As a London preacher and the author of popular discourses, his influence was the greatest outside of the University.† One volume of Whichcot's sermons has some historical interest from its being first published with a preface written by the Earl of Shaftesbury, the author of 'The Characteristics.' Shaftesbury was not yet reckoned a Deist. He called the principles of Hobbes 'atheistic,' and he blamed Hobbes for much of the impiety and irreligion of that age. Shaftesbury never owned to Deism, and Hobbes never owned to Atheism. The charges in both cases were

---

* Εἴδωλον ψυχῆς, literally, the image of the soul.

† Whichcot was Provost of King's College, Cambridge. He was deprived of his Provostship at the Restoration.

CHAP. VI.

Is goodness eternal or only constituted by authority?

only inferential, and, therefore, in both cases unfair. In the case of Hobbes the least fair of the two. The position which Shaftesbury opposed, and which is opposed in the sermons to which he wrote the preface, is that natural goodness is not the goodness recommended in Christianity. This was one phase of the question which has often been discussed,—whether goodness is eternal, or if it is only constituted by authority. What Hobbes said on this subject, when speaking of his 'Commonwealth,' we have already seen. What qualifications or limitations he made we have also seen. But there was another class of people to whom the doctrine of authority was agreeable. Orthodox Christians thought that it would be advantageous to Christianity if it could be shown that man knew nothing of what is right and just and good, without external revelation. Shaftesbury speaks of this as having become a method of Christianity in his time. But it was no new method. It had found advocates among Fathers, Schoolmen, and Reformers, and among these it had also found opponents. It was the same principle which consigned to perdition the good men among the Pagans, and which made Archbishop Cranmer, following St. Augustine instead of his own better judgment, to say, that 'good works' were not acceptable to God unless done by Christians. It was to deny the truth of natural religion, that a place might be found for revealed, or what was called revealed, in contradistinction to what men know by the immediate teaching of God. Like two aspirants to the same throne, it was thought that the one must be put to death if the other is to reign. It was doubtless the bias of Puritanism to vilify human nature. This it learned from Calvin, and Calvin learned it from Augustine. Men were regarded as wholly depraved. Even little children were demons of unrighteousness, to be cast into everlasting burnings, unless they were among the elect, or, as St. Augustine put it, unless they were baptized. Whatever men knew by nature was supposed to be evil. Whatever men knew by external revelation was supposed to be the only measure of

Natural goodness the essence of true religion.

good. Shaftesbury, on the other hand, said that natural goodness was the essence of true religion.* The Pagans

* Whichcot says, 'Gallantly doth the poet tells us, *Remember to reverence* *thyself.* There is much of God in every man. If a man do justly value

called religion piety. It was the best word they had for it. And more than the half of piety consisted in natural affection. All moral works and moral duties are pleasing to God, because they are moral. God shows His approbation of them by the rewards that naturally accompany them. It is a great advantage to the Atheist, Shaftesbury says, to be able to show that 'there is nothing in man that moves him to what is moral, just, and honest, except a prospect of some different good, some advantage of a different sort from what attends the actions themselves.' He will not deny the importance of the external revelation. He fears, however, that many have been led to deny the principle of natural goodness, lest they should seem to under-estimate the need of revelation. 'In this way they have been forced to wound virtue, to be selfish in religion, and to see no happiness in well-doing, except what is in reversion.' Thus the Atheist and the Christian, the one fearing a proof of Deity, the other prejudice to revelation, have made war even with virtue itself. But man's nature, according to Shaftesbury and Whichcot, is not so untoward a thing but that it has a secret sympathy with virtue and honesty. God has so contrived, that if a rational being shall sink into sensuality or any kind of moral pollution, misery and torment shall befal him in this life. Virtue and vice are the foundations of peace and happiness, or sorrow and misery. No power can separate between vice and the punishment which is necessarily and naturally connected with it. Even if God were not to inflict a positive punishment, the vicious man would punish himself. Shaftesbury advocates these views of the foundation of religion and virtue, expressly that he may be better able to defend Christianity.

Virtue brings naturally its own reward, and vice its own punishment.

The first sermon in this volume is on the text, 'Never man spake like this man.' The words of Jesus were full of wisdom. Under pretence of reason, some men dispute the existence of Deity, and some the principal matters of the Christian religion. But the doctrines of Jesus will stand to be tested by reason. Whichcot considers first the

himself, he will not do that which is base, though it be in the dark.'
Again, 'The spirit of man is the candle of the Lord lighted by God, and calling men to God.'

quality of Christ's teaching. It is that which commends itself, that which satisfies the mind concerning its reality and usefulness. It is because we believe this to be the character of the Christian religion that we reject the pretences of the Church of Rome to be the infallible judge. Every man has the capacity to discover, to feel, and to know that Christianity is true. The exercise of the individual judgment is part of the training of every Christian. It is necessary to the attainment of any great progress in the Christian life. The men who are most settled in their belief are those who have most used their own judgments. Truth is self-evident, and so satisfactory to the reason that it will always be received by men whose minds are sincere. Whichcot's arguments are all built on the Platonic doctrine, that there is an absolute reason which is common to the Divine Being and to all rational creatures. Truth is called the soul's health and strength, its true and natural perfection. It is that which speaks to man as uncreated Wisdom speaks to God, saying, 'I was by Him as one brought up with Him. I was daily His delight.' When Truth presents herself, our souls know her as we know the face of an old and familiar friend.

These are general statements. Their meaning becomes definite when we apply them to particular cases. Truth is divided into two kinds. It is either 'of first inscription' or 'of after revelation from God.' The one is 'conatural' to man. It belongs to the soul. It is the 'soul's complexion.' The other is the 'soul's cure.' It supposes the disease of sin, and provides a remedy. It lays down 'terms of recovery and reconciliation.' The one is truth necessarily and absolutely. The other is 'the voluntary results and determination of the divine will.' The one is written, not merely in the Bible or on tables of stone, but in the hearts of men. It is interwoven into our rational being. The other, which is the external law, is given to recall the soul from the apostasy of sin. Had there not been a law in the heart of man, the external law would have been of no value. There are some natural truths to which every man, Whichcot says, must subscribe who has not abused himself, or forced himself from nature. These are reverence of the Deity, sobriety in the government of the body, a moderate use of the pleasures of life, justice and righteousness in men's dealing with each other. These are of the class of natural duties. But the revelation in the Gospel also speaks for itself. It bears a Divine impress. The substance of it is independent of external authority and external circumstances. The men of Samaria said, 'We have heard Him ourselves, and we know that He is the Christ.' This was the answer of souls that felt the truth. The words of Jesus ravish men's hearts. They meet an answer in the universal reason. Men wonder at them, and the world exclaims, 'Never man spake like this man.' 'The great things of revealed truth, though they be not of reason's invention, yet they are of the prepared mind readily entertained and received.'

Revealed religion as well as natural is self-evidencing.

The first step towards receiving the truth, or, indeed, towards knowing it, is sincerity. A desire to regulate our lives by what we know to be just and good is the best evidence that we are in earnest. Light will come in upon us just in proportion as the life of righteousness increases within us. He that is living in a state of eternal death will not easily believe in eternal life. Remission of sins is something incomprehensible to those who love their sins. The true penitent, on the other hand, forgives himself with more difficulty than God forgives him. Before the Gospel revelation, that for which earnest men incessantly craved was the forgiveness of sin. Humanity groaned under the weight of guilt. The cry of every good heathen was, 'Who will deliver me from the body of this death?' That for which the world was waiting and longing the Gospel revealed. Whichcot says that 'the great principles of reason are by awakened minds easily found out,' and 'those of the Gospel by prepared minds fairly admitted and entertained.' The heathen entirely agree with us as to the principles of morality. We have nothing to say as to moral duties which has not been said by them. They often speak and act so as to shame professing Christians. The representations which the Scriptures make of God are such as are worthy of Him. There is a fitness between what is revealed and what the state of man requires. All these things are 'assurances to settle us in the belief of Divine truth.' It is true that there have been men who grossly neglected the materials of natural knowledge. It is also true that there has been great, even invincible, ignorance in several ages and places of the world concerning the chief doctrines of revelation. Yet it may be said that the great principles of morality and the main articles of the Christian faith have received a universal acknowledgment. This is explained 'to mean not received by every individual person,' but 'as the due and even proportion it bears to the universal reason of mankind.' The great differences that have been in the world have not been about necessary or indispensable truths. This is true even of what is revealed in the Bible. All parties agree as to the essential doctrines of Christianity. Whichcot mentions two things that helped to confirm him in the truth of Christianity. One is, that it has existed long. Error and falsehood, he says, never live long. The other was derived from a consideration of the goodness and love of God. It could not be supposed that He would suffer that which was false to be believed in all times and ages of the world. An objection might be made to this argument, especially as it is here stated. Whichcot anticipates the objection, and in answering it explains, or rather limits, his meaning. The religion of Mahomet is widely spread, and has existed for centuries. Mahometanism, so far as it belongs to Mahomet, is not reasonable. All that Whichcot seems to mean is, that in the main God will not suffer man to be deceived. The value of the argument only extends to Christianity so far as it is plainly rational. It is a general faith in God, and the faculties which God has given to men.

Another sermon is on the text, 'I am not ashamed of the gospel of Christ.' It is properly a sequel to the sermon on 'Never man spake like this man.' We are not ashamed of the Gospel for the very reason that it is so full of the wisdom of Christ. Whichcot puts aside all the language common in his day, both among High Churchmen and Puritans, about receiving the Gospel because it is a mystery. If he receives it because it is reasonable, that must be a sufficient cause for rejecting all that is unreasonable. The question has to be determined whether or not the Gospel is mysterious. If it cannot be understood by the human mind, it

We are not ashamed of the Gospel, because it is rational.

cannot be said that we receive it because it commends itself to our reason or conscience. We cannot say that we are not ashamed of it, if, as some of the Fathers said, it is to be believed because it is incredible. If it be true that 'no man ever spake like this man,' those who pronounced this judgment must have understood what was said. All these things are implied in the very nature of Whichcot's argument. He therefore at once sets aside the idea of the Gospel being a mystery. It was so before it was revealed. It was hid for ages, but now the secret is opened; that which was hidden is brought to light. The natural knowledge of God is the product of reason. Revelation is the other part of religion, and reason is the recipient. 'God gives His counsels only to intelligent agents, so that reason has a great place in religion.'

The centre of Whichcot's theology is the inseparability of goodness and blessedness, of vice and misery. To do good is to be like God, and to share in His eternal and glorious existence. To do evil is to fight against God, against the nature of essential being, yea against our own nature, and therefore the result must be misery. Hell rises out of a man's self, and hell's fuel is the guilt of a man's conscience. 'The judgment of God at the last day will be easy, for there will be none to be condemned but what were condemned before. For man's misery arises *out of himself*, and not by *positive infliction*. Men run upon mistakes; the wicked and profane think that, if God *would*, they may please themselves, and no harm done, and that it is the will of God only that limits and restrains them; and they think that they are out of danger if God would forbear a *positive infliction*. This is a great mistake.' Sin brings hell in its train, but not in virtue of the will of God, for right and wrong are independent of the divine will. And well-doing brings blessedness. 'Heaven is an eternal reconciliation to the nature of God, and to the rule of righteousness.' It was objected to Whichcot in his time, that to preach about good and evil with their inevitable consequences was not preaching Christ. He answered, that this was the very thing about which Christ preached. The very thing for which He came into this world was to reveal the connection between righteousness and blessedness, transgression and suffering. We are not to preach Christ as if His name were 'a charm or spell.' By His death we have remission of sins; but, before we can have eternal life, we must have a righteousness within us. Christ cannot save us unless we are righteous. If God were to reckon a man righteous who is not righteous, 'this act of God's would be a wrong act.'

The theology of Calvin was banished from the creed of the Cambridge Platonists. It was irrational. It represented God as doing what it is impossible for Him, consistently with His own nature, to do. Whichcot says, 'Some think of God that He useth His creatures as He will, giving no account of any of His matters to principles of reason and righteousness. But certainly the ways of God are most accountable of anything to righteousness.' With one hand the Cambridge men set aside Calvin, and with the other some favourite doctrines that were popular with Churchmen.

Superstitions connected with the Sacraments. One of Whichcot's sermons is on the Lord's Supper. He shows in some plain and clear words how unnecessary is all the mystery which men throw around this ordinance. Jesus said, 'Do this in remembrance of me.' Here is the action, something to be done; and the explanation of the action, why it is to be done. There is nothing more said. Yet we have a multitude of questions raised about the celebration of the Supper,—some concerning the company, and what preparation; some the time, how often; and the posture. All that Jesus required was that we should observe what was comely, and retain Christian charity. A sacrament is a positive, not a moral duty, and therefore it is no indispensable part of religion. As to the company, Judas was admitted when the Supper was instituted. As to the time, the disciples were met upon another occasion, and not for this business. As to preparation, the disciples were prepared for the Passover, and knew nothing of what Jesus was to do. How often is not set down, nor is the posture mentioned. Jesus took the disciples as He found them. The superstitions about the posture are of later origin. As with the sacrament of the Supper, so with that of Baptism. There was nothing in its institution but the material action; and now it has become a great part of the religion of some

Christians. Men are prone to superstition, but God expects us to act according to His prerogatives of reason and understanding.*

Richard Cumberland, afterwards Bishop of Peterborough, wrote his treatise, 'De Legibus Naturæ,' expressly to refute Hobbes. Hallam says of this work that it makes an epoch in the history of ethical philosophy. The appeal is no longer to the authority of Fathers and Schoolmen, but to experience. Cumberland affirmed the existence of the laws of nature, which Hobbes seemed to deny. A great part of the controversy depended, indeed, on the meaning or use of the word law. Hobbes said that laws of nature are not properly called laws till they are imposed by the civil ruler. John Selden said that they were not properly laws till they were imposed by God as the legislator. They supposed, in strict language, that there was no law without a lawgiver. Cumberland did not see the necessity of authority to make a law. We could discover laws at work in nature. If we observe them carefully in their causes and effects, we may find out for what ends they are working. If we put ourselves in harmony with these laws, the results will be beneficial both to ourselves and to other beings. These laws teach us by their consequences, which are to us their precepts or sanctions, that our duty is to endeavour with all our ability to promote the common good of all rational beings. This is an obligation imposed upon us by the very nature of these laws previous to all questions of civil government. There is a necessary connection between the highest human happiness and acts of universal benevolence. The good of the individual is bound up with the public good. We do not always see the connection in this

---

* The reader of Whichcot's sermons cannot fail to mark the likeness between them and those of Frederick Robertson. It would be easy to quote from Robertson's sermons many passages parallel to this: 'We stand nearer related to God than we do to any being in the world; our souls and bodies are not nearer related than our souls to God. God is more inward to us than our very souls. In Him we live, move, and have our being. God is nearer to us than what is most ourselves.' In another place Whichcot says, 'It is as natural and proper for mind and understanding to tend towards God, as for heavy things to tend towards their centre, for God is the creator of immortal souls. All understandings seek after God, and have a sense and feeling of God. If reason did not apprehend God, religion would not be learned, for there would be nothing to graft on.'

life, but we see enough to convince us that it exists even when we do not see it. In the laws of nature God points out to us what actions will promote the common good. We are assured at the same time that these will be most beneficial to ourselves. The law of nature is nothing else but right reason, or as the ancients justly called it 'eternal reason.'

The Cambridge men derived our knowledge of right from reason and conscience. These were made the guides of human life, and the sure way to blessedness. The fact of external revelation was supposed to have additional evidence from its agreement with the revelation within. But if that agreement was not entire, it followed that the one must regulate the other. Which of the two, then, is to be supreme? This was not the only question at issue. The difference between those who followed external authority, and those who sought the origin of law in immutable natures, reached even to the very essence of God. With Hobbes God was Absolute Will. With Cudworth and those of his school, God was Absolute Wisdom. As wisdom or reason was something in itself independent of the divine will, so, also, was justice, which was an integral part of that wisdom. Evil, then, must bring its own punishment. Strictly speaking, there is no place for forgiveness. Every man must personally bear the punishment of his own sin. If this is proved, it follows that the substitution of one man for another or for all men, is impossible. What, then, is the meaning of the doctrine of sacrifice for sin? In the theology of the Cambridge Platonists, it cannot be the same as it is in the theology of Calvin. It must be understood in such a way as it can be harmonized with what we know of the eternal laws of immutable right. The external revelation must agree with the internal. If not it must be rejected. The priority must always be given to the direct revelation in the soul. The certainty of this is greater than the certainty of any external revelation. If that revelation is agreeable to reason it may be received, and then we have rational Christianity. If it is not agreeable to reason it must be rejected, and at this point of the argument we have the origin of Deism. We say at this point of the argument, for as to time we must go back to another controversy which began where this ended. Even before the publication of the 'Leviathan,' Lord Herbert of Cherbury had taken up the position that external revelation has less certainty than the revelation in the soul.

Dr. Leland makes Lord Herbert of Cherbury the first of the English Deists, and Robert Hall calls him 'the first and purest of our English freethinkers.' The name of Herbert is a name dear to the Church of England. The quaint but devout poet who sung of the priest and the temple was himself the high ideal of the temple priest. He was the representative man of the early Reformed Church of England. His brother, Lord Herbert of Cherbury, was no less the representative of the age in which he lived. He was a man of extensive learning, a brave knight, 'a mirror of chivalry,' as one of his admiring countrymen called him, as familiar with the sword as with the pen, a royal ambassador, a skilful diplomatist, and a refined courtier.* As a child he was sickly. It was a long time before he learned to speak. His first inquiries were concerning his coming into this world. Some laughed, but others wondered at the anxious thoughtfulness of the child. When he grew older, he meditated much on the strange mystery of finding himself in possession of a conscious existence, though oblivious of any sufferings which he might have had at his birth. From this he was comforted by the hope that the agonies of dissolution might be no more than the pains of being born into another world. 'For as I believe,' he said, 'that I shall then be admitted to a more happy state by God's grace, I am confident I shall no more know how I came out of this world than how I came into it.' As he reflected how all the wonderful organs of speech and sense were formed with a prospective adaptation to this life, he concluded that the faculties of hope, faith, love, and joy, which

---

* Herbert wrote his autobiography, in which he records many curious things of himself and of the times in which he lived. He was sent to France as ambassador by James I., with whom he seems to have been a favourite. In the differences between Charles I. and his Parliament, Herbert took the side of the Parliament, and had his castle of Montgomery destroyed by the Royalists. Horace Walpole says of this autobiography, that 'it is, perhaps, the most extraordinary account that was ever given seriously by a wise man of himself.'

are being formed now, and which cannot rest on objects that are perishing and transitory, would find their true satisfaction in the life to come. They reach out beyond the temporal and the finite. They crave the perfect, the eternal, and the infinite. 'The proper object of these faculties,' says Herbert, 'is God only; upon whom faith, hope, and love were never placed in vain, or remain long unrequited.' Again, in one of his poetical pieces, which reminds us of his brother's verses, he says:—

> 'I am most sure
> Those virtuous habits we acquire,
> As being with the soul entire,
> Must with it evermore endure.
>
> * * * *
>
> 'Else should our souls in vain elect—
> And vainer still were Heaven's laws—
> When to an everlasting cause
> They gave a perishing effect.'*

His theology a philosophy. Lord Herbert's theology is of necessity a philosophy, as all natural theology must be. It has its foundation in reason, and is thus connected with a system of metaphysics, or at least a doctrine of mental science. Herbert was an ontologist. He believed in the capacity of the human mind to penetrate the reality of being. Since Nature has gifted us with faculties to discern sounds and colours, which are but the 'fleeting qualities' of things, she must, he thought, have given us the sure means of discovering the truths which are internal, necessary, and everlasting.

---

* Lord Herbert had a chaplain in his house, who read prayers twice a day in his family, and sometimes a sermon, generally one of Smyth's. When he was dying, he requested Archbishop Ussher to give him the sacrament, remarking that it mattered little whether he received it or not; but at the same time saying that if there was good in anything, it was in that. The Archbishop declined to administer it, for which he has been much blamed. He probably took the same view as Herbert, reckoning that the sacrament was of benefit only to those who needed the help of external rites.

The following epitaph was written by Herbert for himself:—

'READER!

'The monument which thou beholdest here
  Presents Edward, Lord Herbert to thy sight:
A man who was so free from either hope or fear
  To have or lose this ordinary light,

'That when to elements his body turned were,
  He knew that as these elements would fight,
So his immortal soul would find above,
  With his Creator, peace, joy, truth, and love.'

Herbert's metaphysics are somewhat abstruse, but that need not trouble us. They have no inseparable connection with his religious system, beyond the general fact that he believed in the capacity of the human mind to know truth. Hallam quotes his axioms and propositions at some length, and then excuses himself for not going into Herbert's arguments. 'Partly,' says Hallam, 'by not thoroughly grasping his subject, partly by writing in Latin, partly perhaps by the "sphalmata et errata in typographo, *quædam fortasse in seipso*,"* of which he complains in the end, Herbert often fails to make himself intelligible.' This obscurity, however, does not affect the great outlines of his system. His religious teaching and the grounds on which it rests are clear and definite.

CHAP. VI.

The difficulty which pressed on Herbert's mind, and which separated him from the Christianity of his day, was the same which meets every reasoning man when he is first told that the Divine Being has in any way limited the salvation of the human race. In his time the religious world was divided into two parties, which seemed to him about equally irrational, and both as corrupters of simple Christianity. These were the Sacerdotalists, who suspended all on the Church, and the Puritans, who resolved the everlasting condemnation of the greater portion of the human race into the mere will of God. If there is no salvation out of the Church, if God has left it to depend on the mere accident of being baptized by a properly ordained priest, or on having received the other sacrament, according to certain prescribed rites and ceremonies, where is the goodness, not to say the justice, of God towards the heathen, and those who are without the pale of the Church? And if He is good and merciful and just, how can He take pleasure in the eternal reprobation of those to whom He never even offers salvation? Herbert laid it down as a first principle that God must, in consistency with His own character, have given to all men the means of being saved. He found that his difficulty was not a new one. Some divines had tried to obviate it by supposing that Christ was revealed to the heathen at the

The divine love must be universal.

* Hallam has facetiously added 'quædam fortasse in seipso.' The words are not in Herbert's postscript.

CHAP. VI. moment of death. Others—the Schoolmen, for instance—taught that saving grace was never wanting to those who did their best. Moreover, he found that many of the ancient Fathers believed the heathen could be saved. This belief seemed not only reasonable, but necessary for the vindication of the universality of Divine Providence.

Starting with the conviction that God must in some way have revealed Himself to all men, Herbert prosecutes the inquiry, how far, and in what way, He has revealed Himself. In his book, 'On Truth as it is distinguished from Revelation, Probability, Possibility, and Falsehood,' he tries to discover what are the truths of reason concerning religion; that is, the truths which are intuitive or innate. These being revealed directly to the mind, he holds for the only certain truths. Some men put faith before reason, but this is to invert the proper order. It is to pronounce judgment before the cause is heard. There is a catholic or universal reason of mankind. What agrees with it is truth. It is catholic truth. Religion is innate in man. It is a *common notice* in the mind. No nation, no age, is without religion in some form. This is the distinguishing mark, 'the ultimate difference,' between man and the brute.* No man, says Herbert, with sound faculties can be an atheist. Religion is as natural to man as faith or hope, love or intellect. It is religion which makes him a man. The universal reason testifies to five articles which are *common notices,* or innate ideas, in the soul. (1.) That there is a God. (2.) That

Five articles of natural religion.

---

* Hallam notices that the same distinction was made by John Wesley, who says that the true difference between man and the brute creatures is not reason, but that we are formed to know God and they are not. George Herbert has said something of the same kind:—

' Of all the creatures, both on sea and land,
　Only to man Thou hast made known Thy ways,
And put the pen alone into his hand,
　And made him secretary of Thy praise.

' Beasts fain would sing, birds ditty to their notes,

Trees would be tuning on their native lute,
To Thy renown: but all their hands and throats
Are brought to man, while they are lame and mute.

' Man is the world's high-priest; he doth present
　The sacrifice for all; while they below
Unto the service mutter an assent,
　Such as springs use that fall, and winds that blow.'

Did not Ovid mean much the same when he says—

' Os homini sublime dedit cælumque
　tueri jussit?'

He ought to be worshipped. (3.) That virtue and piety are the chief parts of worship. (4.) That we are to repent and turn from our sins. (5.) That there are rewards and punishments in another life.

All the heathen nations acknowledged one God. The Romans called him 'greatest and best;' the Greeks, 'God over all, self-produced, beginning and end of all things.' The Mahometans call Him 'Allah,' and the Indians 'Brahma.' It is admitted that in one sense the Pagans were polytheists, yet they all had a supreme God who ruled over all worlds both of gods and men. He was the first of beings, the only true Being, the permanent amid all change; in the words of the Orphic verses, 'the beginning, middle, and end of all things,' corresponding to the words of a New Testament writer, who says, 'Of Him, and to Him, and through Him are all things.' What we know to be good in ourselves as partakers of the divine reason must be supremely in Him whom we call God. Author of all good, He must Himself be good. He is just. There are anomalies in the world which we cannot explain, yet He rules in righteousness. He is wise. All things bear witness to His wisdom. The infinity of space is the infinity of God, for He pervades the boundless universe. His infinity proves His omnipotence, and His omnipotence proves His freedom to will and to do according to His pleasure.

That God ought to be worshipped is the second *notice* in the mind. It is a plain dictate of reason. Our relation to Him, our daily dependence on Him, and the benefits which we receive at His hands, show how natural and becoming are thanksgiving, prayer, and praise. All nations have expressed this in some form or mode of worship, in shrines, in temples, in vows, in sacrifices, and in consultations with the Deity as to future events. There have been indeed many errors connected with religion, and many superstitious ceremonies; yet the catholic reason, or *common notice*, plainly teaches that the chief part of divine worship is virtue joined with piety. This, Herbert says, is, and always has been, considered the essential part of the worship of God. By virtue he seems to mean morality, or a certain rectitude of the whole man in all his faculties and affections. The necessity of repentance is inferred from the dread which always rests on the minds of wicked men, showing that they are not ignorant of their vices. It is true indeed that the priests, both in old times and in the present day, have devised many ways of expiating sin. The Romans had their lustrations, their purifyings. All nations have their sacrifices. The universal consciousness of guilt, the reasonableness of repentance, and the need of atonement, led men to build altars, and to offer oblations to the offended Deity. As to rewards and punishments in a future life, no nation is so barbarous as not to have acknowledged them. Some have pronounced the reward to be in heaven, some in the stars, and some in divine contemplation. The punishment was in the infernal regions, in hell,—either a hell that burned or smoked,—sometimes in metempsychosis, or in death, either temporal or eternal. Conscience, as well as all religion, law, and philosophy, distinctly proclaims that there is a reward to the righteous, a God that judges the earth, and that He will avenge in His own time all the wickedness which escapes punishment in this life.

In his book 'On the Religion of the Gentiles,' Lord Herbert goes to the heathen world to show that these five articles were universally received. This he holds to be a certain proof from simple facts that they are *common notices*, or parts of God's universal revelation to man. Sallust says that the inhabitants of Crete first invented religion, a statement which Herbert indignantly rejects, religion being 'written in the hearts of men.' There is in the world a universal dissatisfaction with this life. Its brevity, its uncertainty, and the sorrows consequent on change and separation, make it not only unsatisfying, but sad. The sun goes down while it is yet day. The fairest promises of life and enjoyment are often blighted, as the early leaves in the spring-time. No man has such satisfaction in this life as to suffer him to believe that he was created for it alone. The mind is greater than the world. It craves something more than the world can give. Even the ancients, who enjoyed the pleasures of sense with all the eagerness of youth, confessed that they were not satisfied with them. The Greek dwelt amid visions of external beauty. He drank in all that pleased the eye and the ear, and yet he longed for something higher. He craved the infinite. He *felt after* the living God. 'And God,' says Herbert, 'inspiring all men with a desire of an eternal and more happy state, tacitly discovered Himself, who is eternal life, and perfectly blessed.'

It is confessed that the Gentiles had many errors concerning the first article of the catholic faith. Yet the wiser among them found their way out of the labyrinth. And even these errors are capable, if not of extenuation, yet of explanation, by a more comprehensive view of the philosophy of religion. The multitude of the Pagan deities is reducible to the manifold names of the one Infinite God, according to the saying of Seneca, that 'God may have as many names as He dispenses benefits.' Each of the greater deities is represented by some of the poets or philosophers as the Pantheus,* or All-God, who was in all, and over all, and through all. Besides the *certain* or known gods, according to Varro's classification, there were *dii incerti*, the gods of whom nothing was sufficiently known to admit of regular worship. That these views of the Divine nature were much nearer the Christian than is generally supposed, we may see from the character of the worship which was rendered to God. 'The polemical writings,' says Herbert, 'of the heathen theologians and philosophers who lived among Christians show that they acknowledged piety and virtue to be the chief part of Divine service. Celsus even dared to challenge the learned Origen to point out anything in the Christian religion that tended more to the establishing of virtue than the Pagans had before acknowledged. They no more doubted that a virtuous man should arrive at the seat of the blessed, though he knew not where it was, than that a traveller going on in the right path which leads to any magnificent city must come to the place he intended.' Plato said, 'We should endeavour to be like God, by prudence, justice, and holiness.' The Christian religion has no

---

* 'Ogygia me Bacchum vocat
   Osirin Ægyptus putat
   Mystæ Phanacen nominant;
   Dionyson Indi existimant;
   Romana sacra Liberum;
   Arabica Gens Adoneum;
   Lucaniacus *Pantheum*.'—AUSONIUS.

higher precept than this, and this was the teaching of many of the philosophers of the heathen world.

There are many passages in the writings of the philosophers which show that the Gentiles had the same ideas of good and evil which we have. They ascribed all sin to anger, malice, concupiscence, and depraved desires. They knew that wars and fightings came from the lusts that war in the members. They knew, also, that repentance was the way to amendment and forgiveness. 'The knowledge of sin is the beginning of salvation,' said Seneca; and, again, 'He that repents of his sins is almost innocent.' They knew, too, from whom forgiveness was to be obtained. Cicero says expressly, 'There is no expiation of sin or impiety to be had from men.' Even Lucretius could feel how terrible was the

> 'Mens sibi conscia facti
> Præmetuens. . . .
> Nec videt interea, qui terminus esse malorum
> Possit; nec qui sit pœnarum denique finis.'

And Ovid could say,—

> 'Ah nimium faciles, qui tristia crimina cædis
> Fluminea tolli posse putatis aquâ.'

The hope of a future life pervades all the literature, and forms a prominent part of all the philosophies of the ancient world. In that life the Gentiles looked for the rewards and punishments which they could not always discover in the present life. To this their Elysium and Tartarus, their good dæmons and their judges in hell, are all witnesses. Philosophers comforted mourners concerning their departed friends, that they had gone to a better world. They were now to complete their happiness, to be rewarded for their virtues and recompensed for their sufferings. Death was even less terrible to them than it is to us. Already they rejoiced in the prospect of victory over the terrible destroyer who triumphs now. 'They did not represent death,' Herbert says, 'as we do, with a meagre countenance, thin-jawed, and deep forehead, but pleasant and composed, the image of sleep; and they generally said,—*Such a one has gone from amongst us*, that the fear of death might not strike terror, and the minds of men be possessed that nothing but their bones remained after this life. For this reason they were more valiant and inclined to the practice of virtue, because death was esteemed by them only as a passage from a good to a better life; thinking it very base and mean that nothing of those who had led exemplary lives here should remain after death.'

Herbert admits that it was with great labour that he found these five articles of religion among the Pagans. But he did find them, and the discovery made him 'more happy than Archimedes.' He had found, as it were, a lever with which to move the world of superstition, and, at the same time, a place on which to stand, from whence he might vindicate the moral character of God. It rejoiced his heart to know that the Divine mercy was not limited to an elect few, to a baptized Church, to Jews or Christians, but that it extended to the whole race of Adam. It was manifested in past ages and in other dispensations. Wherever there were men, there God had left witnesses of Himself, *and in every nation he that did righteousness was accepted of Him*. It is true these five articles were dug, as it were, out of the accumulated superstitions of ages. These superstitions were the work of the priests, who were interested in multiplying ceremonies and keeping the people in ignorance. What priests did of old time they do now. All the perversions of doctrine, all the irrational dogmas that are imposed upon the world, all additions to religion which are not found in the universal or catholic reason of mankind, are the inventions of priests. In all ages priests have claimed supernatural powers, and in all religions they have been the opponents of reason, and of that only pure religion which has its foundation in reason. It was the glory of Christianity that it summed up, so to speak, all that was good in the Pagan world; and when that was placed in contrast with the superstitions superadded by the priests, heathenism naturally expired. It could not withstand the raillery of the Fathers of the Church. 'But,' says Herbert, 'by *their* means other articles were substituted in the room of the former, which gained belief, though very slowly for some ages; yet at last they obtained, and are very universal at

Religion always corrupted by the priests.

this time. *The hierarchy also remained, in which was the authority in sacred matters.'*

Herbert nowhere professes opposition to Christianity, nor even to *revealed* religion, as that expression is generally understood in the religious world. But he wished to rest Christianity upon the internal rather than the external evidence. The five articles which constitute 'the only true catholic religion,' he regarded as embracing the substance of what is taught in the Scriptures. Whatever external revelation adds to these is not so evidently true, yet it is not on that account to be rejected. 'There is,' he says, 'a certain revealed truth which, unless ungrateful, we cannot pass over in silence. But it is not of the same kind with that which is derived from the faculties. It has not the same certainty, for it depends on the authority of the revealer, and is not a truth of the mind.' He lays down several tests of an external revelation, but they are so strict as to leave but little authority for any revelation which is not immediate. A revelation to be believed must be made to oneself. Such a revelation Herbert had when the Divine Being, by a 'gentle noise' in the heavens on a calm summer day, intimated that it would be for the benefit of mankind if he published his book 'De Veritate.'*

The concluding chapters of this book, 'On Probability,

---

* 'Being thus doubtful, in my chamber, one fair day in the summer, my casement being open towards the south, the sun shining clear, and no wind stirring, I took my *De Veritate* in my hands, and kneeling on my knees, devoutly said these words,—*O Thou Eternal God, author of this light which now shines upon me, and giver of all inward illuminations, I do beseech Thee of Thine infinite goodness, to pardon a greater request than a sinner ought to make: I am not satisfied enough whether I shall publish this book. If it be for Thy glory, I beseech Thee give me some sign from heaven; if not, I shall suppress it.* I had no sooner spoken these words, but a loud though gentle noise came forth from the heavens (for it was like nothing on earth), which did so cheer and comfort me that I took my petition as granted, and that I had the sign I demanded; whereupon also I resolved to print my book. This, however strange it may seem, I protest before the eternal God is true; neither am I any way superstitiously deceived herein; since I did not only clearly hear the noise, but in the serenest sky that ever I saw, being without a cloud, did, to my thinking, see the place from whence it came.'

Herbert has been sometimes ridiculed for believing that an external revelation was made to himself, and yet placing internal revelation on higher grounds than external. The ridicule is scarcely just, for part of his argument is, that a revelation made directly to oneself is surer than a revelation made to another and coming to us through the medium of testimony. He believed that his prayer was answered by a voice from heaven. He was more certain of the truth of that fact than that a voice spoke to St. Paul out of heaven. The one voice he heard, the other he knew only by testimony. But the sense of right in the heart was something even

Possibility, and Falsehood,' need scarcely be noticed. Probability is that which depends on the authority of a person or persons, as history or tradition; Possibility concerns things future; and Falsehood is simply that which can neither be said to be probable nor possible, but is so opposed to truth, whether common, probable, or revealed, that it implies some contradiction. To the 'De Veritate,' Herbert appended two tracts, one 'On the Causes of Errors,' and another 'On the Religion of a Layman.' In the latter he shows the difficulty which the layman must have in finding out which is the best religion, when the clergy are advocating a faith scarcely to be distinguished from credulity, and denouncing reason as too depraved to be of any service. He recommends the layman to use his reason in the spirit of faith and prayer, and promises that he will find 'those truths which flourish everywhere, and which must flourish always,' for they are inscribed on the human mind, and depend on 'no tradition, either written or unwritten.' Past things being only among the probable, books professing revelation are to be received with caution, and only that in them which is conformable to right reason. In reading the Holy Scriptures we should be careful to notice that all things spoken there are not of equal authority. More than once Herbert intimates that he is far from desiring to injure Christianity, 'the best religion in the world.' He wishes to establish both it and the universal religion, which, he says, 'answers the ultimate design and end of Holy Scripture, for all the doctrines there taught aim at the establishment of these five articles, as we have often hinted. There is no rite or ceremony there enjoined but what aims, or seems to aim, at the establishment of these five articles.' He concludes his book 'On the Religion of the Gentiles,' with a declaration of his willingness to submit to 'the censure of the catholic or orthodox Church, but not to the impious enemies of universal Divine Providence and the *public peace*.' Herbert was a Parliamentarian, but this is an obvious fling at those of the Puritans who believed *particular grace* was only given to them and a few others.

more certain than the voice he heard himself, or the voice which St. Paul is said to have heard. It is not at all a question of denying external revelation, but only of determining the nature and value of different kinds of evidence.

John Locke disputes Herbert's doctrine of innate ideas.

Though Herbert built his theology on his metaphysics, they were not, as we have already said, necessarily connected with each other. Locke, in his 'Essay on the Human Understanding,' controverted the doctrine of *innate ideas*, or *common notices*; yet he admitted the five articles of religion to be discoverable by reason. It is probable that Herbert would have acceded to the greater part of Locke's criticism. They both seem to mean much the same thing, only Locke contends that ideas which are not found to exist universally —as, for instance, in children and idiots—cannot be called innate. This is like saying that physical strength is not innate, because young children have not yet reached maturity, or that the capacity to know good and evil is not natural because there are men, and perhaps nations, who have not reached the ordinary standard of mankind. Herbert, assuming that the capacity of development existed in every mind, pronounced ideas *innate*. Locke, seeing the existence of the ideas clearly manifested only in the developed mind, ascribed their origin to reason and reflection. 'They equally forsake the truth,' he says, 'who, running into the contrary extremes, either affirm an innate law, or deny that there is a law knowable by the light of nature; *i.e.*, without the help of positive revelation.' Though denying that Herbert's five articles are *common notices*, Locke yet admits them for clear truths of reason. He raises doubts about the meaning of virtue in the Pagan world, and the sins to be repented of, and he cites the case of some nations who are without gods, temples, or idols; yet he admits that the wise men of all nations have arrived at the true conceptions of the unity and infinity of the Divine Being. 'His name being once mentioned to express a powerful, wise, and invisible Being, the suitableness of such an idea to the principle of common reason must everywhere be readily received.' Locke disputed Herbert's axiom, that God must have implanted a knowledge of Himself in the minds of all men, because it seemed suitable to the Divine goodness. The Romanist thinks it best that the Church be infallible, but not on that account is it infallible. Locke's cautious principle is sound: we must rather look to the way in which God works than conclude beforehand *how* He must work. But here again, on the essential question, Locke does not differ from Herbert.

That all men to be responsible must have some religious knowledge, is all for which Herbert contended. Locke admitted the main proposition, but differed as to the mode in which God reveals Himself. For innate ideas he substituted reason, by which man could feel after God, and find Him.

Locke's treatise 'On the Reasonableness of Christianity' is supposed to have been written with special reference to Herbert's system. The title at once suggests the object, which is to inquire concerning the nature of the Christian religion, and how far it is agreeable to reason. The treatment of the subject is only partial. Nothing is said of the grounds on which we are to receive the facts and doctrines in the Scripture, which, though reasonable, are not discoverable by reason. With Locke's usual caution and precision, and, at the same time, with his natural deficiency in comprehensiveness, he limits himself to the question of the reasonableness of Christianity considered as a scheme proposed for our reception on what he regards as good evidence. He is equally severe with Herbert against the priests who, to procure reception for their irrational dogmas, forbid the exercise of reason. Sacerdotalism and Calvinism he regarded as the great corrupters of Christianity; the former as the promoter of superstition, the latter as shaking the foundation of all religion. Eternal punishment for the sin of Adam, whom we never authorized to act as our representative, scarcely falls in with our ideas of what is right. Locke speaks of some who, recoiling from this, went to the other extreme, denying that redemption was necessary, and making Jesus Christ nothing but 'the restorer and preacher of a pure natural religion.' This reference is probably to Herbert, but there is nothing in Herbert's writings to show that he would not have taken the same view of Christianity which was taken by Locke.

Setting aside systems of divinity, Locke restricted his inquiry to the Scriptures. He found that the doctrine of redemption—the chief doctrine of the Gospel—was founded upon the supposition of Adam's fall. The true way, then, to find out what we regain in Christ is to consider what we have lost in Adam. That plainly was immortality, the right to the tree of life, whereby men would have lived for ever. There is nothing unjust in God's permitting us to fall in

Adam. There would have been had He doomed men, or any man, to a state without remedy on this account, because such a state would have been worse than non-being. But as the present existence is better than non-existence, we are still debtors to God. And as to things eternal, He will reward every man according to his works. By sin came death. By Jesus Christ came life. We cannot keep the law of works whereby Adam had life, but God has given us the 'law of faith.' Those who keep this law are saved; that is, they gain immortality. Those who do not keep it lose their souls; that is, according to Locke's interpretation, their lives. But in what does this faith consist? It is said Abraham believed Sarah would have a son, and this was accounted unto him for righteousness. What merit was there in this? Abraham believed something contrary to the usual order of nature. Is the reasonableness of Christianity to be staked on its requiring from us belief in something miraculous? Jesus required that the Jews should believe Him to be the Messiah. Was there any merit in believing except in proportion to the evidence He gave them? We have now to believe in the incarnation, death, resurrection, and ascension of Jesus Christ, on the testimony of the Apostles and Evangelists. But, again, what can be the value of mere belief in testimony? It can only be an historical faith. St. James says that the devils believe and tremble. Locke feels that such objections have some validity. He answers that this historical faith may be a justifying or saving faith if God chooses to make it so. It was never promised to the devils that their faith should be accounted for righteousness. The whole of this seems against the reasonableness of Christianity. It is just the ground on which such as Herbert would have refused belief. It is the great stumbling-block which stands in the way of the reception of Christianity by rational men. It is virtually putting aside reason. It is contrary to all that Locke teaches, in his 'Essay on the Human Understanding,' concerning the relation of reason to revelation. Yet the truth dawns upon him at last, as if unconsciously. He sees that the faith of the Scriptures has more to do with the disposition of those from whom faith is required than with the things to be believed. It must be a faith 'producing fruit'—a faith that has more to do with the heart than the intellect. It is no blind credulity, no spirit of believing whatever is told us; but, from the examples given by the writer of the Epistle to the Hebrews, it is plainly ' a steadfast reliance on the goodness and faithfulness of God for those good things which either the light of nature or particular promises had given ground to hope for.'

But the crucial question remains. Jews and Christians had something proposed to them for belief. They could be divided into the two classes of believers and unbelievers; but what was to become of the heathen who had never heard of the Messiah? Locke had but one answer to this— the answer which Herbert gave; the only answer which reason can give,—they shall be rewarded according to what they have done, and not according to what they have not done. God will not expect ten talents where He gives but one. He will not require that any should believe promises of which they never heard. 'Yet God,' says Locke, 'had by the light of reason revealed to all mankind who would make use of that light, that He was good and merciful, and he that used the candle of the Lord so far as to find what was his duty, could not miss to find also the way to reconciliation and forgiveness when he had failed of his duty.'

Can the heathen be saved?

It is generally supposed that in showing Christianity to be reasonable, Locke eliminated its chief doctrine—that of the atonement. Such a passage as the one just quoted concerning the heathen, may seem to sanction its belief, for it resolves forgiveness simply into the mercy of God. It provides salvation for those who have never heard of Jesus Christ, as well as for those who have believed on His name. And yet Locke did not deny the atonement; he did not try to explain it; he did not know in what it consisted; but he believed there were '*transactions* between God and our Saviour in reference to His kingdom which were out of the reach of our ken and guess.'

Locke on the atonement.

Thomas Halyburton, a minister of the Church of Scotland, and Professor of Divinity in the University of St. Andrew's, wrote an elaborate answer to Herbert's whole system. Halyburton was an entirely different kind of man from Locke. As the advocate of a Calvinistic creed, he had little sympathy with reason in its claims to be the judge and examiner of religious belief. Herbert's great object

Thomas Halyburton replies to Lord Herbert.

was to vindicate the justice of God. Halyburton was satisfied that however unjust it might appear to us that God should sentence the majority of mankind to everlasting misery because of Adam's sin, yet it was perfectly just in God. In other words, we have not capacities to constitute us judges of what is divine justice. From Halyburton's lament of the universal prevalence of Deism, which, he says, was the religion 'in vogue among the great wits' of the time, it would seem that there was a general recoil on the part of all thoughtful and intellectual men from the Sacerdotalism and Calvinism that had been alternately in the ascendency during the course of the seventeenth century. For the present state of the religious world he chiefly blames the great divines of the Church of England, who had preached so much about the reasonableness of religion, and, as he says, 'put ethics in the place of the Gospel.' He calls them Arminians and Socinians, affirming that they made the law of grace nothing but a restitution of the law of nature. He judged that the best way to bring men to accept revealed religion was to show the insufficiency of the natural light. He does not seek to extinguish it. He admits that all nations have some idea of God, and that the more obvious of the divine laws have been known by nature's light. The heathen said some good things. In fact, they knew just enough *to justify the Divine Being in punishing them.* This was all the knowledge that any Calvinist ever required to find in the Pagan world. Concerning Herbert's five articles, Halyburton pronounced the Scotch verdict, 'not proven.' The heathen world was not agreed upon them, and, moreover, 'the best things which are generally ascribed to the light of nature were derived from the tradition of an original universal revelation.'

The question of the heathen world was made the subject of a learned treatise by one of the most earnest and impartial of the great theologians of the Church of England. This was Daniel Whitby, D.D., Chanter of Sarum. Whitby never mentions Herbert, but he evidently had before him the question as it had been raised by Herbert, and continued by those who had replied to Herbert's books. With something of Locke's scholar-like caution, he modestly called his work 'A Discourse on the Necessity and Usefulness of the Christian Revelation by Reason of the Corruption of the Principles of Natural Religion among Jews and Heathens.' This coupling of the Jews with the heathen as equally in need of a new revelation, shows how little Whitby undertook to prove, and how much he assumed as to what constitutes a revelation. All had a knowledge of God at one time, but when Christ came they were in darkness. The Jews' religion was so corrupted that it had ceased to serve the end for which it was given. They had perverted the plainest precepts, and turned even the special favours that had been bestowed upon them to the uses of bigotry and superstition. They imagined that God made the world specially for them, and that while His providence watched over them, the other nations were under the power of the Prince of Darkness. They weakened the doctrine of future rewards and punishments, teaching that as Jews, as Abraham's seed, as hearers of the law, they *must* be saved, while the nations of the earth were doomed to destruction without end. They thought they did well when they kept one precept of the law, though neglecting all the others. They were averse to government, supposing that God was their king. They made void the duties of children by their doctrine of *Corban*, and by causing proselytes of the gate to forsake their relations. They violated the Sixth Commandment in their hatred to others; the Seventh, by their proneness to impurity; the Eighth, by their disposition to rob and plunder; the Ninth, by their common swearing; and the Tenth, by their covetousness and love of the world.

The corruptions of heathendom were corruptions of an original *revelation* as well as those of Judaism. Whitby lays down the wide principle that the doctrines of natural religion are as truly the revelation of God's will to the heathen as Scripture is to the Jews or Christians; and yet he paints a picture of the heathen world as dark as if his object had been the same as Halyburton's. He quotes extensively from the Pagan philosophers to prove how small was their knowledge, and how uncertain they were about the little which they did know. They spoke tragically, indeed, of the miseries of life. They called Nature 'a doleful stepmother.' They said they would not have accepted life had it not been given them when ignorant of its sorrows.

They accounted it the greatest happiness *not to have been born;* and the next after that, *to die soon.* They called death '*the best invention of Nature,*' but never once do they mention in connection with this desponding view of human existence the only satisfactory answer,—the life to come, with its rewards and punishments. Indeed, Socrates testified that but few believed in the soul's immortality, and Cicero says that the most learned men have always despised this doctrine. All the philosophers have spoken of it doubtfully. The only consolation that even a Seneca could give the bereaved concerning the departed was a *beatus aut nullus*— he is either happy or he *is* not. Cicero says that though something may be true, yet we have no certainty concerning good or evil, for 'Nature has hidden the truth in the deep;' and again he says, 'Many things happen which so disturb us as to make us sometimes think there are no gods.' Pliny denied the power of God to raise the dead, and Cicero said that it was impossible for Divine wisdom to know future events. When the philosophers looked at the evils and confusion of the world, they even taunted the gods, saying, 'What apology will Jupiter or Apollo make for these things?' The consequence of this uncertainty was to overthrow the foundations of virtue and religion. Hence the worship of the heathen was imperfect, idolatrous, unbecoming. They were really *without God in the world.* Their religious rites were obscene and filthy, as the Floralia in honour of the impure Flora. They were celebrated in the vilest manner, as the Bacchanalian or Eleusinian solemnities; and yet those initiated were said to be *regenerated,* and after death to be among the blessed, while the uninitiated went to Hades or Tartarus. The vilest things were objects of worship. The philosophers were immoral. The Spartans gave their wives to strangers. Other nations had them in common. This is saying nothing of incest and worse sins, not now to be named, which were generally practised in the heathen world. Whitby does not wish to conclude, from the dark condition of the heathen world, that there are no principles of natural religion, but only the necessity and usefulness of such a revelation as the Christian. He was too wise to argue from the scepticism of some of the philosophers, or even the corrupt condition of the ancient world, against the light of nature. He knew that even Job had cursed the day of his birth, had threatened to come even to the seat of the Almighty to order his cause before Him, and that, excepting the disputed verse about the Redeemer, he had no answer from the hope of a future life to the fact that the righteous were often overtaken by calamities. Whitby knew also that there were men under the dispensation of Christianity who doubted of the existence of the Supreme Being, and as to the future life, trembled on the borders of an unknown land, hoping they might be blessed, and yet fearing lest they should not *be*. He knew also that the argument from the evil lives of the heathen, if directed against natural religion, might be easily turned against the Christian revelation. He testifies concerning the Christians of his day that 'adultery, theft, rapine, lying, swearing, bearing false witness, and coveting what belongs to others, are now become as common as they were formerly among the heathens.' He is satisfied with showing the need of further teaching, of republishing the doctrines of natural religion, and these he identified with the practical precepts of Christianity. He explains them as only the results of natural religion, drawn forth to our advantage in plain rules, adapted to the capacity of the meanest, and recommended to our practice from the most excellent example of our God and Saviour. To these, as constituting the sum of the Christian revelation, he adds ' the articles of the Christian faith which our reason was not able to discover. Moreover,' he continues, 'these laws of nature may be said to be implanted in the hearts of men in general, not that God hath put any innate ideas or natural impressions of them on the souls of all men. The Apostle plainly seems to found them on the *reasonings* of men.' (Rom. ii. 14.) This is quoting St. Paul to show that he agreed with Locke against Herbert, and that St. Paul and Whitby, as well as Locke and Herbert, were agreed on the main question concerning natural religion and its relation to the Christian revelation. Christianity made its way in the world because of its reasonableness. The Apostles showed that its 'doctrines were conformable to the principles of natural religion which were known from the beginning.'

Christianity a republication of natural religion with articles of faith added.

Richard Baxter replies to Lord Herbert.

We have reserved to the last Richard Baxter's remarks on Herbert. They were, however, in the order of time the first. Baxter says expressly that he took notice of Herbert's books, 'lest, having been unanswered, they might be thought unanswerable.' He says at the same time that he is so far from writing against the whole of the 'De Veritate,' that he takes most of Herbert's rules and notions to be of singular use. The 'five articles' he pronounces such 'natural certainties that the denying of them would unman a man.' Baxter had written a work on 'The Reason of the Christian Religion,' in which he made no reference to Herbert. In this book he maintains that we have natural evidence of the being of God, the necessity of holiness, and a future life of retribution; and not only have we natural evidence of them, but he shows, by long citations in the margin, that the wisest heathens confessed the same as we confess, though less distinctly than they might have done. The law of nature is a clear *revelation* of God's will. It tells us to keep our reason clear; to govern our thoughts, affections, passions, senses, words, and actions. It was well said by Plato, 'The temperate man has God for his law; the intemperate, pleasure.'

In proof of the life to come Baxter adduces the constant testimony of conscience in all men 'that have not mastered reason by sensuality.' He appeals also to the universal consent of all that are worthy to be called men in all ages and countries that this is a truth naturally revealed, and most sure. He quotes Seneca, Cicero, Plutarch, Plato, Plotinus, Iamblichus, Proclus, Porphyry, Julian the Apostate, Antoninus, Epictetus, Arrian, and others, as heathens among whom he found 'much good, who had a very great care of their souls, and many of whom exercised great industry in seeking after knowledge, especially in the mysteries of the works of God.' Some of them even 'bent their minds higher to know God and the invisible world.' He considers Theophilus of Antioch to have been very unjust towards the heathen philosophers, and he praises Clement of Alexandria, who said he was certain that philosophy had been blessed to the saving of many souls, for 'the Eternal Word, who is Jesus Christ, gave them light and mercy, though they were unconscious whence it came.'

Admits that Pagans may be saved.

A passage concerning the Scriptures in his book on 'The Reason of the Christian Religion' was animadverted upon by an anonymous writer, which caused Baxter to write another work, called 'More Reasons for the Christian Religion, and No Reason against it.' In the second part of this book were 'Some Animadversions on a Treatise "De Veritate," by Lord Herbert.' The passage concerning the Scriptures was this:—'The Scriptures are so entirely the product of the Spirit's inspiration that there is no word in them which is not infallibly true; no one error or contradiction in any matter can be found in Scripture, but those of the printers, transcribers, and translators.' In Baxter's day it was almost necessary for a man to maintain this position to be within the pale of Christianity. Even Locke had spoken of the Scriptures as 'truth without any mixture of error.' The anonymous writer noticed some evident mistakes in the genealogies of the Bible, such as Matt. ii. 8, 9, where it is said Joram begat Ozias, Ozias begat Joatham, while in Kings and Chronicles there are three generations intervening between Ozias and Joatham. He also pointed out some passages in the Gospels not easy to be reconciled with each other. Baxter himself took every history, chronology, and genealogy in Scripture as certainly true. He made, however, several remarks which are hardly consistent with this assumption; such as that we might have a certainty of the Christian religion if it could not be proved that every word of the Scriptures is true, nor the writers infallible; that the Holy Scriptures contain *all our* religion, and *somewhat more*, that is, the accidents and appurtenances of it, just as the body of a man has its accidents besides the parts which are *essential* and *integral*. He says that a multitude of such-like historical, chronological, topographical, physical, accidental passages are not strictly a part of the Christian faith; that it is possible for a man to believe one part of the Bible to be God's word, and not another part; that the disciples of Christ were not absolutely and in all things infallible; that it is possible for a good Christian to doubt whether those that were but Evangelists, as Mark and Luke, had the same promise of the Spirit's infallible assistance as the Apostles. He compares the words to the *body*, and the meaning to the *soul*, saying that there was

CHAP. VI.
On the Scriptures.

A man may believe one part of the Bible to be God's word and not another part.

more of the Spirit's assistance in the meaning and soul of the Scripture than in the *words* or body, and he adds significantly, 'It is the devil's last method to *undo* by overdoing, and so to destroy the authority of the Apostles by over-magnifying.'

Herbert's inquiries, as we have already remarked, arose from his desire to vindicate the justice of God, especially in opposition to the Calvinist scheme. Baxter had parted with Calvinism, but he had not freed himself entirely from its influence. He looked upon the world as a gaol where all were condemned, and hell the gallows to which all were doomed to be led out. Nor did it shock him that the multitude of mankind should be cast into everlasting fire for the sin of Adam. God has such an infinity of worlds in His universe that He can afford to destroy this. It is but like casting one in a million into prison, or cutting off an excrescence; as if justice did not extend to individuals. But Baxter rises above this. He objects to penitence being the remedy, as Lord Herbert had taught, but he grants that the remedy is universal; and he explains that though the remedy is the death of Christ, and that it is for all men, yet Christ did not appease God or make Him *more merciful.* He admits, too, that it is not universally necessary to believe in Christ to be saved. Christ's redemption is not the *first cause* of our salvation. It was God's love and mercy which gave us Christ as the Redeemer. All mankind are brought by Christ under a covenant of grace. As the covenant of innocency was made with all mankind in Adam, so the covenant of grace was made with all in the promised seed. 'None perish now for the mere sin of Adam, nor merely for want of the innocency required by the first law, but for the refusing and abusing some mercy purchased by Christ, which had an apt tendency to their repentance and recovery.' The question is raised whether any heathens really repent and believe. Baxter escapes with one of those distinctions which only a skilful Puritan could make. He says the heathen have the *power* to believe and repent, but he does not clearly admit that any of them do believe and repent.

Can Pagans be said to believe?

Baxter professes to receive the doctrine of innate ideas as taught by Herbert, but he explains his belief so as to agree with Locke. He calls the understanding 'a bare sheet of paper,' which has no actual innate knowledge. He dissents most from Herbert on the question of testimony, or the value of external evidence. Nothing was so certain to Herbert as the truth which he believed God had inscribed on his mind. Baxter was satisfied of the certainty of this truth, and that it did not require Scripture to discover it. Yet he said, after he had silenced all his doubts about the life to come, he still felt in himself 'an uncouth, unsatisfactory kind of apprehension till he looked to *supernatural* evidence.' He confessed, indeed, that this was but the weakness of 'a soul in flesh,' which desires a sensuous apprehension. This, he says, may be a disease, but it is a disease which shows the need of a physician and of some other satisfying light. He dwells on the mode of revelation by prophecy, by miracles, by inspiration, as these things were understood in his day; and he pronounces the evidence so satisfying, that it is 'beyond our reach to know what could be more satisfying.' With evidence so clear, we should not hesitate to believe the most terrible passages in Scripture, such as those which seem to say that only a few shall be saved, and all the rest tormented for ever and ever.* As to the supernatural evidence, Baxter manifestly spoke as if it had come direct to us, and not through the medium of testimony, which was Herbert's reason for making it secondary to intuitive knowledge. And yet, when all is said, it is not on the external evidence, not on testimony, not on the supernatural that Baxter rests the reason of Christianity. He lays the foundation, first of all, in 'the natural verity and its admirable concord with the Gospel of Christ.' Grace is medicinal to nature; where the natural light endeth, supernatural beginneth. The superstructure which Christ has built upon nature is wonderfully adapted to its foundation. 'The sin and misery of the world,' says Baxter, 'is such that it groaneth for a Saviour, and when I hear of a physician sent from heaven, I easily believe it; when I see the woeful world, mortally diseased and gasping

---

* Fortunately it was only such as Baxter among Protestants, and Massillon among Catholics, who found such passages in the Scriptures. A recent writer in the 'Revue des Deux Mondes' says that Père Lacordaire converted the Catholic Church to the opposite belief.

in its deep distress. The condition of the world is visibly so suitable to the whole office of Christ and to the doctrine of the Gospel, that I am driven to think that if God have mercy for it, some physician and extraordinary help will be afforded it; and when I see none other but Jesus Christ, whom reason will allow me to believe is that physician, it somewhat prepareth my mind to look towards Him with hope.' And again he says:—'As there is no other religion that a man can with any strong show of reason entertain, and seeing that he that will appear a reasonable creature must be of some religion, it followeth that to renounce the Christian religion is to renounce reason, and to doubt of it is to be injurious to reason itself.'

The excellency of the Christian religion becomes its great evidence. Men feel its truth. The Holy Spirit, working faith, holiness, and comfort in the hearts of men is an everlasting witness. It is the main argument by which the Christian religion has been proved, and will be proved, to the world's end. The actual saving of men by the renovation of their hearts and lives is a standing seal and witness of Christ. It is no question of genealogies, or histories, or topographies. There may be no testimony as to Joram's descendants, nor clear proof that Paul left his cloak and parchments at Troas, but there is a witness to the fact of men being reclaimed from selfishness and sensuality, and re-made in the image of God. Christianity is a life. Let men live it, and they will feel its truth. The greater progress we make in righteousness, the clearer will be our view of its everlasting foundations. 'It is God's method,' says Baxter, 'to cause the growth of faith at the root in proportion to its growth and tallness in fruit.' How wide, in one sense, is the difference between Richard Baxter and Lord Herbert! and yet on his better or more rational side how near does the great evangelist of the seventeenth century approach 'the first and purest of our English free-thinkers'!

APPENDIX (A).

This volume embraces a period of about a hundred and thirty years. It does not profess to treat of every work in theology written during that time. Those only are mentioned which were necessary to my object, which is to trace the current of religious thought, and not to write a history of theological literature. I feel, however, that there are many works of which the reader would like to know something, although it has not come within my general plan to notice them. Several are mentioned incidentally in the notes, but there are still some which are not even named. It seems desirable, for the sake of completeness, to mention a few of them here. The first is Bullinger's 'Decades,' which in the Parker Society's publications occupy five large volumes. Though written by a foreigner, they partly belong to Church of England literature. Convocation, in 1586, passed an order enjoining every minister who had a cure, and was under the degree of Master of Arts, to provide himself with a Bible and Bullinger's 'Decades' in Latin and English, and to read over one sermon every week, making notes of it in a paper book, to be shown to some preacher appointed to examine it. The theology of the 'Decades' is the ordinary Swiss theology of that era. Many of the works of English divines, for more than a century after the Reformation, were defences of the Church of England against the Church of Rome. Among those not mentioned in the text are 'The Old Learning and the New Compared Together,' by Dean Turner; Dr. John Olde's 'Acquital; or, Purgation of the most Catholic Christian Prince Edward VI.;' his 'Confession of the most ancient and true Christian Catholic Old Belief;' Dr. John Prime 'On the Sacraments;' Dr. William Fulke's 'Defence of the English Translations of the Scriptures,' and his 'Confutations of the Notes of the Rheims Annotators;' with the great work of Dr. Andrew Willet, called *Synopsis Papismi*. All these books are full of the ordinary Calvinistic Protestantism which prevailed in the Church of England till the rise of Arminian High Churchism. The same theology will be found in the sermons of Arthur Lake, Bishop of Bath and Wells, in the time of King James, and in the writings of Dr. George Downhame, Bishop of Derry in the time of James and Charles. Downhame, like a true Churchman of that age, was a champion of Episcopal discipline, and of Calvin's doctrine. On Episcopacy he was answered by Paul Baynes. His treatise on predestination was suppressed by Archbishop Laud. To these may be added an 'Answer to a Treatise of the Cross,' by Dr. James Calfhill, who died Bishop-Elect of Worcester in 1570, and twelve sermons on 'The Sin against the Holy Ghost,' by Dr. Sebastian Benefield, Margaret Professor of Divinity at Oxford in the time of James. Dr. Robert Abbot, Bishop of Salisbury and brother of the Archbishop of the same name, was also a pillar of Calvinism and Protestantism.

It may seem a great omission that nothing is said of the voluminous works of Dr. Thomas Jackson, Dean of Peterborough, and the once popular sermons of Dr. Donne, Dean of St. Paul's. The works of Jackson are of great value, but his theology is described sufficiently by the word Arminian. He was not properly a High Churchman, if we compare him with Laud, nor was he a Rationalist, if we compare him with Hales or Chillingworth. Donne's sermons are not controversial or doctrinal. They are generally classed with those of Bishop Andrewes. There is a large number of Puritan writers who would have been noticed in the text had there been anything to distinguish them from those that are noticed. William Ames wrote many theological books, and several tracts against the ceremonies of the Church. William Perkins was a learned and voluminous author. He was a very high Calvinist, and a thorough Protestant. His 'Reformed Catholic' was long a standard book. Perkins deserves a place in any history of theology, from the circumstance that Arminius wrote against him on predestination. The works of some of the most celebrated Puritan writers, as Adams, Bolton, Sibbs, Manton, Bates, Flavel, Ambrose, and Charnock, are chiefly of a practical character, and therefore lie outside of the plan of this work.

Theophilus Gale, author of the 'Court of the Gentiles' and the 'Anatomy of Infidelitie,' was one of the ejected ministers of 1662. He is sometimes classed with the Cambridge Platonists; but his affinity with the Puritans was closer than it was with Cudworth or More. George Rust, Bishop of Dromore, was also one of the Cambridge men. He wrote a book on truth, and a remarkable sermon in Latin, on 'The Use of Reason in Matters of Religion.'

The plan of this work excludes many great writers who were Oriental scholars or Scripture commentators, such as Pocock, Casaubon, Matthew Pool, and Henry Ainsworth. There are some other names which ought to be mentioned, as Thomas Barlow, Bishop of Lincoln, 1675, who wrote chiefly on the

Roman Catholic controversy, and William Cowper, Bishop of Galloway in the time of James I., whose works, chiefly on practical subjects, make a large folio. Martin Fotherby, Bishop of Salisbury, 1618, wrote a curious book against atheism, called 'Atheomastix.' Dr. John Howson, who died in 1631, was an eminent polemical writer, chiefly against the Church of Rome. Samuel Harsnet, Archbishop of York, 1628, ought to have been mentioned for a sermon which he preached at St. Paul's Cross, against Calvinism, in the days of Whitgift. Harsnet was then a young man, and had not another opportunity of preaching at St. Paul's Cross while Whitgift lived. This sermon is bound up with three sermons by Richard Stuart. There is a copy of it in Dr. Williams's library. Francis Mason, in the beginning of the seventeenth century, wrote a valuable defence of the orders of the Church of England. A preacher and writer of considerable eminence in his time, was John Smith, Vicar of Clavering, in Essex, author of the 'Essex Dove,' which was published after his death as 'a taste of the works of that reverend, faithful, judicious, learned, and holy minister.' Smith was the successor of Andrewes as Lecturer at St. Paul's. His sentiments are openly Calvinistic and Puritan. The excellent sermons of Henry Smith, Puritan Lecturer at St. Clement Danes, should not be forgotten. It was probably the sermons of Henry Smith which Lord Herbert of Cherbury caused to be read daily in his family.

We have no complete history of our theological literature. The nearest approach to it is Dr. Hook's 'Dictionary of Ecclesiastical Biography,' which is generally accurate, though written with that strong party bias which characterizes all the Dean's early writings. Dr. Cattermole's 'History of Church of England Literature' consists chiefly of extracts from some of our great authors. 'The History of the Church of England,' by the Rev. George G. Perry, is a useful and readable book. In Dr. Pusey's treatise on 'The Doctrine of the Real Presence,' there is a catena of authors, with extracts from them. Dr. Pusey was followed by Dean Goode, a man who understood the spirit of these authors, and of the Church of England, much better than Dr. Pusey does. Dean Goode's work is heavy, but it is thorough, and perfectly trustworthy. A 'Retrospect of Religious Life in England,' by J. J. Tayler, is an elegant and thoughtful work, from the Unitarian point of view. The merits of Mr. Pattison's essay in 'Essays and Reviews,' are well known. It will be read carefully by every sincere student of the history of religious thought in England.

APPENDIX (B).

The Bishops from 1530 to 1660.

CANTERBURY.

Thomas Cranmer	1533
Reginald Pole	1555
Matthew Parker	1559
Edmund Grindal	1575
John Whitgift	1583
Richard Bancroft	1604
George Abbot	1611
William Laud	1633
William Juxon	1660

ST. ASAPH.

William Barlow	1536
Robert Warton or Parfew	1536
Thomas Goldwell	1555
Richard Davies	1559
Thomas Davies	1562
William Hughes	1573
William Morgan	1601
Richard Parry	1604
John Hanmer	1624
John Owen	1629
George Griffith	1660

BANGOR.

John Salcot, *alias* Capon	1534
John Bird	1539
Arthur Bulkeley	1541
William Glynn	1555
Rowland Merrick	1559
Nicholas Robinson	1566
Hugh Bellot	1585
Richard Vaughan	1595
Henry Rowlands	1598
Lewis Bailey	1616
David Dolben	1632
Edmund Griffith	1633
William Roberts	1637

BATH AND WELLS.

John Clerk	1523
William Knight	1541
William Barlow	1548
Gilbert Bourn	1554
Gilbert Berkeley	1560
Thomas Godwin	1584
John Still	1592
James Montague	1608
Arthur Lake	1616
William Laud	1626
Leonard Mawe	1628
Walter Curle	1629
William Pierce	1632

BRISTOL.

Paul Bushe (first bishop)	1542
John Holyman	1554
Richard Cheney	1562
John Bullingham	1581
Richard Fletcher	1589
John Thornborough	1603
Nicholas Felton	1617
Rowland Searchfield	1619
Robert Wright	1622
George Coke	1632
Robert Skinner	1636
Thomas Westfield	1641
Thomas Howel	1644
Gilbert Ironside	1661

CHICHESTER.

Robert Sherburn	1508
Richard Sampson	1536
George Day	1543
John Scory	1552
John Christopherson	1557
William Barlow	1559
Richard Curteys	1570
Thomas Bickley	1585
Anthony Watson	1596
Launcelot Andrewes	1605
Samuel Harsnet	1609
George Carleton	1619
Richard Montagu	1628
Brian Duppa	1638
Henry King	1641

ST. DAVID'S.

Richard Rawlins	1523
William Barlow	1536
Robert Ferrar	1548
Henry Morgan	1553
Thomas Young	1559
Richard Davies	1561
Marmaduke Middleton	1582
Anthony Rudd	1594
Richard Milbourne	1615
William Laud	1621
Theophilus Field	1627
Roger Manwaring	1636
William Lucy	1660

ELY.

Nicholas West	1515
Thomas Goodrich	1534
Thomas Thirlby	1554
Richard Cox	1559

APPENDIX.

Martin Heton 1599
Launcelot Andrewes 1609
Nicholas Felton 1619
John Buckeridge 1628
Francis White 1631
Matthew Wren 1638

EXETER.

John Voysey, *alias* Harman . 1519
Miles Coverdale 1551
John Voysey 1553
James Turberville 1555
William Alley 1560
William Bradbridge 1571
John Walton 1579
Gervase Babington 1594
William Cotton 1598
Valentine Carey 1621
Joseph Hall 1627
Ralph Brownrig 1642
John Gauden 1660

GLOUCESTER.

John Wakeman (first bishop) . 1541
John Hooper 1550
James Brookes 1554
Richard Cheney 1562
John Bullingham 1581
Godfrey Goldsborough . . . 1598
Thomas Ravis 1605
Henry Parry 1607
Giles Thompson 1611
Miles Smith 1612
Godfrey Goodman 1624
William Nicholson 1660

HEREFORD.

Charles Booth 1516
Edward Fox 1535
Edmund Bonner 1538
John Skyp 1539
John Harley 1553
Robert Warton, *alias* Parfew or
 Purfoy 1554
John Scory 1559
Herbert Westfaling 1585
Robert Bennet 1602
Francis Godwin 1617
Augustine Lindsell 1634
Matthew Wren 1634
Theophilus Field 1635
George Coke 1636
Nicholas Monk 1660

LLANDAFF.

George Athequa, *alias* De Attica or Attien 1516
Robert Holgate 1537
Anthony Kitchin or Dunstan . 1545
Hugh Jones 1567
William Blethyn 1575

Gervase Babington 1591
William Morgan 1595
Francis Godwin 1601
George Carleton 1617
Theophilus Field 1619
William Murray 1627
Morgan Owen 1639
Hugh Lloyd 1660

LINCOLN.

John Longland 1520
Henry Holbeach 1547
John Tailour 1552
John Whyte 1554
Thomas Watson 1557
Nicholas Bullingham 1560
Thomas Cowper 1570
William Wickham 1584
William Chaderton 1595
William Barlow 1608
Richard Neyle 1614
George Montaigne 1617
John Williams 1621
Thomas Winniffe 1641
Robert Sanderson 1660

LICHFIELD AND COVENTRY.

Geoffrey Blythe 1503
Rowland Lee 1534
Richard Sampson 1543
Ralph Bayne 1554
Thomas Bentham 1560
William Overton 1580
George Abbot 1609
Richard Neyle 1610
John Overall 1614
Thomas Morton 1619
Robert Wright 1632
Accepted Frewen 1643
John Hacket 1661

LONDON.

John Stokesley 1530
Edmund Bonner 1539
Nicholas Ridley 1550
Edmund Bonner 1553
Edmund Grindal 1559
Edwin Sandys 1570
John Aylmer 1577
Richard Fletcher 1594
Richard Bancroft 1597
Richard Vaughan 1604
Thomas Ravis 1607
George Abbot 1610
John King 1611
George Montaigne 1621
William Laud 1628
William Juxon 1633
George Sheldon 1660

Norwich.

Richard Nikke or Nyx	1501
William Rugge or Repps	1536
Thomas Thirlby	1550
John Hopton	1554
John Parkhurst	1560
Edmund Freke	1575
Edmund Scambler	1585
William Redman	1594
John Jegon	1603
John Overall	1618
Samuel Harsnet	1619
Francis White	1629
Richard Corbet	1632
Matthew Wren	1635
Richard Montagu	1638
Joseph Hall	1641
Edward Reynolds	1660

Oxford.

Robert King (first bishop)	1541
Hugh Curwyn or Coren	1567
John Underhill	1589
John Bridges	1603
John Howson	1618
Richard Corbet	1628
John Bancroft	1632
Robert Skinner	1640

Peterborough.

John Chambers (first bishop)	1541
David Pole or Poole	1557
Edmund Scambler	1561
Richard Howland	1584
Thomas Dove	1600
William Pierce	1630
Augustine Lindsell	1632
Francis Dee	1634
John Towers	1638
Benjamin Laney	1660

Rochester.

John Fisher	1504
John Hilsey	1535
Nicholas Heathe	1540
Henry Holbeach	1544
Nicholas Ridley	1547
John Ponet	1550
John Scory	1551
Maurice Griffin	1554
Edmund Gheast	1559
Edmund Freake	1571
John Piers	1576
John Young	1578
William Barlow	1605
Richard Neyle	1608
John Buckeridge	1610
Walter Curle	1628
John Bowle	1629
John Warner	1637

Salisbury.

Lawrence Campejus	1524
Nicholas Shaxton	1535
John Salcot, or Capon	1539
John Jewel	1559
Edmund Gheast	1571
John Piers	1577
John Coldwell	1591
Henry Cotton	1598
Robert Abbot	1615
Martin Fotherby	1618
Robert Tounson	1620
John Davenant	1621
Brian Duppa	1641
Humphrey Henchman	1660

Westminster.

Thomas Thirlby	1541

Winchester.

Thomas Wolsey	1529
Stephen Gardiner	1531
John Ponet	1551
Stephen Gardiner	1553
John White	1556
Robert Horne	1561
John Watson	1580
Thomas Cooper	1583
William Wickham	1595
William Day	1595
Thomas Bilson	1597
James Montague	1616
Launcelot Andrewes	1619
Richard Neyle	1627
Walter Curle	1632
Brian Duppa	1660

Worcester.

Jerome de Ghinucci	1523
Hugh Latimer	1535
John Bell	1539
Nicholas Heathe	1543
Richard Pate	1555
Edwyn Sandys	1559
Nicholas Bullingham	1571
John Whitgift	1577
Edmund Freake	1584
Richard Fletcher	1592
Thomas Bilson	1596
Gervase Babington	1597
Henry Parry	1610
John Thornborough	1617
John Prideaux	1641
George Morley	1660

York.

Thomas Wolsey	1514
Edward Lee	1531
Robert Holgate	1545
Nicholas Heathe	1555

Thomas Young 1561
Edmund Grindal 1570
Edwyn Sandys 1576
John Piers 1589
Matthew Hutton 1595
Toby Matthews 1606
George Montaigne 1628
Samuel Harsnet 1628
Richard Neyle 1632
John Williams 1641
Accepted Frewen 1660

Carlisle.

John Kite 1521
Robert Aldrich 1537
Owen Oglethorpe 1556
John Best 1561
Richard Barnes 1570
John Mey 1577
Henry Robinson 1598
Robert Snowden 1616
Richard Milbourne 1621
Richard Senhouse 1624
Francis White 1626
Barnabas Potter 1628
James Ussher 1641
Richard Sterne 1660

Chester.

John Bird (first bishop) . . . 1542
George Cotes 1554
Cuthbert Scot 1556
William Downham 1561
William Chaderton 1579
Hugh Bellot 1595
Richard Vaughan 1597
George Lloyd 1604
Thomas Morton 1616
John Bridgeman 1619
Brian Walton 1660

Durham.

Cuthbert Tonstall 1530
James Pilkington 1561
Richard Barnes 1577
Matthew Hutton 1589
Toby Matthews 1595
William James 1606
Richard Neyle 1617
George Montaigne 1627
John Howson 1628
Thomas Morton 1632
John Cosin 1660

Sodor and Man.

Thomas Stanley 1510
Robert Farrer 1545
Henry Man 1546
Thomas Stanley 1558
John Salisbury 1571
James Stanley 1573
John Merrick 1576
George Lloyd 1600
John Philips 1604
William Forster 1634
Richard Parr 1653
Samuel Rutter 1661

END OF VOL. I.

By the same Author.

Demy 8vo, 10s. 6d.

AN ESSAY ON PANTHEISM.

'The work of a man indefatigable in his pursuit of truth, not content with second-hand information where it was accessible to him at the fountain-head, making his task a labour of love, and proclaiming his results fearlessly. There is, we believe, no English treatise bringing together the same amount of information, given where it was possible in the words of his authorities and grouped with an instructive clearness.'—*Contemporary Review.*

'The subject of this book is one which must always interest thinkers. . . . Mr. Hunt gives sufficient proof that he has read much on the subject, and spared no pains to apprehend its bearings. He has traversed a wide field, scattering his materials over it with a liberal hand. . . . We commend the volume to the favourable attention of the reader, as one deserving his perusal. The author is earnest and devout. He shows that he is an orthodox Churchman, as well as a man of reading and reflection. . . . He is no common-place writer; his book is well fitted to stimulate and enlighten the minds of those who are desirous to be introduced into the illustrious company of thinkers who have pondered over the profound problem of being.'—*Athenæum.*

'For particular commendation we should select his account of the doctrine of Scotus Erigena, and especially his vindication, for it amounts to that, of Benedict Spinoza. Mr. Hunt's is a very good style, and well suited for setting before the reader intelligible summaries of philosophical systems which might be laboured into any degree of obscurity. It is concise without being peremptory. . . . He manifests no hostile spirit, and his object is evidently to conciliate. Christianity and Pantheism must be reconciled, otherwise it will be the worse for Christianity.'—*Westminster Review.*

'The Curate of St. Ives has redeemed the credit of his order. The Church of Rome has awarded him its most distinguished honour of the Index, in company with Dr. Pusey, and the author of *Ecce Homo!* and we think he is fairly entitled to the distinction from the ability, the patience, and the honesty with which he has conducted the investigation that he felt called to enter upon. In the straightforward and attractive preface, he explains how he came to undertake the task of resolving the great religious question of the day, and how he gradually awoke to the magnitude of the work he had set himself. . . . Mr. Hunt is quite aware of the danger he incurs by his appeal to reason in these matters, but he is one of the few people who see that there is really no help for it, that a man must use his reason, if it is only for the purpose of making up his mind that he won't. In language that frequently rises into eloquence, he maintains the supremacy of the much abused faculty, and he commends the outcome of his patient labour to the sympathies of those who feel the necessities of the age and appreciate the value of truthful inquiry.'—*Spectator.*

'This learned and elaborate work will be hailed with thankfulness by such theological students as take an interest in tracing out, amongst all nations and in all ages, the struggles and developments of human thought in relation to the being and government of God. It will lead devout readers afresh to adore Him, "*in whom are hid all the treasures of wisdom and knowledge.*"'—*Wesleyan Paper.*

'In passing round and over so wide a field, the author has brought out much that is both interesting and curious. Any reader who wishes to master the subject, will find all the materials brought together to his hand within the single volume before us; and also reference to many original sources of information.'—*Record.*

'It passes over a broad field, and occupies a space in English literature before vacant.'—*Christian Examiner* (American).

STRAHAN & CO., 56, LUDGATE HILL.

www.ingramcontent.com/pod-product-compliance
Lightning Source LLC
Chambersburg PA
CBHW080233170426
43192CB00014BA/2454